DAMRON

ACCOMMODATION

Transit: whether public transit is easily accessible; as well as estimated taxi costs to a nearby airport, bus/ train station, and lesbian/ gay bars

Locale City: not necessarily the exact city in which the accommodation is located; it is the city under which the accommodation wishes to be listed: for instance, many of the accommodations listed under "Russian River" are technically located in "Guerneville"; in Hawaii, accommodations are listed alphabetically by *island*, not by *city*

TAG indicates member of **Travel Alternatives Group (TAG)**; see ad inside front cover

Pickup Service: transportation provided by the accommodation and cost; usually from the nearest airport

Rooms: number of units, and typical in-room amenities – not *all* rooms have all the amenities listed

Wheelchair Access: some units have no steps and wide doorways, including the bathrooms

Kids/ Pets: teens are ages 12 and over

Minimum Stay: often 2 nights for weekends, 3 nights for holiday weeknds, and more for major holidays

Season: prime vacation months in the area

Rates: approximate nightly prices (of course, subject to change), ranging from low to high; usually for two people per room

AC: travel agent's commission paid by the accommodation; sometimes special restrictions apply

Meals: "cont'l brkfst" includes fruit and pastries; "full brkfst" generally includes hot food

Recreation: nearby outdoor activities

Amenities: special perks offered; from cookies & milk at bedtime to letting clothing be only an option

Smoking: don't expect to light up inside unless "ok" appears in the listing

Cancellation: this may list the *standard fee* for all cancellations (usually $10-20 or 10-20% of the deposit); or the *time given* for cancellations (i.e., 24hrs to 30 days); and/ or the percent of the *deposit forfeited* if reservations are cancelled without enough notice (usually 100%)

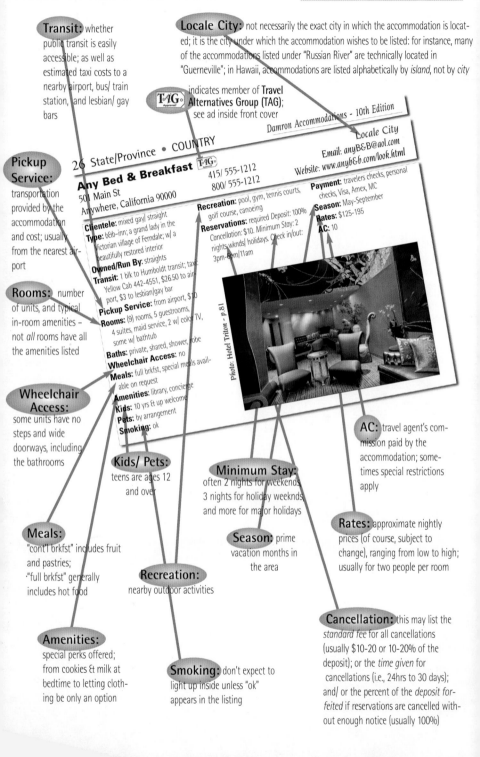

Damron Accommodations - 10th Edition

26 State/Province • COUNTRY

Locale City

Any Bed & Breakfast TAG
501 Main St
Anywhere, California 90000

415/ 555-1212
800/ 555-1212

Email: anyB&B@aol.com
Website: www.anyb&b.com/look.html

Clientele: mixed gay/ straight
Type: b&b-inn; a grand lady in the Victorian village of Ferndale; w/ a beautifully restored interior
Owned/Run By: straights
Transit: 1 blk to Humboldt transit; taxi; Yellow Cab 442-4551, $26.50 to airport, $3 to lesbian/gay bar
Pickup Service: from airport, $10
Rooms: (9) rooms, 5 guestrooms, 4 suites, maid service, w 2 color TV, some w/ bathtub
Baths: private, shared, shower, robe
Wheelchair Access: no
Meals: full brkfst, special meals available on request
Amenities: library, concierge
Kids: 10 yrs & up welcome
Pets: by arrangement
Smoking: ok

Recreation: pool, gym, tennis courts, golf course, canoeing
Reservations: required Deposit: 100%
Cancellation: $10. Minimum Stay: 2 nights wknds/ holidays. Check in/out: 3pm-6pm/11am

Payment: travelers checks, personal checks, Visa, Amex, MC
Season: May-September
Rates: $125-195
AC: 10

Photo: Hotel Triton - p.81

DAMRON
ACCOMMODATIONS

is produced by:

Publisher	Damron Company
Editor-in-Chief	Gina M. Gatta
Managing Editor	Ian Philips
Deputy Editor	Erika O'Connor
Editors	Maya Lara
	Leila Walker
Director of Art/Advertising	Kathleen Pratt
Cover Design	Rick Avila

Board of Directors
Gina M. Gatta, Edward Gatta, Jr., Louise Mock

How to Contact Us:

Mail:	PO Box 422458, San Francisco, CA 94142-2458
Email:	info@damron.com
Web:	www.damron.com
Phone:	415/ 255-0404 & 800/ 462-6654
Fax:	415/ 703-9049

(Cover Image: Hotel Triton, San Francisco)

TABLE OF CONTENTS

TABLE OF CONTENTS

Black Bear Camp Men's Retreat
Auburn

10565 US Hwy 280 W
Waverly, AL 36879
334/ 887-5152
www.blackbearcamp.net

Clientele: men
Type: hostel; clothing-optional campground & bunkhouse on 33 wooded acres; satellite TV, kitchen, central A/C & heat; w/ 10 campsites, 1 RV hookup & 2 private sleeper cabins
Owned/ Run By: gay men
Rooms: 2
Baths: shared

Wheelchair Access: yes, 2 rms
Meals: coffee/tea only
Amenities: free parking, pool, outdoor hot tub, DVDs/ videos, WiFi
Kids: no
Pets: no
Smoking: no
Rates: $5-50

The Tutwiler Wyndham T4G
Birmingham

2021 Park Pl N
Birmingham, AL 35203
205/ 322-2100
www.wyndham.com

Clientele: gay-friendly
Type: hotel; historic luxury property in heart of downtown; also restaurant & lounge
Rooms: 147
Baths: private
Kids: welcome

Pets: welcome
Smoking: ok
Rates: $130+
AC: 10%

Spring Creek Campground & Resort
Geneva

163 Campground Rd
Geneva, AL 36340
334/ 684-3891
www.springcreekcampground.net

Clientele: mostly men
Type: clothing-optional campground & RV park; w/ 100 campsites & 60 RV sites; also deluxe cabins; clubhouse w/ DJ on theme wknds; Cabana Bar & Grill; 1 hr N of Fort Walton & Panama City, FL
Owned/ Run By: gay man

Rooms: 14 (cabins)
Baths: private & shared
Wheelchair Access: yes
Kids: no
Pets: welcome
Rates: $15-60

Berney/ Fly B&B
Mobile

1118 Government St
Mobile, AL 36604
251/ 405-0949
www.berneyflybedandbreakfast.com

Clientele: gay-friendly
Type: b&b; in 1895 Queen Anne Victorian; w/ fish ponds, gazebo; close to gay bars; WiFi inside & poolside
Rooms: 4
Baths: private & shared
Meals: full brkfst

Amenities: free parking, pool, outdoor hot tub, DVDs/ videos, WiFi
Kids: no
Pets: no
Smoking: no (outside only)
Rates: $119-179

Rocky Mount B&B
Montgomery

2364 Rocky Mount Rd
Prattville, AL 36066
334/ 285-0490 800/ 646-3831
www.rockymountbb.com

Clientele: gay-friendly
Type: b&b; located on 50 acres; minutes from downtown Montgomery
Owned/ Run By: straights
Rooms: 2
Baths: private
Meals: full brkfst

Kids: no
Pets: no
Smoking: no
Rates: $120-125

Bluff Creek Falls
Steele

1125 Loop Rd
Steele, AL 35987
256/ 538-0678 205/ 515-7882
www.bluffcreekfalls.com

Clientele: men
Type: campground; 28 campsites & 6 RV hookups & cabins/ bunkhouse; over 200 waterfalls & 3 large natural swimming holes on property; many 40- to 90-foot bluffs to climb; 50 minutes from Birmingham

Owned/ Run By: gay men
Rooms: 2 cabins & 1 bunkhouse (sleeps 14)
Kids: no
Pets: welcome
Smoking: no
Rates: $14-55 + 25 (yearly membership)

A Wildflower Inn B&B
Anchorage

1239 I St
Anchorage, AK 99501
907/ 274-1239 877/ 693-1239
www.alaska-wildflower-inn.com

Clientele: mixed gay/ straight
Type: b&b; convenient downtown location; close to hiking trails & scenic vistas; fun hosts
Owned/ Run By: gay men
Rooms: 3

Baths: private
Meals: full brkfst
Kids: welcome
Pets: no
Rates: $69-129
AC: 10%

Alaska Bear Company B&B
Anchorage

535 E 6th Ave
Anchorage, AK 99501-2639
907/ 277-2327
www.alaska.net/~akbearco

Clientele: mixed gay/ straight
Type: b&b-private home; comfy & cozy house built in mid-1930s & recently renovated; close to downtown businesses, tourist attractions, restaurants
Owned/ Run By: gay men

Rooms: 2
Baths: private & shared
Meals: full brkfst
Rates: $49-85

Alaska Heavenly Lodge
Anchorage

34950 Blakely Rd
Anchorage, AK 99572
907/ 595-2012
www.alaskaheavenly.com

Clientele: gay-friendly
Type: hotel; river & mtn views; billiards rm, stone fireplace, Alaskan library
Owned/ Run By: straights
Rooms: 6
Baths: private

Amenities: free parking, laundry, sauna, outdoor hot tub, massage, DVDs/ videos
Kids: no
Pets: no
Smoking: no
Rates: $199-275

Alaskan Adventures & Outfitters
Anchorage

PO Box 200883
Anchorage, AK 99520
248/ 461-2090 888/ 435-5269461
www.alexandercreek.com

Clientele: gay-friendly
Type: resort; remote fly-in adventure/ fishing lodge; located directly on the banks of Alexander Creek
Owned/ Run By: gay & straight
Rooms: 10
Baths: private & shared

Meals: full brkfst
Kids: kids over 10 yrs welcome
Pets: welcome
Smoking: no
Rates: $605 (all-inclusive)
AC: 15%

Anchorage Jewel Lake B&B
Anchorage

8125 Jewel Lake Rd
Anchorage, AK 99502
907/ 245-7321
www.jewellakebandb.com

Clientele: mixed gay/ straight
Type: b&b-inn
Owned/ Run By: gay men
Rooms: 5
Baths: private
Meals: full brkfst

Kids: welcome
Pets: no
Smoking: no
Rates: $100-250
AC: 10%

City Garden B&B
Anchorage

1352 W 10th Ave
Anchorage, AK 99501
907/ 276-2359
www.citygarden.biz

Clientele: mixed gay/ straight
Type: b&b-private home; beautiful views of Mt McKinley from bdrms; 10-minute walk to downtown area
Owned/ Run By: gay men
Rooms: 3
Baths: private & shared

Meals: expanded cont'l brkfst
Kids: no
Pets: no
Rates: $100-150 + tax
AC: none

Copper Whale Inn
Anchorage

440 L St
Anchorage, AK 99501
907/ 258-7999
www.copperwhale.com

Clientele: mixed gay/ straight
Type: inn; located in downtown Anchorage
Owned/ Run By: gays
Rooms: 15
Baths: private

Rates: $69-189

Gallery B&B
Anchorage

1229 G St
Anchorage, AK 99501
907/ 274-2567

Clientele: mixed gay/ straight
Type: b&b; safe & comfortable; wood flrs,
   big fireplace & custom painting accents
   provide a beautiful setting to relax in
Owned/ Run By: lesbians
Rooms: 7
Baths: shared

Wheelchair Access: yes, 2 rms
Meals: expanded cont'l brkfst
Kids: welcome
Pets: by arrangement
Rates: $35-95
AC: 10%

The Gingerbread House B&B Chalet
Anchorage

28/29 Echo Ridge Dr
Girdwood, AK 99587
907/ 783-1954 877/ 783-7954
www.gingerbreadhousebb.net

Clientele: women
Type: b&b & chalet rental; luxurious
   accommodations in a beautiful setting
Owned/ Run By: women
Rooms: 4
Baths: private & shared
Meals: expanded cont'l brkfst

Amenities: free parking, laundry, massage,
   DVDs/ videos, WiFi
Kids: welcome w/ advance notice
Pets: no
Smoking: no
Rates: $105-350
AC: 10%

Home Suite Home B&B
Anchorage

1611 Cara Loop
Anchorage, AK 99515
907/ 345-2880 888/ 345-2881
www.homesuitehomebnb.com

Clientele: mixed gay/ straight
Type: seasonal; private suite w/ kitchenette;
   cable TV & internet; close to Anchorage
   Int'l Airport
Owned/ Run By: gay men
Rooms: 1 suite
Baths: private

Wheelchair Access: yes, all rms
Meals: expanded cont'l brkfst
Pets: under 15 lbs welcome w/ deposit &
   prior arrangement
Rates: $115 + 12% tax (mention Damron
   for 10% off)
AC: 10%

"Off The Tracks" Women's Guesthouse
Anchorage

342 W 11th Ave
Anchorage, AK 99501
907/ 272-6537
www.offthetracks.com

Clientele: women
Type: guesthouse; "a safe place for women
   to stay"; self-contained w/ private
   entrance & phone; 2 bdrms w/ common
   area & kitchenette
Owned/ Run By: lesbian & straight
Rooms: 2

Baths: private & shared
Meals: cont'l brkfst
Kids: welcome; under 5 yrs free; boys under
   12 yrs only
Pets: welcome; please inquire
Rates: $54-84

Billie's Backpackers Hostel
Fairbanks

2895 Mack Rd
Fairbanks, AK 99709
907/ 479-2034
www.alaskahostel.com

Clientele: gay-friendly
Type: hostel; w/ bunk-style rms & 6
   campsites; open 24 hrs
Owned/ Run By: women
Rooms: 20 (beds)
Baths: private & shared

Kids: welcome
Smoking: ok
Rates: $18

Island Watch B&B   *Homer*

4241 Claudia St
Homer, AK 99603
888/ 235-2711
www.islandwatch.net

Clientele: gay-friendly
Type: b&b-inn; cozy & comfortable cabins w/ modern amenities; internet access; great view; close to town, quiet & woodsy; featured in *Alaska Best Places* guidebook
Owned/ Run By: women
Rooms: 5
Baths: private

Wheelchair Access: yes, 1 rm
Meals: full brkfst
Amenities: hot tub, DVDs/ videos, WiFi
Kids: welcome; under 12 yrs 1/2 price
Pets: welcome; $10 pet fee
Smoking: no
Rates: $100-160 (double)
AC: 10%

Skyline B&B   *Homer*

63540 Skyline Dr
Homer, AK 99603
907/ 235-3823
www.skylinebb.com

Clientele: mixed gay/ straight
Type: b&b; warm Alaskan hospitality w/ magnificent views of bay & glacial mtns; on 10 peaceful wilderness acres; call first about availability of hot tub; now in our 10th year!
Owned/ Run By: lesbian & straight
Rooms: 5

Baths: private
Meals: full brkfst
Amenities: outdoor hot tub, DVDs/ videos
Kids: welcome w/ prior arrangement
Pets: welcome; must stay in garage; $10 deposit ($5 refundable)
Rates: $98-127
AC: 10%

Spit Sister Cafe & B&B   *Homer*

Homer Spit Rd
Homer, AK 99603
907/ 299-6767 907/ 299-6868
carmenpfeil@hotmail.com

Clientele: mixed gay/ straight
Type: b&b; cozy rm; private deck overlooking harbor; dbl & single beds; brkfst in downstairs cafe included
Owned/ Run By: gay & straight
Rooms: 1
Baths: private

Meals: full brkfst
Kids: welcome
Pets: welcome; limit 1 pet
Smoking: no
Rates: $85-140
AC: 10%

A Pearson's Pond Luxury Suites & Adventure Spa   *Juneau*

4541 Sawa Circle
Juneau, AK 99801-8723
907/ 789-3772 888/ 658-6328
www.pearsonspond.com

Clientele: gay-friendly
Type: mini resort/ spa; hot tubs by pond; glacier or garden ceremonies
Owned/ Run By: straights
Rooms: 5
Baths: private
Meals: expanded cont'l brkfst

Amenities: free parking, laundry, outdoor hot tub, massage, DVDs/ videos, gym, WiFi
Kids: 12 yrs & up welcome
Smoking: no
Rates: $109-399
AC: 10%

Anchor Inn by the Sea   *Ketchikan*

4672 S Tongass Hwy
Ketchikan, AK 99901
907/ 247-7117 800/ 928-3308
www.anchorinnbythesea.com

Clientele: gay-friendly
Type: apt; vacation rental; private suites w/ kitchenettes; located so close to the ocean you can view the sealife from the cozy sofa; excellent whale-watching; 1- & 2-bdrm units
Owned/ Run By: straights

Rooms: 3
Baths: private
Meals: coffee/tea only
Smoking: no
Rates: $85-135 (double occupancy)

Ma Johnson's Hotel   *McCarthy*

907/ 554-4402
www.mcarthylodge.com

Type: hotel; "The Living Museum" inside America's largest nat'l park, Wrangell St Elias
Owned/ Run By: gay & straight
Rooms: 20
Wheelchair Access: yes, 2 rms

Meals: full brkfst
Kids: welcome
Pets: welcome; $100 deposit; call ahead
Smoking: no
Rates: $109-159

Alaska Garden Gate B&B   *Palmer*

950 S Trunk Rd
Palmer, AK 99645
907/ 746-2333
www.gardengatebnb.com

Clientele: mixed gay/ straight
Type: b&b-inn; between Anchorage & Denali; 2 minutes from Glenn Parks Hwy junction; "enjoy affordable luxury w/ outstanding mtn views"
Owned/ Run By: lesbian
Rooms: 6
Baths: private & shared

Meals: full brkfst
Amenities: free parking, laundry, hot tub, DVDs/ videos, WiFi
Kids: welcome
Pets: welcome; please reserve in advance
Smoking: no
Rates: $79-159
AC: 10%

A Crescent Harbor Hideaway   *Sitka*

709 Lincoln St
Sitka, AK 99835
907/ 747-4900
www.sitkabedandbreakfast.com

Clientele: gay-friendly
Type: b&b; restored historic waterfront home
Owned/ Run By: straights
Rooms: 2

Baths: private
Meals: expanded cont'l brkfst
Smoking: no
Rates: $90-165

Susa's Serendipity Ranch   *Apache Junction*

4375 E Superstition Blvd
Apache Junction, AZ 85219
480/ 288-9333
www.susasranch.com

Clientele: women
Type: furnished units overlooking Superstition Mtns; semi-secluded yet near downtown Phoenix; game & exercise rms; 2 RV hookups
Owned/ Run By: lesbians
Rooms: 6

Baths: private
Amenities: free parking, laundry, outdoor hot tub, DVDs/ videos
Pets: welcome in some units
Smoking: no
Rates: $60-85/ night; $1,500/ month

Casa de San Pedro B&B   *Bisbee*

8933 S Yell Ln
Hereford, AZ 85615
520/ 366-1300 888/ 257-2050
www.bedandbirds.com

Clientele: gay-friendly
Type: b&b-inn; SE Arizona hacienda on the San Pedro River; ideal for birding, hiking & relaxing
Owned/ Run By: gay men
Rooms: 10
Baths: private
Wheelchair Access: yes, 2 rms
Meals: full brkfst

Amenities: free parking, laundry, pool, outdoor hot tub, WiFi
Kids: over 12 yrs welcome
Pets: 1 rm (must have own pet bed &/ or crate)
Smoking: no
Rates: $139-155+tax
AC: 10%

Copper Queen Hotel   *Bisbee*

PO Drawer CQ
Bisbee, AZ 85603
520/ 432-2216
www.copperqueen.com

Clientele: gay-friendly
Type: hotel; fully restored historical landmark; fine dining, fun staff, elegant surroundings, timeless ambience; "Old World charm in the New West"
Rooms: 48
Baths: private

Wheelchair Access: yes, 1 rm
Amenities: free parking, pool
Kids: welcome
Pets: no
Smoking: ok (in some areas)
Rates: $95-176
AC: 10%

David's Oasis Camping Resort   *Bisbee*

5311 W Double Adobe Rd
McNeal, AZ 85617
520/ 979-6659
azgaycamping.com

Type: private, members-only campground; 21+; located on 120-acre ranch in S Arizona; exclusively LGBT & friends
Kids: no

Pets: welcome on leash
Smoking: ok
Rates: $10-18

Hotel Monte Vista
Flagstaff

100 N San Francisco St
Flagstaff, AZ 86001
928/ 779-6971 800/ 545-3068
www.hotelmontevista.com

Clientele: gay-friendly
Type: hotel; historic lodging, circa 1927, w/ vibrant, lively & colorful past; located in downtown Flagstaff; walk to shops & fine dining
Owned/ Run By: straights
Rooms: 46

Baths: private & shared
Meals: coffee/tea only
Kids: welcome
Pets: welcome; fee
Smoking: ok
Rates: $55-160

Inn at 410
Flagstaff

410 N Leroux St
Flagstaff, AZ 86001-4549
520/ 774-0088 800/ 774-2008
www.inn410.com

Type: elegant 1894 estate home w/ 9 individually designed rms & suites; walk to historic downtown shops, restaurants & bars; summer garden dining; "named best in N Arizona by *Frommer's Grand Canyon*"
Rooms: 9
Baths: private

Wheelchair Access: yes, 1 rm
Meals: full brkfst
Amenities: free parking, DVDs/ videos, WiFi
Kids: over 5 yrs welcome
Smoking: nowhere on property
Rates: $150-210
AC: 10%

Starlight Pines B&B
Flagstaff

3380 E Lockett Rd
Flagstaff, AZ 86004
928/ 527-1912 800/ 752-1912
www.starlightpinesbb.com

Clientele: gay-friendly
Type: b&b-inn; romantic Victorian-styled home w/ Tiffany theme throughout
Owned/ Run By: gay men
Rooms: 4
Baths: private
Meals: full brkfst

Amenities: free parking, DVDs/ videos, WiFi
Kids: call for details
Pets: no
Smoking: no
Rates: $125-155
AC: 10%

The Cottage Inn Jerome
Jerome

PO Box 823
Jerome, AZ 86331
928/ 634-0701 928/ 649-6759
cottageinnjerome.com

Clientele: mixed gay/ straight
Type: b&b; also have apt for longer stays w/ kitchen
Owned/ Run By: gay man
Rooms: 2
Baths: private
Meals: full brkfst

Kids: welcome
Pets: welcome
Smoking: ok
Rates: $75 (b&b) – 95 (apt)
AC: 10%

Kings Inn Best Western
Kingman

2930 E Andy Devine
Kingman, AZ 86401
928/ 753-6101 800/ 750-6101

Clientele: gay-friendly
Type: motel; bakery on premises
Rooms: 101
Baths: private
Wheelchair Access: yes, 3 rms
Meals: expanded cont'l brkfst
Amenities: free parking, laundry, pool,

sauna, indoor hot tub
Kids: welcome
Pets: welcome
Smoking: ok (smokefree rms available)
Rates: $60-95
AC: 10%

Nautical Inn
Lake Havasu City

1000 McCulloch Blvd
Lake Havasu City, AZ 86403
928/ 855-2141 800/ 892-2141
www.nauticalinn.com

Clientele: gay-friendly
Type: hotel; beachfront; full restaurant & bar; private beach & boat launch; close to London Bridge
Rooms: 139
Baths: private

Amenities: free parking, pool, outdoor hot tub
Kids: welcome
Rates: $69-489

Dreamkatchers of Lake Powell B&B

Lake Powell

PO Box 5114
Page, AZ 86040
435/ 675-5828   888/ 479-9419
www.dreamkatchersbandb.com

Clientele: mixed gay/ straight
Type: b&b; sit in outdoor hot tub under the Milky Way & watch the shooting stars; 2 hrs from major nat'l parks; 7 miles from Lake Powell
Owned/ Run By: gay & straight
Rooms: 3

Baths: private
Meals: full brkfst
Amenities: free parking, laundry, outdoor hot tub, DVDs/ videos
Rates: $65-120
AC: 10%

Arizona Royal Villa Complex

Phoenix

4312 N 12th St
Phoenix, AZ 85014

602/ 266-6883
888/ 266-6884

www.RoyalVilla.com

Clientele: men
Type: resort; "largest & most popular property in town"; nonsmoking rms & clothing-optional throughout; $10 day passes
Owned/ Run By: gay men
Nearby Attractions: centrally located to all attractions: walk to bars, restaurants & baths
Transit: near public transit; 10 minutes to airport
Rooms: 19 total, queens, A/C, color TV, cable, wetbar, refrigerator, safer sex supplies, maid service
Baths: private, showers
Amenities: office hrs: 9am-9pm; free parking, laundry, pool, outdoor hot tub, WiFi
Kids: no
Pets: no
Smoking: no
Reservations: required *Cancellation:* cancel by 2 days prior or forfeit 1 night *Check in/ out:* 2pm/ 11am

Payment: cash, travelers checks, Visa, Amex, MC, Diners Club
Season: open yr-round

Rates: $80-130 *Discounts:* weekly, seniors & monthly
AC: 10%

Arizona Sunburst Inn

Phoenix

6245 N 12th Pl
Phoenix, AZ 85014
602/ 274-1474   800/ 974-1474
www.azsunburst.com

Clientele: men
Type: b&b-inn; "a man's b&b in the heart of Phoenix"; close to everything; check out the website
Owned/ Run By: gay men
Rooms: 7
Baths: private & shared

Meals: expanded cont'l brkfst
Amenities: free parking, pool, poolside mist, hot tub, massage, DVDs/ videos
Kids: no
Pets: no
Smoking: no
Rates: $69 & up

Claremont House B&B

Phoenix

502 W Claremont Ave
Phoenix, AZ 85013-1309
602/ 249-2974
www.claremonthousephoenix.com

Clientele: mostly men
Type: b&b-private home; clothing-optional indoors & out
Owned/ Run By: gay men
Rooms: 3
Baths: private & shared
Wheelchair Access: yes, 3 rms

Meals: full brkfst
Amenities: free parking, laundry, pool, outdoor hot tub, DVDs/ videos
Pets: small pets only
Smoking: no
Rates: $70-90

Clarendon Hotel & Suites
Phoenix

401 W Clarendon Ave
Phoenix, AZ 85013
602/ 252-7363
www.theclarendon.net

Clientele: mixed gay/ straight
Type: hotel; modern boutique hotel in midtown, just N of downtown; "in the heart of the action"
Owned/ Run By: gay men
Rooms: 110
Baths: private

Wheelchair Access: yes, 2 rms
Meals: cont'l brkfst
Amenities: free parking, pool, outdoor hot tub
Kids: welcome
Pets: no
Rates: $89-149

Hotel San Carlos
Phoenix

202 N Central Ave
Phoenix, AZ 85004
602/ 253-4121 866/ 253-4121
www.hotelsancarlos.com

Clientele: gay-friendly
Type: hotel; "downtown Phoenix's historic boutique hotel"; rooftop pool, restaurant
Rooms: 121
Baths: private
Wheelchair Access: yes, some rms

Meals: cont'l brkfst
Kids: welcome
Pets: no
Smoking: ok (some nonsmoking rms)
Rates: $79-289

Maricopa Manor B&B Inn
Phoenix

15 W Pasadena Ave
Phoenix, AZ 85013
602/ 274-6302 800/ 292-6403
www.maricopamanor.com

Clientele: mixed gay/ straight
Type: b&b-private home; upscale private estate in heart of N Central Phoenix; close to the gay scene
Owned/ Run By: gay men
Rooms: 7
Baths: private

Wheelchair Access: yes, 6 rms
Meals: expanded cont'l brkfst
Amenities: free parking, pool, outdoor hot tub, DVDs/ videos
Kids: 12 yrs & up welcome
Rates: $99-224
AC: 10%

Yum Yum Tree Guest House
Phoenix

90 W Virginia Ave #1
Phoenix, AZ 85003-1000
602/ 265-2590 877/ 986-8733
www.yytguesthouse.com

Clientele: mixed gay/ straight
Type: guesthouse; recommended by *New York Times*; in historic Central Phoenix; restored Fairhope School; on Nat'l Register of Historic Places
Owned/ Run By: gay men

Rooms: 5
Baths: private
Meals: coffee/tea only
Amenities: free parking, laundry, pool
Rates: $89-139
AC: 10%

Briar Wreath Inn B&B
Prescott

232 S Arizona Ave
Prescott, AZ 86303
928/ 778-6048 877/ 778-6048
www.briarwreath.com

Clientele: mixed gay/ straight
Type: b&b-inn; delightful 1904 Craftsman bungalow w/ an English Country atmosphere; walking distance to downtown
Owned/ Run By: gay men

Rooms: 4
Baths: private
Meals: full brkfst
Amenities: free parking, outdoor hot tub, massage, DVDs/ videos, WiFi
Rates: $110-165

Best Western Scottsdale Airpark Suites
Scottsdale

7515 E Butherus Dr
Scottsdale, AZ 85260
480/ 951-4000
www.scottsdalebestwestern.com

Clientele: gay-friendly
Type: hotel; in North Scottsdale's prestigious resort area, across from Kierland Commons upper-end shopping
Owned/ Run By: gay & straight
Rooms: 120
Baths: private
Wheelchair Access: yes, 2 rms

Meals: full brkfst
Amenities: free parking, laundry, pool, outdoor hot tub, gym, WiFi
Kids: welcome
Pets: no
Smoking: no
Rates: $59-189
AC: 10%

James Hotel
Scottsdale

7353 E Indian School Rd
Scottsdale, AZ 8521
480/ 308-1100 888/ 500-8080
www.jameshotel.com

Clientele: gay-friendly
Type: resort; hip boutique hotel & conference facility; deluxe amenities
Owned/ Run By: gay & straight
Rooms: 194

Baths: private
Amenities: pool, hot tub, gym
Pets: no
Smoking: no

A-Lodge at Sedona—A Luxury B&B Inn
Sedona

125 Kallof Pl
Sedona, AZ 86336
928/ 204-1942 800/ 619-4467
www.lodgeatsedona.com

Clientele: mixed gay/ straight
Type: b&b-inn; health club & heated pool privileges; 5-course gourmet brkfst
Owned/ Run By: straights
Rooms: 14
Baths: private
Wheelchair Access: yes, 1 rm
Meals: full brkfst

Amenities: free parking, pool, hot tub, massage, DVDs/ videos
Kids: 11 yrs & up welcome
Pets: well-behaved dogs w/ written agreement
Smoking: 100% smokefree
Rates: $160-325
AC: 10%

Iris Garden Inn
Sedona

390 Jordan Rd
Sedona, AZ 86336
928/ 282-2552 800/ 321-8988
www.irisgardeninn.com

Clientele: mixed gay/ straight
Type: inn; casual atmosphere; walk to art galleries, shopping & fine restaurants; garden area & views of Red Rock Mtns
Owned/ Run By: gay men
Rooms: 8
Baths: private
Wheelchair Access: yes, 1 rm

Meals: coffee/tea only
Amenities: laundry, hot tub, WiFi
Kids: welcome; under 12 yrs free
Pets: welcome; one-time $50 fee
Smoking: no
Rates: $74-125
AC: 10%

Southwest Inn at Sedona
Sedona

3250 W Hwy 89-A
Sedona, AZ 86336
928/ 282-3344 800/ 483-7422
www.swinn.com

Clientele: gay-friendly
Type: b&b-inn; Santa Fe-style architecture; spa; internet cafe
Owned/ Run By: straights
Rooms: 28
Baths: private
Wheelchair Access: yes, 2 rms
Meals: expanded cont'l brkfst

Amenities: free parking, pool, outdoor hot tub, massage, DVDs/ videos, gym, WiFi
Kids: welcome; under 12 yrs free
Pets: no
Smoking: totally smokefree
Rates: $119-239
AC: 10%

Two Angels Guesthouse
Sedona

PO Box 669
Sedona, AZ 86336
928/ 204-2083
www.twoangelshealing.com

Clientele: mixed gay/ lesbian
Type: guesthouse; red rock mtn views, gardens, private deck; near shopping, dining & outdoor activities; "experience the magic of Sedona's vortex energies!"
Owned/ Run By: lesbians
Rooms: 1

Baths: private
Meals: coffee/tea only
Amenities: hot tub, massage, DVDs/ videos
Kids: please inquire
Smoking: no
Rates: $115

Armory Park Guesthouse
Tucson

219 S 5th Ave
Tucson, AZ 85701
520/ 206-9252
www.armorypark.com

Clientele: gay-friendly
Type: b&b; renovated 1896 owner's residence w/ 2 detached guest units; situated in a lush courtyard garden setting in the historic Armory Park neighborhood
Owned/ Run By: gay men

Rooms: 2 (includes 1 bdrm w/ sitting area & 1 suite w/ kitchenette)
Baths: private
Meals: expanded cont'l brkfst
Amenities: laundry, hot tub, DVDs/ videos
Rates: $60-110

La Casita Del Sol
Tucson

407 N Myer Ave
Tucson, AZ 85701
520/ 623-8882
www.tucsoncasita.com

Clientele: mixed gay/ straight
Type: guesthouse; 2-rm historic 1880s adobe guesthouse; fully equipped w/ bdrm/ sitting rm, kitchen, clawfoot tub/ rain shower, A/C, satellite TV
Owned/ Run By: gay men
Rooms: 1

Baths: private
Kids: no
Pets: welcome w/ prior permission; deposit required
Smoking: no
Rates: $85-95

Catalina Park Inn
Tucson

309 E 1st St
Tucson, AZ 85705
520/ 792-4541 800/ 792-4885
www.catalinaparkinn.com

Clientele: mixed gay/ straight
Type: b&b-inn; historic district mansion, circa 1927; w/ beautiful rms, wonderful gardens, superb central location near U of A
Owned/ Run By: gay men
Rooms: 6

Baths: private
Meals: full brkfst
Kids: 10 yrs & up welcome
Pets: no
Smoking: no
Rates: $126-166

Hacienda del Sol Guest Ranch Resort
Tucson

5601 N Hacienda del Sol Rd
Tucson, AZ 85718
520/ 299-1501 800/ 728-6514
www.haciendadelsol.com

Clientele: gay-friendly
Type: resort; historic resort & delightful escape; private girls school in 1930s then exclusive guest ranch for Hollywood luminaries (a hideaway for Tracy & Hepburn)

Rooms: 31 (includes casitas)
Wheelchair Access: yes
Amenities: free parking, pool, massage
Rates: $99-495

Hotel Congress
Tucson

311 E Congress
Tucson, AZ 85701
520/ 622-8848 800/ 722-8848
www.hotelcongress.com

Clientele: mixed gay/ straight
Type: hotel; historic, railroad era, built in 1919; upscale cafe & busy nightclub on premises
Owned/ Run By: gay & straight
Rooms: 40
Baths: private

Meals: full brkfst
Kids: welcome
Pets: welcome; $10 fee
Smoking: ok
Rates: $59-109
AC: 10%

Milagras Guesthouse
Tucson

11185 W Calle Pima
Tucson, AZ 85743
520/ 578-8577
home.earthlink.net/~milagras/

Clientele: mixed gay/ straight
Type: guesthouse; in rural setting; 30 minutes from Tucson; w/ kitchenette, private patio, central courtyard
Owned/ Run By: lesbians
Rooms: 2 (1 couple at a time)
Baths: private

Wheelchair Access: yes, 1 rm
Amenities: free parking, laundry, outdoor hot tub, DVDs/ videos
Kids: call ahead
Pets: please call ahead to arrange
Smoking: no
Rates: $75-100 (cash or check)

Montecito House
Tucson

PO Box 42352
Tucson, AZ 85733
520/ 795-7592

Clientele: gay-friendly
Type: b&b-private home; "experience the friendly, relaxed atmosphere of Montecito House, my home, not a resort"
Owned/ Run By: lesbians
Rooms: 2
Baths: private & shared

Meals: cont'l brkfst
Kids: please inquire
Smoking: no
Rates: $375/ week

Natural B&B & Retreat   *Tucson*

520/ 881-4582 888/ 295-8500
www.tucsonnatural.com

Clientele: mixed gay/ straight (mostly men)
Type: b&b-private home; private sunbathing; clothing-optional & tantric therapeutic massage
Owned/ Run By: gay man
Rooms: 4
Baths: private & shared

Meals: full brkfst
Amenities: laundry, DVDs/ videos, WiFi
Kids: 6 yrs & up welcome; $15 fee
Pets: please inquire
Smoking: no
Rates: $65-90
AC: 10%

Royal Elizabeth B&B Inn   *Tucson*

204 S Scott Ave
Tucson, AZ 85701
520/ 670-9022 877/ 670-9022
www.royalelizabeth.com

Clientele: mixed gay/ straight
Type: b&b-inn; in historic 1878 downtown mansion; spacious suites; centrally located
Owned/ Run By: gay men
Rooms: 6 (includes 4 two-rm suites)
Baths: private
Meals: full brkfst

Amenities: free parking, laundry, pool, outdoor hot tub, massage, DVDs/ videos
Kids: welcome
Pets: no
Smoking: no
Rates: $115-215
AC: 10%

1905 Basin Park Hotel   *Eureka Springs*

12 Spring St
Eureka Springs, AR 72632
479/ 253-7837 877/ 643-4972
www.basinpark.com

Clientele: mixed gay/ straight
Type: 1905 historic hotel w/ jacuzzi suites & restaurant/ spa access
Owned/ Run By: straights
Rooms: 61
Baths: private
Wheelchair Access: yes, 1 rm

Meals: cont'l brkfst
Amenities: pool, hot tub, massage, WiFi
Kids: welcome
Pets: under 25 lbs in some rms; $10/ night
Smoking: ok
Rates: $89-199
AC: 10%

Candlestick Cottage Inn   *Eureka Springs*

6 Douglas St
Eureka Springs, AR 72632
479/ 253-6813 800/ 835-5184
www.candlestickcottageinn.com

Clientele: gay-friendly
Type: b&b; Victorian home in quiet, wooded hollow; walk to downtown Eureka Springs
Owned/ Run By: lesbians
Rooms: 6
Baths: private

Meals: full brkfst
Amenities: laundry, hot tub, WiFi
Kids: not suitable for small children
Pets: welcome; call first for approval
Rates: $79-145
AC: 10%

Cliff Cottage Inn & Eureka Springs Cottages   *Eureka Springs*

479/ 253-7409 800/ 799-7409
www.cliffcottage.com

Clientele: mixed gay/ straight
Type: b&b-inn; in the very heart of downtown; large jacuzzi suites & hot tub cottages; fireplaces
Owned/ Run By: gay & straight
Rooms: 8
Baths: private
Meals: gourmet brkfst delivered to your door

Amenities: free parking, outdoor hot tub & jacuzzis, massage, DVDs/ videos, WiFi
Kids: 11 yrs & up welcome
Pets: no
Smoking: no
Rates: $189-230
AC: 10% (Mon-Th bookings only)

Eureka House ⌨   *Eureka Springs*

369 County Rd 207
Eureka Springs, AR 72632
479/ 253-4080 800/ 862-6320
www.eurekahouse.com

Clientele: mixed gay/ straight
Type: rental home; private luxury home on 12 acres sleeps up to 6; full kitchen; 2-car garage; entertainment rm; tree-top views
Owned/ Run By: lesbians
Rooms: 2
Baths: private

Amenities: laundry, DVDs/ videos, WiFi
Kids: welcome
Pets: no
Smoking: no
Rates: $165-225
AC: 15%

Gardener's Cottage
Eureka Springs

c/o 11 Singleton
Eureka Springs, AR 72632
479/ 253-9111   800/ 833-3394
www.singletonhouse.com

Clientele: mixed gay/ straight
Type: cottage; private country cottage for 2; jacuzzi tub & separate shower; fireplace, full kitchen, porch w/ hammock & swing; walk to shops, cafes, clubs
Owned/ Run By: woman
Rooms: 1

Baths: private
Meals: coffee/tea only
Kids: well-behaved welcome
Pets: no
Smoking: no
Rates: $125-145
AC: 10%

Heart of the Hills Inn
Eureka Springs

5 Summit
Eureka Springs, AR 72632
479/ 253-7468   800/ 253-7468
www.heartofthehillsinn.com

Type: b&b-inn; built in 1883 & located on historic loop; w/in walking distance or trolley ride of downtown; private decks & entrances
Rooms: 3
Baths: private
Meals: full brkfst

Amenities: hot tub, DVDs/ videos
Kids: welcome w/ prior approval
Pets: no
Smoking: no (porches only)
Rates: $80-139
AC: 5-10%

Ozark Real Log Homes
Eureka Springs

170 W Van Buren
Eureka Springs, AR 72632
479/ 253-7344 (cabin enquiries)
479/ 253-7321 (log homes)
www.ozarkrealloghomes.com

Clientele: women
Type: cabin; quiet & romantic log cabin (sleeps up to 6 but couples preferred); galley kitchen; surrounded by nature walks that lead to lake; private boatdock; canoe & boat rentals

Owned/ Run By: lesbians
Rooms: 1 (cabin)
Baths: private
Amenities: jacuzzi tub for 2
Rates: $125 (for a couple)

Pond Mountain Lodge & Resort
Eureka Springs

1218 Hwy 23 S
Eureka Springs, AR 72632
479/ 253-5877
800/ 583-8043
info@pondmountainlodge.com
www.pondmountainlodge.com

Clientele: mixed gay/ straight
Type: resort; w/ suites & cabins; formerly an estate now designed for relaxation, comfort & romance
Owned/ Run By: lesbian & straight
Nearby Attractions: 3 miles to Passion Play & downtown Eureka Springs
Transit: 2 hrs to Tulsa, OK airport; 1 mile to local trolleys; rental car recommended
Rooms: 8 (includes 3 cabins w/ kitchens & 5 suites w/ kitchen or snack center) total, suites, 4 kings, 4 queens, A/C, color TV, DVD/ VCR, cable TV (5), ceiling fan, fireplace, deck (6), phone (1), refrigerator, maid service, microwave, coffee service
Baths: private, bathtubs, showers, whirlpools, robes
Wheelchair Access: yes, 1 rm
Meals: catered dinners, picnic baskets
Amenities: hot tub, DVDs/ videos, snacks, coffee/ tea, heated swimming pool, fishing ponds, riding stables, billiards rm, meditation sites, hiking trails; also vow/ commitment ceremonies
Kids: welcome in family suites & cabins
Pets: welcome in some units w/ advance notice; $35-50 fee (nonrefundable)

Pets On Premises: 1 dog
Smoking: no
Reservations: recommended (March-Oct) *Deposit:* required, 50%, due at booking, personal check ok *Cancellation:* cancel by 8 days prior or forfeit deposit; all cancellations carry $20 fee *Minimum Stay:* 2 nights (certain wknds)

Payment: cash, travelers checks, personal checks, Visa, MC
Season: open yr-round *High season:* April-Nov
Rates: $89-170 *Discounts:* multiple units, multiple nights
AC: 10% upon invoice

Palace Hotel & Bath House

Eureka Springs

135 Spring St
Eureka Springs, AR 72632
479/ 253-7474
www.palacehotelbathhouse.com

Type: an elegant little hotel w/ suites for 2; the historic bathhouse offers mineral baths, eucalyptus steam treatments & clay masks
Rooms: 8
Baths: private

Meals: cont'l brkfst
Amenities: free parking, hot tub, massage
Smoking: ok
Rates: $140-165
AC: 10%

TradeWinds

Eureka Springs

141 W Van Buren
Eureka Springs, AR 72632
479/ 253-9774 800/ 242-1615
www.eurekatradewinds.com

Clientele: mixed gay/ straight
Type: motel; "traditional Southern hospitality meets midcentury modernism"; a lodge reminiscent of motor inn of the '40s & '50s w/ modern luxuries & elegance
Owned/ Run By: gay men
Rooms: 9
Baths: private

Meals: coffee/tea only
Amenities: free parking, pool, hot tub
Kids: welcome
Pets: no
Smoking: ok
Rates: $49-150

The Veranda Inn B&B

Eureka Springs

38 Prospect Ave
Eureka Springs, AR 72632
479/ 253-7292 888/ 295-2171
www.theverandainn.com

Clientele: mixed gay/ straight
Type: b&b-inn; spacious 1899 Southern Colonial Revival mansion; award-winning residential b&b; located in Historic District; also small weddings & receptions
Owned/ Run By: gay men
Rooms: 5

Baths: private
Meals: 5-course gourmet brkfst
Kids: no
Pets: no
Smoking: no
Rates: $159-195

The Woods Resort

Eureka Springs

50 Wall St
Eureka Springs, AR 72632
479/ 253-8281
www.eureka-usa.com/woods

Clientele: mixed gay/ lesbian
Type: resort; Craftsman-style treehouse cottages: 1- & 2-bdrm; w/ walkout decks; beautiful views of woods & wildlife; fireplaces; treehouse hot tub
Owned/ Run By: gay men
Rooms: 5
Baths: private

Meals: coffee/tea only
Amenities: free parking, hot tub, massage, DVDs/ videos
Kids: no
Pets: welcome w/ prior approval
Smoking: no
Rates: $115-135

Foxglove B&B

Helena

229 Beech
Helena, AR 72342-3401
870/ 338-9391 800/ 863-1926
www.bbonline.com/ar/foxglove

Clientele: gay-friendly
Type: b&b-inn; circa 1900 mansion located on ridge overlooking Helena; luxury rms furnished in antiques
Owned/ Run By: straights
Rooms: 6
Baths: private

Meals: full brkfst
Amenities: free parking, hot tub
Kids: 12 yrs & up welcome
Smoking: no
Rates: $89-119
AC: 10%

The Rose Cottage

Hot Springs

218 Court St
Hot Springs, AR 71901
501/ 623-6449
www.andrea-rose.com

Clientele: gay-friendly
Type: b&b; 117-yr-old historic Victorian row house; for 2 or group; 2 blks from historic downtown; house prepared for 1 night or 1 month
Owned/ Run By: straights
Rooms: 2
Baths: private

Meals: expanded cont'l brkfst
Amenities: free parking, laundry, hot tub, massage
Kids: welcome
Pets: welcome
Smoking: ok
Rates: $185

Legacy Hotel & Suites
Little Rock

625 W Capitol Ave
Little Rock, AR 72201
501/ 374-0100
www.legacyhotel.com

Clientele: gay-friendly
Type: full-service hotel on Historic Register; gourmet coffee shop & lounge; w/in walking distance of LGBT club & bars
Owned/ Run By: straights
Rooms: 92
Baths: private
Wheelchair Access: yes, 4 rms

Meals: cont'l brkfst
Amenities: free parking, laundry, hot tub, massage, DVDs/ videos, WiFi
Kids: welcome; must be w/ an adult
Pets: no
Smoking: ok
Rates: $79-189
AC: 10%

Black Oak Resort
Mountain Home

PO Box 100
Oakland, AR 72661
870/ 431-8363
www.blackoakresort.com

Clientele: mixed gay/ straight
Type: resort; quiet mtn resort bordering Bull Shoals Lake
Owned/ Run By: straights
Rooms: 10
Amenities: free parking, laundry, pool, indoor hot tub

Kids: welcome
Pets: welcome
Smoking: ok
Rates: $87-165

Imperial Hotel
Amador City

PO Box 212
Amador City, CA 95601-0212
209/ 267-9172
www.imperialamador.com

Clientele: gay-friendly
Type: hotel; in brick Victorian from Gold Rush era; home to regionally acclaimed restaurant & Oasis bar (Wed-Sun)
Owned/ Run By: gay men
Rooms: 6

Baths: private
Kids: no
Pets: no
Smoking: no (balconies & patio ok)
Rates: $100-140

Dorrington Inn at Big Trees
Arnold

3450 Hwy 4, PO Box 4446
Dorrington, CA 95223
209/ 795-2164 888/ 874-2164
www.Dorringtoninn.com

Clientele: mixed gay/ straight
Type: b&b; w/ 6 cottages & 2 rms; Gold Country brkfst included
Owned/ Run By: gay men
Rooms: 8
Baths: private

Meals: expanded cont'l brkfst
Kids: very well-behaved only
Pets: dogs welcome in chalet
Rates: $59-229
AC: 10%

Alpine Retreats
Big Bear Lake

433 Edgemoor
Big Bear Lake, CA 92315
909/ 725-4192
909/ 878-4155 (reservations)
www.alpineretreats.com

Clientele: mixed gay/ straight
Type: guesthouse; romantic guesthouses in Old Chapel w/ beautiful mtn decor; also rental homes (sleep up to 15)
Owned/ Run By: gay men
Rooms: 5 (includes 3 one-bdrm units & 2 four-bdrm units)

Baths: private
Amenities: hot tub, DVDs/ videos
Kids: welcome
Pets: small dogs welcome
Smoking: no
Rates: $135-225

Grey Squirrel Resort
Big Bear Lake

39372 Big Bear Blvd
Big Bear Lake, CA 92315
909/ 866-4335 800/ 381-5569
www.greysquirrel.com

Clientele: mixed gay/ straight
Type: private rental homes & cabins; all close to resort, lake & each other in park-like setting; many family reunions
Owned/ Run By: lesbians
Rooms: 20 (cabins) & 30 (vacation homes)
Baths: private

Meals: coffee/tea only
Amenities: laundry, pool, indoor hot tub
Kids: welcome
Pets: welcome; $100 deposit; $10 per night
Smoking: ok (some cabins)
Rates: $85-675
AC: AAA only

Knickerbocker Mansion Country Inn
Big Bear Lake

869 Knickerbocker Rd
Big Bear Lake, CA 92315
909/ 878-9190 877/ 423-1180
www.knickerbockermansion.com

Clientele: mixed gay/ straight
Type: b&b-inn; in historic 1920 log mansion in San Bernardino Mtns; yr-round resort w/ snow & lake skiing; massage by request & booking
Owned/ Run By: gay men
Rooms: 11
Baths: private

Wheelchair Access: yes, 1 rm
Meals: full brkfst
Amenities: hot tub, DVDs/ videos, WiFi
Kids: no
Pets: no
Smoking: no
Rates: $110-250
AC: 10%

Majestic Moose Lodge
Big Bear Lake

39328 Big Bear Blvd
Big Bear Lake, CA 92315
909/ 866-2435 877/ 585-5855
majesticmooselodge.com

Clientele: gay-friendly
Type: resort; beautiful Big Bear Lake & Ski Mtn provide yr-round activities; fully equipped cabins sleep 2-8; some w/ jacuzzis; game rm; groups welcome!
Owned/ Run By: gay & straight
Rooms: 21
Baths: private

Meals: coffee/tea only (in rms)
Amenities: free parking, pool, sauna, hot tub, DVDs/ videos
Kids: welcome
Pets: $10 deposit per pet per night
Smoking: no
Rates: $99-209
AC: 10%

Rainbow View Lodge
Big Bear Lake

2726 View Dr
Running Springs, CA 92382
909/ 867-1810 888/ 868-1810
www.RainbowViewLodge.com

Clientele: mixed gay/ straight
Type: cabin; cottages w/ themed decor
Owned/ Run By: women
Rooms: 6
Baths: private

Kids: welcome
Pets: dogs only; deposit required
Smoking: no
Rates: $69-149

Lucia Lodge
Big Sur

62400 Hwy 1
Big Sur, CA 93920
831/ 667-2391 866/ 424-4787
www.lucialodge.com

Clientele: gay-friendly
Type: rustic cabins (no telephones or televisions) on a cliff 300 ft above sea; unparalleled views; also yr-round restaurant & Rockslide Lounge
Rooms: 10 (cabins)

Baths: private
Meals: cont'l brkfst
Smoking: no
Rates: $100-250

Burney Mountain Guest Ranch
Burney

PO Box 1418
Burney, CA 96013
530/ 335-4087
www.burneymtn.com

Clientele: gay-friendly
Type: cabin; close to casting pond & some of the best fly-fishing in the state; cont'l brkfst & family-friendly buffet dinner served in main lodge
Owned/ Run By: lesbians/ gay men
Rooms: 8
Baths: private

Wheelchair Access: yes, 1 rm
Meals: cont'l brkfst
Kids: welcome
Pets: no
Smoking: no
Rates: $175-300/ night
AC: 10%

Blue Dolphin Inn ⓣⓐⓖ
Cambria

6470 Moonstone Beach Dr
Cambria, CA 93428
805/ 927-3300 800/ 222-9157
www.moonstonehotels.com

Type: inn; romance & charm w/ delightfully uncommon decor on Cambria's Moonstone Beach; choose an oceanfront rm for spectacular views from your patio
Rooms: 20
Baths: private
Wheelchair Access: yes, 1 rm

Meals: cont'l brkfst
Kids: welcome
Pets: no
Smoking: no
Rates: $89-319
AC: 10%

Cambria Pines Lodge
2905 Burton Pl
Cambria, CA 93428

Cambria
info@cambriapineslodge.com
www.moonstonehotels.com

805/ 927-4200
800/ 445-6868

Clientele: gay-friendly
Type: resort; nestled on 25 acres w/ world-class gardens above Cambria's East Village; w/ restaurant, lounge, day spa, hiking trails, garden workshops
Nearby Attractions: Hearst Castle, Big Sur, Piedras Blancas elephant seals, wine-tasting, shopping
Transit: 40 minutes to San Luis Obispo; shuttle: Ride-On Transportation, 800/ 958-7433
Rooms: 152 total, 61 suites, 30 kings, 66 queens, color TV, cable, fireplace (119), deck (42), phone, refrigerator (42), rm service, maid service, range from rustic cabins to deluxe suites featuring 2 fireplaces
Baths: private, bathtubs, showers, whirlpools, hairdryers
Wheelchair Access: yes, 3 rms
Meals: full brkfst
Amenities: indoor hot tub, indoor heated pool, full-service day spa, restaurant w/ homegrown organic produce, lounge w/ nightly entertainment

Recreation: hiking, biking, kayaking, wildlife-viewing
Kids: welcome
Pets: welcome in designated rms; $25 per pet
Pets On Premises: 2 cats
Smoking: no
Reservations: *Cancellation:* cancel by 3 days prior *Minimum Stay:* 2 nights (w/ Sat night) *Check in/ out:* 3pm/ 11am
Payment: cash, travelers checks, Visa, Amex, MC, Discover
Season: open yr-round *High season:* June 15-Sept 15
Rates: $89-329 *Discounts:* check our website for seasonal discounts & packages
AC: 10%

Pelican Cove Inn
6316 Moonstone Beach Dr
Cambria, CA 93428

Cambria
info@pelicansuites.com
www.moonstonehotels.com

805/ 927-1500
800/ 966-6490

Clientele: gay-friendly
Type: b&b-inn; elegance & romance; 4-Diamond service; breathtaking views of Moonstone Beach
Nearby Attractions: Cambria's West Village, Hearst Castle, Paso Robles Wine Country, Piedras Blancas Elephant Seal rookery, sea otter refuge, Morro Rock, Big Sur, wine tasting, antiquing, art galleries
Rooms: 48 total, 27 suites, 41 kings, 6 queens, color TV, DVD/ VCR, cable, ceiling fan, fireplace (26), phone, refrigerator, maid service, all suites & many rms have a patio or balcony w/ full or partial ocean views
Baths: private, bathtubs, showers, whirlpools, robes, hairdryers
Wheelchair Access: yes, 1 rm
Meals: full brkfst
Amenities: pool, massage, DVDs/ videos, afternoon tea & wine-tasting, evening dessert & coffee, concierge service, wine tour reservations
Kids: welcome
Pets: no

Reservations: required *Deposit:* credit card guarantee, due at booking *Cancellation:* cancel by 3 days prior or forfeit a % *Minimum Stay:* check w/ property *Check in/ out:* 3pm/ 11am
Payment: cash, travelers checks, Visa, Amex, MC, Discover

Season: open yr-round *High season:* June-Sept
Rates: $189-329 *Discounts:* check w/ property
AC: 10%

The J Patrick House B&B   *Cambria*

2990 Burton Dr
Cambria, CA 93428
805/ 927-3812 800/ 341-5258
www.jpatrickhouse.com

Clientele: gay-friendly
Type: b&b; award-winning authentic log home in the pines surrounded by country gardens
Owned/ Run By: straights
Rooms: 8
Baths: private

Meals: full brkfst
Kids: 13 yrs & up welcome (2 persons per rm only)
Pets: no
Smoking: no
Rates: $165-205
AC: please inquire

Leopold Cove   *Cambria*

2183 Sherwood Dr
Cambria, CA 93428
805/ 927-5396 800/ 240-2277
www.maisonsdecambria.com

Clientele: gay-friendly
Type: rental home; vacation home on a bluff overlooking the Pacific Ocean; located in the Central Coast wine district
Owned/ Run By: gay men
Rooms: 1

Baths: private
Kids: no
Pets: no
Smoking: no
Rates: $200

Sand Pebbles Inn TAG   *Cambria*

6252 Moonstone Beach Dr
Cambria, CA 93428
805/ 927-5600 800/ 222-9970
www.moonstonehotels.com

Clientele: gay-friendly
Type: b&b-inn; on Cambria's Moonstone Beach; elegant & romantic; each rm features a fireplace; many offer canopy bed & whirlpool tub
Rooms: 24

Baths: private
Wheelchair Access: yes, 1 rm
Kids: welcome
Pets: no
Rates: $89-299
AC: 10%

Sea Otter Inn TAG   *Cambria*

6656 Moonstone Beach Dr
Cambria, CA 93428
805/ 927-5888 800/ 966-6490
www.seaotterinn.com

Clientele: gay-friendly
Type: b&b-inn; all rms offer fireplace & warm country style; heated pool & spa; steps from Cambria's Moonstone Beach
Rooms: 25
Baths: private
Wheelchair Access: yes, 1 rm
Meals: cont'l brkfst

Amenities: free parking, pool, outdoor hot tub, DVDs/ videos
Kids: welcome
Pets: small animals welcome in designated rms; $25
Rates: $79-235
AC: 10%

Capistrano Seaside Inn   *Capistrano Beach*

34862 Pacific Coast Hwy
Capistrano Beach, CA 92624
949/ 496-1399
800/ 252-3224 (reservations only)
www.caposeasideinn.com

Clientele: gay-friendly
Type: b&b-inn; recently renovated & spotlessly clean; cottage-style, terraced rms; 180° ocean views
Owned/ Run By: straights
Rooms: 28
Baths: private
Wheelchair Access: yes, 6 rms

Meals: cont'l brkfst
Amenities: free parking, laundry, hot tub
Kids: welcome
Pets: welcome; fixed sanitation fee
Smoking: ok
Rates: $79-179
AC: 10% (if registration is over $500)

Carmel River Inn TAG   *Carmel*

Hwy 1 at Carmel River Bridge
Carmel, CA 93922
831/ 624-1575 800/ 966-6490
www.moonstonehotels.com

Clientele: gay-friendly
Type: inn & cottages; at the gateway to Big Sur; 1 mile from Carmel Village; rustic cottages on 10 acres of gardens, forest, meadow; pet-friendly
Rooms: 43
Baths: private

Kids: welcome
Pets: welcome in cottages only; $25 per night
Smoking: no
Rates: $79-329
AC: 10%

Edgewater Resort
Clear Lake

6420 Soda Bay Rd
Kelseyville, CA 95451
707/ 279-0208 800/ 396-6224
www.edgewaterresort.net

Clientele: mixed gay/ straight
Type: resort; cabins sleep 4-12 w/ full kitchens; 2 campsites; 59 RV sites w/ full hookup
Owned/ Run By: lesbians
Rooms: 8
Baths: private

Meals: coffee/tea only
Kids: welcome; $5/ day extra after 2 adults
Pets: welcome; $10/ day (cabins)/ $2.50 (camping); dogs must be leashed
Smoking: no
Rates: $30-450
AC: 10%

Lake Vacation Rentals
Clear Lake

601 N Main St
Lakeport, CA 95453
707/ 263-7188
www.clearlakevacations.com

Clientele: gay-friendly
Type: private vacation rentals all around Clear Lake; resort & b&b referrals
Owned/ Run By: gay men
Wheelchair Access: yes, 8 rms
Amenities: free parking, laundry, pool, sauna, outdoor hot tub

Pets: welcome in some units
Smoking: ok
Rates: $110-500
AC: 5-10%

Rocky Point Cottages
Clear Lake

3884 Lakeshore Blvd
Lakeport, CA 95453
707/ 263-5901
www.rockypointcottages.com

Clientele: gay-friendly
Type: resort; private 1920s-style lakefront resort on Clear Lake; cottages w/ private decks & patios; pier, boating, fishing, skiing, wineries, casinos & more
Owned/ Run By: gay & straight
Rooms: 5 (cottages)

Baths: private
Kids: welcome
Pets: welcome in some cottages
Smoking: no
Rates: $135-350

Sea Breeze Resort
Clear Lake

9595 Harbor Dr
Glenhaven, CA 95443
707/ 998-3327
www.seabreeze-resort.com

Clientele: mixed gay/ straight
Type: resort; wonderful lakefront location w/ beautifully landscaped grounds; impeccably clean cottages w/ fully equipped kitchens; super hospitality
Owned/ Run By: gay men
Rooms: 7

Baths: private
Wheelchair Access: yes, all rms
Meals: coffee/tea only
Kids: please inquire
Pets: no
Smoking: no
Rates: $95-140 (2-night minimum)

Asti Ranch
Cloverdale

25750 River Rd
Cloverdale, CA 95425
707/ 894-5960
joanmeisel@worldnet.att.net

Clientele: women
Type: cottage; w/ full kitchen; great privacy; near lake & river in Wine Country; tennis court
Pets: small dogs only

Smoking: no
Rates: $500-750/ week; $250-350/ wknds

Two Bunches Palm Resort & Spa
Desert Hot Springs

67425 Two Bunches Palm Trail
Desert Hot Springs, CA 92240
760/ 329-8791 800/ 472-4334
www.twobunchpalms.com

Clientele: gay-friendly
Type: resort; recently renovated rms, villas & casitas; some full kitchens; clothing-optional sun bins; 5-star restaurant, bar
Owned/ Run By: gay & straight
Rooms: 49
Baths: private
Wheelchair Access: yes, 35 rms

Meals: cont'l brkfst
Amenities: pool, sauna, outdoor hot tub, massage, DVDs/ videos, WiFi
Kids: no; quiet place; speak softly
Pets: service dogs only
Smoking: no
Rates: $150-1,500
AC: please inquire

Bates House B&B   *East Bay*

399 Bellevue Ave
Oakland, CA 94610-3433
510/ 893-3881
www.bateshouse.com

Clientele: mixed gay/ straight
Type: b&b-inn; restored 1907 Colonial revival mansion; located in historic Adams Point District by Lake Merritt & Lakeside Park
Owned/ Run By: gay man
Rooms: 5
Baths: private & shared

Meals: full brkfst
Amenities: free parking, massage, DVDs/ videos, WiFi
Kids: please inquire
Pets: no
Smoking: no
Rates: $99-199

Vacation Home Near San Francisco   *East Bay*

32462 Lake Ree St
Fremont, CA 94555
510/ 449-8255
maritzanevarez48@msn.com

Clientele: mixed gay/ lesbian
Type: rental home; spacious rental home 40 miles from San Francisco; drive to Napa, Half Moon Bay & the Sierras
Owned/ Run By: lesbians
Rooms: 3

Baths: private
Kids: welcome
Pets: welcome
Smoking: no
Rates: $200-300/ week

Washington Inn   *East Bay*

495 10th St
Oakland, CA 94607
510/ 452-1776
thewashingtoninn.com

Clientele: gay-friendly
Type: hotel; old Oakland landmark & historic boutique hotel at Oakland Convention Center; banquet/ mtg facilities; 15 minutes to SF via BART
Owned/ Run By: straights
Rooms: 47

Baths: private
Wheelchair Access: yes, 2 rms
Meals: full brkfst
Kids: welcome
Smoking: no
Rates: $89-178
AC: 10%

Woodfin Suite Hotel   *East Bay*

5800 Shellmound St
Emeryville, CA 94608
510/ 601-5880 888/ 433-9042
www.woodfinsuites.com/emeryville

Clientele: gay-friendly
Type: hotel; suites w/ fully equipped kitchen, dining rm, living rm
Owned/ Run By: gay & straight
Rooms: 202 (1- & 2-bdrm suites)
Baths: private
Wheelchair Access: yes, 3 rms

Meals: full brkfst
Amenities: free parking, laundry, pool, outdoor hot tub, DVDs/ videos
Pets: dogs under 75 lbs welcome
Smoking: no
Rates: $149-299
AC: 10%

Ocean Inn   *Encinitas*

1444 N Hwy 101
Leucadia, CA 92024
760/ 436-1988 800/ 546-1598
www.oceaninnhotel.com

Clientele: gay-friendly
Type: hotel; built in 1990 & located in quiet neighborhood setting; mission-style decor
Owned/ Run By: straights
Rooms: 50
Baths: private
Wheelchair Access: yes, 2 rms

Meals: cont'l brkfst
Kids: welcome
Pets: no
Smoking: ok
Rates: $69-189
AC: 10%

Abigail's Elegant Victorian Mansion B&B   *Eureka*

1406 C St
Eureka, CA 95501
707/ 444-3144
www.eureka-california.com

Clientele: gay-friendly
Type: b&b-inn, reservation service; an interior decorator's award-winning designer showcase; "a spectacular 1878 Nat'l Historic Landmark"
Owned/ Run By: straights
Rooms: 3

Baths: private & shared
Meals: full brkfst
Kids: 14 & up welcome
Pets: no
Smoking: no
Rates: $95-195

Carter House Victorians
Eureka

301 L St
Eureka, CA 95501
707/ 444-8062 800/ 404-1390
www.carterhouse.com

Clientele: gay-friendly
Type: b&b-inn; enclave of 4 unique inns, warm hospitality & opulent accommodations; w/ restaurant, wine/ gift shop
Owned/ Run By: straights
Rooms: 32
Baths: private
Wheelchair Access: yes, 1 rm

Meals: full brkfst
Amenities: free parking, laundry, hot tub, massage, DVDs/ videos
Kids: welcome
Pets: no
Smoking: no
Rates: $155-497
AC: 10%

Trinidad Bay B&B
Eureka

560 Edwards St
Trinidad, CA 95570
707/ 677-0840
www.trinidadbaybnb.com

Clientele: gay-friendly
Type: b&b; Cape Cod-style inn overlooking Trinidad Bay; king-sized beds, private baths, ocean & garden views
Owned/ Run By: gay/ lesbian & straight
Rooms: 4

Baths: private
Meals: full brkfst
Amenities: WiFi
Kids: welcome
Pets: crated/ not in rooms
Rates: $200

Collingwood Inn B&B
Ferndale

831 Main St
Ferndale, CA 95536
707/ 786-9219 800/ 469-1632
www.collingwoodinn.com

Clientele: gay-friendly
Type: b&b; historic Victorian inn; also cottages & houses; relax in the elegance & splendor of the Victorian era
Owned/ Run By: gay men
Rooms: 6 rms & 2 houses & 3 cottages
Baths: private

Wheelchair Access: yes, 1 rm
Meals: full brkfst
Amenities: free parking, laundry, WiFi
Kids: 13 yrs & up welcome
Pets: welcome
Smoking: no
Rates: $100-203

The Gingerbread Mansion Inn
Ferndale

400 Berding St, PO Box 1380
Ferndale, CA 95536
707/ 786-4000 800/ 952-4136
www.gingerbread-mansion.com

Clientele: gay-friendly
Type: b&b-inn; grand lady in the Victorian village of Ferndale w/ a beautifully restored interior
Owned/ Run By: gay/ lesbian & straight
Rooms: 11

Baths: private
Meals: full brkfst
Kids: 10 yrs & up; $40 for third person
Smoking: no
Rates: $130-400
AC: 10%

Aslan Beach House
Fort Bragg

24600 N Hwy 1
Fort Bragg, CA 95437
707/ 964-1952
www.aslanhouse.net

Clientele: gay-friendly
Type: beach house; on 4 acres w/ pond; partial ocean view; romance & privacy on the Mendocino Coast; 5 blks from ocean
Rooms: 2 (suites)
Baths: private

Kids: 10 yrs & up welcome
Pets: no dogs
Smoking: no
Rates: $94-160 + $12 extra person (4 max)
AC: 10% w/ full payment in advance

The Cleone Gardens Inn
Fort Bragg

24600 N Hwy 1
Fort Bragg, CA 95437
707/ 964-2788
800/ 400-2189 (N CA only)
www.cleonegardensinn.com

Clientele: mixed gay/ straight
Type: b&b-inn; romantic country garden retreat on 2.5 acres of gardens, forest, meadow, dunes & pasture; w/ kitchens, fireplaces, courtyards, decks, fountains
Owned/ Run By: gay & straight
Rooms: 10
Baths: private
Wheelchair Access: yes, 1 rm

Amenities: outdoor hot tub, DVDs/ videos
Kids: welcome; some family units; $12 per extra person
Pets: dogs welcome w/ prior approval; $6 fee (designated rms only)
Smoking: no
Rates: $86-130
AC: 10% w/ full payment in advance

The Weller House Inn   *Fort Bragg*

524 Stewart St
Fort Bragg, CA 95437
707/ 964-4415 877/ 893-5537
www.wellerhouse.com

Clientele: gay-friendly
Type: b&b-inn; sumptuous Victorian guest rms, English gardens & ocean views from the water tower; brkfst served in the famous ballroom!
Owned/ Run By: straights
Rooms: 9
Baths: private

Meals: full brkfst
Amenities: free parking, indoor hot tub, massage, DVDs/ videos
Kids: welcome in Karin's Rm only
Pets: no
Smoking: no
Rates: $115-180
AC: 10%

Brandybuck Ranch   *Gualala*

PO Box 266
Point Arena, CA 95468
707/ 882-2269
staplhorse@jps.net

Clientele: mixed gay/ straight
Type: b&b; also cabin w/ full kitchen; in redwoods 1 1/2 miles from beach; woodstove, VCR; 7 miles from Pt Arena & 12 miles from Gualala; seasonal (May-Oct)
Owned/ Run By: woman
Rooms: 1 in B&B & 2-rm cabin

Baths: private
Meals: cont'l brkfst (b&b)
Kids: no
Pets: no
Smoking: no (inside or out)
Rates: $125 (b&b) - 175 (cabin); also weekly rates

Breakers Inn   *Gualala*

39300 S Hwy 1
Gualala, CA 95445
707/ 884-3200 800/ 273-2537
www.breakersinn.com

Clientele: mixed gay/ straight
Type: b&b-inn; oceanfront rms w/ double-size spas, fireplaces, wet bars & decks w/ panoramic views; walk to shops, whale-watching
Owned/ Run By: women
Rooms: 27
Baths: private

Wheelchair Access: yes, 2 rms
Meals: expanded cont'l brkfst
Amenities: free parking, hot tub
Kids: welcome
Smoking: ok (in 2 rms)
Rates: $105-275
AC: 10%

North Coast Country Inn   *Gualala*

34591 S Hwy 1
Gualala, CA 95445
707/ 884-4537 800/ 959-4537
www.northcoastcountryinn.com

Clientele: gay-friendly
Type: b&b; a cluster of weathered bldgs on a forested hillside, overlooking the Mendocino Coast
Owned/ Run By: straights
Rooms: 6
Baths: private

Meals: full brkfst
Amenities: outdoor hot tub, massage
Kids: no
Pets: welcome w/ $50 deposit (refundable)
Smoking: no
Rates: $185-225
AC: 10%

Mill Rose Inn   *Half Moon Bay*

615 Mill St
Half Moon Bay, CA 94019
650/ 726-8750 800/ 900-7673
www.millroseinn.com

Clientele: gay-friendly
Type: b&b-inn; classic European elegance by the sea; AAA 4-Diamond Award for Excellence
Owned/ Run By: straights
Rooms: 6
Baths: private

Meals: full brkfst
Amenities: free parking, laundry, outdoor hot tub, massage, DVDs/ videos, WiFi
Kids: 10 yrs & up welcome
Smoking: no
Rates: $150-360
AC: 10%

Camellia Inn   *Healdsburg*

211 North St
Healdsburg, CA 95448
707/ 433-8182 800/ 727-8182
www.camelliainn.com

Clientele: gay-friendly
Type: b&b-inn; 1869 Italianate Victorian decorated in antiques; on landscaped grounds
Owned/ Run By: straights
Rooms: 9
Baths: private

Meals: full brkfst
Amenities: free parking, pool, hot tub
Kids: please inquire
Smoking: no
Rates: $119-250
AC: 10%

Grape Leaf Inn

Healdsburg

539 Johnson St
Healdsburg, CA 95448
707/ 433-8140 866/ 433-8140
www.grapeleafinn.com

Clientele: gay-friendly
Type: b&b; restored Queen Anne Victorian w/ spa services; surrounded by award-winning gardens; complimentary boutique wine & cheese tastings in secret wine cellar "speakeasy"
Owned/ Run By: straights

Rooms: 12
Baths: private
Meals: full brkfst
Amenities: massage, WiFi
Rates: $200-395

Madrona Manor

Healdsburg

1001 Westside Rd
Healdsburg, CA 95448
707/ 433-4231 800/ 258-4003
www.madronamanor.com

Clientele: gay-friendly
Type: country inn; in elegant Victorian on a lovely estate surrounded by 8 acres of wooded & landscaped grounds
Rooms: 22
Baths: private
Meals: full brkfst

Kids: kids 12 yrs & up welcome in some rms
Pets: no
Smoking: no
Rates: $175-445

Midnight Sun Inn

Healdsburg

428 Haydon St
Healdsburg, CA 95448
707/ 433-1718
www.midnight-sun.com

Clientele: gay-friendly
Type: b&b-inn; in historic home w/ contemporary furnishings; walk to plaza, shops, tasting rms & restaurants
Owned/ Run By: straights
Rooms: 3
Baths: private

Meals: full brkfst
Amenities: free parking, pool, hot tub
Kids: no
Pets: no
Smoking: no
Rates: $145-165

Quality Inn & Suites

Hermosa Beach

901 Aviation Blvd
Hermosa Beach, CA 90254
310/ 374-2666 800/ 553-1145
www.qualityinnsts-hermosa.com

Type: hotel; newly renovated rms; from romantic spa tub rms to family & executive-style suites
Rooms: 68
Baths: private
Wheelchair Access: yes, 3 rms
Meals: expanded cont'l brkfst

Amenities: free parking, laundry, outdoor hot tub, WiFi
Kids: welcome
Rates: $89-139
AC: 10%

Alderwood Cabins

Idyllwild

PO Box 849
Idyllwild, CA 92549
951/ 659-3571
www.alderwoodcabins.com

Clientele: gay-friendly
Type: cabin; vintage 1920s cabins on 2 wooded acres in heart of town; full kitchens
Owned/ Run By: woman
Rooms: 3 (cabins)
Baths: private

Pets: welcome w/ prior approval
Smoking: no

The Cedar Street Inn & Spa

Idyllwild

25870 Cedar St
Idyllwild, CA 92549
951/ 659-4789 877/ 659-4789
www.cedarstreetinn.com

Clientele: gay-friendly
Type: inn & cabins; on-site massage & spa services
Owned/ Run By: straights
Rooms: 9 rms & suites + several cabins
Baths: private
Meals: coffee/tea only

Kids: welcome in cabins only
Pets: welcome in cabins only
Rates: $80-160

Quiet Creek Inn & Vacation Rentals
Idyllwild

26345 Delano Dr
Idyllwild, CA 92549
951/ 659–6110 800/ 450–6110
www.QuietCreekInn.com

Clientele: gay-friendly
Type: cabin; duplex cabins overlooking Strawberry Creek made up of studios & suites; some w/ private spas; also over 15 vacation rental homes available
Owned/ Run By: gay men
Rooms: 10 rms; 21 cabins
Baths: private
Wheelchair Access: yes, 1 rm

Meals: coffee/tea only
Amenities: free parking, private outdoor hot tub, DVDs/ videos, WiFi
Kids: welcome in cabins
Pets: welcome in certain units
Smoking: no
Rates: $80-500
AC: 5% for inn rms

The Rainbow Inn
Idyllwild

54420 S Circle Dr
Idyllwild, CA 92549
951/ 659–0111
www.rainbow-inn.com

Clientele: mixed gay/ straight
Type: b&b-inn; beautiful, natural setting for commitment ceremonies; 2-person jacuzzi tub in 1 rm; also conference center
Owned/ Run By: gay men
Rooms: 5
Baths: private
Meals: full brkfst
Amenities: DVDs/ videos, WiFi

Kids: welcome
Pets: no
Smoking: no
Rates: $90-145

Strawberry Creek Inn B&B
Idyllwild

26370 Hwy 243
Idyllwild, CA 92549
951/ 659–3202 800/ 262–8969
www.strawberrycreekinn.com

Clientele: gay-friendly
Type: b&b-inn; relaxing getaway w/ sundeck, garden & hammocks overlooking Strawberry Creek; Mobil 3 stars & AAA 3 diamonds
Owned/ Run By: gay men
Rooms: 10 (also cottage)
Baths: private
Wheelchair Access: yes, 1 rm

Meals: full brkfst
Amenities: free parking, laundry, indoor hot tub
Kids: no (no more than 2 persons per rm)
Pets: no
Smoking: no
Rates: $120-230

The Homestead at Table Mountain B&B
Jamestown

PO Box 1575
Jamestown, CA 95327
209/ 984–3712
www.homestead-bandb.com

Clientele: gay-friendly
Type: b&b; spacious rms w/ cozy stoves; antique furnishings, great views of the Sierras; restaurants, shops & historical sights nearby; "casual, comfy & very country!"
Owned/ Run By: lesbians
Rooms: 2
Baths: private

Meals: full brkfst
Kids: no
Pets: no
Smoking: no
Rates: $105-115

Joshua Desert Retreats
Joshua Tree Nat'l Park

Witt Rd
Twentynine Palms, CA 92277
310/ 558–5544
www.JoshuaDesertRetreats.com

Clientele: mixed gay/ straight
Type: rental home; Mojave Desert vacation homes on 5+ acres of enhanced desert; 360° mtn views; minutes from Joshua Tree Nat'l Park
Owned/ Run By: gay men
Rooms: 10 (homes)
Amenities: laundry, pool, outdoor hot tub, DVDs/ videos

Kids: welcome
Pets: welcome
Smoking: no
Rates: $1,100-2,200/ week, $2,400-4,500/ month
AC: 10%

Rosebud Ruby Star

Joshua Tree Nat'l Park

PO Box 1116
Joshua Tree, CA 92252-0800
760/ 366-4676 877/ 887-7370
www.rosebudrubystar.com

Clientele: gay-friendly
Type: b&b; artist-owned adobe-style b&b on 5 panoramic acres; also self-catering cabins; seasonal (clsd July-Aug); 2 minutes from scenic west entrance
Owned/ Run By: woman
Rooms: 2 (also 4 cabins)
Baths: private
Meals: full brkfst

Kids: no
Pets: no
Smoking: rms nonsmoking
Rates: $140-155 (b&b) & $275-525 (cabins)
AC: 10%

Spin & Margie's Desert Hideaway

Joshua Tree Nat'l Park

64491 29 Palms Hwy
Joshua Tree, CA 92252
760/ 366-9124
www.deserthideaway.com

Clientele: gay-friendly
Type: hacienda-style b&b on 3 acres; courtyard; suites w/ private patios; cool trading post on-site
Rooms: 4
Baths: private
Meals: cont'l brkfst

Kids: welcome
Pets: no
Smoking: rms nonsmoking
Rates: $115-145
AC: 10%

The Artists' Loft

Julian

PO Box 2408
Julian, CA 92036-2408
760/ 765-0765
www.artistsloft.com

Clientele: gay-friendly
Type: b&b-inn; also 2 cabins; all w/ incredible mtn views & nestled in the mtn community of Julian, E of San Diego
Owned/ Run By: artists
Rooms: inn & 2 cabins
Baths: private
Meals: cont'l brkfst

Kids: no
Pets: no
Rates: $165-280

River View Lodge

Kernville

PO Box 887
Kernville, CA 93238
760/ 376-6019 877/ 885-6333
www.riverviewlodge.net

Clientele: mixed gay/ straight
Type: resort; riverfront; most rms w/ river views
Owned/ Run By: gay men
Rooms: 12
Baths: private
Meals: expanded cont'l brkfst
Amenities: hot tub
Kids: welcome

Pets: welcome
Smoking: no
Rates: $79-129

Rhodes' End B&B

Klamath

115 Trobitz Rd
Klamath, CA 95548
707/ 482-1654
www.rhodes-end.com

Clientele: gay-friendly
Type: b&b-private home; nestled among the majestic redwoods & bordered by the Klamath River
Owned/ Run By: straights
Rooms: 3
Baths: private
Meals: full brkfst
Amenities: free parking, outdoor hot tub, massage

Kids: no
Pets: no
Smoking: no
Rates: $90-120

Best Western Rose Quartz Inn

Lake Almanor

306 Main St
Chester, CA 96020

530/ 258-2002
888/ 571-4885

lfcoast@aol.com
www.rosequartzinn.com

Clientele: gay-friendly
Type: hotel
Owned/ Run By: straights
Nearby Attractions: Lassen Volcanic Nat'l Park, Lake Almanor
Pickup Service: airport pickup; from local regional airport
Transit: 2 hrs to Sacramento airport; 1 hr & 45 minutes to Reno airport; 2 miles to Chester regional airport
Rooms: 50 total, 6 suites, 17 kings, 27 queens, A/C, color TV, DVD/ VCR (6), cable, phone, refrigerator (6), maid service, "incredible beds & linens—better than home"
Baths: private, bathtubs, showers, whirlpools, hairdryers
Wheelchair Access: yes, 4 rms
Meals: cont'l brkfst
Amenities: pool, outdoor hot tub, gym, WiFi, coffee/ tea, conference rm, business center, fitness center, movie theater
Recreation: fishing, boating, sailing, snowmobiling, skiing, hunting
Kids: welcome

Pets: welcome
Pets On Premises: cats, 1 dog
Smoking: ok in 5 rms
Reservations: highly recommended *Deposit:* personal check ok *Cancellation:* cancel by 2 days prior

Payment: cash, travelers checks, personal checks, Visa, Amex, MC, Discover
Season: open yr-round *High season:* May-Oct
Rates: $85-145
AC: 5%

Broken Arrow B&B

Lake Arrowhead

1168 N Hwy 173
Lake Arrowhead, CA 92352
909/ 337-0125 866/ 262-7769
www.brokenarrowbb.com

Clientele: gay-friendly
Type: b&b; w/ feel of mtn lodge; huge redwood deck; 15 miles from Snow Valley Ski Area & 20 miles from Big Bear Lake
Rooms: 5
Baths: private
Meals: full brkfst

Kids: please call first
Pets: welcome w/ prior approval
Smoking: no
Rates: $125-185

Alpine Inn & Spa

Lake Tahoe

920 Stateline Ave
South Lake Tahoe, CA 96150
530/ 544-3340 800/ 826-8885
www.alpineinnlaketahoe.com

Clientele: mixed gay/ straight
Type: motel; clean & quiet accommodations just steps from the casino; 2 blks from private beach; 1 mile to Faces nightclub
Owned/ Run By: gay/ lesbian & straight
Rooms: 38
Baths: private

Meals: coffee/tea only
Amenities: pool, outdoor hot tub
Kids: welcome; no one under 18 yrs in spa rms
Pets: companion animals only
Smoking: ok
Rates: $30-375

Andrea's Grinnin' Bear Cabin

Lake Tahoe

530/ 582-8703
www.sierraviews.com

Clientele: mixed gay/ straight
Type: cabin; 3-bdrm, 2-bath comfortable cabin on pine-treed lot; dogs welcome
Owned/ Run By: women
Rooms: 1 (cabin)
Baths: private

Kids: welcome
Pets: dogs welcome
Smoking: no
Rates: $169-200
AC: 10%

Black Bear Inn
Lake Tahoe

1202 Ski Run Blvd
South Lake Tahoe, CA 96150

530/ 544-4451
877/ 232-7466

info@tahoeblackbear.com
www.tahoeblackbear.com

Clientele: mixed gay/ straight
Type: b&b-inn; small luxury lodge w/ 5 guest rms; plus 3 cabins
Owned/ Run By: gay men
Nearby Attractions: casinos, skiing, resorts
Transit: near public transit; 70 minutes to Reno airport
Rooms: 10 total, kings, A/C, color TV, DVD/ VCR, cable, wetbar (1), fireplace, deck (1), phone, kitchenette (4), refrigerator (4), maid service
Baths: private & shared, bathtubs, showers, robes, hairdryers
Wheelchair Access: yes, 1 rm
Meals: full brkfst, vegetarian meals available
Amenities: office hrs: 10am-6pm; free parking, outdoor hot tub, DVDs/ videos, sunset drinks
Recreation: 30 minutes to nude beach; 1 mile to ski resort, lake, hiking, biking
Kids: no
Pets: no

Pets On Premises: 2 dogs
Smoking: no (outside only)
Reservations: *Deposit:* required, 50%, due at booking, personal check ok *Cancellation:* cancel by 2 weeks prior or forfeit 10% *Minimum Stay:* 2 nights Check

in/ out: 3-6pm/ 11am
Payment: cash, travelers checks, Visa, Amex, MC
Season: open yr-round *High season:* Dec-March/ July-Sept
Rates: $200-500

Heavenly Lodge
Lake Tahoe

930 Park Ave
South Lake Tahoe, CA 96150
530/ 544-2400 800/ 884-4920
www.heavenlylodgetahoe.com

Clientele: mixed gay/ straight
Type: lodge & cabins few blks from South Lake Tahoe's Lakeside Marina & beach
Owned/ Run By: gay men
Rooms: 14 (includes 4 suites)
Baths: private
Wheelchair Access: yes, 7 rms

Meals: cont'l brkfst
Amenities: sauna, hot tub, WiFi
Kids: welcome
Pets: welcome; $15 fee
Smoking: ok (in smoking rms only)
Rates: $75-375
AC: 10%

Holly's Place
Lake Tahoe

PO Box 13197
South Lake Tahoe, CA 96151
800/ 745-7041
www.hollysplace.com

Clientele: mixed gay/ straight
Type: cabins & cottages; on 2 acres of fenced-in property; 2 blks to lake
Owned/ Run By: women
Rooms: 4 cabins (ranging from studios to 3-bdrm)
Baths: private
Meals: coffee/tea & muffins

Amenities: free parking, laundry, outdoor hot tubs, massage, DVDs/ videos, WiFi
Kids: well-behaved welcome
Pets: well-behaved dogs welcome
Smoking: no
Rates: $250-430
AC: 5% or trades

Sierrawood Guest House
Lake Tahoe

PO Box 550187
South Lake Tahoe, CA 96155-0003
530/ 577-6073
www.sierrawoodbb.com

Clientele: mixed gay/ lesbian
Type: guesthouse; cozy chalet in the woods by a rippling mtn stream; great privacy
Owned/ Run By: gay men
Rooms: 6
Baths: private & shared
Meals: brkfst & dinner

Amenities: free parking, laundry, outdoor hot tub, DVDs/ videos
Kids: welcome
Pets: no
Smoking: no
Rates: $95-150
AC: 10%

Tahoe Moon Properties
Lake Tahoe

PO Box 7521
Tahoe City, CA 96145
530/ 581-2771 866/ 581-2771
www.tahoemoonproperties.com

Clientele: gay-friendly
Type: variety of properties available; pet-friendly, clean, many amenities including hot tubs & pool table
Owned/ Run By: straights
Rooms: 200
Baths: private & shared

Amenities: free parking, laundry, pool, sauna, outdoor hot tub, DVDs/ videos
Smoking: no
Rates: $125-1,000
AC: 10%

Tahoe Retreat & Spa
Lake Tahoe

2446 Lake Tahoe Blvd
530/ 544-6776 888/ 824-6378
South Lake Tahoe, CA 96150
www.tahoeretreatspa.com

Clientele: mixed gay/ straight
Type: cabin; traditional mtn cabins set in the heart of South Lake Tahoe; rms range from suites to kitchenettes; rm & spa packages available
Owned/ Run By: gay & straight
Rooms: 16 total

Baths: private
Meals: coffee/tea only
Kids: welcome
Pets: welcome
Smoking: no
Rates: $40-155
AC: 10%

Beachrunners' Inn
Long Beach

231 Kennebec Ave
Long Beach, CA 90803
562/ 856-0202 866/ 221-0001
www.beachrunnersinn.com

Clientele: mixed gay/ straight
Type: b&b-inn; 1913 California Craftsman; 3 blks from beach; walking distance to gay bars & restaurants
Owned/ Run By: straights
Rooms: 5
Baths: private

Meals: expanded cont'l brkfst
Amenities: free parking, laundry, outdoor hot tub, DVDs/ videos
Kids: welcome; please inquire
Pets: no
Smoking: no
Rates: $89-125

The Coast Long Beach Hotel 🏳️‍🌈
Long Beach

700 Queensway Dr
Long Beach, CA 90802
562/ 435-7676
www.coasthotel.com

Clientele: gay-friendly
Type: waterfront resort; views of Long Beach skyline; bay views, balconies, patios
Owned/ Run By: gay & straight
Rooms: 195
Baths: private
Wheelchair Access: yes, 2 rms

Meals: full brkfst
Amenities: pool, gym, WiFi
Kids: welcome
Pets: welcome
Smoking: no
Rates: $104-205 (ask for IGLTA rate)
AC: 10%

Queen Mary
Long Beach

1126 Queens Hwy
Long Beach, CA 90802
562/ 435-3511 800/ 437-2934
queenmary.com

Type: hotel; *The Queen Mary*, the legendary ocean liner, includes attractions, exhibits & award-winning restaurants & shops; also banquet/ catering facilities & day spa
Rooms: 365 (staterms & suites)
Baths: private
Wheelchair Access: yes, 9 rms

Kids: welcome
Pets: companion animals (seeing-eye dogs) only
Smoking: ok
Rates: $119-660
AC: 10%

Turret House B&B 🏳️‍🌈
Long Beach

556 Chestnut Ave
Long Beach, CA 90802
562/ 624-1991 888/ 488-7738
www.turrethouse.com

Clientele: mixed gay/ straight
Type: b&b-inn; restored Victorian home in downtown Long Beach; central to many well-known attractions; DSL access
Owned/ Run By: gay men
Rooms: 5
Baths: private

Meals: expanded cont'l brkfst
Amenities: outdoor hot tub, massage
Kids: no
Pets: well-behaved pets welcome w/ prior approval
Rates: $109-135
AC: 10%

Best Western Beverly Pavilion
Los Angeles

9360 Wilshire Blvd
Beverly Hills, CA 90212
310/ 273-1400 800/ 441-5050
book.bestwestern.com/bestwestern/
productInfo.do?propertyCode=05637

Clientele: gay-friendly
Type: hotel; newly renovated boutique hotel; fitness rm; Wilshire Bar & Grill on-site; high-speed internet; close to Rodeo Dr
Rooms: 110
Baths: private

Wheelchair Access: yes, 7 rms
Meals: coffee/tea only
Kids: welcome
Rates: $159-319
AC: 10%

Chamberlain
Los Angeles

1000 Westmount Dr
Los Angeles, CA 90069
310/ 657-7400 800/ 201-9652
www.chamberlainwesthollywood.com

Clientele: mixed gay/ straight
Type: hotel; metropolitan boutique hotel; high-speed internet throughout; American bistro restaurant & lounge; rooftop pool
Owned/ Run By: gay & straight
Rooms: 112

Baths: private
Wheelchair Access: yes, 2 rms
Meals: expanded cont'l brkfst
Kids: welcome
Pets: welcome; $75 fee (nonrefundable)
Rates: $259-319
AC: 10%

Élan Hotel Modern
Los Angeles

8435 Beverly Blvd
Los Angeles, CA 90048
323/ 658-6663 888/ 611-0398
www.elanhotel.com

Clientele: mixed gay/ straight
Type: hotel; stylish, hip & trendy; centrally located; in-house fitness rm; complimentary wine & cheese happy hour Mon-Fri
Owned/ Run By: gay men
Rooms: 50
Baths: private

Wheelchair Access: yes, 2 rms
Meals: cont'l brkfst
Amenities: massage, DVDs/ videos, WiFi
Kids: welcome
Pets: no
Smoking: no
Rates: $135-215
AC: 10%

The Georgian Hotel
Los Angeles

1415 Ocean Ave
Santa Monica, CA 90401
310/ 395-9945 800/ 538-8147
www.georgianhotel.com

Clientele: gay-friendly
Type: hotel; built in architecturally historic art deco style unique to Los Angeles; spectacular ocean sunsets & panoramic bay views
Owned/ Run By: straights
Rooms: 84
Baths: private

Wheelchair Access: yes, 2 rms
Meals: cont'l brkfst
Kids: welcome; 16 yrs & under free
Pets: 25 lbs or smaller welcome; $250 deposit ($100 nonrefundable)
Smoking: ok
Rates: $195+
AC: 10%

The Grafton on Sunset
Los Angeles

8462 W Sunset Blvd
Los Angeles, CA 90069
323/ 654-4600 800/ 821-3660
www.graftononsunset.com

Clientele: mixed gay/ straight
Type: boutique hotel offering unsurpassed style; in the heart of the Sunset Strip; relax in the private pool or enjoy the scene in Balboa restaurant & lounge
Owned/ Run By: gay/ lesbian & straight
Rooms: 108

Baths: private
Wheelchair Access: yes, 4 rms
Kids: welcome
Pets: welcome; $100 deposit
Smoking: ok
Rates: $139-500
AC: 10%

The Grove Guesthouse
Los Angeles

323/ 876-7778 888/ 524-7683
www.groveguesthouse.com

Clientele: mixed gay/ lesbian
Type: guesthouse; spacious & luxurious 1-bdrm complete villa w/ separate living rm & kitchen; central & quiet, in the heart of gay LA; tropical pool & spa (nudity ok)
Owned/ Run By: gay men
Rooms: 1

Baths: private
Amenities: free parking, pool, outdoor hot tub, DVDs/ videos, WiFi
Kids: by arrangement
Rates: $189 (including tax) & up
AC: 10%

Hollywood Gay Guest House
Los Angeles

323/ 661-1566
www.hollywoodgayguesthouse.com

Clientele: men
Type: b&b-1930s private home w/ hilltop views of the city, mtns & Catalina Island; clothing-optional hot tub
Owned/ Run By: gay men
Rooms: 2
Baths: private & shared

Meals: cont'l brkfst
Amenities: outdoor hot tub, massage
Kids: no
Pets: no
Smoking: no
Rates: $90-120
AC: 5%

Hollywood Metropolitan Hotel
Los Angeles

5825 Sunset Blvd
Los Angeles, CA 90028
323/ 962-5800 800/ 962-5800
www.metropolitanhotel.com

Clientele: gay-friendly
Type: hotel; minutes from Universal Studios, Mann's Chinese Theater, the Hollywood Walk of Fame, the Hollywood Bowl
Owned/ Run By: straights
Rooms: 90
Baths: private

Wheelchair Access: yes, 5 rms
Meals: cont'l brkfst
Kids: welcome; 12 yrs & under free
Pets: no
Smoking: no
Rates: $79-145
AC: 10%

Hotel Sofitel
Los Angeles

8555 Beverly Blvd
Los Angeles, CA 90048
310/ 278-5444 800/ 521-7772
www.sofitel.com

Clientele: gay-friendly
Type: 4-star luxury hotel; 2 blks from Santa Monica Blvd, shopping, theaters; restaurant row across street
Owned/ Run By: gay/ lesbian & straight
Rooms: 311
Baths: private

Wheelchair Access: yes, 11 rms
Kids: welcome
Pets: welcome
Smoking: ok
Rates: $195-1,470
AC: 10%

Hyatt West Hollywood
Los Angeles

8401 Sunset Blvd
Los Angeles, CA 90069
323/ 656-1234 800/ 233-1234
westhollywood.hyatt.com/hyatt/hotels/index.jsp

Clientele: mixed gay/ straight
Type: hotel; in the heart of Sunset Strip, across from The House of Blues & 3 blks from Santa Monica Blvd
Owned/ Run By: gay & straight
Rooms: 262
Baths: private

Wheelchair Access: yes
Amenities: pool, WiFi
Kids: welcome
Pets: no
Smoking: no
Rates: $99-299
AC: 10%

The Inn at Venice Beach
Los Angeles

327 Washington Blvd
Marina Del Rey, CA 90291
310/ 821-2557 800/ 828-0688
www.innatvenicebeach.com

Clientele: gay-friendly
Type: hotel; in European-style inn, close to Venice Beach
Owned/ Run By: gay men
Rooms: 43 (includes singles, doubles, twins, loft suites)
Baths: private

Wheelchair Access: yes, 4 rms
Meals: cont'l brkfst
Amenities: WiFi
Kids: under 12 yrs free w/ existing bedding
Smoking: ok (some nonsmoking rms)
Rates: $99-159
AC: 10%

Le Montrose Suite Hotel
Los Angeles

900 Hammond St
Los Angeles, CA 90069
310/ 855-1115 800/ 776-0666
www.lemontrose.com

Clientele: gay-friendly
Type: hotel; recent 6-million-dollar renovation; all-suite; luxury contemporary-style; celebrity hideaway; located in a quiet residential neighborhood; walk to Santa Monica Blvd
Owned/ Run By: gay & straight
Rooms: 133 (suites)
Baths: private

Wheelchair Access: yes, 2 rms
Meals: full brkfst
Amenities: laundry, pool, sauna, hot tub, massage, DVDs/ videos
Kids: welcome
Pets: welcome; $100 cleaning fee
Smoking: no
Rates: $195-595
AC: 10%

Hollywood Hotel

Los Angeles

1160 N Vermont Ave
Los Angeles, CA 90029

323/ 315–1800
800/ 800–9733

info@hollywoodhotel.net
www.hollywoodhotel.net

Clientele: gay-friendly
Type: hotel; newly renovated; 3-Diamond AAA Award; 3-Star Mobil Travel Guide Award
Owned/ Run By: gay/ lesbian & straight
Nearby Attractions: 3 blks to bars, restaurants, nightclubs, etc
Transit: near public transit; bus at door step; taxi: Community Taxi, 213/ 838-8130
Rooms: 130 total, suites, A/C, color TV, cable, wetbar (some), phone, kitchenette, refrigerator, rm service, maid service
Baths: private
Wheelchair Access: yes, 6 rms
Meals: full brkfst
Amenities: free parking, laundry, pool, sauna, WiFi, coffee/ tea, sundeck, concierge, pharmacy
Recreation: gym on premises
Kids: welcome; under 18 yrs free if in same rm
Pets: dogs & cats under 50 lbs welcome; daily $35 fee
Smoking: no

Reservations: *Deposit:* required, credit card guarantee, due at booking, personal check ok *Cancellation:* cancel by 4pm day of arrival *Check in/ out:* 3pm/ noon
Payment: cash, travelers checks, personal checks, Visa, Amex, MC, Discover

Season: open yr-round
Rates: $90-135 *Discounts:* weekly, monthly, seniors, package deals
AC: 10%

Hotel Angeleno

Los Angeles

170 N Church Ln
Los Angeles, CA 90049

310/ 476-6411
866/ 264-3536

www.hotelangeleno.com

Clientele: mixed gay/ straight
Type: hotel; boutique hotel at crossroads of Brentwood & Bel-Air: "where Sunset meets the 405"
Nearby Attractions: Hollywood, UCLA, Beverly Hills, Santa Monica, J Paul Getty Center, Skirball Cultural Center Geffen Playhouse, Rodeo Dr
Rooms: 209 (including 3 one-bdrm suites) total, A/C, phone (2-line w/ voicemail), rm service, maid service, pillow-top mattresses, 300-thread-count Italian cotton sheets, feather duvet, 30" plasma flat-screen TV, complimentary HBO, CD player, ergonomic chair & work station, each rm w/ private balcony
Baths: private, showers, hairdryers
Amenities: WiFi, pool w/ outdoor fireplace, business center, iPod Nanos w/ person-alized podcasts & music, fitness center, GPS navigational devices for your auto, Italian steakhouse (penthouse level), Angeleno Cafe: coffee & pastry bar in lobby
Smoking: no ($200 penalty if occurs in rm)

Reservations: *Check in/ out:* 3pm/ noon
Payment: cash, travelers checks, Visa, Amex, MC, Discover

Season: open yr-round
Rates: $159+
AC: 10%

Le Parc Suite Hotel 🏳️‍🌈

Los Angeles

733 N West Knoll Dr
Los Angeles, CA 90069

310/ 855-8888
800/ 578-4837

reservations@leparcsuites.com
www.leparcsuites.com

Our private, secluded West Hollywood location is the reason Le Parc is coveted by sophisticated business and leisure travelers as well as world-renowned entertainers.

Our guest amenities are uncommonly generous. Personalized European-style service is evident in our In-Suite Service and at the intimate Knoll at Le Parc—a Mediterranean-style cafe resembling a cozy living room and featuring a separate bar area. You'll appreciate our rooftop heated pool and cabanas, whirlpool spa, lighted tennis court, and Fitness Center with sauna and circuit-training equipment.

Our beautiful, newly remodeled hotel suggests comfort and style. All 154 suites feature special touches like fine art, multiline data phones/ voicemail, terry robes, 2 remote TVs, VCR & DVD players with movie library, and in-room movies/ Nintendo. More desirable amenities include kitchenette with refrigerator and microwave, fireplace, minibar, and private balcony. There is also a free-to-guests business center and in-room DSL.

Le Parc—West Hollywood's great little hotel.

Type: hotel; all suites; located in quiet, residential area w/in walking distance of all gay & lesbian bars & restaurants

Nearby Attractions: Universal Studios, House of Blues, Key Club, downtown Hollywood, Beverly Hills; walk to Santa Monica Blvd, shopping & nightlife

Transit: 11 miles to LAX & Burbank airports; 10 miles to Union Station

Rooms: 154 total, suites, 138 kings, 9 fulls, 7 twins, A/C, color TV, DVD/ VCR, cable, wetbar, fireplace, deck, phone, kitchenette, refrigerator, safer sex supplies, rm service, maid service, all suites have fax, CD player, stereo

Baths: private, bathtubs, showers, robes, hairdryers

Wheelchair Access: yes, 2 rms

Meals: full-service restaurant on-site

Amenities: laundry, pool, sauna, hot tub, massage, DVDs/ videos, restaurant, tennis court, fitness rm, complimentary DSL & business center

Recreation: 1 mile to West Hollywood Park

Kids: welcome; under 17 yrs stay free w/ adults in same rm

Pets: welcome; $75 fee (nonrefundable)

Smoking: ok (designated areas only)

Reservations: required; credit card guarantee *Deposit:* required, 1 night, due 3 days prior (or credit card guarantee) *Cancellation:* cancel by 1 day prior or forfeit deposit *Check in/ out:* 3pm/ noon

Payment: cash, travelers checks, Visa, Amex, MC, Discover, Diners Club

Season: open yr-round

Rates: $300-400 (corp rates from $179) *Discounts:* AAA, AARP, entertainment

AC: 10%

The Linnington

Los Angeles

310/ 422-8825

Clientele: mixed gay/ lesbian
Type: b&b-private home; cozy hideaway in West LA; private entrance, deck w/ view
Owned/ Run By: lesbians
Rooms: 1
Baths: private

Meals: cont'l brkfst
Amenities: free parking, hot tub, massage
Kids: welcome, but limited space
Pets: no
Rates: $70-90

Mondrian

Los Angeles

8440 Sunset Blvd
Los Angeles, CA 90069
323/ 650-8999 800/ 525-8029
www.mondrianhotel.com

Clientele: gay-friendly
Type: home of trendy Sky Bar & Asia de Cuba restaurant (Philippe Starck design); also Agua Bathhouse Spa
Rooms: 237

Baths: private
Amenities: pool, spa, gym
Smoking: ok (nonsmoking rms available)
Rates: $185-425

Ramada Plaza Hotel—West Hollywood

Los Angeles

8585 Santa Monica Blvd
Los Angeles, CA 90069
310/ 652-6400 800/ 845-8585
www.ramadaweho.com

Clientele: gay-friendly
Type: hotel; modern art deco style w/ suites; WiFi poolside
Owned/ Run By: gay & straight
Rooms: 176 rms & 45 suites
Baths: private
Wheelchair Access: yes, 5 rms

Kids: welcome; under 16 yrs stay free in parent's rm
Pets: $100 deposit
Smoking: ok
Rates: $109-275
AC: 10%

San Vicente Inn-Resort ⬚

Los Angeles

845 N San Vicente Blvd
Los Angeles, CA 90069
310/ 854-6915 800/ 577-6915
www.gayresort.com

Clientele: men
Type: resort; historic cottages & executive suites; "the only gay-owned & gay-operated clothing-optional resort in LA & West Hollywood"
Owned/ Run By: gay men
Rooms: 40
Baths: private & shared

Wheelchair Access: yes, 3 rms
Meals: expanded cont'l brkfst
Amenities: free parking, pool, sauna, hot tub, massage, DVDs/ videos
Pets: well-trained & obedient pets welcome; $100 deposit & $20 per day
Rates: $69-269
AC: 10%

Sanborn GuestHouse

Los Angeles

1005 1/2 Sanborn Ave
Los Angeles, CA 90029
323/ 666-3947
www.sanbornhouse.com

Clientele: mixed gay/ lesbian
Type: guesthouse; 2 one-bdrm units w/ shared fully equipped kitchens; in duplex Craftsman cottage in the heart of Silverlake; close to bars & clubs
Owned/ Run By: gay men
Rooms: 2

Baths: private
Meals: coffee/tea only
Amenities: free parking, DVDs/ videos, WiFi
Kids: welcome
Pets: no
Smoking: no
Rates: $59-109

Sunset Marquis Hotel & Villas

Los Angeles

1200 Alta Loma Rd
West Hollywood, CA 90069
310/ 657-1333 800/ 858-9758
www.sunsetmarquishotel.com

Clientele: mixed gay/ straight
Type: hotel; quiet 4-star/ 4-diamond Mediterranean-style hideaway
Owned/ Run By: gay & straight
Rooms: 114
Baths: private
Wheelchair Access: yes, 3 rms
Meals: cont'l brkfst

Amenities: pool, sauna, outdoor hot tub, massage, gym, WiFi
Kids: welcome
Pets: no
Smoking: ok
Rates: $405-3,000
AC: 10%

Valadon Hotel
Los Angeles

8822 Cynthia St
Los Angeles, CA 90069
310/ 854-1114 800/ 835-7997
www.valadonhotel.com

Clientele: gay-friendly
Type: hotel; luxury all-suite; located in the heart of West Hollywood; walking distance to Santa Monica Blvd, nightlife, Hard Rock Cafe & the Sunset Strip
Owned/ Run By: straights
Rooms: 80

Baths: private
Amenities: free parking, laundry, pool, outdoor hot tub, massage, DVDs/ videos
Kids: welcome
Smoking: ok
Rates: $139-265
AC: 10%

Venice Comfort Zone
Los Angeles

310/ 578-5286
www.mohaus.com/vcz

Clientele: gay-friendly
Type: apt; peaceful, lovely studio; full kitchen, bath & hardwood flrs, HBO, satellite TV, cable modem; friendly hosts; monthly; no credit cards; "a very special & healing space"
Owned/ Run By: straights
Rooms: 1 (suite)

Baths: private
Amenities: free parking, laundry, massage, DVDs/ videos, WiFi
Kids: no
Pets: no
Smoking: no
Rates: $700/ wk, $1,750/ month + deposit
AC: 10%

W Los Angeles 🏳️‍🌈
Los Angeles

930 Hilgard Ave
Los Angeles, CA 90024
310/ 208-8765 800/ 421-2317
www.starwoodhotels.com/whotels/
index.html

Clientele: gay-friendly
Type: hotel; situated on a quiet, magnolia-lined residential street in Westwood; 2 heated pools, fitness center, spa, restaurant & terrace cafe
Rooms: 258 (suites)

Baths: private
Amenities: pool, sauna, hot tub
Rates: $219-379

Sea View Inn at the Beach
Manhattan Beach

3400 Highland Ave
Manhattan Beach, CA 90266
310/ 545-1504
www.seaview-inn.com

Clientele: gay-friendly
Type: motel; just steps from the beach in one of LA's safest communities; 3 miles from LAX; close to all SoCal attractions; complimentary bicycle usage
Owned/ Run By: gay & straight
Rooms: 33

Baths: private
Wheelchair Access: yes, 1 rm
Amenities: free parking, pool, WiFi
Kids: welcome
Smoking: ok
Rates: $105-345

Acqua Hotel 🏳️‍🌈
Marin County

555 Redwood Hwy
Mill Valley, CA 94941
415/ 380-0400 888/ 662-9555
www.acquahotel.com

Clientele: gay-friendly
Type: hotel; "Mill Valley's finest luxury boutique hotel"
Owned/ Run By: gay/ lesbian & straight
Rooms: 50
Baths: private
Wheelchair Access: yes, 2 rms
Meals: expanded cont'l brkfst

Amenities: free parking, laundry, massage, DVDs/ videos, gym, WiFi
Kids: welcome
Pets: welcome in 5 rms
Smoking: no
Rates: $189-249
AC: 10%

Beach House, Bolinas CA
Marin County

415/ 454-3371 x2
www.bolinasbeach.net

Clientele: mixed gay/ straight
Type: cottage; on bluffs overlooking Pacific Ocean; surrounded by Point Reyes Nat'l Park & the Golden Gate Nat'l Recreation Area; 1 hr from San Francisco via scenic Hwy 1
Owned/ Run By: lesbians

Rooms: 2-bdrm cottage (rent all)
Baths: shared
Kids: welcome
Pets: no
Smoking: no
Rates: $200-260

The Lodge at Tiburon   *Marin County*

1651 Tiburon Blvd
Tiburon, CA 94920-2511
415/ 435-3133 800/ 762-7770
www.thelodgeattiburon.com

Clientele: gay-friendly
Type: hotel; on 3 acres of landscaped gardens
Owned/ Run By: straights
Rooms: 102
Meals: full brkfst
Amenities: free parking, pool, indoor hot

tub, massage, DVDs/ videos, gym, WiFi
Kids: welcome
Pets: welcome
Smoking: ok
Rates: $219+

Lunar Marine Boat & Breakfast   *Marin County*

3020 Bridgeway #270
Sausalito, CA 94965
415/ 482-8027
www.lalunaboat.com

Type: b&b; 2 staterms, each sleeps 2; galley, deck & bridge privileges; "you haven't lived until you've slept aboard a boat!"
Owned/ Run By: lesbian
Rooms: 2
Baths: shared
Meals: cont'l brkfst

Amenities: free parking, DVDs/ videos, WiFi
Kids: under 12 yrs must wear life preserver while on deck
Pets: no
Smoking: no
Rates: $50-125
AC: 5%

Mill Valley Inn 🏷   *Marin County*

165 Throckmorton Ave
Mill Valley, CA 94941
415/ 389-6608 800/ 595-2100
www.marinhotels.com

Clientele: gay-friendly
Type: hotel; tucked away in a redwood grove at foot of Mt Tamalpais in downtown Mill Valley
Owned/ Run By: gay/ lesbian & straight
Rooms: 25 (includes 1 executive suite & 2 creekside cottages)

Baths: private
Meals: expanded cont'l brkfst
Kids: welcome
Pets: service animals only
Smoking: no
Rates: $165-340

Panama Hotel   *Marin County*

4 Bayview St
San Rafael, CA 94901
415/ 457-3993 800/ 899-3993
www.panamahotel.com

Clientele: gay-friendly
Type: b&b-inn; historic b&b in central San Rafael; also popular local restaurant w/ patio dining
Rooms: 16
Baths: private & shared
Wheelchair Access: yes, 1 rm

Meals: cont'l brkfst
Amenities: WiFi
Kids: welcome
Pets: welcome in 2 rms
Smoking: no
Rates: $75-175

Waters Edge Hotel 🏷   *Marin County*

25 Main St
Tiburon, CA 94920
415/ 789-5999 877/ 789-5999
www.marinhotels.com

Clientele: gay-friendly
Type: boutique hotel; located in historic downtown Tiburon; complimentary evening wine & cheese hour in lobby
Rooms: 23
Baths: private
Wheelchair Access: yes, 1 rm

Meals: expanded cont'l brkfst
Amenities: massage, DVDs/ videos, WiFi
Kids: welcome
Pets: no
Smoking: no
Rates: $169-439
AC: 10%

Agate Cove Inn   *Mendocino*

11201 N Lansing
Mendocino, CA 95460
707/ 937-0551 800/ 527-3111
www.agatecove.com

Clientele: gay-friendly
Type: b&b-inn; 1860s farmhouse; cottages or rms w/ white-water views; 50 ft from the water
Owned/ Run By: straights
Rooms: 10
Baths: private

Meals: full brkfst
Kids: no
Pets: welcome in 2 rms
Smoking: no
Rates: $139-309

The Alegria Quartet
Mendocino

PO Box 803
Mendocino, CA 95460-0803
707/ 937-5150 800/ 780-7905
www.mcelroysinn.com

Clientele: gay-friendly
Type: inn; w/ warm, spacious rms; ocean views; beautiful gardens; in Mendocino Village; close to whale-watching
Owned/ Run By: straights
Rooms: 5

Baths: private
Meals: cont'l brkfst
Kids: welcome
Pets: no
Smoking: no
Rates: $139-279

Bellflower
Mendocino

Box 867
Mendocino, CA 95460
707/ 937-0783
bellflower@bengal-cat.com

Clientele: women
Type: cabin; w/ kitchen, gardens, trampoline; on 10 wooded acres on Mendocino Coast; 2 miles to ocean, 10 minutes to Mendocino
Owned/ Run By: lesbians
Rooms: 1 (cabin w/ 3 rms)

Baths: private
Meals: coffee/tea only
Amenities: free parking, outdoor hot tub
Kids: welcome
Pets: welcome; $5 per night
Smoking: no
Rates: $65-85

Blair House & Cottage
Mendocino

45110 Little Lake St
Mendocino, CA 95460
707/ 937-1800 800/ 699-9269
www.blairhouse.com

Clientele: gay-friendly
Type: 1888 Victorian in Mendocino Village; former "home" of Jessica Fletcher of *Murder, She Wrote*
Rooms: 5 (includes 1 two-rm suite & 1 cottage)

Baths: private & shared
Meals: expanded cont'l brkfst
Smoking: no
Rates: $100-210

Brewery Gulch Inn
Mendocino

9401 Coast Hwy 1 N
Mendocino, CA 95460
707/ 937-4752 800/ 578-4454
www.brewerygulchinn.com

Clientele: gay-friendly
Type: b&b; Mendocino's distinctive inn; features Craftsman-style architecture & decor, ocean views, fireplaces, jacuzzi tubs, private decks, TVs, dataport telephones, gourmet brkfst, wine bar
Owned/ Run By: straights
Rooms: 10
Baths: private

Wheelchair Access: yes, 1 rm
Meals: full brkfst
Amenities: free parking, hot tub, massage, DVDs/ videos, WiFi
Kids: 13 yrs & up welcome
Pets: no
Smoking: no
Rates: $170-396
AC: 10%

Dennen's Victorian Farmhouse
Mendocino

PO Box 661
Mendocino, CA 95460
707/ 937-0697 800/ 264-4723
www.victorianfarmhouse.com

Clientele: gay-friendly
Type: b&b; situated on 2 coastal acres w/ beautiful gardens; luxurious rms w/ featherbeds; gourmet brkfst served in your rm
Owned/ Run By: straights
Rooms: 12

Baths: private
Meals: full brkfst
Amenities: massage, DVDs/ videos
Kids: 12 yrs & up welcome
Pets: no
Smoking: no
Rates: $135-235

Glendeven Inn
Mendocino

8205 N Hwy 1
Little River, CA 95436
707/ 937-0083 800/ 822-4536
www.glendeven.com

Type: b&b; delightful, peaceful 1860 country inn; w/ fireplaces & ocean views; brkfst delivered to your rm; art gallery & beautiful gardens; also private rental home
Rooms: 10
Baths: private

Wheelchair Access: yes, 1 rm
Meals: full brkfst
Kids: no
Pets: no
Smoking: no
Rates: $145-275

John Dougherty House
Mendocino

571 Ukiah St
Mendocino, CA 95460
707/ 937-5266 800/ 486-2104
www.jdhouse.com

Clientele: gay-friendly
Type: b&b; some of the best ocean & bay views in Mendocino; steps away from great restaurants, shopping & art galleries
Owned/ Run By: gay men
Rooms: 8
Baths: private

Meals: expanded cont'l brkfst
Amenities: free parking, hot tub, massage
Kids: over 12 yrs old welcome
Pets: no
Smoking: no
Rates: $130-275

MacCallum House Inn
Mendocino

45020 Albion St
Mendocino, CA 95460
707/ 937-0289 800/ 609-0492
www.maccallumhouse.com

Clientele: mixed gay/ straight
Type: b&b-inn; "the queen of Mendocino Victorians"; also popular restaurant & Grey Whale bar & cafe
Owned/ Run By: straights
Rooms: 19
Baths: private

Wheelchair Access: yes, 1 rm
Meals: gourmet brkfst
Amenities: free parking, hot tub, massage
Kids: welcome
Smoking: no
Rates: $135-395
AC: 10%

Mendocino Hotel & Garden Suites
Mendocino

45080 Main St
Mendocino, CA 95460
707/ 937-0511 800/ 548-0513
www.mendocinohotel.com

Clientele: gay-friendly
Type: hotel; charming full-service; featuring timeless Victorian elegance; located in the heart of Mendocino Village, overlooking the bay & the Pacific Ocean
Rooms: 51
Baths: private & shared

Wheelchair Access: yes, 1 rm
Kids: welcome in garden rms & suites
Pets: welcome
Smoking: no
Rates: $95-395
AC: 10%

Orr Hot Springs
Mendocino

13201 Orr Springs Rd
Ukiah, CA 95482
707/ 462-6277

Clientele: gay-friendly
Type: clothing-optional hot spring resort
Owned/ Run By: gay/ lesbian & straight
Rooms: 21
Baths: private & shared
Wheelchair Access: yes, 1 rm

Amenities: free parking, pool, sauna, outdoor hot tub, massage
Rates: $40 (camping, 1 person) – 185 (cottage, 2 people)

Packard House
Mendocino

45170 Little Lake St
Mendocino, CA 95460
707/ 937-2677 888/ 453-2677
www.packardhouse.com

Clientele: gay-friendly
Type: b&b; shops, beaches, trails & fine dining are all w/in walking distance
Owned/ Run By: gay men
Rooms: 4
Baths: private
Meals: full brkfst

Amenities: free parking, hot tub, massage, DVDs/ videos, WiFi
Kids: over 12 yrs old welcome
Pets: no
Smoking: no
Rates: $225

Sallie & Eileen's Place
Mendocino

PO Box 409
Mendocino, CA 95460
707/ 937-2028
www.seplace.com

Clientele: women
Type: cottage & cabins; 3 miles from Mendocino; close to state parks, beaches, hiking, biking, horseback riding, river canoeing, ocean kayaking; "We are in our 18th year of offering a safe, comfortable place for women!"
Owned/ Run By: lesbians

Rooms: 2 (units)
Baths: private
Amenities: outdoor hot tub, DVDs/ videos
Kids: welcome in cabin only; boy children up to 10 yrs; $10 per day
Pets: welcome in cabin only; $5 per day
Rates: $80-100

Stanford Inn by the Sea & Spa
Mendocino

Coast Hwy 1 & Comptche-Ukiah Rd
Mendocino, CA 95460
707/ 937-5615 800/ 331-8884
www.stanfordinn.com

Clientele: gay-friendly
Type: b&b-inn; redwood lodge overlooking the village & Pacific Ocean
Owned/ Run By: straights
Rooms: 41
Baths: private
Wheelchair Access: yes, 3 rms
Meals: full brkfst, vegetarian dining rm

Amenities: pool, sauna, indoor hot tub, massage, DVDs/ videos, WiFi
Kids: welcome; $30 for extra persons
Pets: welcome; $25 for first pet; $12.50 for each additional
Smoking: no
Rates: $265-320
AC: 10%

Stevenswood Spa Resort T4G
Mendocino

8211 N Hwy 1
Mendocino, CA 95456

707/ 937-2810
800/ 421-2810

stay@stevenswood.com
www.stevenswoodresort.com

Clientele: mixed gay/ straight
Type: resort; w/ gourmet dining & variety of outdoor hot tubs & spas
Owned/ Run By: gay men
Pickup Service: airport pickup; varies; please call
Transit: call us for taxi/ shuttle
Rooms: 30 total, suites, kings, queens, color TV, cable, wetbar, fireplace (wood-burning), deck, phone (cordless, plus speakerphone), refrigerator, safer sex supplies, rm service, maid service
Baths: private, bathtubs, showers, robes,

hairdryers
Wheelchair Access: yes, 4 rms
Meals: full brkfst (5 star!), vegetarian & vegan options available, all ingredients mostly organic
Amenities: sauna, indoor & outdoor hot tub, massage, snacks, coffee/ tea, wine, sunset drinks in summer
Recreation: beach, hiking, kayaking, tennis, golf
Kids: welcome w/ prior approval
Pets: welcome w/ prior approval
Pets On Premises: varies

Smoking: no
Reservations: strongly recommended *Deposit:* required, 1 night + tax, due at booking *Cancellation:* cancel by 3 days prior or forfeit $50
Payment: cash, travelers checks, Visa, Amex, MC, Discover, Carte Blanche, JCB
Season: open yr-round *High season:* spring-fall
Rates: $149-325 *Discounts:* AAA, AARP, Costco
AC: 10%

Gosby House Inn
Monterey

643 Lighthouse Ave
Pacific Grove, CA 93950
831/ 375-1287 800/ 527-8828
www.gosbyhouseinn.com

Type: b&b; exquisite Victorian inn; w/ charming English decor; close to ocean; walking distance to restaurants & shops
Rooms: 22
Baths: private & shared
Meals: full brkfst

Kids: welcome in some rms
Pets: no
Smoking: no
Rates: $100-205
AC: 10%

Monterey Fireside Lodge
Monterey

1131 10th St
Monterey, CA 93940
831/ 373-4172 800/ 722-2624
www.montereyfireside.com

Clientele: gay-friendly
Type: motel; very quiet & very clean
Owned/ Run By: straights
Rooms: 24
Baths: private
Wheelchair Access: yes, 3 rms
Meals: cont'l brkfst

Amenities: free parking, outdoor hot tub
Kids: welcome
Pets: welcome; small fee
Smoking: ok
Rates: $59-399
AC: 10%

The Monterey Hotel ⊞©

406 Alvarado St
Monterey, CA 93940

831/ 375-3184
800/ 727-0960

Monterey

info@montereyhotel.com
www.moonstonehotels.com

Clientele: gay-friendly
Type: hotel; historic turn-of-the-century boutique hotel; w/ hand-carved furnishings, plantation shutters, marble baths; in the heart of downtown Monterey
Nearby Attractions: Monterey Bay Aquarium, Cannery Row, Pebble Beach Golf Course, 17-Mile Drive, Laguna Seca racetrack, Carmel
Transit: near public transit; 20 minutes to Monterey airport
Rooms: 45 total, 6 suites, 15 kings, 17 queens, 5 fulls, 2 twins, color TV, cable, ceiling fan, fireplace (4), phone, refrigerator (4), maid service, elegant yet comfortable decor
Baths: private, bathtubs, showers, hairdryers
Amenities: office hrs: 24hrs; afternoon tea service, bedtime milk & cookies, concierge, gift shop, spa, valet parking
Recreation: kayaking, golf, rollerblading, hiking, biking, deep-sea fishing, whale-watching, diving, nature boat tours, glass-bottom boat tours, sailing & yachting, shopping

Kids: welcome
Reservations: required *Deposit:* credit card guarantee, due at booking *Cancellation:* cancel by 3 days prior or forfeit a % *Minimum Stay:* check w/ property *Check in/ out:* 3pm/ 11am

Payment: cash, travelers checks, Visa, Amex, MC, Discover
Season: open yr-round *High season:* June-Sept
Rates: $89-259
AC: 10%

Giant Redwoods RV & Camp

Myers Flat

PO Box 222/ 455 Boy Scout Camp Rd
Myers Flat, CA 95554
707/ 943-3198
www.giantredwoodsrvcamp.com

Clientele: gay-friendly
Type: RV park; also campground; located off the Avenue of the Giants on the Eel River; w/ clear skies, fresh air & clean water; 25 campsites & 60 RV hookups
Owned/ Run By: straights
Baths: shared

Kids: welcome; $3 per extra person
Pets: welcome; $2 per pet
Rates: $23-35

Beazley House B&B Inn

Napa Valley

1910 First St
Napa, CA 94559
707/ 257-1649 800/ 559-1649
www.beazleyhouse.com

Clientele: gay-friendly
Type: b&b; historic inn located in Victorian neighborhood, steps from Napa River & downtown Napa
Owned/ Run By: straights
Rooms: 11
Baths: private
Wheelchair Access: yes, 1 rm

Meals: full brkfst
Amenities: free parking, WiFi
Kids: welcome
Pets: dogs very welcome; no more than 2 per rm; $25 per pet per night
Smoking: no
Rates: $165-309

Brannan Cottage Inn

Napa Valley

109 Wapoo Ave
Calistoga, CA
707/ 942-4200
www.brannancottageinn.com

Clientele: gay-friendly
Type: b&b; in Victorian cottage
Rooms: 6
Baths: private

Rates: $145-185

The Chanric Inn   *Napa Valley*

1805 Foothill Blvd
Calistoga, CA 94515
707/ 942-4535 877/ 281-3671
www.thechanric.com

Clientele: mixed gay/ straight
Type: b&b-inn; "lush oasis w/ stylish ambience, sensual amenities & tantalizing sustenance"
Owned/ Run By: gay men
Rooms: 7
Baths: private & shared
Meals: full brkfst

Amenities: free parking, pool, sauna, outdoor hot tub, massage, WiFi
Kids: welcome only if book whole inn
Pets: no
Smoking: no
Rates: $209-329
AC: 10%

Chateau de Vie   *Napa Valley*

3250 Hwy 128
Calistoga, CA 94515
707/ 942-6446 877/ 558-2513
www.cdvnapavalley.com

Clientele: mixed gay/ straight
Type: b&b; beautiful, comfortable French chateau w/ lush gardens & incredible mtn views; "quiet understated elegance"
Owned/ Run By: gay men
Rooms: 4
Baths: private

Meals: full brkfst
Amenities: free parking, pool, outdoor hot tub, massage, DVDs/ videos
Pets: welcome w/ prior approval
Smoking: ok
Rates: $209-329
AC: 10%

Garnett Creek Inn   *Napa Valley*

1139 Lincoln Ave
Calistoga, CA 94515
707/ 942-9797
www.garnettcreekinn.com

Clientele: gay-friendly
Type: b&b-inn; in Victorian w/ wraparound porches
Rooms: 5
Baths: private
Wheelchair Access: yes, 1 rm

Meals: cont'l brkfst
Kids: 12 yrs & up welcome
Pets: no
Smoking: no
Rates: $155-295

The Ink House B&B   *Napa Valley*

1575 St Helena Hwy
St Helena, CA 94574
707/ 963-3890
www.inkhouse.com

Clientele: gay-friendly
Type: b&b-inn; in historic & grand 1884 Italianate Victorian among the vineyards; glass observatory w/ 360° view
Owned/ Run By: straights
Rooms: 7

Baths: private & shared
Meals: full brkfst
Kids: no
Smoking: no
Rates: $125-240 + tax
AC: 10%

La Belle Epoque B&B Inn   *Napa Valley*

1386 Calistoga Ave
Napa, CA 94559
707/ 257-2161 800/ 238-8070
www.labelleepoque.com

Clientele: gay-friendly
Type: b&b; in Victorian gem famous for gourmet brkfsts, expansive wine socials & hospitality
Owned/ Run By: straights
Rooms: 9
Baths: private
Meals: full brkfst

Amenities: free parking, hot tub, massage, DVDs/ videos, WiFi
Kids: please inquire
Pets: no
Smoking: no
Rates: $199-420
AC: 10%

Meadowlark Country House   *Napa Valley*

601 Petrified Forest Rd
Calistoga, CA 94515
707/ 942-5651 800/ 942-5651
www.meadowlarkinn.com

Clientele: mixed gay/ straight
Type: b&b-inn; also 2 guesthouses; on secluded 20-acre Napa Valley country estate; clothing-optional mineral pool
Owned/ Run By: gay men
Rooms: 8 (plus 2 guesthouses)
Baths: private
Meals: full brkfst

Amenities: free parking, pool, sauna, indoor & outdoor hot tub; jacuzzi in all rms, massage, DVDs/ videos
Kids: no
Pets: well-behaved dogs w/ prior approval
Smoking: no
Rates: $165-265 & $295-425 (pool house)
AC: 10%

Napa River Inn

Napa Valley

500 Main St
Napa, CA 94559
707/ 251-8500 877/ 251-8500
www.napariverinn.com

Clientele: gay-friendly
Type: hotel; restaurant & spa voted "Best Of" by local residents
Owned/ Run By: gay & straight
Rooms: 66
Baths: private
Wheelchair Access: yes, 5 rms

Meals: full brkfst
Amenities: laundry, massage, gym, WiFi
Kids: welcome
Pets: $25 per night
Rates: $159-499
AC: 10%

Stone Oaks Vineyard B&B

Napa Valley

Silverado Trail
Napa, CA 94558
707/ 226-2462
stoneoaksvineyard@earthlink.net

Clientele: mixed gay/ lesbian
Type: rental home; spacious residence on 5 secluded park-like acres; vineyard, natural pool w/ hot tub; tree house & deck
Owned/ Run By: women
Rooms: 4
Baths: private & shared

Meals: cont'l brkfst
Amenities: free parking, laundry, pool, hot tub, massage, DVDs/ videos, gym
Kids: welcome by prior arrangement
Pets: no
Rates: $150-200
AC: 10%

White Sulphur Springs Resort & Spa

Napa Valley

3100 White Sulphur Springs Rd
St Helena, CA 94574
707/ 963-8588
800/ 593-8873 (in CA & NV only)
www.whitesulphursprings.com

Type: resort; secluded Napa Valley retreat for groups & individuals, featuring 3 pools, ropes course, mtg facilities, redwood forests, natural sulphur pool
Owned/ Run By: straights
Rooms: 37 (includes 9 cabins w/ private baths; 14 rms in inn w/ private baths; 14 rms in Carriage House w/ shared baths)

Baths: private & shared
Meals: cont'l brkfst
Amenities: free parking, pool, sauna, outdoor hot tub, massage
Kids: welcome; though not much to do
Smoking: no
Rates: $95-210
AC: 10%

US Hotel B&B Inn

Nevada City

233 B Broad Street
Nevada City, CA 95959

530/ 265-7999

info@ushotelbb.com
www.ushotelbb.com

Clientele: mixed gay/ straight
Type: b&b-inn; down mattresses, blankets & pillows make your sleep experience a memorable one; "The best beds in Nevada County!"
Owned/ Run By: woman
Nearby Attractions: Grass Valley, Nevada County Fairgrounds, events yr-round
Pickup Service: airport pickup; mileage charge
Transit: 1.5 hrs to Reno airport; 1 hr 15 minutes to Sacramento airport
Rooms: 7 total, 2 kings, 3 queens, 2 double queens, A/C, color TV, cable, ceiling fan, fireplace (3), deck (2), maid service, high ceilings, "largest rms in town"
Baths: private, bathtubs, showers
Meals: full brkfst, special meals available w/ prior arrangements
Amenities: WiFi, snacks, coffee/ tea, kitchen available to guests 24/7
Recreation: Yuba River: trails, hiking; Empire Mine; several lakes

Kids: welcome w/ prior approval
Pets: welcome w/ prior approval
Pets On Premises: yes, but kept out of hotel
Reservations: strongly recommended *Cancellation:* cancel by 10 days prior or forfeit cost of rm *Check in/ out:* 3-6pm/ 11am
Payment: cash, travelers checks, personal checks, Visa, MC, corp checks
Season: open yr-round *High season:* May-Dec
Rates: $99-199 *Discounts:* yes (please inquire)

The Flume's End
Nevada City

317 S Pine St
Nevada City, CA 95959
530/ 265-9665
www.flumesend.com

Clientele: gay-friendly
Type: b&b-inn; in 1860s Victorian next to Gold Run Creek
Owned/ Run By: women
Rooms: 5 + cottage

Baths: private
Meals: full brkfst
Rates: $149-189

Casa Laguna Inn & Spa
Orange County

2510 S Coast Hwy
Laguna Beach, CA 92651
949/ 494-2996 800/ 233-0449
www.casalaguna.com

Clientele: gay-friendly
Type: b&b-inn; romantic mission-style architecture overlooking blue Pacific; charming rms, suites & cottages w/ fireplaces, double-jetted tubs; complimentary wine & cheese
Owned/ Run By: gay & straight
Rooms: 22 (includes 16 guest rms, 5 suites, 1 cottage)

Baths: private
Meals: full gourmet brkfst
Kids: welcome
Pets: welcome; $25 per pet per night
Smoking: no
Rates: $150-590
AC: 10%

The Coast Inn
Orange County

1401 S Coast Hwy
Laguna Beach, CA 92651
949/ 494-7588
800/ 653-2697 (reservations only)
www.boomboomroom.com

Clientele: mixed gay/ lesbian
Type: hotel; also Boom Boom Room bar & cafe: the hottest beach bar in California; located at Laguna Beach
Owned/ Run By: gay men
Rooms: 24

Baths: private
Kids: welcome
Pets: no
Smoking: ok
Rates: $69-99
AC: 10% (1st night lodging)

Laguna Brisas Spa Hotel
Orange County

1600 S Coast Hwy
Laguna Beach, CA 92651
949/ 497-7272 888/ 296-6834
www.lagunabrisas.com

Clientele: mixed gay/ straight
Type: resort; "all-new, lavishly appointed guest rms w/ in-rm spa for 2; parking is free & so is brkfst"
Owned/ Run By: gay & straight
Rooms: 66
Baths: private
Wheelchair Access: yes, 4 rms

Meals: cont'l brkfst
Amenities: pool, outdoor hot tub
Kids: welcome
Pets: welcome; $50 per day pet fee
Smoking: no
Rates: $99-350
AC: 10%

Laguna Cliffs Marriott Resort & Spa
Orange County

25135 Park Lantern
Dana Point, CA 92629
949/ 661-5000 800/ 533-9748
www.marriott.com/SNADP

Clientele: gay-friendly
Type: resort; oceanview rms w/ CD player, minibar, high-speed internet; walk to beach & harbor; minutes from clubs & attractions
Rooms: 347
Baths: private
Wheelchair Access: yes, 11 rms

Meals: coffee/tea only
Amenities: pool, sauna, hot tub, massage
Kids: welcome
Pets: dog & cats up to 50 lbs welcome
Smoking: ok
Rates: $129-438; ask for IGLTA rate
AC: 10%

Laguna Magical Cottages
Orange County

217 & 223 Nyes Pl
Laguna Beach, CA 92651
949/ 494-4554
www.lagunamagicalcottages.com

Clientele: mixed gay/ straight
Type: cottage; charming beach cottages built in the 1930s; restored to perfection; gas-burning fireplaces, open-beam ceilings & gourmet kitchens; just steps to exclusive Victoria Beach
Rooms: 2 (cottages)

Baths: private
Meals: coffee/tea only
Kids: welcome
Pets: welcome
Rates: $975-1,575/ week
AC: 10%

Best Western Lighthouse Hotel
Pacifica

105 Rockaway Beach
Pacifica, CA 94044
650/ 355-6300 800/ 832-4777
bestwesternlighthouse.com

Type: hotel; stay at the only Bay Area hotel right on the Pacific Ocean; only 15 minutes from San Francisco & SFO
Rooms: 97 + 20 suites
Baths: private
Meals: expanded cont'l brkfst

Amenities: free parking, pool, sauna, hot tub, WiFi
Kids: welcome
Smoking: no
Rates: $139-400
AC: 10%

2022 Casa Diego Baristo
Palm Springs

2022 E Baristo Rd
Palm Springs, CA 92262
760/ 320-1124
52-322/ 223-4676 (Mexico #)

Clientele: mixed gay/ lesbian
Type: rental home; short & long-term vacation rental in central Palm Springs; w/ spa & view; near bars; also accommodations in Puerto Vallarta, Mexico

Owned/ Run By: gay men
Rooms: 3
Baths: private

All Worlds Resort
Palm Springs

526 Warm Sands Dr
Palm Springs, CA 92264
760/ 323-7505 800/ 798-8781
www.allworldsresort.com

Clientele: men
Type: resort; newly renovated w/ 44 rms; clothing-optional w/ 4-star features; "the complete gay man's resort!"; *Out & About* raves: "high sexual temperature"
Owned/ Run By: gay men
Rooms: 44 (includes studios, suites, deluxe suites)
Baths: private

Meals: expanded cont'l brkfst
Amenities: free parking, poolside mist, sauna, DVDs/ videos, WiFi
Kids: no
Pets: no
Smoking: ok
Rates: $99-250
AC: 10%

Another World
Palm Springs

526 Warm Sands
Palm Springs, CA 92264
760/ 323-7505 800/ 798-8781
www.anotherworldresort.com

Clientele: men
Type: resort; clothing-optional resort for gay men w/ exquisitely appointed themed suites inspired by Hollywood legends
Owned/ Run By: gay men
Rooms: 6
Baths: private
Meals: expanded cont'l brkfst

Amenities: free parking, pool, poolside mist, sauna, outdoor hot tub, DVDs/ videos, WiFi
Kids: no
Pets: no
Smoking: ok
Rates: $160-250
AC: 10%

Bacchanal Resort
Palm Springs

589 S Grenfall Rd
Palm Springs, CA 92264
760/ 323-0760 800/ 806-9059
www.bacchanal.net

Clientele: men
Type: resort; finely appointed studios & suites surrounding a pool & 9-man hot tub; clothing-optional; in the heart of Warm Sands; luxurious, friendly & fun
Owned/ Run By: gay men
Rooms: 8
Baths: private
Meals: expanded cont'l brkfst

Amenities: free parking, pool, poolside mist, outdoor hot tub, massage, DVDs/ videos
Kids: no
Pets: welcome; $20 fee per stay
Smoking: no
Rates: $99-215
AC: please inquire

Ballantines Hotel
Palm Springs

1420 N Indian Canyon Dr
Palm Springs, CA 92262
760/ 320-1178 800/ 485-2808
www.ballantinesoriginalhotel.com

Type: fabulous retro hotel; theme rms that celebrate the 1950s in Palm Springs
Rooms: 14
Baths: private

Amenities: pool, hot tub, WiFi
Rates: $99-265

BauHouse in the Desert
Palm Springs

2470 S Yosemite Dr
Palm Springs, CA 92264
760/ 320-6800
jfmeagher@aol.com

Clientele: mixed gay/ straight
Type: rental home; 4-bdrm, mid-century modern house w/ 3,750 sq ft; designer-owned; sauna, 20x40 pool & spa on golf course; mtn views
Owned/ Run By: gay & straight
Rooms: 4
Baths: private

Wheelchair Access: yes
Amenities: free parking, pool, sauna, hot tub, DVDs/ videos
Kids: 13 yrs & up welcome
Pets: small pets welcome
Smoking: no (except outside)
Rates: $425-700
AC: 20%

Caliente Tropics Resort
Palm Springs

411 E Palm Canyon Dr
Palm Springs, CA 92264-8805
760/ 327-1391 888/ 277-0999
www.calientetropics.com

Clientele: mixed gay/ straight
Type: resort; newly restored Polynesian & tiki motor hotel; restaurant, tiki bar & full-service spa treatments
Owned/ Run By: gay & straight
Rooms: 90
Baths: private
Wheelchair Access: yes, 40 rms

Meals: expanded cont'l brkfst
Amenities: free parking, pool, hot tub, massage
Kids: welcome
Pets: welcome; $20 per night
Smoking: no
Rates: $69-295
AC: 10%

Calla Lily Inn
Palm Springs

350 S Belardo Rd
Palm Springs, CA 92262
760/ 323-3654 888/ 888-5787
www.callalilypalmsprings.com

Clientele: gay-friendly
Type: resort; a tranquil oasis in the heart of Palm Springs Village; dramatic mtn views; platinum-level amenities
Owned/ Run By: straights
Rooms: 9
Baths: private

Meals: coffee/tea only
Amenities: free parking, pool, outdoor hot tub, massage, WiFi
Kids: adults preferred
Pets: no
Rates: $99-350
AC: 10%

Camp Palm Springs
Palm Springs

1466 N Palm Canyon Dr
Palm Springs, CA 92262

760/ 322-2267
800/ 793-0063 or 747-7969 (CA only)

camper69@aol.com
www.camp-palm-springs.com

Clientele: men
Type: resort; 2 levels built around central courtyard, pool & spa
Owned/ Run By: gay men
Nearby Attractions: Palm Springs tram
Transit: near public transit; taxi: City Cab 760/ 416-2594
Rooms: 29 total, 20 kings, 9 queens, A/C, color TV, DVD/ VCR, cable, deck, phone, kitchenette, refrigerator, safer sex supplies, maid service
Baths: private, showers
Meals: cont'l brkfst
Amenities: free parking, laundry, pool, poolside mist, sauna, outdoor hot tub, massage, DVDs/ videos, gym, WiFi, coffee/ tea, nudity ok
Pets: welcome
Smoking: ok
Reservations: required *Deposit:* required, 100% *Cancellation:* cancel by 3 days prior or forfeit 100% *Minimum Stay:* wknds & holidays *Check in/ out:* 3pm/ noon

Payment: cash, travelers checks, Visa, Amex, MC, Discover
Season: open yr-round *High season:* Oct-June

Rates: $89-199 *Discounts:* 10% weekly
AC: 10%

Canyon Club Hotel

960 N Palm Canyon Dr
Palm Springs, CA 92262

760/ 778-8042
877/ 258-2887

Palm Springs
canyonclubhotel@aol.com
www.canyonclubhotel.com

Clientele: men
Type: clothing-optional; sauna & steam rm
Owned/ Run By: gay men
Nearby Attractions: near museum, water park; walking distance to downtown shops, restaurants & nightlife
Transit: Sunline Bus Service stops in front of hotel; taxi: Budget Taxi, 760/ 864-9357
Rooms: 32 total, 28 kings, 2 queens, 2 fulls, A/C, color TV, DVD/ VCR (8), cable, patio (9), phone, full kitchen (6), kitchenette (2), refrigerator, safer sex supplies, maid service, recently renovated
Baths: private, bathtubs, showers
Meals: cont'l brkfst
Amenities: office hrs: 8am-10pm; free parking, pool, poolside mist, sauna, outdoor hot tub, DVDs/ videos, gym, WiFi, coffee/ tea, sundeck, 4 in-house video channels, public internet access, fireplace in lobby; nudity ok everywhere except the lobby & gym
Recreation: 2 miles to hiking, Aerial Tram, horseback riding
Smoking: ok

Reservations: *Deposit:* required, 2 night, due holidays *Cancellation:* cancel by 72 hrs prior (2 weeks prior for holidays) or forfeit 1 night (2 nights holidays) *Minimum Stay:* most wknds & holidays *Check in/ out:* 2pm/ noon

Payment: cash, travelers checks, Visa, Amex, MC, Discover
Season: open yr-round *High season:* Oct-May
Rates: $89-139 *Discounts:* 5% for 5 nights; 20% for 20 nights

Casa Ocotillo

240 E Ocotillo Ave
Palm Springs, CA 92264

760/ 327-6110
800/ 996-4108

Palm Springs
reservations@casaocotillo.com
www.casaocotillo.com

Clientele: men
Type: guesthouse; private home; intimate & elegant resort-style accommodations in a 1934 Mexican hacienda
Owned/ Run By: gay men
Transit: 10 minutes to airport
Rooms: suites, kings, A/C, color TV, DVD/ VCR, cable, ceiling fan, phone (w/ voicemail), unique, individually decorated bungalows & suites, broadband internet (wireless or plug-in), guest computer, copy & fax service
Baths: private, showers, robes, hairdryers
Amenities: heated salt-water pool & outdoor hot tub w/ fireplace, guest service kitchen & laundry, extensive DVD/ VHS library, electric-gated off-street parking, private patios & gardens
Kids: no
Pets: welcome; please inquire
Pets On Premises: 2 dogs
Smoking: no
Reservations: required *Deposit:* required, 50% of stay, due at booking, personal check ok *Cancellation:* cancel by certain

time (see website) or forfeit deposit *Minimum Stay:* 2 nights on wknds (except holidays & special events)
Payment: cash, travelers checks, personal checks, Visa, Amex, MC, Discover, debit cards

Season: open yr-round
Rates: $129-200 *Discounts:* 10% for 7+ nights
AC: 10%

CCBC Resort Hotel

Palm Springs

68–369 Sunair Rd
Cathedral City, CA 92234

760/ 324–1350
800/ 472–0836

ccbc@earthlink.net
www.ccbc-gay-resort.com

Clientele: men
Type: resort; 3 1/2 acres of very private, park-like grounds; 1,000-ft walks; nude beach & waterfalls; jail & compound, dungeon; tent spaces
Owned/ Run By: gay men
Nearby Attractions: 25 miles to Joshua Tree Nat'l Park; 10 miles to casinos, tramway; 5 miles to canyons, Living Desert Reserve
Pickup Service: airport pickup; free when available
Transit: near public transit; 5 miles to Palm Springs Airport; 10 miles to Greyhound Station
Rooms: 49 total, 4 suites, 34 kings, 6 queens, A/C, color TV, cable, ceiling fan, deck (9), phone, kitchenette, refrigerator, safer sex supplies, maid service
Baths: private, bathtubs, showers, robes
Wheelchair Access: yes, 2 rms
Meals: cont'l brkfst
Amenities: office hrs: 24hrs; free parking, pool, poolside mist, sauna, outdoor hot tub, massage, DVDs/ videos, snacks, coffee/ tea, steam rm; nudity ok by pool
Recreation: volleyball, croquet
Smoking: ok
Reservations: required *Deposit:* required, 1 night, personal check ok *Cancellation:* cancel by 2 weeks prior or forfeit deposit

Check in/ out: 3pm/ 11am
Payment: cash, travelers checks, Visa, Amex, MC
Season: open yr-round
Rates: $79-199; also $39 for tentsites
AC: 10%

Chaps Inn

Palm Springs

312 E Camino Monte Vista
Palm Springs, CA 92262-4711

760/ 327–8222
800/ 445–8916 (also TTY)

info@chapsinn.com
www.chapsinn.com

Clientele: men
Type: hotel; exclusively for gay men; catering mainly to leathermen, leatherbears & bears; most w/ kitchens; TTY facilities
Owned/ Run By: gay men
Nearby Attractions: tramway, Joshua Tree, Living Desert; restaurants w/in walking distance
Transit: near public transit; 2 1/2 hrs to LAX; 1 hr to Ontario; 15 minutes to Palm Springs Airport
Rooms: 10 total, 1 suite, 8 kings, 1 queen, 1 twin, A/C, color TV, DVD/ VCR, cable, deck (5), phone, kitchenette (9), refrigerator, safer sex supplies, down comforters, coffeemakers, microwaves, toaster, large rms, all w/ hooks for slings (available for rent)
Baths: private, bathtubs, showers, hairdryers
Wheelchair Access: yes, 4 rms
Meals: coffee/tea only
Amenities: office hrs: 7am-9pm; free parking, pool, poolside mist, outdoor hot tub, DVDs/ videos, WiFi, coffee/ tea, steam rm, outdoor sling, stocks, St Andrew's Cross
Kids: no
Pets: please inquire
Pets On Premises: cats
Smoking: ok
Reservations: required *Cancellation:* cancel by 2 days prior or forfeit 1 night *Minimum Stay:* 3 nights (major holidays) *Check in/ out:* noon
Payment: cash, travelers checks, personal checks, Visa, Amex, MC, Discover
Season: open yr-round *High season:* Nov-May
Rates: $109-149 *Discounts:* stays over 7 days
AC: 12%

Chestnutz 🏳️‍🌈   *Palm Springs*
641 San Lorenzo Rd   760/ 325-5269   Chestnutz1@aol.com
Palm Springs, CA 92264   800/ 621-6973   www.chestnutz.com

With a relaxed atmosphere and attention to guest comforts, Chestnutz is the perfect place to relax and recharge from the stresses of everyday life. As guests frequently state, staying at Chestnutz is like vacationing with a good friend. Located within easy walking distance of restaurants and bars in the downtown area, the resort is convenient to the excitement, pleasures, and treasures of Palm Springs. The hotel's beautiful garden setting and magnificent mountain views offer a tranquil place to unwind and enjoy the sun and fun of a great vacation experience.

Recently renovated with all-new mattresses, carpeting, and room décor, Chestnutz offers individually decorated rooms that offer all the comforts with an "at home" touch. All rooms have individual climate control, TV/VCR, iron and full-sized ironing board, imported guest toiletries, and guest robes. Room rates include breakfast, along with a variety of complimentary guest items. Grounds are "clothing optional" without restriction, and include pool, Jacuzzi, guest gym, and 24-hour internet station.

Clientele: primarily gay men
Type: resort; w/ relaxed friendly atmosphere & attention to guest comforts, a visit to Chestnutz is like vacationing w/ a good friend"
Owned/ Run By: gay men
Nearby Attractions: the Tram, Joshua Tree Nat'l Park, The Living Desert, Wind Farms, Idyllwild, Moore Botanical Gardens, spas & casinos
Pickup Service: airport pickup; $10
Transit: 10 minutes to Palm Springs Regional Airport; 5 minutes to bus station
Rooms: 12 total, 6 suites, 6 kings, 6 queens, 1 twin, A/C, color TV, DVD/ VCR, cable, ceiling fan, deck (6), phone, kitchenette (6), refrigerator, safer sex supplies, rm service, maid service, all rms individually decorated in a variety of styles
Baths: private, bathtubs, showers, robes, hairdryers
Wheelchair Access: yes, 2 rms
Meals: expanded cont'l brkfst
Amenities: laundry, pool, poolside mist, outdoor hot tub, massage, DVDs/ videos, gym, WiFi, snacks, sunset drinks, soda & juice honor bar, 24hr complimentary coffee/ tea/ cocoa; 24hr free internet station
Kids: no
Pets: welcome w/ prior approval
Pets On Premises: 1 cat, 1 dog
Smoking: no
Reservations: required *Cancellation:* cancel by 2 weeks prior or forfeit full amount *Minimum Stay:* 2 nights (wknds)/ up to 6 nights (holidays)
Payment: cash, travelers checks, Visa, Amex, MC, Discover, Diners Club
Season: open yr-round *High season:* Oct-May
Rates: $99-229 *Discounts:* weekly stays
AC: 10-20%

Casitas Laquita
Palm Springs

450 E Palm Canyon Dr
Palm Springs, CA 92264
760/ 416-9999 877/ 203-3410
www.casitaslaquita.com

Clientele: lesbians
Type: world-class lesbian resort on 1.2 acres; casitas w/ full kitchens; some w/ new spa-hot tub suite, private yard & fireplace
Owned/ Run By: lesbian
Rooms: 15
Baths: private
Wheelchair Access: yes, 1 rm

Meals: cont'l brkfst
Amenities: laundry, pool, poolside mist, outdoor hot tub, massage, DVDs/ videos, WiFi
Pets: small pets welcome
Smoking: no
Rates: $135-350
AC: 10-12%

Century Palm Springs
Palm Springs

598 Grenfall Rd
Palm Springs, CA 92264
760/ 323-9966 800/ 475-5188
www.centurypalmsprings.com

Clientele: men
Type: hotel; modern, hip & comfortable place to enjoy; called "a mid-century masterpiece" by In LA Magazine
Owned/ Run By: gay men
Rooms: 9 (including 3 suites)
Baths: private

Meals: cont'l brkfst
Amenities: free parking, pool, outdoor hot tub, DVDs/ videos
Pets: welcome at proprietors' discretion (guest assumes responsibilities)
Rates: $139-259
AC: 15%

Columns Resort
Palm Springs

537 Grenfall Rd
Palm Springs, CA 92264
760/ 325-0655 800/ 798-0655
www.pscolumns.com

Clientele: men
Type: resort; intimate, friendly & relaxed; w/ pool & spa in a tropical central courtyard; clothing-optional
Owned/ Run By: gay men
Rooms: 7
Baths: private
Wheelchair Access: yes

Meals: expanded cont'l brkfst
Amenities: free parking, pool, poolside mist, sauna, outdoor hot tub, DVDs/ videos
Kids: no
Pets: no
Smoking: ok
Rates: $99-145
AC: 10%

The Desert Bear
Palm Springs

530 Mel Ave
Palm Springs, CA 92262
760/ 325-6767 877/ 464-7695
www.thedesertbear.com

Clientele: men
Type: b&b-inn; clothing-optional; welcomes bears, leathermen & their admirers; "new mgmnt, new look, new attitude!"
Owned/ Run By: gay men
Rooms: 10
Baths: private

Wheelchair Access: yes, all rms
Meals: cont'l brkfst
Amenities: laundry, pool, poolside mist, outdoor hot tub, DVDs/ videos, WiFi
Pets: welcome; $5 each day
Smoking: no
Rates: $89-149

Desert Star Bungalows
Palm Springs

1611 Calle Palo Fierro
Palm Springs, CA 92264
760/ 778-1047 800/ 399-1006
www.desertstarhotel.com

Clientele: gay-friendly
Type: hotel; boutique hotel made up of bungalows w/ fully equipped kitchen & private lounge area
Baths: private

Amenities: pool, WiFi
Kids: no
Pets: no
Rates: $130-180

The East Canyon Hotel & Spa
Palm Springs

288 E Camino Monte Vista
Palm Springs, CA 92262
760/ 320-1928 877/ 324-6835
www.eastcanyonps.com

Clientele: men
Type: hotel; award-winning; luxury accommodations; complete, licensed spa facilities on-site
Owned/ Run By: gay men
Rooms: 15 (includes 1 three-rm suite, 8 jr suites, 6 deluxe double queens)
Baths: private
Wheelchair Access: yes, 1 rm

Meals: expanded cont'l brkfst
Amenities: pool, poolside mist, tented jacuzzi, massage, DVDs/ videos, WiFi
Kids: no
Pets: no
Smoking: no
Rates: $149-359
AC: varies

Desert Moon Resort ☞

2150 N Palm Canyon Dr
Palm Springs, CA 92262

760/ 325-8038
800/ 506-1899

Palm Springs
info@desertmoonresort.com
www.desertmoonresort.com

Clientele: mostly men
Type: resort; lush grounds, surrounded by bougainvillea; citrus-lined courtyard; "come relax w/ us and leave w/ a lifetime of memories"
Owned/ Run By: gay men
Transit: 10 minutes to airport; 5 minutes to bus terminal; taxi: City Cab, 760/416-2594
Rooms: 24 total, 1 suite, queens, A/C, color TV, cable, kitchenette (7), refrigerator (18), safer sex supplies, maid service, 3 rms have 2 queen beds
Baths: private, showers, hairdryers
Wheelchair Access: yes, 1 rm
Meals: expanded cont'l brkfst
Amenities: laundry, pool, poolside mist, outdoor hot tub, massage, WiFi, cocktails, manager's reception on wknds
Kids: welcome
Pets: welcome
Pets On Premises: dog
Smoking: no
Reservations: requested *Cancellation:* cancel by 1 week prior or forfeit 1 night

Minimum Stay: 3 nights holidays/ special events *Check in/ out:* 3pm/ noon
Payment: cash, travelers checks, Visa, MC, Discover

Season: open yr-round *High season:* Oct-May
Rates: $99-159
AC: 10%

Desert Paradise Resort Hotel

615 Warm Sands Dr
Palm Springs, CA 92264

760/ 320-5650
800/ 342-7635

Palm Springs
dparadise@desertparadise.com
www.desertparadise.com

Clientele: men
Type: resort; playful, yet elegant; lushly landscaped; clothing-optional; in the heart of Warm Springs; *Out & About* Editor's Choice Award 1999-2004; "your home away from home"
Owned/ Run By: gay men
Nearby Attractions: close to tram, desert, mtns, gay areas, bars, cruisy areas, casinos
Pickup Service: airport pickup
Transit: 5 minutes to Palm Springs airport
Rooms: 14 total, 12 suites, 14 kings, color TV, DVD/ VCR, cable, wetbar, ceiling fan, deck, phone, kitchenette, refrigerator, safer sex supplies, rm service, maid service, microwaves, iron & ironing board, answering machines, central air & heat
Baths: private, showers, hairdryers
Meals: expanded cont'l brkfst
Amenities: laundry, pool, poolside mist, sauna, hot tub, massage, DVDs/ videos, WiFi, snacks, sunset drinks, coffee/ tea, 30 free adult-video channels, garden shower, fire pit, guest computer & data port
Kids: no

Pets: small dogs welcome w/ prior approval
Smoking: no
Reservations: required; w/ credit card guarantee *Deposit:* required, 1 night *Cancellation:* cancel by 2 weeks prior (30 days prior holidays) or forfeit entire stay & $25 *Check in/ out:* 3pm/ 11am

Payment: cash, travelers checks, Visa, Amex, MC, Discover, personal checks in advance only
Season: open yr-round *High season:* Sept-July 4th
Rates: $99-250 *Discounts:* extended stays

El Mirasol Villas
Palm Springs

525 Warm Sands Dr
Palm Springs, CA 92264
760/ 327-5913 800/ 327-2985
www.elmirasol.com

Clientele: men
Type: resort; deluxe bungalows in a lush garden setting; 2 clothing-optional pools & spa; steam rm; outdoor shower; mtn views; originally built by Howard Hughes
Owned/ Run By: gay men
Rooms: 14
Baths: private

Meals: expanded cont'l brkfst
Amenities: free parking, pool, poolside mist, hot tub, DVDs/ videos, WiFi
Kids: no
Pets: no
Smoking: no
Rates: $95-179
AC: 10%

Honeysuckle Inn
Palm Springs

435 E Avenida Olancha
Palm Springs, CA 92264
760/ 322-5793 888/ 275-9903
www.queenofheartsps.com/honey.html

Clientele: women
Type: b&b; newest extension of the Queen of Hearts Resort (just across the street); studios & suites; w/ picket fence, hammock for 2, pool & breathtaking mtn views
Owned/ Run By: lesbians

Rooms: 3
Baths: private
Meals: cont'l brkfst
Pets: small pets welcome
Rates: $110-150
AC: 10%

Indianola—A Tiki Resort
Palm Springs

354 E Stevens Rd
Palm Springs, CA 92262
760/ 323-3203 866/ 468-8454
www.indianola-tiki.com

Clientele: men
Type: recently renovated '50s-era hotel w/ a tiki twist; clothing-optional
Owned/ Run By: gay men
Rooms: 10
Baths: private
Wheelchair Access: yes, all rms

Meals: expanded cont'l brkfst
Amenities: free parking, pool, poolside mist, outdoor hot tub, DVDs/ videos, WiFi
Pets: welcome; must be house-trained
Smoking: ok
Rates: $79-275
AC: 10%

Inn Exile
Palm Springs

545 Warm Sands Dr
Palm Springs, CA 92264

760/ 327-6413
800/ 962-0186

innexile@earthlink.net
www.innexile.com

Clientele: men
Type: resort; gay men's resort where clothing is always optional
Owned/ Run By: gay men
Nearby Attractions: Aerial Tramway, shopping, downtown, museums, casino, bars
Transit: near public transit; 5 minutes to airport; 1 blk to bus
Rooms: 31 total, suites, kings, A/C, color TV, DVD/ VCR, cable, ceiling fan, fireplace (4), phone, refrigerator, safer sex supplies, maid service, houseman service, modern Southwest decor
Baths: private, bathtubs, showers
Wheelchair Access: yes, 1 rm
Meals: cont'l brkfst, Skivvies Cafe, 6pm-10pm, pizza & salads
Amenities: DVDs/ videos, gym, WiFi, sunset drinks, coffee/ tea, steam rm, 4 pools, 2 jacuzzis, poolside mist, outdoor fireplace; nudity ok
Recreation: tennis, golf, hiking
Kids: no
Pets: no

Smoking: ok
Reservations: required; w/ credit card guarantee *Cancellation:* cancel by 3 days prior or forfeit 1 night *Minimum Stay:* please inquire *Check in/ out:* flexible/ noon (invited to stay after check-out)

Payment: cash, travelers checks, Visa, Amex, MC, Discover, Diners Club, Carte Blanche
Season: open yr-round *High season:* Sept-June
Rates: $94-122 *Discounts:* weekly
AC: 10%

The Hacienda at Warm Sands   *Palm Springs*

586 Warm Sands Dr   760/ 327-8111   info@thehacienda.com
Palm Springs, CA 92264   800/ 359-2007   www.thehacienda.com

The Hacienda at Warm Sands, a member of the World's Foremost Gay Hotels, is honored by its inclusion in *Out & About*'s first-ever list of the "Top 10 North American Gay Guest Houses"–and its listing as one of the "World's Most Romantic Hotels." The Hacienda is also the first 5-Palm-rated resort hotel in Palm Springs, which is the highest Editor's Choice Award issued for "outstanding achievement, excellence and innovation in gay travel."

Among its many comments regarding The Hacienda, this prestigious travel newsletter has stated: "luxurious décor, oodles of space–a real class act" and that it is a "friendly, super-service-oriented property which is setting a new standard for excellence in gay hostelry." We also have the highest staff-to-guest-room ratio of any resort in Palm Springs: one-to-one.

Many others have praised The Hacienda with comments, such as, "the best of the best"–*Instinct* magazine, "the things dreams are made of"–*Our World* magazine, and "the most extravagantly spacious and exclusive resort in the area"–*Genre* magazine.

Clientele: men

Type: resort; all-suite; w/ spacious grounds, unparalleled views, friendly staff, concierge service, 2 beautifully situated pools & jacuzzi; clothing-optional

Owned/ Run By: gay men

Transit: 2 miles to airport & bus station

Rooms: 10 total, 9 suites, 1 rm, kings, A/C, all suites poolside, plasma/ LDC TVs & DVDs (2 in each suite), iPods & iHomes, espresso machine in all kitchens/ bars (10), fireplace (4), free WiFi, cordless phones/ answering machines (2 phones in each rm), living rm sleep sofas, pillow menu, plush linens, French doors w/ plantation shutters, Saltillo tile, lavish furnishings & original art

Baths: private; 2-man showers, Kohler spa showers (4), upscale bath amenities, plush towels, robes, hairdryers

Wheelchair Access: yes, 1 rm

Meals: expanded cont'l brkfst, gourmet sandwiches/ salads served for lunch

Amenities: laundry, poolside mist, hot tub, DVDs/ videos, WiFi, snacks, cocktails, coffee/ tea, 2 swimming pools, in-suite massage, concierge, high staff-to-guest ratio; nudity ok

Kids: no

Pets: no

Smoking: on patios only

Reservations: required; w/ credit card guarantee *Deposit:* personal check ok *Cancellation:* cancel by 2 weeks prior (30 days for holidays) *Minimum Stay:* wknds, holidays & events

Payment: cash, travelers checks, Visa, Amex, MC

Season: open yr-round *High season:* Oct & Feb-May

Rates: $169-399 *Discounts:* summer

AC: 10%

INNdulge Palm Springs

Palm Springs

601 Grenfall Rd   760/ 327-1408   inndulge@ix.netcom.com
Palm Springs, CA 92264   800/ 833-5675   www.inndulge.com

INNdulge Palm Springs is a legendary award-winning gay men's resort located in the heart of Warm Sands, one of the most popular gay areas in Palm Springs. It has also been rated Five Palms by *Out & About*, the most trusted source in gay travel.

Built in 1958 in the midcentury style, the hotel is featured in the *Historic Inns of Palm Springs* guidebook. Twenty-four poolside rooms with custom-designed desert-style furnishings surround a 24-hour heated pool and 12-man Jacuzzi. Clothing is forever optional so you can swim nude at midnight!

INNdulge Palm Springs has also received *Out & About*'s coveted Editor's Choice Award for nine consecutive years. Member World's Foremost Gay Hotels (www.worldsforemost.com). Expanded continental breakfast, in-room safes, TV/ VCR with video library, on-site gym, guest internet stations, and property-wide wireless are all complimentary. Several videos were even filmed on the grounds of INNdulge Palm Springs.

A comfortable environment for gay men. Fun, playful, friendly, INNdulgent!

Clientele: men

Type: guesthouse; caters to gay men; clothing-optional pool & jacuzzi open 24hrs; "Five Palms/ Editor's Choice Award"–*Out & About*

Owned/ Run By: gay men

Nearby Attractions: Palm Springs Tram, Palm Springs Art Museum

Transit: near public transit; 1 mile to Palm Springs airport

Rooms: 24 total, 6 suites, 18 kings, A/C, color TV, DVD/ VCR, cable, phone, kitchenette (12), refrigerator, safer sex supplies, maid service, in-rm safes, poolside rms face clothing-optional pool & jacuzzi

Baths: private, showers, whirlpools, hairdryers

Meals: expanded cont'l brkfst

Amenities: laundry, pool, poolside mist, outdoor hot tub, DVDs/ videos, gym, WiFi, snacks, coffee/ tea, guest internet station

Kids: no

Pets: no

Smoking: no (ok in courtyard)

Reservations: *Deposit:* credit card guarantee, personal check ok *Cancellation:* cancel by 1 week prior

Payment: cash, travelers checks, Visa, Amex, MC, Discover

Season: open yr-round *High season:* Oct-May

Rates: $109-195 *Discounts:* 7th night free, summer specials

AC: 10%

La Dolce Vita Resort 🏳️‍🌈   *Palm Springs*

1491 S Via Soledad
Palm Springs, CA 92264
760/ 325-2686 877/ 644-4111
www.ladolcevitaresort.com

Clientele: men
Type: resort; casually elegant, clothing-optional European-style resort hotel
Owned/ Run By: gay men
Rooms: 19
Baths: private
Wheelchair Access: yes, 12 rms
Meals: expanded cont'l brkfst

Amenities: laundry, poolside mist, sauna, hot tub, massage, DVDs/ videos, WiFi
Kids: no
Pets: by special arrangement only
Smoking: no
Rates: $109-189
AC: 10%

Las Palmas Hotel   *Palm Springs*

1404 N Palm Canyon Dr
Palm Springs, CA 92262
760/ 327-6883 866/ 552-7272
www.laspalmas-hotel.com

Clientele: mostly men
Type: resort; mtn views, pool & jacuzzi, luxurious beds & linens
Owned/ Run By: gay men
Rooms: 17
Baths: private
Meals: expanded cont'l brkfst

Amenities: laundry, pool, poolside mist, hot tub, massage, DVDs/ videos, WiFi
Kids: no
Pets: small, well-behaved pets welcome
Smoking: no
Rates: $129-239
AC: 10%

Mirage   *Palm Springs*

555 Grenfall Rd
Palm Springs, CA 92264
760/ 322-2404 800/ 669-1069
www.mirage4men.com

Clientele: gay men
Type: a Vista Grande Resort; luxurious villas; tropical multileveled gardens; waterfalls, fire pit, steam rm, 18-man spa; nudity ok
Owned/ Run By: gay men
Rooms: 4
Baths: private

Wheelchair Access: yes, 1 rm
Meals: cont'l brkfst
Amenities: free parking, laundry, pool, poolside mist, sauna, hot tub, DVDs/ videos
Smoking: ok
Rates: $175-195
AC: 10%

Mojave   *Palm Springs*

73721 Shadow Mountain Dr
Palm Desert, CA 92260
760/ 346-6121 866/ 846-8358
www.hotelmojave.com

Clientele: gay-friendly
Type: newly renovated, luxury boutique hotel offers the romance, glamour & sophistication of the desert of the 1940s
Owned/ Run By: straights
Rooms: 24
Baths: private
Wheelchair Access: yes, 1 rm

Meals: expanded cont'l brkfst
Amenities: free parking, pool, sauna, outdoor hot tub, massage, DVDs/ videos
Kids: welcome
Smoking: no
Rates: $75-219
AC: 10%

Mountain View Villa   *Palm Springs*

305/ 293-9611 305/ 294-1525 (FL#)
www.vacationdepot.com/
palmspringsmesquiterentals.htm

Clientele: mixed gay/ straight
Type: condo; 1- & 2-bdrm luxury villas w/ full kitchens; at Mesquite Country Club
Owned/ Run By: gay & straight
Rooms: 6 (villas)
Baths: private
Meals: coffee/tea only

Amenities: laundry, pool, hot tub
Kids: welcome
Pets: no
Smoking: no
Rates: $159-259
AC: 10-15%

Ozz Resort   *Palm Springs*

67-580 Hwy 111
Cathedral City, CA 92234
760/ 324-3000 866/ 247-7443
www.ozzresort.com

Clientele: mixed gay/ lesbian
Type: resort; w/ rms facing a central courtyard & pool; full-service bar, nightclub & restaurant; featured in the 1963 film *Palm Springs Weekend*
Owned/ Run By: gay man
Rooms: 29
Baths: private

Wheelchair Access: yes, 14 rms
Meals: cont'l brkfst
Amenities: pool, outdoor hot tub, WiFi
Kids: no
Pets: well-behaved welcome; $10 per day
Smoking: no
Rates: $79-149
AC: 10%

Queen of Hearts Resort
Palm Springs

435 E Avenida Olancha
Palm Springs, CA 92264
760/ 322-5793 888/ 275-9903
www.queenofheartsps.com

Clientele: women
Type: b&b; originally The Desert Knight–
  Palm Springs' first resort catering to
  alternative lifestyles; now completely
  renovated & exclusively for women
Owned/ Run By: lesbians
Rooms: 9

Baths: private
Meals: cont'l brkfst
Rates: $105-160
AC: 10%

The Resort at Palm Springs
Palm Springs

701 E Palm Canyon Dr
Palm Springs, CA 92264
760/ 320-2700 800/ 854-4345
www.theresortatpalmsprings.com

Clientele: mixed gay/ straight
Type: hotel
Owned/ Run By: straights
Rooms: 192
Baths: private
Amenities: free parking, laundry, pool,
  poolside mist, outdoor hot tub

Kids: welcome
Pets: welcome; $50 nonrefundable cleaning
  fee
Smoking: ok
Rates: $79-129
AC: 10%

Rick's Palm Spring Vacation Rentals
Palm Springs

760/ 320-8684

Clientele: gay-friendly
Type: reservation service; condos, cottages,
  modern & midcentury homes; all w/ pools
Owned/ Run By: gay men

Baths: private
Rates: $95+

Ruby Montana's Coral Sands Inn
Palm Springs

210 W Stevens Rd
Palm Springs, CA 92262
760/ 325-4900 866/ 820-8302
www.coralsandspalmsprings.com

Clientele: mixed gay/ straight
Type: resort; 1950s resort close to the Rat
  Pack's original gathering spot near the
  base of Mt San Jacinto; close to
  downtown
Owned/ Run By: lesbians/ gay men
Rooms: 7

Baths: private
Wheelchair Access: yes, 7 rms
Kids: welcome
Pets: welcome
Rates: $107-120
AC: 10%

Santiago Resort
Palm Springs

650 San Lorenzo Rd
Palm Springs, CA 92264
760/ 322-1300 800/ 710-7729
www.santiagoresort.com

Clientele: men
Type: resort; sophisticated & elegant but w/
  casual atmosphere; clothing-optional;
  sauna & shower garden; also
  complimentary lunch
Rooms: 23
Baths: private
Meals: expanded cont'l brkfst

Amenities: laundry, pool, poolside mist,
  sauna, hot tub, DVDs/ videos
Kids: no
Pets: no
Smoking: no
Rates: $139-189
AC: 10%

Sun & Fun Vacation Rentals
Palm Springs

760/ 322-7961
www.sandfvr.com

Clientele: mixed gay/ straight
Type: vacation rental houses/ condos; 1-4-
  bdrms; some w/ pools
Owned/ Run By: gay men
Baths: private

Kids: welcome in certain units
Pets: welcome in certain units
Smoking: no
Rates: $120-350
AC: 5%

Terrazzo Resort

Palm Springs

1600 E Palm Canyon Dr
Palm Springs, CA 92264
760/ 778-5883 866/ 837-7996
www.terrazzo-ps.com

Clientele: men
Type: resort; "intimate & relaxing, clothing-optional men's resort where you can relax & rejuvenate & be completely catered to"
Owned/ Run By: gay men
Rooms: 12
Baths: private
Wheelchair Access: yes, 1 rm

Meals: expanded cont'l brkfst
Amenities: pool, poolside mist, outdoor hot tub, DVDs/ videos, gym, WiFi
Kids: no
Pets: no
Smoking: ok (on property; not in rms)
Rates: $109-219
AC: 10%

The Three Thirty Three B&B

Palm Springs

333 E Ramon Rd
Palm Springs, CA 92264
760/ 320-7744 (9am-8pm PST)
www.333bnb.com

Clientele: mixed gay/ straight
Type: b&b; midcentury modern transformed into small hotel; 8-person spa
Owned/ Run By: gay men
Rooms: 3

Baths: private
Meals: expanded cont'l brkfst (full wknds)
Amenities: free parking, outdoor hot tub
Smoking: no (outside only)
Rates: $85-150

Tortuga del Sol

Palm Springs

715 San Lorenzo
Palm Springs, CA 92264
760/ 416-3111 888/ 541-3777
www.tortugadelsol.com

Clientele: men
Type: resort; unique & intimate clothing-optional resort; "superior guest services, supreme sleeping accommodations & a friendly relaxing atmosphere"
Owned/ Run By: gay men
Rooms: 12
Baths: private

Meals: expanded cont'l brkfst
Amenities: laundry, pool, poolside mist, hot tub, massage, DVDs/ videos, gym, WiFi
Kids: no
Pets: welcome
Smoking: no
Rates: $99-259
AC: 10%

Triangle Inn Palm Springs

Palm Springs

555 San Lorenzo Rd
Palm Springs, CA 92264

760/ 322-7993
800/ 732-7555

triangleinnps@earthlink.net
www.triangle-inn.com

Clientele: men
Type: guesthouse; elegant suites, lush tropical gardens, sparkling pool, soothing jacuzzi, 2 large sundecks, spectacular mtn views; "escape to our unique enclosed compound where clothing is always optional"
Owned/ Run By: gay men
Pickup Service: airport pickup; free
Transit: 5 minutes to airport
Rooms: 9 (plus separate guesthouse that sleeps 8) total, 6 suites, 4 kings, 6 queens, A/C, color TV, DVD/ VCR, cable, ceiling fan (1), phone, kitchenette (2), refrigerator, safer sex supplies, maid service, also 6 full kitchens, stereo/ CD
Baths: private, bathtubs, showers, hairdryers
Meals: expanded cont'l brkfst
Amenities: laundry, pool, poolside mist, outdoor hot tub, DVDs/ videos, snacks, cocktails; nudity ok
Kids: no
Pets: no
Pets On Premises: 1 cat

Smoking: ok
Reservations: required *Deposit:* required, 1 night (plus tax), due at booking, personal check ok *Cancellation:* cancel by varying times or forfeit deposit *Minimum Stay:* applies over holidays

Payment: cash, travelers checks, Visa, Amex, MC, Discover
Season: open yr-round *High season:* Oct-May
Rates: $115-450 *Discounts:* 7+ nights
AC: 10%

The Villa Resort Palm Springs ▣

Palm Springs

67-670 Carey Rd
Cathedral City, CA 92234

760/ 328-7211
877/ 778-4552

reservations@thevilla.com
www.thevilla.com

Clientele: mostly men
Type: resort; totally remodeled; rated "best of the best"; provides 5 acres of fun
Owned/ Run By: gay men
Transit: 1/4 mile to SunBus transit
Rooms: 43 total, 15 kings, 15 queens, 13 fulls, A/C, color TV, DVD/ VCR, cable, wetbar, ceiling fan (3), deck (7), phone, kitchenette (4), refrigerator, safer sex supplies, rm service, maid service, deluxe designer casitas w/ private patios
Baths: private, bathtubs, showers, robes, hairdryers
Meals: cont'l brkfst, also full-service restaurant
Amenities: laundry, pool, poolside mist, sauna, hot tub, massage, DVDs/ videos, gym, WiFi, fine dining indoors & out at Butterfield's Adobe Restaurant; also poolside cocktail bar & our new V Lounge supperclub
Kids: please call ahead
Pets: welcome
Pets On Premises: ducks
Smoking: ok (in some rms)

Reservations: required *Deposit:* required, 1 night, personal check ok *Cancellation:* cancel by 3 days prior (1 week for special events) or forfeit 1 night *Minimum Stay:* holidays only *Check in/ out:* 3pm/ noon
Payment: cash, travelers checks, Visa, Amex, MC, Discover
Season: open yr-round *High season:* Oct-May
Rates: $99-179   *Discounts:* midweek specials
AC: 10%

Warm Sands Villas

Palm Springs

555 Warm Sands Dr
Palm Springs, CA 92264

760/ 323-3005
800/ 357-5695

warmsandsvillas@earthlink.net
warmsandsvillas.com

Clientele: men
Type: resort; Spanish architecture w/ expansive courtyard & lush landscaping; in the heart of Palm Springs; guest rms w/ modern amenities; clothing-optional
Owned/ Run By: gay men
Transit: near public transit; 2 blks
Rooms: 27 total, 8 suites, kings, A/C, color TV, DVD/ VCR, cable, ceiling fan, fireplace (5), phone, kitchenette (16), refrigerator, safer sex supplies, maid service, bungalow-style rms w/ modern amenities including climate control & travertine stone flrs
Baths: private, bathtubs, showers, hairdryers
Wheelchair Access: yes, 16 rms
Meals: expanded cont'l brkfst, coffee/ tea
Amenities: pool, poolside mist, outdoor hot tub, massage, DVDs/ videos, guest internet station, broadband wireless internet access, evening refreshments
Kids: no
Pets: no
Smoking: no
Reservations: required; walk-ins welcome *Deposit:* 1st night, due at booking

Cancellation: cancel by 1 week prior or forfeit deposit *Minimum Stay:* 2 nights; 3 nights (holidays) *Check in/ out:* 3pm/ noon
Payment: cash, travelers checks, personal checks, Visa, Amex, MC, Discover, Optima, Diners Club
Season: open yr-round *High season:* Jan-May
Rates: $109-239   *Discounts:* midweek, weekly, off-season (summer)
AC: 10%

Villa Royale
Palm Springs

1620 Indian Trail
Palm Springs, CA 92264
760/ 327-2314 800/ 245-2314
www.villaroyale.com

Clientele: gay-friendly
Type: resort; "named one of the five best small inns in Southern California by *Sunset Magazine*"
Rooms: 31 (villas)
Baths: private

Meals: full brkfst
Amenities: pool, hot tub
Kids: adults preferred
Pets: no
Rates: $139-279

Vista Grande Villa ⊞G⊞
Palm Springs

574 Warm Sands Dr
Palm Springs, CA 92264
760/ 322-2404 800/ 669-1069
www.mirage4men.com

Clientele: gay men
Type: "mega resort; world-famous clothing-optional exotic male playground; fantastic multilevel tropical gardens & waterfalls; 18-man spa steam rm
Owned/ Run By: gay men
Rooms: 40
Baths: private

Meals: cont'l brkfst
Amenities: free parking, laundry, pool, poolside mist, sauna, outdoor hot tub (jacuzzi), massage, DVDs/ videos
Smoking: ok
Rates: $79-195
AC: 10%

Creekside Inn
Palo Alto

3400 El Camino Real
Palo Alto, CA 94306
650/ 493-2411 800/ 492-7335
www.creekside-inn.com

Clientele: mixed gay/ straight
Type: inn; nestled in a tranquil creekside setting; abundant gardens & trees; close to Stanford University; lounge/ bar, deli, wine hr
Owned/ Run By: gay/ lesbian & straight
Rooms: 136
Baths: private

Wheelchair Access: yes, 4 rms
Meals: coffee/tea only
Amenities: free parking, laundry, pool, WiFi
Kids: welcome
Smoking: no
Rates: $179-259
AC: 10%

Hotel Avante ⊞G⊞
Palo Alto

860 El Camino Real
Mountain View, CA 94040
650/ 940-1000 800/ 538-1600
www.hotelavante.com

Clientele: gay-friendly
Type: hotel; ideally located in bustling heart of Silicon Valley
Owned/ Run By: gay & straight
Rooms: 91
Baths: private
Wheelchair Access: yes
Meals: expanded cont'l brkfst

Amenities: free parking, pool, outdoor hot tub
Kids: welcome
Pets: service animals only
Smoking: no
Rates: $210+
AC: 10%

Costanoa
Pescadero

2001 Rossi Rd
Pescadero, CA 94060
650/ 879-1100 877/ 262-7848
www.costanoa.com

Clientele: mixed gay/ straight
Type: 40-rm coastal lodge & camp w/ tent bungalows & cabins; also restaurant, general store & spa; 1 hr S of San Francisco (close to Año Nuevo reserve, home of the elephant seals)

Kids: welcome
Rates: $40-365

Estancia del Mar
Pescadero

PO Box 58
Pescadero, CA 94060
650/ 879-1500
www.estanciadelmar.com

Clientele: gay-friendly
Type: cottage; 5 non-hosted rental cottages w/ ocean views & fully equipped kitchens; on majestic San Mateo County coast & overlooking Pigeon Point & Año Nuevo
Rooms: 5 (cottages)
Baths: private

Wheelchair Access: yes, 1 rm
Meals: coffee/tea only
Kids: welcome
Pets: welcome; w/ prior approval
Smoking: no
Rates: $150-225

The Palms Inn

Petaluma

2 Liberty St
Petaluma, CA 94952
707/ 658-2554
www.oldpalms.com

Clientele: gay-friendly
Type: b&b; quiet & private Victorian; located in the heart of Petaluma; 5-course gourmet brkfst
Owned/ Run By: straights
Rooms: 6
Baths: private

Wheelchair Access: yes, 1 rm
Meals: full brkfst
Kids: welcome
Pets: no
Smoking: no
Rates: $125-200
AC: please inquire

Cottage Inn by the Sea

Pismo Beach

2351 Price St
Pismo Beach, CA 93449
805/ 773-4617 888/ 440-8400
www.cottage-inn.com

Clientele: gay-friendly
Type: hotel
Rooms: 80
Baths: private
Wheelchair Access: yes, 5 rms
Meals: expanded cont'l brkfst

Amenities: free parking, pool, outdoor hot tub
Kids: welcome
Pets: welcome
Smoking: no
Rates: $99-229
AC: 10%

Sandcastle Inn

Pismo Beach

100 Stimson Ave
Pismo Beach, CA 93449
805/ 773-2422 800/ 822-6606
www.sandcastleinn.com

Clientele: gay-friendly
Type: on the sand in Pismo Beach; ocean- & pier-view rms available; some rms w/ balconies & fireplaces
Rooms: 75
Baths: private
Meals: expanded cont'l brkfst

Amenities: free parking, outdoor hot tub, WiFi
Kids: welcome
Pets: welcome
Rates: $99-359
AC: 10%

Spyglass Inn

Pismo Beach

2705 Spyglass Dr
Pismo Beach, CA 93449
805/ 773-4855 800/ 824-2612
www.spyglassinn.com

Type: hotel; on the bluffs overlooking the Pacific Ocean; open-air dining w/ ocean view
Rooms: 82
Baths: private
Wheelchair Access: yes, 2 rms
Meals: coffee/tea only

Amenities: free parking, pool, WiFi
Kids: welcome
Pets: welcome in smoking rms only
Rates: $99-299
AC: 10%

Albert Shafsky House B&B

Placerville

2942 Coloma St
Placerville, CA 95667
530/ 642-2776
www.shafsky.com

Clientele: gay-friendly
Type: b&b; all the comforts of home; ideal location; walking distance to town
Owned/ Run By: lesbians
Rooms: 3
Baths: private
Meals: full brkfst

Amenities: free parking, DVDs/ videos, WiFi
Kids: welcome; please call
Pets: no
Smoking: no
Rates: $115-145

Rancho Cicada Retreat

Placerville

PO Box 225
Plymouth, CA 95669
209/ 245-4841 877/ 553-9481
www.ranchocicadaretreat.com

Clientele: mostly men
Type: retreat; secluded riverside retreat in the Sierra foothills w/ 8' X 10' two person tent-cabins w/ mattresses & 2 cabins; private group use available
Owned/ Run By: gay man
Rooms: 25 tent-cabins & 2 cabins

Baths: private & shared
Amenities: free parking, outdoor hot tub, massage
Kids: please inquire
Pets: no
Rates: $100-200 (lower during week)

Best Western Sunrise Hotel   *Redondo Beach*

400 N Harbor Dr
Redondo Beach, CA 90277
310/ 376-0746 800/ 334-7384
www.bestwestern-sunrise.com

Clientele: gay-friendly
Type: hotel
Rooms: 111
Baths: private
Wheelchair Access: yes

Meals: expanded cont'l brkfst
Amenities: free parking, pool, outdoor hot tub, WiFi
Kids: welcome
Rates: $119-169

Palos Verdes Inn   *Redondo Beach*

1700 S Pacific Coast Hwy
Redondo Beach, CA 90277
310/ 316-4211 800/ 421-9241
www.palosverdesinn.com

Clientele: gay-friendly
Type: hotel; 3 blks from the beach; located at the tip of the shopping area, Riviera Village & surrounded by great restaurants
Rooms: 110
Baths: private
Wheelchair Access: yes, all rms

Amenities: free parking, pool, hot tub, massage, WiFi
Kids: welcome
Smoking: ok
Rates: $75-125
AC: 10%

Applewood Inn   *Russian River*

13555 Hwy 116
Guerneville, CA 95446
707/ 869-9093 800/ 555-8509
www.applewoodinn.com

Clientele: gay-friendly
Type: b&b-inn; luxury villa compound; also acclaimed restaurant & wine cellar; near wineries, redwoods & Sonoma Coast
Owned/ Run By: gay men
Rooms: 19
Baths: private
Wheelchair Access: yes, 1 rm
Meals: full brkfst

Amenities: free parking, pool, outdoor hot tub, WiFi
Kids: welcome in Piccola Casa or Gate House
Pets: welcome in designated rm
Smoking: no (inside or out)
Rates: $185-345
AC: 10% (off-season only)

Dawn Ranch Lodge [T&G]   *Russian River*

16467 River Rd
Guerneville, CA 95446
707/ 869-0656 800/ 734-3371
www.dawnranch.com

Clientele: gay-friendly
Type: resort; 15 acres of redwoods, rose gardens & meadows; private beach on the Russian River; 2 bars & 1 restaurant
Owned/ Run By: gay man
Rooms: 55
Baths: private
Wheelchair Access: yes, 1 rm

Meals: cont'l brkfst
Amenities: pool, massage, gym, WiFi
Kids: welcome; w/ restrictions
Pets: dogs welcome; $25 per night; must be leashed at all times
Smoking: no
Rates: $89-289
AC: 10%

Eagle's Peak   *Russian River*

11644 Our Peak Rd
Forestville, CA 95436
707/ 887-9218 877/ 891-6466
www.eaglespeak.net

Clientele: men
Type: retreat; 1,500-sq-ft secluded getaway on 26 acres; w/ grand views, large deck, indoor spa, sleeps 8-10 people
Owned/ Run By: gay men

Rooms: 1 (home)
Baths: private
Amenities: free parking, indoor hot tub, massage, DVDs/ videos
Rates: $195-255

Fern Grove Cottages   *Russian River*

16650 River Rd
Guerneville, CA 95446
707/ 869-8105 888/ 243-2674
www.ferngrove.com

Clientele: gay-friendly
Type: b&b-inn; cottages surrounded by redwoods & lush gardens; walk to town; near wineries & ocean
Owned/ Run By: straights
Rooms: 20
Baths: private
Wheelchair Access: yes, 1 rm

Meals: expanded cont'l brkfst
Amenities: free parking, pool, WiFi
Kids: well-behaved kids welcome
Pets: welcome w/ prior approval; spa rms excluded
Smoking: no
Rates: $89-239
AC: 10%

Grandma's House

Russian River

20280 River Blvd
Monte Rio, CA 95462
707/ 865-1865
www.rrgetaways.com/grandmas_1.htm

Clientele: mixed gay/ lesbian
Type: rental home; spacious home on private beach
Owned/ Run By: lesbians
Rooms: 4
Baths: private

Wheelchair Access: yes, 1 rm
Kids: welcome
Pets: welcome
Rates: $600

Highland Dell Resort

Russian River

21050 River Blvd
Monte Rio, CA 95462-0370
707/ 865-2300
www.highlanddell.com

Clientele: gay-friendly
Type: hotel; serene river retreat; restaurant & bar overlooking river; some rms w/ private balconies
Rooms: 15 (includes penthouse rm)
Baths: private

Meals: cont'l brkfst
Amenities: WiFi

Highlands Resort ⓣ🄶

Russian River

14000 Woodland Dr, PO Box 346
Guerneville, CA 95446
707/ 869-0333
www.HighlandsResort.com

Clientele: mixed gay/ lesbian
Type: resort; an adult retreat on 3 wooded acres in Guerneville; w/ casually comfortable cabins & rustic camping (20 campsites); near bars & restaurants
Owned/ Run By: straights
Rooms: 16
Baths: private & shared

Meals: cont'l brkfst
Amenities: free parking, pool, outdoor hot tub, massage
Pets: welcome in certain cabins by arrangement
Smoking: ok
Rates: $45-170
AC: 10%

Huckleberry Springs Country Inn & Spa

Russian River

PO Box 400
Monte Rio, CA 95462
707/ 865-2683 800/ 822-2683
www.huckleberrysprings.com

Clientele: mixed gay/ straight
Type: b&b-inn; cottage accommodations on 56 acres of redwoods; fabulous views from lodge; on-site restaurant & spa treatments
Owned/ Run By: women
Rooms: 4
Baths: private
Meals: full brkfst

Amenities: free parking, pool, outdoor hot tub, massage, DVDs/ videos
Kids: no
Pets: no
Smoking: no
Rates: $145-175

Inn at Occidental

Russian River

3657 Church St
Occidental, CA 95465
707/ 874-1047 800/ 522-6324
www.innatoccidental.com

Clientele: gay-friendly
Type: b&b-inn; also cottage; luxury Sonoma Wine Country inn
Rooms: 18 (includes 1 cottage)
Baths: private
Wheelchair Access: yes

Meals: full brkfst
Kids: welcome w/ prior approval
Pets: no
Smoking: no
Rates: $199-629

Inn at the Willows

Russian River

15905 River Rd
Guerneville, CA 95446
707/ 869-2824 (8am-8pm PST)
800/ 953-2828
www.innatthewillows.com

Clientele: mixed gay/ lesbian
Type: 1945 redwood lodge, campground (75 sites) & spa on 5 riverfront acres w/ dock; in Wine Country & 20 minutes from Pacific Ocean
Rooms: 13
Baths: private & shared
Meals: cont'l brkfst

Amenities: free parking, sauna, outdoor hot tub, massage, DVDs/ videos
Kids: welcome
Pets: welcome
Smoking: no
Rates: $25+ (camping)/ $99-179 (lodge)
AC: 10%

New Dynamic Inn   *Russian River*

14030 Mill St
Guerneville, CA 95446
707/ 869-5082
www.newdynamicinn.com

Clientele: mixed gay/ straight
Type: motel; w/in walking distance of dowtown Guerneville & the Russian River
Owned/ Run By: straights
Rooms: 8
Baths: private

Wheelchair Access: yes, 1 rm
Amenities: free parking, WiFi
Kids: welcome
Pets: welcome in some rms; fee
Smoking: no
Rates: $59-225

Ridenhour Ranch House Inn & Cottages   *Russian River*

12850 River Rd
Guerneville, CA 95446
707/ 887-1033 888/ 877-4466
www.ridenhourranchhouseinn.com

Clientele: gay-friendly
Type: b&b; built in 1906; near redwood forests, wineries & Pacific Ocean
Rooms: 8 (includes 2 rms in cottage)
Meals: full brkfst

Amenities: outdoor hot tub, WiFi
Kids: welcome
Pets: dogs welcome w/ prior approval
Smoking: no
Rates: $139-199

Rio Villa Beach Resort   *Russian River*

20292 Hwy 116
Monte Rio, CA 95462
707/ 865-1143 877/ 746-8455
www.riovilla.com

Clientele: gay-friendly
Type: b&b-inn; relaxing resort on the Russian River; "perfect for weddings & romantic getaways"
Owned/ Run By: gay men
Rooms: 11
Baths: private
Meals: cont'l brkfst

Amenities: free parking, hot tub, massage, DVDs/ videos, WiFi
Kids: welcome
Pets: no
Smoking: no
Rates: $99-229
AC: 10%

River Gem Resort   *Russian River*

20284 Hwy 116
Monte Rio, CA 95462
707/ 865-1467 800/ 865-1467
www.rivergemresort.com

Clientele: mixed gay/ straight
Type: cottage; historic cottages on the Russian River; views of water, redwoods & mtns
Owned/ Run By: straights
Rooms: 6
Baths: private

Meals: coffee/tea only
Amenities: free parking, laundry, DVDs/ videos
Kids: welcome
Pets: welcome
Smoking: no
Rates: $80-160

River Village Resort & Spa   *Russian River*

PO Box 526
Guerneville, CA 95446
707/ 869-8139 888/ 342-2624
www.rivervillageresort.com

Clientele: mixed gay/ straight
Type: resort; 18 intimate cottages & full-service spa; close to downtown Guerneville; cont'l brkfst during high season & holidays
Owned/ Run By: straights
Rooms: 18 (cottages)
Baths: private

Wheelchair Access: yes, 1 rm
Amenities: free parking, laundry, pool, outdoor hot tub, massage, DVDs/ videos
Kids: welcome; please call ahead
Pets: dogs welcome in certain cottages only
Smoking: no
Rates: $90-195
AC: 8%

Russian River Resort/ Triple R Resort   *Russian River*

16390 4th St
Guerneville, CA 95446
707/ 869-0691 800/ 417-3767
www.RussianRiverResort.com

Clientele: mixed gay/ lesbian
Type: resort; full-service w/ spa, pool, bar, live entertainment & superb restaurant; open yr-round
Owned/ Run By: gay men
Rooms: 24
Baths: private

Wheelchair Access: yes, 3 rms
Amenities: free parking, pool, outdoor hot tub, massage, DVDs/ videos
Kids: welcome in restaurant only
Pets: welcome w/ prior approval
Smoking: ok
Rates: $55-195

Tim & Tony's Treehouse
Russian River

PO Box 609
Forestville, CA 95436
707/ 887-9531 888/ 887-9531
www.timntony.com

Clientele: mixed gay/ straight
Type: cottage; on 21 sunny, private, ridgetop acres; w/ wonderful fir, oak & madrone trees & beautiful views; organic garden produce & fresh eggs available seasonally
Owned/ Run By: gay men

Rooms: 1 (cottage)
Baths: private
Amenities: free parking, pool, sauna, hot tub, massage, DVDs/ videos
Smoking: no
Rates: $145+

Village Inn & Restaurant
Russian River

20822 River Blvd
Monte Rio, CA 95462
707/ 865-2304 800/ 303-2303
www.villageinn-ca.com

Clientele: mixed gay/ straight
Type: inn; charming & historic; restaurant w/ full bar; spectacular views; on the Russian River in heart of Sonoma Wine Country
Owned/ Run By: gay men
Rooms: 11
Baths: private

Wheelchair Access: yes, 1 rm
Meals: expanded cont'l brkfst
Kids: primarily adult resort
Pets: welcome in certain rms w/ prior notice
Smoking: no
Rates: $85-195
AC: 10%

Wildwood Retreat
Russian River

PO Box 78
Guerneville, CA 95446
707/ 632-5321
www.wildwoodretreat.com

Clientele: mixed gay/ straight
Type: retreat; 250 acres for seminars, workshops & weddings; 3 meals included in nightly rate; away from city life
Owned/ Run By: gay/ lesbian & straight
Rooms: 20
Baths: shared

Meals: cont'l brkfst
Amenities: free parking, pool, sauna, indoor & outdoor hot tub, massage
Kids: no
Pets: no
Smoking: ok
Rates: $110 + 15%

The Woods Resort
Russian River

16484 4th St
Guerneville, CA 95446

707/ 869-0600
877/ 887-9218

info@rrwoods.com
rrwoods.com

Clientele: mostly men
Type: resort; centrally located in downtown area; cottages, guest cabins & suites; clothing-optional pool; clean, value-priced accommodations
Owned/ Run By: gay men
Nearby Attractions: Wine Country, Armstrong State Redwood Park, Bodega Bay, Charles Schultz "Peanuts" Museum, Luther Burbank Entertainment Center
Pickup Service: airport pickup; $50
Transit: near public transit
Rooms: 19 total, 19 kings, 4 queens, color TV, DVD/ VCR (15), cable, ceiling fan, fireplace (10), deck (15), kitchenette (15), refrigerator, safer sex supplies, maid service
Baths: private, bathtubs, showers, whirlpools
Wheelchair Access: yes, 1 rm
Meals: coffee/tea only
Amenities: pool, massage, DVDs/ videos, coffee/ tea, ice, self-serve snack & soda machine
Recreation: hiking, biking, canoeing, swimming, horseback riding
Kids: no

Pets: no
Smoking: no (in rms; ok on grounds)
Reservations: required *Deposit:* required, final night's stay, due at booking *Cancellation:* cancel by 2 weeks prior or forfeit $25 *Minimum Stay:* 2 nights (wknds) *Check in/ out:* 4pm/ 11am

Payment: cash, travelers checks, Visa, Amex, MC, Discover
Season: open yr-round *High season:* June-Oct
Rates: $55-225
AC: 10%

Governor's Inn　　　　　　　　　　　　　　　*Sacramento*

210 Richards Blvd
Sacramento, CA 95814
916/ 448-7224 800/ 999-6689
www.governorsinn.net

Clientele: gay-friendly
Meals: cont'l brkfst
Amenities: free parking, laundry, pool, outdoor hot tub, WiFi

Smoking: no
Rates: $92-124

Inn & Spa at Parkside　　　　　　　　　　　*Sacramento*

2116 6th St
Sacramento, CA 95818
916/ 658-1818 800/ 995-7275
www.innatparkside.com

Clientele: mixed gay/ straight
Type: b&b-inn; 1936 Mediterranean Revival built as the official US residence for the North American Ambassador from Nationalist China; grand ballrm; gardens
Owned/ Run By: gay men
Rooms: 7
Baths: private

Wheelchair Access: yes, 1 rm
Meals: full brkfst
Amenities: free parking, hot tub, DVDs/ videos, WiFi
Kids: well-behaved welcome; cost increase
Pets: no
Rates: $179-329
AC: 5%

Balboa Park Inn　　　　　　　　　　　　　　*San Diego*

3402 Park Blvd
San Diego, CA 92103
619/ 298-0823 800/ 938-8181
www.balboaparkinn.com

Clientele: gay-friendly
Type: b&b-inn; unique, immaculate & beautifully appointed suites, nestled in a quiet residential area; just steps from Balboa Park & the world-famous San Diego Zoo
Owned/ Run By: gay/ lesbian & straight

Rooms: 26
Baths: private
Meals: expanded cont'l brkfst
Kids: welcome
Smoking: ok
Rates: $99-219
AC: 10%

The Bristol Hotel　　　　　　　　　　　　　　*San Diego*

1055 First St
San Diego, CA 92101
619/ 232-6141 800/ 662-4477
www.thebristolsandiego.com

Clientele: mixed gay/ straight
Type: hotel; contemporary-styled boutique hotel located downtown; close to Gaslamp Quarter & Horton Plaza
Owned/ Run By: gay/ lesbian & straight
Rooms: 102
Baths: private

Wheelchair Access: yes
Kids: welcome
Pets: welcome
Smoking: ok
Rates: $119-239
AC: 10%

Casa Granada　　　　　　　　　　　　　　　*San Diego*

1720 Granada Ave
San Diego, CA 92102
619/ 501-5911 866/ 524-2312
www.casa-granada.com

Clientele: mixed gay/ lesbian/ straight
Type: guesthouse; 3 separate units w/ antique furnishings; hardwood flrs; canyon location; minutes to Hillcrest, San Diego Zoo & Balboa Park
Owned/ Run By: gay man
Rooms: 3

Baths: private
Amenities: free parking, laundry, WiFi
Kids: welcome
Pets: welcome w/ prior approval
Smoking: no
Rates: $109-139

Crown City Inn　　　　　　　　　　　　　　*San Diego*

520 Orange Ave
Coronado Island, CA 92118
619/ 435-3116 800/ 422-1173
www.crowncityinn.com

Clientele: gay-friendly
Type: hotel; small, Mediterranean-style property; near beach; complimentary bicycles; restaurant
Rooms: 35
Baths: private
Wheelchair Access: yes, 1 rm

Amenities: free parking, laundry, pool, WiFi
Kids: welcome
Pets: w/ prior approval; fee
Smoking: ok in some rms
Rates: $99-209
AC: 10%

Gaslamp Vacations
San Diego

PO Box 127671
San Diego, CA 92112
619/ 446-6329
www.gaslampvacations.com

Clientele: mixed gay/ straight
Type: condo; vacation rentals in dowtown San Diego's Gaslamp Quarter, Little Italy & PETCO Park areas
Owned/ Run By: gay & straight
Rooms: 30 individual properties
Wheelchair Access: yes, 2 rms

Amenities: free parking, laundry, pool, outdoor hot tub, DVDs/ videos, gym, WiFi
Kids: welcome
Pets: welcome in some units
Smoking: no
Rates: $149-349

Handlery Hotel & Resort [TAG]
San Diego

950 Hotel Circle N
San Diego, CA 92108
619/ 298-0511 800/ 676-6567
www.handlery.com

Clientele: gay-friendly
Type: hotel; family-owned, resort-style full-service property centrally located in Mission Valley; member of IGLTA & GSDBA
Rooms: 217
Baths: private
Wheelchair Access: yes, 6 rms

Amenities: laundry, pool, hot tub, massage, WiFi
Kids: welcome
Pets: no
Smoking: no
Rates: $89-169
AC: 10%

Hillcrest Inn Hotel
San Diego

3754 5th Ave
San Diego, CA 92103

619/ 293-7078
800/ 258-2280

info@hillcrestinn.net
www.hillcrestinn.net

Clientele: mostly men
Type: hotel; in the heart of Hillcrest; walk to shops, bars & restaurants
Owned/ Run By: gay/ lesbian & straight
Nearby Attractions: San Diego Zoo & Wild Animal Park, Sea World, Tijuana
Transit: near public transit; public transit pickup in front of hotel; shuttle: Public Shuttle, 619/ 990-8770
Rooms: 45 total, 12 kings, 30 queens, 3 fulls, color TV, wetbar, ceiling fan, phone, kitchenette, refrigerator, maid service, microwave, data ports; limited number of deluxe rms w/ balcony, 27" flat-screen TV w/ built-in VCR/ DVD player
Baths: private, bathtubs, showers, hairdryers
Wheelchair Access: yes, 3 rms

Meals: coffee/tea only
Amenities: office hrs: 8am-midnight; laundry, outdoor hot tub, DVDs/ videos, WiFi, coffee/ tea, sundeck, enclosed courtyard
Kids: welcome
Pets: welcome
Smoking: ok
Reservations: required *Deposit:* required, 1 night, due 3 days prior *Cancellation:* cancel by 3 days prior or forfeit deposit *Minimum Stay:* 2 nights (wknds)/ 3 nights (holidays) *Check in/ out:* 2pm/ noon
Payment: cash, travelers checks, Visa, Amex, MC, Discover
Season: open yr-round
Rates: $79-169 *Discounts:* weekly & monthly
AC: 10%

Inn Suites Lafayette Hotel & Suites
San Diego

2223 El Cajon Blvd
San Diego, CA 92104
619/ 296-2101 877/ 343-4648
sandiego.innsuites.com

Clientele: gay-friendly
Type: hotel; Colonial-style mansion that once hosted stars like Bob Hope & Ava Gardner & has a swimming pool designed by Tarzan, Jonny Weissmuller
Rooms: 129
Baths: private
Wheelchair Access: yes, 4 rms

Meals: cont'l brkfst
Amenities: free parking, pool, hot tub, WiFi
Kids: welcome
Pets: welcome; $25 pet fee
Smoking: no
Rates: $99-159
AC: 10%

Keating House

San Diego

2331 2nd Ave
San Diego, CA 92101
619/ 239-8585 800/ 995-8644
www.keatinghouse.com

Clientele: gay-friendly
Type: b&b-inn; graceful, inviting Victorian on Bankers Hill; just 16 blks to Hillcrest, 4 blks to Balboa Park & 12 blks to Gaslamp Square & bay
Owned/ Run By: gay/ lesbian & straight
Rooms: 9

Baths: private
Meals: full brkfst
Kids: welcome
Smoking: no
Rates: $95-155
AC: 10%

Mike's Place

San Diego

1252 Lincoln Ave
San Diego, CA 92103
619/ 992-7466
www.MikesPlace1252.com

Clientele: mostly men
Type: cottage; private entrance & courtyard; Japanese garden; wet bar; high-quality furnishings throughout
Owned/ Run By: gay men
Rooms: 1
Baths: private

Meals: coffee/tea only
Kids: no
Pets: no
Rates: $95/ night; $500/ week

Park Manor Suites ⒯⒢

San Diego

525 Spruce St
San Diego, CA 92103
619/ 291-0999 800/ 874-2649
www.parkmanorsuites.com

Clientele: gay-friendly
Type: hotel; experience old-world charm in gay Hillcrest
Owned/ Run By: gay/ lesbian & straight
Rooms: 75
Baths: private
Wheelchair Access: yes

Meals: expanded cont'l brkfst
Amenities: free parking, laundry, massage, DVDs/ videos, WiFi
Kids: welcome
Smoking: ok
Rates: $99-229
AC: 10%

Sunburst Court Inn

San Diego

4086 Alabama St
San Diego, CA 92104

619/ 294-9665

info@sunburstcourtinn.com
www.sunburstcourtinn.com

Clientele: mixed gay/ straight
Type: all-suite b&b-inn; tastefully refurbished; "conveniently located near all that San Diego has to offer"
Owned/ Run By: gay men
Nearby Attractions: SeaWorld, San Diego Zoo, Gaslamp Quarter, Old Town, San Diego Wild Animal Park, Balboa Park, the Midway
Transit: near public transit; 12 minutes to airport
Rooms: 4 total, suites, kings, color TV, cable, ceiling fan, phone, refrigerator, maid service, all our rms are suites w/ separate bdrms & living rms
Baths: private, bathtubs, showers, hairdryers
Wheelchair Access: yes, 1 rm
Meals: coffee/tea only
Amenities: office hrs: 9am-5pm; free parking, laundry, free local phone calls, complimentary bottled water & snacks
Recreation: beaches, hiking
Kids: no
Pets: no

Pets On Premises: 1 dog, birds
Smoking: no
Reservations: required *Deposit:* credit card charged in full, due at booking *Cancellation:* cancel by 3 days prior or forfeit 1 night *Check in/ out:* 3pm/ 11am

Payment: Visa, MC
Season: open yr-round
Rates: $95

W San Diego TAG

San Diego

421 W B St
San Diego, CA 92101
619/ 231-8220 877/ WHOTELS
(reservations only)
www.whotels.com/sandiego

Clientele: gay-friendly
Type: hotel; modern sophistication & style, merged w/ time-honored service
Rooms: 259
Baths: private
Wheelchair Access: yes, 10 rms
Meals: coffee/tea only

Amenities: pool, massage, DVDs/ videos, WiFi
Kids: welcome
Pets: welcome
Smoking: no
Rates: $249-379
AC: 10%

24 Henry & Village House TAG

San Francisco

24 Henry St & 4080 18th St
San Francisco, CA 94114-1215
415/ 864-5686 800/ 900-5686
www.24Henry.com

Clientele: mixed gay/ lesbian
Type: b&b; elegant gay nonsmoking guesthouses in the Castro District; newly decorated; bars, restaurants, shops & transit w/in 1-2 blks
Owned/ Run By: gay men
Rooms: 10
Baths: private & shared

Meals: expanded cont'l brkfst
Amenities: massage, WiFi
Kids: welcome in rms w/ bath ensuite
Pets: please inquire
Smoking: no
Rates: $75-139
AC: 10%

555 Haight Guesthouse

San Francisco

555 Haight St
San Francisco, CA 94117
415/ 551-2555 800/ 785-5504
www.555haight.net

Clientele: mixed gay/ straight
Type: hostel; located in the Haight; convenient to the Castro, SOMA & downtown
Owned/ Run By: straights
Rooms: 14
Baths: shared

Meals: coffee/tea only
Kids: welcome
Pets: no
Smoking: no
Rates: $20-44

Adante Hotel

San Francisco

610 Geary St
San Francisco, CA 94102
415/ 673-9221 888/ 423-0083
adantehotel.com

Clientele: mixed gay/ straight
Type: hotel; unique boutique hotel centrally located in Union Square/ Theater District; all rms feature hand-painted murals; comfortable amenities & friendly staff
Owned/ Run By: gay & straight
Rooms: 93
Baths: private

Wheelchair Access: yes, 6 rms
Meals: cont'l brkfst
Kids: welcome
Pets: no
Smoking: no
Rates: $89-159
AC: 10%

Andrews Hotel

San Francisco

624 Post St
San Francisco, CA 94109
415/ 563-6877 800/ 926-3739
www.andrewshotel.com

Clientele: gay-friendly
Type: b&b; intimate, European Victorian hotel; centrally located; a jewel in the heart of San Francisco
Owned/ Run By: straights
Rooms: 48
Baths: private

Meals: expanded cont'l brkfst
Kids: welcome; 3 persons max per rm
Pets: no
Smoking: no
Rates: $99-175
AC: 10%

The Archbishop's Mansion TAG

San Francisco

1000 Fulton St
San Francisco, CA 94117
415/ 563-7872 800/ 543-5820
www.thearchbishopsmansion.com

Clientele: gay-friendly
Type: b&b-inn; built in 1904 for the Archbishop himself
Owned/ Run By: gay men
Rooms: 15
Baths: private
Meals: expanded cont'l brkfst

Amenities: free parking, laundry, hot tub, massage, DVDs/ videos
Kids: welcome
Pets: service animals only
Smoking: no
Rates: $145-425
AC: 10%

Joie de Vivre Hotels

Galleria Park Hotel T-IG

191 Sutter St
San Francisco, CA 94104
415/ 781–3060 800/ 792–9639
www.galleriapark.com

Clientele: mixed gay/ straight
Type: boutique hotel; 2 blks from Union Square & gates of Chinatown; close to MUNI & the Castro
Owned/ Run By: gay & straight
Nearby Attractions: SF MOMA, Yerba Buena Center for the Arts, Union Square, cable cars, Chinatown
Transit: near public transit; 25 minutes to SFO
Rooms: 177 total, 14 suites, 68 kings, 44 queens, 50 fulls, A/C, fireplace (3), phone, refrigerator, rm service, maid service, recently renovated w/ dual-line computer access, honor bar, iron & board, double-paned windows, 25" TV w/ Nintendo & on-command movies
Baths: private, bathtubs, showers, robes, hairdryers
Wheelchair Access: yes, 16 rms
Meals: coffee/tea only, full-service restaurant on premises
Amenities: office hrs: 24hrs; WiFi, snacks, cocktails, coffee/ tea, fitness center, full-service concierge; live jazz Wed-Sat
Kids: welcome
Pets: welcome
Smoking: ok (selected rms only)
Reservations: recommended *Deposit:* required, credit card guarantee, due at booking *Cancellation:* cancel by 1 day prior *Check in/ out:* 3pm/ noon
Payment: cash, travelers checks, Visa, Amex, MC, Discover, JCB
Season: open yr-round *High season:* June-Oct
Rates: $99-199
AC: 10%

Hotel Adagio T-IG

550 Geary St
San Francisco, CA 94102
415/ 775–5000 800/ 228–8830
www.thehoteladagio.com

Clientele: gay-friendly
Type: hotel; clean & contemporary design; located in theater, dining & shopping districts
Owned/ Run By: gay/ lesbian & straight
Nearby Attractions: Union Square, cable cars, San Francisco Center, Chinatown, shopping
Transit: near public transit; 30 minutes to SFO
Rooms: 171 total, 2 suites, 46 kings, 46 queens, 19 fulls, color TV, cable, ceiling fan, phone, maid service, Aveda bath amenities
Baths: private, bathtubs, showers, hairdryers
Wheelchair Access: yes, 5 rms
Meals: coffee/tea only
Amenities: office hrs: 24hrs; gym, coffee/ tea, Cortez restaurant on-site, exercise rm, business center, high-speed internet access, morning towncar service to Financial District
Recreation: Embarcadero
Kids: welcome
Pets: service animals only
Smoking: ok
Reservations: required *Cancellation:* cancel by 2 days prior or forfeit a fee *Check in/ out:* 3pm/ noon
Payment: cash, travelers checks, Visa, Amex, MC, Discover
Season: open yr-round *High season:* June-Oct
Rates: $189-249

San Francisco

Hotel Vitale 🏳️‍🌈

8 Mission St
San Francisco, CA 94105
415/ 278-3700 888/ 890-8688
www.hotelvitale.com

Clientele: gay-friendly
Type: hotel; 4-star, full-service waterfront luxury hotel; enjoy our spa, featuring rooftop soaking tubs, & Americano, our restaurant & bar
Nearby Attractions: AT&T Park (baseball), The Embarcadero, Ferry Plaza Farmers Market
Transit: near public transit
Rooms: 199 total, A/C, color TV, cable, phone, rm service, maid service, each guestrm designed w/ nurturing in mind: featuring limestone-covered bathrms; 440-thread-count linens; soothing color scheme; 26- or 30-inch LCD flat-screen televisions; Sealy pillow-top mattress
Baths: private, bathtubs, showers, robes, hairdryers
Wheelchair Access: yes, 10 rms
Meals: coffee/tea only
Amenities: massage, gym, WiFi, coffee/ tea, complimentary yoga class, pillow library
Recreation: Vitality Concierge w/ suggestions of unique wellness-inducing services & activities in the area
Kids: welcome
Pets: welcome
Smoking: no
Reservations: required *Deposit:* required, due at booking *Cancellation:* cancel by 1 day prior or forfeit 1 night *Check in/ out:* 3pm/ noon
Payment: cash, travelers checks, Visa, Amex, MC, Discover
Season: open yr-round
Rates: $199-399
AC: 10%

The Phoenix Hotel

601 Eddy St
San Francisco, CA 94109
415/ 776-1380 800/ 248-9466
www.thephoenixhotel.com

Clientele: mixed gay/ straight
Type: hotel; this 1950s-style motor lodge is a hip, artistic oasis for the creative
Owned/ Run By: gay & straight
Nearby Attractions: 2 miles to Fisherman's Wharf; 7 blks to Union Square
Transit: near public transit; bus lines in front of hotel; 2 blks to BART/ MUNI; taxi: Luxor, 415/ 282-6684
Rooms: 44 total, 3 suites, 17 kings, 24 fulls, color TV, DVD/ VCR, cable, phone, safer sex supplies, maid service, all comfortable, tropical, bungalow-style rms
Baths: private, bathtubs, showers, hairdryers
Meals: cont'l brkfst
Amenities: office hrs: 24hrs; free parking, laundry, pool, massage, DVDs/ videos, WiFi, coffee/ tea, concierge, Bambuddha Lounge & restaurant
Recreation: 2 miles to Golden Gate Park
Kids: welcome; under 12 yrs only if w/ adult
Pets: service animals only
Smoking: ok
Reservations: required *Deposit:* required, due at booking *Cancellation:* cancel by 2 days prior or forfeit 1 night *Check in/ out:* 3pm/ noon
Payment: cash, travelers checks, Visa, Amex, MC, Discover, (credit card is required at check-in)
Season: open yr-round *High season:* summers
Rates: $119+
AC: 10%

Argent Hotel

San Francisco

50 3rd St
San Francisco, CA 94103
415/ 974–6400 877/ 222–6699
www.argenthotel.com

Clientele: gay-friendly
Type: hotel; in downtown San Francisco; hip, contemporary decor w/ flr-to-ceiling windows offering spectacular views; minutes from the Castro
Owned/ Run By: gay & straight
Rooms: 667
Baths: private

Wheelchair Access: yes
Amenities: laundry, massage, DVDs/ videos
Kids: welcome
Pets: no
Smoking: no
Rates: $179-249
AC: 10%

Beck's Motor Lodge

San Francisco

2222 Market St
San Francisco, CA 94114
415/ 621–8212 800/ 955–2325
becksSF@aol.com

Clientele: gay-friendly
Type: motel; renovated classic motor lodge in the heart of the Castro
Rooms: 58
Baths: private
Wheelchair Access: yes, 42 rms
Meals: coffee/tea only

Kids: welcome
Pets: welcome in 2 designated rms
Smoking: ok (some rms)
Rates: $95-114
AC: 10%

Broadway Manor Inn

San Francisco

2201 Van Ness Ave
San Francisco, CA 94109
415/ 776–7900 800/ 727–6239
www.broadwaymanor.com

Clientele: gay-friendly
Type: motel; steps from cable car line; walk to all SF's major tourist attractions
Owned/ Run By: gay/ lesbian & straight
Rooms: 56
Baths: private
Wheelchair Access: yes, 2 rms

Amenities: free parking, microwave/ fridge, WiFi
Kids: welcome
Smoking: ok
Rates: $54-119
AC: 10%

Cartwright Hotel on Union Square

San Francisco

524 Sutter St
San Francisco, CA 94102
415/ 421–2865 800/ 919–9779
www.cartwrighthotel.com

Clientele: gay-friendly
Type: hotel; cozy 1913 Victorian b&b-inn on Union Square furnished in antiques; evening wine reception, complimentary 24hr coffee, tea & cookies
Owned/ Run By: gay & straight
Rooms: 114

Baths: private
Meals: deluxe cont'l brkfst
Kids: welcome; under 17 yrs free w/ adult
Pets: under 25 lbs welcome
Smoking: ok (some rms only)
Rates: $89-219
AC: 10%

Castro Suites

San Francisco

927 14th St
San Francisco, CA 94114
415/ 437–1783
www.castrosuites.com

Clientele: mostly men
Type: apt; 2 furnished 1-bdrm suites for the sophisticated, independent traveler; fully equipped kitchen & washer/ dryer; in quiet but convenient part of Castro
Owned/ Run By: gay men
Rooms: 2 (apts)

Baths: private
Amenities: laundry, DVDs/ videos, WiFi
Kids: welcome; 1 child per unit
Pets: no
Smoking: no
Rates: $200-220
AC: 10%

The Chateau Tivoli

San Francisco

1057 Steiner St
San Francisco, CA 94115
415/ 776–5462 800/ 228–1647
www.chateautivoli.com

Clientele: gay-friendly
Type: b&b; opulently restored Victorian mansion in the heart of SF's Alamo Square District; one of the city's most charming & affordable b&b's
Owned/ Run By: straights
Rooms: 9
Baths: private & shared

Meals: expanded cont'l brkfst
Kids: welcome; under 11 yrs free
Pets: small, quiet pets welcome; only allowed in 2 suites
Smoking: no
Rates: $99-265
AC: 10%

Belvedere House

San Francisco

598 Belvedere St
San Francisco, CA 94117

415/ 731-6654
877/ 226-3273

info@gaybedandbreakfast.net
www.GayBedAndBreakfast.net

San Francisco's #1 gay bed-and-breakfast–within walking distance of the bars, restaurants, dancing, shopping, and all the fun in the Castro district. Bus and streetcar lines to downtown, the Haight-Ashbury district, Ocean Beach, and Golden Gate Park are just around the corner. This is a very popular guesthouse with a high rate of repeat guests.

Guests enjoy full use of the atrium, parlor, dining room, and kitchen. A large continental breakfast buffet is available until noon. Coffee, tea, and pastries are available all day. Laundry service is offered.

Belvedere House is a 1922 Edwardian townhouse with six guestrooms. Rooms are nonsmoking but a stylish smoking atrium is available. All rooms offer individual telephone/modem lines and refrigerators with complimentary refreshments. Free high-speed internet access is available throughout the entire building. Parts of the house present sweeping views of the Golden Gate Bridge and the Pacific Ocean.

Belvedere House is proudly gay-owned and operated.

Clientele: mostly gay/ some straight

Type: b&b; Edwardian home w/ charming & stylish atmosphere; very popular; walking distance to Castro; overlooking Golden Gate Park & Pacific Ocean; German spoken

Owned/ Run By: gay men

Nearby Attractions: Castro District, Golden Gate Park, Twin Peaks, Haight-Ashbury, Cole Valley, Buena Vista Park

Transit: near public transit

Rooms: 6 total, 2 suites, 2 queens, 1 full, 1 twin, color TV, DVD/ VCR (also DVD), phone, refrigerator, writing desk, walk-in closet or armoire, some rms w/ sweeping views of Golden Gate Bridge & Pacific Ocean

Baths: private & shared, bathtubs, showers, robes, hairdryers

Meals: full brkfst

Amenities: laundry, WiFi, snacks, coffee/ tea

Kids: welcome

Pets: welcome

Smoking: no

Reservations: strongly recommended *Deposit:* required, 1 night, due at booking, personal check ok *Cancellation:* cancel by 1 day prior or forfeit deposit

Payment: cash, travelers checks, personal checks, Visa, Amex, MC

Season: open yr-round *High season:* May-Sept

Rates: $115-155 *Discounts:* 10% (if booked 4 weeks in advance)

AC: 10%

Clipper House/ Noe Valley Victorian
San Francisco

164 Clipper St
San Francisco, CA 94114
415/ 821-4872
www.sanfrancisco-victorian.com

Type: rental apt; beautiful self-contained garden flat in owner's home: washer/ dryer, use of gym equipment, piano, private entrance & quiet garden w/ deck; great Noe Valley location; short-term (1-month minimum)
Rooms: 4

Baths: private
Kids: no
Pets: no
Smoking: no
Rates: $2,600

The Commodore Hotel 🏳️‍🌈
San Francisco

825 Sutter St
San Francisco, CA 94108
415/ 923-6800 800/ 338-6848
www.jdvhospitality.com

Clientele: mixed gay/ straight
Type: hotel; an ultra-stylish, fun-filled streetstopper known for its innovative concierge services, warm hospitality, the Red Room cocktail lounge & Canteen restaurant
Owned/ Run By: gay men

Rooms: 110
Baths: private
Kids: welcome
Pets: service animals only
Smoking: ok
Rates: $109-169
AC: 10%

Dakota Hotel
San Francisco

606 Post St
San Francisco, CA 94109
415/ 931-7475
www.hotelsanfrancisco.com

Clientele: gay-friendly
Type: hotel; smaller, newly renovated budget hotel; in the heart of San Francisco; 2 blks from Union Square
Owned/ Run By: straights
Rooms: 40
Baths: private

Kids: welcome
Pets: no
Smoking: ok
Rates: $55+
AC: 10%

Dolores Park Inn
San Francisco

3641 17th St
San Francisco, CA 94114
415/ 621-0482
www.doloresparkinn.net

Clientele: gay-friendly
Type: b&b-private home; in historical 1874 Italianate Victorian mansion; w/ subtropical garden behind a wrought iron fence
Owned/ Run By: gay & straight
Rooms: 5
Baths: private & shared

Meals: full brkfst
Amenities: free parking, indoor hot tub, DVDs/ videos
Kids: 14 yrs & up welcome
Pets: no
Smoking: no
Rates: $99-259
AC: 10% for stays over 3 days

Edward II Inn & Suites
San Francisco

3155 Scott St
San Francisco, CA 94123
415/ 922-3000 800/ 473-2846
www.edwardii.com

Clientele: gay-friendly
Type: European-style b&b; own pub & Cafe Maritime (seafood) next door; "little bit of England in the heart of San Francisco"
Rooms: 30 (including 4 suites)

Baths: private & shared
Meals: expanded cont'l brkfst
Amenities: massage, gym, WiFi
Rates: $69-249

Elements
San Francisco

2516 Mission St
San Francisco, CA 94110
415/ 647-4100 866/ 327-8407
www.elementssf.com

Clientele: mixed gay/ straight
Type: hostel; free internet access, outdoor cafe, rooftop deck w/ views of San Francisco
Baths: private & shared

Amenities: WiFi
Rates: $25-90

Executive Hotel Vintage Court
San Francisco

650 Bush St
San Francisco, CA 94108
415/ 392-4666 800/ 654-1100
www.vintagecourt.com

Clientele: gay-friendly
Type: hotel; "San Francisco's only nonsmoking full-service hotel; a fabulous place to stay for business or pleasure"
Owned/ Run By: straights
Rooms: 107
Baths: private
Wheelchair Access: yes, 8 rms

Meals: cont'l brkfst
Amenities: laundry, WiFi
Kids: welcome; under 12 yrs stay free
Pets: welcome
Smoking: no
Rates: $149-239
AC: 10%

Francisco Bay Inn
San Francisco

1501 Lombard St
San Francisco, CA 94123
415/ 474-3030 800/ 410-7007
www.staysf.com/franciscobay

Clientele: gay-friendly
Type: motel; located on famous Lombard St—home to the Golden Gate & "The Crookedest Street in the World"
Owned/ Run By: gay/ lesbian & straight
Rooms: 40
Baths: private

Meals: cont'l brkfst
Amenities: free parking, WiFi
Kids: welcome
Pets: no
Smoking: no
Rates: $75-169
AC: 10%

Halcyon Hotel
San Francisco

649 Jones St
San Francisco, CA 94102
415/ 929-8033 800/ 627-2396
www.halcyonsf.com

Clientele: gay-friendly
Type: hotel; charming little bldg, where it is necessary to reserve ahead most of the time; rms stylishly furnished
Owned/ Run By: gay & straight
Rooms: 25
Baths: private

Meals: coffee/tea only
Kids: welcome
Pets: welcome
Smoking: smokefree rms available
Rates: $75; $350/ week
AC: 10%

Handlery Union Square Hotel ⊤⁴ᴳ⊃
San Francisco

351 Geary St
San Francisco, CA 94102
415/ 781-7800 800/ 995-4874
www.handlery.com/sf/home.html

Clientele: mixed gay/ straight
Type: hotel; at Union Square; cable car stops at corner; all major department stores & boutiques w/in 1 blk; easy access to Castro
Owned/ Run By: gay/ lesbian & straight
Rooms: 377
Baths: private

Wheelchair Access: yes, 12 rms
Kids: welcome
Pets: no
Smoking: ok (in some rms)
Rates: $194-294
AC: 10%

Harbor Court Hotel ⊤⁴ᴳ⊃
San Francisco

165 Steuart St
San Francisco, CA 94105
415/ 882-1300 866/ 792-6283
www.harborcourthotel.com

Clientele: mixed gay/ straight
Type: hotel; premier waterfront property in the heart of the Financial District
Owned/ Run By: gay & straight
Rooms: 131
Baths: private
Wheelchair Access: yes, 15 rms
Meals: coffee/tea only

Amenities: laundry, pool, sauna, massage, WiFi
Kids: welcome; only 2 people per rm
Pets: welcome
Smoking: ok (in select rms only)
Rates: $139-249
AC: 10%

Hayes Valley Inn
San Francisco

417 Gough St
San Francisco, CA 94102
415/ 431-9131 800/ 930-7999
www.hayesvalleyinn.com

Clientele: mixed gay/ straight
Type: b&b; European-style pensione; newly renovated Victorian rms; close to the opera/ symphony, boutiques, restaurants
Owned/ Run By: straights
Rooms: 28
Baths: shared

Meals: expanded cont'l brkfst
Amenities: laundry, WiFi
Kids: welcome; futon only
Pets: welcome if w/ responsible owner
Smoking: no
Rates: $61-105
AC: 10%

Hotel Bijou ⊤ℐᴳ   *San Francisco*

111 Mason St
San Francisco, CA 94102
415/ 771–1200 800/ 771–1022
www.hotelbijou.com

Clientele: mixed gay/ straight
Type: hotel; inspired by San Francisco's rich cinematic history, each rm is named after a movie filmed here; located in Union Square
Owned/ Run By: gay/ lesbian & straight
Rooms: 65

Baths: private
Meals: cont'l brkfst
Kids: welcome
Pets: service animals only
Smoking: no
Rates: $109-149
AC: 10%

Hotel Carlton ⊤ℐᴳ   *San Francisco*

1075 Sutter
San Francisco, CA 94109
415/ 673–0242 800/ 922–7586
www.carltonhotel.com

Clientele: gay-friendly
Type: originally constructed in 1927; located near Union Square & Theater District; 4-million-dollar renovation in 2004
Owned/ Run By: gay/ lesbian & straight
Rooms: 163

Baths: private
Pets: service animals only

Hotel Del Sol ⊤ℐᴳ   *San Francisco*

3100 Webster St
San Francisco, CA 94123
415/ 921–5520 877/ 433–5765
www.thehoteldelsol.com

Clientele: mixed gay/ straight
Type: motel; located off Lombard St, in the Marina neighborhood, the Hotel Del Sol was created to celebrate the California lifestyle: contemporary decor, vibrant colors, pool, palms & parking
Owned/ Run By: gay/ lesbian & straight
Rooms: 57

Baths: private
Wheelchair Access: yes, 1 rm
Meals: cont'l brkfst
Kids: welcome
Pets: service animals only
Smoking: no
Rates: $129-269
AC: 10%

Hotel Drisco ⊤ℐᴳ   *San Francisco*

2901 Pacific Ave
San Francisco, CA 94115
415/ 346–2880 800/ 634–7277
www.hoteldrisco.com

Clientele: gay-friendly
Type: hotel; 1903 luxury hotel in Pacific Heights
Owned/ Run By: gay/ lesbian & straight
Rooms: 48
Baths: private & shared

Meals: expanded cont'l brkfst
Kids: welcome
Pets: service animals
Smoking: no
Rates: $195-355

Hotel Fusion   *San Francisco*

140 Ellis St
San Francisco, CA 94102
415/ 568–2525 877/ 812–0157
www.hotelfusionsf.com

Clientele: mixed gay/ straight
Type: hotel; elegant fusion of old-world Asian & contemporary American styles; near Union Square
Owned/ Run By: gay & straight
Rooms: 124
Baths: private

Wheelchair Access: yes, 6 rms
Meals: cont'l brkfst
Amenities: gym
Kids: welcome
Pets: no
Smoking: no
Rates: $79-159

Hotel Majestic   *San Francisco*

1500 Sutter St
San Francisco, CA 94109
415/ 441–1100 800/ 869–8966
www.thehotelmajestic.com

Clientele: gay-friendly
Type: hotel; originally built in 1902, this magnificent Edwardian structure was one of SF's earliest grand hotels
Owned/ Run By: gay & straight
Rooms: 58
Baths: private
Wheelchair Access: yes, 3 rms

Meals: cont'l brkfst
Amenities: laundry, WiFi
Kids: welcome
Pets: no
Smoking: no
Rates: $110-235
AC: 10%

Hotel Griffon 🏳️‍🌈

San Francisco

155 Steuart St
San Francisco, CA 94105

415/ 495-2100
800/ 321-2201

reservations@hotelgriffon.com
www.hotelgriffon.com

Clientele: mixed gay/ straight
Type: upscale boutique hotel on San Francisco's Embarcadero; 1 1/2 blks to MUNI to get to Castro District & SOMA; voted "Best Boutique Hotel, Best of the Bay Area" by *San Francisco* magazine
Owned/ Run By: gay & straight
Pickup Service: airport pickup; approximately $55
Transit: 30 minutes to Oakland airport, 20 minutes to San Francisco airport
Rooms: 62 (includes 5 suites) total, 5 suites, 27 kings, 18 queens, 12 fulls, A/C, color TV, DVD/ VCR, cable, wetbar, deck (3), phone, refrigerator, rm service, maid service, original 1906 whitewashed brick walls
Baths: private, bathtubs, showers, robes, hairdryers
Wheelchair Access: yes, 3 rms
Meals: expanded cont'l brkfst, restaurant is very accommodating for special needs
Amenities: massage, WiFi, coffee/ tea, complimentary high-speed internet access, turn-down service, newspaper, Aveda products, morning towncar service in Financial District (Mon-Fri)

Kids: welcome
Pets: no
Smoking: no
Reservations: required *Deposit:* required, 1 night + tax, due at booking *Cancellation:* cancel by 1 day prior or forfeit 1 night + tax *Check in/ out:* 3pm/ noon

Payment: cash, travelers checks, Visa, Amex, MC, Discover
Season: open yr-round *High season:* Sept-Nov
Rates: $139-435 *Discounts:* please call for info
AC: 10%

Hotel Monaco 🏳️‍🌈

San Francisco

501 Geary St
San Francisco, CA 94102
415/ 292-0100 866/ 622-5284
www.monaco-sf.com

Clientele: gay-friendly
Type: hotel; "offers the best of all worlds—a rare combination of high style, sophistication & exemplary service"
Owned/ Run By: gay/ lesbian & straight
Rooms: 201
Baths: private
Wheelchair Access: yes, 11 rms

Meals: coffee/tea only
Amenities: free parking, laundry, sauna, indoor hot tub, massage
Kids: welcome
Pets: welcome
Smoking: ok
Rates: $229-599
AC: 10%

Hotel Palomar 🏳️‍🌈

San Francisco

12 4th St
San Francisco, CA 94103
415/ 348-1111 866/ 373-4941
www.hotelpalomar.com

Clientele: mixed gay/ straight
Type: hotel; "urban luxury & sophistication in downtown San Francisco"
Owned/ Run By: gay & straight
Rooms: 198
Baths: private
Wheelchair Access: yes, 6 rms

Meals: coffee/tea only
Amenities: hot tub, massage, gym, WiFi
Kids: welcome
Pets: dogs only
Smoking: ok (in smoking rms)
Rates: $209-999
AC: 10%

The Hotel Rex 🏳️‍🌈

San Francisco

562 Sutter St
San Francisco, CA 94102
415/ 433-4434 800/ 433-4434
www.thehotelrex.com

Clientele: gay-friendly
Type: hotel; sophisticated & intriguing atmosphere inspired by the arts & literary salons of 1930s San Francisco
Owned/ Run By: gay/ lesbian & straight
Rooms: 94

Baths: private
Kids: welcome
Pets: service animals only
Smoking: ok
Rates: $175-575
AC: 10%

Hotel Nikko San Francisco 🏳️‍🌈 *San Francisco*

222 Mason St   415/ 394-1111   reservations@hotelnikkosf.com
San Francisco, CA 94102   800/ 248-3303   www.hotelnikkosf.com

With a premier location off of Union Square and the Theater District, Hotel Nikko is an oasis within an exciting city: a full-service, four-diamond luxury hotel offering guest room amenities such as large flat-panel television sets, a personal CD stereo, high-speed internet access, two-line speaker phones with data port, complimentary coffee and tea, refreshment center, and 24-hour room service.

The hotel also features an exclusive Nikko Floor with a private lounge. All guests can enjoy the extensive Health Club on the 5th Floor with an indoor swimming pool and Shiatsu massage by appointment. Restaurant ANZU features an innovative menu with a wide range of entrees, including prime aged beef flown in daily from Chicago, and the freshest sushi created by our sushi chefs. The ANZU bar offers cocktails, fine wines and beers, and sixty-five popular Sake martinis.

From our staff's attention to detail to the hotel's unique amenities, it is our goal to make every guest feel the warmth of San Francisco and be left with wonderful memories of their stay at Hotel Nikko, which will make them return time and time again.

Clientele: gay-friendly

Type: hotel

Nearby Attractions: Union Square shopping, Theater District, cable cars, SFMOMA, Castro, Fisherman's Wharf, Asian Art Museum, Alcatraz, AT&T Park

Pickup Service: airport limo pickup service (fee)

Transit: near public transit; 30 minutes to SFO & Oakland airports

Rooms: 532 (including 22 suites) total, suites, kings, queens, fulls (each w/ 2 beds), A/C, TV w/ on-demand movies, cable, phone, CD player, refreshment center, 24hr rm service, daily maid service

Baths: private, bathtubs, showers, robes, hairdryers

Wheelchair Access: yes, 18 rms

Meals: Anzu, full-service restaurant on premises, serves brkfst, lunch, dinner, Sun brunch

Amenities: pool, sauna, indoor hot tub, 24hr health club, massage (by appt), hair salon, restaurant, business center, car rental, multilingual staff

Kids: welcome

Smoking: no

Reservations: required *Deposit:* credit card guarantee only *Cancellation:* cancel by 1 day prior or forfeit deposit *Check in/out:* 3pm/ noon

Payment: cash, travelers checks, Visa, Amex, MC, Discover, Diners Club, JCB

Season: open yr-round

Rates: varies (check website) *Discounts:* yes

AC: yes

Hotel Triton T·G·
San Francisco

342 Grant Ave
San Francisco, CA 94108

415/ 394-0500
800/ 433-6611

reservations@hoteltriton.com
www.hoteltriton.com

Clientele: mixed gay/ straight
Type: hotel; hip, chic & eco-friendly; located in heart of the City's Gallery District & directly across from Chinatown's ornate dragon gate
Owned/ Run By: gay & straight
Nearby Attractions: 10 minutes to the Castro; 3 blks to Union Square; 1/2 blk to Financial District; outside Chinatown's Dragon Gate
Transit: near public transit; 25 minutes to SFO; 1 blk to MUNI; 3 blks to BART; shuttle: Lorrie's, 415/ 334-9000
Rooms: 140 total, 7 suites, 25 kings, 48 queens, 60 fulls, A/C, color TV, cable, phone, refrigerator, rm service, maid service, voicemail, Nintendo
Baths: private
Wheelchair Access: yes, 8 rms
Meals: coffee/ tea only
Amenities: WiFi
Recreation: gym
Kids: welcome
Pets: welcome; please sign agreement

Smoking: ok (in select rms only)
Reservations: required *Deposit:* required, credit card guarantee, personal check ok *Cancellation:* cancel by 1 day prior *Check in/ out:* 3pm/ noon

Payment: cash, travelers checks, Visa, Amex, MC, Discover
Season: open yr-round
Rates: $149-299   *Discounts:* weekly & seniors, 'Out In Style' travelers, AAA
AC: 10%

Howard Johnson Express Inn
San Francisco

385 9th St
San Francisco, CA 94103
415/ 431-5131 800/ 446-4656
www.hojo.com

Clientele: mixed gay/ straight
Type: motel; in the heart of South of Market district; near many gay clubs; limited parking
Rooms: 21
Baths: private
Wheelchair Access: yes, 1 rm

Meals: cont'l brkfst
Amenities: hot tub, WiFi
Kids: welcome
Smoking: ok
Rates: $69-139

Hyatt Regency San Francisco T·G·
San Francisco

5 Embarcadero Center
San Francisco, CA 94111
415/ 788-1234 800/ 233-1234
sanfranciscoregency.hyatt.com

Clientele: gay-friendly
Type: hotel; 4-star waterfront hotel located on Embarcadero waterfront; minutes to Ferry Bldg, Fisherman's Wharf, Chinatown, North Beach, Union Square, the Castro
Rooms: 802
Baths: private

Wheelchair Access: yes, 21 rms
Amenities: laundry, gym, WiFi
Kids: welcome
Smoking: no
Rates: $189-394
AC: 10%

Jackson Court
San Francisco

2198 Jackson St
San Francisco, CA 94115
415/ 929-7670
www.jacksoncourt.com

Clientele: gay-friendly
Type: b&b-inn; cozy 19th-c brownstone mansion in prestigious Pacific Heights; all rms individually decorated; afternoon tea service included
Owned/ Run By: gay/ lesbian & straight
Rooms: 10

Baths: private
Meals: expanded cont'l brkfst
Kids: welcome
Pets: service animals only
Smoking: no
Rates: $160-225
AC: 10%

Inn on Castro

321 Castro St
San Francisco, CA 94114

415/ 861-0321

San Francisco
innkeeper@innoncastro.com
www.innoncastro.com

Clientele: mixed gay/ lesbian
Type: b&b-inn; known for more than 20 yrs for its hospitality & friendly atmosphere
Owned/ Run By: gay men
Transit: near public transit; 100 ft to bus/ train lines
Rooms: 8 total, 2 suites, 4 kings, 3 queens, 1 full, 4 twins, cable, deck, phone, maid service
Baths: private, bathtubs, showers, robes, hairdryers
Wheelchair Access: yes, 1 rm
Meals: full brkfst
Amenities: office hrs: 7:30am-10:30pm; concierge, sundeck, coffee/ tea
Smoking: no
Reservations: required *Deposit:* required, first & last night, due at booking

Cancellation: cancel by 2 weeks prior *Minimum Stay:* 2 nights (wknds)/ 3-4 nights (holidays) *Check in/ out:* noon-10:30pm/ noon
Payment: cash, travelers checks, personal checks, Visa, Amex, MC
Season: open yr-round
Rates: $100-250

The Inn San Francisco

943 S Van Ness Ave
San Francisco, CA 94110

415/ 641-0188
800/ 359-0913

San Francisco
innkeeper@innsf.com
www.innsf.com

Clientele: gay-friendly
Type: b&b-inn; gracious 1872 Victorian mansion in historic residential neighborhood; antiques, fresh flowers, sundeck & lovely English garden; distinct San Francisco hospitality
Owned/ Run By: gay & straight
Nearby Attractions: 5-15 minutes to all San Francisco attractions; 8 blks to South of Market clubs, Noe Valley shops & restaurants, the Castro
Transit: 9 miles to SFO; 1 blk to MUNI buses; 4 blks to BART station
Rooms: 21 total, 16 queens, 5 fulls, 3 twins, color TV, DVD/ VCR (7), cable TV (2), fireplace (4), deck (2), phone, kitchenette (1), refrigerator, maid service
Baths: private & shared, bathtubs, showers, whirlpools, robes
Meals: expanded cont'l brkfst, full buffet brkfst
Amenities: free parking, laundry,

outdoor hot tub, WiFi, concierge, fruit basket, rooftop sundeck, garden, complimentary coffee/ tea/ sherry, fresh flowers
Recreation: jog or play tennis in Dolores Park, horseback ride in Golden Gate Park
Kids: please inquire
Pets: please inquire
Pets On Premises: 1 dog
Smoking: no
Reservations: required *Deposit:* required, 1 night, personal check ok *Cancellation:* cancel by 1 week prior or forfeit deposit *Check in/ out:* 2pm/ noon
Payment: cash, travelers checks, Visa, Amex, MC, Discover, Diners Club, personal checks (US only)
Season: open yr-round *High season:* May-Oct
Rates: $115-295 *Discounts:* negotiable (based on length of stay)
AC: 10%

JW Marriott Hotel San Francisco

San Francisco

500 Post St
San Francisco, CA 94102
415/ 771-8600 800/ 605-6568
sfjw@marriott.com
www.jwmarriottunionsquare.com

Clientele: gay-friendly
Type: hotel; "metropolitan luxury on your terms–service personalized to your taste in the vibrant heart of the City by the Bay"
Owned/ Run By: straights
Nearby Attractions: Union Square shopping, Financial District, Castro & South of Market nightlife, Moscone Center, opera, ballet, symphony, museums
Transit: 20 minutes to SFO ($40 taxi; $25 SuperShuttle; $5 BART); 20 minutes Oakland Int'l ($45 taxi; $7 BART)
Rooms: 338 total, suites, 292 kings, 43 fulls, A/C, color TV, cable, phone (w/ voicemail), refrigerator, rm service, maid service, all have flat-screen TV & granite writing desk, TV in bathrm, in-rm safe
Baths: private, bathtubs, showers, robes, hairdryers
Wheelchair Access: yes, 4 rms
Amenities: laundry, massage, DVDs/ videos, gym, WiFi, coffee/ tea, 24hr personal valet services, pillow preference program, fitness center
Recreation: golf; SF Lincoln, Presidio; hiking/ biking: Marin Headlands (7 miles); boating/ sailing
Kids: welcome
Pets: no
Smoking: no
Reservations: required *Deposit:* required, due at booking *Cancellation:* cancel by 1 day prior or forfeit 1 night + tax *Check in/ out:* 3pm/ noon
Payment: cash, travelers checks, Visa, Amex, MC, Discover
Season: open yr-round *High season:* yr-round
Rates: $229-450

The JW Marriott Hotel San Francisco provides you with a civilized retreat at the end of your day. Whether that means you're returning from sight-seeing at 6pm, or clubbing at 6am, JW Marriott San Francisco is your luxurious, sophisticated choice in the City by the Bay.

Our 338 rooms are appointed with your standards in mind: flat-screen televisions; fine linens; Herman Miller desk chairs; spacious bathrooms with separate tubs and glass-enclosed showers; and Bose Wave Radios.

We are perfectly located for the ultimate San Francisco experience: steps from the world-class shopping, dining, and theater on Union Square. Once the sun goes down, we're minutes from the nightlife of the Castro District and South of Market area. Other nearby attractions include Chinatown, cable cars, Fisherman's Wharf, Moscone Center, SFMOMA, The Asian Art Museum, and the San Francisco Ballet, Symphony, and Opera.

The Laurel Inn 🏳️‍🌈   *San Francisco*

444 Presidio Ave
San Francisco, CA 94115
415/ 567-8467 800/ 552-8735
www.jdvhospitality.com

Clientele: gay-friendly
Type: hotel; renovated '60s sophisticate hotel; in Pacific Heights
Owned/ Run By: gay/ lesbian & straight
Rooms: 49
Baths: private
Meals: cont'l brkfst

Kids: welcome
Pets: welcome
Smoking: no
Rates: $179-209
AC: 10%

The Maxwell Hotel 🏳️‍🌈   *San Francisco*

386 Geary St
San Francisco, CA 94102
415/ 986-2000 888/ 734-6299
www.maxwellhotel.com

Clientele: mixed gay/ straight
Type: hotel; 1908 art deco masterpiece; rms reflect the drama of the Theater District locale; excellent Union Square location
Owned/ Run By: gay/ lesbian & straight
Rooms: 153
Baths: private

Wheelchair Access: yes
Meals: coffee/tea only
Kids: welcome
Pets: guide dogs only
Smoking: ok
Rates: $129-259
AC: 10%

Metro Hotel   *San Francisco*

319 Divisadero St
San Francisco, CA 94117
415/ 861-5364
www.metrohotelsf.com

Clientele: gay-friendly
Type: hotel; quaint European pension w/ charming garden; centrally located near public transportation; rated as best value by Citysearch & featured in *Nat'l Geographic Traveler* magazine
Owned/ Run By: straights

Rooms: 24
Baths: private
Kids: welcome
Smoking: ok
Rates: $66-120
AC: 10%

Monticello Inn 🏳️‍🌈   *San Francisco*

127 Ellis St
San Francisco, CA 94102
415/ 392-8800 866/ 778-6169
www.monticelloinn.com

Clientele: gay-friendly
Type: inn; in charming boutique hotel located in Union Square, the heart of SF's shopping & sight-seeing district; manager's wine hour daily
Owned/ Run By: straights
Rooms: 91

Baths: private
Wheelchair Access: yes, 4 rms
Meals: coffee/tea only
Amenities: free parking, laundry
Kids: welcome
Rates: $139-235
AC: 10%

The Mosser Hotel 🏳️‍🌈   *San Francisco*

54 4th St
San Francisco, CA 94103
415/ 986-4400 800/ 227-3804
www.themosser.com

Clientele: mixed gay/ straight
Type: hotel; premier 1913 landmark near Union Square
Owned/ Run By: gay & straight
Rooms: 166
Baths: private & shared
Amenities: laundry, WiFi

Kids: welcome
Pets: no
Smoking: no
Rates: $69-229
AC: 10%

National Hotel   *San Francisco*

1139 Market St
San Francisco, CA 94102
415/ 864-9343
nationalhotelsf@aol.com

Clientele: gay-friendly
Type: hostel; centrally located; minutes from Castro & just blks to South of Market; directly above subway station for BART & Muni (local light rail)
Rooms: 94

Baths: shared
Kids: no
Pets: no
Smoking: ok
Rates: $35-45

The Parker Guest House

San Francisco

520 Church St   415/ 621-3222   info@parkerguesthouse.com
San Francisco, CA 94114 888/ 520-7275   www.parkerguesthouse.com

San Francisco's Premier Gay Guest House—
The Parker Guest House is a twenty-one-guest-room Edwardian mini-mansion complex, perfectly located in San Francisco's vibrant Castro District. The Guest House is just steps from the Castro's excellent restaurants, bars, and cafes and an easy streetcar ride to the Financial District, Moscone Convention Center, and the City's other major attractions.

Guest services include extended continental breakfast and afternoon wine social as well as use of the property's welcoming public rooms, gardens, sundecks, and steam spa. All rooms come equipped with down comforters, terrycloth robes, private phone, voicemail, WiFi internet, cable TV, new all-tile baths, and first-class amenities. On-site, secure parking is available for $15 per night.

Celebrating 10 years in business, the Parker Guest House is the most highly rated gay and lesbian guest house in San Francisco according to *Out & About*, the Damron guides, and *Fodor's Gay Guide*. Their complete business facilities make them an ideal hotel choice for both leisure and business travelers. Visit them at www.parkerguesthouse.com or call toll-free at 888/ 520-7275.

Clientele: mostly men
Type: beautiful guesthouse complex w/ extensive gardens
Owned/ Run By: gay men
Nearby Attractions: Castro & Mission Districts: extensive bars, cafes & restaurants; Union Square, historic streetcars, Fisherman's Wharf trolley
Transit: near public transit; 15 miles to SFO
Rooms: 21 total, 2 suites, 5 kings, 14 queens, color TV, cable, phone, maid service, down comforters, voicemail, WiFi & DSL, sundecks, new all-tile baths
Baths: private & shared, bathtubs, showers, robes, hairdryers
Meals: expanded cont'l brkfst
Amenities: free parking, sauna, WiFi, spa/ steam area, extensive gardens, afternoon wine social, concierge, computer station w/ DSL
Recreation: tennis in Dolores Park nearby
Pets On Premises: 1 dog
Smoking: no
Reservations: highly suggested *Deposit:* required, 1 night, due at booking, personal check ok *Cancellation:* cancel by 14 days prior or forfeit deposit *Minimum Stay:* wknds *Check in/ out:* 3-9pm/ noon
Payment: cash, travelers checks, Visa, Amex, MC, Discover
Season: open yr-round
Rates: $129-209
AC: 10%

Nob Hill Lambourne
San Francisco

725 Pine St
San Francisco, CA 94108
415/ 433-2287 800/ 274-8466
www.nobhilllambourne.com

Clientele: gay-friendly
Type: hotel; intimate urban retreat w/ spa services available; luxurious, private & tastefully appointed; each rm designed to serve as an office & an elegant place to spend the night
Owned/ Run By: gay men
Rooms: 20

Baths: private
Meals: expanded cont'l brkfst
Kids: welcome; under 12 yrs free
Pets: no
Smoking: no
Rates: $189-350
AC: 10%

Nob Hill Motor Inn
San Francisco

1630 Pacific Ave
San Francisco, CA 94109
415/ 775-8160 800/ 343-6900
www.staysf.com/nobhill

Clientele: gay-friendly
Type: hotel; walking distance of Fisherman's Wharf & cable cars; newly renovated rms w/ microwave, fridge & coffee; free high-speed internet; free parking (!)
Owned/ Run By: gay/ lesbian & straight
Rooms: 30
Baths: private

Wheelchair Access: yes, 2 rms
Meals: cont'l brkfst
Kids: welcome
Pets: no
Smoking: no
Rates: $79-169
AC: 10%

Noe's Nest B&B
San Francisco

1257 Guerrero St
San Francisco, CA 94110
415/ 821-0751
www.noesnest.com

Clientele: mixed gay/ lesbian
Type: b&b; centrally located w/ deck, views & a personal touch
Owned/ Run By: lesbian & straight
Rooms: 6
Baths: private
Meals: expanded cont'l brkfst
Amenities: laundry, outdoor hot tub,

massage, DVDs/ videos
Kids: welcome
Pets: dogs welcome (up to 75 lbs); fee charged
Smoking: no
Rates: $119-249
AC: 10%

Petite Auberge
San Francisco

863 Bush St
San Francisco, CA 94108
415/ 928-6000 800/ 365-3004
www.petiteaubergesf.com

Clientele: gay-friendly
Type: b&b; small hotel nestled between Nob Hill & Union Square
Owned/ Run By: gay/ lesbian & straight
Rooms: 26
Baths: private

Meals: expanded cont'l brkfst
Kids: welcome
Pets: service animals only
Smoking: no
Rates: $159+

The Powell Hotel
San Francisco

28 Cyril Magnin St
San Francisco, CA 94102
415/ 398-3200 800/ 368-0700
www.thepowellhotel.com

Clientele: mixed gay/ straight
Type: boutique hotel w/ newly renovated rms; steps away from world-famous cable-car turnaround
Owned/ Run By: gay/ lesbian & straight
Rooms: 114

Baths: private
Wheelchair Access: yes, 6 rms
Kids: under 12 yrs free w/ existing bedding
Smoking: ok (smokefree rms available)
Rates: $129-179
AC: 10%

Prescott Hotel
San Francisco

545 Post St
San Francisco, CA 94102
415/ 563-0303 866/ 271-3632
www.prescotthotel.com

Clientele: mixed gay/ straight
Type: luxury boutique hotel located on San Francisco's most fashionable street; home to Wolfgang Puck's Postrio restaurant
Rooms: 164
Baths: private
Wheelchair Access: yes, 6 rms

Meals: coffee/tea only
Amenities: laundry, massage, WiFi
Kids: welcome
Pets: welcome
Smoking: ok (smoking rms only)
Rates: $199-340
AC: 10%

Queen Anne Hotel
San Francisco

1590 Sutter St
San Francisco, CA 94109-5395
415/ 441-2828 800/ 227-3970
www.queenanne.com

Clientele: gay-friendly
Type: hotel; award-winning Victorian guesthouse; antique-furnished rms w/ private baths; century-old ambience & charm; some rms w/ fireplaces or jacuzzi
Owned/ Run By: gay men
Rooms: 48
Baths: private
Wheelchair Access: yes, 2 rms

Meals: expanded cont'l brkfst
Amenities: free parking, laundry, massage, WiFi
Kids: welcome; 12 yrs & under free
Pets: no
Smoking: ok
Rates: $139-350 (request Damron discount)
AC: 10%

Radisson Miyako Hotel
San Francisco

1625 Post St
San Francisco, CA 94115
415/ 922-3200 800/ 333-3333
www.miyakohotel.com

Clientele: gay-friendly
Type: hotel; "closest luxury hotel w/ affordable comfort to the Castro District"
Rooms: 218
Baths: private
Wheelchair Access: yes, 7 rms
Meals: full brkfst
Amenities: free parking, laundry, hot tub, massage

Kids: welcome
Smoking: ok
Rates: $179-299
AC: 10%

Ramada Market St
San Francisco

1231 Market St
San Francisco, CA 94103
415/ 626-8000 800/ 227-4747
www.ramadaplazasf.com

Clientele: gay-friendly
Type: hotel; restaurant & Starbucks on-site, very close to Civic Center Plaza (where Pride is held)
Rooms: 456 (includes 13 suites)
Baths: private
Wheelchair Access: yes
Amenities: gym, WiFi

Kids: welcome
Rates: $89+

Renoir Hotel
San Francisco

45 McAllister
San Francisco, CA 94102
415/ 626-5200 800/ 576-3388
www.renoirhotel.com

Clientele: mixed gay/ straight
Type: boutique hotel; downtown location; 3 blks to Folsom St bars & clubs; bar & Brazilian restaurant on-site; close to all public transportation; best views of SF Pride parade
Owned/ Run By: gay/ lesbian & straight
Rooms: 135
Baths: private

Wheelchair Access: yes, 2 rms
Meals: full brkfst
Kids: welcome
Pets: no
Smoking: no
Rates: $89-350
AC: 10% (20% IGLTA members)

Serrano Hotel
San Francisco

405 Taylor St
San Francisco, CA 94102
415/ 885-2500 877/ 294-9709
www.serranohotel.com

Clientele: mixed gay/ straight
Type: newly restored historic hotel in the heart of the Theater District
Owned/ Run By: gay & straight
Rooms: 236
Baths: private
Wheelchair Access: yes, 20 rms
Meals: coffee/tea only
Amenities: sauna, massage, gym, WiFi

Kids: welcome
Pets: small pets only
Smoking: one smoking flr
Rates: $199-350
AC: 10%

Shannon-Kavanaugh Guest House
San Francisco

722 Steiner
San Francisco, CA 94117
415/ 563-2727
www.shannon-kavanaugh.com/rental.html

Clientele: gay-friendly
Type: apt; 1-bdrm apt in garden setting; in house on SF's famous "Postcard Row"
Owned/ Run By: gay men
Rooms: 2
Kids: welcome

Pets: negotiable
Smoking: no
Rates: $150-300
AC: 20%

Sir Francis Drake Hotel
San Francisco

450 Powell St
San Francisco, CA 94102
415/ 392-7755 800/ 795-7129
www.sirfrancisdrake.com

Clientele: mixed gay/ straight
Type: hotel; newly renovated 1928 landmark; w/ grand baroque-style lobby & function rms; famous Scala Bistro restaurant & Starlight Room nightclub on-site
Owned/ Run By: other
Rooms: 417

Baths: private
Wheelchair Access: yes, 14 rms
Kids: welcome
Pets: welcome
Smoking: smoking rms only
Rates: $175-259
AC: 10%

Stanyan Park Hotel
San Francisco

750 Stanyan St
San Francisco, CA 94117
415/ 751-1000
www.stanyanpark.com

Clientele: gay-friendly
Type: b&b-inn; listed on the Nat'l Register of Historic Places, this elegant, thoroughly restored Victorian hotel will take you back to a bygone era of style, grace & comfort
Owned/ Run By: straights
Rooms: 36
Baths: private

Wheelchair Access: yes, 2 rms
Meals: expanded cont'l brkfst
Amenities: WiFi
Kids: welcome
Smoking: no (completely smokefree)
Rates: $130-315
AC: 10%

The Touchstone Hotel
San Francisco

480 Geary St
San Francisco, CA 94102-1223
415/ 771-1600 800/ 620-5889
www.TheTouchstone.com

Clientele: gay-friendly
Type: hotel; located in Union Square/ Theatre District; family-owned for 50 yrs; famous David'd Delicatessen on-site
Owned/ Run By: straights
Rooms: 42
Baths: private

Wheelchair Access: yes, 2 rms
Meals: full brkfst
Kids: welcome
Pets: guide dogs only
Smoking: ok
Rates: $59-99
AC: 10%

Travelodge Central
San Francisco

1707 Market St
San Francisco, CA 94103
415/ 621-6775
800/ 578-7878 (reservations)
www.sanfranciscocentralhotel.com

Clientele: gay-friendly
Type: motel; just steps from the SF LGBT Community Center & popular gay bars & restaurants
Owned/ Run By: women
Rooms: 81
Baths: private

Meals: coffee/tea only
Kids: welcome; under 17 yrs free
Pets: no
Smoking: ok (57 nonsmoking rms)
Rates: $99-179
AC: 10%

Tuscan Inn
San Francisco

425 Northpoint St
San Francisco, CA 94133
415/ 561-1100 888/ 648-4626
www.tuscaninn.com

Clientele: gay-friendly
Type: hotel; one of San Francisco's finest European-style inns; "The best hotel in Fisherman's Wharf"–*Frommer's San Francisco*
Owned/ Run By: gay/ lesbian & straight
Rooms: 221
Baths: private

Wheelchair Access: yes, 7 rms
Meals: coffee/tea only
Kids: welcome w/ existing bedding
Pets: small pets only; $50 deposit (nonrefundable)
Smoking: no
Rates: $129-369
AC: 10%

Terrace Place

San Francisco

PMB 112, 584 Castro St
San Francisco, CA 94114

415/ 241-0425

www.terraceplace.com

Clientele: mixed gay/ lesbian
Type: guesthouse; 1- or 2-bdrm suite; w/ spectacular views, private deck & entrance
Owned/ Run By: gay men
Nearby Attractions: Castro St, Haight St
Transit: near public transit; 15 miles to San Francisco Int'l
Rooms: 4 total, 1 suite, 3 queens, color TV (3), DVD/ VCR (3), cable TV (2), ceiling fan (1), deck, phone, kitchenette (1), refrigerator (1), safer sex supplies, maid service
Baths: private, showers, hairdryers
Meals: coffee/tea only
Amenities: office hrs: 10am-6pm; laundry, DVDs/ videos, WiFi, coffee/ tea, satellite TV, computer, internet access
Recreation: Buena Vista Park, Golden Gate Park
Pets: negotiable; deposit
Pets On Premises: 1 dog
Smoking: ok

Reservations: required *Deposit:* required, 1 night, due 2 weeks prior, personal check ok *Cancellation:* cancel by 2 weeks prior or forfeit 25% *Check in/ out:* 3pm/ noon
Payment: cash, travelers checks, personal checks

Season: open yr-round *High season:* summer, fall, winter
Rates: $99-240 *Discounts:* weekly, monthly
AC: 10%

Villa Florence Hotel

San Francisco

225 Powell St
San Francisco, 94102
415/ 397-7700 866/ 823-4669
www.villaflorence.com

Clientele: mixed gay/ straight
Type: Italian Renaissance boutique hotel w/ unbeatable Union Square location; central to shopping, restaurants & theater district
Owned/ Run By: gay/ lesbian & straight
Rooms: 183
Baths: private

Wheelchair Access: yes, 6 rms
Amenities: free parking, laundry, WiFi
Kids: 4 people max per rm
Rates: $139-199
AC: 10%

W San Francisco

San Francisco

181 Third St
San Francisco, CA 94103
415/ 777-5300
877/ WHOTELS (reservations only)
www.whotels.com/sanfrancisco

Clientele: gay-friendly
Type: hotel; adjacent to SF Museum of Modern Art & directly across from Moscone Center
Rooms: 410
Baths: private
Wheelchair Access: yes

Meals: coffee/tea only
Amenities: laundry, pool, hot tub, massage, DVDs/ videos, WiFi
Kids: welcome
Pets: welcome; $25 daily pet fee
Rates: $229-429
AC: 10%

White Swan Inn

San Francisco

845 Bush St
San Francisco, CA 94108
415/ 775-1755 800/ 999-9570
www.whiteswaninnsf.com

Clientele: gay-friendly
Type: hotel; in Nob Hill/ Union Square area; "visually stunning tribute to the intimate hotels of London"
Owned/ Run By: gay/ lesbian & straight
Rooms: 26
Baths: private

Meals: expanded cont'l brkfst
Kids: welcome
Pets: service animals only
Smoking: no
Rates: $189+

The Willows Inn

710 14th St
San Francisco, CA 94114

415/ 431-4770
800/ 431-0277

innkeeper@WillowsSF.com
www.WillowsSF.com

Clientele: mixed gay/ lesbian
Type: b&b-inn; popular Edwardian inn located in the Castro; noted for a homey atmosphere & friendly, helpful service
Owned/ Run By: lesbians/ gay men
Nearby Attractions: surrounded by the many restaurants, pubs, gyms, clubs & shops of the Castro; walking distance to several parks
Transit: near public transit; Church St MUNI station, street cars, buses across street
Rooms: 12 total, 1 suite, 6 queens, 6 fulls, color TV, DVD/ VCR, cable, refrigerator (mini-fridges), safer sex supplies, rm service, maid service, direct dial phones w/ voicemail, data port, kimono robe, baths shared but private–separate WCs & shower rms
Baths: shared, showers, robes
Meals: expanded cont'l brkfst
Amenities: office hrs: 8am-8pm; DVDs/ videos, WiFi, cocktails, coffee/ tea, kitchen & sitting rm open 24hrs, evening beverage service
Recreation: tennis courts, parks

Smoking: no
Reservations: highly recommended (book by phone or web/ email) *Deposit:* required, 1 night, due at booking *Cancellation:* cancel by 1 week prior or forfeit 100% if rms not rebooked *Check in/ out:* 8am-8pm/ noon

Payment: cash, travelers checks, Visa, Amex, MC, Discover
Season: open yr-round *High season:* June-Oct
Rates: $105-165

The York Hotel

940 Sutter St
San Francisco, CA 94109
415/ 885-6800 800/ 808-9675
www.yorkhotel.com

Clientele: mixed gay/ straight
Type: hotel; a stylish boutique hotel; service-oriented staff w/ city knowledge; home of The Plush Room & Empire Lounge
Owned/ Run By: gay & straight
Rooms: 96
Baths: private

Wheelchair Access: yes, 4 rms
Meals: expanded cont'l brkfst
Amenities: laundry, WiFi
Kids: welcome; 12 yrs & under free when w/ adult & in same rm
Smoking: no
Rates: $129+
AC: 10%

Hotel De Anza

233 W Santa Clara St
San Jose, CA 95113
408/ 286-1000 800/ 843-3700
www.hoteldeanza.com

Type: hotel; art deco gem on the Nat'l Register of Historic Places
Rooms: 101
Baths: private
Wheelchair Access: yes, 5 rms
Meals: coffee/tea only

Kids: welcome
Smoking: no
Rates: $125-329
AC: 10%

Hotel Los Gatos

210 E Main St
Los Gatos, CA 95030
408/ 335-1700 866/ 335-1700
www.hotellosgatos.com

Clientele: gay-friendly
Type: hotel; nestled in the quiet charm of historic downtown Los Gatos at the base of the Santa Cruz Mtns
Owned/ Run By: gay/ lesbian & straight
Rooms: 72
Baths: private

Wheelchair Access: yes
Amenities: free parking, laundry, pool, outdoor hot tub, massage, DVDs/ videos
Kids: welcome
Pets: service animals
Smoking: no
Rates: $219-439

Moorpark Hotel ⬚

San Jose

4241 Moorpark Ave
San Jose, CA 95129
408/ 864-0300 877/ 740-6622
www.moorparkhotel.com

Clientele: gay-friendly
Type: hotel; in heart of Silicon Valley; features billiards loft, heated pool, hot tub, spacious fitness center, business center, conference facilities; also The Park Bar & Grill
Owned/ Run By: gay/ lesbian & straight
Rooms: 80

Baths: private
Wheelchair Access: yes
Amenities: free parking, pool, outdoor hot tub, gym
Kids: welcome
Pets: service animals only
Rates: $149-209

The Madonna Inn

San Luis Obispo

100 Madonna Rd
San Luis Obispo, CA 93405
805/ 543-3000 800/ 543-9666
www.madonnainn.com

Clientele: gay-friendly
Type: inn; a landmark on California's Central Coast for over 40 yrs; each rm is decorated w/ a different theme—check out the online tour!

Rooms: 109
Baths: private
Rates: $168-445

Sycamore Mineral Springs Resort

San Luis Obispo

1215 Avila Beach Dr
San Luis Obispo, CA 93405
805/ 595-7302 800/ 234-5831
www.smsr.com

Clientele: gay-friendly
Type: resort; hot mineral springs spa; integrative retreat center; treatment center; healing arts institute w/ yoga, meditation, Pilates; walking & hiking; award-winning restaurant
Owned/ Run By: gay & straight

Rooms: 74
Baths: private
Amenities: free parking, pool, private mineral spring spas, massage
Smoking: no

Temptation Ranch at Hidden Springs

San Luis Obispo

PO Box 14209
San Luis Obispo, CA 93406
888/ 213-7733
www.temptationranch.com

Clientele: men
Type: historic Central Coast clothing-optional ranch on private lake; hiking; near nude beaches, Hearst Castle & wineries
Owned/ Run By: gay men
Rooms: 6
Baths: private & shared

Meals: cont'l brkfst
Amenities: free parking, outdoor hot tub, DVDs/ videos, gym
Pets: small dogs welcome w/ additional charge
Smoking: no
Rates: $95-210
AC: 10%

Sea Coast Lodge

San Simeon

9135 Hearst Dr
San Simeon, CA 93452
805/ 927-3878 800/ 451-9900
www.seacoastlodge.com

Clientele: gay-friendly
Type: inn; country-inspired rms feature mini-refrigerators, hairdryers, TVs & VCRs; minutes from Hearst Castle & elephant seals; "Gateway to Big Sur"
Rooms: 57
Baths: private

Wheelchair Access: yes, 3 rms
Kids: welcome
Pets: welcome in designated rms; $25
Rates: $69-225
AC: 10%

Fess Parker's DoubleTree Resort ⬚

Santa Barbara

633 E Cabrillo Blvd
Santa Barbara, CA 93103
800/ 879-2929
www.fpdtr.com

Clientele: gay-friendly
Type: resort; directly across from ocean; close to shopping, restaurants & nightlife; all rms have a patio or a balcony
Owned/ Run By: gay & straight
Rooms: 360
Baths: private

Wheelchair Access: yes, 18 rms
Amenities: free parking, laundry, pool, hot tub, massage, DVDs/ videos, WiFi
Kids: welcome
Pets: welcome
Smoking: ok
Rates: $140-1,027

Inn of the Spanish Garden
Santa Barbara

915 Garden St
Santa Barbara, CA 93101
805/ 564-4700 866/ 564-4700
www.spanishgardeninn.com

Clientele: mixed gay/ straight
Type: hotel; only downtown luxury hotel architecturally true to Spanish origins; beautiful gardens & public rms; sensual & serene
Rooms: 23
Baths: private

Wheelchair Access: yes, 1 rm
Meals: cont'l brkfst
Kids: welcome
Smoking: no
Rates: $235-465
AC: 10%

Old Yacht Club Inn
Santa Barbara

431 Corona Del Mar Dr
Santa Barbara, CA 93103
805/ 962-1277 800/ 676-1676
www.oldyachtclubinn.com

Clientele: gay-friendly
Type: b&b-inn; 1 blk to beach; full gourmet brkfst; complimentary wine social; massages can arranged; some rms w/ whirlpool tubs; access to bicycles, beach chairs & towels
Rooms: 14

Baths: private
Meals: full brkfst
Kids: welcome
Pets: no
Smoking: no
Rates: $99-479
AC: 10% (Oct-May, midweek only)

The Orchid Inn at Santa Barbara
Santa Barbara

420 W Montecito St
Santa Barbara, CA 93101
805/ 965-2333 877/ 722-3657
www.orchidinnatsb.com

Clientele: mixed gay/ straight
Type: b&b-inn; early 1900s Queen Anne Victorian; spacious rms, balconies & views; some rms w/ jacuzzis; antiques & fireplaces; daily wine & cheese social
Owned/ Run By: gay & straight
Rooms: 9
Baths: private

Wheelchair Access: yes, 1 rm
Meals: full brkfst in Carriage House
Amenities: free parking, outdoor hot tub
Kids: no
Pets: no
Smoking: no
Rates: $165-295
AC: 10%

Pacifica Suites
Santa Barbara

5490 Hollister Ave
Santa Barbara, CA 93111
805/ 683-6722 800/ 338-6722
www.pacificasuites.com

Clientele: gay-friendly
Type: hotel; Santa Barbara's all-suites hotel; conveniently located
Rooms: 87
Baths: private
Wheelchair Access: yes, 4 rms
Meals: full brkfst

Amenities: free parking, pool, outdoor hot tub, DVDs/ videos, WiFi
Kids: welcome
Pets: welcome; limited rms, $10/ day
Smoking: ok
Rates: $129-209
AC: 10%

Compassion Flower Inn
Santa Cruz

216 Laurel St
Santa Cruz, CA 95060
831/ 466-0420
www.compassionflowerinn.com

Clientele: mixed gay/ straight
Type: b&b; in gorgeously restored 1860s Victorian in vibrant downtown; friendly lesbian innkeepers; lively atmosphere; gourmet brkfst & organic coffee
Owned/ Run By: lesbians
Rooms: 4

Baths: private & shared
Meals: full brkfst
Amenities: free parking, outdoor hot tub, massage
Kids: welcome
Rates: $115-175
AC: 10%

The Grove Women's Country Retreat by the Sea
Santa Cruz

831/ 724-3459
www.grovewomensretreat.com

Clientele: women
Type: 2 secluded cottages; kitchens, fireplaces, stereos & TV/ VCR; ocean view; endless pool; Swedish dry sauna; long uncrowded, spectacular beach; convenient to Santa Cruz & Monterey
Owned/ Run By: woman
Rooms: 2 (cottages)

Baths: private
Meals: coffee/tea only
Amenities: free parking, pool, sauna, outdoor hot tub, massage, DVDs/ videos
Kids: please discuss w/ owner
Pets: please discuss w/ owner
Smoking: no
Rates: $135-195

Pleasure Point Inn
Santa Cruz

3655 E Cliff Dr
nta Cruz, CA 95062
1/ 475–4657
ww.pleasurepointinn.com

Clientele: gay-friendly
Type: Mediterranean-style inn; overlooking Monterey Bay; short drive to Santa Cruz Boardwalk; golf or whale-watching packages
Rooms: 4
Baths: private

Meals: expanded cont'l brkfst
Amenities: outdoor hot tub, massage, WiFi
Kids: no
Pets: no
Smoking: no
Rates: $225-295
AC: 10%

Hyatt Vineyard Creek Hotel
Santa Rosa

70 Railroad St
nta Rosa, CA 95401
7/ 284–1234
ww.vineyardcreek.hyatt.com

Clientele: gay-friendly
Type: resort; 40 miles N of San Francisco; close to the Russian River resorts & wineries; seafood restaurant; spa features steam rms, massage, facials & nail services
Owned/ Run By: straights
Rooms: 155
Baths: private
Wheelchair Access: yes, 6 rms

Meals: full brkfst
Amenities: free parking, pool, sauna, outdoor hot tub, massage, WiFi
Kids: welcome
Pets: welcome; 1 pet under 80 lbs per rm
Rates: $149-249
AC: 10%

Cedars of Sonoma
Sebastopol

203 Barnett Valley Rd
bastopol, CA 95472-9238
7/ 829–1000
ww.cedarsofsonoma.com

Clientele: mixed gay/ straight
Type: cabin; on 20 acres
Owned/ Run By: gay & straight
Rooms: 2

Baths: shared
Kids: welcome
Pets: welcome
Rates: $99-185

Vine Hill Inn B&B
Sebastopol

49 Vine Hill Rd
bastopol, CA 95472
7/ 823–8832
ww.vine-hill-inn.com

Clientele: gay-friendly
Type: b&b-inn; in restored 1897 farmhouse
Rooms: 4
Baths: private
Meals: full brkfst

Kids: please inquire
Pets: please inquire
Smoking: no (ok outside & by pool)
Rates: $150

Organic Gardens B&B
Sequoia Nat'l Park

Box 651
ree Rivers, CA 93271
9/ 561–4610
ww.organicgardens-sequoia.com

Clientele: gay-friendly
Type: b&b; quiet & peaceful; 5 miles from entrance to Sequoia Nat'l Park
Owned/ Run By: lesbian
Rooms: 2
Baths: private
Wheelchair Access: yes, 2 rms

Meals: expanded cont'l brkfst
Amenities: free parking, outdoor hot tub
Kids: 5 yrs & up welcome
Pets: small pets only
Smoking: totally smokefree
Rates: $138

Wine Country Teahouse
Sonoma

56 Frederica Ave
nwood, CA 95452
7/ 833–6998
ww.winecountryteahouse.com

Clientele: mixed gay/ lesbian
Type: guesthouse; in authentic Japanese teahouse
Owned/ Run By: gay men
Rooms: 3
Baths: private

Meals: expanded cont'l brkfst
Amenities: free parking, pool, hot tub, massage, DVDs/ videos
Rates: $225-295
AC: 10%

Beltane Ranch

Sonom

PO Box 395
Glen Ellen, CA 95442
707/ 996-6501
www.beltaneranch.com

Clientele: gay-friendly
Type: b&b-inn; 1892 New Orleans-style ranch house; also cottage; in the Valley of the Moon; private tennis courts & hiking trails
Rooms: 5 + 1 cottage

Baths: private
Meals: full brkfst
Rates: $140-220

Gaige House Inn

Sonom

13540 Arnold Dr
Glen Ellen, CA 95442
707/ 935-0237 800/ 935-0237
www.gaige.com

Clientele: gay-friendly
Type: b&b-inn; small, luxurious inn located in Sonoma Wine Country; w/ large, stylish rms, superior brkfsts & wines; A&E's Top Ten Romantic Spots; T & L's Best B&B
Owned/ Run By: gay & straight
Rooms: 15

Baths: private
Wheelchair Access: yes, 1 rm
Meals: full brkfst
Amenities: free parking, pool, outdoor tub, massage
Rates: $175-695
AC: 10%

Glenelly Inn & Cottages

Sonom

5131 Warm Springs Rd
Glen Ellen, CA 95442
707/ 996-6720
www.glenelly.com

Clientele: gay-friendly
Type: b&b-inn; in 1916 inn; on-site massage & spa services; "ideal for romantic getaways, honeymoons, family reunions"
Rooms: 10 (including 2 cottages)
Baths: private
Meals: full brkfst

Amenities: outdoor hot tub, massage
Kids: welcome
Pets: no
Smoking: no (ok outdoors only)
Rates: $165-295

Magliulo's Rose Garden Inn

Sonom

681 Broadway
Sonoma, CA 95476
707/ 996-1031
www.sonomarose.net

Clientele: gay-friendly
Type: b&b; one of Wine Country's most romantic Victorian b&b's
Owned/ Run By: straights
Rooms: 4

Baths: private & shared
Wheelchair Access: yes, 4 rms
Kids: no
Pets: no
Rates: $115-135

Sonoma Chalet

Sonom

18935 5th St W
Sonoma, CA 95476
707/ 938-3129 800/ 938-3129
www.sonomachalet.com

Clientele: gay-friendly
Type: b&b-inn; cottages; set on 3 1/2 acres in the hillsides of Sonoma Valley; filled w/ a wonderfully eccentric mix of antique collectibles, including extensive Fiestaware

Rooms: 4 rms & 3 cottages
Baths: private & shared
Meals: cont'l brkfst
Amenities: outdoor hot tub
Rates: $110-225

Thistle Dew Inn

Sonom

171 W Spain St
Sonoma, CA 95476
707/ 938-2909 800/ 382-7895
www.thistledew.com

Clientele: gay-friendly
Type: b&b-inn; located in charming Wine Country; whirlpool baths & fireplaces in some rms; free use of bicycles
Owned/ Run By: gay & straight
Rooms: 5
Baths: private
Wheelchair Access: yes, 1 rm

Meals: full brkfst
Amenities: outdoor hot tub, WiFi
Kids: 13 yrs & up
Pets: only service animals welcome
Smoking: no
Rates: $165-300
AC: 10%

Trojan Horse Inn
Sonoma

9455 Sonoma Hwy
Sonoma, CA 95476
707/ 996-2430 800/ 899-1925
www.trojanhorseinn.com

Clientele: gay-friendly
Type: romantic turn-of-the-century inn located in the heart of the California Wine Country
Owned/ Run By: straights
Rooms: 6
Baths: private
Wheelchair Access: yes, 1 rm

Meals: full brkfst
Amenities: outdoor hot tub, massage
Kids: no
Pets: no
Smoking: no
Rates: $175-245
AC: 10%

Warm Springs Getaway
Sonoma

15/ 841-0257
www.warmspringsarts.citymax.com

Clientele: gay-friendly (mostly women)
Type: rental home; sleeps 8 adults; located on 1/2 acre next to new vineyard; beautiful redwood deck & spa area
Owned/ Run By: lesbians
Rooms: 3
Baths: private & shared

Meals: coffee/tea only
Amenities: laundry, hot tub, DVDs/ videos
Kids: please inquire
Pets: please inquire
Smoking: no
Rates: $325-495

Great Energy
Springville

PO Box 473
Springville, CA 93265
559/ 539-2382
www.greatenergy.net/queerlodgings.html

Clientele: mixed gay/ lesbian
Type: b&b-private home; in southern Sierras near Sequoia Nat'l Monument, clothing-optional pool; isolation, peace, quiet
Owned/ Run By: woman
Rooms: 3
Baths: private & shared
Meals: cont'l brkfst

Amenities: free parking, laundry, pool, sauna, hot tub, massage, DVDs/ videos
Kids: welcome as long as no couples already booked
Pets: no
Smoking: no
Rates: $85-125
AC: 5%

Wild Palms Hotel　[TAG]
Sunnyvale

10 E Fremont Ave
Sunnyvale, CA 94087
408/ 738-0500 800/ 538-1600
www.wildpalmhotel.com

Clientele: gay-friendly
Type: hotel
Owned/ Run By: gay & straight
Rooms: 208
Baths: private
Wheelchair Access: yes, 8 rms
Meals: expanded cont'l brkfst

Amenities: free parking, laundry, pool, outdoor hot tub
Kids: welcome
Smoking: ok
Rates: $120+
AC: 10%

The Foxes Inn of Sutter Creek
Sutter Creek

77 Main St
Sutter Creek, CA 95685
209/ 267-5882 800/ 987-3344
www.foxesinn.com

Clientele: gay-friendly
Type: elegant, award-winning inn; located in the heart of the Gold Country & close to the Shenandoah Valley wine region
Owned/ Run By: gay men
Rooms: 7

Baths: private
Meals: full brkfst
Kids: no
Pets: no
Rates: $160-229
AC: 10%

The Brakey House
Ventura

411 Poli St
Ventura, CA 93001
805/ 643-3600
www.brakeyhouse.com

Clientele: gay-friendly
Type: b&b; this 1890 Victorian b&b is the romantic beach getaway of the celebrities; "stay where Barbra stays!"
Owned/ Run By: straights
Rooms: 7
Baths: private

Meals: full brkfst
Amenities: free parking, laundry, hot tub, massage, DVDs/ videos
Kids: 1 rm can accommodate
Pets: 1 rm can accommodate
Rates: $95-235

Black Hawk Weyr
Willits

228 Broad St
San Francisco, CA 94112
415/ 225-2624
callaurose@aol.com

Clientele: mixed gay/ lesbian
Type: private modern vacation cabin; on 20-acre forested mountainside 2.5 hrs N of San Francisco; fully equipped kitchen; luxury bath; sleeps 5
Owned/ Run By: lesbians
Rooms: 4
Baths: shared
Wheelchair Access: yes, 1 rm

Kids: welcome
Pets: call to discuss
Smoking: no
Rates: $85

Apple Tree Inn
Yosemite Nat'l Park

1110 Hwy 41
Fish Camp, CA 93623
559/ 683-5111 888/ 683-5111
www.moonstonehotels.com

Clientele: gay-friendly
Type: b&b-inn; 2 miles from Yosemite Nat'l Park's S Entrance; perfect lodging for your Yosemite adventure
Rooms: 53
Baths: private
Wheelchair Access: yes, 2 rms
Meals: expanded cont'l brkfst

Amenities: free parking, laundry, pool, indoor hot tub, massage, DVDs/ videos
Kids: welcome
Pets: welcome in designated rms; 2 max/ $50 per pet
Rates: $99-239
AC: 10%

Highland House B&B
Yosemite Nat'l Park

3125 Wild Dove Ln
Mariposa, CA 95338
209/ 966-3737
www.highlandhousebandb.com

Clientele: gay-friendly
Type: b&b; charming, quiet retreat in the woods near Yosemite & Sierra Nat'l Forest
Owned/ Run By: straights
Rooms: 3
Baths: private
Meals: expanded cont'l brkfst
Kids: welcome

Pets: no
Rates: $95-135
AC: 10%

The Homestead
Yosemite Nat'l Park

41110 Rd 600
Ahwahnee, CA 93601
559/ 683-0495 800/ 483-0495
www.homesteadcottages.com

Clientele: gay-friendly
Type: 4 cottages, 1 suite & new 2-bdrm house nestled under the oaks on 160 acres; close to restaurants, golf, hiking & biking
Owned/ Run By: straights
Rooms: 6 units
Baths: private
Wheelchair Access: yes, 1 rm

Meals: cont'l brkfst
Kids: 1 cottage can accommodate up to 2 kids; the house up to 4 kids
Pets: no
Smoking: no
Rates: $110-374
AC: 10%

June Lake Villager
Yosemite Nat'l Park

2640 Hwy 158
June Lake, CA
760/ 648-7712 800/ 655-6545
www.junelakevillager.com

Clientele: gay-friendly
Type: b&b-inn; very clean cottages, cabins, suites & rms; walking distance to lakes & trails; 20 minutes from Yosemite
Owned/ Run By: women
Rooms: 25
Baths: private
Meals: expanded cont'l brkfst

Amenities: free parking, laundry, hot tub, massage, DVDs/ videos
Kids: welcome
Pets: welcome
Smoking: no
Rates: $85-225

Narrow Gauge Inn
Yosemite Nat'l Park

48571 Hwy 41
Fish Camp, CA 93623
559/ 683-7720 888/ 644-9050
www.narrowgaugeinn.com

Clientele: gay-friendly
Type: country inn; mtnside lodging & dining; views of forest & Sierras; next door to historic operating steam train
Owned/ Run By: straights
Rooms: 26
Baths: private

Meals: cont'l brkfst
Amenities: pool, outdoor hot tub
Kids: welcome
Pets: welcome; $25 fee
Smoking: no
Rates: $120-205
AC: 10%

Yosemite Big Creek Inn B&B
Yosemite Nat'l Park

1221 Hwy 41
Fish Camp, CA 93623
559/ 641-2828
www.bigcreekinn.com

Clientele: mixed gay/ straight
Type: b&b; "closest b&b to Yosemite Nat'l Park's S entrance"; on Hwy 41
Owned/ Run By: women
Rooms: 3
Baths: private
Meals: full brkfst

Amenities: free parking, outdoor hot tub, massage, DVDs/ videos, WiFi
Kids: no
Pets: no
Smoking: ok
Rates: $100-209

Yosemite's Apple Blossom Inn B&B
Yosemite Nat'l Park

559/ 642-2001 888/ 687-4281
www.sierratel.com/AppleBlossomInn

Clientele: gay-friendly
Type: b&b; 20 minutes from S entrance to Yosemite; quiet country setting situated on mtn ridge overlooking the Oakhurst Valley & the Sierras
Rooms: 4
Baths: private & shared

Wheelchair Access: yes, 1 rm
Amenities: free parking, outdoor hot tub, DVDs/ videos
Kids: welcome; please call for availability
Pets: welcome; please call for availability
Rates: $110-240
AC: 10%

Cottonwood Inn
Alamosa

123 San Juan Ave
Alamosa, CO 81101
719/ 589-3882 800/ 955-2623
www.cottonwoodinn.com

Clientele: gay-friendly
Type: b&b-inn; in heart of the San Luis Valley; golf, train & hot springs packages; Mobil 3-Star rating; great brkfsts
Rooms: 10
Baths: private
Meals: full brkfst

Amenities: free parking, outdoor hot tub, massage, DVDs/ videos
Kids: $15 for each additional person
Pets: welcome; $50 deposit
Smoking: no
Rates: $55-125
AC: 10%

Aspen Mountain Lodge
Aspen

311 W Main St
Aspen, CO 81611
970/ 925-7650 800/ 362-7736
www.aspenmountainlodge.com

Clientele: gay-friendly
Type: b&b; lodge w/in walking distance of downtown & free shuttle buses; après-ski wine & cheese every day of ski season
Rooms: 38
Baths: private

Meals: expanded cont'l brkfst
Amenities: pool, hot tub, DVDs/ videos
Kids: welcome
Pets: welcome; $20 fee
Smoking: no
Rates: $89-359

Hotel Aspen
Aspen

110 W Main St
Aspen, CO 81611
970/ 925-3441 800/ 527-7369
www.hotelaspen.com

Clientele: gay-friendly
Type: hotel; located 3 blks from downtown; fully appointed, spacious rms
Owned/ Run By: straights
Rooms: 45
Baths: private
Meals: expanded cont'l brkfst
Amenities: free parking, pool, outdoor hot tub, DVDs/ videos
Kids: welcome; 2 kids free (12 & under); over 2 kids, additional $20/ night
Pets: welcome; limited to certain rms
Smoking: no
Rates: $109-405
AC: 10%

Hotel Lenado

Aspen

200 S Aspen St
Aspen, CO 81611
970/ 925-6246 800/ 321-3457
www.hotellenado.com

Type: b&b; award-winning architecture & rustic elegance
Rooms: 19
Baths: private
Wheelchair Access: yes, 8 rms
Meals: full brkfst

Kids: welcome
Pets: welcome in rms w/ private entrance (summer only)
Smoking: ok
Rates: $125-525
AC: 10%

Sardy House

Aspen

128 E Main St
Aspen, CO 81611
970/ 920-2525 800/ 321-3457
www.sardyhouse.com

Type: b&b; one of Aspen's finest Victorians
Rooms: 20
Baths: private
Meals: full brkfst
Amenities: free parking, pool, sauna, hot tub, DVDs/ videos

Kids: welcome
Pets: welcome in rm w/ private entrance only
Smoking: ok
Rates: $115-1,075
AC: 10%

Beaver Creek Lodge

Beaver Creek

26 Avondale Ln
Beaver Creek, CO 81620
970/ 845-9800 800/ 583-9615
www.beavercreeklodge.net

Clientele: gay-friendly
Type: resort; all-suite, air-conditioned lodging w/ mtn chic feel; new Rocks Modern Grill featuring great food & views
Owned/ Run By: gay & straight
Rooms: 72
Baths: private
Wheelchair Access: yes, 4 rms

Meals: full brkfst
Amenities: free parking, laundry, pool, sauna, hot tub, DVDs/ videos, gym, WiFi
Kids: welcome
Pets: no
Smoking: no
Rates: $170-699
AC: 10%

The Briar Rose B&B

Boulder

2151 Arapahoe Ave
Boulder, CO 80302
303/ 442-3007 888/ 786-8440
www.briarrosebb.com

Clientele: gay-friendly
Type: "organic b&b"; in the heart of Boulder; offers organic brkfst, fine teas, ecologically conscious hospitality
Rooms: 10
Baths: private
Meals: full brkfst

Amenities: free parking, WiFi
Kids: well-behaved welcome; 5 yrs & under free
Pets: no
Smoking: no
Rates: $129-169
AC: 10%

Allaire Timbers Inn

Breckenridge

9511 Hwy 9, S Main St
Breckenridge, CO 80424
970/ 453-7530 800/ 624-4904
www.allairetimbers.com

Clientele: gay-friendly
Type: b&b-inn; contemporary log inn; daily happy hour, spectacular mtn views
Owned/ Run By: straights
Rooms: 10
Baths: private
Wheelchair Access: yes, 1 rm

Meals: hearty full brkfst
Amenities: outdoor hot tub, DVDs/ videos
Kids: 13 yrs & up welcome
Pets: no
Smoking: no
Rates: $145-390
AC: 10%

The Bunkhouse Lodge

Breckenridge

PO Box 6
Breckenridge, CO 80424
970/ 453-6475
www.bunkhouselodge.com

Clientele: men
Type: b&b-inn; only gay lodge in Colorado w/ private & dorm-style accommodations, nude hot tub, sauna & video rm; includes full brkfst
Owned/ Run By: gay men
Rooms: 4

Baths: shared
Meals: full brkfst
Amenities: free parking, laundry, sauna outdoor hot tub, DVDs/ videos, gym
Smoking: ok (in bar only)
Rates: $30-120
AC: 10%

Valdoro Mountain Lodge
Breckenridge

500 Village Rd
Breckenridge, CO 80424
970/ 453-4880 800/ 436-6780
www.valdoro.com

Clientele: mixed gay/ straight
Type: condo; private couples spa & steam rm on premises
Owned/ Run By: gay/ lesbian & straight
Rooms: 70
Baths: private
Wheelchair Access: yes, 10 rms

Amenities: free parking, laundry, pool, outdoor hot tub, massage, gym, WiFi
Kids: welcome
Pets: no
Smoking: no
Rates: $150-800
AC: 10%

Blue Skies Inn B&B
Colorado Springs

402 Manitou Ave
Manitou Springs, CO 80829
719/ 685-3899 800/ 398-7949
www.blueskiesbb.com

Clientele: mixed gay/ straight
Type: b&b-inn; built by artist/ innkeeper in Gothic Revival style; every suite decorated & painted as individual art project; garden courtyard, gazebo hot tub, gourmet brkfst
Owned/ Run By: straights
Rooms: 10
Baths: private

Wheelchair Access: yes, 1 rm
Meals: full brkfst
Amenities: massage, WiFi
Kids: welcome
Pets: no
Smoking: no
Rates: $135-235
AC: 7%

Old Town Guesthouse
Colorado Springs

115 S 26th St
Colorado Springs, CO 80904
719/ 632-9194 888/ 375-4210
www.OldTown-GuestHouse.com

Clientele: gay-friendly
Type: b&b; urban luxury in historic old town; upscale amenities, 4 rms w/ private outdoor hot tubs, private conference facility; AAA 4-Diamond Award
Owned/ Run By: straights
Rooms: 8
Baths: private

Wheelchair Access: yes, 1 rm
Meals: full brkfst
Amenities: massage, DVDs/ videos, WiFi
Kids: no
Pets: no
Smoking: no
Rates: $99-237
AC: 10%

Pikes Peak Paradise
Colorado Springs

719/ 687-6656 800/ 728-8282
www.pikespeakmall.com/pppbandb

Clientele: gay-friendly
Type: b&b; custom Southern mansion w/ spectacular view of Pikes Peak in Woodland Park
Owned/ Run By: straights
Rooms: 5
Baths: private

Meals: full brkfst
Amenities: indoor & outdoor hot tub
Kids: 10 yrs & up welcome (limited)
Pets: welcome w/ prior approval
Smoking: no
Rates: $110-180
AC: 10% (up to)

Rockledge Country Inn
Colorado Springs

328 El Paso Blvd
Manitou Springs, CO 80829
719/ 685-4515 888/ 685-4515
www.rockledgeinn.com

Clientele: gay-friendly
Type: b&b-private home; in historic 35-acre wooded & gated estate w/ a 9,000-sq-ft Tudor country home built in 1912
Rooms: 4
Baths: private

Meals: full brkfst
Amenities: free parking, outdoor hot tub, DVDs/ videos
Rates: $125-325
AC: 10%

Rodeway Inn & Suites—Garden of the Gods
Colorado Springs

555 W Garden of the Gods
Colorado Springs, CO 80907
719/ 593-9119 800/ 828-4347
www.choicehotels.com

Clientele: mixed gay/ straight
Type: hotel; easy I-25 access; close to all attractions; restaurants w/in walking distance
Owned/ Run By: women
Rooms: 156
Baths: private

Wheelchair Access: yes, 3 rms
Meals: expanded cont'l brkfst
Amenities: free parking, laundry, pool
Kids: welcome; under 18 yrs free
Pets: welcome; $50 refundable deposit
Rates: $50-110
AC: 10%

Two Sisters Inn
Colorado Springs

10 Otoe Pl
Manitou Springs, CO 80829
719/ 685-9684 800/ 274-7466
www.twosisinn.com

Clientele: gay-friendly
Type: "the award-winning Two Sisters Inn is nestled at the base of Pikes Peak in quaint Manitou Springs"
Owned/ Run By: women
Rooms: 5
Baths: private

Meals: full brkfst
Kids: over 10 yrs old welcome
Pets: no
Smoking: no
Rates: $69-138
AC: 10%

Capitol Hill Mansion B&B
Denver

1207 Pennsylvania
Denver, CO 80203
303/ 839-5221 800/ 839-9329
www.capitolhillmansion.com

Clientele: gay-friendly
Type: b&b-inn; circa 1891 Victorian mansion in downtown Denver; walk to Capitol, convention center, 16th St Mall; evening wine social
Owned/ Run By: gay men
Rooms: 8

Baths: private
Meals: full brkfst
Amenities: free parking, laundry, hot tub
Kids: welcome
Pets: no
Rates: $95-175
AC: 10%

The Gregory Inn, LoDo
Denver

2500 Arapahoe St
Denver, CO 80205-2616
303/ 295-6570 800/ 925-6570
www.gregoryinn.com

Clientele: gay-friendly
Type: b&b-inn; luxury inn near convention center & entertainment district
Owned/ Run By: gay & straight
Rooms: 9
Baths: private
Meals: full brkfst

Amenities: free parking, laundry, hot tub, massage
Kids: no
Pets: no
Smoking: no
Rates: $119-259

Hotel Monaco
Denver

1717 Champa St
Denver, CO 80202
303/ 296-1717 800/ 397-5380
www.monaco-denver.com

Clientele: gay-friendly
Type: hotel; deluxe European boutique hotel bringing together luxury w/ a whimsical flair; complimentary evening wine hr
Rooms: 189
Baths: private
Wheelchair Access: yes, 8 rms

Meals: coffee/tea only
Amenities: laundry, massage, WiFi
Kids: welcome
Pets: welcome
Smoking: no
Rates: $125-915
AC: 10%

Lumber Baron Inn
Denver

2555 W 37th Ave
Denver, CO 80211
303/ 477-8205
www.lumberbaron.com

Clientele: gay-friendly
Type: b&b-inn; 8,500-sq-ft historic Victorian mansion restored w/ period antiques
Rooms: 5
Baths: private

Meals: full brkfst
Amenities: hot tub, DVDs/ videos
Rates: $49-235
AC: 10%

Ramada Inn Denver Downtown
Denver

1150 E Colfax Ave
Denver, CO 80218
303/ 831-7700 800/ 272-6232
www.ramadadowntowndenver.com

Clientele: mixed gay/ straight
Type: hotel; full-service hotel in Denver area; in the heart of Capitol Hill; all gay clubs/ bars w/in shuttle service area
Owned/ Run By: gay & straight
Rooms: 149
Baths: private

Wheelchair Access: yes, 3 rms
Meals: full brkfst
Amenities: pool, outdoor hot tub
Pets: welcome; $100 deposit
Rates: $55-99
AC: 10%

Royal Host Motel
Denver

930 E Colfax Ave
Denver, CO 80218
303/ 831-7200

Clientele: gay-friendly
Type: motel; located next door to Charlie's Denver, Colorado's largest gay bar
Owned/ Run By: straights
Rooms: 52

Meals: cont'l brkfst
Kids: welcome
Pets: welcome
Rates: $55+ (double)

Leland House B&B
Durango

721 E 2nd Ave
Durango, CO 81301
970/ 385-1920 800/ 664-1920
www.leland-house.com

Clientele: gay-friendly
Type: b&tb-inn; luxury accommodations w/ Western theme; in restored brick apt bldg across from Rochester Hotel; several 2-rm suites
Owned/ Run By: straights
Rooms: 10
Baths: private

Wheelchair Access: yes, 1 rm
Meals: full brkfst
Kids: welcome
Pets: 1 per rm welcome; $20 fee
Smoking: no
Rates: $109-340
AC: 10%

Rochester Hotel
Durango

726 E 2nd Ave
Durango, CO 81301
970/ 385-1920 800/ 664-1920
www.rochesterhotel.com

Type: b&tb-inn; the warmth & comfort of a country inn w/ the convenience of a downtown hotel
Owned/ Run By: straights
Rooms: 25
Baths: private
Wheelchair Access: yes, 2 rms

Meals: full brkfst
Kids: welcome
Pets: welcome in 2 rms only; $20
Smoking: no
Rates: $109-229
AC: 10%

Greatrental
Keystone

23110 Hwy 6
Keystone, CO 80435
347/ 947-8800
greatrental.home.comcast.net

Clientele: gay-friendly
Type: condo; located in The Gateway Mountain Lodge; 250 yds to the entrance of River Run Village at Keystone Resort; yr-round activities including skiing, golfing, climbing, sailing, shopping, fine dining & more
Rooms: 4

Baths: private
Amenities: free parking, laundry, pool, hot tub
Kids: welcome
Pets: no
Smoking: no
Rates: $265+

Old Mancos Inn
Mancos

200 W Grand Ave
Mancos, CO 81328
970/ 533-9019
www.oldmancosinn.com

Clientele: mixed gay/ straight
Type: inn; 100-yr-old inn w/ individually decorated rms
Owned/ Run By: gay men
Rooms: 14
Baths: private & shared

Meals: coffee/tea only
Pets: please inquire
Rates: $30-50

Colorado Cattle Company & Guest Ranch
New Raymer

70008 WCR 132
New Raymer, CO 80742
970/ 437-5345
www.coloradocattlecompany.com

Clientele: gay-friendly
Type: working cattle ranch; guests participate in cattle work & horseback riding in this Wild West adventure
Owned/ Run By: straights
Rooms: 13
Baths: private

Meals: full brkfst
Kids: no
Pets: welcome
Smoking: no
Rates: $1,497/ week (per person)
AC: 10%

Ouray Chalet Inn
Ouray

PO Box 544
Ouray, CO 81427
970/ 325-4331 800/ 924-2538
www.ouraychaletinn.com

Clientele: gay-friendly
Type: motel; 1 hr to Telluride slopes; near hot springs; hot tub & sundeck; open yr-round; packages available
Owned/ Run By: straights
Rooms: 30
Baths: private

Wheelchair Access: yes, 12 rms
Meals: coffee/tea only
Amenities: outdoor hot tub, WiFi
Kids: welcome
Smoking: no
Rates: $55-104

Patmé Ranch
Trinidad

PO Box 44
Aguilar, CO 81020
719/ 846-5724
sapajane@hotmail.com

Clientele: mostly women
Type: b&b-private home; in large new home on 400 private acres where wildlife abounds; relax, hot tub, camp; 20 campsites & 2 RV hookups; very easy in/ out off I-25; bring your horses to ride!
Owned/ Run By: lesbians
Rooms: 2

Baths: private
Meals: full brkfst
Amenities: free parking, laundry, outdoor hot tub, massage, DVDs/ videos
Kids: welcome w/ active parental control
Pets: welcome w/ active "parental" control
Smoking: no
Rates: $60

Antlers at Vail
Vail

680 W Lionshead Pl
Vail, CO 81657
970/ 476-2471 800/ 843-8245
www.antlersvail.com

Clientele: gay-friendly
Type: condo
Owned/ Run By: straights
Rooms: 91
Baths: private
Amenities: free parking, laundry, pool, sauna, outdoor hot tub, DVDs/ videos

Kids: welcome
Pets: friendly & quiet pets only
Smoking: ok
Rates: $175-1,400
AC: 10%

Bear Paw Inn
Winter Park

871 Bear Paw Dr
Winter Park, CO 80482
970/ 887-1351
www.bearpaw-winterpark.com

Clientele: gay-friendly
Type: b&b-private home; massive log lodge on top of mtn; spectacular views of Rocky Mtn Nat'l Park; luxurious guest rms & 3-course brkfst
Owned/ Run By: straights
Rooms: 2
Baths: private

Meals: full brkfst
Amenities: hot tub, massage, DVDs/ video
Kids: no
Pets: no
Smoking: no (outdoors only)
Rates: $180-235
AC: 7%

Flagship Inn & Suites
Groton

470 Gold Star Hwy, Rte 184
Groton, CT 06340
860/ 445-7458 888/ 800-0770
www.theflagshipinn.com

Clientele: gay-friendly
Type: motel; "near Mystic Seaport & Aquarium & casinos; offers affordable accommodations & discounts"
Owned/ Run By: gay man
Rooms: 60

Wheelchair Access: yes, 2 rms
Kids: welcome
Smoking: ok
Rates: $50-165
AC: 10%

Butternut Farm
Hartford

1654 Main St
Glastonbury, CT 06033
860/ 633-7197
www.butternutfarmbandb.com

Clientele: mixed gay/ straight
Type: b&b; 18th-c architectural jewel furnished w/ period antiques; farm animals in an estate setting; all of CT w/in 1 1/2 hrs
Owned/ Run By: gay & straight

Rooms: 4
Baths: private
Meals: full brkfst
Kids: welcome
Rates: $90-110

The Mansion Inn
Hartford

139 Hartford Rd
Manchester, CT 06040
860/ 646-0453
www.themansioninnct.com

Clientele: gay-friendly
Type: b&b-inn; w/ fireplaces, imaginative decor in flower-garden colors & hundreds of books; Cheney Bros Historic District Preservation Award
Owned/ Run By: straights

Rooms: 5
Baths: private
Meals: full brkfst
Kids: no
Pets: no
Rates: $95-145

Inn at Kent Falls
Kent

107 Kent Cornwall Rd
Kent, CT 06757
860/ 927-3197
www.theinnatkentfalls.com

Clientele: mixed gay/ straight
Type: b&b; in handsome Colonial (main house built 1741) w/ guest books dating back to early 1900s; surrounded by 2.5 lush acres
Owned/ Run By: gay man
Rooms: 6
Baths: private

Wheelchair Access: yes
Meals: cont'l brkfst
Amenities: pool, massage, WiFi
Kids: welcome
Pets: no
Smoking: no
Rates: $175-325

House of 1833 B&B Resort
Mystic

72 N Stonington Rd
Mystic, CT 06355
860/ 536-6325 800/ 367-1833
www.houseof1833.com

Clientele: gay-friendly
Type: b&b-inn; 1833 Greek Revival mansion; nat'l landmark; fireplaces, period furnishings; clay tennis court
Owned/ Run By: gay men
Rooms: 5 (suites)
Baths: private
Meals: full country gourmet brkfst

Amenities: free parking, laundry, pool, hot tub, massage
Kids: welcome
Pets: no
Smoking: no
Rates: $139-249
AC: 10%

Mermaid Inn of Mystic
Mystic

2 Broadway
Mystic, CT 06355
860/ 536-6223 877/ 692-2632
www.mermaidinnofmystic.com

Clientele: mixed gay/ lesbian
Type: b&b; private Italian-granite bathrms, bidets, baby grand piano, village location, river views; straight-friendly
Owned/ Run By: lesbians
Rooms: 3
Baths: private

Meals: full brkfst
Amenities: free parking, outdoor hot tub, DVDs/ videos, WiFi
Kids: welcome
Pets: no
Smoking: ok
Rates: $175-225

The Old Mystic Inn
Mystic

52 Main St
Old Mystic, CT 06372
860/ 572-9422
www.oldmysticinn.com

Clientele: gay-friendly
Type: b&b-inn; 1784 Colonial carriage house; owned/ run by culinary chef; offers warm New England hospitality
Owned/ Run By: gay men
Rooms: 8
Baths: private

Meals: full brkfst
Amenities: free parking, massage
Kids: no
Pets: no
Smoking: no
Rates: $115-195

Three Chimneys Inn at Yale University
New Haven

1201 Chapel St
New Haven, CT 06511
203/ 789-1201
800/ 443-1554 (outside CT only)
www.threechimneysinn.com

Clientele: mixed gay/ straight
Type: b&b; 1876 Victorian 1 blk from Yale; in boutique area of theaters, museums, shops, restaurants & cafes; eclectic collectible furnishings w/ full amenities
Owned/ Run By: gay & straight
Rooms: 11
Baths: private

Meals: full brkfst
Amenities: free parking, laundry, DVDs/ videos, gym, WiFi
Kids: 7 yrs & up welcome
Pets: no
Smoking: no (ok on veranda)
Rates: $195-215
AC: 10%

Manor House B&B
Norfolk

69 Maple Ave
Norfolk, CT 06058
860/ 542-5690 866/ 542-5690
www.manorhouse-norfolk.com

Clientele: gay-friendly
Type: b&b-inn; elegant & romantic 1898 Victorian Tudor estate w/ Tiffany windows
Owned/ Run By: straights
Rooms: 9
Baths: private
Meals: full brkfst

Amenities: free parking, hot tub, massage
Kids: 12 yrs & up welcome
Pets: no
Smoking: no
Rates: $130-255
AC: 10%

Antiques & Accommodations
North Stonington Village

32 Main St
North Stonington Village, CT 06359
800/ 554-7829
www.mysticbb.com

Clientele: gay-friendly
Type: b&b; 2 restored historic village homes; surrounded by gardens; minutes from Mystic, CT, Foxwoods Casino, Mohegan Sun & sandy beaches
Owned/ Run By: straights
Rooms: 7

Baths: private
Meals: full candlelight brkfst
Kids: welcome; please inquire
Pets: welcome; please inquire
Smoking: no
Rates: $110-229
AC: 10%

Silk Orchid
Norwalk

203/ 847-2561

Clientele: women
Type: b&b-private home; in historic, scenic area of Fairfield County; large rms—each w/ private entrance & bath, cable TV/ VCR
Owned/ Run By: lesbians
Rooms: 2

Baths: private
Meals: cont'l brkfst
Amenities: free parking, pool, hot tub, DVDs/ videos
Rates: $100-125

The Copper Beech Inn
Old Saybrook

46 Main St
Ivoryton, CT 06442
860/ 767-0330 888/ 809-2056
www.copperbeech.com

Clientele: gay-friendly
Type: inn; new French grande dame of fine dining & lodging; impeccable staff & romantic setting; Zagat-rated food, decor & service: "extraordinary to perfection"
Owned/ Run By: gay & straight
Rooms: 13
Baths: private
Wheelchair Access: yes, 2 rms

Meals: full brkfst
Amenities: hot tub, massage, DVDs/ videos
Kids: no
Pets: welcome; under 25 lbs
Smoking: no
Rates: $165-350
AC: $10 per booking

An Inn by the Bay
Rehoboth Beach

205 Savannah Rd
Lewes, DE 19958
302/ 644-8878 866/ 833-2565
www.aninnbythebay.com

Clientele: mixed gay/ straight
Type: b&b-inn; lovely Victorian w/ views of the Delaware Bay
Owned/ Run By: gay men
Rooms: 6
Baths: private

Meals: expanded cont'l brkfst
Amenities: free parking, outdoor hot tub
Kids: 12 yrs & up welcome
Smoking: no
Rates: $55-275

At Melissa's B&B
Rehoboth Beach

36 Delaware Ave
Rehoboth Beach, DE 19971
302/ 227-7504 800/ 396-8090
www.atmelissas.com

Clientele: mixed gay/ straight
Type: b&b; in town location 1 1/2 blks to beach; towels, chairs, umbrellas & more provided; walk to dining & shopping; open yr-round
Owned/ Run By: straight woman
Rooms: 6

Baths: private
Meals: expanded cont'l brkfst
Kids: well-behaved welcome
Pets: no
Smoking: no
Rates: $95-285

Breakers Hotel & Suites
Rehoboth Beach

105 Second St
Rehoboth Beach, DE 19971
302/ 227-6688 800/ 441-8009
www.thebreakershotel.com

Clientele: gay-friendly
Type: hotel; adjacent to Lake Gerar; all rms w/ private balconies; rooftop pool
Rooms: rms & 1-2-bdrm suites
Baths: private
Wheelchair Access: yes

Pets: welcome in standard rms
Rates: $65-265

Cabana Gardens B&B
Rehoboth Beach

20 Lake Ave
Rehoboth Beach, DE 19971
302/ 227-5429
www.cabanagardens.com

Clientele: mixed gay/ lesbian
Type: b&b; a quiet retreat in the heart of downtown gay Rehoboth Beach
Owned/ Run By: gay man
Rooms: 8
Baths: private
Wheelchair Access: yes, 3 rms

Meals: cont'l brkfst
Kids: 13 yrs & up welcome
Pets: no
Smoking: no
Rates: $75-250

Canalside Inn
Rehoboth Beach

Canal at 6th
Rehoboth Beach, DE 19971
302/ 226-2006 866/ 412-2625
www.canalside-inn-rehoboth.com

Clientele: mixed gay/ straight
Type: guesthouse; charming inn located w/in walking distance of beach, restaurants & boardwalk
Owned/ Run By: gay men
Rooms: 12
Baths: private

Wheelchair Access: yes, 1 rm
Meals: cont'l brkfst
Amenities: free parking, pool, outdoor hot tub, massage, DVDs/ videos, WiFi
Pets: welcome in deluxe rms
Smoking: no
Rates: $70-235

Delaware Inn B&B
Rehoboth Beach

55 Delaware Ave
Rehoboth Beach, DE 19971
302/ 227-6031 800/ 246-5244
www.delawareinn.com

Clientele: gay-friendly
Type: b&b-inn; country-inn atmosphere in great downtown location; AAA-approved; just steps to the beach, fine dining, shops, bars
Owned/ Run By: gay men
Rooms: 9

Baths: private & shared
Meals: full brkfst
Kids: 13 yrs & up welcome
Rates: $80-210

The Homestead at Rehoboth B&B
Rehoboth Beach

35060 Warrington Rd
Rehoboth Beach, DE 19971
302/ 226-7625
www.homesteadatrehoboth.com

Clientele: gay-friendly
Type: b&b; "country charm at the beach"
Owned/ Run By: lesbians
Rooms: 4
Baths: private
Wheelchair Access: yes, 1 rm

Meals: expanded cont'l brkfst
Kids: no
Pets: dogs welcome w/ prior approval
Smoking: no
Rates: $80-185

Lazy L at Willow Creek
Rehoboth Beach

16061 Willow Creek Rd
Lewes, DE 19958
302/ 644-7220
www.lazyl.net

Clientele: mixed gay/ straight
Type: b&b; on 8 secluded acres just outside the beach-resort town of Lewes; 10 minutes from gay-friendly Rehoboth Beach
Owned/ Run By: lesbians
Rooms: 6
Baths: private

Meals: full brkfst
Amenities: free parking, pool, outdoor hot tub, DVDs/ videos, gym, WiFi
Kids: 11 yrs & up welcome
Pets: very welcome; dog run for off-leash play
Smoking: no
Rates: $75-165

The Lighthouse Inn B&B   *Rehoboth Beach*

20 Delaware Ave
Rehoboth Beach, DE 19971
302/ 226-0407
www.lighthouseinn.net

Clientele: mixed gay/ straight
Type: b&b-inn; in heart of Rehoboth Beach; 1/2 blk to beach; nautical motif
Owned/ Run By: gay men
Rooms: 4 (plus 1 cottage)
Baths: private

Meals: expanded cont'l brkfst
Amenities: massage, DVDs/ videos, WiFi
Kids: 12 yrs & up welcome
Pets: welcome (off-season only)
Smoking: no
Rates: $135-195

Rehoboth Guest House   *Rehoboth Beach*

40 Maryland Ave
Rehoboth Beach, DE 19971
302/ 227-4117 800/ 564-0493
www.rehobothguesthouse.com

Clientele: mixed gay/ lesbian
Type: guesthouse; charming Victorian beach house; steps from the boardwalk, beach & Atlantic Ocean, the "heart of gay Rehoboth"; porches w/ outdoor showers
Owned/ Run By: gay men
Rooms: 14
Baths: private & shared

Meals: expanded cont'l brkfst
Amenities: free parking, WiFi
Kids: 16 yrs & up welcome
Pets: no
Smoking: no
Rates: $75-215
AC: 10%

Sea Witch Manor Inn & Spa   *Rehoboth Beach*

71 Lake Ave
Rehoboth Beach, DE 19971
302/ 226-9482 866/ 732-9482
www.seawitchmanor.com

Clientele: mixed gay/ straight
Type: 3-house b&b: Sea Witch Manor is a traditional Victorian; decor of Bewitched is based on the '60s TV show; Bedazzled is an homage to Hollywood glamour
Owned/ Run By: lesbians/ gay men
Rooms: 17
Baths: private

Wheelchair Access: yes, 1 rm
Meals: full brkfst
Amenities: hot tub, massage, DVDs/ videos
Kids: no
Pets: no
Smoking: no
Rates: $79-325
AC: 10%

Shore Inn at Rehoboth   *Rehoboth Beach*

703 Rehoboth Ave
Rehoboth Beach, DE 19971

302/ 227-8487
800/ 597-8899

theshoreinn@aol.com
www.shoreinn.com

Clientele: men
Type: b&b-inn; 1/2 mile from Poodle Beach & short drive to hundreds of brand-name outlet stores; pool & hot tub are clothing-optional; open yr-round; voted Best B&B for 3 yrs (gaydelaware.com)
Owned/ Run By: gay men
Nearby Attractions: walk to gay bars & restaurants; short drive to outlets
Transit: near public transit
Rooms: 15 (plus 4-bdrm cottage) total, 2 suites, 1 king, 2 queens, 10 fulls, A/C, color TV, DVD/ VCR (4), cable, ceiling fan (1), fireplace (1), deck, phone, refrigerator, safer sex supplies, maid service, also 4-bdrm/ 2-bath cottage w/ pool, 1 blk from Shore Inn & Double L bar
Baths: private, bathtubs, showers, robes
Meals: expanded cont'l brkfst
Amenities: pool, outdoor hot tub, massage, DVDs/ videos, cocktails, coffee/ tea, hot spa, lounge/ sundeck (clothing-optional), festive happy hour Fri-Sat
Recreation: 1/2 mile to gay beaches
Kids: no

Pets: well-behaved welcome
Pets On Premises: 1 cat
Smoking: ok
Reservations: required *Deposit:* required, 1/2 reservation, due at booking, personal check ok *Cancellation:* cancel by 1 week

prior *Minimum Stay:* 2 nights (wknds in-season) *Check in/ out:* 2pm/ 11am
Payment: cash, travelers checks, Visa, Amex, MC, Discover
Season: open yr-round
Rates: $65-235

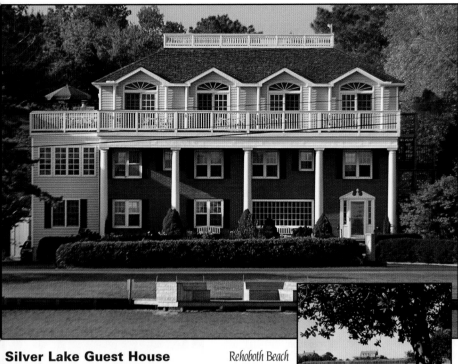

Rehoboth Beach

Silver Lake Guest House

133 Silver Lake Dr   302/ 226-2115   info@silverlakeguesthouse.com
Rehoboth Beach, DE 19971   800/ 842-2115   www.silverlakeguesthouse.com

S ilver Lake is one of the "Top 10 North American Guest Houses" (*Out & About*), "the best of the bunch" (*Fodor's Gay Guide*), "one of the most attractive and best-run gay properties in the country" (*Our World*), and "the jewel of the Delaware shore" (*The Washington Post*).

Located in a tranquil setting in the midst of a waterfowl preserve on Rehoboth Beach's most scenic drive, this beautiful waterfront home, with its spectacular views, offers its guests much more than a conventional bed-and-breakfast. It is also the resort's closest guesthouse to gay "Poodle Beach," and is just a short walk to the best restaurants, shops, and clubs.

Clientele: mixed gay/ lesbian

Type: b&b-inn; offers panoramic lake & ocean views, boat dock, private balconies & luxurious accommodations close to the gay beach

Owned/ Run By: gay men

Nearby Attractions: 150 outlet stores, antique shops, many recreational water sports

Transit: 120 miles to Philadelphia Int'l, Baltimore/ Washington Int'l & Washington Nat'l; 50 miles to Salisbury, MD airport; 10 blks to bus

Rooms: 17 (includes 2 two-bdrm apts w/ living rm, kitchen & dining area) total, 6 kings, 11 queens, A/C, color TV, DVD/ VCR

(10), cable, ceiling fan (8), deck, refrigerator (8), safer sex supplies, maid service

Baths: private, bathtubs, showers, hairdryers

Wheelchair Access: yes, 2 rms

Meals: expanded cont'l brkfst

Amenities: free parking, WiFi, coffee/ tea, outside shower, ice, soft drinks, beach towels & chairs, sundecks, fax

Recreation: ocean beach, bbq grills, biking, jogging, water sports, lake w/ private dock

Pets: dogs welcome in apts w/ prior approval

Smoking: no (ok on decks only)

Reservations: required *Deposit:* required, 50%, due at booking, personal check ok *Cancellation:* cancel by 2 weeks prior or forfeit 50% *Minimum Stay:* in-season (please call) *Check in/ out:* 3pm/ 11am

Payment: cash, travelers checks, personal checks, Visa, Amex, MC, Discover

Season: open yr-round *High season:* June-Sept

Rates: $80-350 *Discounts:* weekly

Summer Place Hotel   *Rehoboth Beach*

30 Olive Ave
Rehoboth Beach, DE 19971
302/ 226-0766 800/ 815-3925
www.rehobothsummerplace.com

Type: guesthouse; newly renovated in the heart of gay Rehoboth; 1 blk to ocean; rms sleep 2-3; also apts (that sleep 4-5) w/ kitchens
Rooms: 27

Baths: private
Pets: no
Smoking: ok
Rates: $39-175

Bloomingdale Inn   *Washington*

2417 1st St NW
Washington, DC 20001
202/ 319-0801
www.BloomingdaleInn.com

Clientele: gay-friendly
Type: b&b; Victorian townhouse; uniquely decorated, comfortable rms; easy access to transportation; friendly inkeepers & resident cats
Owned/ Run By: gay & straight
Rooms: 9

Baths: shared
Meals: expanded cont'l brkfst
Amenities: laundry, DVDs/ videos
Kids: no
Pets: no
Smoking: ok
Rates: $90-120

Comfort Inn Downtown DC—Convention Center [T/G]   *Washington*

1201 13th St NW   202/ 682-5300   comfortinnDC601gm@baywoodhotels.com
Washington, DC 20005   877/ 424-6423   www.choicehotels.com/hotel/DC601

Clientele: mixed gay/ straight
Type: hotel; featuring European-style rms; convenient to metro service & Dupont Circle
Owned/ Run By: gay & straight
Nearby Attractions: Dupont Circle, 17th-St corridor, DC Eagle all nearby; 5 blks to White House, Capitol Bldg, Smithsonian, Washington Monument, Spy Museum, World War II & Vietnam Veterans Memorials
Transit: near public transit; 30 miles to BWI; 27 miles to Dulles; 4 miles to Reagan Int'l; 1 mile to Union Station
Rooms: 100 total, 40 kings, 18 queens, 42 fulls, A/C, color TV, cable, phone, maid service, elegantly appointed rms w/ cherry wood furniture & bright sunny views of downtown DC skyline; all w/ free high-speed internet access
Baths: private, bathtubs, showers, hairdryers

Wheelchair Access: yes
Meals: expanded cont'l brkfst
Amenities: snacks, coffee/ tea, fitness rm, valet parking service
Recreation: Nat'l Mall (park), Rock Creek State Park, Georgetown Waterfront, tennis, cycling, golf
Kids: welcome
Pets: no
Smoking: no
Reservations: required *Deposit:* required, 1 night + tax, due at booking *Cancellation:* cancel by 6pm day of arrival *Minimum Stay:* 1 night *Check in/ out:* 3pm/ 11am
Payment: cash, travelers checks, Visa, Amex, MC, Discover, personal checks only 22 days prior to arrival
Season: open yr-round
Rates: $99-179 *Discounts:* groups (please contact hotel sales dept)
AC: 10%

DC GuestHouse   *Washington*

1337 10th St NW
Washington, DC 20001
202/ 332-2502
www.dcguesthouse.com

Clientele: mixed gay/ straight
Type: b&b-private home; located in one of Washington DC's oldest, most elegant & convenient neighborhoods; spacious rms, contemporary furnishings, loads of charm
Owned/ Run By: gay men
Rooms: 5

Baths: private & shared
Meals: full brkfst
Amenities: free parking, DVDs/ videos, WiFi
Pets: pet day care required & available
Smoking: ok
Rates: $225-275
AC: 10%

The Bed & Breakfast at the William Lewis House

1309 R St NW   202/ 462-7574   info@wlewishous.com
Washington, DC 20009   800/ 465-7574   www.wlewishous.com

Welcome to the Bed and Breakfast at the William Lewis House, Washington DC's premier gay bed-and-breakfast with ten beautifully furnished rooms in the late Victorian/early Edwardian style. We're conveniently located near both tourist and gay attractions—easy access by foot, automobile, and subway.

We're located just off Logan Circle, virtually on the corner of R and 13th Streets. Originally opened as a single house after an extensive ten-year restoration, we expanded in 1999 to include the house next door and the lot between them. The three lots provide space for the owners to create a wonderfully landscaped courtyard that includes a large sitting porch, hot tub, water garden, limited off-street parking, and a large deck to connect the houses. Each weekday morning enjoy a continental breakfast and, on Saturday and Sunday, a full hardy American breakfast.

The Bed and Breakfast at the William Lewis House is owner-occupied and open year-round.

Clientele: mostly men
Type: b&b-private home; authentically restored Victorian full of antiques; near gay neighborhoods, Metro & tourist attractions
Owned/ Run By: gay men
Nearby Attractions: very close to Nat'l Mall, Dupont Circle, 17th St & Metro
Transit: near public transit; short taxi ride to Nat'l Airport; to Baltimore or Dulles take Super Shuttle (800/ BLUEVAN)
Rooms: 10 total, 6 queens, 4 fulls, A/C,

ceiling fan, fireplace (2), phone, maid service, color TV & VCR in living rm, voicemail & data ports in all rms
Baths: shared, robes
Meals: expanded cont'l brkfst, full brkfst Sat-Sun; happy hour cocktails Fri-Sat
Amenities: laundry, outdoor hot tub, snacks, coffee/ tea
Pets On Premises: 1 dog
Reservations: required *Deposit:* required *Cancellation:* cancel by 1 week prior *Minimum Stay:* some wknds/ holidays

(please inquire) *Check in/ out:* 4pm/ 1pm
Payment: cash, travelers checks, Visa, Amex, MC, Discover
Season: open yr-round *High season:* Sept-Nov
Rates: $69-139 *Discounts:* longer stays
AC: 10%

Dupont at The Circle

Washington

1604 19th St NW
Washington, DC 20009
202/ 332-5251 888/ 412-0100
www.dupontatthecircle.com

Clientele: mixed gay/ straight
Type: b&b-inn; AAA-rated Victorian at Dupont Circle; 1/2 blk from Metro; historical neighborhood
Owned/ Run By: straights
Rooms: 8
Baths: private

Meals: expanded cont'l brkfst
Amenities: hot tub, DVDs/ videos, WiFi
Kids: 14 yrs & up welcome
Pets: no
Smoking: no
Rates: $150-475
AC: 10%

Embassy Suites Alexandria

Washington

1900 Diagonal Rd
Alexandria, VA 22314
703/ 684-5900 800/ 362-2779
www.embassysuitesdcmetro.com

Clientele: mixed gay/ straight
Type: hotel; 2-rm suites; cocktail reception every evening; tropical garden atrium; Hilton Honors Points & Miles
Owned/ Run By: gay/ lesbian & straight
Rooms: 268
Baths: private

Wheelchair Access: yes, all rms
Meals: full brkfst
Amenities: laundry, pool, sauna, hot tub
Kids: welcome; under 18 free w/ parents
Smoking: ok
Rates: $119-269
AC: 10%

Embassy Suites Washington, DC

Washington

1250 22nd St NW
Washington, DC 20037
202/ 857-3388 800/ 362-2779
www.embassysuites.com

Clientele: gay-friendly
Type: all-suite, full-service luxury hotel; located between Dupont Circle & Georgetown; complimentary cocktails
Owned/ Run By: gay & straight
Rooms: 318
Baths: private

Wheelchair Access: yes
Meals: cook-to-order brkfsts
Amenities: laundry, pool, sauna, hot tub
Kids: welcome
Smoking: ok
Rates: $119-319
AC: 10%

Hotel Helix

Washington

1430 Rhode Island Ave NW
Washington, DC 20005

202/ 462-9001
800/ 706-1202

reservations@hotelhelix.com
www.hotelhelix.com

Clientele: gay-friendly
Type: hotel; designer full-service boutique hotel; spacious, fun guest rms, fashionable Helix Lounge; 4 blks to Metro; "Washington's newest pop sensation"
Owned/ Run By: other
Nearby Attractions: Dupont Circle shopping & nightlife, Smithsonian, Nat'l Gallery, White House & US Capitol
Transit: 45 miles to BWI; 30 miles to Dulles; 5 miles to Reagan Nat'l; 2 miles Union Station
Rooms: 178 total, 18 suites, 124 kings, 36 queens, A/C, cable, phone, kitchenette (4), refrigerator, safer sex supplies, rm service, maid service, CD stereo, flatscreen TV, DVD (4), full mini-bar, complimentary high-speed internet
Baths: private, showers, robes, hairdryers
Wheelchair Access: yes, 9 rms
Amenities: sunset drinks, coffee/ tea, fitness center w/ state-of-the-art equipment, Helix Lounge menu features modern spin on favorite classics, evening complimentary bubbly hour

Kids: welcome
Pets: welcome
Smoking: ok
Reservations: required; all must be guaranteed w/ credit card *Cancellation:* cancel by 1 day prior

Payment: cash, travelers checks, personal checks, Visa, Amex, MC, Discover
Season: open yr-round *High season:* spring & fall
Rates: $129-359 *Discounts:* AAA
AC: 10%

Hotel Madera 🏳️‍🌈   *Washington*

1310 New Hampshire Ave NW
Washington, DC 20036
202/ 296-7600 800/ 430-1202
www.hotelmadera.com

Clientele: gay-friendly
Type: full-service boutique hotel located in
  chic Dupont Circle; spacious guest rms,
  attentive service
Owned/ Run By: gay & straight
Rooms: 82
Baths: private

Wheelchair Access: yes, 3 rms
Amenities: massage, WiFi
Kids: welcome
Pets: welcome
Smoking: ok in bar only
Rates: $139-259
AC: 10%

Hotel Monaco Washington DC 🏳️‍🌈   *Washington*

700 F St NW
Washington, DC 20004
202/ 628-7177 800/ 649-1202
www.monaco-dc.com

Clientele: gay-friendly
Type: luxury 4-diamond boutique hotel in
  historic landmark bldg; complimentary
  wine reception evenings
Owned/ Run By: gay & straight
Rooms: 184
Baths: private

Wheelchair Access: yes, 9 rms
Meals: coffee/tea only
Kids: welcome
Pets: welcome
Smoking: ok
Rates: $129-350
AC: 10%

Hotel Rouge 🏳️‍🌈   *Washington*

1315 16th St NW
Washington, DC 20036
202/ 232-8000 800/ 368-5689
www.rougehotel.com

Clientele: gay-friendly
Type: high-tech luxury hotel on Embassy
  Row; steps away from business district &
  Dupont Circle
Owned/ Run By: gay/ lesbian & straight
Rooms: 137
Baths: private
Wheelchair Access: yes, 6 rms

Meals: cont'l brkfst
Amenities: massage, WiFi
Kids: welcome
Pets: welcome
Smoking: ok
Rates: $139-249
AC: 10%

Kalorama Guest House at Kalorama Park   *Washington*

1854 Mintwood Pl NW
Washington, DC 20009

202/ 667-6369

www.kaloramaguesthouse.com

Clientele: mixed gay/ straight
Type: b&b-inn; charming Victorian; provides
  a cozy home away from home in
  Washington's most cosmopolitan
  neighborhood
Owned/ Run By: gay & straight
Nearby Attractions: 20 minutes to White
  House, Capitol & other tourist attractions;
  15 minutes to Dupont Circle & art
  galleries; 10 minutes to Nat'l Zoo; dozens
  of restaurants & cafes w/in walking
  distance
Transit: near public transit; 5 miles to Nat'l
  airport; 5 blks to Woodley Park Metro stop;
  1/2 blk to Metro Bus stop
Rooms: 29 total, 5 suites, 4 queens, 15 fulls,
  5 twins, A/C, DVD/ VCR (6), cable TV (7),
  ceiling fan (15), deck (2), phone (6),
  kitchenette (1), refrigerator (1), maid
  service, radio alarm clocks, antiques
Baths: private & shared, bathtubs, showers
Meals: expanded cont'l brkfst
Amenities: office hrs: 8am-8pm; laundry,
  WiFi, sunset drinks, coffee/ tea, fruit basket
Recreation: Rock Creek Park, Nat'l Zoo

Kids: 5 yrs & up welcome
Reservations: required; w/ credit card
  guarantee *Deposit:* required, amount &
  date vary *Cancellation:* cancel by 2 weeks
  prior *Minimum Stay:* please inquire *Check
  in/ out:* 2pm/ 11am

Payment: cash, travelers checks, Visa, Amex,
  MC, Discover
Season: open yr-round *High season:*
  March-June & Sept-Nov
Rates: $60-120 *Discounts:* weekly, seniors
AC: 10%

Kalorama Guest House at Woodley Park
Washington

2700 Cathedral Ave NW
Washington, DC 20008

202/ 328-0860

www.kaloramaguesthouse.com

Clientele: mixed gay/ straight
Type: b&b-inn; cozy home away from home at a very moderate rate; located in one of Washington's most fashionable neighborhoods; just 3 blks to Metro
Owned/ Run By: gay & straight
Nearby Attractions: 20 minutes to White House & Smithsonian Museums
Transit: near public transit; 2 blks to Woodley Park/ Zoo Metro stop
Rooms: 18 total, 2 suites, 5 queens, 10 fulls, 1 twin, A/C, deck (2), maid service, radio alarm clocks, antiques, desks, reading material
Baths: private & shared, bathtubs
Meals: expanded cont'l brkfst
Amenities: office hrs: 8am-8pm; WiFi, sunset drinks, coffee/ tea, fruit basket, cookies, afternoon aperitif
Recreation: Rock Creek Park, Nat'l Zoo
Kids: 6 yrs & up welcome
Smoking: no
Reservations: required; w/ credit card guarantee *Deposit:* required, amount &

date vary *Cancellation:* cancel by 1 week prior *Minimum Stay:* please inquire *Check in/ out:* 1-8pm/ 11am
Payment: cash, travelers checks, Visa, Amex, MC, Discover

Season: open yr-round *High season:* March-June & Sept-Nov
Rates: $55-105 *Discounts:* weekly, seniors
AC: 10%

Morrison-Clark Historic Inn & Restaurant
Washington

Massachusetts Ave NW
Washington, DC 20001
202/ 898-1200 800/ 322-7898
www.morrisonclark.com

Clientele: gay-friendly
Type: hotel; "b&b in style, but full hotel in service"; built in 1864 as 2 separate Victorian town houses, today the Inn has 54 rms & boasts one of the best restaurants in DC
Owned/ Run By: diverse group of people
Rooms: 54

Baths: private
Meals: cont'l brkfst
Kids: welcome
Pets: no
Smoking: ok
Rates: $155-325
AC: 10%

Otis Place B&B
Washington

1003 Otis Place NW
Washington, DC 20010
202/ 483-0241 877/ 893-3233
ww.bedandbreakfastdc.com

Clientele: mixed gay/ straight
Type: b&b-private home; newly-renovated 1910 Victorian townhouse; original woodwork, antique lighting fixtures & fireplace in living rm; back deck; A/C; 2 cats in residence; 3-minute walk from metro

Owned/ Run By: gay men
Rooms: 2
Baths: private
Meals: cont'l brkfst
Kids: welcome
Pets: no
Rates: $75-150

Radisson Barcelo Hotel Washington
Washington

2121 P St NW
Washington, DC 20037
202/ 448-1831 800/ 546-7866
www.hotelpalomar-dc.com

Clientele: mixed gay/ straight
Type: hotel; deluxe property located in the unique neighborhood of Dupont Circle; surrounded by chic galleries, boutiques & nightlife
Owned/ Run By: gay & straight
Rooms: 335
Baths: private

Wheelchair Access: yes, 16 rms
Meals: coffee/tea only
Kids: welcome
Pets: welcome
Smoking: ok
Rates: $175-440
AC: 10%

Swann House Historic B&B   *Washington*

1808 New Hampshire Ave NW
Washington, DC 20009
202/ 265-4414
www.swannhouse.com

Clientele: mixed gay/ straight
Type: b&b-inn; 1883 Victorian mansion in heart of Dupont Circle w/ 9 unique guest rms; fireplaces & jacuzzis in select rms; walk to Metro, restaurants, shops, nightlife
Owned/ Run By: gay & straight

Rooms: 9
Baths: private
Meals: expanded cont'l brkfst
Kids: 12 yrs & up welcome
Rates: $150-345
AC: call

Topaz Hotel 🏷️   *Washington*

1733 N St NW
Washington, DC 20036
202/ 393-3000 800/ 424-2950
www.topazhotel.com

Clientele: gay-friendly
Type: hotel; full-service boutique hotel; playful rms, sophisticated design, personalized service, unique amenities; energy-filled Topaz Bar open daily; 2 blks to Dupont Circle Metro
Owned/ Run By: gay & straight
Rooms: 99

Baths: private
Wheelchair Access: yes, 5 rms
Amenities: sauna, WiFi
Kids: welcome
Pets: welcome
Smoking: ok in lounge only
Rates: $139-249
AC: 10%

Washington Plaza   *Washington*

10 Thomas Cir NW
Washington, DC 20005
202/ 842-1300 800/ 424-1140
www.washingtonplazahotel.com

Clientele: gay-friendly
Type: hotel; ideally located for business & pleasure; modern decor, large outdoor pool, 12,000-sq-ft mtg facilities
Owned/ Run By: gay/ lesbian & straight
Rooms: 340 (includes 15 junior suites & 19 ADA rms)
Baths: private

Wheelchair Access: yes, 8 rms
Meals: full brkfst
Amenities: pool, WiFi
Kids: welcome
Pets: welcome
Smoking: ok
Rates: $99-299
AC: 10%

Mermaid's Tale   *Alligator Point*

703/ 426-1936 866/ 794-9640
www.mermaids-tale.us

Clientele: mostly women
Type: rental home; elegant, waterfront 2-bdrm/ 2-bath vacation-home; private 1-acre on the Gulf of Mexico; every amenity for luxury living
Owned/ Run By: lesbians

Rooms: 2
Baths: private
Kids: welcome
Pets: please inquire
Smoking: no
Rates: $920-1,920/ week

Ash Street Inn   *Amelia Island*

102 S 7th St
Amelia Island, FL 32034
904/ 277-6660 800/ 277-6660
www.ashstreetinn.net

Clientele: mixed gay/ straight
Type: b&b; nestled in the historic seaport of Fernandina Beach, the Ash Street Inn features 11 beautifully appointed guest rms
Owned/ Run By: straights
Rooms: 11
Baths: private
Wheelchair Access: yes, 2 rms

Meals: full brkfst
Amenities: free parking, pool, hot tub, massage, DVDs/ videos, WiFi
Kids: welcome
Pets: dogs under 25 lbs welcome
Smoking: no
Rates: $129-299
AC: 10%

Florida House Inn   *Amelia Island*

20 S 3rd St
Amelia Island, FL 32034
904/ 261-3300 800/ 258-3301
www.floridahouseinn.com

Clientele: gay-friendly
Type: b&b; in Florida's oldest surviving hotel; 2 restaurants & bar & grille
Owned/ Run By: straights
Rooms: 15
Baths: private

Meals: full brkfst
Kids: welcome
Pets: welcome
Smoking: ok
Rates: $99-319

The Hoyt House
Amelia Island

804 Atlantic Ave
Amelia Island, FL 32034
904/ 277-4300 800/ 432-2085
www.hoythouse.com

Clientele: gay-friendly
Type: b&b; in magnificently restored 1905 Queen Anne mansion; wraparound porches
Owned/ Run By: straights
Rooms: 10
Baths: private

Wheelchair Access: yes
Meals: full brkfst
Amenities: pool, WiFi
Kids: please inquire
Pets: please inquire
Smoking: no
Rates: $139-219

Coombs House Inn
Apalachicola

80 6th St
Apalachicola, FL 32320
850/ 653-9199 888/ 244-8320
www.coombshouseinn.com

Clientele: gay-friendly
Type: b&b; "the most elegant Victorian B&B on the Panhandle of Florida"
Owned/ Run By: straights
Rooms: 19 + 1 apt
Baths: private
Wheelchair Access: yes, all rms

Meals: full brkfst
Kids: please call first
Pets: no
Smoking: no (outside smoking areas)
Rates: $89-225

Summer House
Bradenton

111 & 113 36th St
Holmes Beach, FL 34217
941/ 778-2333 800/ 431-0278
ESPBeachRentals.com

Clientele: gay-friendly
Type: inn; includes studio apt, 1-bdrm apt, 2-bdrm apt & 4-bdrm cottage (sleeps 8-10)
Rooms: 4 (rentals)
Baths: private
Amenities: free parking, laundry, pool

Kids: welcome
Pets: please inquire
Smoking: no (outside only)
Rates: $130-250 & $800-1,400/ weekly
AC: 3%

Hampton Inn Clearwater/ St Petersburg Airport
Clearwater

3655 Hospitality Ln
Clearwater, FL 33762
727/ 577-9200
www.hamptoninnclearwater.com

Clientele: gay-friendly
Type: hotel; off I-275; close to many attractions, including gay bars
Rooms: 118
Baths: private
Wheelchair Access: yes, 2 rms
Meals: expanded cont'l brkfst

Amenities: free parking, laundry, pool, sauna, outdoor hot tub
Kids: welcome
Pets: no
Smoking: ok (not in lobby)
Rates: $49-99
AC: 10%

Holiday Inn Select
Clearwater

3535 Ulmerton Rd
Clearwater, FL 33762
727/ 577-9100
www.hiselect.com/clw-stpete

Clientele: gay-friendly
Type: hotel; close to airport & beach; restaurant & lounge; all welcome
Rooms: 176
Baths: private
Wheelchair Access: yes, 10 rms
Amenities: free parking, laundry, pool,

outdoor hot tub
Kids: welcome
Pets: no
Smoking: ok (in guest rms)
Rates: $60-119
AC: 10%

Beach Place Guesthouse
Cocoa Beach

1445 S Atlantic Ave
Cocoa Beach, FL 32931
321/ 783-4045
www.BeachPlaceGuesthouses.com

Clientele: gay-friendly
Type: on 200' of pristine Atlantc shoreline; "we provide the perfect backdrop to relaxation, rejuvenation & reconnection"
Owned/ Run By: gay men
Rooms: 16
Baths: private

Meals: coffee/tea only
Amenities: free parking, laundry, WiFi
Kids: welcome
Pets: no
Smoking: no
Rates: $175-350

Best Western Mayan Inn Beachfront
Daytona Beach

103 S Ocean Ave
Daytona Beach, FL 32118
386/ 252-2378 800/ 443-5323
bwmayaninn.com

Type: hotel; all rms have ocean views; most have balconies
Rooms: 112
Baths: private
Wheelchair Access: yes, 4 rms
Meals: cont'l brkfst

Amenities: free parking, laundry, pool, hot tub
Kids: welcome
Smoking: ok
Rates: $79-215
AC: 10%

Lilian Place B&B
Daytona Beach

111 Silver Beach Ave
Daytona Beach, FL 32118
386/ 323-9913 877/ 893-7579
www.lilianplace.com

Clientele: mixed gay/ straight
Type: b&b; in oldest beachside home on Daytona Beach
Owned/ Run By: straights
Rooms: 6
Baths: private
Wheelchair Access: yes, 1 rm
Meals: full brkfst

Amenities: free parking, laundry, hot tub, DVDs/ videos
Kids: no
Pets: no
Smoking: no
Rates: $135+
AC: 5%

Mermaid Cottage
Daytona Beach

127 Arlington Wy
Ormond Beach, FL 32176
404/ 784-4447
www.mermaidcottage.net

Clientele: mixed gay/ straight
Type: cottage; 1938 Craftsman bungalow w/ fully equipped kitchen & courtyard
Owned/ Run By: lesbian
Rooms: 3

Baths: private
Kids: please inquire
Pets: please inquire
Smoking: no
Rates: $1,195-3,195/ week

The Villa B&B
Daytona Beach

801 N Peninsula Dr
Daytona Beach, FL 32118

386/ 248-2020
888/ 248-7060

thevillabb@aol.com
www.thevillaBB.com

Clientele: gay-friendly
Type: b&b-private home; elegant accommodations in historic Spanish mansion—a private, gated estate w/ old-world charm
Owned/ Run By: gay men
Nearby Attractions: 1 hr to St Augustine, Disney World & Space Coast; 25 miles to Canaveral Nat'l Seashore; Daytona USA, historic museums, flea market nearby
Pickup Service: airport pickup
Transit: 5 miles to Daytona Beach airport
Rooms: 6 (also 3-bdrm cottage) total, 1 king, 3 queens, 2 fulls, A/C, color TV, DVD/ VCR, cable, ceiling fan (5), fireplace (1), deck (3), refrigerator (1), maid service
Baths: private & shared, bathtubs, showers, robes, hairdryers
Meals: expanded cont'l brkfst
Amenities: outdoor hot tub, DVDs/ videos, snacks, sunset drinks, coffee/ tea, spa, bike usage, formal public rms, estate is fenced & gated; clothing-optional heated pool & spa area, see mgr
Kids: no
Pets: no

Pets On Premises: 1 cat, 1 dog
Smoking: no
Reservations: required; w/ credit card guarantee *Deposit:* required, 1 night, personal check ok *Cancellation:* cancel by 1 week prior *Minimum Stay:* special events *Check in/ out:* 2-6pm/ 11am

Payment: cash, travelers checks, Visa, Amex, MC
Season: open yr-round *High season:* Dec-May
Rates: $85-250 *Discounts:* off-season
AC: 10%

Miss Pat's Inn B&B
Daytona Beach

1209 S Peninsula Dr
Daytona Beach, FL 32118
386/ 248-8420 866/ 464-7772
misspatsinn.com

Clientele: gay-friendly
Type: b&b-inn; in historic Victorian 1 blk from ocean
Rooms: 7
Baths: private
Meals: full brkfst

Kids: no
Pets: no
Smoking: ok
Rates: $110-350

Crane's BeachHouse
Delray Beach

82 Gleason St
Delray Beach, FL 33483
561/ 278-1700 866/ 372-7263
www.cranesbeachhouse.com

Clientele: gay-friendly
Type: hotel; island-inspired tropical rms, cabanas & veranda suites w/ kitchenettes & private patios, 2 swimming pools; "we specialize in group-themed wknds!"
Owned/ Run By: straights
Rooms: 27
Baths: private

Wheelchair Access: yes, 1 rm
Kids: welcome
Pets: under 25 lbs welcome; must be crated when guests are away
Smoking: no (outdoors only)
Rates: $135-485
AC: 10%

Blue Skies Cottage
Destin

4442 Oceanview Dr
Destin, FL 32541
251/ 608-7262 888/ 299-6009
www.destingetaways.com

Clientele: gay-friendly
Type: rental home; adorable 2-bdrm/ 2-bath cottage; 1 blk from the beach; community pool; close to shopping & dining
Owned/ Run By: straight man
Rooms: 6
Baths: private

Kids: welcome; 6 person max
Smoking: no
Rates: $117-266

Alhambra Beach Resort
Fort Lauderdale

3021 Alhambra St
Fort Lauderdale, FL 33304
954/ 525-7601 866/ 309-4014
www.alhambrabeachresort.com

Clientele: mixed gay/ straight
Type: resort; steps from the famous St Sebastian gay beach; close to restaurants, clubs & shops
Owned/ Run By: gay men
Rooms: 12
Baths: private

Meals: cont'l brkfst
Kids: no
Pets: no
Smoking: no
Rates: $89-209
AC: 10%

Bamboo Resort
Fort Lauderdale

2733 Middle River Dr
Fort Lauderdale, FL 33306
954/ 565-7775 800/ 479-1767
www.thebambooresort.com

Clientele: men
Type: guesthouse; award-winning; located w/in short walking or driving distance of Fort Lauderdale's best places
Owned/ Run By: gay men
Rooms: 8
Baths: private

Meals: expanded cont'l brkfst
Kids: no
Pets: welcome; under 15 lbs
Smoking: no
Rates: $99-299
AC: 10%

The Blue Dolphin
Fort Lauderdale

725 N Birch Rd
Fort Lauderdale, FL 33304
954/ 565-8437 800/ 893-2583
www.bluedolphinhotel.com

Clientele: men
Type: hotel; minutes' walk to Fort Lauderdale's beach; offers hotel rms, efficiencies & 1-bdrm apts for the discerning gay traveler
Owned/ Run By: gay men
Rooms: 18

Baths: private
Wheelchair Access: yes, 1 rm
Meals: cont'l brkfst
Pets: small pets only; $10 charge
Smoking: ok
Rates: $79-169
AC: 10%

Alcazar Resort
555 N Birch Rd
Fort Lauderdale, FL 33304

954/ 567-2525
888/ 830-9931

Fort Lauderdale

info@alcazarresort.com
www.alcazarresort.com

Welcome and thank you for considering The Alcazar Resort on Fort Lauderdale Beach. The Alcazar opened in early 2006 and is owned and operated by the Worthington Guesthouse, with both resorts located in the same compound.

Guests of the Alcazar and the Worthington share the same outdoor amenities, including two clothing-optional heated pools and hot tubs, which are open 24 hours for guests' enjoyment. Guests may also go back and forth from one property to the other through garden walkways. Both resorts cater to an all-male clientele and tend to draw an interesting mix of US and international travelers.

The Alcazar is located on the Barrier Islands, just two short blocks from the sandy shores of Fort Lauderdale Beach. A short walk along the seawall brings you to the well-known Sebastian Street gay beach. The resort is close to all Gay Fort Lauderdale's nightlife, shopping, and a wide variety of restaurants. Wilton Manors, where some of the most popular gay bars, restaurants, and novelty stores are located, is only minutes away.

Clientele: men only
Type: resort; affordable lodging at the beach; clothing-optional; owned/ run by the Worthington Guesthouse
Owned/ Run By: gay men
Transit: 8 miles to airport; 5 miles to bus
Rooms: 20 total, 4 suites, 12 kings, 4 twins, DVD/ VCR, cable, phone, kitchenette (4), refrigerator, safer sex supplies, maid service

Baths: private, bathtubs, showers
Meals: cont'l brkfst, special meals available Fri, Sat & Sun afternoon
Amenities: pool, outdoor hot tub, DVDs/ videos, WiFi, cocktails
Recreation: gay beach
Kids: no
Pets: no
Smoking: no

Reservations: required *Deposit:* required, 30%, personal check ok *Cancellation:* cancel by 2 weeks prior *Minimum Stay:* holidays *Check in/ out:* 3pm/ noon
Payment: travelers checks, Visa, Amex, MC, Discover
Season: open yr-round *High season:* Dec-May
Rates: $79-129 *Discounts:* extended stays
AC: 10%

The Cabanas

Fort Lauderdale

2209 NE 26th St   954/ 564-7764 info@TheCabanasGuesthouse.com
Fort Lauderdale, FL 33305   866/ 564-7764 www.TheCabanasGuesthouse.com

E xperience "Paradise." This gated enclave is a 15-room, award-winning, tropical hideaway snuggled in the heart of gay Fort Lauderdale. It is ideally located on a beautiful waterfront property minutes from pristine beaches, shopping, and the famous nightlife.

Indulge yourself in our sun-drenched, clothing-optional pool and 10-man Jacuzzi, or release your stress in our 8-man steam room with aromatherapy and dual raindrop showers. For our adventurous guests, we offer kayaks and bicycles to explore the city by water or land.

All cabanas boast goose-down comforters, plush mattresses, coffee bars, refrigerators, DSL high-speed data ports and wireless internet, and DVD players. A complimentary DVD library is also available for your viewing pleasure. The internet café offers expanded daily continental breakfast, happy hour, and a computer for your cyber-delight.

Attention to detail, our friendly staff, and our "no attitude" approach are what truly set us apart from the rest. Whatever you choose, The Cabanas Guesthouse has something for everyone. This is why we have left no stone unturned in our quest to make your stay in "paradise" a most memorable one.

Clientele: mostly men

Type: guesthouse; ideally located on beautiful riverfront property at the edge of Wilton Manors; near gay bars, restaurants & shops

Owned/ Run By: gay men

Transit: 45 minutes to Miami Int'l; 15 minutes to Fort Lauderdale Int'l & Amtrak; 10 minutes to bus station

Rooms: 17 total, 1 suite, 4 kings, 11 queens, 1 full, A/C, color TV, DVD/ VCR, cable, ceiling fan, deck (4), phone, kitchenette (8), refrigerator, safer sex supplies, maid service, beautifully appointed, goose-down comforters; suite features formal living/ dining rm & kitchen; Premium Queen Rooms feature waterfront private decks

Baths: private, showers, robes

Meals: expanded cont'l brkfst

Amenities: pool, sauna, outdoor hot tub w/ waterfall, massage, WiFi, snacks, cocktails, sunset drinks, coffee/ tea, DVD/ videos, steam rm w/ outdoor shower area, 10-man Roman-style jacuzzi w/ waterfall, bikes & kayaks available for rent

Kids: no

Pets: 20 lbs & under welcome w/ $50 nonrefundable pet fee

Smoking: no

Reservations: required *Deposit:* required, 50%, due at booking *Cancellation:* cancel by 30 days prior/ 21 days prior (off-season) or forfeit 1 night (whole deposit if less than 7 days)

Payment: cash, travelers checks, Visa, Amex, MC, Discover

Season: open yr-round *High season:* Dec-May

Rates: $119-269 *Discounts:* check website for special promotions

AC: IGLTA standard/ 10%

Cheston House
Fort Lauderdale

520 N Birch Rd
Fort Lauderdale, FL 33304
954/ 566-7950 866/ 566-7950
www.chestonhouse.com

Clientele: men
Type: guesthouse; architecturally unique, upscale, clothing-optional gay men's resort; located on Fort Lauderdale Beach; "where elegance meets affordability"
Owned/ Run By: gay man
Rooms: 16
Baths: private

Meals: expanded cont'l brkfst
Kids: no
Pets: welcome
Smoking: no
Rates: $99-250
AC: 10%

Coconut Cove Guesthouse
Fort Lauderdale

3012 Granada St
Fort Lauderdale, FL 33304
954/ 523-3226 888/ 414-3226
www.coconutcoveguesthouse.com

Clientele: men
Type: guesthouse; closest gay guesthouse to the beach; morning newspapers; evening cocktails at the poolside bar or on veranda overlooking lush courtyard
Owned/ Run By: gay men
Rooms: 12
Baths: private

Meals: expanded cont'l brkfst
Kids: no
Pets: no
Rates: $99-265

Comfort Suites Airport & Cruise Port T4G
Fort Lauderdale

1800 S Federal Hwy
Fort Lauderdale, FL 33316
954/ 767-8700 800/ 760-0000
www.comfortsuitesftlauderdale.com

Clientele: mixed gay/ straight
Type: hotel; recently renovated; centrally located for beaches & gay nightlife
Owned/ Run By: gay & straight
Rooms: 111
Baths: private
Wheelchair Access: yes, 2 rms
Meals: expanded cont'l brkfst

Kids: welcome
Smoking: ok
Rates: $69-209
AC: 10%

Coral Reef Guesthouse
Fort Lauderdale

2609 NE 13th Ct
Fort Lauderdale, FL 33304
954/ 568-0292 888/ 365-6948
www.coralreefguesthouse.com

Clientele: men
Type: guesthouse; near beach, restaurants & the Galleria Mall; rms scrupulously clean, tastefully decorated & overlook clothing-optional pool & jacuzzi
Owned/ Run By: gay men
Rooms: 8
Baths: private
Meals: expanded cont'l brkfst

Amenities: free parking, pool, hot tub, massage, DVDs/ videos
Kids: no
Pets: no
Smoking: no
Rates: $120-259
AC: 10%

Deauville Inn
Fort Lauderdale

2916 N Ocean Blvd
Fort Lauderdale, FL 33308
954/ 568-5000
www.thedeauvilleinn.com

Clientele: men
Type: guesthouse; friendly, clean clothing-optional inn; near shopping, restaurants & clubs
Owned/ Run By: gay
Rooms: 11
Baths: private
Wheelchair Access: yes, 1 rm
Meals: cont'l brkfst

Amenities: free parking, laundry, pool, WiFi
Kids: no
Pets: small pets ok; fee
Smoking: no
Rates: $79-139
AC: 10%

The Dunes Guest House 🏳️‍🌈

Fort Lauderdale

2835 Terramar St
Fort Lauderdale, FL 33304

954/ 568-6161
800/ 425-8105

info@dunesguesthouse.com
www.dunesguesthouse.com

Clientele: men
Type: guesthouse; unique charm, friendly service; sun, pool & spa; "the fabulous gay guesthouse on Fort Lauderdale Beach"
Owned/ Run By: gay men
Nearby Attractions: Las Olas Blvd, Beach Place shopping center, Sawgrass Mills, Wilton Manors; 3 blks to beach; walking distance to gay beach
Transit: near public transit; 3 blks to bus line
Rooms: 10 total, 5 suites, 4 kings, 1 full, A/C, color TV, DVD/ VCR, cable, ceiling fan, deck, phone, kitchenette (5), refrigerator, safer sex supplies, maid service, all recently redecorated & refurnished
Baths: private, bathtubs, showers, robes, hairdryers
Meals: expanded cont'l brkfst
Amenities: laundry, hot tub, massage, DVDs/ videos, WiFi, cocktails, coffee/ tea, heated clothing-optional pool & spa, soft drinks, brkfst bar, beach towels, complimentary sun lotions, poolside refreshments, sundeck, tropical gardens, fountains
Kids: no

Pets: no
Smoking: no
Reservations: required; by phone, fax, or online *Deposit:* required, 33%, due at booking *Cancellation:* cancel by 21 days prior (w/ $25 fee) or forfeit deposit *Minimum Stay:* 3 nights (in season)

Payment: cash, travelers checks, Visa, Amex, MC
Season: open yr-round *High season:* Dec-May
Rates: $99-179
AC: 5%, $100 max

Elysium Resort

Fort Lauderdale

552 N Birch Rd
Fort Lauderdale, FL 33304
954/ 564-9601 800/ 533-4744
www.elysiumresort.net

Clientele: mostly men
Type: hotel; city's largest boutique hotel; intimate art deco environment; large suites & studios; 200 yds from beach; 2 pools, 18' jacuzzi, free local & 800# calls
Owned/ Run By: gay men
Rooms: 36
Baths: private
Meals: cont'l brkfst

Amenities: free parking, laundry, pool, outdoor hot tub, gym, massage, DVDs/ videos, WiFi
Kids: no
Pets: welcome; not in public areas
Smoking: no
Rates: $109-209
AC: 10%

Embassy Suites Hotel 🏳️‍🌈

Fort Lauderdale

1100 SE 17th St
Fort Lauderdale, FL 33316
954/ 527-2700 800/ 362-2779
www.embassysuitesftl.com

Clientele: gay-friendly
Type: hotel; 2 miles from Sebastian Beach & downtown; 1/2 mile from Port Everglades; 3 miles to Wilton Manors
Owned/ Run By: other
Rooms: 358
Baths: private
Wheelchair Access: yes, 10 rms
Meals: full brkfst

Amenities: laundry, pool, outdoor hot tub, gym
Kids: welcome; kids under 18 free
Pets: welcome; fee
Smoking: ok
Rates: $129-369
AC: 10%

The Flamingo—Inn Amongst the Flowers

2727 Terramar St   954/ 561-4658
Fort Lauderdale, FL 33304   800/ 283-4786   www.theflamingoresort.com

The Flamingo—Inn Amongst the Flowers boasts soothing fountains, delicately manicured gardens, lush tropical palms and flowers, and a sparkling heated swimming pool. Beds are turned down at night, continental breakfast is served each morning, complimentary cocktails at happy hour are served daily, and the office extends full concierge service to make your dinner reservations, gym requests, tour bookings, car rentals, and more.

The romantic hotel is proud of its reputation as one of the leading luxury gay hotels and is often referred to as Florida's first boutique hotel serving the gay community. With luxury in mind, the completely renovated Flamingo has received awards for Best Indoor Decor from the Florida Superior Small Lodging Association and is an *Out&About* 5 Palm-rated resort.

Located in the heart of Fort Lauderdale's gay lodging district and only three blocks from the famous Fort Lauderdale Beach, The Flamingo is an ideal oasis from which to enjoy the outstanding attractions available to the discriminating gay traveler in South Florida.

Clientele: men

Type: guesthouse; "The award-winning Flamingo—Inn Amongst the Flowers is proud to be one of the leading boutique hotels serving the international gay community."

Owned/ Run By: gay men

Nearby Attractions: 5 minutes to gay area of town; Swimming Hall of Fame, Bonnet House, Center for Performing Arts, Galleria Center

Transit: near public transit; 15 minutes to airport; 20 minutes to train/ bus

Rooms: 15 total, 4 suites, 8 kings, 3 queens, A/C, color TV, cable, ceiling fan, phone, kitchenette (7), refrigerator, safer sex supplies, maid service, radio/ CD player, VHS/ DVD, wireless internet, in-rm coffee service, all recently refurbished, w/ 4-poster beds & French doors overlooking or adjacent to heated pool

Baths: private, bathtubs, showers, robes, hairdryers

Meals: expanded cont'l brkfst

Amenities: laundry, pool, hot tub, massage, DVDs/ videos, WiFi, snacks, cocktails, sunset drinks, coffee/ tea, concierge service

Smoking: no

Reservations: recommended *Deposit:* required, 40% or 1 night, due at booking, personal check ok *Cancellation:* cancel by 2 weeks prior or forfeit $20 *Minimum Stay:* 4 nights (in-season) & 5 nights Xmas & New Year's

Payment: cash, travelers checks, personal checks, Visa, Amex, MC

Season: open yr-round *High season:* Dec-April

Rates: $130-330 *Discounts:* extended stays

AC: 10%

The Grand Resort & Spa

Fort Lauderdale

539 N Birch Rd
Fort Lauderdale, FL 33304
954/ 630-3000 800/ 818-1211
info@grandresort.net
www.grandresort.net

Clientele: men
Type: resort
Owned/ Run By: gay men
Nearby Attractions: Las Olas Blvd,
Sawgrass Mills, Museum of Art, Port
Everglades, water taxis
Transit: 15 minutes to airport
Rooms: 33 total, 20 suites, 12 kings, 1
queen, A/C, color TV, DVD/ VCR, cable,
wetbar, ceiling fan, deck, phone,
kitchenette (24), refrigerator, safer sex
supplies, maid service
Baths: private, bathtubs, showers, robes,
hairdryers
Wheelchair Access: yes, 1 rm
Meals: cont'l brkfst
Amenities: office hrs: 24hrs; free parking,
laundry, pool, outdoor hot tub, massage,
DVDs/ videos, WiFi, coffee/ tea, fitness
center, oceanview sundeck, poolside
refreshments, T-1 line, 24hr staff, full-
service   spa,   bicycle   rentals,
clothing-optional area, Fri-Sat evening
cocktail receptions
Recreation: 2 blks to beach
Kids: no
Pets: no
Smoking: no
Reservations: *Deposit:* required, 1 night
+ tax, due at booking, personal check ok
Cancellation: cancel by 2 weeks prior or
forfeit deposit *Check in/ out:* after 3pm/
11am
Payment: cash, travelers checks, Visa,
Amex, MC, Discover, Diners Club
Season: open yr-round *High season:* Dec-
April
Rates: $95-380 *Discounts:* airline, corp,
students, military
AC: 10%

The Grand Resort and Spa is Fort Lauderdale Beach's largest men's hotel. We're just steps from the powder-white sand and soothing Atlantic Ocean. You will sense a very special friendliness and warmth each time you visit.

Our spacious, meticulously clean accommodations feature cable TV, VCRs, DVDs, Hi-Fi CD music systems, voicemail, iron and ironing boards, hairdryer, coffeemaker, refrigerator, and gourmet pantry area. All rooms have either wireless or DSL internet access.

Step outside of your room to enjoy our oceanview sundeck, oversized heated pool, secluded tropical clothing-optional courtyard with a 10-man Jacuzzi, fitness center, and club room. Be sure to pamper yourself in our full-service Day Spa, featuring an array of customized and specialty facials, body wraps, body scrubs, and massages, as well as spa manicures and pedicures.

Inn Leather Guesthouse

Fort Lauderdale

610 SE 19th St #4
Fort Lauderdale, FL 33316
954/ 467-1444 877/ 532-7729
www.innleather.com

Clientele: men
Type: guesthouse; catering to the leather/ levi community; most amenities; sling in each rm
Owned/ Run By: gay man
Rooms: 11
Baths: private

Wheelchair Access: yes, 2 rms
Meals: cont'l brkfst
Amenities: free parking, laundry, pool, outdoor hot tub, massage, DVDs/ videos
Smoking: ok
Rates: $114-194

Liberty Apartment & Garden Suites TAG

Fort Lauderdale

1501 SW 2nd Ave
Dania Beach, FL 33004-4263
954/ 927-0090 877/ 927-0090
www.LibertySuites.com

Clientele: mixed gay/ lesbian
Type: all-suite apt hotel; fully furnished & equipped; full kitchens; weekly rentals for seasonal vacation or extended stays
Owned/ Run By: gay men
Rooms: 20
Baths: private
Wheelchair Access: yes, 8 rms

Amenities: free parking, laundry, pool, hot tub, massage, DVDs/ videos, WiFi
Kids: no
Pets: welcome
Smoking: ok
Rates: $350-995/ week
AC: 10%

The Mangrove Villas

Fort Lauderdale

1100 N Victoria Park Rd
Fort Lauderdale, FL 33304
954/ 527-5250 800/ 238-3538
www.mangrovevillas.com

Clientele: men
Type: guesthouse; individually decorated villas & apts w/ full kitchens; clothing-optional pool & sundeck
Owned/ Run By: gay men
Rooms: (includes 1 queen studio, 3 villas, 3 extended-stay apts)
Baths: private

Wheelchair Access: yes, 1 rm
Amenities: laundry, pool, WiFi
Kids: no
Pets: no
Smoking: no
Rates: $85-230
AC: 10%

Mary's Resort

Fort Lauderdale

1115 Tequesta/ SW 4th St
Fort Lauderdale, FL 33312

954/ 523-3500
866/ 805-6570

info@marysresort.com
www.marysresort.com

Clientele: men only
Type: guesthouse; recently restored & renovated resort; 4 unique Key West-style structures separated by tropical gardens; perfect score from Superior Small Lodging w/ "White Glove Status"
Owned/ Run By: gay men
Transit: 37 minutes to Miami Int'l airport; 13 minutes to Fort Lauderdale airport
Rooms: 11 total, 3 suites, 1 king, 7 queens, A/C, ceiling fan, deck (6), phone (all cellphones), kitchenette, refrigerator, safer sex supplies, maid service, all new in 2006 w/ LCD flat-panel color TV w/ cable & DVD players, luxury linens & towels; no 2 rms are alike
Baths: private & shared, bathtubs, showers, whirlpools, hairdryers
Meals: expanded cont'l brkfst, special meals available by outside caterers
Amenities: laundry, pool, outdoor hot tub, DVDs/ videos, WiFi, snacks, sunset drinks, coffee/ tea, business center, DVD library, daily papers, massage & spa services; we feature Aveda products exclusively

Kids: no
Pets: welcome, but please inquire for details
Smoking: no
Reservations: required *Deposit:* required, 50% *Cancellation:* cancel by 2 weeks prior
Payment: Visa, Amex, MC, Discover

Season: open yr-round *High season:* Dec 15–April 30
Rates: $99-399 *Discounts:* military, students, seniors, 10%
AC: 10%

Manor Inn
Fort Lauderdale

2408 NE 6th Ave
Wilton Manors, FL 33305
954/ 566-8223 866/ 682-7456
www.wiltonmanorsinn.com

Clientele: men
Type: b&b; small, clothing-optional b&b in center of the gay area of Fort Lauderdale; lots of gay businesses w/in 3 blks
Owned/ Run By: gay men
Rooms: 3
Baths: private

Meals: cont'l brkfst
Amenities: pool, outdoor hot tub, WiFi
Kids: no
Pets: no
Smoking: no (inside & out)
Rates: $75-125
AC: 20%

The New Zealand House B&B T&G
Fort Lauderdale

908 NE 15th Ave
Fort Lauderdale, FL 33304
954/ 523-7829 888/ 234-5494
www.newzealandhouse.com

Clientele: men
Type: guesthouse; Key West-style
Owned/ Run By: gay men
Rooms: 8
Baths: private
Wheelchair Access: yes, 1 rm

Meals: cont'l brkfst
Amenities: pool, massage, WiFi
Kids: no
Pets: welcome
Smoking: ok
Rates: $99-165

Orton Terrace
Fort Lauderdale

606 Orton Ave
Fort Lauderdale, FL 33304
954/ 566-5068 800/ 323-1142
www.ortonterrace.com

Clientele: men
Type: guesthouse; 1- & 2-bdrm apts; heated, clothing-optional pool; tropical landscaping; free DSL internet access
Owned/ Run By: gay men
Rooms: 13
Baths: private

Wheelchair Access: yes
Meals: cont'l brkfst
Kids: boys over 14 yrs welcome
Pets: cats & small dogs welcome
Smoking: ok
Rates: $84-345
AC: 10%

Pineapple Point Guest House T&G
Fort Lauderdale

315 NE 16th Terr
Fort Lauderdale, FL 33301

954/ 527-0094
888/ 844-7295

info@pineapplepoint.com
www.pineapplepoint.com

Clientele: men
Type: guesthouse; luxurious accommodations in private & secure Old Florida compound; located in the heart of Fort Lauderdale's gay section; *Out & About* 5-Palm Rating
Owned/ Run By: gay men
Nearby Attractions: Las Olas Blvd & world-class shopping, Miami Beach, gay beaches, nightlife & fine restaurants
Transit: 10 minutes to Fort Lauderdale Int'l
Rooms: 21 (includes deluxe 1 & 2-bdrm suites) total, 4 suites, kings, 1 twin, A/C, color TV, DVD/ VCR, cable, ceiling fan, deck, phone, kitchenette (4), refrigerator, safer sex supplies, maid service, abundance of luxury amenities
Baths: private, bathtubs, showers, robes, hairdryers
Wheelchair Access: yes, 1 rm
Meals: expanded cont'l brkfst, meals delivered or catered by outside caterers
Amenities: pool, outdoor hot tub, massage, DVDs/ videos, gym, WiFi, snacks, cocktails, sunset drinks, coffee/ tea, guest computer, 10-man spa, complimentary happy hour, complimentary bikes; clothing-optional around heated pool & spa
Reservations: required; online or by telephone *Deposit:* required, 50%, due at booking, personal check ok *Cancellation:* cancel by 2 weeks prior
Payment: cash, travelers checks, Visa, Amex, MC

Season: open yr-round *High season:* Dec-April
Rates: $215-449
AC: 10%

Palm Plaza Resort

2801 Rio Mar St
Fort Lauderdale, FL 33304

954/ 260-6568
877/ 707-5588

Fort Lauderdale

palmplazaresort@aol.com
www.palmplazaresort.com

Our beautiful tropical garden with outdoor tables, swing, and chaises is the perfect place to sit, relax, and socialize, while lounging in the sun and listening to our music mixes. The clothing-optional heated swimming pool is never closed. Outdoor gas BBQ for easy cookouts. We are steps from Fort Lauderdale's beach and popular gay section.

Complimentary WiFi hotspot connections throughout our resort for your laptop.

Our attractive, air-conditioned accommodations (+ fans) come with daily complimentary breakfast baskets. Our well-equipped hotel rooms feature color TV, digital cable with 9 HBO channels, CD/DVD/VCR, telephone (voicemail and data port), refrigerator, coffeemaker, microwave; studios also include full kitchens; and our large 1-bedroom suites include a spacious living room and a second TV. Central icemaker, washer and dryer, off-street parking.

Your host is the Greek manager Georgios.

Clientele: men

Type: resort; w/ beautiful tropical garden, steps from the gay beach; suites & studios w/ kitchens; heated clothing-optional pool

Owned/ Run By: gay men

Nearby Attractions: 30 miles to South Beach; 4 blks to gay beach; close to mall, restaurants, bars & shops

Transit: near public transit; 1 hr to West Palm Beach airport; 50 minutes to Miami airport; 15 minutes to Fort Lauderdale

Rooms: 14 (includes 6 suites, 4 studios & 4 rooms) total, A/C, color TV, DVD/ VCR, cable, ceiling fan, deck, phone (w/ voicemail & data port), refrigerator, maid service, free local calls; suites & studios have full kitchen & rms have refrigerator, microwave, coffeemaker

Baths: private, bathtubs, showers

Meals: expanded cont'l brkfst

Amenities: laundry, DVDs/ videos, WiFi, coffee/ tea, clothing-optional heated pool, outdoor gas bbq, hammock, DVD/ video CD/ music CD/ MP3 CD player

Recreation: steps to Fort Lauderdale Beach: parasailing, boating, biking, water & jet skiing, gay beach; Intercoastal Waterway across street w/ water taxi

Kids: no

Pets: no

Smoking: ok

Reservations: required *Deposit:* required, 25% (1-night minimum), due at booking *Cancellation:* cancel by 2 weeks prior or forfeit deposit *Check in/ out:* 1pm/ 11am

Payment: cash, travelers checks, Visa, Amex, MC

Season: open yr-round *High season:* Dec-May

Rates: $89-179 *Discounts:* 1 night free for 3 or more paid nights; special weekly rates

The Royal Palms Resort ⚐

Fort Lauderdale

2901 Terramar St
Fort Lauderdale, FL 33304
954/ 564-6444 800/ 237-7256
info@royalpalms.com
www.royalpalms.com

Clientele: mostly men
Type: resort; rated one of the top gay accommodations in the US; winner of the 1994-2005 *Out & About* Editor's Choice & 1996-2006 5-Palm Award; winner of the 1993 City of Fort Lauderdale Beautification Award; winner of the 1997 & 2002 Award of Excellence from the City of Fort Lauderdale; recipient of the Superior Small Lodging 2005 White Glove Award; voted the 2006 PlanetOut Best Gay Resort in North America; "for those whose standards of exclusive luxury accommodations are higher than most"
Owned/ Run By: gay men
Transit: near public transit
Rooms: 12 total, 4 suites, 6 kings, 2 queens, A/C, color TV, DVD/ VCR, cable, ceiling fan, deck (3), phone, kitchenette (3), refrigerator, safer sex supplies, maid service, all rms are computer-accessible & have voicemail, safes & Bose CD players
Baths: private, showers, robes, hairdryers
Meals: expanded cont'l brkfst
Amenities: pool, poolside mist, hot tub, massage, DVDs/ videos, WiFi, snacks, cocktails, coffee/ tea, spa, sundeck, hammock, Lucy's Lounge guest bar, Guest Services Business Center w/ high-speed & wireless internet; nudity ok poolside
Smoking: no
Reservations: required *Deposit:* required, 1/3 reservation, due at booking, personal check ok *Cancellation:* cancel by 30 days prior (90 days prior Xmas & New Year's) or forfeit deposit *Minimum Stay:* 4 nights (in peak season) *Check in/ out:* 3pm/ 11am
Payment: cash, travelers checks, Visa, Amex, MC
Season: open yr-round *High season:* Dec 25 - April 30
Rates: $199-349
AC: 10%

Located right in the heart of Fort Lauderdale Beach, The Royal Palms is rated by travel experts as the #1 gay accommodation in North America.

Out & About, the gay travel experts, say, "This stunning 5-Palm property, and winner of a flock of Editor's Choice Awards, has us scampering eagerly south as often as we are allowed. The decor is delicious, the service exceptional and amenities without parallel in the gay guesthouse world."

Winner of the 1993 City of Fort Lauderdale Beautification Award and the 1997 and 2002 Award of Excellence . Also recipient of the 2005 Superior Small Lodging White Glove Award and named the Best Gay Resort in North America for 2006 by PlanetOut. You will be delighted and mesmerized with The Royal Palms "passion for perfection."

Andy Collins of Fodors Guide Books and *Travel & Leisure* says that The Royal Palms is "One of the nation's classiest gay resorts! The Royal Palms–and its charming owner, Richard Gray–set in motion Fort Lauderdale's emergence as Florida's premier gay playground."

The Royal Palms is a proud member of World's Foremost Gay & Lesbian Hotels (www.foremostgayhotels.com).

Villa Venice Resort

Fort Lauderdale

2900 Terramar St
Fort Lauderdale, FL 33304
954/ 564-7855 877/ 284-5522
villaven@bellsouth.net
www.villavenice.com

Clientele: men
Type: resort; Fort Lauderdale's newest premier men's resort, located just steps from our famous beaches
Owned/ Run By: gay men
Nearby Attractions: Las Olas riverfront, Jungle Queen, gay beach, shopping mall
Transit: near public transit; 15 minutes to airport; Yellow Cab: 954/ 777-7777
Rooms: 22 total, 9 suites, 8 kings, 5 queens, A/C, color TV, DVD/ VCR, cable, fireplace (8), deck, phone, kitchenette (9), refrigerator, safer sex supplies, maid service, all spacious & w/ tropical flavor
Baths: private, bathtubs, showers, robes
Wheelchair Access: yes, all rms
Meals: expanded cont'l brkfst
Amenities: office hrs: 8am-6pm; free parking, laundry, pool, poolside mist, outdoor hot tub, massage, DVDs/ videos, WiFi, snacks, sunset drinks, coffee/ tea, guest business center
Recreation: Fort Lauderdale beach
Kids: no
Pets: no
Smoking: no
Reservations: *Deposit:* required, 1/3 or 1 night, due at time of reservation *Cancellation:* cancel by 30 days in season (60 days holidays) or forfeit deposit *Minimum Stay:* 4 nights (high season) *Check in/ out:* 3pm/ 11am
Payment: cash, travelers checks, Visa, Amex, MC, Discover, Diners Club
Season: open yr-round *High season:* Dec 15th–April 15th
Rates: $149-455 *Discounts:* please inquire
AC: 10%

Where Leisure is elevated to an Artform–
Villa Venice Men's Resort has become, unquestionably, THE premier accommodation in Fort Lauderdale for the most discriminating gay travelers worldwide.

Located 2 blocks from the beach, Villa Venice offers 23 rooms and suites, artfully decorated in a tropical motif featuring Italian tile and marble baths. Each includes luxury linens, cable television, DVD/CD players (the DVD library is sure to please every man's viewing pleasure!), refrigerator, coffee bar, microwave, electronic safe, telephone with dataport, and individual climate control. Whether a Deluxe Room or the palatial Murano or Venetian Suites, be assured of only the highest caliber of furnishings, amenities, and ambience at Villa Venice!

Most rooms overlook a spacious courtyard featuring a clothing-optional waterfall-fed tropical pool, a 15-man Spa (available 24 hours), and exquisite landscaping with bubbling fountains, exotic orchids, and colorful birds. For the ultimate indulgence, the pool is heated in the cooler months and chilled during the warm ones. Poolside misters ensure total comfort.

Café Torino offers an exquisite continental breakfast, Guest Business Centre, a welcoming atmosphere to greet old friends and make new ones. During an occasional inclement day, curl up with a book from the library, enjoy some televison, and generally luxuriate--perhaps a game of cribbage or Monopoly--all are available at the Café! Bicycles are available to explore Fort Lauderdale by "pedal power"!

Sandra Lee Inn
Fort Lauderdale

2307 NE 33rd Ave
Fort Lauderdale, FL 33305
954/ 249-0565
www.sandraleeinn.com

Clientele: straight-friendly
Type: apts in 1960s-style motel; w/ full living rm, dining rm, kitchen; short walk to beach
Owned/ Run By: gay men
Rooms: 9

Baths: private
Amenities: pool
Kids: welcome
Pets: no
Smoking: no
Rates: $95-135

The Schubert Resort
Fort Lauderdale

855 NE 20th Ave
Fort Lauderdale, FL 33304
954/ 763-7434 866/ 763-7435
www.schubertresort.com

Clientele: men
Type: resort; "full-service gay resort in the heart of the city"
Owned/ Run By: gay men
Rooms: 31
Baths: private
Wheelchair Access: yes, 1 rm

Meals: expanded cont'l brkfst
Amenities: pool, outdoor hot tub, WiFi
Kids: no
Pets: no
Smoking: no
Rates: $99-299
AC: 15%

Sea Grape House Inn
Fort Lauderdale

1109 NE 16th Pl
Fort Lauderdale, FL 33305
954/ 525-6586 800/ 377-8802
www.seagrape.com

Clientele: mostly men
Type: b&b-inn; located in new gay epicenter of Wilton Manors; 2 clothing-optional pools, 7-man jacuzzi & gardens
Owned/ Run By: gay men
Rooms: 6
Baths: private & shared
Meals: cont'l brkfst

Amenities: laundry, pool, poolside mist outdoor hot tub, massage, WiFi
Kids: no
Pets: no
Smoking: no
Rates: $89-159
AC: 10%

Soberano Resort La Casa Del Mar
Fort Lauderdale

3003 Granada St
Fort Lauderdale, FL 33304

954/ 467-2037
866/ 467-2037

lacasadelmarbnb@hotmail.com
www.lacasadelmar.com

Clientele: mixed gay/ lesbian
Type: resort; Mediterranean villa only minutes from the beach; complete renovation in 2005
Owned/ Run By: gay men
Nearby Attractions: Las Olas Blvd, world-class shopping, Miami & South Beach, restaurants, bars & clubs
Transit: near public transit; 15 minutes to airport; taxi: Yellow Cab, 954/ 777-7777
Rooms: 13 total, 4 suites, 6 kings, 3 queens, A/C, color TV, DVD, cable, ceiling fan, deck, phone, kitchenette, refrigerator, safer sex supplies, maid service
Baths: private, bathtubs, showers, whirlpools, robes, hairdryers
Wheelchair Access: yes, 2 rms
Meals: cont'l brkfst
Amenities: office hrs: 9am-8pm; free parking, laundry, pool, massage, DVDs/ videos, WiFi, cocktails, coffee/ tea
Recreation: beach, snorkeling, parks, trails
Kids: no
Pets: no

Smoking: no
Reservations: required *Deposit:* required, 50%, due at booking *Cancellation:* cancel by 1 week prior or forfeit deposit ($25 fee before 1 week) *Minimum Stay:* 3 nights (special events) *Check in/ out:* 3pm/ 11am

Payment: cash, travelers checks, Visa, Amex MC, Discover
Season: open yr-round *High season:* Nov-May
Rates: $79-199 *Discounts:* specials
AC: 10%

The Worthington Guest House [M·G] Fort Lauderdale

543 N Birch Rd
Fort Lauderdale, FL 33304

954/ 563-6819
800/ 445-7036

info@theworthington.com
www.theworthington.com

The Worthington is one of Fort Lauderdale's most popular all-male, clothing-optional resorts on the beach, and we are proud to be an international host to the gay community.

Spend your day relaxing in our sun-kissed courtyard while meeting new friends and enjoying music that suits all tastes. Start your day with a calming morning music mix, and then as the day progresses, enjoy an eclectic mix from the '80s and '90s up through today's latest remixes. And don't forget the evening cocktail parties on Fridays, Saturdays, and Sundays–a perfect setting in which to meet fellow guests and make new friends.

Whether feeling fun and frisky or romantic and affectionate, The Worthington offers the perfect atmosphere for all. Our sparkling heated pool and 12-man Jacuzzi are open 24 hours for your total enjoyment. And our large private courtyard allows you to sit back and take in the overall beauty of our tropical palms, exotic flowers, and soothing fountains.

Clientele: men

Type: resort; an enticing, intimate men's resort; just steps from the ocean in the heart of Fort Lauderdale's gay beach district

Owned/ Run By: gay men

Nearby Attractions: Los Olas Blvd, Galleria Mall, Sebastian Gay Beach

Transit: near public transit; 10 minutes to airport; taxi: Yellow Cab, 954/ 777-7777

Rooms: 15 total, 3 suites, kings, A/C, color TV, DVD/ VCR, cable, ceiling fan, phone, kitchenette (5), refrigerator, safer sex supplies, maid service, down comforters, CD stereo, safe, pool views, all recently redecorated

Baths: private, showers

Meals: expanded cont'l brkfst

Amenities: office hrs: 8am-10pm; free parking, laundry, DVDs/ videos, snacks, cocktails, sunset drinks, coffee/ tea, 24hr heated swimming pool & 12-man hot tub

Recreation: beach

Kids: no

Pets: no

Smoking: no

Reservations: recommended *Deposit:* required, 33-50%, due at booking, personal check ok *Cancellation:* cancel by 14 days prior (60 days holidays/ Xmas/ New Year's) or forfeit $25 *Minimum Stay:* 3 nights (holidays) *Check in/ out:* 3pm/ noon

Payment: cash, travelers checks, Visa, Amex, MC, Discover

Season: open yr-round *High season:* Dec-May

Rates: $119-250 *Discounts:* return guests, referrals

AC: 10%

Sheraton Yankee Trader Beach Hotel

Fort Lauderdale

321 N Fort Lauderdale Beach Blvd
Fort Lauderdale, FL 33304
954/ 467-1111   888/ 627-7109
www.sheratontrader.com

Clientele: gay-friendly
Type: hotel
Rooms: 457

Baths: private
Rates: $230+

The Westin Fort Lauderdale

Fort Lauderdale

400 Corporate Dr
Fort Lauderdale, FL 33334

954/ 772-1331
800/ 937-8461

cypre@westin.com
www.westin.com/fortlauderdale

Clientele: gay-friendly
Type: hotel; all rms feature the "Heavenly Bed & Bath"; "conveniently located near the best gay beaches, dining & nightlife in South Florida"
Owned/ Run By: gay & straight
Nearby Attractions: Broward Center for the Performing Arts, Wilton Manors/ Five Points, Galleria Mall, Office Depot Center; over 100 gay-owned/ run businesses w/in 6 miles
Transit: near public transit; 9 miles to Fort Lauderdale airport; shuttle: Tri-County Airport Express, 954/ 561-8888
Rooms: 293 total, 13 suites, 111 kings, 145 fulls, A/C, color TV, cable, phone, rm service, maid service
Baths: private, showers, robes, hairdryers
Wheelchair Access: yes, 14 rms
Meals: full brkfst, special meals available on request
Amenities: pool, sauna, outdoor hot tub, DVDs/ videos, health club use, fitness rm, jogging trail
Recreation: 6 miles to Las Olas riverfront; 5 miles to Sebastian Beach; 2 miles to Mills

Pond Park & Palm Aire Country Club (5 golf courses & 38 tennis courts)
Kids: welcome
Pets: up to 15 lbs welcome
Smoking: no
Reservations: required *Cancellation:* cancel by 1 day prior or forfeit 1 night *Check in/ out:* 3pm/ 1pm

Payment: cash, travelers checks, personal checks, Visa, Amex, MC, Discover
Season: open yr-round *High season:* Oct-March
Rates: $109-259
AC: 10%

Windamar Beach Resort

Fort Lauderdale

543 Breakers Ave
Fort Lauderdale, FL 33304-4129
954/ 561-0039   866/ 554-6816
www.windamar.com

Clientele: mostly men
Type: guesthouse; small, clean, quiet & friendly; just steps to the ocean
Owned/ Run By: gay men
Rooms: 15
Baths: private
Meals: cont'l brkfst

Amenities: free parking, laundry, pool, hot tub, massage, DVDs/ videos, WiFi
Kids: no
Pets: welcome
Smoking: ok in certain rms
Rates: $99-329
AC: 10%

The Hibiscus House B&B

Fort Myers

2135 McGregor Blvd
Fort Myers, FL 33901
239/ 332-2651
www.thehibiscushouse.net

Clientele: gay-friendly
Type: b&b; "nestled between the Edison-Ford Winter Estate & the Old Fort Myers Downtown area"
Owned/ Run By: straights
Rooms: 5

Baths: private
Wheelchair Access: yes, 1 rm
Kids: 5 yrs & up welcome
Smoking: no

Holiday Inn Gulfside
Fort Myers

6890 Estero Blvd
Fort Myers Beach, FL 33931
239/ 463-5711 800/ 690-9350
www.ichotelsgroup.com/h/d/hi/
1/en/hd/fmybe

Clientele: gay-friendly
Type: resort; beachfront; 1 mile N of Lovers Key State Park
Owned/ Run By: gay & straight
Rooms: 103
Baths: private
Wheelchair Access: yes, 4 rms

Meals: coffee/tea only
Kids: welcome
Pets: no
Smoking: ok
Rates: $69-249
AC: 10%

Lighthouse Resort Inn & Suites
Fort Myers

1051 5th St
Fort Myers Beach, FL 33931
239/ 463-9392 800/ 778-7748
www.lighthouseislandresort.com

Clientele: gay-friendly
Type: resort; across the street from Fort Myers beach; 2 heated pools; also Tiki Bar & Grill restaurant
Rooms: 82
Baths: private

Wheelchair Access: yes
Amenities: pool, WiFi
Kids: welcome
Pets: please call first
Rates: $52-135
AC: 5%

Grady House
High Springs

420 NW 1st Ave
High Springs, FL 32655
386/ 454-2206
www.gradyhouse.com

Clientele: gay-friendly
Type: b&b; in historic 1917 Craftsman home; w/ extensive gardens w/ koi pond
Rooms: 6 (including 2-bdrm cottage)
Baths: private

Meals: full brkfst
Kids: 8 yrs & up welcome
Pets: no
Smoking: no (outside only)
Rates: $90-210

Camp David
Inverness

2000 S Bishop's Point Rd
Inverness, FL 34450
352/ 344-3445
www.campdavidflorida.com

Clientele: men
Type: campground; 16-acre RV & tent retreat; private membership, all male, clothing-optional; shallow pool; massage (in winter); characteristic of central FL landscape: containing 3 small lakes & heavily wooded

Amenities: free parking, laundry, hot tub, DVDs/ videos
Kids: no
Pets: welcome; must be on leash & picked up after (RV & tent only)
Smoking: ok
Rates: $22+

Casa Morada
Islamorada

136 Madeira Rd
Islamorada, FL 33036
305/ 664-0044 888/ 881-3030
www.casamorada.com

Clientele: gay-friendly
Type: resort; all-suite intimate hotel, tucked away on quiet side street; offers luxury-style service in beautiful Islamorada; close to shopping, state parks & great restaurants; w/ private island w/ pool & gazebo
Owned/ Run By: woman
Rooms: 16

Baths: private
Meals: cont'l brkfst
Amenities: free parking, laundry, pool, hot tub, massage, DVDs/ videos
Kids: welcome
Pets: friendly dogs welcome
Smoking: ok
Rates: $209-659
AC: 10%

Lookout Lodge Resort
Islamorada

87770 Overseas Hwy, mile marker 88
Islamorada, FL 33036
305/ 852-9915 800/ 870-1772
www.LookoutLodge.com

Clientele: gay-friendly
Type: resort; intimate waterfront resort; all suites & studios w/ kitchenettes
Owned/ Run By: straights
Rooms: 10
Baths: private

Kids: welcome; under 25 yrs must be accompanied by guardian
Pets: welcome; 3 pets maximum on property at any time
Smoking: ok
Rates: $79-375

Hilton Garden Inn Jacksonville JTB/ Deerwood Park   *Jacksonville*

9745 Gate Pkwy
Jacksonville, FL 32246
904/ 997-6600 877/ 782-9444
www.jacksonvillejtbdeerpark.gardeninn.com

Clientele: gay-friendly
Type: hotel; surrounded by 25 restaurants, bars & movie theater; shopping w/in walking distance; 15 minutes to beach & downtown Jacksonville
Owned/ Run By: gay & straight
Rooms: 119
Baths: private

Wheelchair Access: yes
Amenities: free parking, laundry, pool, hot tub, gym, WiFi
Kids: welcome
Pets: no
Smoking: ok
Rates: $79-149
AC: 10%

Spring Hill Suites Jacksonville   *Jacksonville*

4385 Southside Blvd
Jacksonville, FL
904/ 997-6650 888/ 287-9400
www.marriott.com/JAXSH

Clientele: gay-friendly
Type: hotel; spacious studio suite rms w/ fridge, microwave; 25 restaurants w/in walking distance; movie theater next door
Owned/ Run By: gay & straight
Rooms: 102
Baths: private

Wheelchair Access: yes, 10 rms
Amenities: free parking, laundry, pool, hot tub
Kids: welcome
Smoking: ok
Rates: $89-114
AC: 10%

Alexander Palms Court   *Key West*

715 South St
Key West, FL 33040
305/ 296-6413 800/ 858-1943
www.alexanderpalms.com

Clientele: gay-friendly
Type: guesthouse; charming & affordable accommodations in a tropical setting
Owned/ Run By: gay men
Rooms: 12 (includes 3 efficiencies)
Baths: private

Amenities: pool, outdoor hot tub
Kids: welcome
Pets: no
Rates: $90-300
AC: 10%

Alexander's Guest House   *Key West*

1118 Fleming St
Key West, FL 33040
305/ 294-9919 800/ 654-9919
www.alexghouse.com

Clientele: mixed gay/ lesbian
Type: b&b-inn; Alexander's has been awarded *Out & About* magazine's Editor's Choice award
Owned/ Run By: gay man
Rooms: 17
Baths: private

Wheelchair Access: yes, 1 rm
Meals: expanded cont'l brkfst
Amenities: pool, outdoor hot tub, WiFi
Smoking: ok
Rates: $105-340
AC: 10%

Andrews Inn   *Key West*

Zero Whalton Ln
Key West, FL 33040
305/ 294-7730 888/ 263-7393
www.andrewsinn.com

Clientele: gay-friendly
Type: b&b-inn; perfectly located: just steps from the legendary Duval St, yet set back in a tranquil, tropical courtyard
Owned/ Run By: straights
Rooms: 10
Baths: private

Meals: expanded cont'l brkfst
Amenities: free parking, pool, hot tub, WiFi
Kids: welcome in cottages
Pets: welcome in cottages
Smoking: no
Rates: $125-199
AC: 10%

Author's Key West   *Key West*

725 White St
Key West, FL 33040
305/ 294-7381 800/ 898-6909
www.authorskeywest.com

Clientele: gay-friendly
Type: guesthouse; private, tropical, lush & inviting; entrance on Petronia
Rooms: 12
Baths: private
Meals: expanded cont'l brkfst

Kids: no
Pets: no
Smoking: no
Rates: $85-150
AC: 10%

Coral Tree Inn/ Oasis/ Coconut Grove Guest House

817 & 822 & 823 Fleming St   305/ 296-2131   oasisct@aol.com
Key West, FL 33040   800/ 362-7477   www.keywest-allmale.com

Come explore the comforts and conveniences that make the Oasis the most sought-after all-male guesthouse on the island; 20 immaculate rooms, handsome tropically landscaped grounds, a 24-man hot tub, and an instantly responsive staff. An easy camaraderie is a specialty of the house. Fellow guests grow into friends.

Across the street from the Oasis and the Coconut Grove is the Coral Tree–a fine hotel in its services–a guesthouse in its 11-room intimacy–and it is unrivalled on the island or perhaps the world. Located just a few blocks from the excitements of Duval Street, this all-male inn is an ideal base for both adventure and relaxation.

Now we've added the completely renovated Coconut Grove Guest House with 17 more rooms! An adjoining oasis with pool, Jacuzzi, flat-screen TV, wireless internet, and our Presidential Suite.

Enjoy the facilities of all 3 resorts.

"We only compete with ourselves."

Clientele: men

Type: b&b-inn; expansive sundecks; extensive amenities; warm & friendly; "after all these yrs, still Key West's most sought-after all-male clothing-optional gay guesthouse"

Owned/ Run By: gay men

Nearby Attractions: gay bars & restaurants just 5 blks away

Pickup Service: airport pickup; $38 (round trip)

Transit: near public transit

Rooms: 48 total, 4 suites, 24 kings, 8 queens, 4 fulls, 7 twins, A/C, color TV, DVD/

VCR, cable, ceiling fan, deck, phone, refrigerator, safer sex supplies, maid service, in-rm wall safe

Baths: private, bathtubs, showers, whirlpools, hairdryers

Wheelchair Access: yes, 1 rm

Meals: expanded cont'l brkfst

Amenities: laundry, pool, DVDs/ videos, WiFi, sunset drinks, coffee/ tea, 24-man hot tub, sunset hors d'oeuvres; nudity ok poolside & sundeck

Kids: no

Pets: under 10 lbs welcome

Pets On Premises: 2 cats

Smoking: no

Reservations: required *Deposit:* required, 33%, due at time of booking *Cancellation:* cancel by 30 days in winter & 21 days in summer or forfeit 1/3 of stay *Minimum Stay:* holidays/ special events

Payment: cash, travelers checks, Visa, Amex, MC, Discover, Diners Club

Season: open yr-round *High season:* Dec 16–April 30

Rates: $129-289 *Discounts:* 10% weekly (off-season) for 7 night stays

AC: 10%

Big Ruby's Guesthouse   *Key West*

409 Appelrouth Ln
Key West, FL 33040-6534
305/ 296-2323 800/ 477-7829
www.bigrubys.com

Clientele: mostly men
Type: guesthouse; secluded tropical paradise; friendly, exclusively gay
Owned/ Run By: gay men
Rooms: 17
Baths: private & shared
Wheelchair Access: yes, 2 rms
Meals: full brkfst

Amenities: free parking, laundry, pool, hot tub, massage, DVDs/ videos, gym, WiFi
Kids: no
Pets: welcome
Smoking: ok
Rates: $112-549
AC: 10%

Blue Parrot Inn   *Key West*

916 Elizabeth St
Key West, FL 33040
305/ 296-0033 800/ 231-2473
www.blueparrotinn.com

Clientele: gay-friendly
Type: b&b-inn; beautifully restored 1884 Bahamian Home; gingerbread balconies, lush tropical gardens, heated pool; immaculate, quiet & tasteful
Owned/ Run By: gay men
Rooms: 10

Baths: private
Wheelchair Access: yes, 1 rm
Meals: expanded cont'l brkfst
Smoking: ok
Rates: $85-180
AC: 10%

Casa de Luces   *Key West*

422 Amelia St
Key West, FL 33040
305/ 296-3993 800/ 432-4849
www.casadeluces.com

Clientele: gay-friendly
Type: b&b-inn; built in the early 1800s, this historic inn has rms & suites all w/ private entrances along the wraparound veranda
Owned/ Run By: straights
Rooms: 8
Baths: private & shared

Wheelchair Access: yes, 2 rms
Amenities: free parking, hot tub, massage
Kids: welcome
Smoking: ok
Rates: $99-269
AC: 10%

Chelsea House   *Key West*

707 Truman Ave
Key West, FL 33040
305/ 296-2211 800/ 845-8859
www.chelseahousekw.com

Clientele: mixed gay/ straight
Type: guesthouse; restored 19th-c 2-story Victorian home only 2 blks from famous Duval St
Owned/ Run By: gay men
Rooms: 21
Baths: private

Wheelchair Access: yes, 1 rm
Meals: expanded cont'l brkfst
Pets: welcome; $15 per night
Rates: $84-275
AC: 10%

Curry House   *Key West*

806 Fleming St
Key West, FL 33040
305/ 294-6777 800/ 633-7439
www.curryhousekeywest.com

Clientele: mixed gay/ straight
Type: b&b; comfortable beds, friendly staff, great home-cooked brkfsts
Owned/ Run By: straights
Rooms: 9
Baths: private & shared

Meals: full brkfst
Kids: no
Pets: no
Smoking: no (outside only)
Rates: $110-245
AC: 10%

Cypress House & Guest Studios   *Key West*

601 Caroline
Key West, FL 33040
305/ 294-6969 800/ 525-2488
www.cypresshousekw.com

Clientele: gay-friendly
Type: b&b-inn; enjoy the friendly, relaxed comfort of our historic inn; only steps away from the scenic harbor, Duval St, major attractions & nightlife; all welcome
Owned/ Run By: gay & straight
Rooms: 22
Baths: private & shared

Wheelchair Access: yes, 1 rm
Meals: expanded cont'l brkfst
Amenities: pool, outdoor hot tub
Kids: no
Pets: no
Rates: $120-360
AC: 10%

Eaton Lodge

Key West

511 Eaton St
Key West, FL 33040
305/ 292-2170 800/ 294-2170
www.eatonlodge.com

Clientele: gay-friendly
Type: b&b-inn; 1886 mansion, carriage house & Conch house; all adjacent to Duval St
Owned/ Run By: gay/ lesbian & straight

Rooms: 16
Baths: private
Amenities: pool, outdoor hot tub
Rates: $115-325
AC: 10%

Equator Guest House

Key West

818 Fleming St
Key West, FL 33040

305/ 294-7775
800/ 278-4552

www.equatorresort.com

Clientele: men
Type: guesthouse; upscale plush tropical hideaway in the middle of "Guest House Row"; brand-new interiors & exteriors; clothing-optional; complimentary brkfst & happy hour
Owned/ Run By: gay men
Nearby Attractions: near Hemingway House, Little White House, aquarium, lighthouse, Mallory Square, Maritime Museum, Dick Dock, Duval St
Transit: 5 minutes to airport
Rooms: 12 total, 1 suite, 7 kings, 2 queens, 2 fulls, A/C, color TV, DVD/ VCR, cable, wetbar (3), ceiling fan, deck (2), phone, kitchenette (3), refrigerator, safer sex supplies, maid service, also all-tile flrs, low-voltage lighting, cathedral ceilings, feather pillows, voicemail, in-rm movies
Baths: private, showers, whirlpools, robes, hairdryers
Wheelchair Access: yes, 1 rm
Meals: expanded cont'l brkfst
Amenities: laundry, outdoor hot tub, massage, DVDs/ videos, WiFi, snacks, cocktails, sunset drinks, coffee/ tea, heated black pool, sunning garden

Kids: no
Pets: no
Smoking: no
Reservations: *Deposit:* required, 35%, due at booking, personal check ok *Cancellation:* cancel by 2 weeks prior or forfeit deposit *Minimum Stay:* 3 nights (wknds) *Check in/ out:* 2pm/ 11am

Payment: cash, travelers checks, Visa, Amex, MC, Discover, personal checks ok for deposit if recv'd 3 weeks prior
Season: open yr-round *High season:* Jan-April
Rates: $120-237 *Discounts:* 7 & 14 days
AC: 10%

Heartbreak Hotel

Key West

716 Duval St
Key West, FL 33040
305/ 296-5558
www.heartbreakhotel.org

Clientele: mixed gay/ lesbian
Type: hotel; located in Duval Street's gay district; newly renovated, immaculately clean rms w/ fully equipped kitchens; walk to everything
Owned/ Run By: lesbians/ gay men

Rooms: 6
Baths: private
Kids: no
Pets: no
Smoking: ok
Rates: $43-199

Key West Harbor Inn B&B

Key West

219 Elizabeth St
Key West, FL 33040
305/ 296-2978 800/ 608-6569
www.keywestharborinn.com

Clientele: mixed gay/ straight
Type: guesthouse; beautiful home in the heart of Old Town; next to the harbor & 2 blks to Duval St
Owned/ Run By: gay & straight
Rooms: 14
Baths: private

Wheelchair Access: yes, 1 rm
Meals: expanded cont'l brkfst
Amenities: pool, hot tub
Smoking: no
Rates: $115-400
AC: 15%

Knowles House B&B   *Key West*

1004 Eaton St
Key West, FL 33040
305/ 296-8132 800/ 352-4414
www.knowleshouse.com

Clientele: mixed gay/ straight
Type: b&b; intimate, elegantly decorated, historic home w/ clothing-optional sundeck, heated pool; friendly, attentive staff offers exceptional personal service
Owned/ Run By: gay men
Rooms: 8
Baths: private

Meals: expanded cont'l brkfst
Amenities: pool, outdoor hot tub
Kids: no
Pets: no
Smoking: no
Rates: $109-229
AC: 10%

La Te Da   *Key West*

1125 Duval St
Key West, FL 33040
305/ 296-6706 877/ 528-3320
www.lateda.com

Clientele: mixed gay/ straight
Type: hotel; in the heart of Old Town, complete w/ its own cabaret, theater & gourmet restaurant
Owned/ Run By: gay men
Rooms: 15
Baths: private

Wheelchair Access: yes, 1 rm
Meals: full brkfst
Kids: no
Pets: no
Smoking: no
Rates: $100-310
AC: 10%

Lightbourn Inn   *Key West*

907 Truman Ave
Key West, FL 33040
305/ 296-5152 800/ 352-6011
www.lightbourn.com

Clientele: mixed gay/ straight
Type: b&b-inn; award-winning, historic Victorian; newly restored; elegance of a bygone era w/ comforts expected today
Owned/ Run By: gay men
Rooms: 10
Baths: private

Meals: expanded cont'l brkfst
Kids: 15 yrs & up welcome
Pets: no
Smoking: no
Rates: $98-328
AC: 10%

Marquesa Hotel   *Key West*

600 Fleming St
Key West, FL 33040
305/ 292-1919 800/ 869-4631
www.marquesa.com

Clientele: gay-friendly
Type: hotel; small luxury hotel w/ tropical courtyard surrounding 2 pools; 4 Diamond award for 15 yrs
Owned/ Run By: gay & straight
Rooms: 27

Baths: private
Wheelchair Access: yes, 1 rm
Kids: 12 yrs & up welcome
Smoking: ok
Rates: $175-430
AC: 10%

The Mermaid & the Alligator   *Key West*

729 Truman Ave
Key West, FL 33040
305/ 294-1894 800/ 773-1894
www.kwmermaid.com

Clientele: mixed gay/ straight
Type: b&b-inn; "Key West's finest traditional b&b"; located in heart of Old Town; walking distance to world-famous Duval St
Owned/ Run By: gay men
Rooms: 9
Baths: private

Meals: full brkfst
Amenities: free parking, pool, WiFi
Kids: 16 yrs & up welcome
Pets: no
Smoking: no
Rates: $128-278
AC: 10%

Nassau House   *Key West*

1016 Fleming St
Key West, FL 33040
305/ 296-8513 800/ 296-8513
www.nassauhouse.com

Clientele: gay-friendly
Type: b&b-inn; wonderful example of Conch architecture, built in 1894; fully restored in 2004 to feature 9 lovely rms & suites on 3 flrs; 5 blks to Duval St
Owned/ Run By: gay men
Rooms: 9
Baths: private

Wheelchair Access: yes, 1 rm
Amenities: free parking, pool, outdoor hot tub, massage
Kids: 15 yrs & up welcome
Pets: no
Smoking: no
Rates: $109-199
AC: 10%

Island House [TAG]   *Key West*

1129 Fleming St   305/ 294-6284   IHKeyWest@aol.com
Key West, FL 33040   800/ 890-6284   www.islandhousekeywest.com

Island House is an award-winning gay resort in Old Town Key West, set in a completely secure private compound where the choice to wear something, or nothing at all, is yours. Our large heated pool and Jacuzzi are open 24 hours a day. Our cafe serves breakfast, lunch, and dinner poolside, as well as beer, wine, and cocktails.

All of our rooms have luxurious feather beds, CD players, a color TV/VCR with cable service, air-conditioning with ceiling fan, direct-dial phone with data ports, a security safe, and a refrigerator.

Our new health club includes a complete gym with machines, free weights, and cardio equipment. There is a changing room with lockers, a shower and dressing area, sauna, steam room, and Jacuzzi. The Health Club is free for Island House guests and is open day and night

Island House was recently named "The best gay men's resort in the world" by *Out Traveler* magazine.

Clientele: men

Type: resort; private, enclosed compound w/ sauna, gym, steam rm, video rm & cafe; clothing-optional

Owned/ Run By: gay men

Transit: near public transit; 10 minutes to airport

Rooms: 34 total, 3 suites, 4 kings, 21 queens, 6 fulls, A/C, color TV, DVD/ VCR, cable, wetbar (12), ceiling fan, phone, kitchenette (13), refrigerator, safer sex supplies, rm service, maid service, feather beds, data ports, high-speed internet, in-rm safes

Baths: private & shared, showers, hairdryers

Wheelchair Access: yes, 1 rm

Amenities: office hrs: 24hrs; free parking, pool, poolside mist, sauna, indoor & outdoor hot tub, massage, DVDs/ videos, gym, sunset drinks, coffee/ tea, health club, gym (free weights, machines, aerobic equipment), steam rm, erotic video rm

Kids: no

Pets: under 20 lbs welcome

Pets On Premises: cats

Smoking: no

Reservations: required *Deposit:* required, varies *Cancellation:* cancel by 15 days prior or forfeit deposit *Minimum Stay:* holidays & special events *Check in/ out:* 2pm/ 11am

Payment: cash, travelers checks, Visa, Amex, MC, Discover, Diners Club

Season: open yr-round *High season:* Dec-April

Rates: $79-419   *Discounts:* military, students

AC: 10%

Pearl's Rainbow

Key West

525 United St
Key West, FL 33040
305/ 292-1450
800/ 749-6696
www.pearlsrainbow.com

Clientele: women
Type: resort; Key West's distinctive resort for women; a rambling historic guesthouse amid lush tropical vegetation
Owned/ Run By: lesbians
Nearby Attractions: 2 blks from Southernmost Point in cont'l US; 1 blk to Duval St, Atlantic Ocean, Butterfly Conservatory, Old Town Trolley stop; walking distance to all attractions
Transit: near public transit; 10 minutes from airport; taxi: Maxi Taxi, 305/ 296-6666
Rooms: 38 total, 5 suites, 6 kings, 32 queens, A/C, color TV, cable, ceiling fan, deck, phone, kitchenette, refrigerator, rm service, maid service, eclectic decor
Baths: private, bathtubs, showers, hairdryers
Wheelchair Access: yes, 1 rm
Meals: light cont'l brkfst
Amenities: office hrs: 9am-10pm; pool, poolside mist, outdoor hot tub, massage, WiFi, coffee/ tea, some free parking, concierge, poolside bar, restaurant sundeck; nudity ok
Recreation: biking, sailing, snorkeling, scuba diving, fishing, parasailing, golf & tennis
Kids: no
Pets: welcome in some rms; please inquire
Pets On Premises: some outdoor cats
Smoking: no
Reservations: required; online booking available at www.pearlsrainbow.com *Deposit:* required, 50%, due at booking, personal check ok *Cancellation:* cancel by 15 days prior (30 days holidays) or forfeit deposit *Minimum Stay:* 2 nights (wknds)/ 3 nights (long wknds)/ 5 nights (holidays & special events) *Check in/ out:* 2pm/ 11am
Payment: cash, travelers checks, Visa, Amex, MC, Discover
Season: open yr-round *High season:* Dec-April
Rates: $99-379 *Discounts:* for long-term stays & frequent guests
AC: 10%

At the quiet end of Duval Street, steps away from the Atlantic, you'll find Pearl's Rainbow, the only guesthouse in paradise designed especially for women. Like Key West, it's lush, relaxing, comfortable, and historic, from our award-winning, renovated main building–a cigar factory built in 1889–to our quaint cigar-makers' cottages, to our newest building, the former Surf Motel from 1950.

With two pools, two outdoor spas, on-site massage, concierge service, wireless internet access, Pearl's Patio bar and The Strand restaurant, Pearl's is a full-service resort. We offer 38 rooms and suites to suit a variety of budgets, all with private bath, cable TV, air conditioning, hairdryers–all the amenities you'd find in any hotel. But what you won't find anywhere else is the warm welcome of our friendly staff and a relaxed environment created for women in America's Caribbean.

Winner, 2005 *Out & About* Editor's Choice Award; Winner, 2005 *Out Traveler* Reader's Choice for Best Lesbian Property; Member, World's Foremost Gay & Lesbian Hotels.

Pier House Resort & Caribbean Spa

Key West

1 Duval St
Key West, FL 33040
305/ 296-4600 800/ 327-8340
www.pierhouse.com

Clientele: mixed gay/ straight
Type: resort; located on the Gulf of Mexico in the heart of Old Town; 4 bars, 3 restaurants, private beach, spa & fitness center
Rooms: 142
Baths: private

Wheelchair Access: yes, 5 rms
Amenities: laundry, pool, sauna, outdoor hot tub, massage, DVDs/ videos
Kids: under 18 accompanied by an adult
Smoking: no
Rates: $200-1,800
AC: 10%

Sheraton Suites Key West

Key West

2001 S Roosevelt Blvd
Key West, FL 33040
305/ 292-9800 800/ 452-3224

Clientele: gay-friendly
Type: resort; Key West's only all-suite hotel; across from Smather's Beach, the island's only natural beach, walk to many water sports; free shuttle to downtown & airport
Owned/ Run By: straights
Rooms: 180
Baths: private

Wheelchair Access: yes, 10 rms
Amenities: laundry, pool, outdoor hot tub
Kids: welcome; must be accompanied by an adult; 17 yrs & under stay free
Smoking: ok
Rates: $179-349
AC: 10%

Simonton Court Historic Inn & Cottages

Key West

320 Simonton St
Key West, FL 33040
305/ 294-6386 800/ 944-2687
www.simontoncourt.com

Clientele: gay-friendly
Type: b&b-inn; romantic, secluded, 26-unit compound built in 1880s close to everything in town; also cottages
Owned/ Run By: gay/ lesbian & straight
Rooms: 26
Baths: private

Meals: expanded cont'l brkfst
Amenities: 4 pools, hot tub, massage
Kids: no
Pets: no
Smoking: ok
Rates: $150-540
AC: 10%

Sunset Motel

Lakeland

2301 New Tampa Hwy
Lakeland, FL 33815
863/ 683-6464

Clientele: gay-friendly
Type: motel; also apts & private home; all sharing 3 acres; near Disney World, Busch Gardens, Bok Tower
Owned/ Run By: gay man
Rooms: 23

Baths: private
Wheelchair Access: yes, 1 rm
Pets: welcome w/ owner; 100% + fee
Smoking: ok
Rates: $55-100
AC: 15%

Swan Park Inn B&B

Lakeland

118 E Park St
Lakeland, FL 33803-1328
863/ 248-2235 888/ 211-1671
www.swan-park-inn.com

Clientele: mixed gay/ straight
Type: remodeled 1915 Four Square in historic district; totally barrier-free access on 1st flr & grounds for patrons w/ disabilities; clothing-optional pool/ spa; near Tampa/ Orlando attractions
Owned/ Run By: gay men
Rooms: 3
Baths: private & shared

Wheelchair Access: yes, 1 rm
Meals: full brkfst
Amenities: free parking, pool, outdoor hot tub, massage, DVDs/ videos
Kids: no
Pets: service animals only
Smoking: no
Rates: $95-150

The Mystic Lake Manor

Madison

2398 W US90
Madison, FL 32340
850/ 973-8435
www.mysticlakemanor.com

Clientele: mostly men
Type: b&b-inn; also 4 RV hookups
Owned/ Run By: gay men
Rooms: 10
Baths: private & shared
Wheelchair Access: yes, 1 rm
Meals: full brkfst

Amenities: free parking, pool, indoor hot tub, DVDs/ videos
Kids: no
Pets: no
Smoking: ok
Rates: $40-85

Tropical Cottages   *Marathon*

243 61st St Gulf
Marathon, FL 33050
305/ 743-6048
www.tropicalcottages.com

Clientele: mixed gay/ straight
Type: cottage; quiet vintage motorcourt-style resort; 11 campsites; near kayaking/ diving/ sailing adventures
Owned/ Run By: gay men
Rooms: 11
Baths: private

Wheelchair Access: yes, 2 rms
Amenities: free parking, laundry, outdoor hot tub, massage, DVDs/ videos
Pets: welcome
Smoking: no
Rates: $99-150+11.5% tax
AC: 10%

Beach Bungalow   *Melbourne*

312 Wavecrest Ave
Indialantic by the Sea, FL 32903
321/ 984-1330
www.1stBeach.com

Clientele: gay-friendly
Type: rental home; beachfront villas w/ private patios & inground spas
Owned/ Run By: straights
Rooms: 3 (2-bdrm villas)
Baths: private

Amenities: outdoor hot tub
Kids: welcome
Pets: dogs welcome
Smoking: ok (nonsmoking rms available)
Rates: $1,400-1,500/wk

Crane Creek Inn B&B   *Melbourne*

907 E Melbourne Ave
Melbourne, FL 32901
321/ 768-6416
www.cranecreekinn.com

Clientele: gay-friendly
Type: b&b-inn; waterfront; near downtown's fine shops & restaurants
Owned/ Run By: straights
Rooms: 5
Baths: private
Meals: full brkfst

Amenities: free parking, pool, outdoor hot tub, WiFi
Kids: no
Pets: dogs welcome
Smoking: no
Rates: $139-199
AC: 10%

Miami River Inn   *Miami*

118 SW S River Dr
Miami, FL 33130
305/ 325-0045 800/ 468-3589
www.miamiriverinn.com

Clientele: gay-friendly
Type: Miami's only b&b located in the ethnically diverse Miami River neighborhood of East Little Havana; 4 three-story cottages decorated w/ period antiques
Owned/ Run By: woman
Rooms: 40
Baths: private & shared

Wheelchair Access: yes, 3 rms
Meals: cont'l brkfst
Amenities: laundry, pool, hot tub
Kids: welcome; 12 yrs & under free w/ accompanying adult
Pets: welcome
Rates: $89-199
AC: 10%

The AAA Shelborne Beach Resort—South Beach   *Miami Beach*

1801 Collins Ave
Miami Beach, FL 33139
305/ 531-1271 800/ 327-8757
www.shelborne.com

Clientele: gay-friendly
Type: resort; full-service, first-class hotel, featuring new guest rms & executive suites; located in the Art Deco District of South Beach, directly on the ocean
Owned/ Run By: straights
Rooms: 200
Baths: private

Wheelchair Access: yes, 1 rm
Amenities: free parking, laundry, pool, sauna, outdoor hot tub
Kids: welcome
Pets: no
Smoking: ok
Rates: $145-300
AC: 10%

Aqua Hotel & Lounge   *Miami Beach*

1530 Collins Ave
Miami Beach, FL 33139
305/ 538-4361
www.aquamiami.com

Clientele: mixed gay/ straight
Type: hotel; *The Jetsons* meets *Jaws* in this new, cheap & chic hotel
Owned/ Run By: gay & straight
Rooms: 50
Baths: private
Meals: expanded cont'l brkfst

Amenities: laundry, pool, hot tub, massage
Kids: welcome
Pets: welcome; $10/ day per pet
Smoking: ok
Rates: $95-395
AC: 10%

Beachcomber Hotel
Miami Beach

1340 Collins Ave
Miami Beach, FL 33139
305/ 531-3755 888/ 305-4683
www.beachcombermiami.com

Clientele: gay-friendly
Type: hotel; art deco in the heart of South Beach; recently renovated; modern style w/ art deco details
Owned/ Run By: gay & straight
Rooms: 29
Baths: private

Wheelchair Access: yes, 1 rm
Meals: cont'l brkfst
Kids: welcome
Pets: no
Smoking: no
Rates: $65-140
AC: 10%

The Cardozo Hotel
Miami Beach

1300 Ocean Dr
Miami Beach, FL 33139
305/ 535-6500 800/ 782-6500
www.cardozohotel.com

Clientele: gay-friendly
Type: hotel; elegantly restored 1939 deco landmark; well-appointed guest rms & suites; on the beach in the heart of South Beach; walk to nightlife, restaurants & shopping
Rooms: 43
Baths: private

Wheelchair Access: yes, 2 rms
Kids: welcome; must be accompanied by an adult
Pets: no
Smoking: ok
Rates: $160-460
AC: 10%

The Century
Miami Beach

140 Ocean Dr
Miami Beach, FL 33139
305/ 674-8855 888/ 982-3688
www.centurysouthbeach.com

Clientele: gay-friendly
Type: hotel; designed in 1939 & highly regarded for its alluring charm & exceptional service; aura of casual elegance
Rooms: 31

Baths: private
Meals: expanded cont'l brkfst
Kids: welcome
Smoking: ok
Rates: $80-195
AC: 10%

Circa 39
Miami Beach

3900 Collins Ave
Miami Beach, FL 33140

305/ 538-4900
877/ 824-7223

www.circa39.com

Clientele: mixed gay/ straight
Type: hotel; near beaches, South Beach & Ocean Drive; art deco hotel built in 1939, formerly Copley Plaza; in-house bistro & massage cabanas; hip & romantic, stylish & chic
Owned/ Run By: gay & straight
Nearby Attractions: Key West, Parrot Jungle, Everglades, aquarium, Vizcaya, Art Deco District
Transit: near public transit; 15 minutes to airport
Rooms: 86 total, 15 suites, 27 kings, 25 queens, 4 fulls, 15 twins, A/C, DVD/ VCR, cable, phone, kitchenette, refrigerator
Baths: private, bathtubs, showers, robes, hairdryers
Wheelchair Access: yes, 10 rms
Meals: full brkfst
Amenities: free parking, laundry, pool, massage, gym, WiFi, coffee/ tea, bar & bistro
Recreation: beach, golf course, scuba diving, water sports
Kids: welcome

Pets: welcome
Smoking: no
Reservations: *Cancellation:* cancel by 2 days prior *Check in/ out:* noon
Payment: cash, travelers checks, Visa, Amex, MC

Season: open yr-round *High season:* winter months
Rates: $95-395
AC: 10%

The Colony Hotel
Miami Beach

736 Ocean Dr
Miami Beach, FL 33139
305/ 673-0088 800/ 226-5669
colonymiami.com

Clientele: gay-friendly
Type: hotel; oceanfront art deco accommodations; in the heart of South Beach on Ocean Dr
Owned/ Run By: gay/ lesbian & straight
Rooms: 50
Baths: private

Wheelchair Access: yes, 3 rms
Meals: cont'l brkfst
Kids: welcome
Smoking: ok
Rates: $129-256
AC: 10%

Delano Hotel
Miami Beach

1685 Collins Ave
Miami Beach, FL 33139
305/ 672-2000 800/ 697-1791
www.delanohotelmiamibeach.com

Type: resort; hip hotel designed by Philippe Starck; great bar scene (see & be seen)
Rooms: 208
Baths: private
Wheelchair Access: yes, 20 rms

Kids: welcome
Smoking: ok
Rates: $350-950
AC: 10%

Delores Guesthouse
Miami Beach

1420 Collins Ave
Miami Beach, FL 33139
305/ 673-0800
www.hoteldelores.com

Clientele: mixed gay/ straight
Type: guesthouse; stay in the heart of South Beach; 1 blk from the ocean & w/in walking distance of world-famous nightclubs & restaurants
Owned/ Run By: gay & straight
Rooms: 27

Meals: coffee/tea only
Kids: welcome
Pets: welcome
Smoking: ok
Rates: $60-115
AC: 10-15%

The European Guesthouse
Miami Beach

721 Michigan Ave
Miami Beach, FL 33139
305/ 673-6665
www.europeanguesthouse.com

Clientele: mixed gay/ lesbian
Type: b&b; tropical garden w/ bar; 2 sundecks, jacuzzi; close to beaches, bars & restaurants
Owned/ Run By: gay men
Rooms: 12
Baths: private & shared

Meals: full brkfst
Amenities: outdoor hot tub
Kids: no
Pets: no
Rates: $99-199
AC: 10%-15%

Golden Tulip Casablanca Hotel (now called New Casablanca)
Miami Beach

6345 Collins Ave
Miami Beach, FL 33141
305/ 868-0010 800/ 813-6676
www.casablancaontheocean.com

Clientele: mixed gay/ straight
Type: hotel; located in the heart of Millionaires Row, directly on the beach
Owned/ Run By: gay & straight
Rooms: 150
Baths: private
Wheelchair Access: yes, 3 rms

Kids: welcome
Pets: no
Smoking: ok
Rates: $99-187
AC: 10-15%

The Hotel
Miami Beach

801 Collins Ave
Miami Beach, FL 33139
305/ 531-2222 877/ 843-4683
www.thehotelofsouthbeach.com

Clientele: gay-friendly
Type: hotel; South Beach gem w/ an interior redesign by designer Todd Oldham; rooftop pool; restaurant & bar; fitness studio

Rooms: 52
Baths: private
Rates: $255-425

Island House Miami Beach

Miami Beach

82nd St
Miami Beach, FL

305/ 864–2422
800/ 382–2422

www.islandhousesouthbeach.com

Clientele: mixed gay/ lesbian
Type: guesthouse; rms, studios & suites; our original location is just off the beaten track; tropical, intimate setting; nude sunbathing permitted
Nearby Attractions: 10 minutes to South Beach & gay nightlife
Transit: near public transit; 25 minutes to Miami or Fort Lauderdale airport
Rooms: 7 (includes 4 studios) total, 2 suites, 3 kings, 5 queens, A/C, color TV, DVD/ VCR, cable, ceiling fan, phone, refrigerator, maid service
Baths: private, bathtubs, showers, hairdryers
Meals: coffee/tea only
Amenities: office hrs: 9am-6pm; free parking, laundry, hot tub, massage, free local calls; nudity ok while sunbathing
Recreation: 5 minutes to Haulover gay nude beach; 4 blks to North Shore State Rec Area
Pets: no
Smoking: no

Reservations: recommended *Deposit:* required, 50%, due at booking, personal check ok *Cancellation:* cancel by 2 weeks prior *Minimum Stay:* holidays & special events *Check in/ out:* 2pm/ 11am

Payment: cash, travelers checks, Visa, Amex, MC, Discover, Diners Club
Season: open yr-round *High season:* Dec-April
Rates: $49-239 *Discounts:* airline
AC: 10%

Island House South Beach

Miami Beach

1428 Collins Ave
Miami Beach, FL 33139

305/ 864–2422
800/ 382–2422

ihsobe@bellsouth.net
www.islandhousesouthbeach.com

Clientele: men
Type: guesthouse; South Beach's largest gay guesthouse
Nearby Attractions: in the heart of the Art Deco Historical District: walk to all bars, restaurants & shops
Transit: near public transit; 35 minutes to Fort Lauderdale airport; 15 minutes to Miami Airport
Rooms: 26 (includes 10 studios) total, 1 suite, 11 kings, 17 queens, 7 fulls, A/C, color TV, cable, wetbar (11), ceiling fan (13), phone, kitchenette (11), refrigerator (20), maid service
Baths: private & shared, bathtubs, showers, hairdryers
Meals: full brkfst
Amenities: office hrs: 9am-11pm; massage, wknd & holiday happy hour
Recreation: 2 blks to Lincoln Rd Mall; 1 blk to the beach & Ocean Dr
Pets: no
Smoking: ok (nonsmoking rms available)

Reservations: recommended *Deposit:* required, 50%, due at booking, personal check ok *Cancellation:* cancel by 2 weeks prior *Minimum Stay:* holidays & special events *Check in/ out:* 2pm/ 11am

Payment: cash, travelers checks, Visa, Amex, MC, Discover, Diners Club
Season: open yr-round *High season:* Dec-April
Rates: $49-239 *Discounts:* airline, military
AC: 10%

Hotel Astor
Miami Beach

956 Washington Ave
Miami Beach, FL 33139
305/ 531-8081 800/ 270-4981
www.hotelastor.com

Clientele: gay-friendly
Type: hotel; "a South Beach jewel from its inception, the Hotel Astor was designed to be a truly unique, service-oriented, chic & intimate property for discerning corporate & leisure travelers"
Owned/ Run By: man

Rooms: 40
Baths: private
Wheelchair Access: yes, 2 rms
Kids: welcome
Smoking: ok
Rates: $125-900
AC: 10%

Hotel Nash
Miami Beach

1120 Collins Ave
Miami Beach, FL 33139
305/ 674-7800 800/ 403-6274
www.hotelnash.com

Clientele: gay-friendly
Type: hotel; "South Beach's premier boutique hotel"; "masterfully reconfigured by Peter Page"; 1 blk to beach
Rooms: 50
Baths: private
Wheelchair Access: yes, 3 rms

Meals: cont'l brkfst
Kids: welcome
Pets: no
Smoking: no
Rates: $155-1,400
AC: 10%

Hotel Ocean
Miami Beach

1230-38 Ocean Dr
Miami Beach, FL 33139
305/ 672-2579 800/ 783-1725
www.hotelocean.com

Clientele: mixed gay/ straight
Type: hotel; small, pet-friendly, luxury hotel, 21st-c amenities w/ the timeless European tradition of service; exquisite, sound-proofed suites w/ ocean views
Owned/ Run By: straights
Rooms: 27
Baths: private

Wheelchair Access: yes, 1 rm
Meals: cont'l brkfst
Amenities: hot tub, massage, DVDs/ videos
Kids: welcome
Pets: welcome; no large cats
Smoking: ok
Rates: $199-750
AC: 10%

Hotel Shelley
Miami Beach

844 Collins Ave
Miami Beach, FL 33139
305/ 531-3341
www.hotelshelley.com

Clientele: mixed gay/ straight
Type: hotel; 1930s renovated art deco hotel in the heart of South Beach; w/in walking distance to all the hot spots of SoBe
Owned/ Run By: gay & straight
Rooms: 50
Baths: private

Wheelchair Access: yes, 2 rms
Meals: expanded cont'l brkfst
Kids: welcome
Pets: no
Smoking: ok
Rates: $89-249
AC: 10%

The Indian Creek Hotel
Miami Beach

2727 Indian Creek Dr
Miami Beach, FL 33140
305/ 531-2727 800/ 491-2772
www.indiancreekhotel.com

Clientele: gay-friendly
Type: hotel; quaint retreat where a European boutique hotel meets a Key West guesthouse
Owned/ Run By: straights
Rooms: 61
Baths: private

Wheelchair Access: yes, 2 rms
Meals: cont'l brkfst
Kids: welcome
Smoking: ok
Rates: $89-299
AC: 10%

The Kent
Miami Beach

1131 Collins Ave
Miami Beach, FL 33139
305/ 604-5068 866/ 826-5368
www.thekenthotel.com

Clientele: mixed gay/ straight
Type: hotel; original art deco property w/ charm & style; clean & spacious rms w/ original bath tiling; great personal service
Owned/ Run By: gay/ lesbian & straight
Rooms: 54
Baths: private

Wheelchair Access: yes, 4 rms
Kids: welcome
Pets: welcome; $75 minimum fee (nonrefundable)
Rates: $79+
AC: 10%

The Loft Hotel
Miami Beach

952 Collins Ave
Miami Beach, FL 33139
305/ 534–2244
www.thelofthotel.com

Clientele: mixed gay/ straight
Type: world-class boutique hotel; recently renovated & featuring distinctive European styling; in the heart of South Beach Art Deco District; lush, tropical courtyard; 1 blk to beach
Owned/ Run By: gay & straight

Rooms: 20 (includes junior suites)
Baths: private
Kids: welcome
Pets: small pets welcome; $10 deposit daily
Smoking: ok
Rates: $99+

Marlin Hotel
Miami Beach

1200 Collins Ave
Miami Beach, FL 33139
305/ 604–3595
www.marlinhotel.com

Clientele: mixed gay/ straight
Type: hotel; art deco gem; one of the original restored properties on South Beach
Owned/ Run By: gay/ lesbian & straight
Rooms: 13

Baths: private
Kids: welcome
Pets: welcome; $150 minimum fee (nonrefundable)
Rates: $175–1,100
AC: 10%

The Nassau Suite Hotel
Miami Beach

1414 Collins Ave
Miami Beach, FL 33139
305/ 532–0043 866/ 859–4177
www.nassausuite.com

Clientele: mixed gay/ straight
Type: hotel; beautiful art deco all-suite; over-sized spaces w/ full kitchen in each unit; parking on-site
Owned/ Run By: gay/ lesbian & straight
Rooms: 22 (suites)
Baths: private

Meals: cont'l brkfst
Kids: welcome
Pets: no
Smoking: no
Rates: $109-290
AC: 10%

The National Hotel
Miami Beach

1677 Collins Ave
Miami Beach, FL 33139
305/ 532–2311 800/ 327–8370
www.nationalhotel.com

Type: resort; oceanfront luxury art deco hotel w/ spectacular gourmet restaurant & 5-star amenities (205-ft-long infinity pool, poolside massage, etc); located in South Beach
Rooms: 136

Baths: private
Wheelchair Access: yes, 8 rms
Kids: welcome
Smoking: ok
Rates: $255-450
AC: 10%

Ocean Surf Hotel
Miami Beach

7436 Ocean Terrace
Miami Beach, FL 33141
305/ 866–1648 800/ 555–0411
www.theoceansurfhotel.com

Clientele: gay-friendly
Type: hotel; boutique-style art deco hotel; located on a secluded stretch of sand in quiet & uncrowded North Beach...an intimate escape from hectic South Beach!
Owned/ Run By: straights
Rooms: 49
Baths: private

Wheelchair Access: yes, 2 rms
Meals: cont'l brkfst
Kids: welcome
Pets: no
Smoking: ok (in restricted areas)
Rates: $80-150
AC: 10%

The Pelican
Miami Beach

826 Ocean Dr
Miami Beach, FL 33139
305/ 673–3373 800/ 773–5422
www.pelicanhotel.com

Clientele: mixed gay/ straight
Type: hotel; funky yet deluxe oceanfront property; w/ eclectic theme rms designed by Diesel Jeans, including James Bond penthouses
Owned/ Run By: straights
Rooms: 32

Baths: private
Kids: welcome
Smoking: ok
Rates: $135-430
AC: 10%

The Raleigh, Miami Beach   *Miami Beach*

1775 Collins Ave
Miami Beach, FL 33139
305/ 534-6300 800/ 848-1775
www.raleighhotel.com

Clientele: gay-friendly
Type: hotel; restored classic art deco; w/ "Florida's most beautiful swimming pool," restaurant & several bars (great martinis)
Rooms: 104
Baths: private

Wheelchair Access: yes, 4 rms
Kids: welcome
Pets: small pets welcome
Smoking: ok
Rates: $225-550
AC: 10%

Royal South Beach   *Miami Beach*

758 Washington Ave
Miami Beach, FL 33139
305/ 673-9009 888/ 394-6835
www.royalsouthbeach.com

Clientele: mixed gay/ straight
Type: hotel; "funkadelic" 1930s hotel restored to retro fabulousness & infused w/ 21st-century amenities by Jordan Mozer; flat-screen TVs, digital safes, internet, kitchenettes; in heart of gay Deco District
Owned/ Run By: gay & straight

Rooms: 40
Baths: private
Wheelchair Access: yes, 2 rms
Kids: welcome
Pets: no
Smoking: ok
Rates: $119+
AC: 10%

SoBeYou   *Miami Beach*

1018 Jefferson Ave
Miami Beach, FL 33139

305/ 534-5247
877/ 599-5247

www.sobeyou.us

Clientele: mixed gay/ straight
Type: b&b; all rms face lush tropical pool & garden; "the service & pampering of a 5-star hotel w/out the 5-star prices"
Owned/ Run By: lesbians
Nearby Attractions: Ocean Dr, Lincoln Rd Mall, Wolfsonian Museum, Parrot Jungle, New World Symphony
Transit: 15 minutes to Miami Int'l; 30 minutes to Ft Lauderdale airport; 5 minutes to Port of Miami; 1 blk to bus line
Rooms: 10 total, 2 suites, 7 kings, 3 queens, A/C, color TV, DVD/ VCR, cable, ceiling fan, phone, refrigerator, maid service, CD players, iron & ironing boards, luxurious pima cotton linens, towels & robes
Baths: private & shared, bathtubs, showers, robes, hairdryers
Wheelchair Access: yes, 3 rms
Meals: full brkfst
Amenities: free parking, pool, jacuzzi, massage, DVDs/ videos, WiFi
Recreation: next to park (public pool & tennis courts); beautiful sunny beaches
Kids: welcome

Pets: welcome
Smoking: no
Reservations: required *Cancellation:* cancel by 1 week prior *Check in/ out:* 3pm/ noon

Payment: cash, travelers checks, Visa, Amex, MC
Season: open yr-round
Rates: $105-325 *Discounts:* stays of 1 week or longer
AC: 10%

Adora Inn   *Mt Dora*

352/ 383-0633

Clientele: mixed gay/ straight
Type: b&b-inn; renovated historic home; boutique hotel-style rms; in historic town; gourmet dinner available
Owned/ Run By: gay men
Rooms: 5
Baths: private
Amenities: free parking, massage

Meals: full brkfst
Kids: over 5 yrs welcome
Pets: no
Smoking: no
Rates: $135-225 (mention Damron for discount)
AC: please inquire

Night Swan B&B
New Smyrna Beach

512 S Riverside Dr
New Smyrna Beach, FL 32168
386/ 423-4940 800/ 465-4261
www.nightswan.com

Clientele: gay-friendly
Type: b&b; in 3-story 1906 home; on the Intracoastal Waterway
Owned/ Run By: straights
Rooms: 15
Baths: private
Wheelchair Access: yes, all rms

Meals: full brkfst
Kids: welcome
Pets: please call first
Smoking: ok (nonsmoking rms available)
Rates: $100-200

Clarion Hotel Universal
Orlando

7299 Universal Blvd
Orlando, FL 32819
407/ 351-5009 800/ 445-7299
www.clarionuniversal.com

Clientele: gay-friendly
Type: hotel; full-service; just outside Universal Studios
Rooms: 300
Baths: private
Wheelchair Access: yes

Kids: welcome
Pets: no
Smoking: ok (some nonsmoking rms)
Rates: $69-119

Embassy Suites Orlando Downtown
Orlando

191 E Pine St
Orlando, FL 32801
407/ 841-1000 800/ 362-2779
embassyorlandodowntown.com

Clientele: gay-friendly
Type: hotel; all-suite; close to trendy Thornton Park
Rooms: 167
Baths: private
Wheelchair Access: yes

Meals: full brkfst
Kids: welcome
Pets: no
Smoking: ok (some nonsmoking rms)
Rates: $119-169

Grand Bohemian Hotel Orlando
Orlando

325 S Orange Ave
Orlando, FL 32801
407/ 313-9000 866/ 663-0024
www.grandbohemianhotel.com

Clientele: gay-friendly
Type: luxury hotel in downtown Orlando; 24hr fitness center, restaurant, lounge & Starbucks
Rooms: 250
Baths: private
Wheelchair Access: yes

Kids: welcome
Pets: no
Smoking: ok (some nonsmoking rms)
Rates: $129-209

Holiday Villas
Orlando

2928 Vineland Rd
Kissimmee, FL 34746
407/ 397-0700 800/ 344-3959
www.holidayvillas.com

Clientele: gay-friendly
Type: condo; 2- & 3-bdrm fully equipped luxury villas; just 5 miles from Walt Disney World; great for families & couples traveling together
Owned/ Run By: straights
Rooms: 260

Baths: private
Amenities: free parking, laundry, pool, sauna, outdoor hot tub, DVDs/ videos
Kids: welcome
Smoking: ok
Rates: $99-249
AC: 10%

Parliament House Motor Inn
Orlando

410 N Orange Blossom Tr
Orlando, FL 32805
407/ 425-7571
www.parliamenthouse.com

Clientele: mostly men
Type: resort; the world's largest gay resort w/ 5 bars on premises
Owned/ Run By: gay men
Rooms: 127
Baths: private

Meals: full brkfst
Smoking: ok
Rates: $64-104 + tax
AC: 10% (billable after checkout)

Sheraton Studio City T+G

Orlando

5905 International Dr
Orlando, FL 32819

407/ 351-2100
800/ 327-1366

reservations@sheratonstudiocity.com
www.sheratonstudiocity.com

Clientele: gay-friendly
Type: hotel; world-class amenities are combined w/ the elegance & sophisticated excitement of 1940s & 1950s Hollywood
Owned/ Run By: gay & straight
Nearby Attractions: Universal Studios Orlando, Wet 'N Wild Waterpark, Sea World of Florida, Belz Factory Outlet Mall
Transit: near public transit; 12 miles to Orlando Int'l; shuttle: Mears Transportation, 407/ 423-5566
Rooms: 301 total, 1 suite, 5 kings, 295 queens, A/C, color TV, cable, phone, rm service, maid service, extraordinary rms w/ distinctive art deco decor (most w/ 2 queen beds)
Baths: private, bathtubs, showers, hairdryers

Wheelchair Access: yes, 12 rms
Amenities: laundry, pool, poolside bar & cafe, game rm, car rental, complimentary transportation to all theme parks
Kids: welcome
Pets: no
Smoking: no
Reservations: required *Cancellation:* cancel by 3 days prior or forfeit 1 night *Check in/ out:* 3pm/ 11am
Payment: cash, travelers checks, Visa, Amex, MC, Discover
Season: open yr-round
Rates: $89-399
AC: 10%

The Perri House Inn

Orlando

10417 Vista Oaks Ct
Orlando, FL 32836

407/ 876-4830 800/ 780-4830
www.perrihouse.com

Clientele: gay-friendly
Type: b&b-inn; 3 miles from downtown Disney & 5 miles from The Magic Kingdom
Rooms: 8
Baths: private
Meals: cont'l brkfst
Amenities: free parking, pool, outdoor hot

tub
Kids: welcome
Smoking: ok (all bdrms nonsmoking rms)
Rates: $99-143

Rick's B&B

Orlando

PO Box 22318,
Orlando, FL 32830

407/ 396-7751 407/ 414-7751 (cell)
www.ricksbedandbreakfast.com

Clientele: mostly men
Type: b&b-private home; private, personal & upscale accommodations; adjacent to Walt Disney World, Orlando Convention Center, Universal Studios, Sea World & gay beaches
Owned/ Run By: gay man
Rooms: 2

Baths: private & shared
Meals: full brkfst
Amenities: free parking, laundry, pool, massage, DVDs/ videos, WiFi
Kids: no
Pets: no
Smoking: outside patio only
Rates: $150-350

The Winter Park Sweet Lodge

Orlando

271 S Orlando Ave
Winter Park, FL 32789

407/ 644-6099

Clientele: mixed gay/ straight
Type: motel; on Hwy 17/92 on bus route; walk to lake; close to fine dining, shopping, bars; 30 minutes to Disney World; 5 minutes to gay area
Owned/ Run By: gay men
Rooms: 12

Baths: private
Kids: welcome
Pets: no
Smoking: ok
Rates: $49-59/ night; $189-239/ week

Heart of Palm Beach

Palm Beach

160 Royal Palm Wy
Palm Beach, FL 33480
561/ 655-5600
800/ 521-4278 (reservations)
heartofpalmbeach.com

Clientele: gay-friendly
Type: hotel; on the Island of Palm Beach; w/ fresh-water pool, self-parking garage & restaurant; 1/2 blk from the ocean; full-service salon & spa
Rooms: 88
Baths: private

Wheelchair Access: yes
Meals: expanded cont'l brkfst
Kids: welcome
Pets: welcome
Rates: $99-299
AC: 10%

Beach Vacation Rentals

Panama City

770/ 569-9215
www.TheCapeEscape.com

Clientele: gay-friendly
Type: condo; pet-friendly townhouse; near pet-friendly beach on Florida panhandle
Owned/ Run By: straights
Rooms: 2
Baths: private

Amenities: free parking, laundry, pool, DVDs/ videos
Kids: welcome
Pets: well-behaved dogs welcome
Smoking: no
Rates: $700-1,300

Casa de Playa

Panama City

20304 Front Beach Rd
Panama City Beach, FL 32413
850/ 236-8436
casadeplayapcb@aol.com

Clientele: mixed gay/ lesbian
Type: guesthouse; w/ living & dining areas, full kitchen; private, secluded tropical paradise; sundecks & tropical gardens; steps from beach
Owned/ Run By: gay men
Rooms: 2

Baths: shared
Amenities: free parking, laundry, pool, outdoor hot tub, DVDs/ videos
Pets: no
Smoking: no
Rates: $150-175

Wisteria Inn

Panama City

20404 Front Beach Rd
Panama City Beach, FL 32413
850/ 234-0557
www.wisteria-inn.com

Clientele: mixed gay/ straight
Type: inn; secluded in a tropical setting; steps from the beach; beautifully furnished; limo & boat for cocktail cruises; enormous hot tub & heated pool
Owned/ Run By: straights
Rooms: 14
Baths: private
Meals: cont'l brkfst

Amenities: free parking, pool, poolside mist, outdoor hot tub
Kids: no
Pets: welcome; must be caged if puppies or prone to scratching or chewing when left alone
Smoking: no
Rates: $69-149
AC: 10%

The Cypress

Sarasota

621 Gulfstream Ave S
Sarasota, FL 34236
941/ 955-4683
www.cypressbb.com

Clientele: gay-friendly
Type: b&b; enjoy this charming Florida home overlooking beautiful Sarasota Bay
Owned/ Run By: lesbian & straight
Rooms: 4
Baths: private

Meals: full brkfst
Amenities: free parking, indoor hot tub
Kids: no
Pets: no
Smoking: no (ok on porches)
Rates: $150-260

Siesta Holidays

Sarasota

1017 Seaside Dr & 1011 Crescent St
Siesta Key, FL 34242
941/ 312-9882 800/ 720-6885
www.siestaholidays.com

Clientele: gay-friendly
Type: condo; 2 locations; lavish, colorful, fully furnished; just steps from world-famous Crescent Beach & a few blks from Sarasota's friendliest gay bars
Owned/ Run By: straights
Rooms: 9

Baths: private
Kids: welcome
Pets: no
Smoking: no
Rates: $475-1,425/ week
AC: 10%

Vera's Place
Sarasota

941/ 351-3171 941/ 359-8881

Clientele: men
Type: b&b-private home; w/ private entrance & patio for each rm; clothing-optional
Owned/ Run By: gay men
Rooms: 2
Baths: private

Meals: expanded cont'l brkfst
Amenities: free parking, laundry, pool, DVDs/ videos, WiFi
Pets: welcome
Smoking: covered patio only
Rates: $75-85
AC: 10%

Alexander Homestead
St Augustine

14 Sevilla St
St Augustine, FL 32084
904/ 826-4147 888/ 292-4147
www.alexanderhomestead.com

Clientele: gay-friendly
Type: b&b; Victorian inn in St Augustine's historic district
Owned/ Run By: straights
Rooms: 5
Baths: private

Meals: full brkfst
Kids: please call first
Pets: no
Smoking: no
Rates: $159-209

Casa Monica
St Augustine

95 Cordova St
St Augustine, FL 32084
904/ 827-1888 800/ 648-1888
www.casamonica.com

Clientele: gay-friendly
Type: resort; historic 1888 hotel, restored for $25 million in 2000; w/ upscale restaurant, piano bar, fitness center, spa, oceanfront beach club
Rooms: 138

Baths: private
Wheelchair Access: yes
Kids: welcome
Pets: please inquire
Smoking: ok (nonsmoking rms available)
Rates: $99-1,000

Eve's Web Guest House & Retreat
St Augustine

904/ 823-9660
www.evesweb.com

Clientele: mostly women
Type: guesthouse; retreat by the beach, in FL nature; "a truly peaceful refuge, surrounded by beautiful waters, between the ocean & intracoastal"
Owned/ Run By: lesbians
Rooms: 6 (2 bdrms)

Baths: shared
Meals: expanded cont'l brkfst
Amenities: free parking, laundry, hot tub, massage, DVDs/ videos
Kids: welcome
Smoking: no
Rates: $120/ night; $700/ week

Our House B&B
St Augustine

7 Cincinnati Ave
St Augustine, FL 32084
904/ 824-9204
www.ourhousestaugustine.com

Clientele: mixed gay/ straight
Type: b&b; in renovated Victorian home; located in antiques district; private verandas
Owned/ Run By: gay man
Rooms: 3
Baths: private

Meals: full brkfst
Amenities: free parking, WiFi
Kids: 14 yrs & up
Pets: no
Smoking: no (outside only)
Rates: $149-230

Saragossa Inn B&B
St Augustine

34 Saragossa St
St Augustine, FL 32084
904/ 808-7384 877/ 808-7384
www.saragossainn.com

Clientele: mixed gay/ straight
Type: b&b-inn; 1920 Craftsman-style bungalow located in the historic district; all w/ private entrances; full gourmet brkfst daily
Rooms: 6 (includes 2-bdrm suite)
Baths: private

Meals: full brkfst
Kids: 12 yrs & up welcome; please call first
Pets: no
Rates: $109-250
AC: 10%

Bay Palm Resort
St Petersburg

4237 Gulf Blvd
St Petersburg Beach, FL 33706
727/ 360-7642
www.baypalmresort.com

Clientele: gay-friendly
Type: motel
Owned/ Run By: gay men
Rooms: 14
Baths: private
Meals: coffee/tea only

Amenities: free parking, laundry, pool, WiFi
Kids: welcome
Pets: welcome
Smoking: no
Rates: $55-180

Berwin Oak Guesthouse
St Petersburg

5103 28th Ave S
Gulfport, FL 33707
727/ 321-4272
www.berwinoak-of-gulfport.com

Clientele: men
Type: guesthouse; comprised of 3 furnished apts; tropical courtyard w/ deck, bar & hot tub; clothing-optional; exercise rm; DVD & VCR; coin-operated laundry
Owned/ Run By: gay men
Rooms: 3

Baths: private
Amenities: free parking, laundry, outdoor hot tub
Kids: no
Pets: welcome
Smoking: no
Rates: $300/ week; $800/ month

Boca Ciega B&B
St Petersburg

727/ 381-2755

Clientele: women
Type: b&b-private home; in quiet & safe neighborhood in sub-tropical setting near gay beaches, bars & businesses; minutes from sight-seeing, shopping, dining & entertainment
Owned/ Run By: lesbians

Rooms: 1
Baths: private
Meals: cont'l brkfst
Pets: no
Rates: $40-50

Changing Tides Cottages
St Petersburg

225 Boca Ciega Dr
Madeira Beach, FL 33708

727/ 397-7706

women@changingtidescottages.com
www.changingtidescottages.com

Clientele: mixed gay/ lesbian
Type: cottage; fully equipped, individual cottages on the harbor; decorated around theme of famous women; 1/2 blk to beach
Owned/ Run By: lesbian & straight
Nearby Attractions: outstanding restaurants & local bars
Transit: near public transit; 30 minutes to Tampa Int'l & St Petersburg
Rooms: 10 cottages (1- & 2-bdrm) total, A/C, color TV, DVD/ VCR (5), cable, ceiling fan, deck, phone, kitchenette, refrigerator, maid service
Baths: private, bathtubs, showers
Wheelchair Access: yes, 5 rms
Amenities: office hrs: 9am-7pm; free parking, courtyard, picnic tables, bbqs, bikes, boats
Recreation: beaches: diving, fishing, jet skiing, sight-seeing (sunsets), boating, powersailing; golf & tennis
Kids: please inquire
Pets: welcome; must be friendly

Pets On Premises: dog
Smoking: ok
Reservations: required *Deposit:* required, 50%, personal check ok *Cancellation:* cancel by 10 days prior or forfeit 3% *Check in/ out:* 10:30am/ 2:30pm

Payment: cash, travelers checks, personal checks, Visa, MC, Discover
Season: open yr-round *High season:* all year
Rates: $95-175

Dicken's House B&B
St Petersburg

335 8th Ave NE
St Petersburg, FL 33701
727/ 822-8622 800/ 381-2022
www.dickenshouse.com

Clientele: mixed gay/ straight
Type: b&b; 3-story 1912 Arts & Crafts home; preservation awards; Egyptian linens, business center
Owned/ Run By: gay man
Rooms: 5
Baths: private

Meals: full brkfst
Amenities: free parking, laundry, hot tub, DVDs/ videos, WiFi
Kids: 9 yrs & up welcome
Rates: $95-210
AC: 10%

Inn at the Bay B&B
St Petersburg

126 4th Ave NE
St Petersburg, FL 33701
727/ 822-1700 888/ 873-2122
www.innatthebay.com

Clientele: gay-friendly
Type: b&b-inn; king & queen feather beds (allergy-free), double whirlpool tubs
Owned/ Run By: straights
Rooms: 12
Baths: private
Wheelchair Access: yes, 1 rm

Meals: full brkfst
Amenities: free parking, hot tub
Kids: 12 yrs & up welcome
Pets: no
Smoking: no
Rates: $125-270
AC: 10%

Mansion House
St Petersburg

105 Fifth Ave NE
St Petersburg, FL 33701
727/ 821-9391 800/ 274-7520
www.mansionbandb.com

Clientele: gay-friendly
Type: b&b-inn; in heart of St Petersburg's Old Northeast; 5-15 minutes to Bay or beaches
Rooms: 12
Baths: private

Meals: full brkfst
Amenities: pool, hot tub
Kids: welcome
Pets: please inquire
Rates: $99-220
AC: 10%

Pass-A-Grille Beach Co-op
St Petersburg

709 Gulf Wy
St Pete Beach, FL 33706
727/ 367-4726
PAGBeachMotel@msn.com

Clientele: gay-friendly
Type: condo; fully furnished efficiency, 1- & 2-bdrm apts by the week or month; on beautiful Pass-A-Grille beach; 2-night minimum
Owned/ Run By: straights

Rooms: 15
Baths: private
Kids: welcome
Pets: small pets accepted in some units
Rates: $60-95

Sea Oats by the Gulf
St Petersburg

12625 Sunshine Lane
Treasure Island, FL 33706
727/ 367-7568 866/ 715-9595
www.flainns.com/seaoats

Clientele: gay-friendly
Type: motel; cozy efficiencies & 1- or 2-bdrm units w/ kitchens; on the Gulf of Mexico; walk to day-cruises, restaurants, shops, para-sailing & clubs
Owned/ Run By: straights
Rooms: 6
Baths: private

Wheelchair Access: yes, 4 rms
Meals: coffee/tea only
Kids: welcome
Pets: welcome; $30 fee (one-time charge)
Smoking: ok
Rates: $250-795/ week
AC: 10%

Twelve Oaks B&B
Tallahassee

984 Boston Hwy/ County Rd 149
Monticello, FL 32344
850/ 997-0333
www.12oaksresort.com

Clientele: mixed gay/ straight (mostly men)
Type: b&b; Victorian plantation b&b on private 6-acre complex; tennis court; clothing-optional
Owned/ Run By: gay/ lesbian & straight
Rooms: 9
Baths: private

Meals: full brkfst
Amenities: free parking, laundry, pool, outdoor hot tub, massage, DVDs/ videos
Kids: welcome
Pets: no
Smoking: ok
Rates: $85-150
AC: 10%

Suncoast Resort [T-IG]
St Petersburg

000 34th St S/ Hwy 19 S
t Petersburg, FL 33711

727/ 867-1111
www.suncoastresort.com

The Suncoast Resort is the world's largest all-gay resort and entertainment complex. You'll find 120 hotel rooms and suites, 6 bars (including a large dance bar, a leather/ Levi's cruise bar, a piano bar, a poolside tiki bar, a show bar with cabaret, and a large open porch bar), large convention facilities, a 30-store shopping mall, 9 tennis courts, 2 volleyball courts, 2 restaurants, a heated pool, and plenty of free on-site parking.

The resort features internationally famous recording artists and touring shows, lots of live entertainment every week, and the Sunday courtyard Tea Dance is packed with thousands of fun-seekers every Sunday all year.

The resort covers four city blocks and is only minutes from one of the top ten beaches in the world. Check out the website at www.suncoastresort.com. Call 727/ 867-1111 for reservations.

Clientele: mixed gay/ lesbian

Type: resort; world's largest all-gay resort & entertainment complex: 120 rms & suites, 6 bars, 2 restaurants, 9 tennis courts, 2 volleyball courts; also conference & convention facilities, heated pool & shopping center

Owned/ Run By: gay men

Transit: near public transit; 30 minutes to Tampa Airport; 20 minutes to St Petersburg Airport

Rooms: 120 total, 24 suites, 22 kings, 29 queens, 45 fulls, A/C, color TV, cable, wetbar (24), deck (24), phone, refrigerator (72), safer sex supplies, rm service, maid service, large deluxe rms; all suites w/ wet bar, microwave & refrigerator

Baths: private, bathtubs, showers

Wheelchair Access: yes, 2 rms

Meals: full brkfst, special meals available on request

Amenities: office hrs: 24hrs; free parking, pool, massage, coffee/ tea

Recreation: 1 1/2 hrs to Disney World; 30 minutes to Busch Gardens; only minutes to some of the finest beaches in the world

Smoking: ok

Reservations: *Deposit:* required, 1 night, due at booking, personal check ok *Cancellation:* cancel by 2 days prior *Minimum Stay:* varies (holidays only) *Check in/ out:* 3pm/ 11am

Payment: cash, travelers checks, Visa, MC

Season: open yr-round *High season:* all year

Rates: $49-89 *Discounts:* inquire; stays over 7 days

Gram's Place Hostel

Tampa

3109 N Ola Ave
Tampa, FL 33603
813/ 221-0596
www.Grams-Inn-Tampa.com

Clientele: mixed gay/ straight/ bi
Type: b&b; Tampa's only alternative lodging w/ music-themed rms; in the center of Tampa, 2 miles NW of historic Ybor City; clean & restful
Owned/ Run By: other
Rooms: 7

Baths: private & shared
Meals: cont'l brkfst
Kids: 10 yrs & up welcome
Pets: welcome in some rms w/ additional charge
Smoking: no
Rates: $22.50-68

Our Country Home

Tampa

813/ 388-3313

Clientele: mixed gay/ lesbian
Type: rental home; private home on 5 acres; near bike trails & canoeing
Owned/ Run By: gay men
Rooms: 2
Baths: private

Wheelchair Access: yes, 2 rms
Kids: no
Pets: welcome
Smoking: no
Rates: $400/ 3-day wknd

Sawmill Camping Resort

Tampa

21710 US Hwy 98
Dade City, FL 33523
352/ 583-0664
www.flsawmill.com

Clientele: mixed gay/ lesbian
Type: resort; all-gay clothing-optional camping (membership required); RV & tent sites (175), cabins (25), camping store; theme wknds w/ live entertainment
Owned/ Run By: gay men
Rooms: 25 (cabins)

Baths: private & shared
Wheelchair Access: yes, 1 rm
Meals: coffee/tea only
Kids: no
Pets: leashed & quiet welcome
Smoking: no
Rates: $10.25-129

Grandma Jean's B&B

Venice

PO Box 415
Laurel, FL 34272
305/ 394-7547
jprobinsky@yahoo.com

Clientele: mostly women
Type: b&b-private home
Owned/ Run By: woman
Rooms: 2
Baths: private
Meals: cont'l brkfst
Amenities: free parking, laundry, pool,

sauna, outdoor hot tub, DVDs/ videos
Kids: no
Pets: welcome
Smoking: no
Rates: $55-65

Camp Mars

Venus

326 Goff Rd
Venus, FL 33960
863/ 699-6277
www.campmars.com

Clientele: mostly men
Type: campground; cabins, tents, 50 RV hookups; all-gay clothing-optional campground 2 hrs from Fort Lauderdale & Miami
Owned/ Run By: gay men
Rooms: 8 (cabins)
Baths: private & shared

Meals: coffee/tea only
Kids: no
Pets: welcome; must be leashed at all time
Smoking: ok
Rates: $10-85
AC: 10%

Grandview Gardens B&B

West Palm Beach

1608 Lake Ave
West Palm Beach, FL 33401
561/ 833-9023
www.grandview-gardens.com

Clientele: gay-friendly
Type: b&b; historical 1923 Spanish-Mediterranean home nestled in tropical garden paradise; walking distance to downtown
Owned/ Run By: gay men
Rooms: 5

Baths: private
Wheelchair Access: yes, 1 rm
Meals: full brkfst
Kids: welcome
Pets: welcome; on request
Rates: $105-180
AC: 10%

Hibiscus House B&B
West Palm Beach

501 30th St
West Palm Beach, FL 33407
561/ 863-5633 800/ 203-4927
www.hibiscushouse.com

Clientele: mixed gay/ straight
Type: b&b-private home; rated by the *Miami Herald* as one of the 10 best in Florida; tropical elegance at its best
Owned/ Run By: gay men
Rooms: 7
Baths: private

Meals: full brkfst
Amenities: free parking, laundry, pool, hot tub, DVDs/ videos
Pets: by arrangement
Smoking: no
Rates: $95-270
AC: 10%

Scandia Lodge
West Palm Beach

625 S Federal Hwy
Lake Worth, FL 33460
561/ 586-3155
www.scandialodge.net

Clientele: mixed gay/ straight
Type: hotel; quality rms w/ personalized service; walk to downtown Lake Worth & the beach; 10-minute drive to West Palm Beach
Owned/ Run By: gay men
Rooms: 23

Baths: private
Wheelchair Access: yes, 11 rms
Pets: welcome
Smoking: no
Rates: $75-95

The Whimsy
West Palm Beach

561/ 686-1354

Clientele: women
Type: feminist/ women's land; camping, RV spaces (4), picnicking & 3-rm guesthouse; feminist-friendly men welcome
Owned/ Run By: lesbians

Wheelchair Access: yes
Kids: no
Pets: please inquire
Smoking: no
Rates: $seasonal/ sliding scale $25-65

Ranch House Motor Inn
Winter Haven

1911 Cypress Gardens Blvd
Winter Haven, FL 33884
863/ 324-5994 800/ 366-5996
www.ranchhousemotel.com

Clientele: gay-friendly
Type: motel; IHOP on premises
Rooms: 50
Baths: private
Wheelchair Access: yes
Kids: welcome

Pets: dogs & cats welcome
Smoking: ok (some nonsmoking rms)
Rates: $49-82

Ansley Inn B&B
Atlanta

253 15th St
Atlanta, GA 30309
404/ 872-9000 800/ 446-5416
www.ansleyinn.com

Clientele: mixed gay/ straight
Type: b&b-inn; an unrivaled blend of comfort & elegance; 1999 Best B&B of Atlanta
Rooms: 22
Baths: private
Meals: full brkfst

Amenities: free parking, hot tub, DVDs/ videos
Kids: well-behaved welcome
Pets: no
Smoking: no
Rates: $120-250
AC: 10%

The Georgian Terrace Hotel
Atlanta

659 Peachtree St
Atlanta, GA 30308
404/ 897-1991 800/ 555-8000
www.thegeorgianterrace.com

Clientele: gay-friendly
Type: hotel; historic luxury hotel; hosted the world premier reception for *Gone With the Wind* in 1939
Rooms: 319
Baths: private
Wheelchair Access: yes

Meals: coffee/tea only
Kids: welcome
Pets: companion animals welcome only
Smoking: ok
Rates: $119-299
AC: 10%

Glenn Hotel
Atlanta

110 Marietta St NW
Atlanta, GA 30303
404/ 521–2250 866/ 404–5366
www.glennhotel.com

Clientele: mixed gay/ straight
Type: boutique hotel, contemporary design; also restaurant & rooftop lounge
Rooms: 110
Baths: private
Wheelchair Access: yes, 6 rms

Amenities: gym, WiFi
Kids: welcome
Pets: welcome
Smoking: ok in smoking rms only

Hello B&B
Atlanta

1865 Windemere Dr
Atlanta, GA 30324
404/ 892–8111
members.aol.com/hellobnb

Clientele: mixed gay/ lesbian
Type: b&b; beautiful place in quiet, wooded neighborhood in heart of Atlanta; inside the gay hub
Owned/ Run By: gay men
Rooms: 7
Baths: private & shared

Meals: cont'l brkfst
Amenities: free parking, laundry, outdoor hot tub, massage, DVDs/ videos, WiFi
Kids: welcome
Smoking: no
Rates: $75-155
AC: 10%

Hill Street Resort B&B
Atlanta

729 Hill St SE
Atlanta, GA 30315
404/ 627–4281
www.hillstreetresort.com

Clientele: mixed gay/ straight
Type: b&b-private home
Owned/ Run By: gay men
Rooms: 4
Baths: private

Meals: full brkfst
Amenities: free parking, pool, poolside mist, outdoor hot tub
Rates: $109-129

In the Woods Campground & Resort
Atlanta

142 Casey Ct
Canon, GA 30520
706/ 246–9504
www.inthewoodscampground.com

Clientele: mostly men
Type: RV park; private-membership, clothing-optional; 1 hr to Atlanta; 36 campsites & 20+ RV hookups; located at GA Hwy 327 & GA Hwy 51
Owned/ Run By: gay men
Rooms: 13 (including 4 sleepers & 3-bdrm cabin)

Baths: private & shared
Amenities: free parking, laundry, pool, outdoor hot tub, DVDs/ videos
Kids: no (must be 21 yrs & up)
Pets: welcome; must be leashed
Smoking: some smoking rms
Rates: $14-120

Midtown Guest House
Atlanta

845 Penn Ave
Atlanta, GA 30308
404/ 931–8791
midtowninn@aol.com

Clientele: mixed gay/ straight
Type: in the heart of midtown; walk to gay bars, restaurants, shopping, subway & Piedmont Park
Owned/ Run By: gay men
Rooms: 4
Baths: private & shared

Meals: coffee/tea only
Kids: no
Pets: no
Rates: $80-170
AC: 5%

W Atlanta
Atlanta

111 Perimeter Center W
Atlanta, GA 30346
770/ 396–6800
877/ WHOTELS (reservations only)
www.whotels.com/atlanta

Clientele: gay-friendly
Type: hotel; in upscale northern suburb of Atlanta; 20 minutes from Buckhead District & 45 minutes from Hartsfield Int'l Airport
Rooms: 275
Baths: private
Wheelchair Access: yes, 13 rms

Meals: coffee/tea only
Amenities: laundry, pool, sauna, hot tub, massage, DVDs/ videos, WiFi
Kids: welcome
Pets: welcome
Smoking: no
Rates: $125-399
AC: 10%

Parliament Resort

Augusta

11250 Gordon Hwy
Augusta, GA 30901
706/ 722-1155
www.p-house.com

Clientele: men
Type: motel; "world's largest all-male gay resort"; membership required; pride/ gift shop, steam rm, cafe; 18+ yrs
Owned/ Run By: gay men
Rooms: 70
Baths: private
Meals: coffee/tea only

Amenities: free parking, pool, sauna, outdoor hot tub, DVDs/ videos, WiFi
Kids: no (18 yrs & up)
Pets: small, lap-sized pets welcome; $15 fee (nonrefundable)
Smoking: ok
Rates: $43-74 (higher holidays)

Black Bear Cabin Rentals

Blue Ridge

706/ 632-4794 888/ 902-2246
www.blackbearcabinrentals.com

Clientele: gay-friendly
Type: cabin; 32 cabins in the Blue Ridge Mountains
Owned/ Run By: straights
Rooms: 32
Baths: private

Amenities: free parking, WiFi
Kids: welcome
Pets: welcome
Smoking: ok
Rates: $115-250

Buckaroos Cabin Rental

Blue Ridge

160 Doyle Carder Pkwy
Blue Ridge, GA 30513
404/ 876-2677
www.buckarooscabin.com

Clientele: mixed gay/ straight
Type: cabin; 90 minutes N of Atlanta; 7 lakes, streams & hiking on property; close to Lake Blue Ridge, boating/ rafting, art galleries, shopping & theater
Meals: cont'l brkfst

Kids: welcome
Pets: no
Smoking: no
Rates: $120

Mountain Laurel Creek

Dahlonega

202 Talmer Grizzle Rd
Dahlonega, GA 30533
706/ 867-8134
www.mountainlaurelcreek.com

Clientele: mixed gay/ straight
Type: b&b-inn; tucked away in the foothills of the Blue Ridge Mtns in the heart of Georgia's Wine Country
Owned/ Run By: gay men
Rooms: 4
Baths: private

Meals: full brkfst
Amenities: hot tub
Kids: no
Pets: no
Smoking: no
Rates: $120-157

Swiftwaters Womanspace

Dahlonega

830 Swiftwaters Rd
Dahlonega, GA 30533
706/ 864-3229 888/ 808-5021
www.swiftwaters.com

Clientele: women
Type: campground; also summer cabins & Honeymoon Suite; lovely, forested, riverside retreat in the Blue Ridge Mtns
Owned/ Run By: women
Rooms: 1
Baths: private
Meals: full brkfst

Amenities: free parking, indoor hot tub, DVDs/ videos
Kids: welcome; camping only
Pets: friendly dogs only
Smoking: no
Rates: $50-95 (indoors)/ $15 (camping)
AC: 10%

The River's Edge

Dewy Rose

32311 Pulliam Mill Rd
Dewy Rose, GA 30634-7939
706/ 213-8081
www.camptheriversedge.com

Clientele: mostly men
Type: campground; private membership; cabins & over 100 campsites & 100 RV hookups; 1 1/2 hrs from Atlanta
Rooms: 22
Baths: shared
Wheelchair Access: yes, 6 rms

Amenities: free parking, laundry, pool, hot tub, massage
Kids: no
Pets: welcome; must be leashed, remain at campsite & owner cleans up
Smoking: no
Rates: $15-98

1st Class B&B Kona Hawaii
Hawaii (Big Island)

77-6504 Kilohana St
Kailua-Kona, HI 96740
808/ 329-8778 888/ 769-1110
www.dolbandb.com

Clientele: gay-friendly
Type: b&b; studio & cottage; luxury accommodations; gourmet brkfst; ocean views; restaurants & beaches nearby
Rooms: 2 (suites)
Baths: private
Meals: full brkfst

Amenities: free parking, WiFi
Kids: no
Pets: no
Smoking: no
Rates: $140-150
AC: 10%

Absolute Paradise B&B
Hawaii (Big Island)

808/ 965-1828 888/ 285-1540
www.absoluteparadise.tv

Clientele: mostly men
Type: b&b; all rms w/ ocean views; clothing-optional pool, hot tub & patio; walk to naturist black sand beach; close to active volcano & lava flow
Owned/ Run By: gay men
Rooms: 4
Baths: private & shared

Meals: cont'l brkfst
Amenities: pool, outdoor hot tub, WiFi
Kids: no
Pets: no
Smoking: no
Rates: $90-165
AC: 10%

Affordable Hawaii at Pomaika'i (Lucky) Farm B&B
Hawaii (Big Island)

83-5465 Mamalahoa Hwy
Captain Cook, HI 96704
808/ 328-2112 800/ 325-6427
www.luckyfarm.com

Clientele: mixed gay/ straight
Type: b&b; working, century-old Kona farm; enjoy a brkfst of Kona coffee, homemade jams & breads
Owned/ Run By: straights
Rooms: 4
Baths: private

Meals: full brkfst
Kids: welcome
Pets: no
Smoking: no
Rates: $70-85 + 11.25% tax
AC: 10%

Aloha Healing Women
Hawaii (Big Island)

PO Box 1850
Pahoa, HI 96778
888/ 967-8622
www.healthretreats.info

Clientele: women only
Type: hotel; all-inclusive health center; holistic retreats: reiki, accupuncture, gourmet meals, healing-life workshops, tours & more; free ground transportation from Hilo
Owned/ Run By: women
Rooms: 5

Baths: private
Meals: full brkfst
Kids: no
Pets: no
Smoking: no
Rates: $150-295
AC: 10%

Areca Palms Estate B&B
Hawaii (Big Island)

PO Box 489
Captain Cook, HI 96704
808/ 323-2276 800/ 545-4390
www.konabedandbreakfast.com

Clientele: gay-friendly
Type: b&b-private home; immaculate rm furnished w/ antiques & fresh flowers; hearty Hawaiian brkfst
Owned/ Run By: straights
Rooms: 4
Baths: private

Meals: full brkfst
Amenities: outdoor hot tub, massage
Kids: welcome; $25 each additional person
Smoking: no
Rates: $110-145
AC: 10% (registered agents who've booked before)

Big Island Cabanas
Hawaii (Big Island)

12-7007 Kamoamoa Homestead Rd
Pahoa, HI 96778
808/ 965-7056
www.BigIslandCabanas.com

Clientele: mostly men
Type: cottage; tropically landscaped, clothing-optional compound
Owned/ Run By: gay men
Rooms: 3
Baths: private
Wheelchair Access: yes, 1 rm

Amenities: free parking, pool, outdoor hot tub, massage, DVD/ videos
Kids: no
Pets: no
Smoking: no
Rates: $81-90

The Chalet Kilauea Collection
                                    Hawaii (Big Island)

350 Lehua St
Hilo, HI 96720
808/ 967-7786 800/ 937-7786
www.volcano-hawaii.com

Clientele: gay-friendly
Type: b&b-inn; wide range of accommodations in the fern forest; vacation homes, inns & lodges
Owned/ Run By: straights
Rooms: 33
Baths: private & shared

Meals: expanded cont'l brkfst
Amenities: free parking, hot tub, DVDs/ videos
Kids: welcome; $15 fee
Smoking: no
Rates: $49-399
AC: 10%

Diver Dan's B&B Hawaii
                                    Hawaii (Big Island)

81633 Papio Dr
Captain Cook, HI 96704
808/ 328-9546
www.flex.com/~hdc/diverdan

Clientele: mostly men
Type: b&b; beautiful new home w/ view of Kona coastline; includes access to private nude beach
Owned/ Run By: gay men

Rooms: 2
Baths: private & shared
Wheelchair Access: yes, 1 rm
Rates: $88-115
AC: 13%

Dragonfly Ranch Healing Arts Center
                                    Hawaii (Big Island)

PO Box 675
Honaunau-Kona, HI 96726
808/ 328-2159
www.dragonflyranch.com

Clientele: mixed gay/ straight
Type: eco-spa; luxuriously rustic upscale treehouse; also vacation cottage rental
Owned/ Run By: straights
Rooms: 5
Baths: private
Wheelchair Access: yes, 1 rm
Meals: healthy wheat-free cont'l brkfst

Amenities: free parking, laundry, sauna, outdoor hot tub, massage, DVDs/ videos, WiFi
Kids: well-behaved welcome
Pets: welcome
Smoking: no
Rates: $100-300
AC: 10%

Green Fire Productions
                                    Hawaii (Big Island)

RR2 Box 3898
Pahoa, HI 96778
808/ 934-9205
www.greenfireproductions.com

Clientele: women
Type: b&b-private home; on ocean w/ warm artesian pond; proprietor performs commitment ceremonies, telepathic sessions & Hawaiian magic
Owned/ Run By: lesbians
Rooms: 2

Baths: shared
Meals: expanded cont'l brkfst
Amenities: pool, outdoor hot tub, massage
Kids: no
Pets: no
Smoking: no
Rates: $125-150

The Hala Kahiki Guesthouse
                                    Hawaii (Big Island)

PO Box 72,
Volcano Village, HI 96785
808/ 985-9851
www.halakahikiguesthouse.com

Clientele: gay-friendly
Type: guesthouse; also b&b; newly renovated home; fireplace; designed to showcase Hawaiian arts & crafts
Owned/ Run By: lesbians
Rooms: 3
Baths: private & shared

Meals: expanded cont'l brkfst
Amenities: outdoor hot tub, massage
Kids: welcome
Pets: no
Smoking: no
Rates: $80-95 (b&b); $165 (guesthouse)
AC: 20%

Hale Lana at Kealakekua Bay
                                    Hawaii (Big Island)

82-6277 Kahauloa St
Captain Cook, HI 96704
808/ 328-7338
hawaiihalelana@yahoo.com

Clientele: gay-friendly
Type: rental home; luxurious pole house near snorkeling at Kealakekua Bay
Owned/ Run By: gay men
Rooms: 5
Baths: private
Amenities: free parking, laundry, hot tub

Kids: no
Pets: no
Smoking: no
Rates: $125-250
AC: 10%

Hale O Luna
Hawaii (Big Island)

963181 Pikake St
Pahala, HI 96777
808/ 640-1113
www.pahala.info

Clientele: mixed gay/ straight
Type: b&b; grand restored plantation home on the sunny side of Volcano
Owned/ Run By: gay men
Rooms: 2

Baths: private
Kids: welcome
Pets: no
Smoking: no
Rates: $65-125

Hawaiian Dream Vacation
Hawaii (Big Island)

808/ 965-9523
tweek.net/hawaiianvacation

Clientele: mixed gay/ straight
Type: cottage; clean, well-designed space for peaceful, simple stay; walk to Kehana beach & attractions
Owned/ Run By: women
Rooms: 1
Baths: private

Meals: cont'l brkfst
Amenities: free parking, outdoor hot tub, massage
Kids: please inquire
Pets: no
Smoking: no
Rates: $85/ night

Hawaiian Oasis B&B
Hawaii (Big Island)

74-4958 Kiwi St
Kailua-Kona, HI 96740
808/ 327-1701
www.hawaiianoasis.com

Clientele: gay-friendly
Type: secluded b&b on 2 acres; tennis court, workout rm, internet access; private entrance
Owned/ Run By: gay & straight
Rooms: 4
Baths: private
Wheelchair Access: yes, 3 rms

Meals: expanded cont'l brkfst
Amenities: free parking, laundry, pool, outdoor hot tub, massage
Kids: welcome depending on number & age; please call first
Pets: welcome: please call first
Smoking: no
Rates: $140-190

Horizon Guest House
Hawaii (Big Island)

PO Box 268
Honaunau, HI 96726
808/ 328-2540 888/ 328-8301
www.horizonguesthouse.com

Clientele: mixed gay/ straight
Type: b&b; 40-acre setting w/ 20 miles of coastline views; gated entry; private
Owned/ Run By: gay men
Rooms: 4
Baths: private
Wheelchair Access: yes, all rms

Meals: full brkfst
Amenities: laundry, pool, outdoor hot tub
Kids: please inquire
Pets: no
Smoking: no
Rates: $250
AC: 10%

Isle of You–Hawaii Farm & Retreat
Hawaii (Big Island)

PO Box 587
Pahoa, HI 96778
808/ 965-1639
www.isleofyou-hawaii.com

Clientele: mostly men
Type: cabin & yurts; naturist farm retreat where everyone is welcome; ocean views; 70 acres of rainforest, banana groves & solitude
Owned/ Run By: gay men
Rooms: 2

Baths: shared
Meals: fruit basket on arrival
Kids: welcome
Pets: no
Smoking: no
Rates: $55-75
AC: 10%

Kalani Oceanside Retreat
Hawaii (Big Island)

RR2 Box 4500
Pahoa, HI 96778
808/ 965-7828 800/ 800-6886
www.kalani.com

Clientele: mixed gay/ straight
Type: secluded rural gay retreat; also 20 campsites; nudity ok after 7pm in pool area or during naturist events
Owned/ Run By: gay/ lesbian & straight
Rooms: 48
Baths: private & shared

Wheelchair Access: yes, 8 rms
Amenities: free parking, pool, sauna outdoor hot tub, massage
Kids: welcome
Smoking: no
Rates: $60-240; $20-30 (camping)
AC: 10%

KonaLani Coffee Plantation Inn

Hawaii (Big Island)

76-5917H Mamalahoa Hwy
Holualoa, HI 96725
808/ 324-0793
www.konalani.com

Clientele: mixed gay/ lesbian
Type: b&b & condo units; on 3-acre tropical garden/ coffee plantation; coastline views
Owned/ Run By: gay men
Rooms: 6
Baths: private & shared
Wheelchair Access: yes, 1 rm

Meals: full brkfst
Amenities: gym, hot tub, WiFi
Kids: welcome in suites only
Pets: no
Smoking: no
Rates: $80-175
AC: negotiable

Kulana: The Affordable Artists Sanctuary

Hawaii (Big Island)

PO Box 190
Volcano Village, HI 96785
808/ 985-9055
www.panpolynesia.net/kulana

Clientele: mostly women (mixed gay/ straight)
Type: artist retreat; cabins, guest rms & camping; no smoking, drugs or alcohol
Owned/ Run By: women
Rooms: 4 (includes 2 cabins, 2 guest rms)
Baths: shared

Meals: coffee/tea only
Kids: welcome
Pets: cats & birds welcome; dogs negotiable
Smoking: no
Rates: $15 (campers) & $20-30 (cabin); $325/ month

Margo's Corner

Hawaii (Big Island)

near South Point
Na'alehu, HI
808/ 929-9614
www.margoscorner.com

Clientele: mixed gay/ straight
Type: b&b-private home; southernmost B&B in the US; homecooked organic brkfst & dinner
Owned/ Run By: lesbians
Rooms: 4
Baths: private & shared
Wheelchair Access: yes, 4 rms

Meals: full brkfst
Amenities: free parking, laundry, sauna, massage, DVDs/ videos, WiFi
Kids: please inquire
Pets: no
Smoking: no
Rates: $35-125

Mele Kohola

Hawaii (Big Island)

15-991 Paradise Dr
Hilo, HI 96749
808/ 965-0400
www.melekohola.com

Clientele: gay-friendly
Type: rental home; oceanfront w/ stunning views; seasonal whale-watching; near Hawaii Volcano Nat'l Park, rain forest, natural hot ponds & gay beach
Owned/ Run By: gay & straight
Rooms: 4 (rent whole house)

Baths: private & shared
Amenities: laundry, hot tub, DVDs/ videos
Kids: welcome
Pets: no
Smoking: no
Rates: $225-375
AC: please inquire

Pamalu—Hawaiian Country House

Hawaii (Big Island)

RR 2 Box 4023
Pahoa, HI 96778
808/ 965-0830
www.gayhawaiivacations.com

Clientele: mixed gay/ straight
Type: retreat; tropical treasure on 5 private acres; on Puna Coast; near clothing-optional, black-sand beach
Owned/ Run By: gay men
Rooms: 4
Baths: private

Meals: expanded cont'l brkfst
Kids: welcome if family rents whole house
Pets: no
Smoking: no
Rates: $75-125
AC: 15%

Pu'ukala Lodge B&B

Hawaii (Big Island)

PO Box 2967
Kailua-Kona, HI 96745
808/ 325-1729 888/ 325-1729
www.Puukala-lodge.com

Clientele: mixed gay/ lesbian/ straight
Type: b&b; located on the slopes of Mt Hualalai; w/ gorgeous coastal views & spectacular sunsets
Owned/ Run By: gay men
Rooms: 4
Baths: private & shared

Meals: full brkfst
Kids: please call first
Pets: no
Smoking: no (except on lanais & outdoors)
Rates: $95-165
AC: negotiable

Rainbow Dreams Cottage   Hawaii (Big Island)

13-6412 Kalapana Beach Rd
Pahoa, HI 96778
415/ 824-7062
www.rainbowdreamscottage.com

Clientele: mixed gay/ straight
Type: rental home; oceanfront cottage; romantic & quiet; near warm springs & black-sand beach
Owned/ Run By: gay men
Rooms: 4
Baths: private

Kids: by arrangement
Pets: no
Smoking: no
Rates: $600/ week; $1,850/ month
AC: 10%

Royal Kona Resort   Hawaii (Big Island)

75-5852 Alii Dr
Kailua-Kona, HI 96740-1334
808/ 329-3111   800/ 222-5642
www.royalkona.com

Clientele: gay-friendly
Type: resort; oceanfront setting, overlooking spectacular Kailua Bay on Hawaii's Big Island
Owned/ Run By: straights
Rooms: 452
Baths: private

Wheelchair Access: yes, 5 rms
Kids: welcome; under 18 yrs stay free in rm w/ parents using existing bedding
Rates: $105-250
AC: 10%

Seascape Gardens B&B   Hawaii (Big island)

2107 A Kaiwiki Rd
Hilo, HI 96720
808/ 961-3036
www.seascapegardens.com

Clientele: women
Type: b&b-private home; 2-bdrm suite; panoramic views from Puna Coast & volcanic range; 1300 ft above Hilo; close to beaches & restaurants
Owned/ Run By: women
Rooms: 4

Baths: shared
Meals: full brkfst
Kids: welcome
Pets: no
Smoking: no
Rates: $95-190
AC: 10%

17 Palms Kauai   Kauai

808/ 822-5659 888/ 725-6799
www.17palmskauai.com

Clientele: mixed gay/ straight
Type: 2 secluded cottages 200 steps from beach, restaurants & shopping; *Condé Nast Traveler*'s: "One of 20 perfect places to stay in Hawaii"
Owned/ Run By: gay men
Rooms: 2 (1- & 2-bdrm) cottages

Baths: private
Wheelchair Access: yes, 2 rms
Kids: welcome
Pets: no
Smoking: no
Rates: $110-165

Aliomanu Palms—A Beachfront Vacation Rental   Kauai

PO Box 675
Anahola, HI 96703
831/ 438-2800
www.aliomanupalms.com

Clientele: mixed gay/ straight
Type: b&b-private home; located right on the beach in a quiet, gay-friendly residential area
Owned/ Run By: gay men
Rooms: 3

Baths: private
Meals: cont'l brkfst
Kids: no
Pets: no
Rates: $500/ night, 2,500/ week
AC: 10%

Anuenue Plantation B&B   Kauai

PO Box 226
Kapaa, HI 96746-0226
808/ 823-8335 888/ 371-7716
www.anuenue.com

Clientele: mostly men
Type: b&b; in plantation estate house & cottage w/ 360° ocean & mtn views
Owned/ Run By: gay men
Rooms: 2
Baths: private
Meals: full brkfst

Amenities: free parking, DVDs/ videos, Wi
Kids: no
Pets: no
Smoking: no
Rates: $80
AC: 10%

Kalanikai B&B   *Kauai*

PO Box 1001
Kalaheo, HI 96741
808/ 332-5149 888/ 552-2777
www.kalanikai.com

Clientele: mostly men
Type: b&b; clothing-optional guest home; "come share the beauty of Kauai the way nature intended—naturally"
Owned/ Run By: gay man
Rooms: 3
Baths: private

Meals: expanded cont'l brkfst
Amenities: free parking, laundry, pool, 2 hot tubs, massage, WiFi
Kids: welcome w/ prior approval
Smoking: no
Rates: $99-129
AC: 10-20%

Kauai Oceanfront Condo   *Kauai*

5300 Ka Haku Rd
Princeville, HI 96722
10/ 793-7539
www.alohasooz.com

Clientele: mixed gay/ straight
Type: condo; deluxe oceanfront vacation rental overlooking the ocean & Bali Hai Mtn; breathtaking views
Owned/ Run By: straights
Amenities: free parking, laundry, pool, sauna, hot tub, massage

Kids: welcome
Smoking: no
Rates: $1,365-1,540/ week
AC: 10%

Kauai Waterfall B&B 🏳️‍🌈   *Kauai*

6783 Haaheo St
Kapaa, HI 96746
808/ 823-9533 800/ 996-9533
www.kauaiwaterfall.com

Clientele: mixed gay/ lesbian
Type: b&b-private home; elegant private b&b, overlooking Wailua River State Park waterfall
Owned/ Run By: gay men
Rooms: 3
Baths: private & shared
Meals: expanded cont'l brkfst

Amenities: free parking, laundry, pool, outdoor hot tub, DVDs/ videos
Kids: no
Pets: no
Smoking: no
Rates: $80+tax (single); 90+tax (double)
AC: 10%

Mahina's Women's Guest House on Kaua'i   *Kauai*

4433 Panihi Rd
Kapaa, HI 96746
808/ 823-9364
www.mahinas.com

Clientele: women
Type: guesthouse; beach house on Kauai; w/ shared kitchen, baths, living/ dining areas; sunrise beach walks outside your door
Owned/ Run By: women
Rooms: 4

Baths: shared
Meals: coffee/tea only
Rates: $65-110
AC: 10%

Mohala Ke Ola B&B Retreat   *Kauai*

5663 Ohelo Rd
Kapaa, HI 96746
808/ 823-6398 888/ 465-2824
www.waterfallbnb.com

Clientele: gay-friendly
Type: b&b-private home; safe, quiet place for people to rest, relax & just be themselves
Owned/ Run By: gay man
Rooms: 4
Baths: private

Meals: expanded cont'l brkfst
Amenities: free parking, laundry, pool, outdoor hot tub, massage
Kids: no
Smoking: no
Rates: $100-125
AC: 20%

Poipu Plantation Resort 🏳️‍🌈   *Kauai*

1792 Pe'e Rd
Poipu Beach, HI 96756
808/ 742-6757 800/ 634-0263
www.poipubeach.com

Clientele: mixed gay/ straight
Type: b&b-inn; small b&b & cottage-style rental property; across from the ocean on the sunny shore of Kauai
Owned/ Run By: gay men
Rooms: 14
Baths: private

Wheelchair Access: yes, 2 rms
Meals: full brkfst
Amenities: free parking, laundry, outdoor hot tub
Kids: welcome in cottages only
Rates: $99-190
AC: 10%

ResortQuest Waimea Plantation Cottages   *Kauai*

940 Kaumualii Highway
Waimea, HI 96796
808/ 338-1625 866/ 774-2924
www.waimeacottages.com

Clientele: gay-friendly
Type: cottage; private seaside cottages on Kauai set amidst a 27-acre coconut grove; this oceanfront resort created from renovated historic plantation homes
Rooms: 61
Baths: private

Amenities: free parking, laundry, pool, hot tub, DVDs/ videos
Kids: welcome
Rates: $150-455

Anfora's Dreams   *Maui*

323/ 467-2991
800/ 788-5046

mauicondo@earthlink.net
home.earthlink.net/~mauicondo

Clientele: mixed gay/ straight
Type: condo; completely furnished condo vacation rentals
Owned/ Run By: gay men
Transit: rental car recommended
Rooms: A/C, color TV, ceiling fan, phone, refrigerator, full kitchen
Baths: private, bathtubs, showers
Amenities: free parking, laundry, pool, outdoor hot tub, coffee/ tea, tennis courts
Recreation: Little Beach
Kids: welcome
Pets: no
Smoking: ok
Reservations: required *Deposit:* required, 50%, due at booking, personal check ok *Cancellation:* cancel by 30 days prior or forfeit $100 *Minimum Stay:* 4 nights *Check in/ out:* 2pm/ noon

Payment: cash, personal checks, Visa, MC, out-of-state checks must be received 30 days prior

Season: open yr-round
Rates: $89-135
AC: 10%

Best Western Maui Oceanfront Inn   *Maui*

2980 S Kihei Rd
Kihei, HI 96752
808/ 879-7744 800/ 263-3387
www.mauioceanfrontinn.com

Clientele: mixed gay/ straight
Type: hotel; $6 million renovation in 2001; located on one of Hawaii's most romantic beaches
Owned/ Run By: gay & straight
Rooms: 72
Baths: private

Kids: welcome
Smoking: ok
Rates: $112-250
AC: 10%

Hale Ho'okipa Inn B&B   *Maui*

32 Pakani Pl
Makawao, HI 96768
808/ 572-6698 877/ 572-6698
www.maui-bed-and-breakfast.com

Clientele: gay-friendly
Type: b&b-inn; "Upcountry Maui's historic b&b"; also Kipa Cottage
Owned/ Run By: woman
Rooms: 5 + 1 cottage
Baths: private
Wheelchair Access: yes, 4 rms
Meals: expanded cont'l brkfst

Amenities: free parking, massage, WiFi
Kids: welcome
Smoking: no
Rates: $95-165 + tax; cottage: $160/ night & $2,900/ month
AC: 10-20%

Hale Kumulani (House at the Horizon)   *Maui*

874 Kumulani Dr
Kihei, HI 96753
808/ 891-0425
www.cottagemaui.com

Clientele: gay-friendly
Type: cottage & suites; elegant & private; on lush, gated property; all close to best beaches; welcome basket
Owned/ Run By: straights
Rooms: 3 (1 private garden cottage, 2 waterfall suites)
Baths: private
Wheelchair Access: yes, 2 rms

Amenities: free parking, laundry, massage, DVDs/ videos, WiFi
Kids: welcome; crib & youth bed available
Pets: no
Smoking: no
Rates: $175-205 (waterfall suite); $155 (garden cottage)
AC: 15%

Hana Accommodations   *Maui*

PO Box 564
Hana, HI 96713
808/ 248-7868 800/ 228-4262
www.hana-maui.com

Clientele: mixed gay/ straight
Type: private studios & cottages conveniently located in serene settings on the beautiful Hana coast; great rates & no minimum stay

Rooms: 4
Baths: private
Kids: welcome
Rates: $68-150
AC: 10%

Ke Kala's Hula Hale Studio   *Maui*

PO Box 458
Makawao, HI 96768
808/ 572-0664 877/ 787-4440
www.ikekala.com

Clientele: mostly women
Type: studio; peaceful Polynesian decor; private 19-jet outdoor jacuzzi; guest discounts at restaurant & wellness center
Owned/ Run By: lesbians
Rooms: 1
Baths: private

Wheelchair Access: yes, 1 rm
Meals: coffee/tea only
Pets: no
Smoking: no
Rates: $70-80
AC: 10%

Maluhia Kai Guesthouse   *Maui*

808/ 283-8966
weddingsbymakamae.com

Clientele: women
Type: b&b; self-contained private rm w/ awesome ocean view; lesbian commitment ceremonies on-site; also 2 campsites ($35; includes use of pool, shower & toilet)
Owned/ Run By: lesbians
Rooms: 3

Baths: private
Meals: cont'l brkfst
Amenities: free parking, laundry, outdoor hot tub, massage, DVDs/ videos
Kids: welcome
Pets: no
Rates: $95 (2-night minimum)
AC: 10%

Maui Sunseeker Resort ⬤   *Maui*

551 S Kihei Rd
Kihei, HI 96753
808/ 879-1261 800/ 532-6432
www.mauisunseeker.com

Clientele: mostly men (women welcome)
Type: hotel; unique beachfront island hideaway; Maui's largest gay resort
Owned/ Run By: gay men
Rooms: 16
Baths: private
Amenities: free parking, laundry, outdoor

hot tub, massage, DVDs/ videos, WiFi
Kids: no
Pets: welcome
Smoking: no
Rates: $85-205
AC: 10%

Milo's Vacation Rentals   *Maui*

808/ 298-9350
www.milosvacationrentals.com

Clientele: mixed gay/ straight
Type: rental home; sweeping views of the N & W shores, including the islands of Molokai, Lanai & Kahoolawe; watch the sun set from 1,500 sq ft deck
Owned/ Run By: gay men
Rooms: 7

Baths: private
Amenities: laundry, hot tub, DVDs/ videos
Kids: no
Pets: no
Smoking: no
Rates: $1,400-2,800/ week
AC: 10%

Na Pualani 'Ohana   *Maui*

PO Box 118
Hana, HI 96713
808/ 248-8935 800/ 628-7092
moreinfo@randm.com

Clientele: mixed gay/ straight
Type: guesthouse; deluxe studios & suites; Napualani 'Ohana is on 4 acres of flowers & plants
Owned/ Run By: gay men
Rooms: 11
Baths: private

Wheelchair Access: yes, 5 rms
Meals: coffee/tea only
Kids: welcome
Pets: welcome
Smoking: ok
Rates: $60-85
AC: 10-15%

ResortQuest Maui Kaanapali Villas   *Maui*

45 Kai Ala Dr
Lahaina, HI 96761
808/ 667-7791 866/ 774-2924
www.rqkaanapalivillas.com

Clientele: gay-friendly
Type: resort; condo resort "fronting the best stretch of beach in West Maui"; offers privacy & comfort amidst 11 acres of landscaped grounds
Rooms: 260

Baths: private
Kids: welcome

The Royal Lahaina Resort   *Maui*

2780 Kekaa Dr
Kaanapali, HI 96761
808/ 661-3611 800/ 447-6925
www.2maui.com

Clientele: gay-friendly
Type: full-service resort along Ka'anapali, Maui's best beach; casually elegant
Owned/ Run By: straights
Rooms: 592
Baths: private
Wheelchair Access: yes, 4 rms

Meals: full brkfst
Amenities: free parking, laundry, pool, outdoor hot tub, massage, DVDs/ videos
Kids: welcome; under 18 yrs free w/ parents when using existing bedding
Rates: $149-790
AC: 10%

Wavecrest Oceanfront Condo   *Molokai*

808/ 218-0408

Clientele: mixed gay/ straight
Type: condo; oceanfront 1-bdrm; sleeps 2; on most beautiful, peaceful & tropical side of Molokai
Owned/ Run By: lesbians
Rooms: 1 (condo)
Baths: private

Kids: welcome; 3 people max
Pets: no
Smoking: no
Rates: $75/ night; 473/ week + $60 one-time cleaning fee
AC: 10%

Ali'i Bluffs Windward B&B   *Oahu*

46-251 Ikiiki St
Kane'ohe, HI 96744
808/ 235-1124 800/ 235-1151
www.hawaiiscene.com/aliibluffs

Clientele: mixed gay/ straight
Type: b&b; sweeping views over Kaneohe Bay; 40 minutes from Waikiki—but more like less-developed islands
Owned/ Run By: gay men
Rooms: 2
Baths: private

Meals: expanded cont'l brkfst
Kids: 16 yrs & up welcome
Pets: no
Smoking: no
Rates: $65-80
AC: 15%

Ilima Hotel [TAG]   *Oahu*

445 Nohonani St
Honolulu, HI 96815
808/ 923-1877 800/ 801-9366
www.ilima.com

Clientele: gay-friendly
Type: hotel; spacious condo-style studios & suites w/ full kitchens, private lanai
Owned/ Run By: straights
Rooms: 99
Baths: private
Wheelchair Access: yes, 4 rms

Amenities: free parking, laundry, pool, sauna, hot tub
Kids: welcome
Pets: no
Smoking: ok
Rates: $119-355
AC: 10%+

The Cabana at Waikiki [MG]   *Oahu*

2551 Cartwright Rd   808/ 926-5555
Honolulu, HI 96815   877/ 902-2121   www.cabana-waikiki.com

The Cabana is a place where both men and women can relax, make friends, and enjoy all the amenities our newly remodeled 1-bdrm suites have to offer. Our goal is to provide personal attention in a relaxed, intimate atmosphere.

The Cabana is a 4-story, 15-suite property ideally situated one block from world-renowned Waikiki Beach and is gay-owned and operated.

Each suite features custom-made furniture, a queen-size bed plus a day bed, a private lanai, a kitchenette, and an entertainment center. Relax in our 8-person spa, or walk to Queen's Surf Beach (the gay beach) and Honolulu's best shops and restaurants. We're just steps from Hula's, Waikiki's world-famous gay bar, and a short hop from Angles and Fusion nightclubs.

The Cabana at Waikiki is THE gay place to stay in Waikiki. Wonderfully friendly. Exclusively gay.

Clientele: mostly men
Type: hotel; a quiet respite yet close to everything
Owned/ Run By: gay men
Nearby Attractions: Waikiki!; close to Hula's gay bar
Transit: near public transit; 10 miles to airport
Rooms: 15 total, suites, A/C, color TV, DVD/ VCR, cable, wetbar, ceiling fan, phone, refrigerator, safer sex supplies, maid service, all w/ queen-size bed, separate living area, entertainment system, kitchen & private lanai
Baths: private, bathtubs, showers, hairdryers
Meals: cont'l brkfst
Amenities: office hrs: 8am-midnight; laundry, hot tub, coffee/ tea, spa, tropical veranda, complimentary cocktail parties
Recreation: next to Kapiolani Park & 1 blk from Queen's Surf (the gay beach), close to 24hr Fitness
Pets: no

Reservations: required *Deposit:* required, 1 night (off-season) & 2 nights (in-season), due 21 days prior *Cancellation:* cancel by 21 days prior or forfeit full deposit *Minimum Stay:* 2 nights (in-season) *Check in/ out:* 3pm/ noon
Payment: Visa, Amex, MC, Discover
Season: open yr-round *High season:* Dec 20-Jan 7
Rates: $129-175 *Discounts:* groups
AC: 10%

Kolohe's B No B   *Oahu*

441 Kanekapolei St #102A
Oahu, HI 96815
808/ 923-2408
www.kolohekea.com

Clientele: men
Type: b&b-private home; in heart of Waikiki
Owned/ Run By: gay men
Rooms: 1
Baths: private
Kids: no

Pets: no
Smoking: ok
Rates: $50/ night, $320/ week, (higher
  holidays) tax inclusive

ResortQuest Coconut Plaza Hotel   *Oahu*

450 Lewers St
Honolulu, HI 96815
808/ 923-8828 877/ 997-6667
www.rqcoconutplaza.com

Clientele: gay-friendly
Type: boutique hotel in the heart of Waikiki,
  near the Kuhio (gay) District
Rooms: 80
Baths: private

Wheelchair Access: yes, 2 rms
Meals: cont'l brkfst
Kids: welcome
AC: 10-15% (depending on season)

ResortQuest Waikiki Joy Hotel   *Oahu*

320 Lewers St
Honolulu, HI 96815
808/ 923-2300 866/ 774-2924
www.rqwaikikijoy.com

Clientele: gay-friendly
Type: Waikiki's premier boutique hotel;
  tropical landscaping & personalized
  service
Rooms: 93
Baths: private
Wheelchair Access: yes, 4 rms

Meals: cont'l brkfst
Amenities: laundry, pool, sauna, hot tub
Kids: welcome
Pets: no
Smoking: ok
AC: 10%

Vivian's 605   *Oahu*

1911 Kalakaua Ave #605
Honolulu, HI 96815

808/ 344-3866
760/ 567-6634

Clientele: mixed gay/ lesbian
Type: condo; 1-bdrm condo; sleeps up to 4;
  near beach; in heart of Waikiki
Owned/ Run By: gay men
Nearby Attractions: beach, Ala Moana
  Center, walk to lots of shops & eateries
Transit: near public transit; 17 miles to
  airport; lots of taxis & shuttles; garage
  parking $15 per day
Rooms: 1 (condo) total, A/C, color TV (2),
  DVD/ VCR, cable, ceiling fan, deck, phone,
  kitchenette, refrigerator, really cute condo
  w/ 6th flr views of downtown
Baths: private, bathtubs, showers
Wheelchair Access: yes
Amenities: laundry, DVDs/ videos, world-
  famous Eggs 'N Things restaurant
  downstairs
Recreation: parks, Queen's Beach
Kids: welcome
Pets: no (companion animals only)
Smoking: no

Reservations: required *Deposit:* required,
  30%, due at booking, personal check ok
  Cancellation: cancel by 45 days prior or
  forfeit deposit *Minimum Stay:* 1 day @
  $109 *Check in/ out:* 4pm/ noon

Payment: cash, bank checks, PayPal
Season: open yr-round *High season:* Dec-
  Feb
Rates: $109/ night, $595/ week, $2,200/
  month

Bed & Buns
Boise

10325 Victory Rd
Boise, ID 83709
208/ 866-2759
www.bedandbuns.com

Clientele: men
Type: b&b; large, beautiful colonial home w/ very private grounds; clothing-optional inside & out; hot tub close to downtown, bars & airport
Owned/ Run By: gay men
Rooms: 3
Baths: private

Meals: cont'l brkfst
Amenities: free parking, laundry, outdoor hot tub, massage, DVDs/ videos, WiFi
Kids: no
Pets: welcome
Smoking: no
Rates: $65-85

The Clark House on Hayden Lake
Coeur d'Alene

5250 E Hayden Lake Rd
Hayden Lake, ID 83835
208/ 772-3470 800/ 765-4593
www.clarkhouse.com

Clientele: gay-friendly
Type: b&b-inn; in magnificent mansion on a wooded 12-acre estate, a reminder of its glorious past
Owned/ Run By: gay men
Rooms: 10

Baths: private
Meals: full brkfst
Amenities: free parking, outdoor hot tub
Smoking: no
Rates: $125-275
AC: 10%

Lava Hot Springs Inn
Lava Hot Springs

94 E Portneuf Ave
Lava Hot Springs, ID 83246
208/ 776-5830 800/ 527-5830
www.lavahotspringsinn.com

Type: b&b-inn; a great, friendly place to relax; w/ mineral pools & massage
Owned/ Run By: straights
Rooms: 26
Baths: private & shared
Wheelchair Access: yes, 4 rms
Meals: full brkfst

Amenities: free parking, pool, outdoor hot tub, massage, DVDs/ videos
Kids: welcome
Pets: welcome
Smoking: no
Rates: $69-195
AC: 10%

Rainbow Ranch Gay Campsite
Carbondale

90 Old Cape Rd
Jonesboro, IL 62952-2497
618/ 833-7926 877/ 518-4377
gaycampers.com/rainbowranch

Clientele: men
Type: nudist campground; sundeck; w/ 10 primitive creekside campsites; tent, pop-up camper & small travel trailer RV compatible (30 & 50 Amps); 5 RV hookups
Owned/ Run By: gay men
Baths: shared

Amenities: free parking, laundry, pool, hot tub, DVDs/ videos
Kids: welcome
Pets: welcome; must be leashed
Smoking: no
Rates: $20-35

Allegro Chicago
Chicago

171 W Randolph
Chicago, IL 60601
312/ 236-0123 800/ 643-1500
www.allegrochicago.com

Clientele: gay-friendly
Type: hotel; sophisticated, lively accommodations designed by interior designer Cheryl Rowley
Owned/ Run By: straights & gays
Rooms: 483
Baths: private
Wheelchair Access: yes, 12 rms

Meals: coffee/tea only
Amenities: laundry, massage, gym, WiFi
Kids: welcome
Pets: welcome
Smoking: ok (in designated areas)
Rates: $139-399
AC: 10%

The Ardmore House
Chicago

1248 W Ardmore Ave
Chicago, IL 60660
773/ 728-5414
www.ardmorehousebb.com

Clientele: mostly men
Type: b&b-private home; located 4 short blks from fabulous Lake Shore Dr & just a 10-minute ride from Boystown, this Victorian b&b offers all the comforts of home
Owned/ Run By: gay men

Rooms: 3
Baths: shared
Meals: full brkfst
Amenities: free parking, hot tub, DVDs/ videos
Rates: $89-139
AC: 10%

Best Western Hawthorne Terrace [T-IG]
Chicago

3434 N Broadway
Chicago, IL 60657

773/ 244-3434
888/ 675-2378

14151@hotel.bestwestern.com
www.hawthorneterrace.com

Clientele: gay-friendly
Type: hotel; located in the heart of Chicago's gay community; charming accommodations in picturesque period architecture; fully restored to modern convenience
Owned/ Run By: gay & straight
Nearby Attractions: near all gay attractions; Wrigley Field, Lincoln Park Zoo, Halsted St, theatres & nightlife—just 10 minutes from downtown
Transit: near public transit; 10 miles to O'Hare & Midway airports; Red Line to Blue Line Trains to O'Hare; 4 blks to station
Rooms: 59 total, 10 suites, 9 kings, 20 queens, 20 fulls, A/C, color TV, cable TV (satellite), phone (2-lines w/ data port), refrigerator, rm service, maid service, in-rm modem, coffeemakers, iron & ironing boards (microwaves in many rms)
Baths: private, bathtubs, showers, whirlpools, hairdryers

Wheelchair Access: yes, 4 rms
Meals: expanded cont'l brkfst
Amenities: laundry, sauna, indoor hot tub, gym, WiFi, coffee/ tea, business center
Kids: welcome; 12 yrs & under free
Pets: welcome on case-by-case basis
Smoking: ok (designated rms only)
Reservations: required
Cancellation: cancel by 6pm the day before or forfeit 1 night
Check in/ out: 2pm/ noon
Payment: cash, travelers checks, Visa, Amex, MC, Discover, Diners Club
Season: open yr-round *High season:* April-Oct
Rates: $139+ *Discounts:* AAA, AARP
AC: 10%

Chicago Sisters' Place
Chicago

773/ 542-9126

Clientele: women
Type: apt; furnished rms for rent in 3-bdrm 2nd-flr women artists' flat
Owned/ Run By: lesbians
Rooms: 3

Baths: shared
Meals: coffee/tea only
Kids: no
Pets: no
Rates: $45-55

City Suites Hotel
Chicago

933 W Belmont Ave
Chicago, IL 60657
773/ 404-3400 800/ 248-9108
www.cityinns.com

Clientele: gay-friendly
Type: hotel; affordable, comfortable & convenient accommodations w/ a touch of European style
Rooms: 45
Baths: private
Wheelchair Access: yes

Meals: expanded cont'l brkfst
Kids: welcome; under 12 yrs free
Pets: no
Smoking: ok
Rates: $139-179
AC: 10%

Flemish House of Chicago
Chicago

68 E Cedar St
Chicago, IL 60611
312/ 664-9981
www.innchicago.com

Clientele: mixed gay/ straight
Type: b&b; furnished studio & 1-bdrm apts in 1890s greystone row house; in Gold Coast, near Michigan Ave
Owned/ Run By: gay men
Rooms: 7
Baths: private

Meals: cont'l brkfst
Amenities: laundry, WiFi
Rates: $125-200 + tax
AC: 10%

Comfort Inn & Suites Downtown
Chicago

15 E Ohio St
Chicago, IL 60611

312/ 894-0900
888/ 775-4111

reservations@chicagocomfortinn.com
www.chicagocomfortinn.com

Clientele: gay-friendly
Type: charming boutique hotel; stylish art deco decor; in the heart of downtown
Owned/ Run By: straights
Nearby Attractions: gay nightlife, Michigan Ave shopping, Navy Pier, Art Institute, Adler Planetarium, Shedd Aquarium, Millennium Park, numerous bars, restaurants, nightclubs & theaters
Transit: 17 miles to Chicago O'Hare; 15 miles to Chicago Midway; 1 mile to Union Station (train) & Greyhound Bus terminal; public transit adjacent to hotel
Rooms: 130 total, 25 suites, 8 kings, 79 queens, 18 twins, A/C, color TV, cable, wetbar (49), phone, refrigerator (49), maid service, microwave (51), in-rm safes, high-speed internet access, morning paper, bedside CD player, upgraded bath amenities
Baths: private, bathtubs, showers, hairdryers
Wheelchair Access: yes, 7 rms
Meals: expanded cont'l brkfst
Amenities: laundry, sauna, indoor hot tub, gym, WiFi, coffee/ tea, fitness center, sauna, express check-out

Kids: welcome
Smoking: ok
Reservations: required; credit card guarantee *Deposit:* required, 1 night + tax, due at booking *Cancellation:* cancel by 1 day prior or forfeit deposit
Payment: cash, travelers checks, Visa, Amex,

MC, Discover, Diners Club
Season: open yr-round *High season:* May-Oct
Rates: $149-349 *Discounts:* AAA, seniors/ AARP, travel agents
AC: 10%

The Hotel Burnham
Chicago

One W Washington St
Chicago, IL 60602

312/ 782-1111
877/ 294-9712

www.burnhamhotel.com

Clientele: gay-friendly
Type: hotel; a Chicago landmark transformed into an elegant haven of vibrant design; excellent location at State & Washington
Owned/ Run By: gay/ lesbian & straight
Nearby Attractions: Michigan Ave, State St shopping, Navy Pier, The Art Institute, theatre district
Transit: near public transit; 15 miles to Midway Airport; 17 miles to O'Hare Airport; Airport Express arranged through concierge
Rooms: 122 total, 19 suites, 13 kings, 72 queens, 18 fulls, A/C, color TV, cable, phone, refrigerator, rm service, maid service, guest rms decorated in a midnight blue/ gold scheme w/ plush furnishings & mahogany hardwood pieces
Baths: private, bathtubs, showers, robes, hairdryers
Wheelchair Access: yes, 3 rms

Meals: through restaurant
Amenities: laundry, fitness rm, restaurant/ bar, 24hr rm service, daily newspaper, twice-daily maid service, turndown service, overnight shoe-shine, complimentary morning coffee/ tea service, evening wine reception, high-speed internet access
Kids: welcome
Pets: welcome
Reservations: required *Deposit:* credit card guarantee, due at booking, personal check ok *Cancellation:* cancel by 1 day prior or forfeit 1 night *Check in/ out:* 3pm/ noon
Payment: cash, travelers checks, personal checks, Visa, Amex, MC, Discover
Season: open yr-round *High season:* May-June, Aug-Oct
Rates: $179+ *Discounts:* yes
AC: 10%

The Willows
Chicag

555 W Surf St
Chicago, IL 60657
773/ 528-8400 800/ 787-3108
www.cityinns.com

Clientele: mixed gay/ straight
Type: hotel; charming French Country-style hotel nestled on a quiet tree-lined street in the heart of Lincoln Park
Rooms: 55
Baths: private
Meals: expanded cont'l brkfst

Kids: welcome; under 12 yrs free
Pets: some exceptions made
Smoking: ok (in designated rms only)
Rates: $109-379
AC: 10%

The Pit
Du Quoin

7403 Persimmon Rd
Du Quoin, IL 62832
618/ 542-9470
hdbr@onecliq.net

Clientele: mixed gay/ lesbian
Type: campground; primitive camping w/ 125 campsites; deep clear strip pit; 3/4 miles of water: fishing, swimming, snorkeling, boats allowed w/ electric trolling motors; 18 yrs + only

Owned/ Run By: gay men
Rates: $5 per person (holiday wknds only free otherwise

The Fahnestock House
Galesburg

591 N Prairie St
Galesburg, IL 61401
309/ 344-0270
www.innkeepers-coffee.com

Clientele: mixed gay/ straight
Type: b&b-private home; in Queen Anne Victorian w/ 3-story turret, bow window, beveled glass, veranda; suite includes: bdrm, living rm, private bath, pantry
Owned/ Run By: gay men
Rooms: 2

Baths: private
Meals: full brkfst
Amenities: free parking, pool
Kids: welcome
Pets: no
Smoking: no
Rates: $150

Priapus Pines
Iuka

618/ 822-2559
www.priapuspines.com

Clientele: men
Type: campground; clothing-optional campground on 60 acres; RV hookups, nearby fish & boating
Owned/ Run By: gay men

Amenities: pool, hot tub
Kids: no
Pets: must be leashed

The Henry Mischler House
Springfield

802 E Edwards St
Springfield, IL 62703
217/ 525-2660 800/ 525-2660
www.mischlerhouse.com

Clientele: gay-friendly
Type: b&b; overlooks Lincoln's home, a nat'l historic site; original fixtures; available for private parties
Owned/ Run By: gay men
Rooms: 5
Baths: private

Meals: full brkfst
Kids: 12 yrs & up welcome
Smoking: no
Rates: $85-115 (10% gay discount)
AC: 10%

The State House, a Clarion Collection Hotel
Springfield

101 E Adams
Springfield, IL 62701
217/ 528-5100
www.thestatehouseinn.com

Clientele: gay-friendly
Type: recently renovated; just 3 blks from the busiest gay bar, The Station House; free high-speed internet
Owned/ Run By: gay & straight
Rooms: 125
Baths: private
Wheelchair Access: yes, 7 rms

Meals: full brkfst
Amenities: gym
Kids: welcome
Pets: welcome
Smoking: ok
Rates: $89-159
AC: 10%

Worthington Mansion B&B
Fort Wayne

305 W Wayne St
Fort Wayne, IN 46802
260/ 424-6564
www.worthingtonmansion.com

Clientele: mixed gay/ straight
Type: b&b; newly restored luxury Queen Anne mansion; intimate historic atmosphere; in the heart of historic West Central neighborhood
Owned/ Run By: gay men
Rooms: 4
Baths: shared

Meals: full brkfst
Amenities: free parking, laundry, massage, DVDs/ videos, WiFi
Kids: welcome; please notify in advance
Pets: please inquire
Smoking: no
Rates: $75-150

Sibley Court Yard Inn
Hammond

529 Sibley St
Hammond, IN 46320
219/ 933-9604
www.sibleybaths.com

Clientele: men
Type: gay men's guesthouse w/ bathhouse facilities; private courtyard; clothing-optional
Owned/ Run By: gay men
Rooms: 26
Baths: private
Meals: cont'l brkfst

Amenities: free parking, laundry, sauna, indoor hot tub, DVDs/ videos
Kids: no
Pets: welcome; fee
Smoking: ok
Rates: $23-32 + tax

The Gray Goose Inn B&B
Indiana Dunes

350 Indian Boundary Rd
Chesterton, IN 46304
219/ 926-5781 800/ 521-5127
www.graygooseinn.com

Clientele: mixed gay/ straight
Type: English country inn; fireplace & jacuzzi suites; gourmet brkfsts
Rooms: 8
Baths: private
Meals: full brkfst
Amenities: free parking, DVDs/ videos, WiFi

Kids: 12 yrs & up welcome
Smoking: smoking allowed in common rms only
Rates: $100-190
AC: 10%

East Lake Retreat
Indianapolis

335 W Lakeview Dr
Nineveh, IN 46164
812/ 376-0784
kbolte@alumni.indiana.edu

Type: rental home; fully furnished 2 bdrm plus loft, 2 bathrms; 30 minutes from Indianapolis; wooded lot, waterfall, lake access (boating, swimming), firepit
Owned/ Run By: lesbians
Kids: welcome

Pets: no
Smoking: no
Rates: $200-300/ wknd; $500-700/ week

Sycamore Knoll B&B
Indianapolis

10777 Riverwood Ave
Noblesville, IN 46062
317/ 776-0570
www.sycamoreknoll.com

Clientele: mixed gay/ straight
Type: b&b; fully restored 1886 estate near the White River w/ perennial gardens & apple orchard
Owned/ Run By: lesbians
Rooms: 2
Baths: private

Meals: full brkfst
Amenities: free parking, DVDs/ videos, WiFi
Kids: no
Pets: no
Smoking: no
Rates: $95

Yellow Rose Inn
Indianapolis

1441 N Delaware St
Indianapolis, IN 46202
317/ 636-7673
www.yellowroseinn.com

Clientele: mixed gay/ straight
Type: restored Georgian Revival Colonial; roof deck w/ 6-person hot tub; in restored historical district
Rooms: 4 (suites)
Baths: private
Meals: full brkfst

Amenities: free parking, hot tub, massage, DVDs/ videos
Kids: no
Pets: no
Smoking: no
Rates: $175-250

Inn Town B&B

Lowell

1651 E Commercial Ave
Lowell, IN 46356
219/ 696-3338
www.inntownbedandbreakfast.com

Clientele: gay-friendly
Type: b&b-private home; "experience hopitality that will make you want to return again & again"
Owned/ Run By: women
Rooms: 2
Baths: private

Meals: full brkfst
Amenities: free parking, laundry, massage, DVDs/ videos, WiFi
Kids: welcome
Pets: welcome w/ prior approval
Smoking: no
Rates: $75-110

Duneland Beach Inn & Restaurant

Michigan City

3311 Pottawattamie Trail
Michigan City, IN 46360
219/ 874-7729 800/ 423-7729
www.dunelandbeachinn.com

Clientele: gay-friendly
Type: b&b; also restaurant/ bar; only 1 blk away from Lake Michigan & private beach; 60 miles outside of Chicago; jacuzzi suites available
Owned/ Run By: gay & straight
Rooms: 9

Baths: private
Meals: full brkfst
Amenities: hot tub
Rates: $129-189

Tryon Farm Guest House

Michigan City

1400 Tryon Rd
Michigan City, IN 46360
219/ 879-3618
www.tryonfarmguesthouse.com

Clientele: gay-friendly
Type: b&b; 1896 farmhouse on 170 acres of prairie, woods, meadow & wetlands
Owned/ Run By: women
Rooms: 5
Baths: private
Meals: full brkfst

Amenities: free parking, laundry, outdoor hot tub, massage, DVDs/ videos
Kids: welcome
Pets: welcome
Smoking: no
Rates: $98-170

Council Oak Inn

South Bend

near airport
South Bend, IN
574/ 273-6416 574/ 315-7098
stevea@michiana.org

Clientele: men
Type: b&b-private home; clothing-optional; private decks
Owned/ Run By: gay men
Rooms: 2
Baths: private & shared

Meals: full brkfst
Kids: no
Pets: no
Smoking: no
Rates: $65

Arrowhead Motel, Inc

Burlington

2520 Mt Pleasant St
Burlington, IA 52601-2118
319/ 752-6353
ww.arrowheadia.com

Clientele: gay-friendly
Type: motel; guest rms & 1- to 3-bdrm suites; "privacy respected or we will tend to your wishes"
Owned/ Run By: gay man
Rooms: 30
Baths: private
Wheelchair Access: yes, 2 rms

Amenities: free parking, laundry, indoor hot tub
Kids: welcome if w/ adult
Pets: welcome w/ prior approval
Smoking: ok
Rates: $48-84
AC: 10%

The Cottage B&B

Des Moines

1094 28th St
Des Moines, IA 50311
515/ 277-7559
thecottagedsm.com

Clientele: gay-friendly
Type: b&b; 1929 Georgian brick house in historic Drake neighborhood; gardens & fountain; mtg & small reception facilities available
Owned/ Run By: gay men
Rooms: 4

Baths: private
Meals: full brkfst
Amenities: free parking, outdoor hot tub
Rates: $89-119

Hotel Fort Des Moines   *Des Moines*

1000 Walnut St
Des Moines, IA 50309
515/ 243-1161 800/ 532-1466
www.hotelfortdesmoines.com

Clientele: gay-friendly
Type: hotel; historic landmark; near Gateway West & Temple Theatre; walking distance to dining, skyway connection; 24hr free shuttle service
Rooms: 238
Baths: private
Wheelchair Access: yes, 12 rms

Meals: full brkfst
Amenities: laundry, pool, sauna, hot tub, gym, WiFi
Kids: welcome if accompanied by guardian 21+
Pets: no
Smoking: ok
Rates: $99-400

The Renaissance Savery Hotel   *Des Moines*

401 Locust St
Des Moines, IA 50309
515/ 244-2151 800/ 798-2151
www.shanerhotels.com

Type: hotel
Rooms: 224
Baths: private
Wheelchair Access: yes, 7 rms

Amenities: pool, sauna, hot tub, massage
Kids: welcome
Rates: $99-695
AC: 10%

La Corsette Maison Inn   *Newton*

629 1st Ave E
Newton, IA 50208
641/ 792-6833
www.lacorsette.com

Clientele: gay-friendly
Type: b&b-inn; architectural masterpiece on the Nat'l Register of Historical Places; elegant but comfortable; gourmet dining, fireplaces, swirling whirlpools
Owned/ Run By: straight woman
Rooms: 7

Baths: private
Meals: full brkfst
Amenities: free parking, hot tub
Kids: welcome w/ prior approval
Pets: welcome w/ prior approval
Smoking: no
Rates: $90-225

The Bear & Boar B&B Resort   *Lexington*

PO Box 2602
London, KY 40743
606/ 862-6557
www.BearandBoar.com

Clientele: men
Type: elegant b&b & rugged camping resort; multiple decks & balconies overlooking beautiful 900 acres at Wood Creek Lake; parties
Owned/ Run By: gay men
Rooms: 3 suites

Baths: private & shared
Meals: expanded cont'l brkfst
Kids: no
Pets: welcome outdoors
Smoking: ok
Rates: $15-125

Bernheim Mansion B&B   *Louisville*

1416 S 3rd St
Louisville, KY 40208
502/ 638-1387 800/ 303-0053
www.BernheimMansion.com

Clientele: mixed gay/ straight
Type: b&b; Victorian mansion w/ original woodwork & 3-story stained glass
Owned/ Run By: gay men
Rooms: 5
Baths: private & shared
Meals: full brkfst

Amenities: free parking, laundry, pool, hot tub, DVDs/ videos
Kids: no
Pets: no
Smoking: no
Rates: $139-225
AC: 10%

Columbine B&B   *Louisville*

1707 S 3rd St
Louisville, KY 40208
502/ 635-5000 800/ 635-5010
www.thecolumbine.com

Clientele: gay-friendly
Type: b&b-private home; elegant 1896 Victorian mansion; incredible food, hospitality & gracious atmosphere
Owned/ Run By: gay/ lesbian & straight
Rooms: 6
Baths: private

Meals: full brkfst
Kids: no
Pets: no
Smoking: no
Rates: $105-165
AC: 10%

Inn at the Park   *Louisville*

1332 S 4th St
Louisville, KY 40208
502/ 637-6930
www.innatpark.com

Type: b&b; beautifully restored mansion in historic Old Louisville; whirlpools, balconies & fireplaces
Rooms: 7
Baths: private

Meals: full brkfst
Smoking: no
Rates: $119-199
AC: 10%

Mansion at River Walk   *Louisville*

704 E Main St
New Albany, IN 47150
812/ 941-8100

Clientele: gay-friendly
Type: b&b; Italianate home on Mansion Row in New Albany, Indiana; gourmet brkfst daily
Rooms: 6
Baths: private & shared

Meals: full brkfst
Kids: 12 yrs & up welcome
Pets: no
Smoking: ok
Rates: $95-145

Mark Palmer Guest Retreat   *Paducah*

524 Harrison St
Paducah, KY 42001
270/ 444-2056
www.markpalmergallery.com

Clientele: all welcome
Type: guest accommodations located above contemporary art gallery/ artist residence in Historic Lowertown Arts District
Rooms: 1
Baths: private
Amenities: free parking

Kids: welcome
Pets: welcome
Smoking: no
Rates: $65-100

Maison des Amis   *Breaux Bridge*

111 Washington St
Breaux Bridge, LA 70517
337/ 507-3399
www.maisondesamis.com

Clientele: gay-friendly
Type: b&b-inn; charming 1870 Creole/ Caribbean residence overlooking legendary Bayou Teche; lush gardens, gazebo, sun porch; tour info
Owned/ Run By: women
Rooms: 4

Baths: private
Meals: full Cajun/ Creole brkfst
Kids: ages 12 yrs & up welcome
Pets: no
Rates: $100-200

Chez des Amis B&B   *Natchitoches*

910 Washington St
Natchitoches, LA 71457
318/ 352-2647
www.chezdesamis.com

Clientele: mixed gay/ straight
Type: b&b; 1923 Arts & Crafts bungalow; city where *Steel Magnolias* was filmed; resident ghost
Owned/ Run By: gay men
Rooms: 3
Baths: private
Meals: full brkfst

Amenities: free parking, DVDs/ videos, WiFi
Kids: no
Pets: under 15 lbs welcome w/ prior approval
Smoking: no
Rates: $90-150
AC: 10%

1227 Easton House   *New Orleans*

1227 N Rendon St
New Orleans, LA 70119
504/ 324-5077
www.eastonhouse1227.com

Clientele: mixed gay/ straight
Type: b&b; perfect for visiting couples; the best location for seeing the French Quarter & touring surrounding attractions
Owned/ Run By: gay men
Rooms: 4
Baths: private

Meals: full brkfst
Smoking: no
Rates: $85-210

1850s Creole Cottage
New Orleans

504/ 527–5360 888/ 523–5235
www.innthequarter.com/
la_maison_creole.htm

Clientele: mixed gay/ straight
Type: apt; at corner of Bourbon & Dumaine; kitchen; complimentary bottle of champagne
Owned/ Run By: gay & straight
Rooms: 2
Baths: private

Meals: coffee/tea only
Kids: welcome
Pets: small dogs welcome
Smoking: ok
Rates: $125-330
AC: 10%

1896 O'Malley House B&B
New Orleans

120 S Pierce St
New Orleans, LA 70119
504/ 488–5896 866/ 226–1896
www.1896omalleyhouse.com

Clientele: mixed gay/ straight
Type: b&b; private bathrooms w/ granite countertops; most units have whirlpool tubs; internet access; local artists' work on display
Owned/ Run By: gay men
Rooms: 8
Baths: private

Wheelchair Access: yes, 1 rm
Meals: expanded cont'l brkfst
Amenities: free parking, hot tub
Kids: welcome
Pets: welcome w/ pet carrier
Rates: $89-195
AC: 10%

5 Continents B&B
New Orleans

1731 Esplanade Ave
New Orleans, LA 70116
504/ 943–3536 800/ 997–4652
www.fivecontinentsbnb.com

Clientele: mixed gay/ straight
Type: b&b; circa 1895 Greek Revival mansion w/in walking distance of the French Quarter & all bars
Owned/ Run By: gay men
Rooms: 3 (plus 1 cottage)
Baths: private

Meals: full brkfst
Amenities: free parking, hot tub, WiFi
Kids: welcome, although house is not really child-friendly
Pets: small pets welcome
Rates: $100-300
AC: 10%

A Creole House
New Orleans

1013 St Ann
New Orleans, LA 70116
504/ 524–8076 800/ 535–7858
www.acreolehouse.com

Clientele: mixed gay/ straight
Type: guesthouse; you'll love the offbeat charm of our petite historical property located right in the French Quarter; friendly 24hr staff
Owned/ Run By: gay & straight
Rooms: 31

Baths: private & shared
Meals: cont'l brkfst
Kids: welcome
Smoking: no
Rates: $49-225
AC: 10%

Aaron Ingram Haus
New Orleans

1012 Elysian Fields Ave
New Orleans, LA 70117
504/ 949–3110
www.ingramhaus.com/ct.htm

Clientele: mixed gay/ straight
Type: guesthouse; suites accommodating up to 4 people in the heart of the gay area; 6 blks to Bourbon St
Owned/ Run By: gay man
Rooms: 4
Baths: private

Meals: coffee/tea only
Amenities: free parking, laundry, WiFi
Kids: no
Pets: no
Smoking: ok
Rates: $68-175
AC: 15%

Antebellum Guest House
New Orleans

1333 Esplanade Ave
New Orleans, LA 70116
504/ 943–1900
www.antebellumguesthouse.com

Clientele: mixed gay/ straight
Type: b&b; historic circa 1830s Grand Revival just 2 1/2 blks from French Quarter; lush antique interiors
Owned/ Run By: gay men
Rooms: 5
Baths: private
Meals: full brkfst

Amenities: free parking, laundry, outdoor hot tub
Kids: no
Pets: no
Smoking: no
Rates: $100-175
AC: 10%

Ashton's B&B   *New Orleans*

2023 Esplanade Ave
New Orleans, LA 70116
504/ 942–7048 800/ 725–4131
www.ashtonsbb.com

Clientele: gay-friendly
Type: b&b; 1860s Greek Revival mansion; quiet location; 9 blks to French Quarter
Owned/ Run By: straights
Rooms: 8
Baths: private
Meals: full brkfst

Amenities: free parking, laundry, hot tub, WiFi
Kids: up to rm capacity
Smoking: ok
Rates: $120-180
AC: 10%

Auld Sweet Olive B&B   *New Orleans*

2460 N Rampart
New Orleans, LA 70117
504/ 947–4332 877/ 470–5323
www.sweetolive.com

Clientele: mixed gay/ straight
Type: b&b; fabulous & relaxing; internet access; easy walk to bars & major attractions
Rooms: 5
Baths: private

Meals: expanded cont'l brkfst
Amenities: free parking, laundry, DVD/ videos, WiFi
Kids: 13 yrs & up welcome
Smoking: no
Rates: $85-150

Big Easy/ French Quarter Lodging   *New Orleans*

233 Cottonwood Dr
Gretna, LA 70056
504/ 433–2563 800/ 368–4876
fqlodging.com

Clientele: mixed gay/ straight
Type: reservation service; for b&bs, guesthouses, studios, condos
Owned/ Run By: gay men
Baths: private
Meals: coffee/tea only
Amenities: hot tub

Kids: welcome
Pets: welcome
Smoking: ok
Rates: $69-400
AC: 5%

Biscuit Palace Guest House   *New Orleans*

730 Dumaine
New Orleans, LA 70116
504/ 525–9949
www.biscuit-palace.com

Clientele: gay-friendly
Type: guesthouse; pristinely restored 1820 Creole mansion; 50 ft from Bourbon St; all privately accessed
Rooms: 8
Baths: private
Wheelchair Access: yes, 1 rm

Meals: coffee/tea only
Amenities: free parking, laundry, WiFi
Kids: welcome
Pets: no
Smoking: ok
Rates: $105-150
AC: 10%

Block-Keller House   *New Orleans*

3620 Canal St
New Orleans, LA 70119
504/ 483–3033
www.blockkellerhouse.com

Clientele: mixed gay/ straight
Type: b&b-inn; in meticulously restored Classical Revival villa w/ antiques; near French Quarter
Owned/ Run By: gay men
Rooms: 5
Baths: private

Meals: expanded cont'l brkfst
Amenities: free parking, hot tub, massage
Kids: no
Pets: dogs welcome
Smoking: no
Rates: $90-135
AC: 10%

Bon Maison Guest House   *New Orleans*

835 Bourbon St
New Orleans, LA 70116
504/ 561–8498
www.bonmaison.com

Clientele: mixed gay/ straight
Type: guesthouse; well-appointed & located in the heart of New Orleans' French Quarter; steps away from bars, restaurants & Jackson Square
Owned/ Run By: gay men
Rooms: 5 (including 2-bdrm suite)

Baths: private
Kids: no
Pets: no
Smoking: no (except courtyard)
Rates: $95-300

Bourgoyne Guest House
New Orleans

839 Bourbon St
New Orleans, LA 70116
504/ 524-3621 504/ 525-3983
www.damron.com/homepages/
BourgoyneGuestHouse

Clientele: mixed gay/ straight
Type: apt; an 1830s Creole mansion near the excitement of Bourbon St, coupled w/ a courtyard retreat
Rooms: 5
Baths: private

Pets: no
Smoking: ok
Rates: $93-190
AC: 10%

The Burgundy B&B
New Orleans

2513 Burgundy St
New Orleans, LA 70117
504/ 942-1463 800/ 970-2153
www.theburgundy.com

Clientele: mixed gay/ straight
Type: cozy b&b w/ in walking distance of the French Quarter; clothing-optional hot tub & sunbathing
Owned/ Run By: gay men
Rooms: 4
Baths: private
Meals: cont'l brkfst

Amenities: free parking, laundry, outdoor hot tub, DVDs/ videos, WiFi
Kids: please inquire
Pets: no
Smoking: no
Rates: $80-90
AC: 10%

Bywater B&B
New Orleans

1026 Clouet St
New Orleans, LA 70117
504/ 944-8438
bywaterbnb.com

Clientele: gay-friendly
Type: b&b; late Victorian "double shotgun" cottage; short distance downriver from French Quarter
Owned/ Run By: lesbians/ gay men
Rooms: 4
Baths: private & shared

Meals: cont'l brkfst
Kids: welcome
Pets: no
Smoking: no
Rates: $75-125

The Chimes B&B
New Orleans

Constantinople at Coliseum
New Orleans, LA
504/ 342-4861 800/ 729-4640
www.historiclodging.com/chimes

Clientele: gay-friendly
Type: b&b-inn; 5 quaint guest suites & rms sit on the brick courtyard of an 1876 home
Owned/ Run By: straights
Rooms: 5
Baths: private

Meals: expanded cont'l brkfst
Kids: welcome
Pets: by arrangement
Smoking: no
Rates: $85-155
AC: 10%

Creole Inn
New Orleans

2471 Dauphine St
New Orleans, LA 70117
504/ 948-3230
www.creoleinn.com

Clientele: mixed gay/ straight
Type: b&b-private home; in the gay Marigny w/ quick access to the French Quarter & convention center
Owned/ Run By: gay men
Rooms: 5
Baths: private

Meals: cont'l brkfst
Amenities: free parking, DVDs/ videos, WiFi
Kids: 12 yrs & up welcome
Pets: no
Smoking: no (except in garden)
Rates: $83-188
AC: 10%

Crescent City Guest House
New Orleans

612 Marigny St
New Orleans, LA 70117
504/ 944-8722 877/ 203-2140
www.crescentcitygh.com

Clientele: mixed gay/ straight
Type: b&b-private home; many restaurants & nightclubs w/in walking distance; daily maid service
Owned/ Run By: gay men
Rooms: 4
Baths: private

Meals: cont'l brkfst
Amenities: free parking, outdoor hot tub, DVDs/ videos
Pets: please inquire
Smoking: ok
Rates: $89-159
AC: 10%

The Degas House
New Orleans

2306 Esplanade Ave
New Orleans, LA 70119
504/ 821-5009 800/ 755-6730
www.degashouse.com

Clientele: gay-friendly
Type: b&b-inn; immerse yourself in the home of French Impressionist painter Edgar Degas (1872-1873) for a wknd & see the rm believed to be the artist's studio
Owned/ Run By: straights
Rooms: 9
Baths: private

Meals: full brkfst
Amenities: free parking, laundry, hot tub, WiFi
Kids: no
Pets: no
Rates: $99-250
AC: 10%

Elysian Guest House
New Orleans

1008 Elysian Fields Ave
New Orleans, LA 70117
504/ 324-4311
www.elysianguesthouse.com

Clientele: mixed gay/ lesbian
Type: guesthouse; renovated "double shotgun" home; gardens & hot tub, luxuriously furnished
Owned/ Run By: gay men
Rooms: 5 (includes 3 one-bdrm suites & 2 studios)
Baths: private

Meals: cont'l brkfst
Amenities: laundry, outdoor hot tub, DVDs/ videos
Kids: welcome w/ good parental supervision
Pets: small dogs welcome
Smoking: ok
Rates: $80-200
AC: 10%

Empress Hotel
New Orleans

1317 Ursulines Ave
New Orleans, LA 70116
504/ 529-4100 888/ 524-9200
www.empreshotel.com

Clientele: gay-friendly
Type: hotel; small Euro-style; located 2 blks from the French Quarter in the historic Treme neighborhood
Owned/ Run By: gay/ lesbian & straight
Rooms: 36

Baths: private
Meals: coffee/tea only
Kids: welcome w/ deposit
Pets: welcome w/ deposit
Smoking: ok
Rates: $25-65

Garden District B&B
New Orleans

2418 Magazine St
New Orleans, LA 70130
504/ 895-4302
www.gardendistrictbedandbreakfast.com

Clientele: gay-friendly
Type: b&b; "100+-yr-old Victorian home nestled in one of the most beautiful neigborhoods of the South"; located less than 2 miles from French Quarter
Owned/ Run By: straights
Rooms: 5

Baths: private
Meals: cont'l brkfst
Kids: welcome
Pets: no
Rates: $80-150

The Gillham Pierce House B&B
New Orleans

1407 Esplanade Ave
New Orleans, LA 70116
504/ 944-2115 866/ 226-6392
www.gillhampiercehouse.com

Clientele: mixed gay/ straight
Type: b&b; restored circa 1877 mansion just 3 blks from French Quarter
Owned/ Run By: gay men
Rooms: 4
Baths: private

Meals: cont'l brkfst
Kids: 12 yrs & up welcome
Pets: welcome w/ deposit & daily fee
Smoking: no
Rates: $110-225
AC: 10-15%

The Green House Inn
New Orleans

1212 Magazine St
New Orleans, LA 70130
504/ 525-1333 800/ 966-1303
www.thegreenhouseinn.com

Clientele: mixed gay/ straight
Type: b&b-inn; tropical oasis, comfortable rms, king beds, lush garden; friendly hospitality
Owned/ Run By: gay men
Rooms: 7
Baths: private
Meals: expanded cont'l brkfst

Amenities: free parking, laundry, pool, outdoor hot tub, massage, DVDs/ videos
Kids: no
Pets: welcome w/ advance reservations; daily charge
Smoking: no
Rates: $69-199
AC: 10%

HH Whitney House on the Historic Esplanade
New Orleans

1923 Esplanade Ave
New Orleans, LA 70116-1706
504/ 948-9448 877/ 944-9448
www.hhwhitneyhouse.com

Clientele: mixed gay/ straight
Type: b&b; circa 1865 Italianate beauty; located just blks from the historic French Quarter
Owned/ Run By: gay men
Rooms: 5
Baths: private & shared
Meals: full brkfst

Amenities: free parking, laundry, outdoor hot tub
Kids: well-behaved kids welcome
Pets: no
Smoking: no
Rates: $95-250
AC: 10%

Historic Rentals
New Orleans

800/ 537-5408
www.historicrentals.com

Clientele: mixed gay/ straight
Type: reservation service; 1-bdrm apts in French Quarter historic properties; near bars & tourist sights
Owned/ Run By: gay/ lesbian & straight

Rooms: 12
Baths: private
Meals: coffee/tea only
Rates: $75-140
AC: 10%

Hotel de la Monnaie
New Orleans

405 Esplanade Ave
New Orleans, LA 70116
504/ 947-0009
www.hoteldelamonnaie.com

Clientele: gay-friendly
Type: hotel; built 10 yrs ago to duplicate Victorian all-suite hotel (time share)
Owned/ Run By: straights
Baths: private
Wheelchair Access: yes, all rms
Meals: coffee/tea only

Amenities: free parking, laundry, indoor hot tub
Rates: $140-190

Hotel St Pierre
New Orleans

911 Burgundy St
New Orleans, LA 70116
504/ 524-4401 800/ 225-4040
www.hotelsaintpierre.com

Clientele: gay-friendly
Type: hotel; European-style; courtyards & swimming pools; 2 blks off Bourbon St
Rooms: 77
Baths: private
Meals: cont'l brkfst

Amenities: pool, outdoor hot tub
Kids: welcome
Rates: $90-179

Kerlerec House
New Orleans

928 Kerlerec
New Orleans, LA 70016
504/ 944-8544
www.kerlerec.com

Clientele: mixed gay/ straight
Type: guesthouse; 1 blk from the French Quarter; gardens; kitchen in each suite
Owned/ Run By: gay men
Rooms: 6
Baths: private
Wheelchair Access: yes, 1 rm

Meals: coffee/tea only
Amenities: laundry, hot tub, WiFi
Kids: welcome
Pets: no
Smoking: no
Rates: $75-450

La Maison Marigny B&B on Bourbon
New Orleans

1421 Bourbon St
New Orleans, LA 70116
504/ 948-3638 800/ 570-2014
www.lamaisonmarigny.com

Clientele: mixed gay/ straight
Type: b&b; one of *Travel & Leisure*'s "Top 10 in the US"; perfectly located at Bourbon & Esplanade; just steps from clubs, restaurants & more
Owned/ Run By: gay men
Rooms: 4
Baths: private

Meals: expanded cont'l brkfst
Amenities: free parking, massage, DVDs/ videos, WiFi
Kids: 12 yrs & over welcome
Pets: no
Smoking: no
Rates: $95-199
AC: $25 flat fee

Lanata House
New Orleans

1226 Chartres St
New Orleans, LA 70116
504/ 581–9060 866/ 881–9060
www.lanatahouseapts.com

Clientele: mixed gay/ straight
Type: guesthouse; fine accommodations in the French Quarter
Owned/ Run By: gay man
Rooms: 3
Baths: private

Kids: no
Pets: seeing-eye dogs only
Rates: $125-275

Le Papillon Guesthouse
New Orleans

2011 N Rampart St
New Orleans, LA 70116
504/ 948–4993 504/ 884–4008 (cell)
www.lepapillonguesthouse.com

Clientele: mixed gay/ straight
Type: guesthouse; restored 1830s slave quarters w/ period furnishings & modern amenities, private entrances, courtyard, backyard
Owned/ Run By: gay men
Rooms: 2

Baths: private
Meals: coffee/tea only
Kids: no
Pets: welcome
Rates: $65-135

Lions Inn
New Orleans

2517 Chartres St
New Orleans, LA 70117
504/ 945–2339 800/ 485–6846
www.lionsinn.com

Clientele: mixed gay/ straight
Type: b&b; in handsome 1850s home; beautifully & tastefully restored w/ all modern conveniences; semitropical patio; clothing-optional
Owned/ Run By: gay men
Rooms: 9

Baths: private & shared
Meals: cont'l brkfst
Amenities: pool, outdoor hot tub, WiFi
Kids: no
Pets: welcome
Smoking: no
Rates: $50-165

Magnolia Mansion
New Orleans

2127 Prytania St
New Orleans, LA 70130
504/ 412–9500 888/ 222–9235
www.magnoliamansion.com

Clientele: mixed gay/ straight
Type: b&b; enchanting antebellum mansion w/ uniquely themed guestrms; located in historic Garden District; minutes from French Quarter
Owned/ Run By: gay & straight
Rooms: 9

Baths: private
Meals: cont'l brkfst
Kids: no
Pets: no
Smoking: no
Rates: $150-550
AC: 10%

Maison Dupuy Hotel
New Orleans

1001 Toulouse St
New Orleans, LA 70112
504/ 586–8000 800/ 535–9177
www.maisondupuy.com

Clientele: gay-friendly
Type: hotel; luxury boutique hotel; on *Condé Nast Traveler*'s "Gold List"; also fine dining at Dominique's restaurant
Baths: private

Amenities: pool, outdoor hot tub
Rates: $99-489

Marigny Guest House
New Orleans

621 Esplanade
New Orleans, LA 70116
504/ 944–9700 (Lamothe House #)
888/ 696-9575
www.lamothehouse.com/
marigny_house.html

Clientele: mixed gay/ straight
Type: b&b-inn; 1860s home converted to 9-rm guesthouse in super location
Owned/ Run By: gay & straight
Rooms: 9
Baths: private
Meals: cont'l brkfst

Amenities: free parking, pool, outdoor hot tub
Kids: welcome
Smoking: no
Rates: $49-175
AC: 10%

Marigny Manor House

2125 N Rampart St
New Orleans, LA 70116
504/ 943-7826 877/ 247-7599
www.marignymanorhouse.com

Clientele: mixed gay/ straight
Type: b&b-private home; in historic 1850s Greek Revival House; w/ beautiful courtyard & secret garden; 1 blk to 3 gay bars
Owned/ Run By: gay men
Rooms: 4
Baths: private

Meals: expanded cont'l brkfst
Amenities: free parking, outdoor hot tub
Kids: no
Pets: no
Smoking: no
Rates: $89-129
AC: 10%

The McKendrick-Breaux House

1474 Magazine St
New Orleans, LA 70130
504/ 586-1700 888/ 570-1700
www.mckendrick-breaux.com

Type: b&b; upscale 1860s restored Greek Revival; located in the heart of the Lower Garden District; private courtyard & patio w/ pond
Rooms: 9
Baths: private

Meals: expanded cont'l brkfst
Amenities: free parking, hot tub
Kids: welcome
Pets: no
Smoking: no
Rates: $145-235

Mentone B&B

1437 Pauger St
New Orleans, LA 70116-1600
504/ 943-3019
www.mentonebandb.com

Clientele: gay-friendly
Type: b&b-private home; suite w/ private entrance; in a Victorian house 1 blk from the French Quarter
Owned/ Run By: women

Rooms: 1
Baths: private
Meals: expanded cont'l brkfst
Smoking: no
Rates: $125-175

New Orleans B&B/ French Quarter Accommodations

328 Royal St, Ste 259
New Orleans, LA 70116
504/ 561-0447 888/ 240-0070
www.neworleansbandb.com

Type: reservation service; w/ condos & apts in French Quarter & Marigny, b&bs in Garden District & Uptown; 1-3 bdrm plus multiple unit properties
Rooms: 40
Baths: private
Amenities: pool, hot tub, WiFi

Kids: welcome if accompanied by parent at all times
Pets: welcome in certain long-term rentals
Rates: $100-500
AC: please inquire

New Orleans Guest House

1118 Ursulines Ave
New Orleans, LA 70116
504/ 566-1177 800/ 562-1177
www.neworleans.com/nogh

Clientele: mixed gay/ straight
Type: brick, gable-sided 1848 Creole cottage; 3 blks to Bourbon St
Owned/ Run By: gay men
Rooms: 14
Baths: private

Meals: cont'l brkfst
Kids: welcome
Pets: no
Smoking: ok
Rates: $99-139

Olde Victorian Inn & Spa—French Quarter

914 N Rampart St
New Orleans, LA 70116
504/ 522-2446 800/ 725-2446
www.oldevictorianinn.com

Clientele: mixed gay/ straight
Type: b&b-private home; antiques, clawfoot tubs, jazz brkfst; full-service day spa; one of the nation's Top 10 on inns-msn.com
Owned/ Run By: gay men
Rooms: 6
Baths: private

Meals: full brkfst
Kids: no
Pets: no
Smoking: no
Rates: $99-250
AC: 10% (for 7 nights or more)

The Olivier House

New Orleans

828 Toulouse
New Orleans, LA 70112
504/ 525-8456 866/ 525-9748
www.olivierhouse.com

Clientele: gay-friendly
Type: hotel; in 3 Greek Revival townhouses filled w/ period antiques & beautiful architectural touches; lush courtyards; in the heart of the French Quarter
Rooms: 42

Baths: private
Kids: welcome
Pets: welcome
Rates: $135-450

The Pontchartrain Hotel

New Orleans

2031 St Charles Ave
New Orleans, LA 70140
504/ 524-0581 800/ 777-6193
www.pontchartrainhotel.com

Clientele: gay-friendly
Type: hotel; offering the splendor of a bygone era w/ luxurious modern amenities; "Old World elegance meets Southern hospitality"
Rooms: 118
Baths: private
Wheelchair Access: yes

Amenities: free parking, laundry, saun hot tub, massage
Kids: welcome
Pets: no
Smoking: ok
Rates: $59-429
AC: 10%

Royal Street Courtyard

New Orleans

2438 Royal St
New Orleans, LA 70117
504/ 943-6818 888/ 846-4004
www.RoyalStreetCourtyard.com

Clientele: mixed gay/ straight
Type: b&b; 1850s Greek Revival exudes elegance & decadence of old Creole Louisiana; w/ courtyard
Owned/ Run By: gay men
Rooms: 9
Baths: private
Meals: expanded cont'l brkfst

Amenities: free parking, outdoor hot tu WiFi
Pets: welcome
Smoking: no
Rates: $55-164

St Peter House Hotel

New Orleans

1005 St Peter St
New Orleans, LA 70116
504/ 524-9232 800/ 535-7815
www.stpeterhouse.com

Clientele: mixed gay/ straight
Type: guesthouse; tropical, brick courtyards w/ broad iron-lace balconies; authentic New Orleans flavor w/ a friendly local touch
Owned/ Run By: gay & straight
Rooms: 29

Baths: private
Meals: cont'l brkfst
Kids: welcome
Pets: no
Smoking: ok
Rates: $49-259
AC: 10%

Sully Mansion

New Orleans

2631 Prytania St
New Orleans, LA 70130
504/ 891-0457 800/ 364-2414
www.sullymansion.com

Clientele: gay-friendly
Type: b&b; 1890s home designed by renowned architect Thomas Sully; furnished w/ antiques; in the heart of the Garden District
Owned/ Run By: gay men
Rooms: 7

Baths: private
Meals: cont'l brkfst
Pets: no
Smoking: no
Rates: $90-250

Sun Oak Museum & Guesthouse

New Orleans

2020 Burgundy St
New Orleans, LA 70116-1606
504/ 250-6630
www.sunoaknola.com

Clientele: mixed gay/ straight
Type: guesthouse; restored Greek Revival Creole cottage w/ fine antiques; city of New Orleans landmark
Owned/ Run By: gay men
Rooms: 2
Baths: private

Meals: cont'l brkfst
Kids: no
Pets: no
Smoking: no
Rates: $75-150
AC: 10%

Ursuline Guest House

New Orleans

708 Ursuline St
New Orleans, LA 70116
504/ 525–8509 800/ 654–2351
www.ursulineguesthouse.com

Clientele: mixed gay/ straight
Type: guesthouse; charming 18th-c guesthouse in French Quarter; "proudly serving our community since 1964"
Owned/ Run By: gay & straight
Rooms: 13
Baths: private

Meals: cont'l brkfst
Amenities: outdoor hot tub
Pets: well-groomed & quiet welcome; $50 damage deposit
Smoking: ok
Rates: $85-125

W New Orleans 🏷

New Orleans

333 Poydras St
New Orleans, LA 70130
504/ 525–9444
877/ WHOTELS (reservations only)
www.whotels.com/neworleans

Clientele: gay-friendly
Type: hotel; unconditionally dedicated to service; offers 24hr concierge & rm service; "we'll help you have an unforgettable New Orleans experience"
Rooms: 423
Baths: private
Wheelchair Access: yes

Amenities: laundry, pool, DVDs/ videos, WiFi
Kids: welcome
Pets: welcome
Smoking: ok
Rates: $239-479
AC: 10%

Twenty-Four Thirty-Nine Fairfield

Shreveport

2439 Fairfield Ave
Shreveport, LA 71104
318/ 424-2424 877/ 251-2439
www.shreveportbedandbreakfast.com

Clientele: gay-friendly
Type: b&b; 1905 Victorian nestled among oak trees; in historic district; English rose & herb gardens, Victorian swing, gazebo, water fountain; private balconies
Rooms: 4

Baths: private
Meals: gourmet brkfst
Pets: welcome
Smoking: no

Magic Pond Wildlife Sanctuary & Guest House

Aroostook County

PO Box 174
Blaine, ME 04734
207/ 429-8787 207/ 947-2240
www.magicpondmaine.com

Clientele: mostly women
Type: cottage; exceptional skiing at Bigrock; artist-owned; comfortable for women traveling alone
Owned/ Run By: lesbians
Rooms: 1 (cottage)
Baths: private

Kids: welcome w/ prior approval
Pets: welcome w/ prior approval
Smoking: no
Rates: $595/ week
AC: $50 (per week)

Annabessacook Farm

Augusta

192 Annabessacook Rd
Winthrop, ME 04364
207/ 377-3276
hometown.aol.com/abcfarmbandb/

Clientele: mixed gay/ straight
Type: b&b; restored 1810 farmhouse on 25 acres; 10 miles W of Augusta; lakefront; ideal for weddings, commitment ceremonies, retreats, writers & artists
Owned/ Run By: gay men

Rooms: 5 (including 1 suite)
Baths: private & shared
Meals: full brkfst
Pets: pets may be boarded in barn
Smoking: no
Rates: $65-300

Maple Hill Farm B&B Inn

Augusta

11 Inn Road
Hallowell, ME 04347
207/ 622-2708 800/ 622-2708
www.MapleBB.com

Clientele: mixed gay/ straight
Type: b&b-inn; spacious farmhouse; 130 acres; farm menagerie; dbl jacuzzis, fireplaces, private decks in some rms; secluded clothing-optional swimming hole; 1 campsite
Owned/ Run By: gay men
Rooms: 8
Baths: private

Wheelchair Access: yes, 1 rm
Meals: full brkfst
Amenities: free parking, massage, DVDs/ videos, WiFi
Kids: 10 yrs & up welcome
Pets: no
Smoking: no
Rates: $75-195
AC: 10%

Central House Inn   *Bar Harbor*

51 Clark Point Rd
Southwest Harbor, ME 04679
207/ 244-0100 877/ 205-0289
www.centralhouseinn.com

Clientele: mixed gay/ straight
Type: b&b-inn; located in Southwest harbor; DSL internet; fireplaces
Owned/ Run By: gay men
Rooms: 3
Baths: private

Meals: full brkfst
Amenities: free parking, hot tub
Kids: welcome; 2 persons max per rm
Pets: no
Rates: $85-175

Manor House Inn   *Bar Harbor*

106 West St
Bar Harbor, ME 04609
207/ 288-3759 800/ 437-0088
www.barharbormanorhouse.com

Clientele: gay-friendly
Type: b&b-inn; in restored 1887 Victorian summer cottage; close to town & Acadia Nat'l Park
Rooms: 17

Baths: private
Meals: full brkfst
Amenities: free parking, hot tub
Rates: $75-250

The Galen C Moses House   *Bath*

1009 Washington St
Bath, ME 04530
207/ 442-8771 888/ 442-8771
www.galenmoses.com

Clientele: mixed gay/ straight
Type: b&b-private home; beautifully restored 1874 Victorian mansion on the Nat'l Register of Historic Homes; antique-filled rms; porches; AAA 3-Diamonds
Owned/ Run By: gay men
Rooms: 4

Baths: private
Meals: full brkfst
Kids: well-controlled & over 12 yrs welcome; 2 persons per rm
Smoking: no
Rates: $99-259

The Inn at Bath   *Bath*

969 Washington St
Bath, ME 04530
207/ 443-4294 800/ 423-0964
www.innatbath.com

Clientele: mixed gay/ straight
Type: b&b-inn; an elegant, comfortable, antique-filled 1810 b&b on the midcoast of Maine
Owned/ Run By: gay & straight
Rooms: 9
Baths: private
Wheelchair Access: yes, 1 rm

Meals: full brkfst
Amenities: free parking, hot tub, DVDs videos
Kids: welcome if quiet & under control
Pets: welcome if quiet & continent
Smoking: no
Rates: $125-200
AC: 7%

Hodgdon Island Inn   *Boothbay Harbor*

PO Box 603
Boothbay, ME 04571
207/ 633-7474 800/ 314-5160
www.hodgdonislandinn.com

Clientele: mixed gay/ straight
Type: b&b; in restored 1810 sea captain's home; located on a private cove w/ water views
Owned/ Run By: gay men
Rooms: 8
Baths: private

Meals: full brkfst
Kids: please inquire
Smoking: no
Rates: $125-175

Sur La Mer Inn   *Boothbay Harbor*

18 Eames Rd, PO Box 663
Boothbay Harbor, ME 04538
207/ 633-7400 800/ 791-2026
www.surlamerinn.com

Clientele: gay-friendly
Type: b&b-inn; luxury b&b w/ 650' of ocean front; short walk to town; oceanfront terrace w/ hot tub, dock, float, small beach; also visit the Boat House Bistro restaurant
Owned/ Run By: gay man
Rooms: 14

Baths: private & shared
Meals: cont'l brkfst
Amenities: free parking, outdoor hot tub
Kids: welcome
Pets: no
Smoking: no
Rates: $85-300

Norumbega

Camden

63 High St
Camden, ME 04843-1733
207/ 236-4646
www.norumbegainn.com

Clientele: gay-friendly
Type: hotel
Rooms: 13
Baths: private
Meals: full brkfst

Amenities: free parking, hot tub
Kids: 7 yrs & up welcome
Rates: $95-475
AC: 5%

The Black Duck Inn on Corea Harbor

Corea

PO Box 39
Corea, ME 04624
207/ 963-2689
www.blackduck.com

Clientele: mixed gay/ straight
Type: b&b-inn; in restored farmhouse; filled w/ art & antiques; overlooking harbor; also rental cottages
Owned/ Run By: gay men
Rooms: 6
Baths: private
Meals: full brkfst

Amenities: free parking
Kids: under 1 yr & over 8 yrs welcome
Pets: no
Smoking: no
Rates: $120-180
AC: 10%

The Royalsborough Inn

Freeport

290 Royalsborough Rd
Durham, ME 04222
207/ 865-6566 800/ 765-1772
www.royalsboroughinn.coom

Clientele: mixed gay/ straight
Type: b&b-inn; relax in the peace & tranquility of this beautifully renovated historic home
Owned/ Run By: lesbians
Rooms: 8
Baths: private

Wheelchair Access: yes, 1 rm
Meals: full brkfst
Kids: welcome
Smoking: no
Rates: $105-175
AC: 10%

Pleasant Street Inn at Moosehead Lake

Greenville

26 Pleasant St
Greenville, ME 04441
207/ 695-3400
www.pleasantstinn.com

Clientele: mixed gay/ straight
Type: b&b; in romantic, elegant 1889 home; located in the village; 1/2 blk from Maine's largest lake, Moosehead Lake
Owned/ Run By: gay men
Rooms: 6
Baths: private

Meals: full brkfst
Smoking: no
Rates: $110-260

Arundel Meadows Inn

Kennebunkport

1024 Portland Rd
Arundel, ME 04046
207/ 985-3770 888/ 985-3770
www.arundelmeadowsinn.com

Clientele: gay-friendly
Type: b&b-private home; charming 19th-c farmhouse near Ogunquit
Owned/ Run By: gay men
Rooms: 7
Baths: private
Meals: full brkfst

Amenities: free parking, pool, indoor hot tub
Kids: teens welcome
Pets: no
Smoking: no
Rates: $110-140
AC: 10%

White Barn Inn

Kennebunkport

37 Beach St
Kennebunkport, ME 04046
207/ 967-2321
www.whitebarninn.com

Clientele: gay-friendly
Type: inn
Rooms: 25 (includes 16 guest rms, 9 suites)
Baths: private
Meals: expanded cont'l brkfst

Rates: $320-820
AC: 10%

Ware Street Inn B&B
Lewiston

52 Ware St
Lewiston, ME 04240
207/ 783-8171 877/ 783-8171
www.warestreetinn.com

Clientele: gay-friendly
Type: b&b-inn; in elegant, gracious 1940 Colonial; caters to business travelers & college crowd; unpretentious & hospitable; award-winning chef
Owned/ Run By: straights
Rooms: 6
Baths: private

Meals: full brkfst
Amenities: free parking, DVDs/ videos, WiFi
Kids: well-behaved & well-supervised welcome
Pets: no
Smoking: no
Rates: $70-175

Lambs Mill Inn
Naples

131 Lambs Mill Rd
Naples, ME 04055
207/ 693-6253
www.lambsmillinn.com

Clientele: mixed gay/ straight
Type: b&b-inn; small country inn; in the foothills of the White Mtns
Owned/ Run By: lesbians
Rooms: 6
Baths: private

Meals: full brkfst
Amenities: free parking, indoor hot tub, DVDs/ videos, WiFi
Kids: 12 yrs & up welcome
Rates: $110-150
AC: 10%

The Tipsy Butler B&B
Newcastle

11 High St
Newcastle, ME 04553
207/ 563-3394
www.thetipsybutler.com

Clientele: gay-friendly
Type: b&b; wonderful New England b&b in beautiful coastal fishing village
Rooms: 4
Baths: private
Meals: full brkfst

Kids: 12 yrs & up welcome
Pets: no
Smoking: no
Rates: $90-150

Abalonia
Ogunquit

268 Main St
Ogunquit, ME 03907
207/ 646-4804
www.abalonia.com

Clientele: mostly men
Type: b&b; 1840s-style New England farmhouse; centrally located; truly walk to everything
Owned/ Run By: gay men
Rooms: 16
Baths: private & shared

Meals: cont'l brkfst
Kids: please inquire; best accommodated off-season
Pets: no
Smoking: no
Rates: $58-200

Admiral's Inn Resort Hotel
Ogunquit

87 Main St
Ogunquit, ME 03907
207/ 646-7093 888/ 263-6318
www.theadmiralsinn.com

Clientele: mostly men
Type: hotel; Ogunquit's premier gay accommodations; close to nightlife, restaurants & beach
Owned/ Run By: gay men
Rooms: 18
Baths: private & shared

Meals: cont'l brkfst
Amenities: free parking, pool, outdoor hot tub
Kids: no
Pets: no
Smoking: no
Rates: $69-169

Beaver Dam Campground
Ogunquit

551 School St, Rte 9
Berwick, ME 03901
207/ 698-2267
www.beaverdamcampground.com

Clientele: gay-friendly
Type: quiet family campground; w/ 60 campsites & 60 RV hookups; on beautiful 20-acre spring-fed pond
Owned/ Run By: women
Amenities: free parking, laundry, pool, WiFi
Kids: welcome

Pets: welcome; must be leashed & nonaggressive
Rates: $26-39

Black Boar Inn
Ogunquit

277 Main St
Ogunquit, ME 03907
207/ 646–2112
www.blackboarinn.com

Clientele: mixed gay/ lesbian
Type: b&b-inn; built in 1674; also weekly cottages; 50-ft terrace overlooking garden
Owned/ Run By: gay man
Rooms: 6 (+ 3 cottages)
Baths: private

Meals: full brkfst & afternoon tea
Amenities: free parking, outdoor hot tub
Kids: welcome
Pets: no
Smoking: no
Rates: $100-205

The Carriage Trade Inn
Ogunquit

254 Shore Rd, PO Box 1793,
Ogunquit, ME 03907
207/ 646–0650 866/ 500–0650
www.carriagetradeinn.com

Clientele: mixed gay/ lesbian
Type: b&b; walking distance to Perkins Cove, the Village, the beach, clubs & restaurants
Owned/ Run By: gay men
Rooms: 7 (includes 1 suite)
Baths: private
Meals: expanded cont'l brkfst

Amenities: free parking, DVDs/ videos, WiFi
Kids: no
Pets: no
Smoking: no
Rates: $85-250

Distant Sands B&B
Ogunquit

PO Box 148, 632 Main St
Ogunquit, ME 03907
207/ 646-8686
www.distantsands.com

Clientele: mixed gay/ straight
Type: b&b; restored 18th-c farmhouse overlooking the Ogunquit River; eclectic motif, antiques & artwork; also weekly cottage rentals
Owned/ Run By: gay men
Rooms: 6
Baths: private & shared

Meals: full brkfst
Amenities: free parking, hot tub, DVDs/ videos
Kids: no
Pets: no
Smoking: no
Rates: $95-195

The Heritage of Ogunquit
Ogunquit

PO Box 1788
Ogunquit, ME 03907
866/ 623-2647
www.heritageogunquit.com

Clientele: mostly women
Type: b&b; in Victorian reproduction; 5-10-minute walk to beach, town & cove; also efficiencies; gay men welcome, mostly women
Owned/ Run By: lesbian
Rooms: 5
Baths: private

Meals: full brkfst
Amenities: free parking, indoor hot tub, DVDs/ videos
Kids: welcome; up to $20 fee
Pets: no, but boarding close by
Smoking: no
Rates: $80-145
AC: 3%

The Inn at Tall Chimneys
Ogunquit

PO Box 2286
Ogunquit, ME 03907
207/ 646-8974

Clientele: mixed gay/ lesbian
Type: b&b-inn; open April-Nov
Owned/ Run By: gay men
Rooms: 8

Baths: private & shared
Meals: cont'l brkfst
Amenities: outdoor hot tub
Rates: $50-95

Leisure Inn
Ogunquit

PO Box 2113
Ogunquit, ME 03907-2113
207/ 646-2737
www.theleisureinn.com

Clientele: mixed gay/ straight
Type: b&b-inn; "the warmth that is Maine & the special ambience that is the Leisure Inn"; everything w/in walking distance
Rooms: 6
Baths: private
Meals: expanded cont'l brkfst

Amenities: free parking, WiFi
Kids: welcome
Pets: no
Smoking: no
Rates: $99-229

Meadowmere Resort   *Ogunquit*

74 S Main St
Ogunquit, ME 03907
207/ 646-9661 800/ 633-8718
www.meadowmere.com

Clientele: gay-friendly
Type: resort; elegant yr-round accommodations; fireplace & jacuzzi suites; health club & spa
Owned/ Run By: gay & straight
Rooms: 145
Baths: private
Wheelchair Access: yes, 115 rms

Meals: expanded cont'l brkfst
Amenities: free parking, laundry, pool, sauna, indoor (yr-round) & outdoor hot tub (seasonal), massage, gym, WiFi
Kids: welcome
Pets: no
Smoking: no
Rates: $64-359

Moon Over Maine B&B   *Ogunquit*

Berwick Rd
Ogunquit, ME 03907
207/ 646-6666 800/ 851-6837
www.moonovermaine.com

Clientele: mixed gay/ lesbian
Type: b&b; Cape-style house built in 1839; recently renovated & furnished
Owned/ Run By: gay men
Rooms: 9
Baths: private
Meals: expanded cont'l brkfst

Amenities: free parking, outdoor hot tub, DVDs/ videos, WiFi
Kids: welcome
Pets: no
Smoking: no
Rates: $70-150

Ogunquit Beach Inn   *Ogunquit*

67 School St
Ogunquit, ME 03097
207/ 646-1112 888/ 976-2463
www.ogunquitbeachinn.com

Clientele: mostly men
Type: b&b-inn; affordable rms in heart of gay Ogunquit; "Ogunquit's favorite gay guesthouse"
Owned/ Run By: gay men
Rooms: 8
Baths: private & shared

Meals: expanded cont'l brkfst
Amenities: free parking, DVDs/ videos, WiFi
Kids: 12 yrs & up welcome; in cottages only
Pets: no
Smoking: no
Rates: $89-169

The Ogunquit Inn & Cottages   *Ogunquit*

PO Box 1883
Ogunquit, ME 03907
207/ 646-3633 866/ 999-3633
www.ogthouse.com

Clientele: mixed gay/ straight
Type: b&b-inn; Victorian home & cottages; w/ beautiful gardens
Owned/ Run By: gay men
Rooms: 10 (includes 6 rms & 4 cottages)
Baths: private & shared
Meals: expanded cont'l brkfst

Kids: 12 yrs & up welcome; in cottages only
Pets: welcome in cottages only
Smoking: no
Rates: $49-189

Yellow Monkey Guest Houses/ Hotel   *Ogunquit*

280 Main St
Ogunquit, ME 03907
207/ 646-9056
www.yellowmonkeyguests.com

Clientele: mixed gay/ straight
Type: b&b-inn; inn consists of 6 houses; rms, cabins & apts; short walk to beach
Owned/ Run By: gay men
Rooms: 48
Baths: private & shared
Wheelchair Access: yes, 2 rms

Meals: cont'l brkfst
Amenities: free parking, hot tub
Kids: welcome
Pets: welcome; 2 max (small to medium)
Smoking: ok
Rates: $90-150
AC: 10%

Auberge by the Sea B&B   *Portland*

103 East Grand Ave
Old Orchard Beach, ME 04064
207/ 934-2355
www.aubergebythesea.com

Clientele: gay-friendly
Type: b&b; in quaint, quiet beach house
Owned/ Run By: straights
Rooms: 4
Baths: private
Meals: expanded cont'l brkfst
Kids: no

Pets: no
Smoking: no
Rates: $79-159
AC: 10%

Two Village Square

PO Box 864
Ogunquit, ME 03907

207/ 646-5779
412/ 606-2007 (winter #)

Ogunquit

www.twovillagesquare.com

Two Village Square, located in the heart of Ogunquit, is a 17-room inn nestled on a wooded hillside perch overlooking the town square and Atlantic Ocean.

It is large enough to offer the space and amenities you are looking for, yet small enough to maintain the charm and personal attention found at a B&B.

The laid-back and congenial atmosphere of our extensively renovated 1886 inn is complemented by its close proximity to all the resort activities of this seaside getaway. Casually appointed common areas and rooms, a heated pool, 12-person spa, and attentive staff all offer a friendly invitation to kick back and relax after a day of antiquing, whale-watching, hiking, or sunning on the convenient three miles of unspoiled white-sand beach.

A Sunday cocktail party, Wednesday happy hour, and an expanded continental breakfast are all included at this Ogunquit getaway.

Clientele: mostly men

Type: b&b-inn; in oceanview Victorian; perched on 3 acres of wooded hillside; just minutes' walk to beach, shops, clubs & restaurants

Owned/ Run By: gay men

Nearby Attractions: art galleries, antiquing, LL Bean outlet shopping, beach

Transit: near public transit; 65 miles to Boston; 60 miles to Manchester, NH (Southwest Airlines); 35 miles to Portland; 16 miles to Portsmouth (PanAm); 7 miles to Wells, ME (Amtrak from Boston)

Rooms: 17 total, 5 kings, 12 queens, A/C, color TV, cable, ceiling fan, maid service

Baths: private & shared, bathtubs, showers

Meals: expanded cont'l brkfst

Amenities: pool, outdoor 12-person hot tub, DVDs/ videos, WiFi, coffee/ tea, guest kitchen, piano, fireplace, cocktail party Sun (in-season), Pool Party Wed (in-season)

Recreation: tennis, whale-watching, sailing, sea kayaking, golf, biking

Pets: dogs under 30 lbs & socialized welcome

Pets On Premises: 2 dogs

Smoking: no

Reservations: recommended *Deposit:* required, 1/3, due w/in 2 weeks, personal check ok *Cancellation:* cancel by 30 days prior (in-season) or forfeit a fee *Minimum Stay:* in-season

Payment: cash, travelers checks, Visa, MC

Season: *High season:* late June-Labor Day *Closed:* Nov-April

Rates: $120-179 *Discounts:* off-season weeknights, groups

The Danforth
Portland

163 Danforth St
Portland, ME 04102
207/ 879-8755 800/ 991-6557
www.danforthmaine.com

Clientele: gay-friendly
Type: b&b-inn; historic 1821 mansion overlooking Portland's waterfront; featuring gracious accommodations & working fireplaces
Owned/ Run By: women
Rooms: 10

Baths: private
Kids: welcome
Pets: welcome w/ prior approval
Smoking: no
Rates: $119-359

The Inn at St John
Portland

939 Congress St
Portland, ME 04102
207/ 773-6481 800/ 636-9127
www.innatstjohn.com

Clientele: mixed gay/ straight
Type: b&b-inn; most unique 100-yr-old inn; noted for its European charm & quiet gentility; centrally located
Owned/ Run By: gay men
Rooms: 37
Baths: private & shared

Wheelchair Access: yes, 2 rms
Meals: expanded cont'l brkfst
Kids: welcome
Pets: please call first
Smoking: ok
Rates: $50-190
AC: 10%

The Inn by the Sea
Portland

40 Bowery Beach Rd
Cape Elizabeth, ME 04107
207/ 799-3134 800/ 888-4287
www.innbythesea.com

Clientele: gay-friendly
Type: condo-style suites w/ ocean views
Owned/ Run By: woman
Rooms: 43
Baths: private
Wheelchair Access: yes, 2 rms
Kids: welcome

Pets: well-behaved dogs on leashes welcome
Smoking: no
Rates: $179-709
AC: 10% of rack rate

The Percy Inn
Portland

15 Pine St
Portland, ME 04102
207/ 871-7638 888/ 417-3729
www.percyinn.com

Clientele: gay-friendly
Type: b&b-inn; 1830 brick row house at Longfellow Square; owned by hotel critic; amenity-rich guest rms
Rooms: 10
Baths: private
Meals: expanded cont'l brkfst

Kids: no
Pets: no
Smoking: no
Rates: $89-199
AC: 10%

Sea View Motel
Portland

65 W Grand Ave
Old Orchard Beach, ME 04064
207/ 934-4180 800/ 541-8439
www.seaviewgetaway.com

Clientele: mixed gay/ straight
Type: motel; yr-round oceanfront motel; close to local attractions
Rooms: 49
Baths: private
Wheelchair Access: yes, 1 rm
Meals: coffee/tea only

Amenities: free parking, pool, WiFi
Kids: welcome
Pets: welcome (seasonal)
Smoking: no
Rates: $52-280

West End Inn
Portland

146 Pine St
Portland, ME 04102
207/ 772-1377 800/ 338-1377
www.westendbb.com

Clientele: gay-friendly
Type: b&b-inn; our quiet location & comfortable bdrms invite a good night's sleep
Owned/ Run By: women
Rooms: 6
Baths: private

Meals: full brkfst
Kids: 10 & up welcome
Smoking: no
Rates: $99-209

Wild Iris Inn   *Portland*

273 State St
Portland, ME 04101
207/ 775-0224 800/ 600-1557
www.wildirisinn.com

Clientele: gay-friendly
Type: b&b; cozy b&b in historic neighborhood; conveniently located w/in walking distance of the art district & old port
Owned/ Run By: women
Rooms: 7

Baths: private & shared
Meals: expanded cont'l brkfst
Kids: 6 yrs & up welcome
Pets: no
Smoking: no
Rates: $85-190

Captain Lindsey House Inn   *Rockland*

5 Lindsey St
Rockland, ME 04841
207/ 596-7950 800/ 523-2145
www.lindseyhouse.com

Clientele: gay-friendly
Type: "picture a lovely Old English inn magically blended w/ a 19th-c Maine sea captain's home"
Owned/ Run By: lesbian & straight
Rooms: 9
Baths: private

Wheelchair Access: yes, 1 rm
Meals: expanded cont'l brkfst
Kids: 10 yrs & up welcome
Pets: no
Smoking: no
Rates: $85-195
AC: 10%

Wildflower Inn   *Searsport*

2 Black Rd S/ US Rte 1
Searsport, ME 04974
207/ 548-2112 888/ 546-2112
www.wildflowerinnme.com

Clientele: mixed gay/ straight
Type: b&b; located conveniently on US Coastal Rte 1 midway between Rockland & Bar Harbor; close to hiking, kayaking, biking & antiquing; 40 minutes to Bangor, 2.5 hrs to Portland
Owned/ Run By: lesbians
Rooms: 4

Baths: private
Meals: full brkfst
Amenities: free parking, DVDs/ videos, WiFi
Kids: 12 yrs & older welcome
Pets: no
Smoking: no
Rates: $79-149

Mountain Village Inn   *White Mtns*

164 Main St
Kingfield, ME 04947

207/ 265-2030
866/ 577-0741

innkeeper@mountainvillageinn.com
www.mountainvillageinn.com

Clientele: gay-friendly
Type: b&b; circa 1850 cape-style farmhouse on 17 acres renovated into upscale b&b; views of Mt Abraham & Longfellow Range; Trailside Cafe on-site
Owned/ Run By: woman
Nearby Attractions: White Mtns, resorts, shopping, dining
Transit: 2 hrs to Portland or Bangor Int'l
Rooms: 7 total, 2 suites, 1 king, 4 queens, 2 twins, cable TV (1), ceiling fan (1), fireplace (1), kitchenette (1), refrigerator (1)
Baths: private, bathtubs, showers, whirlpools, robes, hairdryers
Wheelchair Access: yes, 1 rm
Meals: full brkfst, vegan meals available
Amenities: free parking, laundry, DVDs/ videos, WiFi, coffee/ tea, snowmobile trail, x-country skiing
Recreation: Sugarloaf: skiing, golfing, hiking, fly-fishing, boating, swimming
Kids: welcome
Pets: welcome
Pets On Premises: 3 dogs

Smoking: no
Reservations: *Deposit:* required, 50%, due at booking *Cancellation:* cancel by 2 weeks prior or forfeit $20 *Check in/ out:* 3pm-7pm/ 11am

Payment: cash, travelers checks, personal checks, Visa, Amex, MC, Discover
Season: *High season:* Nov-April
Rates: $75-160 *Discounts:* yes

Two-O-One B&B
Annapolis

201 Prince George St
Annapolis, MD 21401
410/ 268-8053
www.201bb.com

Clientele: mixed gay/ straight
Type: b&b; in elegant Georgian-style town house on quiet street; very private, convenient location
Owned/ Run By: gay men
Rooms: 4
Baths: private

Meals: full brkfst
Amenities: free parking, hot tub, DVDs/ videos, WiFi
Smoking: no

William Page Inn B&B
Annapolis

8 Martin St
Annapolis, MD 21401
410/ 626-1506 800/ 364-4160
www.williampageinn.com

Clientele: mixed gay/ straight
Type: b&b-inn; elegantly renovated 1908 home in the historic district; AAA 3 Diamonds
Owned/ Run By: gay men
Rooms: 5
Baths: private & shared

Meals: full brkfst
Amenities: free parking, WiFi
Kids: 12 yrs & up welcome
Pets: no
Smoking: no
Rates: $150-270
AC: 10%

1870 Guest House
Baltimore

21 S Stricker St
Baltimore, MD 21223
410/ 947-4622
www.innsite.com/inns/a005349

Clientele: gay-friendly
Type: b&b-private home; spacious guest suite includes full private kitchen; in restored Italianate row house on historic park close to Inner Harbor
Owned/ Run By: straights
Rooms: 1

Baths: private
Meals: full brkfst
Kids: welcome
Pets: no
Smoking: no
Rates: $115-125

Abacrombie Fine Food & Accommodations
Baltimore

58 W Biddle St
Baltimore, MD 21201
410/ 244-7227 888/ 922-3437
www.abacrombie.net

Clientele: mixed gay/ straight
Type: b&b-inn; 19th-c house next to Meyerhoff Symphony Hall; in the heart of Baltimore's cultural center
Rooms: 12
Baths: private

Meals: expanded cont'l brkfst
Kids: 10 yrs & up welcome
Smoking: no
Rates: $88-185
AC: 8%

Biltmore Suites
Baltimore

205 W Madison St
Baltimore, MD 21201
410/ 728-6550 800/ 868-5064
www.biltmoresuites.com

Clientele: gay-friendly
Type: turn-of-the-century Victorian hotel; located in Mt Vernon District; 10 blks from Inner Harbor, convention center & Camden Yards
Owned/ Run By: straights
Rooms: 25
Baths: private

Meals: cont'l brkfst
Kids: welcome
Pets: welcome; $25 charge per 3 nights
Smoking: ok (in some rms)
Rates: $69-179
AC: 8% for new agents & 10% for prior agents

Harbor Inn Pier 5
Baltimore

711 Eastern Ave
Baltimore, MD 21202
410/ 539-2000
www.thepier5.com

Clientele: mixed gay/ straight
Type: waterfront boutique hotel; w/ personally designed rms; also 3 restaurants, cigar bar & nightclub
Owned/ Run By: straights
Rooms: 65

Baths: private
Wheelchair Access: yes, 3 rms
Kids: welcome
Rates: $219-1,495
AC: 10%

Park Avenue B&B

Baltimore

2018 Park Avenue
Baltimore, MD 21217
410/ 523-2625
www.parkavenuebedandbreakfast.com

Clientele: mixed gay/ straight
Type: b&b-private home; in historic Reservoir Hill; easy access to I-83; close to downtown
Owned/ Run By: gay men
Rooms: 2

Baths: private & shared
Meals: expanded cont'l brkfst
Kids: no
Pets: no
Smoking: no
Rates: $135-145

Radisson Plaza Lord Baltimore Hotel

Baltimore

20 W Baltimore St
Baltimore, MD 21201
410/ 539-8400 800/ 333-3333
www.radisson.com/lordbaltimore

Clientele: mixed gay/ straight
Type: hotel; "Baltimore's only historic, landmark hotel; offers modern-day convenience in an Old World atmosphere"
Owned/ Run By: gay & straight
Rooms: 439
Baths: private
Wheelchair Access: yes, 9 rms

Meals: cont'l brkfst
Amenities: laundry, sauna, indoor hot tub
Kids: welcome
Smoking: ok (only in lobby lounge & smoking rms)
Rates: $179-259
AC: $5-10

Tremont Park Hotel

Baltimore

8 E Pleasant St
Baltimore, MD 21202
800/ 873-6668
www.tremontsuitehotels.com

Clientele: mixed gay/ straight
Type: hotel; "Baltimore's only all-suites hotel"; outdoor pool 1 blk away at Tremont Plaza
Owned/ Run By: straights
Rooms: 58
Baths: private

Wheelchair Access: yes, 2 rms
Kids: welcome
Pets: welcome
Smoking: ok
Rates: $99-349
AC: 10%

Red Lamp Post B&B

Cumberland

849 Braddock Rd
Cumberland, MD 21502
301/ 777-7476
khummel@allconet.org

Clientele: mixed gay/ lesbian
Type: b&b; antique-filled home; TV/ VCR in each rm; complimentary cocktails
Owned/ Run By: lesbians/ gay men
Rooms: 3
Baths: shared

Amenities: free parking, laundry, hot tub, DVDs/ videos, gym
Kids: no
Pets: no
Smoking: no
Rates: $65-75

Rocky Gap Lodge & Golf Resort

Cumberland

16701 Lakeview Rd NE
Flintstone, MD 21530
301/ 784-8400 800/ 724-0828
www.rockygapresort.com

Clientele: gay-friendly
Type: resort; expansive 243-acre property w/ forests, lake & elegantly rustic lodge
Owned/ Run By: straights
Meals: coffee/tea only

Amenities: free parking, laundry, pool, indoor hot tub, massage
Pets: welcome
Rates: $110+

La Clé D'Or

Havre de Grace

226 N Union Ave
Havre de Grace, MD 21078-2907
410/ 939-6562 888/ 484-4837
www.lacledorguesthouse.com

Clientele: mixed gay/ straight
Type: b&b; 1868 home of the Johns Hopkins family
Owned/ Run By: gay men
Rooms: 3
Baths: private

Meals: full brkfst
Kids: 12 yrs & up welcome; please call first
Pets: welcome; limited rms
Smoking: ok (limited rms)
Rates: $120-140 (double)
AC: 10%

The Alexander House Booklovers B&B
Princess Anne

30535 Linden Ave
Princess Anne, MD 21853
410/ 651-5195
www.bookloversbnb.com

Clientele: gay-friendly
Type: b&b; literary-themed b&b; in historic town close to Atlantic Ocean & Chesapeake Bay; "we celebrate books, writers & diversity!"
Owned/ Run By: straights
Rooms: 3

Baths: private
Meals: full brkfst
Kids: 14 yrs & up welcome
Pets: no
Smoking: no
Rates: $80-150
AC: 5%

Tallulah's on Main
Rock Hall

5750 Main St
Rock Hall, MD 21661
410/ 639-2596
www.tallulahsonmain.com

Clientele: mixed gay/ straight
Type: hotel; suites w/ kitchens; in quiet fishing village on E shore of Chesapeake Bay; 3 blks to harbor
Owned/ Run By: gay men
Rooms: 5
Baths: private

Wheelchair Access: yes, 1 rm
Meals: coffee/tea only
Kids: well-behaved & supervised welcome
Pets: welcome w/ prior approval
Smoking: no
Rates: $115-150
AC: 10%

Ivy House B&B
Amherst

1 Sunset Ct
Amherst, MA 01002
413/ 549-7554
ivyhouse@usermail.com

Clientele: mixed gay/ straight
Type: b&b-inn; in handsomely restored Colonial Cape (portions circa 1740); voted "Best B&B" in the Valley
Owned/ Run By: gay man
Rooms: 2
Baths: private

Meals: full brkfst
Kids: no
Pets: no
Smoking: no
Rates: $60-90
AC: 10%

Jenkins Inn & Restaurant
Barre

7 West St/ Rte 122
Barre, MA 01005
978/ 355-6444 800/ 378-7373
www.jenkinsinn.com

Clientele: gay-friendly
Type: b&b-inn; located at the center of Massachusetts; 4-star restaurant on premises serving gourmet lunch & dinner w/ daily specials, homemade desserts & full bar
Owned/ Run By: gay men
Rooms: 4

Baths: private
Meals: full brkfst
Amenities: free parking, DVDs/ videos, WiFi
Kids: 12 yrs & up welcome
Pets: by arrangement
Smoking: no
Rates: $160-190

Winterwood
Barre

19 N Main St
Petersham, MA 01366
978/ 724-8885
www.winterwoodinn.com

Clientele: gay-friendly
Type: b&b-inn; elegantly restored 1842 Greek Revival mansion; fireplaces; available for weddings & cocktail receptions
Owned/ Run By: straights
Rooms: 6
Baths: private

Meals: full brkfst
Amenities: free parking
Kids: welcome; no cribs available
Pets: no
Smoking: no
Rates: $139

The B&B at Howden Farm
Berkshires

303 Rannapo Rd
Sheffield, MA 01257
413/ 229-8481
www.howdenfarm.com

Clientele: mixed gay/ straight
Type: b&b-private home; working farm on 250 acres whose main crop is pumpkins—the Howden Pumpkin & Howden Biggie; berry picking & a flock of chickens too!
Owned/ Run By: gay men

Rooms: 4
Baths: private & shared
Meals: full brkfst
Smoking: no
Rates: $89-179

Broken Hill Manor
Berkshires

771 West Rd
Sheffield, MA 01257
413/ 528-6159 877/ 535-6159
www.brokenhillmanor.com

Clientele: gay-friendly
Type: b&b-inn; tranquil Edwardian manor; 12 hilltop acres; minutes from downtown Great Barrington
Owned/ Run By: gay men
Rooms: 8
Baths: private

Wheelchair Access: yes
Meals: full brkfst
Kids: 13 yrs & up welcome
Pets: no
Smoking: no
Rates: $125-200
AC: 10%

Cornell Inn
Berkshires

203 Main St
Lenox, MA 01240
413/ 637-0562 800/ 637-0562
www.cornellinn.com

Clientele: gay-friendly
Type: b&b-inn; located minutes from all cultural venues in the Berkshires; same-sex wedding ceremonies happily facilitated; pub on-site
Owned/ Run By: straights
Rooms: 28

Baths: private
Wheelchair Access: yes, 2 rms
Meals: full brkfst
Amenities: free parking, hot tub, WiFi
Kids: no
Pets: no
Rates: $80-350

The Old Post Inn
Berkshires

32 Old Post Rd
Worthington, MA 01098
413/ 238-0170
www.oldpostinn.com

Clientele: mixed gay/ straight
Type: b&b; in 18th-c restored farmhouse
Owned/ Run By: lesbians
Rooms: 2
Baths: private & shared
Meals: cont'l brkfst

Amenities: free parking, outdoor hot tub, WiFi
Kids: no
Pets: no
Smoking: no
Rates: $65-95

The Rookwood Inn
Berkshires

11 Old Stockbridge Rd
Lenox, MA 01240
413/ 637-9750 800/ 223-9750
www.rookwoodinn.com

Clientele: mixed gay/ straight
Type: b&b-inn; Victorian fairy-tale inn w/ luxurious modern amenities; near Tanglewood, theater, skiing; walk to town; packages available
Owned/ Run By: women
Rooms: 21
Baths: private

Meals: full brkfst
Amenities: free parking, massage, WiFi
Kids: welcome
Pets: welcome; please ask about policies
Smoking: no
Rates: $125-400
AC: 10% (in off-season)

Topia Inn
Berkshires

10 Pleasant St
Adams, MA 01220
413/ 743-9605 888/ 868-6742
www.topiainn.com

Clientele: mixed gay/ straight
Type: b&b-inn; eco-friendly; organic gourmet brkfst
Owned/ Run By: lesbians
Rooms: 10
Baths: private
Wheelchair Access: yes, 1 rm

Meals: full brkfst
Amenities: free parking, laundry, indoor hot tub, massage, DVDs/ videos, WiFi
Kids: welcome
Pets: no
Smoking: no
Rates: $125-160

Windflower Inn
Berkshires

684 S Egremont Rd
Great Barrington, MA 01230
413/ 528-2720 800/ 992-1993
www.windflowerinn.com

Clientele: gay-friendly
Type: b&b-inn; gracious antique-filled country inn; set on 10 acres
Owned/ Run By: straights
Rooms: 13
Baths: private

Meals: full brkfst
Kids: welcome
Pets: no
Smoking: no
Rates: $100-215
AC: varies

463 Beacon St Guest House   *Boston*

463 Beacon St
Boston, MA 02115

617/ 536-1302

info@463beacon.com
www.463beacon.com

Clientele: mixed gay/ straight
Type: guesthouse; modestly priced nightly, weekly & monthly accommodations; conveniently located in Boston's Back Bay
Owned/ Run By: gay & straight
Nearby Attractions: walking distance to Prudential/ Hynes Convention Center, Copley Place, restaurants, nightlife
Transit: near public transit; 3 blks to "T" (mass transit)
Rooms: 20 total, 3 kings, 3 queens, 13 fulls, 1 twin, A/C, color TV, cable, phone, kitchenette, refrigerator
Baths: private & shared
Meals: coffee/tea only
Amenities: office hrs: 8am-9pm; laundry, WiFi, coffee/ tea, fax service
Kids: 13 yrs & up welcome
Pets: no

Smoking: no
Reservations: *Deposit:* required, 50% *Cancellation:* cancel by 14 days prior or forfeit $10 *Check in/ out:* 1pm/ noon
Payment: cash, travelers checks, personal checks, Visa, MC, Discover, JCB
Season: open yr-round
Rates: $79-169   *Discounts:* 10-15% weekly
AC: 10%

82 Chandler B&B   *Boston*

82 Chandler St
Boston, MA 02116
617/ 482-0408
www.82chandler.com

Clientele: mixed gay/ straight
Type: b&b-inn; 4-story brick town house; located in downtown Boston, just off famous Copley Square in the city's historic South End; w/in walking distance or a short subway ride to all Boston attractions
Owned/ Run By: gay men

Rooms: 5 (includes 2 studios for 7+ day stays)
Baths: private
Meals: cont'l brkfst
Amenities: WiFi
Smoking: no
Rates: $95-175

Appleton Studio   *Boston*

30 Appleton St
Boston, MA 02116
617/ 720-0522 800/ 347-5088
www.bnbboston.com/
boston-bnbs/b&bs_5b.htm

Clientele: gay-friendly
Type: studio; spacious 2nd-flr studio apt; w/ fully equipped kitchen, bay window, private entry; close to Copley Square; also weekly/ monthly rentals
Owned/ Run By: gay man

Rooms: 1 (studio)
Baths: private
Amenities: WiFi
Smoking: no
Rates: $100-160

The Charles Street Inn   *Boston*

94 Charles St
Boston, MA 02114
617/ 314-8900 877/ 772-8900
www.charlesstreetinn.com

Clientele: mixed gay/ straight
Type: b&b-inn; circa 1860 town house; original fireplaces; antique furnishings; large rms w/ seating areas & whirlpool tubs; DSL-internet access
Owned/ Run By: lesbians
Rooms: 9
Baths: private

Wheelchair Access: yes, 1 rm
Meals: expanded cont'l brkfst
Amenities: hot tub, DVDs/ videos
Kids: welcome
Pets: welcome, if well-behaved & quiet
Smoking: no
Rates: $225-375
AC: 10%

Chandler Inn ⏏ℭ   *Boston*

26 Chandler St
Boston, MA 02116
617/ 482-3450 800/ 842-3450
inn3450@ix.netcom.com
www.chandlerinn.com

Clientele: gay-friendly
Type: hotel; European-style hotel in the heart of the city; "enjoy our comfortable accommodations, superb location & competitive rates"
Owned/ Run By: gay/ lesbian & straight
Nearby Attractions: 1/4-2 miles to all Boston attractions
Transit: near public transit; Back Bay/ South End subway station nearby; taxi: Boston Cab, 617/ 536-3200
Rooms: 55 total, 14 queens, 28 fulls, 14 twins, A/C, color TV, cable, phone, maid service, all renovated in 2000
Baths: private, bathtubs, showers, hairdryers
Wheelchair Access: yes, all rms
Meals: coffee/tea only
Amenities: office hrs: 24hrs; WiFi, coffee/ tea, Fritz bar on-site
Kids: welcome; no cots available
Pets: w/ manager's approval only (dogs under 20 lbs)
Smoking: ok (in guest rms only)
Reservations: recommended; personal checks ok if recv'd 2 weeks prior *Deposit:* personal check ok *Cancellation:* cancel by 2 days prior or forfeit 1 night *Minimum Stay:* 2 nights (some wknds) *Check in/ out:* 3pm/ 11am
Payment: cash, travelers checks, Visa, Amex, MC, Discover, Diners Club
Season: open yr-round *High season:* April- Nov
Rates: $89-169
AC: 10%

T he Chandler Inn Hotel offers European-style accommodations in Boston's historic South End.

Great rates put you no more than a short walk from fashionable Newbury Street, Copley Square, the Theater District, and the convention center. Here you will find a lively collection of restaurants and shops to explore and enjoy.

The Chandler Inn's comfortable accommodations, friendly and knowledgeable staff, outstanding location, and great rates make us the ideal choice for lodging in Boston.

Clarendon Square Inn
Boston

198 W Brookline St
Boston, MA 02118
617/ 536-2229
www.clarendonsquare.com

Clientele: mixed gay/ straight
Type: b&b-inn; hip, historic property in Boston's South End offering personal attention in a relaxed, stylish atmosphere
Owned/ Run By: gay men
Rooms: 3

Baths: private
Meals: expanded cont'l brkfst
Amenities: outdoor hot tub, WiFi
Kids: welcome
Smoking: no
Rates: $125-328

The College Club
Boston

44 Commonwealth Ave
Boston, MA 02116
617/ 536-9510
www.thecollegeclubofboston.com

Clientele: gay-friendly
Type: b&b; located in the heart of Boston's historic Back Bay neighborhood; offers guests Old World charm & modern convenience
Rooms: 12
Baths: private & shared

Wheelchair Access: yes
Meals: cont'l brkfst
Amenities: WiFi
Kids: welcome
Pets: no
Smoking: no
Rates: $75-175

Encore B&B
Boston

116 W Newton St
Boston, MA 02118
617/ 247-3425
www.encorebandb.com

Clientele: gay-friendly
Type: b&b; located on the upper flrs of a 19-c town house in Boston's historic South End neighborhood
Owned/ Run By: gay men
Rooms: 3
Baths: private

Meals: expanded cont'l brkfst
Kids: 12 yrs & up welcome
Pets: no
Smoking: no
Rates: $130-190
AC: 10%

Hotel 140
Boston

140 Clarendon St
Boston, MA 02116
617/ 585-5600
www.hotel140.com

Clientele: gay-friendly
Type: hotel; "boutique hotel offering contemporary rms, Terra Cotta Cafe, fitness & business centers at a price you wouldn't expect in the Back Bay"; close to pride festival & parade
Owned/ Run By: women
Rooms: 40

Baths: private
Wheelchair Access: yes, 3 rms
Meals: cont'l brkfst
Kids: welcome
Pets: no
Smoking: no
Rates: $99-329
AC: 10%

Nine Zero Hotel
Boston

90 Tremont St
Boston, MA 02108
617/ 772-5800 866/ 646-3937
www.ninezerohotel.com

Clientele: gay-friendly
Type: luxury hotel; in center of downtown; warm, welcoming, sexy, unique & intimate
Owned/ Run By: gay & straight
Rooms: 189
Baths: private
Wheelchair Access: yes, 5 rms
Meals: full brkfst

Amenities: free parking, laundry, hot tub, massage
Kids: welcome
Pets: welcome
Smoking: ok
Rates: $239-3,000
AC: 10%

Oasis Guest House
Boston

22 Edgerly Rd
Boston, MA 02115
617/ 267-2262 800/ 230-0105
www.oasisgh.com

Clientele: mixed gay/ straight
Type: guesthouse; attractive & affordable; in prime Back Bay location; walk to sights, shopping, nightlife
Owned/ Run By: gay men
Rooms: 30
Baths: private & shared

Wheelchair Access: yes, 1 rm
Meals: cont'l brkfst
Kids: no
Pets: no
Smoking: no
Rates: $69-150
AC: 10%

Taylor House B&B
Boston

50 Burroughs St
Jamaica Plain, MA 02130
617/ 983-9334 888/ 228-2956
www.taylorhouse.com

Clientele: mixed gay/ straight
Type: b&b-private home; Italianate Victorian home; near restaurants, parks, public transit
Owned/ Run By: gay men
Rooms: 3
Baths: private

Meals: expanded cont'l brkfst
Amenities: free parking, massage, DVDs/ videos, WiFi
Kids: in 3rd floor suite only
Pets: welcome, if well-behaved & quiet
Smoking: no
Rates: $119-210

15 Park Square
Cape Cod

15 Park Square
Hyannis, MA 02601
508/ 771-4760
www.15parksquare.com

Clientele: gay-friendly
Type: guesthouse; antique-furnished; beautiful gardens; close to Cape Cod beaches, bars & transit
Owned/ Run By: gay man
Rooms: 6
Baths: shared

Meals: coffee/tea only
Kids: no
Pets: no
Smoking: no
Rates: $50-100
AC: 10%

The Blue Heron
Cape Cod

464 Pleasant Lake Ave
Harwich, MA 02645
508/ 430-0219
www.theblueheronbb.com

Clientele: mixed gay/ lesbian
Type: vacation rental; restored 19th-c Colonial; on the Cape's scenic bicycle path & steps from a private beach on Long Pond; weekly rentals only; sleeps 10
Owned/ Run By: lesbians
Rooms: 5

Baths: private & shared
Pets: no
Smoking: no
Rates: $1,900-3,000/ week

Cape Cod Gay Guest House
Cape Cod

83 Old Barnstable Rd
Falmouth, MA 02536
508/ 540-9998
www.capecodguesthouse.com

Clientele: men
Type: guesthouse; clothing-optional; close to shopping, steamship authority, antique shops & beaches; 1 hr from Provincetown
Owned/ Run By: gay men
Rooms: 2

Baths: private & shared
Meals: cont'l brkfst
Kids: no
Pets: small pets welcome
Smoking: no
Rates: $65-150

The Capeside Cottage B&B
Cape Cod

320 Woods Hole Rd
Woods Hole, MA 02540
508/ 548-6218 800/ 320-2322
www.capesidecottage.com

Clientele: gay-friendly
Type: b&b-inn
Rooms: 6
Baths: private
Meals: full brkfst
Kids: 2 yrs & up welcome

Pets: please inquire
Smoking: no
Rates: $90-160
AC: 10%

The Crow's Nest of West Dennis
Cape Cod

230 Main St
West Dennis, MA 02670
508/ 760-3335 877/ 240-2769
www.thecrowsnestinn.com

Clientele: mixed gay/ straight
Type: b&b; romantic Victorian-Greek Revival home for visitors to Cape Cod since the 1800s; also upscale restaurant
Owned/ Run By: gay men
Rooms: 3

Baths: private
Meals: expanded cont'l brkfst
Kids: no
Pets: welcome
Rates: $105-145

Private Cape Cod Cottage
Cape Cod

35 Rolling Ln
Eastham, MA 02651
631/ 689-9456
jfivefeet@optonline.net

Clientele: mostly women
Type: cottage; immaculate 2-bdrm summer rental; 20 minutes from Provincetown; 1/2 mile to beaches; seasonal
Owned/ Run By: lesbians
Rooms: 2
Baths: private

Kids: 10 yrs & up welcome
Pets: no
Smoking: no
Rates: $800-1,075/ week

The Sleepy Rooster Guesthouse
Cape Cod

125 Sea St
Cape Cod, MA 02601
508/ 771-5731
www.thesleepyrooster.com

Clientele: gay-friendly
Type: 1830s garden guesthouse; decorated w/ vintage furniture; walk to beach & historic Hyannis Main St restaurants & shops
Owned/ Run By: gay man
Rooms: 3

Baths: private & shared
Amenities: free parking, DVDs/ videos, WiFi
Kids: over 12 yrs welcome
Pets: no
Smoking: no
Rates: $99-149

Brandt House
Greenfield

29 Highland Ave
Greenfield, MA 01301
413/ 774-3329 800/ 235-3329
www.brandthouse.com

Clientele: gay-friendly
Type: b&b-inn; 16-rm estate high on a hill; clay tennis court, wraparound porches
Owned/ Run By: woman
Rooms: 9
Baths: private & shared
Meals: full brkfst

Kids: welcome
Pets: dogs by arrangement
Smoking: no (outdoor porches only)
Rates: $110-325
AC: 10%

The Charlemont Inn
Greenfield

Rte 2, Mohawk Trail
Charlemont, MA 01339
413/ 339-5796
www.charlemontinn.com

Clientele: gay-friendly
Type: charming country inn; restaurant & bar; entertainment wknds; skiing, hiking, biking, fishing, rafting & kayaking all w/in 1 mile
Owned/ Run By: lesbians
Rooms: 14

Baths: shared
Kids: welcome
Pets: welcome w/ some restrictions
Smoking: no
Rates: $60-150

Thoreau's Walden B&B
Lincoln

2 Concord Rd
Lincoln, MA 01773
781/ 259-1899

Clientele: mixed gay/ straight
Type: b&b-private home; across the road & w/in sight of historic Walden Pond; surrounded by hiking trails on conservation land; x-country skiing from residence; 18 miles to Boston
Owned/ Run By: straight woman

Rooms: 2
Baths: private
Meals: full brkfst
Kids: welcome
Pets: no
Smoking: no
Rates: $75-100

Arbor Inn
Martha's Vineyard

222 Upper Main St
Edgartown, MA 02539
508/ 627-8137 888/ 748-4383
www.arborinn.net

Clientele: mixed gay/ straight
Type: b&b; typically New England in decor; rms furnished w/ antiques; brkfst indoors or in on-site gardens
Rooms: 8
Baths: private & shared

Meals: expanded cont'l brkfst
Rates: $125-250

Martha's Vineyard Surfside

Martha's Vineyard

PO Box 2507
Oak Bluffs, MA 02557
508/ 693-2500 800/ 537-3007
mvsurfside.com

Clientele: gay-friendly
Type: motel; some ocean views; heat & A/C; broadband internet
Owned/ Run By: gay & straight
Rooms: 38
Baths: private
Wheelchair Access: yes, 2 rms

Meals: coffee/tea only
Amenities: free parking, jacuzzi (some rms)
Kids: welcome
Pets: welcome; $15 per night pet fee
Smoking: ok in some rms
Rates: $75-355
AC: 10%

The Shiverick Inn

Martha's Vineyard

5 Pease's Pt Wy, Edgartown
Martha's Vineyard, MA 02539
508/ 627-3797 800/ 723-4292
www.shiverickinn.com

Clientele: mixed gay/ straight
Type: b&b-inn; 1840s elegant mansion embellished w/ beautiful antiques, 9 fireplaces, garden & drawing rms, terrace & formal garden
Owned/ Run By: gay men
Rooms: 10

Baths: private
Meals: full brkfst
Kids: 12 yrs & up welcome
Smoking: no
Rates: $130-385
AC: 10%

The Chestnut House

Nantucket

3 Chestnut St
Nantucket, MA 02554
508/ 228-0049
www.chestnuthouse.com

Clientele: gay-friendly
Type: b&b, cottage
Owned/ Run By: straights
Rooms: 6
Baths: private
Meals: full brkfst (off premises)
Kids: welcome

Pets: no
Smoking: no
Rates: $85-325
AC: 10%

Apple Valley Log Cabin

Northampton

619/ 542-1664
www.vacationrentals.com/
vacation-rentals/7259.html

Clientele: mixed gay/ straight
Type: cabin; deck w/ views of the Berkshires; near hiking, skiing, rafting, canoeing; 20 minutes from Northampton

Owned/ Run By: lesbians
Rates: $150-320

Canterbury Trails B&B

Northampton

2 Laurel Rd
Haydenville, MA 01039
413/ 687-8453
www.canterburytrailsbandb.com

Clientele: mixed gay/ straight
Type: b&b; near walking trails & rivers
Owned/ Run By: lesbians
Rooms: 2
Baths: shared
Meals: full brkfst

Kids: welcome
Pets: no
Smoking: no
Rates: $75

Corner Porches

Northampton

82 Baptist Corner Rd
Ashfield, MA 01330
413/ 628-4592

Clientele: mixed gay/ straight
Type: b&b-private home; informal 1880s farmhouse in rural New England town, high in Berkshire Hills; fall foliage; country walks; pets in residence
Owned/ Run By: woman
Rooms: 4

Baths: shared
Meals: full brkfst
Kids: welcome; must be supervised; babysitting available; cots & cribs $5-15
Smoking: no
Rates: $65-80

The Hotel Northampton   *Northampton*

36 King St
Northampton, MA 01060
413/ 584-3100 800/ 547-3529
www.hotelnorthampton.com

Clientele: gay-friendly
Type: hotel; in the heart of downtown; cafe
   & historic tavern; gym
Rooms: 99
Baths: private

Kids: welcome
Smoking: ok
Rates: $99-325

The McKinley House   *Northampton*

3 McKinley Ave
Easthampton, MA 01027
413/ 695-6599
webpages.charter.net/mckinleyhouse

Clientele: mixed gay/ lesbian
Type: b&b-private home; in restored 1900s
   Colonial; 3 miles S of Northampton;
   gourmet brkfst
Owned/ Run By: gay men
Rooms: 2
Baths: private & shared

Meals: full brkfst
Amenities: free parking, hot tub
Kids: 12 yrs & up welcome
Smoking: no
Rates: $95-155
AC: 10%

Symphony Hollow B&B   *Plymouth*

127 Brook St
Plympton, MA 02367-1720
781/ 585-7823 888/ 655-1200
www.symphonyhollow.com

Clientele: mixed gay/ straight
Type: b&b; in enchanting 1720 Cape house
   on 7 acres; just 7 miles to Plymouth Rock;
   gardens, art & antiques
Owned/ Run By: gay men
Rooms: 3

Baths: private
Meals: full brkfst
Rates: $105-135
AC: 10%

1807 House   *Provincetown*

54 Commercial St
Provincetown, MA 02657
508/ 487-2173 888/ 522-1807
www.1807House.com

Clientele: mixed gay/ lesbian
Type: guesthouse; charming historic home;
   most units w/ kitchens & private
   entrances; just across from bay beach;
   btwn downtown & gay beach
Owned/ Run By: gay men
Rooms: 8 (includes 5 apts: no brkfst)
Baths: private

Meals: expanded cont'l brkfst
Amenities: free parking, DVDs/ videos, WiFi
Kids: welcome (off-season only)
Pets: no
Smoking: no
Rates: $70-225
AC: 10% (except high season)

Admiral's Landing Guest House   *Provincetown*

158 Bradford St
Provincetown, MA 02657
508/ 487-9665 800/ 934-0925
www.admiralslanding.com

Clientele: mostly men
Type: b&b-inn; centrally located captain's
   house from 1860; guest rms & studio
   efficiencies w/ fireplaces, hot tub & WiFi
Owned/ Run By: gay men
Rooms: 8 (includes 6 bdrms & 2 house-
   keeping studio efficiencies)
Baths: private

Meals: cont'l brkfst
Amenities: free parking, outdoor hot tub,
   DVDs/ videos, WiFi
Kids: no
Pets: no
Smoking: no
Rates: $55-150
AC: 10% (pre-paid only)

Aerie House & Beach Club   *Provincetown*

184 Bradford St
Provincetown, MA 02657
508/ 487-1197 800/ 487-1197
www.aeriehouse.com

Clientele: mixed gay/ lesbian
Type: guesthouse; spectacular bay views
   from our hilltop guesthouse & bayfront
   beach club; airport/ pier pickup; open yr-
   round
Owned/ Run By: gay men
Rooms: 11

Baths: private & shared
Meals: expanded cont'l brkfst
Amenities: free parking, laundry, outdoor
   hot tub, DVDs/ videos, WiFi
Pets: dogs welcome
Rates: $30-290

Ampersand Guesthouse
Provincetown

6 Cottage St
Provincetown, MA 02657
508/ 487-0959 800/ 574-9645
www.ampersandguesthouse.com

Clientele: mostly men
Type: guesthouse; mid-19th-c Greek Revival; in neighborly West End; great views & ambience; sundeck w/ water views
Owned/ Run By: gay men

Rooms: 11 (includes 1 studio apt)
Baths: private
Meals: cont'l brkfst
Smoking: no
Rates: $90-190
AC: 10% (off-season)

Anchor Inn Beach House
Provincetown

175 Commercial St
Provincetown, MA 02657
508/ 487-0432 800/ 858-2657
www.anchorinnbeachhouse.com

Clientele: mixed gay/ straight
Type: b&b-inn; offers the best of Provincetown: rms have all the amenities, central location, close to T-dance, private beach & spectacular view of the harbor
Owned/ Run By: lesbian & straight
Rooms: 23
Baths: private
Wheelchair Access: yes, 2 rms

Meals: expanded cont'l brkfst
Amenities: free parking, hot tub, DVDs/ videos
Kids: welcome
Pets: no
Smoking: no
Rates: $115-385
AC: 10%

Bayshore
Provincetown

493 Commercial St
Provincetown, MA 02657
508/ 487-9133
www.bayshorechandler.com

Clientele: mixed gay/ straight
Type: cottage; unique complex on the water; beautifully furnished w/ fully equipped kitchens, private decks & patios; beautiful gardens & private beach
Owned/ Run By: gay/ lesbian & straight
Baths: private

Pets: dogs & declawed cats welcome
Smoking: ok
Rates: $95-210/ night (off-season); $1,350-3,295/ week (in-season)

Beaconlight Guest House
Provincetown

12 Winthrop St
Provincetown, MA 02657
508/ 487-9603 800/ 696-9603
www.beaconlightguesthouse.com

Clientele: mixed gay/ lesbian
Type: guesthouse; open yr-round; located in center of town; award-winning romantic, luxurious accommodations
Owned/ Run By: gay men
Rooms: 10
Baths: private
Meals: expanded cont'l brkfst

Amenities: free parking, laundry, outdoor hot tub, WiFi
Kids: please call first
Pets: no
Smoking: no
Rates: $75-345
AC: 10%

Benchmark Inn & Central
Provincetown

6-8 Dyer St
Provincetown, MA 02657
508/ 487-7440 888/ 487-7440
www.benchmarkinn.com

Clientele: mixed gay/ lesbian
Type: b&b; total luxury: 14 fireplaces; whirlpool tubs; heated pool; spa & sauna rm; stunning water views
Owned/ Run By: gay men
Rooms: 14
Baths: private
Wheelchair Access: yes, 1 rm

Meals: expanded cont'l brkfst
Amenities: free parking, laundry, pool, sauna, indoor hot tub, DVDs/ videos, WiFi
Kids: 6 yrs & up welcome at Central
Pets: welcome in 3 rooms
Smoking: no
Rates: $110-425
AC: 10%

The Black Pearl Inn
Provincetown

11 & 18 Pearl St
Provincetown, MA 02657
508/ 487-0302 800/ 761-1016
www.theblackpearlinn.com

Clientele: mixed gay/ lesbian
Type: restored 19th-c captain's house located near center of town; off-street parking, A/C, some fireplaces
Owned/ Run By: gay men

Rooms: 10
Baths: private
Meals: cont'l brkfst
Amenities: outdoor hot tub
Pets: welcome

Boatslip Resort

Provincetown

161 Commercial St
Provincetown, MA 02657
508/ 487-1669 877/ 786-9662
www.glresorts.com

Clientele: mostly men
Type: resort; beachfront; w/ restaurant, several bars & pool; hosts New England's largest waterfront T-dance
Owned/ Run By: gay men
Rooms: 45

Baths: private
Meals: coffee/tea only
Smoking: ok
Rates: $115-255
AC: 10%

The Bradford Carver House

Provincetown

70 Bradford St
Provincetown, MA 02657-1363
508/ 487-4966 800/ 826-9083
www.bradfordcarver.com

Clientele: mixed gay/ lesbian
Type: guesthouse; restored mid-19th-c house, located in heart of Provincetown; *Out & About* newsletter says, "Highly recommended"
Owned/ Run By: gay men
Rooms: 5

Baths: private
Meals: cont'l brkfst
Kids: no
Pets: no
Smoking: no
Rates: $49-259
AC: 10%

Brass Key Guesthouse TAG

Provincetown

67 Bradford St
Provincetown, MA 02657

508/ 487-9005
800/ 842-9858

www.brasskey.com

Clientele: mixed gay/ lesbian
Type: b&b-inn; "meticulously restored to its original charm"; w/ 2 pools & spacious, sunny courtyards
Owned/ Run By: gay men
Nearby Attractions: whale-watching, dune tours, shopping
Transit: 2 miles to airport; 1/2 mile to bus & ferry
Rooms: 42 total, 15 kings, 17 queens, 1 twin, A/C, color TV, DVD/ VCR, cable, ceiling fan (1), fireplace (10), deck (3), refrigerator, maid service, Bose radios, phones w/ data port & voicemail
Baths: private, bathtubs, showers, whirlpools, robes, hairdryers
Wheelchair Access: yes, 1 rm
Meals: expanded cont'l brkfst
Amenities: laundry, pool, outdoor hot tub, DVDs/ videos, WiFi, sunset drinks, coffee/ tea

Recreation: 1 mile to gay beach; bike trails
Kids: no
Pets: no
Smoking: no
Reservations: *Deposit:* required, 50%, due at booking, personal check ok *Cancellation:* cancel by 3 weeks prior or forfeit 50% *Minimum Stay:* varies
Payment: cash, travelers checks, Visa, Amex, MC, Discover
Season: *High season:* June-Sept *Closed:* Dec-March
Rates: $100-475
AC: 10%

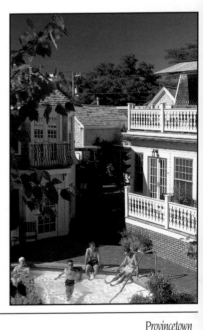

Captain's House B&B

Provincetown

350-A Commercial St
Provincetown, MA 02657
508/ 487-9353 800/ 457-8885
www.captainshouseptown.com

Clientele: mostly men
Type: guesthouse; in the center of town; w/ common rm & private patio serving home-baked cont'l brkfst
Owned/ Run By: gay men
Rooms: 10

Baths: private & shared
Meals: expanded cont'l brkfst
Amenities: hot tub, DVDs/ videos
Pets: no
Smoking: no
Rates: $49-129

Carpe Diem Guesthouse
Provincetown

12 Johnson St
Provincetown, MA 02657
508/ 487-4242 800/ 487-0132
www.carpediemguesthouse.com

Clientele: mixed gay/ lesbian
Type: guesthouse; elegant yet casual; cozy common rms; secluded patios; some rms w/ fireplaces & whirlpool tubs
Owned/ Run By: gay men
Rooms: 14
Baths: private
Meals: full brkfst

Amenities: free parking, laundry, outdoor hot tub, DVDs/ videos, WiFi
Kids: welcome if they're old enough to stay in their own rm
Pets: no
Smoking: no
Rates: $95-345
AC: 10%

Chicago House
Provincetown

6 Winslow St
Provincetown, MA 02657
508/ 487-0537 800/ 733-7869
www.chicagohse.com

Clientele: mixed gay/ lesbian
Type: guesthouse; quaint Cape-style; in middle of town
Owned/ Run By: gay man
Rooms: 9
Baths: private & shared

Meals: expanded cont'l brkfst
Amenities: outdoor hot tub, DVDs/ videos
Kids: no
Pets: no
Smoking: no
Rates: $54-164

Christopher's by the Bay
Provincetown

8 Johnson St
Provincetown, MA 02657
508/ 487-9263 877/ 487-9263
www.christophersbythebay.com

Clientele: mixed gay/ lesbian
Type: b&b; 19th-c Victorian inn on quiet side street in the heart of town; relax by the fireplace or in the private garden
Owned/ Run By: gay men
Rooms: 10
Baths: private & shared
Meals: expanded cont'l brkfst

Amenities: free parking, laundry, DVDs/ videos, WiFi
Kids: not during high season; 15 yrs & up (off-season)
Pets: no
Smoking: no
Rates: $65-180
AC: please call

The Clarendon House
Provincetown

118 Bradford St
Provincetown, MA 02657
508/ 487-1645 800/ 669-8229
www.clarendonhse.com

Clientele: mixed gay/ straight
Type: b&b-inn; 1823 guesthouse; roof deck; "right under the monument—you don't get any more central than this"
Rooms: 7
Baths: private & shared

Amenities: hot tub, DVDs/ videos
Kids: well-behaved welcome
Pets: well-behaved welcome
Smoking: no
Rates: $75-185
AC: yes

The Commons Guest House & Bistro
Provincetown

386 Commercial St
Provincetown, MA 02657
508/ 487-7800 800/ 487-0784
www.commonsghb.com

Clientele: mixed gay/ straight
Type: b&b-inn; in renovated 1840s house; garden setting; w/ 14 recently renovated rms; all have private baths; full-service restaurant on premises
Owned/ Run By: gay men

Rooms: 14
Baths: private
Meals: expanded cont'l brkfst
Pets: welcome; $10
Rates: $99-235
AC: yes

Crowne Pointe Historic Inn
Provincetown

82 Bradford St
Provincetown, MA 02657
508/ 487-6767 877/ 276-9631
www.crownepointe.com

Clientele: mixed gay/ lesbian
Type: b&b-inn; luxurious inn, 2 large jacuzzis, heated pool; spa & restaurant; "five stars w/out the price tag"—*NY Daily News*
Owned/ Run By: gay men
Rooms: 40
Baths: private

Wheelchair Access: yes, 1 rm
Meals: full brkfst
Amenities: free parking, laundry, outdoor hot tub, massage, DVDs/ videos
Smoking: no
Rates: $125-469
AC: 10%

Crown & Anchor

247 Commercial St
Provincetown, MA 02657

508/ 487-1430

frontdesk@onlyatthecrown.com
www.onlyatthecrown.com

Clientele: mixed gay/ lesbian
Type: hotel; waterfront hotel in the heart of Provincetown; whirlpool tubs, fireplaces, spacious decks overlooking Provincetown Harbor; 6 bars & restaurant also in complex
Owned/ Run By: gay men
Nearby Attractions: at the heart of Provincetown's entertainment
Transit: near public transit
Rooms: 18 total, 8 suites, 5 kings, 5 fulls, A/C, color TV, DVD/ VCR, cable, wetbar (6), fireplace (6), deck (6), phone, kitchenette (6), refrigerator (6), maid service
Baths: private, showers, whirlpools
Wheelchair Access: yes, 1 rm
Meals: cont'l brkfst
Amenities: pool, WiFi, full-service restaurant, 6 bars, cabaret & show spaces, nightclub
Kids: no
Pets: no
Smoking: no

Reservations: required *Deposit:* required, 50%, due at booking, personal check ok *Cancellation:* cancel by 3 weeks prior or forfeit $75 *Minimum Stay:* varies; please call *Check in/ out:* 3pm/ 11am

Payment: cash, travelers checks, Visa, Amex, MC
Season: open yr-round *High season:* June-Sept
Rates: $85-285
AC: 10%

Fairbanks Inn

90 Bradford St
Provincetown, MA 02657

508/ 487-0386
800/ 324-7265

info@fairbanksinn.com
www.fairbanksinn.com

Clientele: mixed gay/ lesbian
Type: b&b-inn; rated 5 Palms & awarded Editor's Choice by *Out & About* 10 yrs running. "Exceptional...Exquisite...Unbeatable charm & warmth"
Owned/ Run By: lesbians
Nearby Attractions: Nat'l Seashore, Pilgrim Monument
Transit: near public transit; 3 miles to Cape Air shuttle to Boston
Rooms: 14 total, 3 suites, A/C, color TV, DVD/ VCR, cable, fireplace (10), deck (2), phone, refrigerator (3), maid service
Baths: private & shared, bathtubs, showers, hairdryers
Meals: expanded cont'l brkfst
Amenities: office hrs: 9am-7pm; free parking, DVDs/ videos, WiFi, snacks, coffee/ tea
Recreation: bike trails, whale-watching, beach
Kids: 16 yrs & up welcome
Pets: no
Smoking: no

Reservations: walk-ins welcome but reservations recommended *Deposit:* required, 50%, due at booking, personal check ok *Cancellation:* cancel by 21 days prior or forfeit varying amounts plus $50 for all refunds *Minimum Stay:* varies

Payment: cash, travelers checks, Visa, Amex, MC
Season: open yr-round *High season:* June-Sept
Rates: $65-295
AC: 10%

Dexter's Inn

Provincetown

6 Conwell St
Provincetown, MA 02657
508/ 487-1911 888/ 521-1999
www.ptowndextersinn.com

Clientele: mixed gay/ lesbian
Type: b&b-inn; in traditional Cape Cod guesthouse; the perfect place for your all-season vacation; in the heart of Provincetown
Owned/ Run By: gay men
Rooms: 15

Baths: private & shared
Meals: expanded cont'l brkfst
Kids: 14 yrs & up welcome
Smoking: no
Rates: $60-150

Gabriel's Apartments & Guest Rooms

Provincetown

102 Bradford St
Provincetown, MA 02657-1440
508/ 487-3232 800/ 969-2643
www.gabriels.com

Clientele: mostly women
Type: b&b-inn; luxury animal-friendly inn w/ beautiful gardens; "where every detail has been tailored to your well-being"
Owned/ Run By: lesbians/ gay men
Rooms: 8
Baths: private

Meals: expanded cont'l brkfst
Amenities: free parking, DVDs/ videos, WiFi
Kids: welcome
Pets: companion animals welcome
Smoking: no
Rates: $100-350
AC: 10%

The Gallery Inn

Provincetown

3 Johnson St
Provincetown, MA 02657
508/ 487-3010 800/ 676-3010
www.galleryinnptown.com

Clientele: mostly men
Type: guesthouse; located in the heart of Provincetown
Rooms: 11
Baths: shared

Meals: cont'l brkfst
Rates: $45-165

Gifford House Inn

Provincetown

9 Carver St
Provincetown, MA 02657
508/ 487-0688 800/ 434-0130
www.giffordhouse.com

Clientele: mixed gay/ lesbian
Type: b&b-inn; housed in grand bldg w/ views of Provincetown Harbor; on-site restaurant, lounge & dance club
Owned/ Run By: gay men
Rooms: 26
Baths: private

Meals: cont'l brkfst
Kids: welcome
Smoking: ok (in rms only)
Rates: $60-275
AC: 10% (off-season only)

Gracie House

Provincetown

152 Bradford St
Provincetown, MA 02657-2313
508/ 487-4808
home.att.net/~graciehouse

Clientele: mixed gay/ lesbian
Type: b&b; spacious, restored 1890s Queen Anne; w/ A/C; central location; great porch for watching the street scene
Owned/ Run By: women
Rooms: 3
Baths: shared

Meals: expanded cont'l brkfst
Kids: no
Pets: no
Smoking: no
Rates: $115-140
AC: varies

Grand View Inn

Provincetown

4 Conant St
Provincetown, MA 02657
508/ 487-9193 888/ 268-9169
www.grandviewinn.com

Clientele: mixed gay/ lesbian
Type: guesthouse; 1870s renovated sea captain's home; in West End; 1 blk from beach; wonderful water views
Owned/ Run By: gay men
Rooms: 12
Baths: private & shared

Meals: expanded cont'l brkfst
Kids: welcome Sept 15-June 15
Pets: welcome yr-round
Smoking: no
Rates: $40-160
AC: 10%

Harbor Hill at Provincetown
Provincetown

4 Harbor Hill Rd
Provincetown, MA 02657
508/ 487-0541
www.harborhill.com

Clientele: gay-friendly
Type: condo; condominium resort in West End, 500 yds from Cape Cod Nat'l Seashore; both 1- & 2-bdrm luxury condos w/ full kitchen
Rooms: 30 (condos)
Baths: private

Amenities: laundry, outdoor hot tub
Kids: welcome
Pets: no
Smoking: ok (nonsmoking rms available)
Rates: $100-275

Heritage House
Provincetown

7 Center St
Provincetown, MA 02657
508/ 487-3692
www.heritageh.com

Clientele: mixed gay/ lesbian
Type: guesthouse; "grand old Provincetown home w/ views of Cape Cod Bay; relax on the veranda, enjoy the delicious brkfst & make our home your home"
Owned/ Run By: lesbians
Rooms: 8 (includes 2 king, 2 queen, 2

double, 2 twin)
Baths: shared
Meals: expanded cont'l brkfst
Kids: welcome; ages 12 & up
Pets: no
Smoking: no
Rates: $70-125

The Inn at Cook Street
Provincetown

7 Cook St
Provincetown, MA 02657
508/ 487-3894 888/ 266-5655
www.innatcookstreet.com

Clientele: mixed gay/ straight
Type: b&b; in small, intimate country inn in Provincetown's charming East End Gallery District
Rooms: 6
Baths: private

Meals: expanded cont'l brkfst
Pets: no
Smoking: no
Rates: $115-225

John Randall House
Provincetown

140 Bradford St
Provincetown, MA 02657
508/ 487-3533 800/ 573-6700
www.johnrandallhouse.com

Clientele: mixed gay/ lesbian
Type: b&b-inn; handsome turn-of-the-century home; conveniently located 1 blk from center of town
Owned/ Run By: gay men
Rooms: 12
Baths: private & shared

Meals: expanded cont'l brkfst
Kids: welcome
Smoking: no
Rates: $69-179
AC: 10%

Labrador Landing
Provincetown

47 Commercial St
Provincetown, MA 02657
917/ 597-1500
www.labradorlanding.com

Clientele: mixed gay/ lesbian
Type: cottage; private-owned West End waterfront compound w/ pet-friendly luxury cottages; newly renovated; open yr-round
Owned/ Run By: gay men
Rooms: 2 cottages ("Boat House" & "Two

Story"—each sleeps 2-4 adults)
Baths: private
Kids: welcome
Pets: welcome
Rates: $2,000-3,500/ week
AC: please inquire

Lotus Guest House
Provincetown

296 Commercial St
Provincetown, MA 02657
508/ 487-4644 888/ 508-4644
www.provincetown.com/lotus

Clientele: mixed gay/ lesbian
Type: guesthouse; beautiful Victorian in heart of town; near beaches, bus & ferry
Owned/ Run By: lesbians/ gay men
Rooms: 13 (also 2-bdrm suite)
Baths: private & shared
Meals: coffee/tea only

Kids: 13 yrs & up welcome
Pets: no
Smoking: ok
Rates: $90-275
AC: 10-12%

Moffett House
Provincetown

296-A Commercial St
Provincetown, MA 02657
508/ 487-6615 800/ 990-8865
www.moffetthouse.com

Clientele: mostly men
Type: guesthouse; in Three-Quarter Cape Cod-style house w/ TVs, patios; in the heart of town; near beaches, bus & ferry
Owned/ Run By: gay men
Rooms: 11

Baths: private & shared
Meals: coffee/tea only
Rates: $55-165
AC: 10%

Officers Quarters
Provincetown

164 Commercial St
Provincetown, MA 02657
508/ 487-1850 800/ 400-2278
www.provincetownvacations.com

Clientele: mixed gay/ straight (mostly men)
Type: guesthouse; 19th-c sea captain's house; ocean views, newly decorated rms, new renovations & amenities; near the Boatslip
Owned/ Run By: gay men
Rooms: 6

Baths: private & shared
Meals: expanded cont'l brkfst
Amenities: outdoor hot tub, DVDs/ videos
Kids: welcome
Pets: welcome in certain rms only
Smoking: ok (in common areas only)
Rates: $75-260

Pilgrim House Hotel
Provincetown

336 Commercial St
Provincetown, MA 02657
508/ 487-6424
www.thepilgrimhouse.com

Clientele: mostly women
Type: b&b-inn; in heart of Provincetown; walking distance to beach, shops, restaurants; also Vixen Nightclub, fine wine bar, cafe
Owned/ Run By: gay/ lesbian & straight
Rooms: 20

Baths: private
Wheelchair Access: yes, 2 rms
Kids: welcome
Pets: welcome in some rms
Smoking: ok
Rates: $99-139
AC: 10%

The Ranch Guestlodge
Provincetown

198 Commercial St
Provincetown, MA 02657
508/ 487-1542 800/ 942-1542
www.theranch.ws

Clientele: men
Type: guesthouse; the choice for men; *Out & About* agrees, "a simple, fun place smack in the middle of the nightlife zone"
Owned/ Run By: gay men
Rooms: 20
Baths: shared

Meals: cont'l brkfst
Amenities: DVDs/ videos, WiFi
Kids: no
Pets: no
Smoking: no
Rates: $75-139
AC: 10%

Ravenwood Guest House
Provincetown

462 Commercial St
Provincetown, MA 02657
508/ 487-3203
www.provincetown.com/ravenwood/

Clientele: mixed gay/ lesbian
Type: 1830 Greek Revival home offering guest rms, apts & cottage; private fenced-in yard; beach access; 5-minute walk to town center
Owned/ Run By: lesbians
Rooms: 5 (includes 1 one-bdrm Cape Cod cottage)

Baths: private
Wheelchair Access: yes, cottage only rms
Kids: welcome; ground level & cottage only
Pets: no
Smoking: no
Rates: $85-175
AC: yes

The Red Inn
Provincetown

15 Commercial St
Provincetown, MA 02657
508/ 487-7334 866/ 473-3466
www.theredinn.com

Clientele: mixed gay/ straight
Type: hotel; luxury boutique hotel on the beach
Owned/ Run By: gay men
Rooms: 8
Baths: private

Wheelchair Access: yes, 2 rms
Meals: coffee/tea only
Kids: no
Pets: no
Smoking: no
Rates: $135-525

Revere Guesthouse

14 Court St
Provincetown, MA 02657

508/ 487-2292
800/ 487-2292

info@reverehouse.com
www.reverehouse.com

Clientele: mixed gay/ lesbian
Type: b&b; restored captain's home, circa 1830; centrally located
Owned/ Run By: gay men
Nearby Attractions: whale-watching
Transit: near public transit
Rooms: 8 (includes 2-bdrm suite & 1-bdrm apt) total, 1 suite, 1 king, 3 queens, 3 fulls, A/C, color TV, DVD/ VCR, cable, fireplace (4), deck (1), phone, kitchenette (1), refrigerator, maid service
Baths: private & shared, bathtubs, showers, whirlpools
Meals: cont'l brkfst
Amenities: office hrs: 8:30am-8pm; free parking, outdoor hot tub, DVDs/ videos
Recreation: beach, pool, biking, tennis, water sports
Kids: no
Pets: no
Pets On Premises: 2 dogs
Smoking: no

Reservations: recommended *Deposit:* required, 50%, due at booking, personal check ok *Cancellation:* cancel by 21 days prior or forfeit $50 *Minimum Stay:* wknds; 5 nights (summers) *Check in/ out:* 2-8pm/ 11am

Payment: cash, travelers checks, Visa, Amex, MC
Season: *High season:* June-Aug *Closed:* Nov-April
Rates: $85-295
AC: 10%

Roomers

8 Carver St
Provincetown, MA 02657
508/ 487-3532
www.roomersptown.com

Clientele: mostly men
Type: guesthouse; centrally located restored Greek Revival in lush garden setting; artfully appointed rms w/ fridges, cable & ceiling fans
Owned/ Run By: gay men
Rooms: 10

Baths: private
Meals: expanded cont'l brkfst
Pets: please call first
Smoking: ok
Rates: $70-185
AC: 10%

Rose Acre

5 Center St
Provincetown, MA 02657
508/ 487-2347
roseacreguests.com

Clientele: women
Type: apts & cottage; a wonderful women's hideaway; tucked down a private drive in the center of P'town; decorated for the artist in all of us
Owned/ Run By: women

Rooms: 4 (suites)
Baths: private
Pets: no
Smoking: no
Rates: $125-200

Rose & Crown Guest House

158 Commercial St
Provincetown, MA 02657
508/ 487-3332
www.provincetown.com/rosecrown

Clientele: mixed gay/ straight
Type: guesthouse; 206-yr-old captain's home
Owned/ Run By: lesbians
Rooms: 8 (includes 2 apts)
Baths: private & shared
Wheelchair Access: yes, 3 rms

Meals: cont'l brkfst
Kids: welcome in cottage only
Pets: welcome in back cottage only
Smoking: ok
Rates: $40-210 (rms)/ $160-230 (cottage)
AC: 10-12%

Sandbars
Provincetown

570 Shore Rd, Beach Pt
North Truro, MA 02652
800/ 223-0088 x160
www.sandbars.com

Clientele: mixed gay/ straight
Type: studio; 16 newly renovated deluxe studio units; w/ full kitchen; directly on private beach; minutes from Provincetown
Owned/ Run By: other

Rooms: 16
Baths: private
Smoking: ok
Rates: $89-219

Seasons, An Inn for All
Provincetown

160 Bradford St
Provincetown, MA 02657
508/ 487-2283 800/ 563-0113
www.provincetownseasons.com

Clientele: mixed gay/ lesbian
Type: b&b-inn; conveniently located Victorian w/ antique furnishings; sumptuous full brkfsts
Owned/ Run By: gay men

Rooms: 5
Baths: private
Meals: full brkfst
Smoking: no
Rates: $80-145

The Secret Garden Inn
Provincetown

300-A Commercial St
Provincetown, MA 02657
508/ 487-9027 866/ 786-9646
www.secretgardenptown.com

Clientele: mixed gay/ lesbian
Type: guesthouse; in heart of Provincetown; gardens, porches & a comfortable homelike atmosphere; "we're near everything"
Owned/ Run By: bisexuals
Rooms: 5
Baths: private & shared

Meals: expanded cont'l brkfst
Amenities: free parking, outdoor hot tub, DVDs/ videos
Kids: welcome
Pets: no
Smoking: no
Rates: $60-170
AC: 10%

Shiremax Inn
Provincetown

5 Tremont St
Provincetown, MA 02657
508/ 487-1233 888/ 744-7362

Clientele: mixed gay/ lesbian
Type: b&b-inn; turn-of-the-century bldg; attractively decorated rms, offering more amenities than most
Owned/ Run By: gay men
Rooms: 7 (also 2 apts)
Baths: private & shared

Meals: expanded cont'l brkfst
Pets: welcome; must be quiet; $10 per day
Smoking: ok
Rates: $70-115 (rms); $700-950/ week (apts)
AC: 10-12%

Snug Cottage
Provincetown

178 Bradford St
Provincetown, MA 02657
508/ 487-1616 800/ 432-2334
www.snugcottage.com

Clientele: mixed gay/ straight
Type: b&b; historic 19th-c inn; luxurious rms w/ wood-burning fireplaces, A/C, CTV/VCR/DVD, telephones w/ data ports & voicemail
Owned/ Run By: gay men
Rooms: 8
Baths: private

Meals: expanded cont'l brkfst
Amenities: free parking, DVDs/ videos, WiFi
Kids: 7 yrs & up
Pets: no
Smoking: no
Rates: $90-235
AC: 10%

Somerset House
Provincetown

378 Commercial St
Provincetown, MA 02657
508/ 487-0383 800/ 575-1850
www.somersethouseinn.com

Clientele: mixed gay/ lesbian
Type: guesthouse; "Provincetown's only hip & trendy boutique-style guesthouse"
Owned/ Run By: gay men
Rooms: 13
Baths: private
Meals: full hot brkfst

Amenities: free parking, hot tub, WiFi
Kids: no
Pets: no
Smoking: no
Rates: $75-285
AC: 10%

Sunset Inn

Provincetown

142 Bradford St
Provincetown, MA 02657
508/ 487-9810 800/ 965-1801
www.sunsetinnptown.com

Clientele: mixed gay/ lesbian
Type: b&b-inn
Owned/ Run By: gay man
Rooms: 20
Baths: private & shared

Meals: cont'l brkfst
Smoking: no
Rates: $60-175
AC: 10%

Surfside Hotel & Suites

Provincetown

543 Commercial
Provincetown, MA 02657

508/ 487-1726
800/ 421-1726

surfsideinnptown@aol.com
www.surfsideinn.cc

Clientele: mixed gay/ straight
Type: hotel; newly renovated waterfront guest rms; conveniently located near downtown shopping, restaurants, activities; new Lighthouse Bar; private beach
Owned/ Run By: other
Nearby Attractions: Pilgrim Monument, whale-watching, Herring Cove Beach, Race Point Beach, lighthouses, wineries
Transit: near public transit; 120 miles to Boston's Logan
Rooms: 86 total, 2 suites, 41 kings, 13 queens, 2 fulls, 28 twins, A/C, color TV, cable, deck, phone, kitchenette (2), maid service, hair dryers, robes, refrigerators, microwaves & coffeemakers in waterfront rms
Baths: private, bathtubs, showers, robes, hairdryers
Meals: expanded cont'l brkfst
Amenities: office hrs: 7am-1am; free parking, coffee/ tea, heated swimming pool, private beach, safes available at front desk, WiFi in lobby
Recreation: biking, kayaking, shopping, dune tours
Kids: welcome

Pets: welcome; fee
Smoking: ok
Reservations: required *Deposit:* required, 50%, due at booking, personal check ok *Cancellation:* cancel by 28 days prior or forfeit 50% *Minimum Stay:* sometimes *Check in/ out:* after 3pm/ before 11am

Payment: cash, travelers checks, Visa, Amex, MC, Discover, personal checks (only in advance)
Season: *High season:* June-Sept *Closed* Nov 1-March 31
Rates: $139-329 *Discounts:* AAA, AARP
AC: 10%

The Tucker Inn

Provincetown

12 Center St
Provincetown, MA 02657
508/ 487-0381 800/ 477-1867
www.thetuckerinn.com

Clientele: mixed gay/ lesbian
Type: guesthouse; gently restored admiral's house; all modern amenities; on quiet side street in center of town
Owned/ Run By: gay men
Rooms: 9 (includes 1 cottage)
Baths: private

Meals: full brkfst
Amenities: free parking, outdoor hot tub, DVDs/ videos, WiFi
Kids: 2 people max per rm
Pets: welcome in private cottage
Smoking: no
Rates: $125-225

Watermark Inn

Provincetown

603 Commercial St
Provincetown, MA 02657
508/ 487-0165
watermark-inn.com

Clientele: mixed gay/ straight
Type: inn; spacious suites w/ kitchenettes; located on waterfront in quiet East End; open yr-round
Owned/ Run By: straights
Rooms: 10

Baths: private
Kids: welcome
Pets: no
Smoking: no
Rates: $85-265/ night (off-season) $1,200-2,510/ weekly (in-season)

Watership Inn   *Provincetown*

7 Winthrop St
Provincetown, MA 02657
508/ 487-0094 800/ 330-9413
www.watershipinn.com

Clientele: mostly men
Type: b&b-inn; 1820s sea captain's house; 1/2 blk from Provincetown harbor; spacious common rm w/ fireplace; yard w/ volleyball & croquet sets
Owned/ Run By: gay men
Rooms: 17
Baths: private

Meals: expanded cont'l brkfst
Amenities: free parking, WiFi
Kids: welcome
Pets: no
Smoking: ok
Rates: $45-225
AC: 10% (off-season)

West End Inn   *Provincetown*

44 Commercial St
Provincetown, MA 02657
508/ 487-9555 800/ 559-1220
www.westendinn.com

Clientele: mostly men
Type: b&b-inn; meticulously restored 1840s Greek Revival captain's house; w/ luxury rms, apts & suites
Owned/ Run By: gay men
Rooms: 7 (includes 2 apts)

Baths: private
Meals: expanded cont'l brkfst
Smoking: ok
Rates: $79-259
AC: 8%

White Wind Inn   *Provincetown*

174 Commercial St
Provincetown, MA 02657
508/ 487-1526 888/ 449-9463
www.whitewindinn.com

Clientele: mixed gay/ lesbian
Type: b&b-inn; the perfect yr-round retreat; cozy up in the "great rm" w/ fireplace & grand piano, or relax outside on the veranda–considered the best in town
Owned/ Run By: gay men
Rooms: 12

Baths: private
Meals: expanded cont'l brkfst
Pets: by arrangement; limited rm options
Rates: $95-265
AC: 10%

Applesauce Inn B&B   *Bellaire*

7296 S M-88
Bellaire, MI 49615
231/ 533-6448 888/ 533-6448
www.applesauceinn.com

Clientele: gay-friendly
Type: b&b; beautifully restored 100-yr-old four-square farmhouse; 5 minutes from world-famous Torch Lake, Shanty Creek Ski Resort, Bellaire, Alden & Grass River Natural Area
Owned/ Run By: straights

Rooms: 3
Baths: private & shared
Meals: full brkfst
Kids: please inquire
Pets: well-behaved dogs welcome; $10 fee
Smoking: ok
Rates: $75-115

Bellaire B&B   *Bellaire*

212 Park St
Bellaire, MI 49615
231/ 533-6077 800/ 545-0780
www.bellairebandb.com

Clientele: mixed gay/ straight
Type: b&b-inn; in stately 1879 home; w/ large porches overlooking expansive grounds
Owned/ Run By: gay men
Rooms: 9
Baths: private

Meals: full brkfst
Amenities: free parking, hot tub, DVDs/ videos, WiFi
Kids: 13 yrs & up welcome
Smoking: no
Rates: $95-225
AC: 10%

Big Bay Depot Motel   *Big Bay*

PO Box 61
Big Bay, MI 49808
906/ 345-9350
www.bigbayonline.com/depot

Clientele: gay-friendly
Type: motel; converted 1905 train depot; access to Lake Independence; 1 mile from Lake Superior
Owned/ Run By: lesbians
Rooms: 6 (rms w/ full kitchen)
Baths: private

Meals: coffee/tea only
Kids: well-supervised welcome
Pets: welcome
Smoking: ok
Rates: $60

Big Bay Point Lighthouse B&B

Big Bay

3 Lighthouse Rd
Big Bay, MI 49808
906/ 345–9957
www.bigbaylighthouse.com

Clientele: mixed gay/ straight
Type: b&b-inn; 100-yr-old working lighthouse on Lake Superior
Owned/ Run By: gay/ lesbian & straight
Rooms: 7
Baths: private

Meals: full brkfst
Kids: 16 yrs & up welcome
Smoking: no
Rates: $99-185
AC: 10%

My Sister's Place

Cadillac

231/ 775–9730

Clientele: mostly women & children
Type: women's resort on 500-acre all-sports lake; b&b rms & campsites
Owned/ Run By: lesbians
Rooms: 5
Baths: private & shared

Meals: expanded cont'l brkfst
Kids: we are geared for kids of all ages
Pets: welcome; on occasion
Smoking: no (but rm available in house)
Rates: $25-135

Jeralan's Farm B&B

Copemish

18361 Viaduct Rd
Copemish, MI 49625
231/ 378–2926 866/ 250–8444
www.bbonline.com/mi/jeralansfarm/

Clientele: gay-friendly
Type: b&b; in restored & expanded 1872 farmhouse on 120 acres of woods & ponds
Owned/ Run By: straights
Rooms: 4

Baths: private
Meals: full brkfst
Kids: no
Pets: no
Smoking: no
Rates: $100-150

Shorecrest Motor Inn

Detroit

1316 E Jefferson Ave
Detroit, MI 48207
313/ 568–3000 800/ 992–9616
www.shorecrestmi.com

Type: hotel; family-owned/ run motel located in the heart of downtown; 2 blks E of Renaissance Center
Rooms: 54
Baths: private
Wheelchair Access: yes, 1 rm

Kids: welcome
Smoking: ok
Rates: $69-159
AC: 10%

Woodbridge Star B&B

Detroit

3985 Trumbull Ave
Detroit, MI 48208-2940
313/ 831–9668
www.woodbridgestar.com

Clientele: mixed gay/ straight
Type: b&b; Victorian nestled in one of city's oldest neighborhoods; Greenfield Village packages
Owned/ Run By: gay men
Rooms: 6 (includes 3 suites)
Baths: private

Meals: full gourmet brkfst
Amenities: laundry, outdoor hot tub, massage, DVDs/ videos
Kids: well-behaved welcome
Pets: by special arrangement only
Smoking: no (outside ok)
Rates: $125-175

Wayfarer Lodgings

Frankfort

1912 S Scenic Hwy (M-22)
Frankfort, MI 49635
231/ 352–9264 800/ 735–8564
www.wayfarerlodgings.com

Clientele: gay-friendly
Type: cottage; minutes from Frankfort, Lake Michigan & the Betsie River
Owned/ Run By: straights
Rooms: 10 (cottages)
Baths: private
Amenities: free parking

Kids: welcome
Pets: welcome w/ prior approval
Smoking: ok
Rates: $42-80

Duneswood
Glen Arbor

PO Box 457
Glen Arbor, MI 49636
231/ 334-3346
www.duneswood.org

Clientele: women
Type: resort; Northwoods-style retreat; on 7 acres of wooded land at Sleeping Bear Dunes
Owned/ Run By: lesbians
Rooms: 11 (includes 5 rms w/ shared kitchen, 5 self-sufficient rms, 1 two-bdrm trailer)

Baths: private
Kids: welcome in 2-bdrm trailer
Smoking: no
Rates: $50-95

Labrys Wilderness Resort
Honor

231/ 882-5994
www.labryswoods.com

Clientele: women
Type: "home away from home"; situated on a small, wild lake in the Sleeping Bear Dunes Nat'l Lakeshore
Owned/ Run By: lesbians
Rooms: 4 (cottages)

Baths: private & shared
Amenities: free parking, outdoor hot tub
Kids: girls only
Pets: pet fee, please inquire
Rates: $50-80

The Leaven Center
Lansing

PO Box 97
Lyons, MI 48851
989/ 855-2606
www.leaven.org

Clientele: mixed gay/ straight
Type: retreat & study center; offering spirituality & justice programming; available for rentals up to 20 people
Owned/ Run By: nonprofit
Rooms: 9

Baths: shared
Wheelchair Access: yes, 4 rms
Kids: please inquire
Pets: only companion animals welcome
Smoking: no

Windover Resort
Owendale

4596 Blakely Rd
Owendale, MI 48754
989/ 375-2586
www.windoverresort.com

Clientele: women
Type: private resort for women "located in the thumb of Michigan"; campsites & RV hookups, rental trailers, showers & flush toilets; "friendly, safe, inclusive for all women"

Owned/ Run By: women
Rates: $25/ yr membership fee; $15-20 camping fee

Coach House Inn
Petoskey

1011 N US 31
Petoskey, MI 49770
231/ 347-8281 877/ 347-8088
www.coachhousemotel.com

Clientele: mostly men
Type: motel; features nicely decorated rms w/ double beds, A/C, cable TV, telephones w/ free local calls
Owned/ Run By: gay men
Rooms: 21
Baths: private

Meals: full brkfst
Kids: welcome
Pets: welcome
Smoking: ok
Rates: $39-105
AC: 10%

Beechwood Manor Inn
Saugatuck

736 Pleasant St
Saugatuck, MI 49453
269/ 857-1587 877/ 857-1587
www.beechwoodmanorinn.com

Clientele: mixed gay/ straight
Type: b&b; upscale inn just blks from the heart of downtown Saugatuck; open yr-round
Owned/ Run By: gay men
Rooms: 3
Baths: private

Meals: full brkfst
Amenities: free parking, WiFi
Kids: no
Pets: no
Smoking: no
Rates: $150-225

The Belvedere Inn & Restaurant
Saugatuck

3656 63rd St
Saugatuck, MI 49453
269/ 857-5777
www.thebelvedereinn.com

Clientele: gay-friendly
Type: b&b-inn; European-style boutique inn in restored 1913 mansion on 5 acres of serene manicured gardens; full gourmet brkfst; fine-dining restaurant on-site
Owned/ Run By: gay men
Rooms: 10

Baths: private
Meals: full brkfst
Pets: no
Smoking: no
Rates: $180-295

Campit Outdoor Resort
Saugatuck

PO Box 444
Saugatuck, MI 49453-0444
269/ 543-4335 877/ 226-7481
www.campitresort.com

Clientele: mixed gay/ lesbian
Type: membership resort w/ 120 sites for RVs (90) & tenting (30); pool, clubhouse, volleyball, trails; men's, women's & mixed areas available; also cabins & b&b
Owned/ Run By: lesbians/ gay men

Amenities: free parking, laundry, pool, gym, WiFi
Kids: welcome for family events only
Pets: welcome; must be leashed
Rates: $19-50

Douglas House B&B
Saugatuck

41 Spring St
Douglas, MI 49406
269/ 857-1119 248/ 478-9392

Clientele: mostly men
Type: b&b; restored Queen Anne; in downtown Douglas, sister city of Saugatuck & on Lake Michigan
Owned/ Run By: gay men
Rooms: 4

Baths: private
Meals: expanded cont'l brkfst
Kids: no
Pets: no
Smoking: no
Rates: $125-145

The Dunes Resort
Saugatuck

333 Blue Star Hwy
Douglas, MI 49406

269/ 857-1401

info@dunesresort.com
www.dunesresort.com

Clientele: mixed gay/ lesbian
Type: resort; located on over 20 acres in the resort village of Douglas; across the river from Saugatuck; "we're the largest gay/ lesbian resort in the Midwest"
Owned/ Run By: gay men
Nearby Attractions: Saugatuck, Lake Michigan, Kalamazoo River, Dunes State Park, Holland
Transit: 45 miles to Grand Rapids airport; 10 miles to Holland train/ bus stations
Rooms: 80 (includes 12 cottages & 5 suites) total, 15 suites, 20 kings, 5 queens, 41 fulls, A/C (50), color TV (50), DVD/ VCR (14), cable TV (50), ceiling fan (39), fireplace (2), deck (12), phone (50), kitchenette (1), refrigerator (27), safer sex supplies, maid service, newly remodeled motel rms; also cottages & dorm-style rms available
Baths: private & shared, bathtubs, showers, whirlpools
Wheelchair Access: yes, 2 rms
Meals: at Blue Frog To Go 11am-5pm Wed-Mon
Amenities: hot tub, West Michigan's largest dance bar, bistro, cabaret, game rm, swimming pool & pool bar

Kids: no
Pets: welcome; $10 fee
Smoking: ok
Reservations: required *Deposit:* required, 1st night, due 1 week after booking, personal check ok *Cancellation:* cancel by 1 week prior or pay $20 (forfeit deposit if less than 1 week) *Minimum Stay:* 2 nights June; 3 nights July-Aug
Payment: cash, travelers checks, Visa, Amex, MC, Discover
Season: open yr-round *High season:* May-Sept
Rates: $50-275

The Glenn Country Inn
Saugatuck

1286 64th St
Fennville, MI 49408
269/ 227-3045 888/ 237-3009
www.glenncountryinn.com

Clientele: mixed gay/ straight
Type: b&b; "SW Michigan's #1 pet-friendly B&B"
Owned/ Run By: gay men
Rooms: 5
Meals: full brkfst

Kids: no
Pets: welcome
Rates: $89-200

Hidden Garden Cottages & Suites
Saugatuck

247 Butler St
Saugatuck, MI 49453
269/ 857-8109 888/ 857-8109
www.hiddengardencottages.com

Clientele: gay-friendly
Type: cottage; luxuriously decorated cottages & suites designed for two, tucked away in downtown Saugatuck
Rooms: 4 (2 cottages & 2 suites)
Baths: private
Meals: cont'l brkfst

Kids: no
Pets: no
Smoking: no (ok on porches only)
Rates: $125-195
AC: 10%

Hooten Inn
Saugatuck

6541 Blue Star Hwy
Saugatuck, MI
269/ 857-1039
www.HootenInn.com

Clientele: mixed gay/ straight
Type: motel; boutique motel featuring cozy themed rms
Owned/ Run By: straights
Rooms: 9
Baths: private
Meals: coffee/tea only

Amenities: free parking, WiFi
Kids: welcome
Smoking: no
Rates: $75-280
AC: 5%

J Paules Fenn Inn
Saugatuck

2254 S 58th St
Fennville, MI 49408
269/ 561-2836 877/ 561-2836
www.jpaulesfenninn.org

Clientele: gay-friendly
Type: b&b; nestled in SW Michigan countryside; 6 miles from Lake Michigan; Reiki sessions available; close to winter sports
Owned/ Run By: straights
Rooms: 5

Baths: private & shared
Meals: full brkfst
Kids: welcome
Pets: welcome
Smoking: no
Rates: $95-135

The Kingsley House B&B
Saugatuck

626 West Main St
Fennville, MI 49408
269/ 561-6425 866/ 561-6425
www.kingsleyhouse.com

Clientele: gay-friendly
Type: b&b; in elegant, award-winning Victorian Queen Anne mansion; minutes from Holland, Saugatuck & South Haven
Owned/ Run By: gay man
Rooms: 8

Baths: private
Meals: full brkfst
Kids: please inquire
Pets: no
Rates: $95-195

Lake Street Commons
Saugatuck

790 Lake St
Saugatuck, MI 49453
269/ 857-1680
www.lakestreetcommons.com

Clientele: gay-friendly
Type: 1- & 2-bdrm suites w/ private decks & full kitchens; 8-person Jacuzzi; 3-night minimum in season
Owned/ Run By: gay men
Rooms: 2

Baths: private
Amenities: hot tub
Pets: no
Smoking: no
Rates: $95-175

Lynn Dee Lea Boat & Breakfast, LLC
Saugatuck

868 Holland St, Slip #1
Saugatuck, MI 49453
309/ 360-7498
www.lynndeeleabandb.com

Clientele: mostly women
Type: b&b; refurbished 52'x14' houseboat w/ 10'x10' bdrm on upper deck; walk to restaurants, shopping, pubs
Owned/ Run By: straights
Rooms: 2

Baths: shared
Meals: full brkfst
Kids: 12 yrs & older w/ prior approval
Pets: no
Smoking: no
Rates: $100-130

The Newnham SunCatcher Inn
Saugatuck

131 Griffith
Saugatuck, MI 49453
269/ 857-4249
www.suncatcherinn.com

Clientele: gay-friendly
Type: b&b-inn; built at the turn-of-the-century; features family antiques & wraparound porch; 1 blk to business district
Owned/ Run By: lesbians
Rooms: 7

Baths: private & shared
Meals: full brkfst
Amenities: free parking, pool, outdoor hot tub
Rates: $85-145

The Park House Inn B&B
Saugatuck

888 Holland St
Saugatuck, MI 49453
269/ 857-4535 866/ 321-4535
www.parkhouseinn.com

Clientele: gay-friendly
Type: b&b; in Saugatuck's oldest residence; some rms w/ hot tub/ whirlpool; "Celebrating 20 yrs of excellence!"
Rooms: 10
Baths: private
Wheelchair Access: yes, 1 rm

Meals: full brkfst
Amenities: hot tub, WiFi
Kids: in 2 rooms only
Pets: please inquire
Smoking: no
Rates: $115-195
AC: 10%

The Pines Motor Lodge
Saugatuck

56 Blue Star Hwy
Douglas, MI 49406
269/ 857-5211
www.thepinesmotorlodge.com

Clientele: mixed gay/ straight
Type: newly renovated boutique retro lodging; easy walk to beaches, bars, clubs, restaurants, antiquing
Owned/ Run By: gay men
Rooms: 14

Baths: private
Meals: cont'l brkfst
Kids: varies (off-season only)
Pets: varies (off-season only)
Smoking: no
Rates: $75-195

The Spruce Cutter's Cottage
Saugatuck

6670 126th Ave
Fennville, MI 49408
269/ 543-4285 800/ 493-5888
www.sprucecutters.com

Clientele: mixed gay/ straight
Type: b&b; in quiet cottage in the country; surrounded by acres of spruce trees; w/ charming rms, 2 fireplaces; close to beach
Owned/ Run By: gay men
Rooms: 3

Baths: private
Meals: full brkfst
Kids: welcome
Pets: welcome
Smoking: ok
Rates: $100-200

Yelton Manor B&B
South Haven

140 North Shore Dr
South Haven, MI 49090
269/ 637-5220
www.yeltonmanor.com

Clientele: mixed gay/ straight
Type: b&b-inn; w/ award-winning gardens, lake views, wonderful food, pampering service
Owned/ Run By: straights
Rooms: 17
Baths: private

Wheelchair Access: yes, 1 rm
Meals: full brkfst
Amenities: free parking, hot tub, massage, DVDs/ videos
Smoking: no
Rates: $100-295

Budget Host Inn & Suites
St Ignace

700 N State St
St Ignace, MI 49781
906/ 643-9666 800/ 872-7057
www.mackinaclodging.com

Clientele: gay-friendly
Type: hotel; w/in walking distance to restaurants, museums, shops, ferries & beach; also brkfst bar
Rooms: 58
Baths: private
Wheelchair Access: yes, 55 rms

Meals: expanded cont'l brkfst
Amenities: free parking, laundry, pool, indoor hot tub, WiFi
Kids: welcome
Pets: welcome (in smoking rms only)
Smoking: ok
Rates: $58-157

Elegant Retreat
Traverse City

810 Cottageview Dr
Traverse City, MI 49684
231/ 947-6913
www.MargaretDodd.com

Clientele: gay-friendly
Type: condo; infamous historic landmark; marble flrs; 12' ceilings; Japanese soaking tub; large porch
Owned/ Run By: women
Rooms: 5
Baths: private
Meals: coffee/tea only

Amenities: free parking, laundry, indoor hot tub, WiFi
Kids: no
Pets: no
Smoking: no
Rates: $180-225/ night; $700-800/ week
AC: 5%

Blue Fish Guest House & Cottage
Union Pier

16070 Lake Shore Rd
Union Pier, MI 49129
269/ 469-0468 x112
www.bluefishcottages.com

Clientele: mixed gay/ straight
Type: charming 5-bdrm guesthouse or cozy 1-bdrm cottage; both w/ fireplace; walking distance to Lake Michigan
Owned/ Run By: gay men
Kids: welcome

Pets: $20 fee per stay
Smoking: no
Rates: $800-1,900/ week

Fire Fly Resort
Union Pier

15657 Lakeshore Rd
Union Pier, MI 49129
269/ 469-0245
www.fireflyresort.com

Clientele: mixed gay/ straight
Type: resort; 1- & 2-bdrm cottages w/ living rm, bdrm, kitchen & bath; also new 5-bdrm guesthouse; just steps from the beautiful beaches of Lake Michigan
Owned/ Run By: gay men
Rooms: 18

Baths: private
Kids: welcome
Pets: welcome
Smoking: no
Rates: $80-150

Sanctuaire
Union Pier

773/ 454-8318
www.michigansanctuaire.com

Clientele: mixed gay/ lesbian
Type: rental home; secluded yr-round getaway; pristine natural surroundings
Owned/ Run By: lesbians/ gay men
Rooms: 7
Baths: private
Meals: coffee/tea only

Amenities: outdoor hot tub
Kids: well-behaved kids welcome
Pets: only exceptional dogs welcome
Smoking: no
Rates: $399-3,499
AC: 10%

Farm Island Lake Resort & Campground
Aitkin

29551 Pioneer Ave
Aitkin, MN 56431
218/ 927-3841

Type: simple resort & campgrounds; clean & restful; canoes, pontoons, paddle bikes for rent; 40 campsites & 26 RV hookups
Rooms: 9 (cabins)
Baths: private

Kids: must be supervised
Pets: welcome (except in cabins)
Smoking: ok
Rates: $22 (camp); $375-575 (cabins)

The Olcott House B&B Inn
Duluth

2316 E 1st St
Duluth, MN 55812
218/ 728-1339 800/ 715-1339
www.olcotthouse.com

Clientele: gay-friendly
Type: b&b-inn; historic 1904 Georgian colonial mansion; complimentary wine & cheese; near Lake Superior
Owned/ Run By: gay men
Rooms: 6
Baths: private

Meals: full brkfst
Amenities: free parking, DVDs/ videos, WiFi
Kids: 16 yrs & up welcome
Pets: no
Smoking: no
Rates: $145-195

Log Cabin Hideaways
Ely

1321 N Hwy 21
Ely, MN 55731
218/ 365-6045
www.logcabinhideaway.com

Clientele: gay-friendly
Type: secluded log cabins, w/ homemade furniture, appliances, no running water/ electricity; adjacent to Boundary Waters Wilderness; all on different lakes
Owned/ Run By: straights

Amenities: sauna, outdoor hot tub
Kids: welcome
Pets: welcome; per day fee
Smoking: no
Rates: $433-1,350/ week

Classic Rosewood
Hastings

620 Ramsay
Hastings, MN 55033
651/ 437-3297 888/ 846-7966
www.thorwoodinn.com

Clientele: gay-friendly
Type: inn; 1880 Nat'l Register mansion; 7 of 8 rms have double whirlpools & fireplaces; gourmet in-house dinners available
Rooms: 8
Baths: private

Meals: full brkfst
Kids: please inquire
Pets: please inquire
Smoking: no
Rates: $97-277
AC: 10%

Dakota Lodge B&B
Hinckley

40497 State Hwy 48
Hinckley, MN 55037
320/ 384-6052
www.dakotalodge.com

Clientele: mixed gay/ straight
Type: b&b-inn; private luxury cabins/ guesthouse on 6 beautiful acres; fireplaces
Owned/ Run By: straights
Rooms: 5
Baths: private
Wheelchair Access: yes, all rms
Meals: full brkfst

Amenities: free parking, hot tub, DVDs/ videos, WiFi
Kids: 10 yrs & up welcome; $10 per night
Pets: welcome in guest house; dependent on size & behavior
Smoking: no
Rates: $109-145
AC: 10%

Dancing Winds Farmstay Retreat
Kenyon

6863 County 12 Blvd
Kenyon, MN 55946-4125
507/ 789-6606
www.dancingwinds.com

Clientele: mixed gay/ straight
Type: farmstay; "experience life on 20-acre sustainable working farm w/ cashmere & boer goats; chores optional (!); outdoor labyrinth; deck; pond; stargazing, hiking, biking, canoeing"
Owned/ Run By: lesbians
Rooms: 2 (guesthouse & loft)

Baths: private
Meals: stocked refrigerator & pantry
Kids: well-mannered w/ interest in animal welcome
Pets: welcome w/ prior approval
Smoking: no
Rates: $95-150

Cover Park Manor
Minneapolis/ St Paul

15330 58th St N
Stillwater, MN 55082-6508
651/ 430-9292 877/ 430-9292
www.coverpark.com

Clientele: gay-friendly
Type: b&b-inn; 1850s b&b; suites w/ private double whirlpools & fireplaces; secluded location, yet minutes from historic downtown Stillwater; 4-course brkfst delivered to the privacy of your rm
Rooms: 4 (suites)

Baths: private
Meals: full brkfst
Kids: welcome (in 1 suite)
Smoking: no
Rates: $119-195
AC: 10%

Millennium Hotel Minneapolis
Minneapolis/ St Paul

1313 Nicollet Mall
Minneapolis, MN 55403
612/ 332-6000 866/ 866-8086
www.millennium-hotels.com

Type: hotel; 14-story deluxe hotel in heart of downtown & connected by skyway; walking distance to theater, shopping & restaurants
Rooms: 321
Baths: private
Wheelchair Access: yes, 8 rms

Kids: welcome
Pets: welcome; fee applies
Smoking: ok
Rates: $99-289
AC: 10%

Nan's B&B
Minneapolis/ St Paul

2304 Fremont Ave S
Minneapolis, MN 55405
612/ 377-5118
www.virtualcities.com/mn/nan.htm

Clientele: gay-friendly
Type: b&b-private home; 1895 Victorian family home; guest rms furnished w/ antiques
Owned/ Run By: straights
Rooms: 3

Baths: shared
Meals: full brkfst
Kids: welcome; $5 extra bed fee
Pets: no
Smoking: no
Rates: $60-70

Quill & Quilt
Minneapolis/ St Paul

615 Hoffman St W
Cannon Falls, MN 55009
507/ 263-5507 800/ 488-3849
www.quillandquilt.com

Clientele: gay-friendly
Type: b&b; 100-yr-old colonial revival home; on-site spa treatments
Owned/ Run By: gay men
Rooms: 5
Baths: private
Meals: full brkfst

Amenities: free parking, indoor hot tub, massage, DVDs/ videos, WiFi
Kids: 11 yrs & up welcome
Pets: no
Smoking: no
Rates: $89-219
AC: 10%

Water Street Inn
Minneapolis/ St Paul

101 S Water St
Stillwater, MN 55082
651/ 439-6000
www.waterstreetinn.us

Clientele: gay-friendly
Type: b&b-inn; historic; in heart of downtown, next to historic Lift Bridge & overlooking St Croix River; also restaurant & pub & mtg/ banquet rms
Owned/ Run By: straights
Rooms: 41
Baths: private

Wheelchair Access: yes, 3 rms
Meals: full brkfst
Amenities: free parking, hot tub, massage
Kids: welcome
Pets: no
Smoking: ok (in 3 rms & pub)
Rates: $129-299
AC: 10%

Windswept Inn
Rushford

207 N Mill St
Rushford, MN 55971
507/ 864-2545
aldave722@yahoo.com

Clientele: mixed gay/ straight
Type: motel
Owned/ Run By: gay men
Rooms: 8
Baths: private
Wheelchair Access: yes, 4 rms

Kids: welcome
Pets: welcome
Smoking: ok
Rates: $40-50

Grand Superior Lodge
Two Harbors

2826 Hwy 61 E
Two Harbors, MN 55616
218/ 834-3796 800/ 627-9565
www.grandsuperior.com

Clientele: mixed gay/ straight
Type: resort; log cabins on N shore of Lake Superior
Owned/ Run By: straights
Rooms: 80
Baths: private
Wheelchair Access: yes

Amenities: free parking, pool, sauna, hot tub, massage, DVDs/ videos
Kids: welcome
Pets: welcome in some units; please inquire
Smoking: ok
Rates: please inquire

Nella's RV Park
Bay Saint Louis

16145 Hwy 603
Kiln, MS 39556
228/ 586-0053
www.geocities.com/nella_rvpark

Clientele: mixed gay/ straight
Type: RV park; friendly & clean w/ 30-ft fishing dock; casino nearby; close to New Orleans; 42 campsites & 42 RV hookups
Owned/ Run By: gay & straight
Wheelchair Access: yes

Kids: welcome
Pets: welcome
Smoking: ok
Rates: $300/ month; inquire if nightly available

Lofty Oaks Inn
Biloxi

17288 Hwy 67
Biloxi, MS 39552
228/ 392-6722 800/ 280-4361
www.bbhost.com/loftyoaksinn

Clientele: gay-friendly
Type: b&b-private home; w/ 2 in-room jacuzzis; outdoor jacuzzi in gazebo sits 5
Owned/ Run By: straight woman
Rooms: 4 (3 rms & 1 cottage)
Baths: private
Wheelchair Access: yes, cottage rms
Meals: full brkfst

Amenities: free parking, laundry, pool, outdoor hot tub, DVDs/ videos
Kids: welcome
Pets: welcome; $10 per pet per day
Smoking: ok
Rates: $125
AC: 15%

The Antebellum Music Room B&B at the Joseph Newman Stone House
Natchez

804 Washington St
Natchez, MS 39120
601/ 445-7466
www.discoverourtown.com/webs/
natchezms/billiard/

Clientele: gay-friendly
Type: b&b; antebellum Greek Revival home in downtown Natchez; on Nat'l Historic Register; classical music concert w/ complimentary wine; gallery of rare maps, prints, books & American arts
Owned/ Run By: gay man
Rooms: 1 master bdrm & 1 cottage

Baths: private
Meals: full brkfst
Amenities: free parking, laundry, WiFi
Kids: welcome
Smoking: on porches only
Rates: $95-125
AC: 12%

Historic Oak Hill Inn B&B
Natchez

409 S Rankin St
Natchez, MS 39120
601/ 446-2500
www.historicoakhill.com

Clientele: mixed gay/ straight
Type: b&b-inn; antebellum mansion near the Mississippi River
Owned/ Run By: gay men
Rooms: 3
Baths: private

Meals: full brkfst
Kids: over 10
Pets: no
Smoking: no
Rates: $100-135
AC: 15%

Camp Sister Spirit
Ovett

444 East Side Dr
Ovett, MS 39464
601/ 344-1411
www.campsisterspirit.com

Clientele: mixed gay/ straight
Type: retreat; on 120 acres; w/ full kitchen, dining hall, library, fire pits; RV hookups; please no illegal drugs or alcohol & no violence in word or deed
Owned/ Run By: lesbian & straight
Rooms: 60 (beds)

Baths: shared
Wheelchair Access: yes, 1 rm
Amenities: laundry, hot tub, DVDs/ videos
Kids: welcome
Pets: no
Smoking: no
Rates: $10-20 (suggested donation)

Cactus Canyon Campground
Ava

PO Box 266
Ava, MO 65608
417/ 683-9199
www.cactuscanyoncampground.com

Clientele: men
Type: campground; private, clothing-optional; w/ 100 campsites & 36 RV hookups; creek swimming; theme wknds & dances; reservations req'd from Nov-March, open March 1-Nov 1
Owned/ Run By: gay men
Rooms: 7

Baths: private & shared
Amenities: laundry, sauna, outdoor hot tub
Kids: no
Pets: must be leashed; no barking dogs
Smoking: ok
Rates: $13-16 (camping) & $40-75 (rooms cabins/ lodge)

Eden Roc Resort Motel
Branson

2652 State Hwy 176
Rockaway Beach, MO 65740
417/ 561-4163

Clientele: gay-friendly
Type: motel; located 9 miles from Branson on Lake Taneycomo; all rms w/ lake views; pool overlooking lake; fruit basket on arrival
Owned/ Run By: gay men

Rooms: 11
Baths: private
Kids: welcome
Pets: welcome; one-time $10 charge
Smoking: ok
Rates: $45-80

Rose Bed Inn
Cape Girardeau

611 S Sprigg St
Cape Girardeau, MO 63703
573/ 332-7673 866/ 767-3233
www.rosebedinn.com

Clientele: mixed gay/ straight
Type: b&b-inn; elegant; also features gourmet dining by reservation
Owned/ Run By: gay men
Rooms: 8
Baths: private
Wheelchair Access: yes, 2 rms

Meals: full brkfst
Amenities: free parking, laundry, indoor hot tub, massage, DVDs/ videos, gym, WiFi
Smoking: no
Rates: $85-200
AC: 10%

Ramada Inn Columbia
Columbia

1100 Vandiver Dr
Columbia, MO 65202
573/ 449-0051
www.ramadainncolumbia.com

Clientele: gay-friendly
Type: hotel
Rooms: 160
Baths: private
Wheelchair Access: yes, 12 rms
Meals: expanded cont'l
Amenities: free parking, laundry, pool,

gym, WiFi
Kids: welcome
Pets: welcome
Smoking: ok
Rates: $49-89
AC: 10%

Healing Stone Retreat & Spa
Hermann

5 Danuser Dr
Hermann, MO 65041
573/ 486-5000
www.healingstoneretreat.com

Clientele: gay-friendly
Type: a retreat b&b for spiritual & physical healing; attached to the historic Katy Trail; hiking & biking, spa facilities, yoga, healthy cooking classes & dining
Owned/ Run By: women
Rooms: 13
Baths: private & shared

Meals: full brkfst
Amenities: free parking, sauna, indoor hot tub, massage
Kids: no
Pets: no
Smoking: no
Rates: $125-255
AC: 10%

40th St Inn
Kansas City

1007 E 40th St
Kansas City, MO 64110
816/ 561-7575
www.40thstreetinn.com

Clientele: mixed gay/ straight
Type: b&b
Owned/ Run By: gay men
Rooms: 3
Meals: cont'l brkfst

Kids: no
Pets: no
Smoking: no
Rates: $65-90

The Concourse Park B&B
Kansas City

300 Benton Blvd
Kansas City, MO 64124
816/ 231-1196
austindue@sbcglobal.net

Clientele: mostly men
Type: grand Victorian b&b in historic NE Kansas City, Missouri; able to host large groups or events
Owned/ Run By: gay men
Rooms: 12
Baths: private & shared

Meals: expanded cont'l brkfst
Amenities: free parking, laundry, DVDs/ videos
Kids: welcome
Pets: welcome
Smoking: no
Rates: $60-120

Hydes Guesthouse   *Kansas City*

816/ 561–1010
www.hydeskc.com

Clientele: mostly men
Type: guesthouse; 1908 Shirtwaist in historic Hyde Park; close to plaza, shopping, galleries & bars
Owned/ Run By: gay men
Rooms: 3
Baths: private & shared

Meals: cont'l brkfst
Amenities: free parking, WiFi
Kids: no
Pets: no
Smoking: no
Rates: $65-90

LaFontaine Inn   *Kansas City*

4320 Oak St
Kansas City, MO 64111
816/ 753–4434 888/ 832–6000
www.lafontainebb.com

Clientele: gay-friendly
Type: b&b; beautifully restored 1910 Georgian Colonial; in cultural center of Kansas City
Owned/ Run By: gay men
Rooms: 5
Baths: private

Meals: full brkfst
Amenities: free parking, outdoor hot tub
Kids: will consider
Pets: no
Smoking: no
Rates: $139-184
AC: 10%

The Porch Swing Inn   *Kansas City*

702 East St
Parkville, MO 64152
816/ 587–6282 866/ 587–6282
www.theporchswinginn.com

Clientele: gay-friendly
Type: b&b; minutes from downtown; "experience the simple comforts & down-home cooking of our b&b"
Owned/ Run By: lesbians
Rooms: 4
Baths: private
Meals: full brkfst

Amenities: free parking, indoor hot tub, DVDs/ videos, WiFi
Kids: welcome; please call first
Pets: welcome (outdoor kennel available); please call first
Rates: $85-160
AC: 1 free night for every 10 nights booked

Quarterage Hotel   *Kansas City*

560 Westport Rd
Kansas City, MO 64111
816/ 931–0001 800/ 942–4233
www.quarteragehotel.com

Clientele: gay-friendly
Type: hotel; located in historic Westport district, close to shopping & clubs
Meals: expanded cont'l brkfst

Amenities: free parking, WiFi
Kids: welcome
Rates: $89+

Su Casa B&B   *Kansas City*

9004 E 92nd St
Kansas City, MO 64138
816/ 965–5647 816/ 916–3444 (cell)
www.sucasabb.com

Clientele: gay-friendly
Type: b&b-private home; spacious w/ Southwestern decor; on 5 acres; in-home theater, game rm & guest kitchen
Owned/ Run By: woman
Rooms: 3
Baths: private

Meals: expanded cont'l brkfst wkdays & full wknds
Amenities: pool, hot tub, DVDs/ videos
Kids: well-behaved welcome
Pets: well-behaved dogs & horses
Smoking: no
Rates: $100-145

A St Louis Guesthouse   *St Louis*

1032–38 Allen Ave
St Louis, MO 63104
314/ 773–1016
www.stlouisguesthouse.com

Clientele: mostly men
Type: guesthouse; located in historic Soulard, a restored neighborhood built in pre-Civil War era
Owned/ Run By: gay men
Rooms: 5
Baths: private

Meals: coffee/tea only
Amenities: free parking, laundry, outdoor hot tub, DVDs/ videos
Kids: no
Pets: no
Smoking: no
Rates: $75-110

Brewers House B&B
St Louis

1829 Lami St
St Louis, MO 63104
314/ 771-1542 888/ 767-4665
www.brewershouse.com

Clientele: mixed gay/ lesbian
Type: b&b-inn; Civil War vintage home in South St Louis; close to several breweries
Owned/ Run By: gay men
Rooms: 2
Baths: private
Meals: expanded cont'l brkfst
Amenities: free parking, laundry, outdoor

hot tub, DVDs/ videos
Kids: no
Pets: by arrangement
Smoking: no
Rates: $85
AC: 10%

Dwell 912 B&B
St Louis

912 Hickory St
St Louis, MO 63104
314/ 599-3100
www.dwell917.com

Clientele: gay-friendly
Type: b&b; modern home; 2nd-flr suite; separate entrance; 1st-flr lounge & kitchen; walking distance to town attractions
Owned/ Run By: lesbians
Rooms: 1

Baths: private
Meals: expanded cont'l brkfst
Amenities: free parking, DVDs/ videos, WiFi
Kids: no
Pets: no
Smoking: no
Rates: $125-175

Lafayette Park B&B
St Louis

1415 Missouri Ave
St Louis, MO 63104
314/ 771-9700 866/ 338-1415
lafayetteparkbedandbreakfast.com

Clientele: mixed gay/ straight
Type: b&b-private home; elegant; in historic neighborhood w/ decks & garden
Owned/ Run By: gay man
Rooms: 3
Baths: private
Meals: full brkfst

Amenities: free parking, hot tub, WiFi
Kids: welcome
Pets: no
Smoking: no (outside only)
Rates: $89-119
AC: 10%

Napoleon's Retreat B&B
St Louis

1815 Lafayette Ave
St Louis, MO 63104
314/ 772-6979 800/ 700-9980
www.napoleonsretreat.com

Clientele: mixed gay/ straight
Type: b&b-inn; elegant 1880 vintage town house; historic neighborhood near downtown
Owned/ Run By: gay men
Rooms: 5
Baths: private

Meals: full brkfst
Amenities: hot tub
Kids: 10 yrs & up welcome
Pets: service dogs only w/ prior approval
Smoking: no
Rates: $99-150
AC: 10%

Park Avenue Mansion—A B&B Guesthouse
St Louis

2007 Park Ave
St Louis, MO 63104
314/ 588-9004 866/ 588-9004
www.parkavenuebandb.com

Clientele: mixed gay/ straight
Type: b&b-inn; elegant 1870s mansion; helpful & friendly hosts; perfect venue for business or pleasure
Owned/ Run By: straights
Rooms: 5

Baths: private
Meals: full brkfst
Amenities: hot tub, DVDs/ videos
Kids: no
Pets: no
Rates: $89-225

Boulder Hot Springs Inn & Retreat
Boulder

31 Hot Springs Rd
Boulder, MT 59632
406/ 225-4339
www.boulderhotsprings.com

Clientele: gay-friendly
Type: b&b-inn; 100-yr-old grand inn at the foot of the Elkhorn Mtns; indoor & outdoor natural hot spring pools
Owned/ Run By: straights
Rooms: 12
Baths: private & shared

Wheelchair Access: yes
Meals: full brkfst
Kids: welcome; 1/2 price for 12 yrs & under
Pets: no
Smoking: no
Rates: $55-129

Gallatin Gateway Inn
Bozeman

PO Box 376
Gallatin Gateway, MT 59730
406/ 763-4672 800/ 676-3522
www.GallatinGatewayInn.com

Clientele: gay-friendly
Type: inn; "stunningly restored elegant railroad hotel, listed on the National Register of Historic Places"; located in the heart of Yellowstone Country
Rooms: 33

Baths: private
Wheelchair Access: yes
Kids: welcome
Smoking: ok (some smokefree rms)
Rates: $89-245

Lehrkind Mansion B&B
Bozeman

719 N Wallace Ave
Bozeman, MT 59715
406/ 585-6932 800/ 992-6932
www.bozemanbedandbreakfast.com

Clientele: mixed gay/ straight
Type: b&b; historic 1897 Queen Anne Victorian brewmaster's mansion; near downtown & many attractions
Owned/ Run By: gay men
Rooms: 8
Baths: private

Meals: full brkfst
Amenities: free parking, outdoor hot tub
Kids: well-supervised welcome
Pets: please call to discuss
Smoking: no
Rates: $119-169

Copper King Hotel & Convention Center
Butte

4655 Harrison Ave
Butte, MT 59701
406/ 494-6666 800/ 332-8600
www.copperkinghotel.com

Clientele: mixed gay/ straight
Type: hotel; located off I-15/I-90 junction near Bert Mooney Airport
Owned/ Run By: gay/ lesbian & straight
Rooms: 148
Baths: private
Wheelchair Access: yes, 75 rms

Meals: expanded cont'l brkfst
Amenities: free parking, laundry, pool, sauna, indoor hot tub
Kids: welcome
Pets: welcome
Smoking: in some areas
Rates: $85-196

Happy Horse Ranch B&B
Hamilton

273 Fox Run Trail
Hamilton, MT 59840
406/ 961-6893 877/ 817-0422
www.happyhorseranch.net

Clientele: mixed gay/ straight
Type: b&b; located on 10 acres in spectacular Bitterroot Valley; farm-fresh gourmet brkfst
Owned/ Run By: gay & straight
Rooms: 2

Baths: private
Meals: full brkfst
Kids: welcome; 10 yrs & up
Pets: welcome; well-behaved dogs only
Rates: $85-95

Cottonwood Hill Farm Inn
Kalispell

2928 Whitefish Stage Rd
Kalispell, MT 59901
406/ 756-6404 800/ 458-0893
www.cottonwoodhillfarm.com

Clientele: mixed gay/ straight
Type: b&b-private home; renovated farmhouse; on 14 acres in the Flathead Valley; 25 minutes from Glacier Nat'l Park & Big Mtn
Owned/ Run By: straights
Rooms: 3

Baths: private
Meals: full brkfst
Kids: 12 yrs & up welcome
Smoking: no
Rates: $65-135
AC: 10%

Yellowstone River Inn Cabins
Livingston

4950 Hwy 89 S
Livingston, MT 59047
406/ 222-2429 888/ 669-6993
www.yellowstoneriverinn.com

Clientele: mixed gay/ straight
Type: cozy cabins & a sheepherder's wagon on 5 acres; all 40 ft from the Yellowstone River
Owned/ Run By: women
Rooms: 2 (cabins)
Baths: private

Meals: full brkfst
Kids: 9 yrs & up welcome
Pets: by arrangement
Smoking: no
Rates: $110-135
AC: 10%

Brooks St Motor Inn
Missoula

3333 Brooks St
Missoula, MT 59801
406/ 549-5115 800/ 538-3260

Clientele: gay-friendly
Type: motel; close to local shops &
restaurants; whirlpool suites
Owned/ Run By: gay & straight
Rooms: 61
Baths: private
Wheelchair Access: yes, 3 rms

Meals: cont'l brkfst
Amenities: free parking, laundry, indoor
hot tub
Kids: welcome; 11 yrs & under free
Smoking: ok (some smokefree rms)
Rates: $40-125

Foxglove Cottage B&B
Missoula

2331 Gilbert Ave
Missoula, MT 59802
406/ 543-2927
www.foxglovecottage.net

Clientele: mixed gay/ straight
Type: b&b; cozy 100-yr-old home
surrounded by a lovely garden; near
downtown & the University; airport
pickup; complimentary drinks
Owned/ Run By: gay men
Rooms: 4

Baths: private & shared
Meals: full brkfst
Kids: well-behaved welcome
Pets: no
Smoking: no
Rates: $85-135

Lake Upsata Guest Ranch
Ovando

PO Box 6
Ovando, MT 59854
406/ 793-5890 800/ 594-7687
www.upsata.com

Clientele: gay-friendly
Type: guest ranch; full-service & all-
inclusive; rates include meals, lodging,
riding, fishing, hiking, hunting (fall),
snowmobiling (winter)
Rooms: 8 (cabins)
Baths: private

Amenities: laundry, hot tub
Kids: welcome; no horseback riding for
under 6 yrs
Pets: welcome
Smoking: no
Rates: $90-255
AC: 10%

Holland Lake Lodge
Swan Valley

1947 Holland Lake Rd
Swan Valley, MT 59826
406/ 754-2282 877/ 925-6343
www.hollandlakelodge.com

Clientele: gay-friendly
Type: resort; authentic western resort in NW
Montana; on mtn lake; lodge & guest
cabins; restaurant w/ gourmet chef & full
bar
Owned/ Run By: gay men
Rooms: 15
Baths: private & shared

Wheelchair Access: yes, 5 rms
Meals: full brkfst
Amenities: free parking, laundry, sauna,
outdoor hot tub, massage, DVDs/ videos
Kids: welcome
Pets: no
Rates: $105-125

Castle Unicorn
Omaha

712/ 527-5930
www.castleunicorn.com

Clientele: mixed gay/ straight
Type: b&b; in sprawling European stone &
brick castle; on 400-acre private estate in
Iowa's Loess Hills
Owned/ Run By: gay men
Rooms: 4
Baths: private & shared

Meals: full brkfst
Amenities: free parking, laundry, sauna,
hot tub, massage, DVDs/ videos, WiFi
Kids: please inquire
Pets: outdoor kennel available
Smoking: no
Rates: $169-189

The Cornerstone Mansion Inn
Omaha

140 N 39th St
Omaha, NE 68131
402/ 558-7600 888/ 883-7745
www.cornerstonemansion.com

Clientele: gay-friendly
Type: b&b-inn; restored 1894 mansion in
Omaha's historic Gold Coast; features
large library, sitting rm, formal dining rm &
sunporch
Rooms: 7
Baths: private

Meals: expanded cont'l brkfst
Amenities: free parking, DVDs/ videos, WiFi
Kids: welcome w/ prior approval
Pets: no
Smoking: no
Rates: $85-150

Blue Moon Resort

2651 Westwood Dr
Las Vegas, NV 89109

702/ 361-9099
866/ 798-9194

info@bluemoonlv.com
www.bluemoonlasvegas.com

Clientele: men
Type: resort; Las Vegas' only all-male private resort; w/ amenities second to none; steam rm & jacuzzi grotto; tour & travel desk; close to gay nightlife, swimming pool & city attractions; 3 blks to The Strip
Owned/ Run By: gay men
Pickup Service: airport pickup
Transit: near public transit
Rooms: 45 total, 11 suites, 39 kings, 5 fulls, A/C, deck, phone, safer sex supplies, maid service, satellite TV & free in-house adult channels, tile flrs 1st flr, carpet 2nd & 3rd flr; deluxe rm: 400 square ft; suite: 800 square ft
Baths: private, bathtubs, showers, whirlpools, hairdryers
Wheelchair Access: yes, 5 rms
Meals: expanded cont'l brkfst
Amenities: office hrs: 24hrs; free parking, massage, DVDs/ videos, WiFi, lagoon pool, 10' waterfall, 10-man jacuzzi, 400-sq-ft steam rm, coffeehouse, sight-seeing tour
Kids: no
Pets: small dogs welcome w/ $50 deposit

Smoking: ok (in rms only)
Reservations: required *Deposit:* required, 50%, due at booking, personal check ok *Cancellation:* cancel by 2 days prior (5 days holidays) or forfeit deposit
Payment: cash, travelers checks, personal

checks, Visa, Amex, MC, Discover
Season: open yr-round *High season:* March-June & Sept-Nov
Rates: $79-179 *Discounts:* travel agent, military, flight attendant
AC: 10%

Lucky You B&B

702/ 384-1129

haven00069@aol.com

Clientele: men
Type: b&b-private home; "the inside of my home features a unique, European decor while outside tropical plants & trees surround the pool area"
Owned/ Run By: gay man
Nearby Attractions: Las Vegas Strip
Pickup Service: airport pickup; $10 each way
Transit: near public transit; 15-minute ride to airport; local transit around the corner
Rooms: 4 total, 1 king, 3 queens, A/C, color TV, DVD/ VCR, cable, ceiling fan (3), fireplace (1), phone, refrigerator (2), safer sex supplies, rm service, maid service
Baths: private & shared, bathtubs, showers, whirlpools, robes, hairdryers
Meals: full brkfst, Liberace's former chef will cater to your every culinary desire
Amenities: free parking, laundry, pool, poolside mist, sauna, outdoor hot tub, DVDs/ videos, snacks, cocktails, coffee/ tea
Recreation: Lake Mead, Hoover Dam, nude beach, Valley of Fire, Grand Canyon
Pets: small pets only

Pets On Premises: 1 small dog
Reservations: required *Deposit:* required, 50%, due at booking, personal check ok *Cancellation:* cancel by 1 week *Check in/ out:* flexible

Payment: cash, travelers checks, personal checks
Season: open yr-round
Rates: $59-79 *Discounts:* 1 night free after 6 nights
AC: 10%

West Walker Motel
Carson City

106833 Hwy 395
Coleville, CA 96107
530/ 495-2263
www.westwalkermotel.com

Clientele: gay-friendly
Type: motel; near West Walker River, 770 acres of riparian habitat
Owned/ Run By: women
Rooms: 10
Baths: private

Meals: coffee/tea only
Amenities: free parking, DVDs/ videos, WiFi
Kids: welcome
Pets: dogs & cats
Smoking: ok
Rates: $45-75

F Ranch
Gerlach

PO Box 269
Gerlach, NV 89412
775/ 557-2804
www.f-ranch.com

Clientele: gay-friendly (mostly women)
Type: B&B on a beautiful, remote working horse/ cattle ranch in Gerlach, N of Reno & bordering the Black Rock Desert; 3 campsites & 3 RV hookups under shade trees w/in ranch headquarters
Owned/ Run By: straight women
Rooms: 4

Baths: private & shared
Meals: all meals included
Kids: welcome; no special activities but plenty of frogs, dogs & ranch explorations
Pets: no
Smoking: no
Rates: $2,500-3,500 (double occupancy)
AC: 15%

Three Chimneys Inn
Durham

17 Newmarket Rd
Durham, NH 03824
603/ 868-7800 888/ 399-9777
www.threechimneysinn.com

Clientele: gay-friendly
Type: historic b&b inn; near Portsmouth; w/ fireplaces, in-rm jacuzzi, fine dining, tavern, gardens, banquets
Owned/ Run By: straights
Rooms: 23
Baths: private

Wheelchair Access: yes, 6 rms
Meals: full brkfst
Kids: over 6 yrs welcome
Pets: no
Smoking: no (except on terrace)
Rates: $139-209
AC: 10%

Hannah Davis House
Fitzwilliam

106 NH Rte 119 W
Fitzwilliam, NH 03447
603/ 585-3344
www.hannahdavishouse.com

Clientele: mixed gay/ straight
Type: b&b-private home; 1820 Federal bldg in historic district in Currier & Ives corner of NH
Owned/ Run By: straights
Rooms: 6
Baths: private

Meals: full brkfst
Kids: welcome; very young only in suites
Pets: no
Smoking: no
Rates: $70-190
AC: 5-10%

E F Lane Hotel
Keene

30 Main St
Keene, NH
603/ 357-7070 888/ 300-5056
info@eflane.com

Clientele: gay-friendly
Type: hotel
Rooms: 40
Baths: private
Wheelchair Access: yes, 2 rms
Meals: expanded cont'l brkfst

Amenities: free parking, hot tub
Kids: welcome
Pets: no
Smoking: ok (in select guestrms)
Rates: $139-315

The Inn on Newfound Lake
Newfound Lake

1030 Mayhew Tpke Rte 3-A
Bridgewater, NH 03222
603/ 744-9111 800/ 745-7990
www.newfoundlake.com

Clientele: mixed gay/ straight
Type: b&b-inn; Victorian w/ renowned restaurant, private beach & boat dock; say you saw us here for special rates
Owned/ Run By: gay men
Rooms: 31
Baths: private & shared

Meals: cont'l brkfst
Amenities: free parking, hot tub, DVDs/ videos
Rates: $105-345
AC: 10%

Federal House Inn Historic B&B
Plymouth

27 Rte 25
Plymouth, NH 03264-0147
603/ 536-4644 866/ 536-4644
www.FederalHouseInnNH.com

Clientele: mixed gay/ straight
Type: b&b-inn; at base of Tenney Mtn; guest rms w/ utmost in amenities; unsurpassed brkfst
Owned/ Run By: gay men
Rooms: 5
Baths: private & shared

Meals: full brkfst
Amenities: free parking, outdoor hot tub, DVDs/ videos
Kids: 12 yrs & up welcome
Pets: no
Rates: $99-180
AC: 12%

The Surry House
Surry

50 Village Rd
Surry, NH 03431
603/ 352-2268
www.thesurryhouse.com

Clientele: mixed gay/ straight
Type: b&b-private home; large circa 1885 home; close to Surry Recreation Area; minutes to Keene, NH
Owned/ Run By: lesbians
Rooms: 3 (1 king w/ private bath; 1 queen & 1 double w/ shared)

Baths: private & shared
Meals: full brkfst
Amenities: free parking, pool
Kids: well-behaved welcome
Pets: well-behaved welcome
Smoking: no
Rates: $75-100

Brookhill B&B
White Mtns

PO Box 221
North Conway, NH 03860
603/ 356-3061 888/ 356-3061
www.brookhillbb.com

Clientele: mixed gay/ straight
Type: 2-bdrm luxury suite w/ spectacular mtn views, private terrace, gardens, fireplace, deep-soaking tub & kitchen; 1.5 miles from North Conway village
Owned/ Run By: straights
Rooms: 2-bdrm suite w/ 1 bath

Meals: full brkfst
Amenities: free parking, indoor hot tub, massage
Kids: 17 yrs & up welcome
Pets: no
Smoking: no
Rates: $219-389

The Bungay Jar B&B
White Mtns

791 Easton Valley Rd
Franconia, NH 03580
603/ 823-7775 800/ 421-0701
www.bungayjar.com

Clientele: gay-friendly
Type: b&b-inn; restored 1800s post & beam barn on 8 acres of gardens/ woodland; views of the White Mtns
Owned/ Run By: gay men
Rooms: 8
Baths: private

Meals: full brkfst
Amenities: free parking, sauna, hot tub, massage
Kids: 8 yrs & up welcome
Pets: no
Smoking: no
Rates: $140-245

The Horse & Hound Inn
White Mtns

205 Wells Rd
Franconia, NH 03580
603/ 823-5501 800/ 450-5501
www.horseandhoundnh.com

Clientele: gay-friendly
Type: b&b; renovated in 1946 from an 1830 farmhouse to an old-fashioned New England b&b; also restaurant & pub
Owned/ Run By: gay men
Rooms: 9
Baths: private

Meals: full brkfst
Amenities: free parking, DVDs/ videos, WiFi
Kids: welcome
Pets: welcome; $8.50 per pet
Smoking: ok
Rates: $90-150
AC: 10%

Inn at Crystal Lake
White Mtns

Rte 153 Eaton Center
North Conway, NH 03832
603/ 447-2120 800/ 343-7336
www.innatcrystallake.com

Clientele: mixed gay/ straight
Type: b&b-inn; located in a quiet village, yet close to everything, this 1884 Victorian is the perfect place for relaxation
Owned/ Run By: gay men
Rooms: 11
Baths: private

Meals: full brkfst
Kids: 9 yrs & up welcome
Pets: dogs only welcome (1 rm)
Smoking: no
Rates: $109-239

Highlands Inn 🏳️‍🌈   *White Mtns*

PO Box 118 Valley View Ln
Bethlehem, NH 03574

603/ 869-3978
877/ LES-B-INN (537-2466)

www.highlandsinn-nh.com

Clientele: women
Type: b&tb-inn; Lesbian Paradise: 19 rms; 100 acres; "One of the most romantic lesbian destinations on the planet!"—*PlanetOut*
Owned/ Run By: lesbians
Rooms: 19 (includes 1 cottage) total, 1 suite, 4 kings, 8 queens, 6 fulls, A/C, color TV, DVD/ VCR, fireplace (4), deck (5), kitchenette (6), refrigerator, maid service, 2-person spa (2), individually decorated w/ antiques & comfortable furniture
Baths: private, bathtubs, showers, whirlpools, hairdryers
Wheelchair Access: yes, 3 rms
Meals: full brkfst
Amenities: massage, snacks, coffee/ tea, indoor & outdoor spas, large heated swimming pool w/ sundeck & adjacent gazebo, 15 miles of trails for x-country skiing, snowshoeing, hiking & mtn-biking, extensive lesbian/ gay video collection, guest computer w/ high-speed internet access, WiFi in common areas, spectacular sunsets, commitment ceremonies, many special events including free concerts & holiday events
Kids: welcome

Pets: w/ prior approval; 6 rms available
Pets On Premises: 1 dog
Reservations: recommended; our sign always says No Vacancy–ignore it! *Deposit:* required, 50%, due at booking, personal check ok *Cancellation:* cancel by 8 days prior for deposit refund; $25 cancellation fee *Check in/ out:* 3pm/ 11am

Payment: cash, travelers checks, personal checks, Visa, MC
Season: open yr-round *High season:* summer & fall; winter wknds
Rates: $110-200 *Discounts:* 10-15% weekly (except holidays), midweek
AC: 10%

Mulburn Inn at Bethlehem   *White Mtns*

2370 Main St/ Rte 302
Bethlehem, NH 03574

603/ 869-3389
800/ 457-9440

info@mulburninn.com
www.mulburninn.com

Clientele: mixed gay/ straight
Type: b&tb; in historic Woolworth family English Tudor mansion; w/ hardwood flrs, stained glass & fireplaces; Cary Grant, Thomas Edison & the Rockefellers all vacationed here
Owned/ Run By: women
Rooms: 8 total, 1 suite, 4 kings, 4 queens, A/C, cable TV (1), fireplace (1), maid service
Baths: private, bathtubs, showers, hairdryers
Meals: full brkfst
Amenities: outdoor hot tub, WiFi, coffee/ tea, wraparound porches, in-rm massage, 2 fireplaces in living rms, spectacular sunsets, many special dinners & events throughout year, gift shop, piano
Kids: welcome
Pets: please inquire
Pets On Premises: 2 dogs
Smoking: no
Reservations: recommended *Deposit:* 50% *Cancellation:* cancel by 2 weeks prior or forfeit $25 *Minimum Stay:* possible during high season

Payment: cash, travelers checks, personal checks, Visa, MC, Discover
Season: open yr-round *High season:* Sept-Oct & Xmas–New Year's

Rates: $85-175 *Discounts:* 10% TAC
AC: 10%

The Notchland Inn   White Mtns

Rte 302
Hart's Location, NH 03812
603/ 374-6131 800/ 866-6131
www.Notchland.com

Clientele: mixed gay/ straight
Type: b&b-inn; comfortable, elegant 1860s granite mansion; surrounded by nat'l forest; romantic 5-course dinner & hearty country brkfsts; "a magical location"
Owned/ Run By: gay men
Rooms: 14

Baths: private
Amenities: outdoor hot tub, massage
Kids: 12 yrs & up welcome
Pets: welcome only in River View Cottage
Smoking: no
Rates: $195-340
AC: 10%

Riverbend Inn B&B   White Mtns

273 Chocorua Mtn Hwy
Chocorua, NH 03817
603/ 323-7440 800/ 628-6944
www.riverbendinn.com

Clientele: mixed gay/ straight
Type: b&b; luxurious award-winning inn on 15 wooded acres on the Chocorua River
Owned/ Run By: gay men
Rooms: 10
Baths: private & shared
Meals: full brkfst

Amenities: free parking, massage, WiFi
Kids: over 10 yrs welcome
Pets: no
Smoking: no
Rates: $99-229
AC: 10% (except foliage season)

Wildcat Inn & Tavern   White Mtns

PO Box T
Jackson, NH 03846
603/ 383-4245 800/ 228-4245
www.wildcattavern.com

Type: b&b; suites available; also full bar & dining rm
Rooms: 12 (also 1 cottage)
Baths: private & shared
Meals: full brkfst
Kids: welcome; no more than 3 people/ rm
Pets: no

Smoking: ok (in designated rms & tavern)

The Carisbrooke Inn   Atlantic City

105 S Little Rock Ave
Ventnor, NJ 08406
609/ 822-6392
www.carisbrookeinn.com

Clientele: gay-friendly
Type: on a beach blk; 1 mile from Atlantic City
Owned/ Run By: gay & straight
Rooms: 8
Baths: private & shared

Meals: full brkfst
Amenities: free parking, DVDs/ videos
Smoking: no
Rates: $79-260
AC: 15%

Ocean House   Atlantic City

127 S Ocean Ave
Atlantic City, NJ 08401-7202
609/ 345-8203
oceanhouseatlanticcity.com

Clientele: men
Type: guesthouse; large turn-of-the-century home; exclusively for gay men; clothing-optional; intimate atmosphere; 200 yds from beach & boardwalk; open yr-round
Owned/ Run By: gay men

Rooms: 14
Baths: private & shared
Meals: coffee/tea only
Kids: no
Pets: no
Smoking: ok
Rates: $42-150

Surfside Resort Hotel   Atlantic City

18 S Mt Vernon Ave
Atlantic City, NJ 08401
609/ 347-7873 888/ 277-7873
www.surfsideresorthotel.com

Clientele: mixed gay/ straight
Type: resort; small, upscale, straight-friendly; w/ piano lounge & poolside bar
Owned/ Run By: gay men
Rooms: 50
Baths: private
Meals: cont'l brkfst

Kids: no; must be 21 or older
Pets: no
Smoking: ok
Rates: $51-225
AC: 10%

Beauclaires B&B Inn
Cape May

23 Ocean Ave
Cape May, NJ 08204
609/ 889-1222
www.beauclaires.com

Clientele: mixed gay/ straight
Type: b&b-inn; 2 blks from downtown shopping & restaurants; 1/2 blk from ocean; oceanview rms available
Owned/ Run By: gay & straight
Rooms: 6
Baths: private

Meals: full brkfst
Amenities: free parking
Kids: no
Pets: no
Smoking: no
Rates: $125-245

Cottage Beside the Point
Cape May

609/ 204-0549
www.cottagebesidethepoint.com

Clientele: mixed gay/ straight
Type: studio; beautiful, private setting overlooking gardens w/ lots of bird life & naturally landscaped pond; ideal for romantic getaways
Owned/ Run By: lesbians

Rooms: 1 (studio apt)
Baths: private
Amenities: free parking, DVDs/ videos
Kids: welcome
Smoking: no
Rates: $115-135

Highland House
Cape May

609/ 898-1198
www.highlandhousecapemay.com

Clientele: gay-friendly
Type: b&b-inn; relaxed, comfortable accommodations; open yr-round; guests encouraged to enjoy the porch, gazebo & living rm
Owned/ Run By: gay & straight
Baths: private & shared

Meals: expanded cont'l brkfst
Amenities: free parking
Kids: welcome
Pets: welcome
Smoking: no
Rates: $110-155

The Virginia Hotel
Cape May

25 Jackson St
Cape May, NJ 08204
609/ 884-5700 800/ 732-4236
www.virginiahotel.com

Clientele: gay-friendly
Type: hotel; small, European boutique-style hotel; in the heart of Cape May's historic district
Owned/ Run By: gay & straight
Rooms: 24
Baths: private

Meals: cont'l brkfst
Kids: welcome
Pets: no
Smoking: ok (except in public areas)
Rates: $85-425
AC: 10%

The Pillars of Plainfield B&B
Plainfield

922 Central Ave
Plainfield, NJ 07060-2311
908/ 753-0922
www.pillars2.com

Clientele: mixed gay/ straight
Type: b&b; luxury private bath suites in restored Victorian mansion; easy access to NYC, New Hope, Sandy Hook & Newark airport
Owned/ Run By: straights
Rooms: 7
Baths: private
Meals: full brkfst

Amenities: free parking, laundry, DVDs/ videos, WiFi
Kids: welcome; under 2 yrs free; 3-17 yrs 1/2 price
Pets: only dogs & by arrangement
Smoking: no
Rates: $125-250
AC: 8%

Woolverton Inn
Stockton

6 Woolverton Rd
Stockton, NJ 08559
609/ 397-0802 888/ 264-6648
www.woolvertoninn.com

Clientele: gay-friendly
Type: b&b; grand estate 5 minutes from Lambertville, NJ & New Hope, PA
Owned/ Run By: gay/ lesbian & straight
Rooms: 13
Baths: private
Wheelchair Access: yes, 1 rm

Meals: full brkfst
Amenities: free parking, hot tub, massage
Kids: 13 yrs & up welcome
Pets: no
Smoking: no
Rates: $130-425

Brittania & W E Mauger Estate B&B 🏳️‍🌈

Albuquerque

701 Roma Ave NW
Albuquerque, NM 87102

505/ 242-8755
800/ 719-9189

info@maugerbb.com
www.maugerbb.com

Clientele: gay-friendly
Type: b&b-inn; 1897 restored Victorian b&b (listed on Nat'l Register of Historic Places); 3-Star rating from Mobil; 3-Diamond rating from AAA
Owned/ Run By: straight
Nearby Attractions: historic Old Town, Biopark, zoo, museums, historic Route 66, Indian pueblos
Transit: 15 minutes to Albuquerque Int'l
Rooms: 8 total, 1 suite, 2 king, 7 queens, 1 twin, A/C, color TV, DVD/ VCR, cable, ceiling fan, fireplace (1), deck (1), phone, refrigerator, maid service, down comforters, snack baskets, all large comfortable rms
Baths: private, showers, robes, hairdryers
Meals: full brkfst, most restricted diets can be accommodated (diabetic, wheat-free, etc)
Amenities: WiFi, snacks, cocktails, sunset drinks, coffee/ tea
Kids: welcome
Pets: dogs welcome in 1 rm; $30 fee
Pets On Premises: 2 dogs
Smoking: no

Reservations: required *Deposit:* required, 1 night, due at booking, personal check ok *Cancellation:* cancel by 10 days prior or forfeit $25 *Check in/ out:* 4-7pm/ 11am
Payment: cash, travelers checks, personal checks, Visa, Amex, MC, Discover, Diners Club

Season: open yr-round *High season:* March-Oct
Rates: $89-189 *Discounts:* AAA, corp, gov't, military
AC: 10%

Casitas at Old Town

Albuquerque

1604 Old Town Rd NW
Albuquerque, NM 87104

505/ 843-7479

bratotown@aol.com
www.oldtowncasitas.com

Clientele: mixed gay/ straight
Type: guesthouse; suites in a classic adobe bldg on the secluded edge of Albuquerque's oldest historical area
Owned/ Run By: gay man
Nearby Attractions: 25 minutes to Mtn Tram; 5 minutes to zoo, botanical garden & aquarium; 3 blks to Old Town & museums
Pickup Service: airport pickup
Transit: near public transit; 20 minutes to airport; 5 minutes to bus/ train station
Rooms: 2 total, suites, 1 queen, 1 full, A/C, fireplace, deck, kitchenette, refrigerator, traditional New Mexican furnishings
Baths: private, showers
Meals: coffee/ tea only
Amenities: free parking, coffee/ tea, private patios
Recreation: Petroglyph Nat'l Monument, Albuquerque Nature Center, bike & jogging trails
Kids: no

Pets: no
Smoking: no
Reservations: *Deposit:* required, $85, due at booking, personal check ok *Cancellation:* cancel by 2 days prior or forfeit 1 night *Check in/ out:* flexible
Payment: cash, travelers checks, personal checks
Season: open yr-round
Rates: $85 *Discounts:* for extended stay
AC: 10%

8 Dwelling
Albuquerque

6800 Vista Del Norte Unit 1928
Albuquerque, NM 87113
800/ 941-6759
www.8dwelling.com

Clientele: mixed gay/ straight
Type: condo; private balcony
Owned/ Run By: lesbians
Rooms: 3
Baths: private & shared
Amenities: free parking, laundry, pool, gym, WiFi

Kids: welcome
Pets: no
Smoking: no
Rates: $149/ night, $2000/ month

El Peñasco
Albuquerque

PO Box 846
Placitas, NM 87043
505/ 771-8909 888/ 576-2726
www.purpleroofs.com/listingpictures/
e/elpenasco-nm.html

Clientele: mostly women
Type: guesthouse; "your own adobe house in the mtns between Albuquerque & Santa Fe"
Owned/ Run By: lesbians
Rooms: 2
Baths: private

Meals: full brkfst
Amenities: free parking, outdoor hot tub (on private patio), massage, DVDs/ videos
Kids: welcome
Pets: no
Smoking: no
Rates: $80-100

Hacienda Antigua B&B
Albuquerque

6708 Tierra Dr NW
Albuquerque, NM 87107
505/ 345-5399 800/ 201-2986
www.haciendantigua.com

Clientele: mixed gay/ straight
Type: b&b-inn; 200-yr-old compound; w/ courtyard, pool, gardens & fireplaces
Owned/ Run By: straights
Rooms: 8
Baths: private
Meals: full brkfst

Amenities: free parking, pool, outdoor hot tub
Kids: welcome
Pets: welcome
Smoking: no
Rates: $149-300
AC: 10%

Hacienda of Old Town B&B
Albuquerque

Central at Laguna
Albuquerque, NM 87104
505/ 245-7838
oldtownhacienda@aol.com

Clientele: gay-friendly
Type: charming adobe condos; enclosed courtyards; daily, weekly, or monthly rental
Owned/ Run By: gay & straight
Rooms: 4
Baths: private

Wheelchair Access: yes
Meals: cont'l brkfst
Kids: welcome
Smoking: no
Rates: $99-149

Wyndham Albuquerque Hotel
Albuquerque

2910 Yale Blvd SE
Albuquerque, NM 87106
505/ 843-7000 800/ 227-1117
www.wyndhamalbuquerque.com

Clientele: gay-friendly
Type: hotel
Owned/ Run By: gay & straight
Rooms: 295
Baths: private
Kids: welcome

Pets: no
Smoking: ok
Rates: $179-209
AC: 10%

Casa Escondida B&B
Chimayo

PO Box 142
Chimayo, NM 87522
505/ 351-4805 800/ 643-7201
www.casaescondida.com

Clientele: gay-friendly
Type: b&b; an intimate & serene b&b nestled on 6 acres; located in the mtns just 35 minutes from Santa Fe
Rooms: 8
Baths: private
Meals: full brkfst

Amenities: free parking, outdoor hot tub
Kids: welcome
Pets: welcome; must be arranged in advance
Smoking: no
Rates: $95-155

Good Life Inn B&B & Wedding Chapel
Cloudcroft

164 Karr Canyon Rd
High Rolls, NM 88325
505/ 682-5433 866/ 543-3466
www.goodlifeinn.com

Clientele: mixed gay/ straight
Type: b&b-inn; 10 minutes from Cloudcroft, 2 hrs from El Paso & Las Cruces; luxurious mtn setting; wedding packages
Owned/ Run By: lesbians
Rooms: 3
Baths: private
Meals: full brkfst

Amenities: free parking, hot tub, massage DVDs/ videos, gym, WiFi
Kids: 14 yrs & up welcome
Pets: no
Smoking: no
Rates: $125-175
AC: 5%

High Rolls Hideaway
Cloudcroft

PO Box 711
High Rolls, NM 88325
505/ 682-5433 866/ 543-3466
www.goodlifeinn.com/
highrollshideaway.html

Clientele: mixed gay/ straight
Type: quaint 1-bdrm/ 1-bath cottage; newly remodeled; sleeps 4; wraparound front porch; cable TV/ DVD; fully equipped kitchen
Owned/ Run By: gay & straight
Rooms: 1

Baths: private
Amenities: free parking, massage
Kids: welcome
Pets: no
Smoking: no
Rates: $99-130
AC: 5%

Days Inn
Farmington

1901 E Broadway
Farmington, NM 87401
505/ 325-3700

Type: hotel; new property w/ 9 suites & I jacuzzi suite
Rooms: 63
Baths: private
Wheelchair Access: yes, 3 rms

Meals: cont'l brkfst
Kids: welcome
Pets: welcome
Rates: $39-99
AC: 10%

Madrid Lodging
Madrid

14 Opera House Rd
Madrid, NM 87010
505/ 471-3450
www.madridlodging.com

Clientele: gay-friendly
Type: b&b; relaxed, creative atmosphere; w/ friendly owners; suites offer views & balconies
Rooms: 2 (suites)
Baths: private
Wheelchair Access: yes, 1 rm

Meals: full brkfst
Amenities: free parking, outdoor hot tub DVDs/ videos, WiFi
Kids: welcome
Pets: welcome w/ advance notice; $15 fee
Smoking: no
Rates: $85-100

El Morro RV Park, Cabins & Cafe
Ramah

4018 Hwy 53
Ramah, NM 87321
505/ 783-4612
www.el-morro-nm.com

Clientele: mixed gay/ straight
Type: cabin, RV park; located in Zuni Mtns among piñon & ponderosa pine trees; near El Morro Nat'l Monument, ice caves, El Malpais Nat'l monument & hiking & biking trails
Owned/ Run By: lesbians
Rooms: 6

Baths: private & shared
Wheelchair Access: yes, 2 rms
Meals: full brkfst
Kids: welcome
Pets: welcome
Smoking: no
Rates: $65-75

Bishop's Lodge Resort & Spa
Santa Fe

1297 Bishops Lodge Rd
Santa Fe, NM 87501
505/ 983-6377 800/ 419-0492
www.bishopslodge.com

Clientele: gay-friendly
Type: resort; on 450 tranquil acres 8 minutes from historic Plaza
Owned/ Run By: straights
Rooms: 110
Baths: private
Wheelchair Access: yes, 3 rms

Amenities: free parking, pool, outdoor hot tub, massage
Kids: welcome
Pets: welcome
Smoking: ok
Rates: $149-389
AC: 10%

Four Kachinas Inn
Santa Fe

512 Webber St
Santa Fe, NM 87501
505/ 988-1631 888/ 634-8782
www.fourkachinas.com

Clientele: mixed gay/ straight
Type: b&b-inn; built around a quiet courtyard; near historic Plaza; exquisite decor & great service
Owned/ Run By: gay men
Rooms: 5
Baths: private
Wheelchair Access: yes, 1 rm

Meals: expanded cont'l brkfst
Amenities: free parking, laundry, outdoor hot tub, WiFi
Kids: welcome
Pets: no
Smoking: no
Rates: $110-215
AC: 10%

Hacienda Las Barrancas
Santa Fe

27 Country Rd 84-D
Santa Fe, NM 87506
505/ 455-2197 866/ 455-2197
www.haciendalasbarrancas.com

Clientele: gay-friendly
Type: b&b; in adobe hacienda; comfortable, relaxing atmosphere; full brkfst
Owned/ Run By: straights
Rooms: 4
Baths: private
Meals: full brkfst

Amenities: free parking, laundry, outdoor hot tub, DVDs/ videos, WiFi
Kids: well-behaved kids welcome
Pets: no
Smoking: no
Rates: $110-175
AC: 10%

Heart Seed B&B Retreat & Spa
Santa Fe

PO Box 867
Cerrillos, NM 87010
505/ 471-7026
www.heart-seed.com

Clientele: gay-friendly
Type: retreat; in spectacular mtn setting on 60 acres; day spa offers variety of massage & spa treatments
Owned/ Run By: lesbians
Rooms: 6
Baths: private

Meals: full brkfst
Amenities: outdoor hot tub, massage
Kids: welcome
Pets: no
Smoking: no
Rates: $85-129
AC: 10%

Inn of the Anasazi
Santa Fe

113 Washington Ave
Santa Fe, NM 87501
505/ 988-3030 800/ 688-8100
www.innoftheanasazi.com

Clientele: gay-friendly
Type: inn; small luxury hotel located 1/2 blk from Santa Fe's historic Plaza; rms beautifully decorated in Southwestern style
Rooms: 57
Baths: private

Wheelchair Access: yes, 1 rm
Kids: welcome
Pets: no
Smoking: ok
Rates: $269-525
AC: 10%

La Tienda Inn & Duran House
Santa Fe

445-447 W San Francisco St
Santa Fe, NM 87501
505/ 989-8259 800/ 889-7611
www.latiendabb.com

Clientele: gay-friendly
Type: b&b-inn; romantic adobe compound w/ historic bldgs; 4 blks to historic downtown plaza
Owned/ Run By: gay/ lesbian & straight
Rooms: 13
Baths: private

Wheelchair Access: yes, 5 rms
Meals: expanded cont'l brkfst
Kids: welcome
Pets: no
Smoking: no
Rates: $85-175
AC: 10%

Las Palomas
Santa Fe

460 W San Francisco St
Santa Fe, NM 87501
505/ 982-5560 877/ 982-5560
www.laspalomas.com

Clientele: gay-friendly
Type: charming inn w/ 38 "casitas"; 3 blks from Santa Fe's Plaza; beautiful garden; paths lead to each lovely rm; w/ wood or gas fireplace
Owned/ Run By: man
Rooms: 37 (8 studios & 29 casitas)
Baths: private

Meals: expanded cont'l brkfst
Amenities: sauna, outdoor hot tub
Kids: welcome
Pets: welcome
Smoking: ok
Rates: $139-269
AC: 10%

Inn of the Turquoise Bear B&B

Santa Fe

342 E Buena Vista St
Santa Fe, NM 87505-2623
505/ 983-0798 800/ 396-4104
bluebear@newmexico.com
www.turquoisebear.net

Clientele: mixed gay/ lesbian
Type: b&b-inn; at historic Witter Bynner estate in park-like setting; close to Plaza; *Out & About*'s Editor's Choice 1999-2003; Heritage Preservation Awards 1999 & 2000
Owned/ Run By: gay men
Nearby Attractions: 10-20 miles to Indian pueblos; 7 miles to Santa Fe opera; 8 blks to gay bar; 7 blks to Plaza & Indian markets; 5-15 blks to museums, rodeos, festivals; 3-15 blks to galleries & architectural tours
Transit: near public transit; 55 miles to Albuquerque airport; 5 miles to Santa Fe airport; 15 miles to train station
Rooms: 11 (includes 1 double) total, 2 suites, 3 kings, 7 queens, A/C (1), color TV, DVD/ VCR, cable, fireplace, deck (1), phone, refrigerator (2), safer sex supplies, maid service, each rm is unique
Baths: private & shared, bathtubs, showers, robes, hairdryers
Wheelchair Access: yes, 1 rm (outside main building which is not) rms
Meals: expanded cont'l brkfst
Amenities: free parking, massage, DVDs/ videos, snacks, sunset drinks, coffee/ tea, newspapers, gift shop
Recreation: 10 miles to hiking, skiing & rafting; 5 miles to horseback riding, Japanese spa, hot-air balloon rides
Kids: welcome; please inquire
Pets: welcome; 50-lb limit & $20 cleaning fee
Pets On Premises: 2 cats
Smoking: no
Reservations: recommended *Deposit:* required, 1 night, due 5 days after booking, personal check ok *Cancellation:* cancel by 2 weeks prior ($20 cancellation fee) or forfeit 100% *Minimum Stay:* 2 nights (some wknds & holidays) *Check in/ out:* 3pm/ noon
Payment: cash, travelers checks, personal checks, Visa, Amex, MC, Discover
Season: open yr-round *High season:* April-Oct & Dec
Rates: $99-325 *Discounts:* 7+ days (high season excluded)
AC: 10%

On an acre of secluded gardens astride the Santa Fe Trail, a short stroll from the Plaza and Santa Fe's gay nightlife, stands The Turquoise Bear, the historic adobe home of the poet Witter Bynner.

Renowned for "setting the standard for being gay in Santa Fe" in the 1920s, Bynner entertained famous guests in this house, including Igor Stravinsky, Stephen Spender, Robert Frost, Edna St. Vincent Millay, Errol Flynn, Ansel Adams, and Christopher Isherwood. D. H. Lawrence slept here his first night in New Mexico–and now you can too.

The Turquoise Bear, your headquarters for fun and adventure in the Land of Enchantment, is the gay alternative in Santa Fe.

The Madeleine Inn
Santa Fe

106 Faithway St
Santa Fe, NM 87501
505/ 982-3465 888/ 877-7622
www.madeleineinn.com

Clientele: mixed gay/ straight
Type: b&b; elegant 1886 Queen Anne Victorian in secluded garden setting near Plaza
Owned/ Run By: gay & straight
Rooms: 8
Baths: private & shared
Meals: full brkfst

Amenities: free parking, laundry, hot tub, massage, DVDs/ videos
Kids: 12 & up welcome in main house; any age in suites
Smoking: no
Rates: $110-220
AC: 10%

The Triangle Inn—Santa Fe
Santa Fe

14 Arroyo Cuyamungue
Santa Fe, NM 87506

505/ 455-3375
877/ 733-7689

Stay@TriangleInn.com
www.triangleinn.com

Clientele: mixed gay/ lesbian
Type: b&b-inn; authentic adobe compound w/ 7 private casitas & first-class amenities; caters exclusively to the lesbian & gay communities
Owned/ Run By: lesbians
Nearby Attractions: 12 miles to Santa Fe; close to world-renowned shopping, galleries, opera & restaurants; ideally located near Indian ruins, fabulous sightseeing
Transit: 60 miles to airport; rental car recommended
Rooms: 7 (includes 3 studios, 3 one-bdrms & 1 two-bdrm house) total, 7 suites, 2 kings, 5 queens, color TV, DVD/ VCR, wetbar, fireplace (4), phone, kitchenette, refrigerator, safer sex supplies, maid service, stereo/ CD players
Baths: private, bathtubs, showers, robes, hairdryers
Wheelchair Access: yes, 1 rm
Meals: expanded cont'l brkfst, includes home-baked muffins & concierge services
Amenities: office hrs: 24hrs; free parking, outdoor hot tub, DVDs/ videos, snacks, sunset drinks, coffee/ tea, outdoor grill, sundeck, courtyards, portal w/ outdoor, yr-round fireplace

Recreation: hiking, horseback riding, x-country & downhill skiing, mtn biking, river rafting
Kids: welcome
Pets: well-behaved only
Pets On Premises: 2 dogs (in main house)
Smoking: ok
Reservations: required *Cancellation:* cancel by 2 weeks prior or forfeit 100% (unless re-rented) *Minimum Stay:* 3 nights

(holidays) *Check in/ out:* 4-6pm/ noon
Payment: cash, travelers checks, personal checks, Visa, MC
Season: open yr-round *High season:* May-Oct & winter holidays
Rates: $70-160 *Discounts:* weekly, 10% to New Mexicans
AC: 10%

Villas de Santa Fe
Santa Fe

400 Griffin St
Santa Fe, NM 87501
505/ 988-3000 800/ 424-1943
www.villasdesantafe.com

Clientele: mixed gay/ straight
Type: hotel; all-suite property w/in walking distance of the Plaza; free shuttle to downtown
Owned/ Run By: gay/ lesbian & straight
Rooms: 105
Baths: private
Wheelchair Access: yes, 5 rms

Meals: coffee/tea only
Amenities: free parking, laundry, pool, outdoor hot tub
Kids: welcome
Pets: no
Rates: $130-220
AC: 10%

The Water Street Inn

Santa Fe

427 W Water St
Santa Fe, NM 87501
505/ 984–1193 800/ 646-6752
www.waterstreetinn.com

Clientele: gay-friendly
Type: b&b-inn; intimate, historic adobe inn; w/ warm Southwestern decor
Owned/ Run By: gay/ lesbian & straight
Rooms: 12
Baths: private
Wheelchair Access: yes, 9 rms
Meals: expanded cont'l brkfst

Amenities: free parking, outdoor hot tub, massage, DVDs/ videos, WiFi
Kids: welcome
Pets: welcome
Smoking: no
Rates: $100-258
AC: 10%

Adobe & Stars B&B

Taos

PO Box 2285
Taos, NM 87571

505/ 776–2776
800/ 211–7076

www.TaosAdobe.com

Clientele: mixed gay/ straight
Type: b&b; features traditional Southwestern Taos architecture, luxury & Southwestern hospitality
Owned/ Run By: woman
Nearby Attractions: Taos Pueblo, Martinez Hacienda, San Francisco de Assis Church; Millicent Rogers & Harwood Museum; day trips to Abiquiu & around the Enchanted Circle
Transit: 2 1/2 hrs to Albuquerque Int'l
Rooms: 8 total, 1 suite, 6 kings, 2 queens, 2 twins, wetbar (1), ceiling fan, fireplace, deck (2), phone, refrigerator (1), maid service, high-speed internet/ wireless access (7); luxurious guest rms w/ Southwestern furniture, regional art & great views
Baths: private, bathtubs, showers, whirlpools, robes, hairdryers
Wheelchair Access: yes, 1 rm
Meals: full brkfst, vegetarian meals available w/ advance notice

Amenities: office hrs: 8am-9pm; free parking, outdoor hot tub, massage, snacks, sunset drinks, coffee/ tea, concierge services
Recreation: white-water rafting, hiking, hot-air ballooning, downhill & x-country skiing, swimming, mtn-biking, fishing, ski-mobiling
Kids: well-behaved welcome
Pets: please inquire
Pets On Premises: 1 cat
Smoking: no
Reservations: recommended; we welcome walk-ins if space available *Deposit:* required, 50%, due at booking, personal check ok *Cancellation:* cancel by 30 days prior or forfeit 100% *Minimum Stay:* on holidays only *Check in/ out:* 4pm-6pm/ 11am
Payment: cash, travelers checks, personal checks, Visa, Amex, MC
Season: open yr-round *High season:* July-Oct & Dec-March
Rates: $120-190
AC: 10%

Brooks Street Inn

Taos

119 Brooks St
Taos, NM 87571
505/ 758–1489 800/ 758–1489
www.brooksstreetinn.com

Clientele: gay-friendly
Type: b&b-inn; comfortable & casual; convenient to shops, galleries, restaurants, the historic Taos Plaza, Toas Pueblo & Taos Ski Valley
Owned/ Run By: women
Rooms: 6
Baths: private

Meals: full brkfst
Amenities: free parking, DVDs/ videos, WiFi
Kids: 10 yrs & up welcome
Pets: welcome in some rms w/ prior approval
Smoking: no
Rates: $89-169 (double)
AC: 10%

Casa Benavides B&B   *Taos*

137 Kit Carson Rd
Taos, NM 87571
505/ 758-1772 800/ 552-1772
www.taos-casabenavides.com

Clientele: gay-friendly
Type: b&b; fireplaces, extensive garden, mtn views
Rooms: 39
Baths: private
Wheelchair Access: yes, 1 rm

Meals: full brkfst
Amenities: outdoor hot tub, DVDs/ videos
Kids: welcome
Pets: no
Smoking: no
Rates: $89-300

Casa Europa Inn & Gallery   *Taos*

840 Upper Ranchitos Rd
Taos, NM 87571
505/ 758-9798 888/ 758-9798
www.casaeuropanm.com

Clientele: mixed gay/ straight
Type: b&b-inn; elegant 18th-c adobe building surrounded by willow & cottonwood trees; country setting 1.5 miles from Taos Plaza
Owned/ Run By: straights
Rooms: 7

Baths: private
Meals: full brkfst
Amenities: free parking, sauna, hot tub
Kids: in apt only
Pets: in apt only
Smoking: no
Rates: $120-200

Casa Gallina   *Taos*

PO Box 63
Taos, NM 87571
505/ 758-2306
www.casagallina.net

Clientele: mixed gay/ straight
Type: guesthouse; 3 separate adobe casitas are part of this charming guesthouse in a quiet pastoral setting
Owned/ Run By: gay man
Rooms: 3

Baths: private
Wheelchair Access: yes, 1 rm
Kids: welcome
Pets: no
Smoking: no
Rates: $125-185

Dreamcatcher B&B   *Taos*

416 La Lomita Rd
Taos, NM 87571
505/ 758-0613 888/ 758-0613
dreambb.com

Clientele: gay-friendly
Type: b&b-inn; adobe home in wooded area; 10-minute walk from Taos Plaza
Owned/ Run By: straights
Rooms: 7
Baths: private
Wheelchair Access: yes, 2 rms

Meals: full brkfst
Amenities: free parking, outdoor hot tub
Kids: 10 yrs & up welcome
Pets: no
Smoking: no
Rates: $89-129
AC: 10%

Orinda B&B   *Taos*

461 Valverde St
Taos, NM 87571
505/ 758-8581 800/ 847-1837
www.orindabb.com

Clientele: mixed gay/ straight
Type: b&b-private home; on adobe estate; spectacular views & country privacy, yet walking distance to Taos Plaza
Owned/ Run By: straights
Rooms: 5
Baths: private

Meals: full brkfst
Amenities: hot tub, massage, DVDs/ videos
Kids: 6 yrs & up welcome
Pets: dogs under 50 lbs only
Smoking: no
Rates: $80-130
AC: 10%

San Geronimo Lodge   *Taos*

1101 Witt Rd
Taos, NM 87571
505/ 751-3776 800/ 894-4119
www.SanGeronimoLodge.com

Clientele: mixed gay/ straight
Type: b&b; circa 1925 lodge; quiet 2.25 acres;
Owned/ Run By: "a friendly person"
Rooms: 18
Baths: private
Wheelchair Access: yes, 2 rms
Meals: full brkfst

Amenities: free parking, laundry, pool, outdoor hot tub, massage, WiFi
Kids: welcome
Pets: welcome in 2 rms
Smoking: no
Rates: $95-160
AC: 10%

The Bay Beach House
Adirondack Mtns

518/ 361-2375

Clientele: mixed gay/ lesbian
Type: 2-bdrm cottage w/ private beach on Upper Hudson River; sleeps up to 4
Owned/ Run By: women
Rooms: 2
Baths: shared

Kids: welcome
Pets: extra security deposit required
Smoking: no
Rates: $120-190
AC: 10%

The Cornerstone Victorian
Adirondack Mtns

3921 Main St (Rte 9)
Warrensburg, NY 12885
518/ 623-3308
www.cornerstonevictorian.com

Clientele: gay-friendly
Type: b&b; located in the Adirondacks close to skiing, hiking, Saratoga & more; 5-course gourmet brkfst; whirlpool bath & fireplace in some of the rms; beautiful gardens & wraparound porch
Owned/ Run By: straights

Rooms: 5
Baths: private
Meals: full brkfst
Rates: $78-179

Country Road Lodge B&B
Adirondack Mtns

115 Hickory Hill Rd
Warrensburg, NY 12885-3912
518/ 623-2207
www.countryroadlodge.com

Clientele: gay-friendly
Type: b&b-private home; secluded riverside retreat at the end of a country road; since 1974
Owned/ Run By: straights
Rooms: 4
Baths: private

Meals: full brkfst
Kids: 10 yrs & up welcome
Pets: no
Smoking: no
Rates: $74-116
AC: 10%

Falls Brook Yurts in Adirondacks
Adirondack Mtns

PO Box 2681
Glens Falls, NY 12801
518/ 761-6187
www.fallsbrookyurts.com

Clientele: gay-friendly
Type: yurts; sleep up to 8; "a unique backcountry experience" in a private, beautiful Adirondack setting; access to hiking, fishing & boating; skydome to view stars; private composting outhouses

Owned/ Run By: straights
Rooms: 20 (yurts)
Rates: $95

The Merrill Magee House
Adirondack Mtns

3 Hudson St
Warrensburg, NY 12885
518/ 623-2449 888/ 664-4661
www.merrillmageehouse.com

Clientele: gay-friendly
Type: b&b-inn; cozy Victorian country inn w/ spacious grounds & lovely gardens; 5 miles from Lake George
Owned/ Run By: women
Rooms: 10
Baths: private

Wheelchair Access: yes, 1 rm
Meals: full brkfst
Kids: 12 yrs & up welcome
Pets: no
Smoking: no
Rates: $115-145
AC: 10%

Rainbow Woods Campgrounds
Adirondack Mtns

134 Rte 74
Schroon Lake, NY 12870
518/ 532-9728
www.rainbowwoodscampgrounds.com

Clientele: men
Type: wooded campground for summer; 110 sites & 28 RV hookups; scheduled wknd events
Owned/ Run By: gay & straight
Rooms: 3

Baths: private
Amenities: free parking, laundry, hot tub, DVDs/ videos
Pets: welcome in campgrounds; must be leashed
Rates: $22-66

Saranac Club & Inn
Adirondack Mtns

371 Park Ave
Adirondack Mtns, NY 12983
518/ 891-7212 866/ 595-9800
www.SaranacClubandInn.com/gay.htm

Clientele: mixed gay/ straight
Type: b&b-inn; beautifully restored mansion; "the only Adirondack property that is accepted into Small Elegant Hotels of the World"; mention Damron at booking for free bottle of wine
Owned/ Run By: gay & straight
Rooms: 13
Baths: private

Meals: full brkfst
Amenities: free parking, laundry, hot tub, massage, DVDs/ videos, WiFi
Kids: no
Pets: welcome in beach club only
Smoking: no
Rates: $99-269
AC: 5%

Tea Island Resort
Adirondack Mtns

3020 Lake Shore Dr
Lake George, NY 12845
518/ 668-2776
www.teaislandresort.com

Clientele: gay-friendly
Type: motel; small family-owned; private beach; located 1/2 mile outside of Lake George Village
Owned/ Run By: gay & straight

Rooms: 18
Kids: welcome
Pets: no
Smoking: ok
Rates: $110-210

Jones Pond Campground
Angelica

9835 Old State Rd
Angelica, NY 14709
716/ 567-8100
www.jonespond.com

Clientele: men
Type: campground; located in rural Allegany County in southern tier of NY state; 170 campsites & 25 RV hookups
Owned/ Run By: gay men

Rooms: 3 (in guesthouse)
Baths: private & shared
Pets: welcome; no more than 2 per site
Rates: $10-110

Serenity Farms
Binghamton

PO Box 1216
Oxford, NY 13830
607/ 656-4659
www.geocities.com/serenityofny/SERENITY

Clientele: mixed gay/ straight
Type: b&b-inn, campground; on 100 acres; 30 minutes N of Binghamton; 50 campsites & 2 RV hookups; heated 20' x 40' pool
Owned/ Run By: gay men
Rooms: 12
Baths: private & shared
Meals: full brkfst

Amenities: free parking, laundry, pool, outdoor hot tub, DVDs/ videos
Pets: welcome (an AKC Labrador breeder)
Smoking: ok (some rms)
Rates: $65-89
AC: 10-15%

Dreamer's B&B
Capital District

48 Oneida St
Cohoes, NY 12047
518/ 233-7155
www.gtown-ny.com

Clientele: mixed gay/ straight
Type: b&b; located near Albany & the Saratoga racetrack; family atmosphere; adjacent to the Big G's gay-themed complex
Owned/ Run By: lesbians
Rooms: 6

Baths: private & shared
Meals: full brkfst
Amenities: free parking, indoor hot tub
Pets: no
Smoking: no
Rates: $50-125

The Morgan State House
Capital District

393 State St
Albany, NY 12210
518/ 427-6063 888/ 427-6063
www.statehouse.com

Clientele: gay-friendly
Type: b&b-inn; 1800s town house; "voted best b&b in the Capital & Saratoga Springs regions for the last 4 yrs"
Owned/ Run By: gay & straight
Rooms: 16

Baths: private
Meals: expanded cont'l brkfst
Smoking: no
Rates: $135-260
AC: 10%

Carrier House B&B
Catskill Mtns

64 Carrier St
Liberty, NY 12754
845/ 292-9742
www.carrierhouseny.com

Clientele: mixed gay/ straight
Type: b&b; retro '50s decor; w/ full kitchens; walk to hiking trails on Walnut Mtn; ask about writers' retreat rates
Owned/ Run By: gay men
Rooms: 2 (suites)
Baths: private & shared

Meals: cont'l brkfst
Amenities: free parking, DVDs/ videos, WiFi
Kids: welcome; by arrangement
Pets: no
Smoking: no
Rates: $120-150

Country Suite
Catskill Mtns

PO Box 700
Windham, NY 12496
518/ 734-4079 888/ 883-0444
www.countrysuite.com

Clientele: gay-friendly
Type: b&b-private home; in renovated 150-yr-old farmhouse; furnished w/ antiques & heirlooms; "country elegance w/ urban flair"
Owned/ Run By: women
Rooms: 6

Wheelchair Access: yes, 1 rm
Meals: full brkfst
Kids: well-behaved welcome
Smoking: no
Rates: $69-159

ECCE B&B
Catskill Mtns

19 Silverfish Rd
Barryville, NY 12719
845/ 557-8562 888/ 557-8562
www.eccebedandbreakfast.com

Clientele: mixed gay/ straight
Type: b&b; newly renovated; located 300 ft above Upper Delaware River; majestic views; 60 acres; 2 hrs from NYC
Owned/ Run By: gay men
Rooms: 5
Baths: private

Meals: full brkfst
Amenities: free parking, hot tub, DVDs/ videos, WiFi
Kids: 12 yrs & up welcome
Pets: no
Smoking: no
Rates: $150-250

Fifth Floor Farm B&B
Catskill Mtns

26 Mill St
Jeffersonville, NY 12748
845/ 482-3126
www.fifthfloorfarmkitchen.com

Clientele: mixed gay/ straight
Type: b&b; in an old mill; art by Lynda Geyer & Salvatore Scalisi; overlooks Callicoon Creek
Rooms: 3

Meals: full brkfst
Pets: no
Smoking: no
Rates: $125-225

Full Moon Resort
Catskill Mtns

Valley View Rd
Oliverea, NY 12410
845/ 254-5117
www.fullmooncentral.com

Clientele: mixed gay/ straight
Type: resort; on 100 acres; cabins available; 20 campsites; country weddings/ commitment ceremonies a specialty
Owned/ Run By: straights
Rooms: 25 (+ 5 cabins)
Baths: private & shared

Kids: welcome
Pets: no
Smoking: no
Rates: $75-165

The Herbal Bear Catskill Cabin Rental
Catskill Mtns

State Rte 23
Grand Gorge, NY 12434
212/ 532-9322
www.catskillcabin.com

Clientele: mixed gay/ straight
Type: cabin; on 30 private acres in the Catskills, sleeps up to 4
Owned/ Run By: gay & straight
Rooms: 1
Baths: private
Amenities: free parking, pool, outdoor hot tub

Kids: no
Pets: welcome
Smoking: no
Rates: $750/ wknd

Kate's Lazy Meadow Motel
Catskill Mtns

5191 Rte 28
Mt Tremper, NY 12457
845/ 688–7200
www.lazymeadow.com

Clientele: gay-friendly
Type: deluxe cabins & cottages; owned by Kate Pierson of the B-52s; mtn views; groovy modern decor; "the Mod-dest of Mid-century Design Marvels"
Rooms: 8 (suites, plus new cabin)
Baths: private

Amenities: free parking, outdoor salt spa under the stars, massage, DVDs/ videos, WiFi
Pets: welcome
Smoking: no
Rates: $150-275

The Roxbury
Catskill Mtns

2258 County Hwy 41
Roxbury, NY 12474
607/ 326–7200
www.gaycatskillslodging.com

Clientele: mixed gay/ straight
Type: hotel; "an innovative, hip twist on the old country motel experience"
Owned/ Run By: gay men
Rooms: 11
Baths: private

Wheelchair Access: yes, 1 rm
Meals: coffee/tea only
Kids: welcome
Pets: no
Rates: $85-190
AC: 10%

The Wild Rose Inn
Catskill Mtns

66 Rock City Rd
Woodstock, NY 12498
845/ 679–8783
www.thewildroseinn.com

Clientele: gay-friendly
Type: b&b; beautifully renovated Victorian; sumptuous rms w/ private whirlpool tubs
Owned/ Run By: woman
Rooms: 5
Baths: private

Meals: expanded cont'l brkfst
Kids: welcome
Pets: no
Smoking: no
Rates: $99-250

Hillcrest Manor B&B
Corning

227 Cedar St
Corning, NY 14830
607/ 936–4548
www.corninghillcrestmanor.com

Clientele: gay-friendly
Type: b&b; elegant 1890 neo-classical mansion in quiet neighborhood; close to Corning Museum of Glass & Watkins Glen, home of NASCAR racing
Owned/ Run By: gay men
Rooms: 5
Baths: private

Meals: full brkfst
Amenities: free parking, laundry, DVDs/ videos, WiFi
Kids: 13 yrs & up welcome
Pets: no
Smoking: no
Rates: $145-175
AC: 10%

Rufus Tanner House B&B
Corning

60 Sagetown Rd
Pine City, NY 14871-9502
607/ 732–0213
www.rufustanner.com

Clientele: mixed gay/ straight
Type: b&b; 1864 Greek Revival farmhouse sheltered by century-old sugar maples
Owned/ Run By: woman
Rooms: 4
Baths: private
Wheelchair Access: yes, 1 rm

Meals: full brkfst
Amenities: free parking, laundry, hot tub
Kids: 12 yrs & up welcome
Pets: welcome w/ prior approval
Smoking: no
Rates: $77-135
AC: 12%

Alexander Hamilton House
Croton-on-Hudson

49 Van Wyck St
Croton-on-Hudson, NY 10520
914/ 271–6737 888/ 414–2539
www.alexanderhamiltonhouse.com

Clientele: mixed gay/ straight
Type: b&b-inn; romantic 1889 Victorian; river views
Owned/ Run By: women
Rooms: 8
Baths: private
Meals: full brkfst

Amenities: free parking, pool, hot tub, massage, DVDs/ videos
Kids: well-behaved welcome
Pets: no
Smoking: no
Rates: $120-300 (includes tax + gratuity)
AC: 10%

Blue Heron Inn
Findley Lake

PO Box 588
Findley Lake, NY 14736
716/ 769-7852
www.theblueheroninn.com

Clientele: gay-friendly
Type: b&b-inn; overlooking scenic Findley Lake; restaurant & eclectic shops on premises; close to Peek 'n Peak Resort & the shore of Lake Erie & Chautauqua Lake; open yr-round
Owned/ Run By: straights

Rooms: 4
Baths: private
Meals: full brkfst
Kids: welcome
Pets: no
Smoking: no
Rates: $110-145

A Summer Place Realty
Fire Island

Bayview Walk
Cherry Grove, NY 11782
631/ 597-6140
www.asummerplacerealty.com

Clientele: mixed gay/ lesbian
Type: rentals; private homes & apts; short & long-term
Owned/ Run By: lesbians/ gay men

Belvedere Hotel
Fire Island

Box 4026
Cherry Grove, NY 11782
631/ 597-6448
www.belvederefireisland.com

Clientele: men
Type: guesthouse; a Venetian palace on the water; gardens, fountains, statuary, antiques, towers & terraces
Owned/ Run By: gay men
Rooms: 40
Baths: private & shared

Wheelchair Access: yes, 6 rms
Amenities: pool, outdoor hot tub, gym
Kids: no
Pets: no
Smoking: ok
Rates: $125-250

Dune Point Guesthouse
Fire Island

PO Box 78
Cherry Grove, NY 11782
631/ 597-6261
www.dunepointfireisland.com

Clientele: gay-friendly
Type: resort; spotless rms, studios & apts to rent, (short- or long-term); w/ private ocean decks; open yr-round
Owned/ Run By: gay/ lesbian & straight
Rooms: 24 (studios & apts)
Baths: private

Amenities: indoor & outdoor hot tubs
Kids: welcome
Pets: welcome
Smoking: ok
Rates: $75-425
AC: 10%

GroveHotel
Fire Island

PO Box 537
Sayville, NY 11782
631/ 597-6600
www.grovehotel.com

Clientele: mixed gay/ lesbian
Type: hotel; in heart of town; just steps away from a spectacular beach; lounge by our Olympic-size pool; visit the Ice Palace Bar & Disco
Owned/ Run By: gay men
Rooms: 58

Baths: private
Wheelchair Access: yes, 4 rms
Kids: no
Pets: no
Smoking: ok
Rates: $40-500
AC: 20%

Belhurst
Geneva

PO Box 609, Rte 14 S
Geneva, NY 14456
315/ 781-0201
www.belhurst.com

Type: historic 1880s castle overlooking Seneca Lake in the heart of the Finger Lakes Wine Region
Owned/ Run By: family-owned
Rooms: 13
Baths: shared
Meals: expanded cont'l brkfst

Amenities: hot tub
Kids: not unwelcome but experience not geared toward them
Smoking: ok
Rates: $65-365

Glens Falls Inn   *Glens Falls*

25 Sherman Ave
Glens Falls, NY 12801
646/ 824-8379
www.glensfallsinn.com

Clientele: gay-friendly
Type: b&b; 19th-c Victorian; located half-way between Saratoga Springs & Lake George
Rooms: 6

Baths: private
Meals: full brkfst
Amenities: WiFi
Rates: $130-342

Barclay Heights B&B   *Hudson Valley*

158 Burt St
Saugerties, NY 12477
845/ 246-3788
www.outstandinghospitality.com

Type: b&b; cozy Victorian cottage; proprietors are professional chefs; personalized brkfst; private jacuzzi tubs; concierge service
Owned/ Run By: straights
Rooms: 6

Baths: private & shared
Meals: full brkfst
Kids: no
Pets: no
Smoking: no
Rates: $135-195

The Country Squire B&B   *Hudson Valley*

251 Allen St
Hudson, NY 12534
518/ 822-9229
www.countrysquireny.com

Clientele: mostly men
Type: b&b-private home; recently restored Queen Anne; 2 blks from antiques, galleries, restaurants & shops; Victorian elegance, contemporary sophistication; convenient to Amtrak
Owned/ Run By: gay man

Rooms: 5
Baths: private
Meals: cont'l brkfst
Kids: welcome
Smoking: no
Rates: $115-195

The Day House   *Hudson Valley*

260 Main St
Catskill, NY 12414
518/ 943-4751
www.thedayhouse.us

Clientele: gay-friendly
Type: b&b; meticulously restored & decorated Georgian brick mansion in the heart of the upper Hudson Valley
Owned/ Run By: gay men
Rooms: 2 or 1 en suite
Baths: shared

Meals: full brkfst
Kids: welcome
Pets: no
Smoking: no
Rates: $125-325

Hudson City B&B   *Hudson Valley*

326 Allen St
Hudson, NY 12534
518/ 822-8044
www.hudsoncitybnb.com

Clientele: mixed gay/ straight
Type: b&b; 18th-c Victorian mansion in historic antique district; plus new 3 guest-rm cottage
Owned/ Run By: gay men
Rooms: 6 (+ 3-rm cottage)
Baths: private

Meals: cont'l brkfst
Kids: well-behaved welcome
Pets: no
Smoking: no
Rates: $100-199
AC: 10%

Inn at Applewood & The Would Restaurant   *Hudson Valley*

120 North Rd
Highland, NY 12528
845/ 691-2516
thewould.com

Clientele: mixed gay/ straight
Type: b&b-inn; wonderful mtn views; commitment ceremonies on premises & cater off-site; wheelchair accessible restaurant w/ New American cuisine
Rooms: 8
Baths: private

Meals: full brkfst
Kids: 11 yrs & up welcome
Pets: no
Smoking: no
Rates: $95

Lefèvre House B&B
Hudson Valley

14 Southside Ave
New Paltz, NY 12561
845/ 255-4747
www.lefevrehouse.com

Clientele: mixed gay/ straight
Type: b&b; 1890s Victorian renovated w/ modern European design; located in the heart of historic New Palz
Owned/ Run By: lesbians/ gay men
Rooms: 5
Baths: private
Meals: 3-course gourmet brkfst

Amenities: free parking, sauna, indoor hot tub, also outdoor hot tub on terrace, massage, WiFi
Kids: welcome
Pets: welcome; dogs only
Smoking: no
Rates: $165-225

Van Schaack House
Hudson Valley

20 Broad St
Kinderhook, NY 12106
518/ 758-6118
www.vanschaackhouse.com

Clientele: gay-friendly
Type: b&b-private home; luxurious mansion reputed to be the 1st law school in New York state
Owned/ Run By: gay men

Rooms: 4
Baths: private
Meals: full brkfst
Smoking: no
Rates: $120-185

Frog Haven Women's B&B
Ithaca

578 W King Rd
Ithaca, NY 14850
607/ 272-3238
www.froghavenbb.com

Clientele: women
Type: b&b-private home; modern log-sided home; on 4 quiet acres w/ swimmable pond, wildlife; reiki massage offered
Owned/ Run By: women
Rooms: 2

Baths: private
Meals: expanded cont'l brkfst
Kids: welcome
Pets: no
Smoking: no
Rates: $73-86 + 11% tax

William Henry Miller Inn
Ithaca

303 N Aurora St
Ithaca, NY 14850
607/ 256-4553 877/ 256-4553
www.millerinn.com

Clientele: gay-friendly
Type: b&b; comfortably elegant 1880 Victorian/ Queen Anne mansion; 2 blks from Ithaca Commons
Owned/ Run By: straights
Rooms: 9
Baths: private
Wheelchair Access: yes, 1 rm

Meals: full brkfst
Amenities: free parking, hot tub, WiFi
Kids: kids over 12 yrs welcome
Pets: no
Smoking: no
Rates: $125-205
AC: 10%

Fairmount Motel
Jamestown

138 W Fairmount (Rte 394)
Jamestown, NY 14750
716/ 763-9550
www.fairmountmotel.com

Clientele: gay-friendly
Type: charming roadside motel 10 minutes from Lake Chautauqua
Owned/ Run By: gay men
Rooms: 8

Baths: private
Kids: welcome
Pets: no
Smoking: ok
Rates: $40-70

The Country Place
Long Island

29 Hands Creek Rd
East Hampton, NY 11937
631/ 324-4125
www.webhampton.com/thecountryplace

Clientele: mixed gay/ straight
Type: b&b; on 3 acres w/ pond; all w/ private entrance, bath, cable TV, A/C, beach pass; minutes to beach
Owned/ Run By: gay & straight
Rooms: 4
Baths: private

Meals: expanded cont'l brkfst
Kids: no
Pets: no
Smoking: no (except outside)
Rates: $95-225 + tax

Cozy Cottages

Long Island

395 Montauk Hwy
East Hampton, NY 11975
631/ 537-1160
hamptsonescape@aol.com

Clientele: mixed gay/ lesbian
Type: cottage; bike to beautiful LGBT ocean beach; across street from LGBT bar & restaurant; tranquil setting to relax & socialize; beach pass included
Owned/ Run By: gay men
Rooms: 2

Baths: private
Meals: cont'l brkfst
Amenities: free parking, laundry, outdoor hot tub
Pets: hypoallergenic pets welcome
Smoking: no
Rates: $60-375

East Hampton Village B&B

Long Island

172 Newtown Ln
East Hampton, NY 11937
631/ 324-1858
www.easthamptonvillagebandb.com

Clientele: mixed gay/ straight
Type: b&b; in lovely turn-of-the-century home; walk to restaurants, boutiques, art galleries; beach permit included
Rooms: 4

Baths: private
Meals: cont'l brkfst
Pets: no
Smoking: no
Rates: $145-425

Hampton Resorts & Hospitality

Long Island

1655 Country Rd 39
Southampton, NY 11968
631/ 283-6100
www.hrhresorts.com

Clientele: gay-friendly
Type: very chic boutique motels in the heart of the Hamptons; "ce n'est pas un motel"
Owned/ Run By: straights
Rooms: 132
Baths: private
Wheelchair Access: yes, 1 rm

Meals: cont'l brkfst
Amenities: free parking, pool, hot tub, DVDs/ videos
Kids: welcome
Pets: welcome; $40 per night
Rates: $120-550
AC: 5% (except in summer months)

Mill House Inn

Long Island

31 N Main St
East Hampton, NY 11937
631/ 324-9766
www.millhouseinn.com

Clientele: gay-friendly
Type: b&b-inn; splendid suites & gracious hospitality in the heart of historic East Hampton Village
Owned/ Run By: straights
Rooms: 10
Baths: private
Wheelchair Access: yes, 1 rm

Meals: full brkfst
Amenities: free parking, WiFi
Kids: welcome in appropriate rms
Pets: welcome in suites
Smoking: no
Rates: $200-1,200
AC: 5% (off-season)

Stirling House B&B

Long Island

104 Bay Ave
Greenport, NY 11944
631/ 477-0654 800/ 551-0654
www.stirlinghousebandb.com

Clientele: gay-friendly
Type: b&b; breathtaking water views from every rm; Victorian home in maritime Greenport; walking distance to beaches, shopping & fine dining
Owned/ Run By: gay men
Rooms: 3

Baths: private
Meals: full brkfst
Amenities: free parking, hot tub, DVDs/ videos
Smoking: no
Rates: $150-265

Best Western Inn at Hunt's Landing

Middletown

120 Rtes 6 & 209
Matamoras, PA 18336
570/ 491-2400 800/ 528-1234
www.bestwesternhuntslanding.com

Clientele: gay-friendly
Type: hotel; in Pocono foothills, along the Delaware River; "perfect place for meetings, retreats, reunions, or wknd getaways"; also gourmet restaurant & bar
Owned/ Run By: straights
Rooms: 109
Baths: private

Wheelchair Access: yes, 4 rms
Meals: full brkfst
Amenities: free parking, laundry, pool, sauna, indoor hot tub, gym, WiFi
Kids: welcome
Pets: up to 50 lbs welcome
Smoking: ok
Rates: $90-210

The Borland House B&B   *Montgomery*

130 Clinton St
Montgomery, NY 12549
845/ 457-1513
www.theborlandhouse.com

Type: b&b-private home; stately Greek Revival home; in the heart of a historic village; 1 blk away from 4 critically acclaimed restaurants
Rooms: 3
Baths: private

Meals: full brkfst
Kids: welcome
Pets: please inquire
Smoking: no
Rates: $95-165

Abingdon Guesthouse   *New York City*

13 8th Ave
New York City, NY 10014
212/ 243-5384
www.abingdonguesthouse.com

Clientele: mixed gay/ straight
Type: guesthouse; conservative, quiet clientele; registered guests only in rms after 9pm
Owned/ Run By: gay & straight
Rooms: 9
Baths: private

Wheelchair Access: yes, please call for details of rms
Kids: please inquire
Pets: no
Smoking: no
Rates: $159-254

Algonquin Hotel   *New York City*

59 W 44th St
New York City, NY 10036
212/ 840-6800 888/ 304-2047
www.algonquinhotel.com

Clientele: gay-friendly
Type: hotel; a true landmark, w/ a tradition of elegance; home of Oak Room Cabaret
Rooms: 174
Baths: private
Wheelchair Access: yes, 9 rms
Kids: welcome

Pets: welcome; under 50 lbs
Smoking: ok (in designated rms only)
Rates: $179+
AC: 10%

Belvedere Hotel   *New York City*

319 W 48th St
New York City, NY 10036
212/ 245-7000 888/ 468-3558
www.belvederehotelnyc.com

Clientele: gay-friendly
Type: hotel; boutique-style guest rms & suites provide charm & understated elegance; also renowned Brazilian steak house Churrascaria Plataforma
Owned/ Run By: gay & straight
Rooms: 400
Baths: private

Wheelchair Access: yes, 2 rms
Kids: welcome; please inquire about restrictions
Pets: no
Smoking: ok
Rates: $160+
AC: 10%

Buckingham Hotel   *New York City*

101 W 57th St
New York City, NY 10019
212/ 246-1500 888/ 511-1900
www.buckinghamhotel.com

Type: all-suite hotel; located in the heart of Manhattan across the street from Carnegie Hall; kitchens, VCRs, fitness center
Rooms: 133
Baths: private
Kids: welcome

Pets: 1 pet per rm; no dogs over 40 lbs
Smoking: ok
Rates: $149+
AC: 10%

Chelsea Inn   *New York City*

46 W 17th St
New York City, NY 10011
212/ 645-8989 800/ 640-6469
www.chelseainn.com

Clientele: gay-friendly
Type: guesthouse; European-style inn; 2 town houses offer studio rms, guest rms, shared bath & suites
Owned/ Run By: straights
Rooms: 28
Baths: private & shared

Meals: cont'l brkfst
Kids: welcome; $10 per crib
Smoking: ok
Rates: $79-259 + tax
AC: 10%

Chelsea Pines Inn   *New York City*

317 W 14th St
New York City, NY 10014
212/ 929-1023 888/ 546-2700
cpiny@aol.com
www.chelseapinesinn.com

Clientele: mostly men
Type: b&b-inn; described by *Out & About* as one of the top 10 gay accommodations in the Northeast & winner of their Editor's Choice Award for "Outstanding Achievement in Gay Travel"
Owned/ Run By: gay men
Transit: near public transit; bus & subway on corner; 30-40 minutes to all major airports
Rooms: 25 total, 22 queens, 3 fulls, A/C, color TV, cable, phone, refrigerator, safer sex supplies, maid service, free HBO & Showtime, voicemail, irons & boards (limited # of rms w/ 2 beds; please inquire when booking)
Baths: private & shared, showers, hairdryers
Meals: expanded cont'l brkfst
Amenities: office hrs: 24hrs; snacks, coffee/ tea, free internet access, lovely garden to enjoy brkfst (seasonal) & yr-round greenhouse
Pets On Premises: cat
Smoking: ok
Reservations: recommended
Deposit: required, 1 night via credit card
Cancellation: cancel by 1 week prior or forfeit deposit (unless space is rebooked) *Check in/ out:* 2pm/ noon
Payment: cash, travelers checks, Visa, Amex, MC, Discover, Diners Club, Carte Blanche
Season: open yr-round *High season:* March-Dec
Rates: $109-169 *Discounts:* weekly & midweek rates available
AC: 10%

Welcome to Chelsea Pines Inn, the premier bed-and-breakfast in the heart of "Gay New York." Each year we are awarded *Out & About*'s Editor's Choice Award for outstanding achievement in gay travel. And recently, we were named "one of the hottest hotels in NYC" by *New York Magazine*.

The Inn is on the border between Greenwich Village and Chelsea, the two major gay areas in Manhattan. Chelsea Pines is located in a renovated 1850 row house, just a short walk from many of the gay bars, restaurants, clubs, and shops in the City.

Our rooms and common areas are decorated with vintage movie posters, highlighting the "Golden Age" of Hollywood films.

Be our guest for the expanded continental breakfast, featuring homemade bread, fresh fruit, and freshly delivered donuts, in our charming breakfast lounge, lovely flower-filled garden (in season), or our year-round greenhouse.

Our helpful staff will provide you with information, guidebooks, and theater discounts in our effort to make your stay in New York City a memorable one.

Chelsea Mews Guest House

344 W 15th St
New York, NY 10011-5901
212/ 255-9174

Clientele: men
Type: guesthouse; quaint, cozy, old Colonial town house; located in the heart of Chelsea & Greenwich Village
Owned/ Run By: gay men
Rooms: 8
Baths: private & shared

Meals: coffee/tea only
Kids: no
Pets: no
Smoking: no
Rates: $100-200
AC: 5%

The Chelsea Savoy Hotel

204 W 23rd St
New York City, NY 10011
212/ 929-9353 866/ 929-9353
www.chelseasavoyNYC.com

Clientele: gay-friendly
Type: hotel; walk to SoHo's galleries, Greenwich Village, Empire State Bldg, museums, 5th Avenue shopping & fine restaurants
Rooms: 90

Baths: private
Wheelchair Access: yes, 5 rms
Kids: welcome
Smoking: ok
Rates: $99-275

Colonial House Inn

318 W 22nd St
New York City, NY 10011
212/ 243-9669 800/ 689-3779
www.colonialhouseinn.com

Clientele: mixed gay/ lesbian
Type: b&b-inn; in historic Chelsea; renovated circa 1850 brownstone; walking distance to Greenwich Village; rooftop sundeck; internet access; "free premium satellite TV in all rms"
Owned/ Run By: gay/ lesbian & straight
Rooms: 20

Baths: private & shared
Meals: expanded cont'l brkfst
Kids: welcome
Pets: no
Smoking: ok
Rates: $85-150
AC: 10%

Country Inn the City

W 77th St
New York City, NY
212/ 580-4183
www.countryinnthecity.com

Clientele: gay-friendly
Type: b&b-inn; studio apts in restored 1891 landmark limestone town house
Owned/ Run By: gay & straight
Rooms: 4
Baths: private
Meals: cont'l brkfst

Kids: 12 yrs & up welcome
Pets: no
Smoking: no
Rates: $150-300
AC: 10%

Greenwich Village Home

877/ 878-2263
www.greenwichvillagehome.com

Clientele: mixed gay/ lesbian
Type: private guest cottage w/ separate entrance attached to circa 1800s town house in historic Greenwich Village
Owned/ Run By: lesbians
Rooms: 1

Baths: private
Meals: expanded cont'l brkfst
Kids: welcome
Rates: $165

The Harlem Flophouse

212/ 662-0678
www.harlemflophouse.com

Type: guesthouse; charming brownstone located on a safe, quiet street; catering to traveling artists, dancers, musicians & performers; artist-owned
Rooms: 4
Baths: shared
Amenities: free parking, antique claw-foot tubs

Kids: welcome
Pets: no
Smoking: no
Rates: $100-150
AC: 5%

Hotel 17

225 E 17th St
New York City, NY 10003
212/ 475-2845
www.hotel17ny.com

Clientele: gay-friendly
Type: hotel; "East Village chic" budget hotel; no frills but fun
Rooms: 120

Baths: shared
Rates: $100+

Hotel 57

130 E 57th St
New York City, NY 10022
212/ 753-8841 800/ 497-6028
www.hotel57.com

Clientele: mixed gay/ straight
Type: upscale budget hotel in the heart of Manhattan; near MOMA, Rockefeller Center & Fifth Ave
Owned/ Run By: straights
Rooms: 314
Baths: private & shared

Kids: welcome
Rates: $295+
AC: 10%

Hotel Newton

2528 Broadway
New York City, NY 10025
212/ 678-6500 800/ 643-5553
www.newyorkhotel.com

Clientele: mixed gay/ straight
Type: hotel; totally renovated little secret on Upper West Side; 1/2 blk to subway; nearest hotel to Columbia University
Rooms: 105
Baths: private
Wheelchair Access: yes, 3 rms

Kids: welcome
Pets: no
Smoking: ok
Rates: $105-185
AC: 10%

Incentra Village House

32 8th Ave
New York City, NY 10014
212/ 206-0007
www.iloveinns.com/
incentravillagehouse.inn

Clientele: mixed gay/ straight
Type: guesthouse; 2 red-brick bldgs built in 1841; both in walking distance to all the Village & Chelsea have to offer
Owned/ Run By: gay men
Rooms: 12
Baths: private

Kids: no
Pets: no
Smoking: no
Rates: $119-259

Ivy Terrace

230 E 58th St
New York City, NY 10022
516/ 662-6862
www.ivyterrace.com

Clientele: mixed gay/ lesbian
Type: b&b-inn; studio suites w/ private entrance
Owned/ Run By: lesbians
Rooms: 3 (suites)
Baths: private
Meals: expanded cont'l brkfst

Kids: w/ advance notice
Pets: welcome; $150 deposit
Smoking: no
Rates: $180-300
AC: 10%

Lambda Mews

212/ 213-8798
www.AtHomeUS.com

Clientele: mixed gay/ lesbian
Type: b&b-private home; fabulous loft w/ views of Empire State Bldg, near Chelsea & Midtown; also hosted guestrooms
Owned/ Run By: gay men
Rooms: 3
Baths: shared

Wheelchair Access: yes, 3 rms
Meals: cont'l brkfst
Kids: welcome
Rates: $140-550

The Loralei B&B
New York City

667 Argyle Rd
New York City, NY 11230
646/ 228-4656
www.loraleinyc.com

Clientele: mixed gay/ straight
Type: b&b; 3-story, 1904 Victorian
Owned/ Run By: gay men
Rooms: 2
Baths: private
Meals: cont'l brkfst

Kids: no
Pets: no
Smoking: no
Rates: $125-150

W New York
New York City

541 Lexington Ave
New York City, NY 10022
212/ 755-1200
877/ WHOTELS (reservations only)
www.whotels.com/newyork

Clientele: mixed gay/ straight
Type: hotel; the 1st W Hotel; also Heartbeat restaurant & popular Whiskey Blue bar
Rooms: 688
Baths: private
Wheelchair Access: yes, 36 rms
Amenities: laundry, massage, DVDs/

videos, WiFi
Kids: welcome
Pets: welcome; restrictions apply
Smoking: ok (smoking rms only)
Rates: $249-569

The Mansion
Saratoga Springs

801 Rte 29
Rock City Falls, NY 12863
518/ 885-1607 888/ 996-9977
www.themansionsaratoga.com

Clientele: gay-friendly
Type: b&b-inn; romantic 1860 Victorian mansion; on private grounds yet near Saratoga action
Owned/ Run By: gay men
Rooms: 10
Baths: private

Wheelchair Access: yes, 1 rm
Meals: full brkfst
Pets: welcome in outdoor kennels
Smoking: no
Rates: $100-325
AC: 10%

Saratoga B&B/ Saratoga Motel
Saratoga Springs

434 Church St
Saratoga Springs, NY 12866
518/ 584-0920
www.saratogabnb.com

Clientele: gay-friendly
Type: b&b, motel; beautifully restored; the only gay-owned b&b in Saratoga; located on 5 acres; 2 miles from downtown
Owned/ Run By: gay men
Rooms: 14

Baths: private
Meals: full brkfst
Kids: 9 yrs & up welcome
Smoking: no
Rates: $120-239
AC: 10%

Saratoga Rose Inn & Restaurant
Saratoga Springs

4136 Rockwell St
Hadley, NY 12835
518/ 696-2861 800/ 942-5025
www.saratogarose.com

Clientele: mixed gay/ straight
Type: b&b-inn; 6 guest rms, 4 in the mansion; Victorian-styled rms; fine-dining on site
Owned/ Run By: gay men
Rooms: 6
Baths: private

Meals: full brkfst
Amenities: free parking, hot tub
Kids: 13 yrs & up welcome
Pets: no
Smoking: no
Rates: $165-205
AC: 5% if booked by phone

American Hotel
Sharon Springs

PO Box 121, Main St
Sharon Springs, NY 13459
518/ 284-2105
www.americanhotelny.com

Clientele: mixed gay/ straight
Type: hotel; 1847 Nat'l Register Hotel & restaurant near Cooperstown; featured on Food Network & HGTV's *Restore America*
Owned/ Run By: gay men
Rooms: 9
Baths: private

Wheelchair Access: yes, 1 rm
Meals: full brkfst
Amenities: free parking, massage, WiFi
Kids: welcome
Pets: ok in 1 rm
Smoking: no
Rates: $170-180

Edgefield
Sharon Springs

153 Washington St (PO Box 152)
Sharon Springs, NY 13459
518/ 284-3339
www.sharonsprings.com/edgefield.htm

Clientele: mixed gay/ straight
Type: b&b-inn; well-appointed English Country house; near Cooperstown & Glimmerglass Opera; featured in *Colonial Homes* & *Condé Naste Traveler* magazines
Owned/ Run By: gay man
Rooms: 5

Baths: private
Meals: full brkfst
Kids: welcome; only 2 people per rm
Smoking: no
Rates: $135-185 (double)
AC: 10% ltd

New Yorker Guest House & Spa
Sharon Springs

110 Center St
Sharon Springs, NY 13459
518/ 284-2126
www.nyguesthouse.com

Clientele: gay-friendly
Type: b&b-inn
Rooms: 10
Baths: private
Meals: full brkfst

Kids: well-behaved kids welcome
Pets: no
Smoking: no
Rates: $135-250

The TurnAround Spa
Sharon Springs

105 Washington St
Sharon Springs, NY 13459
518/ 284-9708 212/ 628-9008
turnaroundspa@yahoo.com

Clientele: mixed gay/ lesbian
Type: small hotel/ health spa; fully furnished in-rm kitchen; perfect for longer stays; mineral waters; tranquil setting
Owned/ Run By: gay/ lesbian & straight
Rooms: 7 (studios)
Meals: full brkfst

Amenities: free parking, indoor hot tub, massage
Kids: welcome
Pets: welcome; no large dogs
Smoking: no
Rates: $35-85
AC: 10-15%

Yellow Lantern Kampground
Syracuse

1770 Rte 13 N
Cortland, NY 13045
607/ 756-2959
YLKinCort@aol.com

Clientele: gay-friendly
Type: campground; short drive from Syracuse or Ithaca; 205 campsites & RV hookups
Owned/ Run By: straights

Kids: welcome
Pets: welcome
Rates: $21-25

27 Blake Street
Asheville

27 Blake St
Asheville, NC 28801
828/ 252-7390
www.sheville.org/27blake.html

Clientele: women
Type: b&b-private home; gorgeous Victorian surrounded by gardens; romantic suite; private entrance; reasonable rates
Owned/ Run By: woman
Rooms: 1

Baths: private
Meals: coffee/tea only
Kids: no
Pets: no
Smoking: no
Rates: $75

A Bird's Nest Bed & Kitchen
Asheville

41 Oak Park Rd
Asheville, NC 28801
828/ 251-2002 800/ 770-9055
www.seeasheville.com

Clientele: mixed gay/ lesbian
Type: b&b-private home; comfortable, secluded & private; this early 1900s 10-rm home is light, spacious & w/in walking distance of downtown; 1 or 2 bdrms/ baths available; high-speed internet; owner prefers to be contacted by email
Owned/ Run By: lesbians
Rooms: 2

Baths: private
Meals: coffee/tea only; catering on request
Kids: welcome
Pets: no
Smoking: no
Rates: $135+
AC: 10%

1889 WhiteGate Inn & Cottage
173 E Chestnut St
Asheville, NC 28801

828/ 253-2553
800/ 485-3045

Asheville
InnKeeper@whitegate.net
www.whitegate.net

Clientele: mixed gay/ straight
Type: b&b; in shingle-style home; also cottage w/ full kitchen
Owned/ Run By: gay men
Nearby Attractions: Biltmore Estate, Chimney Rock, Harrah's Casino, shopping, antiques, winery
Transit: near public transit
Rooms: 6 (includes 3 suites w/ sitting rms & cottage w/ balcony, living rm & kitchen) total, 3 suites, 1 king, 5 queens, A/C, color TV, DVD/ VCR, cable, wetbar (1), ceiling fan (2), fireplace (5), deck, phone, kitchenette (1), refrigerator (1), maid service, custom decorated
Baths: private, bathtubs, showers, robes, hairdryers
Meals: full brkfst, special meals available on request
Amenities: massage, DVDs/ videos, snacks, coffee/ tea, greenhouse, waterfalls, koi pond
Kids: 15 yrs & up welcome
Pets: please inquire; dogs 30 lbs & under only

Reservations: required *Deposit:* required, 1 night, due at booking, personal check ok *Cancellation:* cancel by 30 days prior or forfeit $35 *Minimum Stay:* 2 nights on wknds *Check in/ out:* 3pm/ 11am
Payment: cash, travelers checks, personal checks, Visa, Amex, MC
Season: open yr-round *High season:* June-Dec
Rates: $180-340 *Discounts:* AAA (midweek only)

The 1900 Inn on Montford
296 Montford Ave
Asheville, NC 28801

828/ 254-9569
800/ 254-9569

Asheville
info@innonmontford.com
www.innonmontford.com

Clientele: gay-friendly
Type: b&b-inn; Arts & Crafts property located 5 blks from dowtown in Montford Historic District; whirlpools, steam baths, fireplaces, king-size beds
Owned/ Run By: straights
Nearby Attractions: 1 mile to downtown; close to Biltmore Estate
Pickup Service: airport pickup
Transit: 2 hrs to Charlotte, NC airport; 1 hr to Greenville, SC airport; 15 minutes to Asheville airport
Rooms: 8 total, 3 suites, 7 kings, 1 queen, A/C, color TV, DVD/ VCR, cable, wetbar (1), ceiling fan (3), fireplace, deck (1), phone, kitchenette (4), refrigerator, maid service
Baths: private, bathtubs, showers, whirlpools, robes, hairdryers
Meals: full brkfst, can accommodate most dietary restrictions
Amenities: sauna, hot tub, massage, DVDs/ videos, WiFi, snacks, sunset drinks, coffee/ tea
Kids: welcome
Pets: welcome in Griffin Cottage

Pets On Premises: 1 cat
Smoking: no
Reservations: *Deposit:* required, 1 night or 50%, due at booking *Cancellation:* cancel by 2 weeks prior (30 days in Oct) or forfeit $40 *Minimum Stay:* 2 nights (wknds)
Payment: cash, travelers checks, personal checks, Visa, Amex, MC, Discover
Season: open yr-round *High season:* May-Dec
Rates: $175-650
AC: 10%

Acorn Cottage B&B
Asheville

25 St Dunstans Cir
Asheville, NC 28803
828/ 253-0609 800/ 699-0609
www.acorncottagebnb.com

Clientele: mixed gay/ straight
Type: b&b-inn; 1925 granite Arts & Crafts bungalow; 4 individually decorated rms
Owned/ Run By: woman
Rooms: 4
Baths: private

Meals: full brkfst
Smoking: no
Rates: $90-130
AC: 10%

Another Point of View
Asheville

99 Booter Rd
Fairview, NC 28730
828/ 628-0005

Clientele: mixed gay/ lesbian
Type: private apt on equestrian farm in Cane Creek Valley outside Asheville; spectacular views; private bath & entrance
Owned/ Run By: gay men
Rooms: 2

Baths: private
Meals: cont'l brkfst
Kids: no
Pets: no
Smoking: no
Rates: $90-120

Asheville's Downtown Loft
Asheville

55 1/2 Broadway St
Asheville, NC 28801
828/ 251-2002 800/ 770-9055
www.seeasheville.com

Clientele: mixed gay/ straight
Type: studio loft; "first & only in the heart of downtown Asheville"; high-speed internet; sleeps up to 6 people
Owned/ Run By: lesbians
Rooms: 2
Baths: private

Meals: coffee/tea only
Kids: welcome w/ prior approval
Pets: no
Smoking: no
Rates: $135+
AC: 10%

Biltmore Village Inn
Asheville

119 Dodge St
Asheville, NC 28803
828/ 274-8707 866/ 274-8779
www.biltmorevillageinn.com

Clientele: gay-friendly
Type: b&b-inn; in historic landmark built for George Vanderbilt's lawyer in 1892; "just a stone's throw from the gates of the Biltmore Estate"
Rooms: 6

Baths: private
Amenities: DVDs/ videos, WiFi
Pets: dogs ok in 1 suite
Smoking: no
Rates: $185-295
AC: 10%

Ceili's Porch
Asheville

PO Box 2835
Asheville, NC 28801
828/ 215-2915
www.ceilisporch.com

Clientele: women
Type: women's guesthouse; lovely original home; in older neighborhood
Owned/ Run By: lesbians
Rooms: 2
Baths: private
Meals: cont'l brkfst

Amenities: free parking, DVDs/ videos, WiFi
Kids: no
Pets: no
Smoking: no
Rates: $60
AC: 5%

Compassionate Expressions Mtn Inn & Spa
Asheville

828/ 683-6633
www.compassionatexpression.com/
healing_sanctuary_&_inn.htm

Clientele: mostly women
Type: inn; also cabins; RV hookups; views of Blue Ridge Mtns; 30 minutes from Asheville; quality spa services
Owned/ Run By: lesbians
Rooms: 4
Baths: private
Wheelchair Access: yes, 1 rm

Meals: coffee/tea only
Amenities: free parking, hot tub, massage
Kids: 10 yrs & up welcome
Pets: no
Smoking: no
Rates: $60-120; rooms & cabins
AC: 5%

Lofty Notions Campsite
Asheville

377 Arrowood Rd
Rutherfordton, NC 28139
828/ 287-0069
loftynotions2@yahoo.com

Clientele: mixed gay/ lesbian
Type: campground; 1 private campsite w/ RV hookup overlooking beautiful 12-foot waterfall; SE of Asheville; w/ fire ring, trails, fairy circle, spiral path, fishing & swimming

Owned/ Run By: lesbians
Kids: welcome
Pets: please call first
Rates: $200/ week

Lovers' Loop Retreat
Asheville

828/ 296-0660
www.loversloopretreat.com

Clientele: mixed gay/ straight
Type: apt; private guest suite w/ own living rm, dining area, ping-pong; on wooded acre
Owned/ Run By: lesbians
Rooms: 1 suite

Baths: private
Meals: coffee/tea only
Kids: no
Pets: no
Smoking: no
Rates: $60-70

Monthaven Guest Suite Apartments
Asheville

21 Arborvale Rd #4
Asheville, NC 28801
828/ 236-9089
www.monthavenapartments.com

Clientele: mixed gay/ straight
Type: apt; 1920s brick apt bldg in historic neighborhood adjacent to downtown, 2-night minimum stay
Owned/ Run By: gay men
Rooms: each apt 2-bdrm

Baths: private
Kids: no
Pets: no
Smoking: no
Rates: $90
AC: 5%

Owl's Nest Inn & Engadine Cabins
Asheville

2630 Smokey Park Hwy
Candler, NC 28715

828/ 665-8325
800/ 665-8868

info@engadineinn.com
www.engadineinn.com

Clientele: mixed gay/ straight
Type: b&b-inn; 1885 Victorian inn on 12 acres w/ beautiful mtn views; Biltmore packages, murder mystery wknds, union ceremonies; also cabins
Owned/ Run By: woman
Nearby Attractions: Biltmore Estate & Winery, Blue Ridge Pkwy, Cherokee Indian Reservation w/ casino, Chimney Rock Park, Thomas Wolfe Memorial, Carl Sandburg Home, Great Smoky Mtn Railway
Transit: 14 miles to Asheville; 20 miles to Asheville reg'l airport
Rooms: 5 (+ 3 cabins) total, 1 suite, 4 kings, 4 queens, 1 twin, A/C, color TV, DVD/ VCR (3), cable, ceiling fan, fireplace, deck (2), phone, kitchenette (2), refrigerator (3), maid service, 1885 watercloset, 2-person whirlpool, sitting area
Baths: private, bathtubs, showers, whirlpools, robes, hairdryers
Meals: full brkfst, vegetarian & diabetic diets can be accommodated; day-trip & gourmet picnic baskets
Amenities: hot tub, snacks, sunset drinks, coffee/ tea, CCTV, CD players, sound machines
Recreation: white-water rafting, hiking, golf, fishing, horseback riding, snow skiing

Kids: welcome in cabins; 13 yrs & up in inn
Pets: welcome in cabins only; nonrefundable pet fee
Pets On Premises: 2 dogs
Reservations: required; by phone only *Deposit:* required, 1 night or 50%, due at booking, personal check ok *Cancellation:* cancel by 2 weeks prior (30 days for cabins) or forfeit deposit *Minimum Stay:* 2 nights

(wknds & Oct); 3 nights (major holidays)
Payment: cash, travelers checks, personal checks, Visa, Amex, MC, Discover
Season: open yr-round *High season:* April-Dec
Rates: $145-225 *Discounts:* 10% for 4+ nights; midweek, pkgs
AC: 10%

Tanbark Ridge B&B
Asheville

828/ 298-5879
www.tanbarkweb.com

Clientele: men
Type: b&b-private home; log home in secluded area w/ beautiful views; licensed massage therapist
Owned/ Run By: gay men
Rooms: 3
Baths: private
Wheelchair Access: yes, 1 rm

Meals: full brkfst
Amenities: free parking, laundry, outdoor hot tub, massage, DVDs/ videos
Kids: no
Pets: no
Smoking: no
Rates: $60-100

The Tree House
Asheville

190 Tessie Ln
Black Mountain, NC 28711
828/ 669-3889
HollyFairy@juno.com

Clientele: mixed gay/ lesbian/ transgender
Type: cottage; private, sunny mtn house w/ cathedral ceilings & full kitchen; 5 decks; sweat lodge
Owned/ Run By: lesbian/ trans
Rooms: 1 bdrm & 1 sleeping loft

Baths: private & shared
Meals: homestyle brkfst
Kids: no
Pets: no
Smoking: no
Rates: $50-75

Palm Suites of Atlantic Beach
Atlantic Beach

602 W Ft Macon Rd
Atlantic Beach, NC 28512
252/ 247-6400 800/ 972-3297
www.palmsuites.com

Clientele: gay-friendly
Type: condo; rental condos near beach; 9 boatslips
Owned/ Run By: straights
Rooms: 90 (condos)
Baths: private

Amenities: free parking, pool
Wheelchair Access: yes, 4 rms
Kids: welcome
Pets: no
Smoking: no
Rates: $95-125

Blowing Rock Cabins
Blowing Rock

PO Box 989
Blowing Rock, NC 28605
828/ 278-0102
www.blowingrockcabins.com

Clientele: gay-friendly
Type: cabin; 1-, 2- & 3-bdrm log cabins; w/ gas fireplaces & whirlpools for 2 in bath, full kitchens, covered porches
Owned/ Run By: gay men
Rooms: 4
Baths: private

Amenities: free parking, laundry, indoor hot tub
Kids: welcome
Pets: welcome w/ prior approval
Smoking: no
Rates: $119-189
AC: 10%

Blowing Rock Victorian Inn
Blowing Rock

242 Ransom St
Blowing Rock, NC 28605
828/ 295-0034
www.blowingrockvictorianinn.com

Clientele: gay-friendly
Type: b&b; elegantly restored Victorian home nestled in the heart of Blowing Rock
Owned/ Run By: gay men
Rooms: 6
Baths: private
Meals: full brkfst

Amenities: free parking, hot tub
Kids: welcome in cottage rms only; please inquire
Pets: welcome in cottage rms only; please inquire
Rates: $119-199

Twin Oaks Campground
Bonlee

PO Box 173
Bonlee, NC 27213
919/ 742-3203
www.ourtwinoaks.com

Clientele: men
Type: campground; on 26 scenic acres; open to men over 21 yrs old; 15 campsites & 6 RV hookups
Owned/ Run By: gay & straight
Amenities: free parking, sauna, hot tub

Kids: no
Pets: welcome
Smoking: ok
Rates: $12-60 + registration fee

Stonecliff/ Blue Ridge Mountain Cabin
Boone

182 Laurel Trail
Fleetwood, NC 28626

954/ 205-6594

stonecliff@att.net
stonecliff.home.att.net

Clientele: gay-friendly
Type: cabin; mountain cabin w/ giant, stone, wood-burning fireplace; large wraparound deck w/ gas grill; close to river, hiking & local activities
Owned/ Run By: lesbians
Nearby Attractions: Grandfather Mtn, Tweetsie Railroad, New River Zoo
Transit: 2 hrs to Charlotte, NC airport
Rooms: 3 total, color TV (1), DVD/ VCR (1), cable TV (1), ceiling fan (2), fireplace (1), deck (1), phone (1), refrigerator (1), 1 master bdrm w/ queen & private bath, 1 bdrm w/ queen bed & 1 bdrm w/ 2 twin beds
Baths: private & shared, bathtubs, showers
Amenities: free parking, laundry, DVDs/ videos, wraparound porch w/ hammock & rockers, outdoor dining (w/ gas grill), game rm w/ ping-pong, foozball & darts, dishwasher, washer/ dryer
Recreation: Blue Ridge Mtns, hiking, parks, caverns, falls, fishing, horseback riding, golf, rafting/ tubing
Kids: welcome

Pets: no
Smoking: no
Reservations: required *Deposit:* required, $100 + 1 night's stay, due at booking *Cancellation:* cancel by 2 weeks prior or forfeit $50 *Minimum Stay:* 2 nights

Check in/ out: 2pm/ 11am
Payment: cash, travelers checks, Visa, MC
Season: open yr-round *High season:* June-Oct
Rates: $135

Cabin Branch
Burnsville

828/ 628-0005

Clientele: mixed gay/ straight
Type: brand-new log cabin at Mt Mitchell lands; 2-bdrm/ 2-bath; fully equipped house; screened porch along stream
Owned/ Run By: gay men
Rooms: 2
Baths: private

Meals: coffee/ tea only
Amenities: free parking, laundry
Kids: no
Smoking: no
Rates: $150/ night (up to 4 people), $800/ week, $2,500/ month

Jane's Aerie Cottage
Cashiers

PO Box 1811
Cashiers, NC 28717
828/ 743-9002
janesaerie@aol.com

Clientele: gay-friendly (mostly women)
Type: modern cottage on old family estate; private, quiet location, in deep woods near town; hiking from doorstep
Owned/ Run By: women
Rooms: 3
Baths: private

Meals: coffee/ tea only
Kids: 2 people max
Rates: $100/ night; $500/ week

The Morehead Inn
Charlotte

1122 E Morehead St
Charlotte, NC 28204
704/ 376-3357 888/ 667-3432
www.moreheadinn.com

Clientele: gay-friendly
Type: b&b
Owned/ Run By: gay & straight
Rooms: 12
Baths: private
Wheelchair Access: yes, 1 rm
Meals: expanded cont'l brkfst

Rates: $125-199

VanLandingham Estate
Charlotte

2010 The Plaza
Charlotte, NC 28205
704/ 334-8909 888/ 524-2020
www.vanlandinghamestate.com

Clientele: gay-friendly
Type: b&b-inn; on wonderful urban estate w/ 5 acres of manicured, formal gardens; luxurious rms
Owned/ Run By: gay & straight
Rooms: 9
Baths: private

Meals: full brkfst
Amenities: free parking, hot tub, WiFi
Kids: welcome
Smoking: no
Rates: $125-199
AC: 10%

Advice 5¢, a B&B
Duck

111 Scarborough Ln
Duck, NC 27949
252/ 255-1050 800/ 238-4235
www.advice5.com

Clientele: gay-friendly
Type: b&b-private home; welcoming seaside cottage in Duck on North Carolina's Outer Banks
Rooms: 5
Baths: private

Meals: expanded cont'l brkfst
Kids: 16 yrs & up welcome
Pets: no
Smoking: no
Rates: $135-245

Phoenix Nest
Franklin

850/ 421-1984
www.geocities.com/tippys_cabin/index.html

Clientele: mixed gay/ lesbian
Type: cabin; Mystical Mtn retreat; sleeps 4; fully equipped kitchen, deck, wood stove; w/ spectacular view & wooded privacy; clsd Dec-Feb
Owned/ Run By: lesbians
Rooms: 4 (includes 1 double bed in bdrm &

1 double sleeper sofa & 1 queen futon in living rm)
Wheelchair Access: yes, all rms
Kids: welcome
Pets: welcome if on flea program
Smoking: no
Rates: $85/ night; $385/ week

Rainbow Acres (Honey's)
Franklin

850/ 997-8847

Clientele: mixed gay/ straight
Type: rental home; since 1987, Rainbow Acres is available for whole-house rentals; sleeps 9; "knock-your-socks-off view!"
Owned/ Run By: women
Rooms: 4

Baths: private & shared
Kids: well-mannered welcome w/ weekly rentals of the whole house
Pets: no
Smoking: no
Rates: $750/ week + 9 1/2% NC tax

Rose Creek Campground & Cabins
Franklin

828/ 524-3225
rosecreekcamp.com

Clientele: gay-friendly
Type: RV park; "come visit us for Smoky Mtn fun"; 34 campsites & 22 RV hookups
Owned/ Run By: lesbians
Rooms: 2 cabins
Baths: private & shared

Amenities: laundry, pool, DVD/ videos
Kids: welcome
Pets: welcome
Smoking: no
Rates: $12-85

Biltmore Greensboro Hotel
Greensboro

111 W Washington St
Greensboro, NC 27401
336/ 272-3474 800/ 332-0303
biltmorehotelgso@aol.com

Clientele: mixed gay/ straight
Type: European boutique hotel in historic district of Greensboro; minutes from clubs
Owned/ Run By: gay men
Rooms: 27
Baths: private
Meals: expanded cont'l brkfst

Amenities: free parking, laundry, DVDs/ videos, gym, WiFi
Kids: welcome
Pets: dogs welcome
Smoking: ok
Rates: $69-139
AC: 10%

O Henry Hotel ⊞🏳️‍🌈   *Greensboro*

624 Green Valley Rd
Greensboro, NC 27408
336/ 854-2000 800/ 965-8259
www.ohenryhotel.com

Type: hotel; "AAA 4-Diamond hotel" w/ oversized rms, gracious amenities, attentive staff & lively restaurant & bar popular w/ local gay community
Rooms: 131
Baths: private

Wheelchair Access: yes, 131 rms
Meals: full brkfst
Kids: welcome
Smoking: ok
Rates: $219-500
AC: 10%

The Duckett House Inn   *Hot Springs*

PO Box 441
Hot Springs, NC 28743
828/ 622-7621
www.duckethouseinn.com

Clientele: mixed gay/ straight
Type: b&b-inn; Victorian-period farmhouse; on 5 wooded acres; close to white-water rafting, hiking, hot mineral baths, Appalachian Trail, Smoky Mtns
Owned/ Run By: gay men
Rooms: 5
Baths: shared

Meals: full brkfst
Amenities: free parking, massage, DVDs/ videos, WiFi
Kids: 12 yrs & up welcome
Smoking: no
Rates: $105-130
AC: 10%

Serendipity Cabin   *Mt Mitchell*

2160 S Toe River Rd
Burnsville, NC 28714
954/ 448-8371
www.mtmitchell-cabin.com

Clientele: mixed gay/ straight
Type: rental cabin at base of Mt Mitchell, just off the Blue Ridge Pkwy; 1 hr from Asheville
Owned/ Run By: gay & straight
Rooms: 2

Baths: shared
Kids: welcome
Pets: welcome; 3 maximum
Smoking: no
Rates: $95-125

Harmony House Inn   *New Bern*

215 Pollock St
New Bern, NC 28560
252/ 636-3810 800/ 636-3113
www.harmonyhouseinn.com

Clientele: gay-friendly
Type: b&b-inn; Greek Revival circa 1850; decorated w/ authentic antiques & locally made reproductions
Owned/ Run By: straights
Rooms: 10 (7 rms, 3 suites, 2 w/ jacuzzis)
Baths: private

Meals: full brkfst
Kids: welcome
Pets: no
Smoking: no
Rates: $99-175
AC: 10%

Fickle Creek Farm B&B   *Raleigh/Durham/Chapel Hill*

919/ 304-6287
home.mebtel.net/~ficklecreek

Clientele: mixed gay/ straight
Type: b&b; farm getaway near Duke/ Durham, UNC/ Chapel Hill, Burlington; 2 campsites; stand-alone studio
Owned/ Run By: gay men
Rooms: 2
Baths: private & shared
Meals: full brkfst

Amenities: free parking, laundry, hot tub, massage, DVDs/ videos
Kids: welcome
Pets: well-behaved welcome
Smoking: no
Rates: $80-90
AC: 10%

Morehead Manor B&B   *Raleigh/Durham/Chapel Hill*

914 Vickers Ave
Durham, NC 27701
919/ 687-4366 888/ 437-6333
www.moreheadmanor.com

Clientele: mixed gay/ straight
Type: b&b-private home; 1910 Colonial Revival-style mansion w/ contemporary decor; walk to great restaurants & area attractions; available for special events
Rooms: 4
Baths: private
Meals: full brkfst

Amenities: free parking, massage, DVDs/ videos
Kids: 12 yrs & up welcome
Pets: no
Smoking: no
Rates: $135-450
AC: 10%

The Oakwood Inn B&B
Raleigh/Durham/Chapel Hill

411 N Bloodworth St
Raleigh, NC 27604
919/ 832-9712 800/ 267-9712
www.oakwoodinnbb.com

Clientele: gay-friendly
Type: b&b-inn; Victorian retreat nestled in the heart of Raleigh; beautiful antiques
Owned/ Run By: straights
Rooms: 6
Baths: private

Meals: full brkfst
Kids: welcome
Rates: $129-175
AC: 10%

Blue Waters Mountain Lodge
Robbinsville

292 Pine Ridge Rd
Robbinsville, NC 28771
828/ 479-8888 888/ 828-3978
www.bluewatersmtnl.com

Clientele: gay-friendly
Type: relaxing escape or outdoor adventure
Owned/ Run By: straights
Rooms: 9
Baths: private
Wheelchair Access: yes, 1 rm

Meals: full brkfst
Amenities: free parking, DVDs/ videos, WiFi
Kids: welcome
Smoking: no
Rates: $145-165
AC: 5%

Shepherd's Ridge
Spruce Pine

1280 Chestnut Mtn Rd
Spruce Pine, NC 28777
828/ 765-7809
ljspots@vol.com

Clientele: mostly lesbians & straight women
Type: guesthouse; woman-built; located in country w/ mtns; complete kitchen; views & garden; hiking trails & Penland School of Craft nearby
Owned/ Run By: woman

Rooms: 1
Baths: private
Meals: cont'l brkfst
Kids: welcome
Pets: welcome w/ prior approval
Smoking: no
Rates: $70/ night; $350/ week

Madelyn's in the Grove
Statesville

1836 W Memorial Hwy
Union Grove, NC 28689
704/ 539-4151 800/ 948-4473
www.madelyns.com

Clientele: mixed gay/ straight
Type: b&b; 1934 inn; on 9 serene acres in Yadkin Valley wine region
Owned/ Run By: straights
Rooms: 5
Baths: private
Meals: full brkfst

Amenities: free parking, hot tub, DVDs/ videos, WiFi
Kids: 12 yrs & up welcome
Pets: no
Smoking: no
Rates: $85-190
AC: 10%

The Old Traphill Mill Inn & Resort
Wilkesboro

452 Traphill Mill Rd
Traphill, NC 28685
336/ 957-3713
www.oldtraphillmill.com

Clientele: gay-friendly
Type: cabin, campground; 30-acre rustic mtn retreat; cabins & campsites; clothing-optional; swimming in spring-water ponds; reservations req'd

Owned/ Run By: gay man
Amenities: outdoor hot tub
Pets: extra fee
Rates: $15-100

Best Western Coastline Inn
Wilmington

503 Nutt St
Wilmington, NC 28401
910/ 763-2800 800/ 617-7732
coastlineinn.com

Clientele: mixed gay/ straight
Type: inn; in historic riverfront district; close to all attractions; internet access
Owned/ Run By: gay men
Rooms: 53
Baths: private
Wheelchair Access: yes, 3 rms

Meals: expanded cont'l brkfst
Kids: welcome
Pets: size of a beagle or smaller welcome
Smoking: no
Rates: $69-169
AC: 10%

Flex Cleveland

Cleveland

2600 Hamilton Ave
Cleveland, OH 44114

216/ 812-3004

cleveland@flexbaths.com
www.flexbaths.com

Clientele: men
Type: hotel; "biggest bathhouse in the world"
Owned/ Run By: gay men
Nearby Attractions: Rock & Roll Hall of Fame, Great Lakes Science Center, Theater District, art galleries, The Flats, Gateway District
Transit: 13 miles to airport; 2 miles to train; 1 mile to bus; taxi: Yellow Taxi, 216/623-1550
Rooms: 113 total, 1 suite, 3 kings, 12 queens, 16 fulls, A/C, color TV, cable, phone, safer sex supplies
Baths: private & shared, bathtubs, showers
Wheelchair Access: yes, 2 rms
Meals: cont'l brkfst
Amenities: free parking, pool, sauna, indoor hot tub, massage, gym, WiFi
Recreation: Cleveland Lakefront State Park
Kids: no
Pets: no
Smoking: no

Reservations: not required but desired
Deposit: required, 50%, due at booking
Cancellation: cancel by 1 day prior or forfeit deposit *Check in/ out:* 2pm/ 11am

Payment: cash, travelers checks, Visa, MC
Season: open yr-round
Rates: $90-250

Glendennis B&B

Cleveland

2808 Bridge Ave
Cleveland, OH 44113
216/ 589-0663
www.glendennis.com

Clientele: mixed gay/ straight
Type: apt, b&b-private home; private 3-rm suite plus full bath & garage parking
Owned/ Run By: straights
Rooms: 1 (suite)
Baths: private

Meals: full brkfst
Kids: welcome
Pets: crated pets welcome
Smoking: no
Rates: $100+tax (single); $115+tax (double)
AC: 10%

Radisson Hotel Cleveland—Gateway

Cleveland

651 Huron Rd
Cleveland, OH 44115
216/ 377-9000 800/ 333-3333
www.radisson.com/clevelandoh_gateway

Clientele: gay-friendly
Type: hotel; full-service gay-friendly hotel directly across from Q Arena & Jacobs Field; featuring Sleep Number beds & featherbed duvets
Rooms: 142
Baths: private

Wheelchair Access: yes, 11 rms
Amenities: WiFi
Kids: welcome; under 18 yrs free
Pets: no
Smoking: ok
Rates: $94-149 + tax

Stone Gables B&B

Cleveland

3806 Franklin Blvd
Cleveland, OH 44113
216/ 961-4654 877/ 215-4326
www.stonegables.net

Clientele: mixed gay/ straight
Type: b&b-inn; located in historic Ohio City; blks from bars, Club Cleveland & downtown
Owned/ Run By: gay men
Rooms: 5
Baths: private

Meals: full brkfst
Amenities: free parking, laundry, sauna, hot tub, DVDs/ videos, WiFi
Kids: welcome
Pets: welcome
Rates: $100-150

The Brewmaster's House   *Columbus*

1083 S High St
Columbus, OH 43206

614/ 449-8298

brewmastershouse@compuserve.com
www.damron.com/homepages/brewmastershouse/

Clientele: men
Type: b&b; in grand 1909 house w/ original features intact; historic fireplaces & woodwork
Owned/ Run By: gay man
Nearby Attractions: located in German Village & Brewery District—rated top 2 tourist destinations by Fodors; walk to architecture, antiques, restaurants, 8 gay bars; clusters of 4-5 gay bars each in downtown (5 minutes) & Short North (7 minutes) are a short drive & all easy to find along High St
Transit: 15 minutes to airport; 5 minutes to Greyhound bus station
Rooms: 4 total, 3 kings, 1 full, A/C, color TV, cable, fireplace (2), safer sex supplies
Baths: shared
Meals: full brkfst
Amenities: free parking, laundry, iron, fax, modems, large yard, pond
Pets On Premises: 1 dog
Smoking: ok
Reservations: required; 72 hrs in advance (no walk-ins); actual reservations must be

made by phone for security reasons
Deposit: required, 100% w/ credit card imprint, due at booking, personal check ok
Cancellation: cancel by 3 days prior or forfeit 100% *Check in/ out:* around 3pm/ around noon

Payment: cash, travelers checks
Season: open yr-round
Rates: $75-100
AC: 10%

Glenlaurel—A Scottish Country Inn & Cottages   *Logan*

14940 Mt Olive Rd
Rockbridge, OH 43149-9736
740/ 385-4070 800/ 809-7378
www.Glenlaurel.com

Clientele: mixed gay/ straight
Type: b&b-inn; high-end country inn w/ fine dining; on 133 acres
Owned/ Run By: gay/ lesbian & straight
Rooms: 19
Baths: private
Wheelchair Access: yes, 1 rm
Meals: full brkfst

Amenities: free parking, outdoor hot tub, massage, DVDs/ videos
Kids: no
Pets: no
Smoking: no
Rates: $119-319
AC: 10% (1st night lodging)

Fourth St B&B   *Marietta*

614/ 638-1187

Clientele: mixed gay/ straight
Type: b&b-private home; in walking distance of Ohio River & downtown
Owned/ Run By: gay men
Rooms: 3
Baths: private & shared

Meals: cont'l brkfstt
Amenities: laundry, massage, DVDs/ videos
Kids: welcome
Pets: no
Smoking: no
Rates: $69-99

Hotel Seagate   *Toledo*

141 N Summit St
Toledo, OH 43604
419/ 242-8885 866/ 744-5711
www.hotelseagate.com

Clientele: gay-friendly
Type: hotel; in business district; across the river & attached to Seagate Convention Center
Owned/ Run By: gay man
Rooms: 212
Baths: private
Wheelchair Access: yes, 8 rms

Meals: coffee/tea only
Amenities: laundry, pool, jacuzzi suites
Kids: welcome
Pets: welcome; $25 fee
Smoking: ok (on smoking flrs)
Rates: $79-199
AC: 5%

Southern Oaks Resort & Spa
Grand Lake

PO Box 310
Langley, OK 74350
918/ 782-9346
www.southernoaksresort.com

Clientele: gay-friendly
Type: cabins & RV hookups on 30 acres w/ hot tubs on back decks; "enjoy a relaxing couples massage in our spa"
Owned/ Run By: gay men
Rooms: 19 (cabins); 25 RV sites
Baths: private

Wheelchair Access: yes, 1 rm
Amenities: free parking, pool, hot tub, massage
Kids: welcome
Pets: please inquire
Smoking: no
Rates: $59-189

America's Crossroads B&B
Oklahoma City

PO Box 270642
Oklahoma City, OK 73137
405/ 495-1111
www.cimarron.net/usa/ok/rdac.html

Clientele: mostly men
Type: b&b-private home; private rms available in network of private homes across metro Oklahoma City; "only exclusively gay accommodations in OKC"
Owned/ Run By: gay men
Rooms: 7
Baths: private & shared
Wheelchair Access: yes, some rms

Meals: expanded cont'l brkfst
Amenities: free parking, pool, poolside mist, sauna, outdoor hot tub, DVDs/ videos, gym, WiFi
Kids: no
Pets: by arrangement; fee
Smoking: no (except in smoking areas)
Rates: $35-55

Habana Inn
Oklahoma City

2200 NW 39th Expwy
Oklahoma City, OK 73112
405/ 528-2221
800/ 988-2221 (reservations only)
www.habanainn.com

Clientele: mixed gay/ lesbian
Type: resort/ hotel complex; w/ 2 pools, full-service restaurant, 2 clubs, piano bar & gift shop; in heart of gay district
Owned/ Run By: gay/ lesbian & straight
Rooms: 180

Baths: private
Wheelchair Access: yes, 6 rms
Meals: coffee/tea only
Pets: please inquire
Smoking: no
Rates: $40-108

The Hollywood Hotel & Suites
Oklahoma City

3535 NW 39 Expwy
Oklahoma City, OK 73112
405/ 947-2351
www.hollywoodhotelokc.com

Clientele: mostly men
Type: hotel; the midwest's largest gay/ lesbian resort; newly remodeled extended-stay rms available; 12 blks from gay area
Owned/ Run By: gay & straight
Rooms: 264

Baths: private
Wheelchair Access: yes, 2 rms
Pets: welcome with $50 deposit
Smoking: ok
Rates: $42-72

Holiday Inn Select
Tulsa

5000 East Skelly Dr
Tulsa, OK 74135
918/ 622-7000 800/ 836-9635
www.hiselect.com/tulsa-select

Type: hotel; located in the heart of Tulsa's "midtown"
Rooms: 313
Baths: private
Wheelchair Access: yes, 8 rms

Kids: welcome
Pets: welcome; $25 fee
Smoking: ok (in designated areas)
Rates: $69-109
AC: 10%

The Arden Forest Inn
Ashland

261 W Hersey St
Ashland, OR 97520
541/ 488-1496 800/ 460-3912
www.afinn.com

Clientele: mixed gay/ straight
Type: b&b-inn; Ashland's premier theater-oriented inn offers lively discussions of theater in a casually elegant setting; 5 blks to theater; expansive gardens
Owned/ Run By: gay men
Rooms: 5

Baths: private
Wheelchair Access: yes, 2 rms
Meals: full brkfst
Kids: 10 yrs & up welcome
Smoking: no
Rates: $110-200

Blue Moon B&B
Ashland

312 Helman St
Ashland, OR 97520
541/ 482-9228 800/ 460-5453
www.bluemoonbandb.com

Clientele: mixed gay/ straight
Type: b&b; casual, contemporary & entertaining; 1890s farmhouse w/ spa amenities, 3 blks from downtown
Owned/ Run By: gay men
Rooms: 6

Baths: private
Meals: full brkfst
Kids: welcome w/ prior approval
Pets: welcome in cottage only
Smoking: no
Rates: $90-195

Country Willows Inn
Ashland

1313 Clay St
Ashland, OR 97520
541/ 488-1590 800/ 945-5697
www.countrywillowsinn.com

Clientele: gay-friendly
Type: ultimate country inn; snuggled against a rolling hillside on a lush 5 acres of farmland
Rooms: 9
Baths: private
Wheelchair Access: yes, 1 rm
Meals: full brkfst

Amenities: free parking, pool, outdoor hot tub, DVDs/ videos, WiFi
Kids: 12 yrs & up welcome
Pets: no
Smoking: no
Rates: $125-245
AC: 10%

Lithia Springs Inn
Ashland

2165 W Jackson Rd
Ashland, OR 97520
541/ 482-7128 800/ 482-7128
www.ashlandinn.com

Clientele: mixed gay/ straight
Type: b&b-inn; hot-springs-fed whirlpool in each cottage, suite & rm; on 8 garden acres; 2 miles from plaza
Owned/ Run By: straights
Rooms: 17
Baths: private

Wheelchair Access: yes, 1 rm
Meals: full brkfst
Amenities: hot tub, massage, DVDs/ videos
Kids: 12 yrs & up welcome
Smoking: no
Rates: $129-250
AC: 10%

Romeo Inn B&B
Ashland

295 Idaho St
Ashland, OR 97250
541/ 488-0884 800/ 915-8899
www.romeoinn.com

Clientele: gay-friendly
Type: b&b-private home; in quiet, residential neighborhood near downtown; Mobil & *Northwest Best Places* 3 Stars
Owned/ Run By: straights
Rooms: 6
Baths: private

Meals: full brkfst
Amenities: free parking, pool, hot tub, WiFi
Kids: 12 yrs & up welcome
Pets: no
Smoking: no
Rates: $80-200
AC: 10%

Dawson House Lodge
Bend

109455 Hwy 97 N
Chemult, OR 97731
541/ 365-2232 888/ 281-8375
www.dawsonhouse.net

Clientele: gay-friendly
Type: b&b-inn; rustic inn w/ modern amenities; near Crater Lake; the "newest old hotel" in central Oregon
Owned/ Run By: gay men
Rooms: 9
Baths: private

Meals: cont'l brkfst
Amenities: free parking, DVDs/ videos, WiFi
Kids: welcome
Pets: welcome
Smoking: no
Rates: $50-99
AC: 10%

C'est La Vie Inn
Eugene

1960 Willamette St
Eugene, OR 97405
541/ 302-3014 866/ 302-3014
www.cestlavieinn.com

Clientele: gay-friendly
Type: small luxurious b&b; walk to U of O, Hult Center, restaurants, coffee shops & shopping district; whirlpool tubs
Owned/ Run By: straight woman
Rooms: 3
Baths: private & shared

Meals: full brkfst
Amenities: free parking, DVDs/ videos, gym, WiFi
Kids: please inquire
Pets: please inquire
Smoking: no
Rates: $85-145

WomanShare
Grants Pass

PO Box 411
Murphy, OR 97533
541/ 862-2807
billiemiracle@hotmail.com

Clientele: women
Type: cabin; country retreat: private cabins w/ wood heat on women's land (since 1974); shared kitchen
Owned/ Run By: lesbians
Rooms: 4
Baths: shared

Amenities: free parking, outdoor hot tub, DVDs/ videos
Kids: girls only
Pets: welcome but please call first; must be under control or on leash
Smoking: no
Rates: $15-35 (per person per night)

The Touvelle House
Jacksonville

455 N Oregon St
Jacksonville, OR 97530
541/ 899-8938 800/ 846-8422
www.touvellehouse.com

Clientele: mixed gay/ straight
Type: b&b-private home; 1916 Craftsman home on 1 1/2 acres; 2 blks to historic shopping & Britt Grounds
Owned/ Run By: gay & straight
Rooms: 6
Baths: private

Meals: full brkfst
Amenities: pool, sauna, DVDs/ videos, WiFi
Kids: 12 yrs & up welcome
Pets: no
Smoking: no
Rates: $145-185
AC: 6%

The Beach House B&B
Newport

107 SW Coast St
Newport, OR 97365
541/ 265-9141
www.beachhousebb.com

Clientele: mixed gay/ straight
Type: b&b-private home; Victorian-style; ocean view; in-rm whirlpools; in friendly community of historic Nye Beach; also 2-bdrm rental house
Owned/ Run By: lesbians
Rooms: 3
Baths: private

Wheelchair Access: yes, 1 rm
Meals: full brkfst
Amenities: hot tub, DVDs/ videos
Kids: welcome
Pets: welcome
Smoking: no
Rates: $110-125

Cliff House B&B
Newport

1450 SW Adahi Rd
Waldport, OR 97394
541/ 563-2506
www.cliffhouseoregon.com

Clientele: gay-friendly
Type: b&b-private home; hot tub on 65' glass-fronted deck overlooking ocean & bay
Rooms: 4
Baths: private
Meals: full brkfst

Amenities: free parking, outdoor hot tub, massage, DVDs/ videos
Kids: no
Pets: no
Smoking: no
Rates: $110-225
AC: yes

The Ace Hotel
Portland

1022 SW Stark St
Portland, OR 97205
503/ 228-2277
www.theacehotel.com

Clientele: mixed gay/ straight
Type: hotel; attracts cultural influencers & opinion leaders on a budget
Owned/ Run By: gay/ lesbian & straight
Rooms: 79
Baths: private & shared

Amenities: laundry, DVDs/ videos, WiFi
Kids: welcome
Pets: welcome
Smoking: no
Rates: $85-195

Forest Springs B&B
Portland

3680 SW Towle Ave
Gresham, OR 97080
503/ 674-8992 877/ 674-9282
www.ForestSpring.com

Clientele: mixed gay/ straight
Type: b&b; 1907 English Cottage-style b&b; at the base of 1000+ acres of forest; hill-top views; also weddings & commitment ceremonies
Owned/ Run By: gay man

Rooms: 4
Baths: private & shared
Kids: welcome
Pets: no
Smoking: no
Rates: $55-100

The Grand Ronde Place   Portland

150 NE Tomahawk Island Dr, Slip A-15
Portland, OR 97217
503/ 808-9048 866/ 330-7245
www.thegrandrondeplace.com

Clientele: mixed gay/ straight
Type: stay overnight "aboard a beautiful Hunter 34-ft yacht" in McCuddy's Marina; Sun brunch, dockside dinner & dinner cruises; WiFi
Owned/ Run By: gay men
Rooms: 2

Baths: private
Meals: expanded cont'l brkfst
Kids: no
Pets: no
Smoking: ok on deck only
Rates: $128-219 + 12.5% tax
AC: 15%

Jupiter Hotel   TAG→   Portland

300 E Burnside
Portland, OR 97214
503/ 230-9200 877/ 800-0004
www.jupiterhotel.com

Clientele: gay-friendly
Type: hotel; "exciting, affordable boutique hotel & cutting edge entertainment experience; Doug Fir restaurant & lounge (7am-4am)
Rooms: 80
Baths: private

Wheelchair Access: yes, 3 rms
Amenities: laundry, massage, WiFi
Kids: welcome
Pets: no
Smoking: no
Rates: $89-139
AC: 10%

MacMaster House   Portland

1041 SW Vista Ave
Portland, OR 97205
503/ 223-7362 800/ 774-9523
www.macmaster.com

Clientele: gay-friendly
Type: b&b-private home; in historic mansion on prestigious King's Hill; near the Rose Gardens, cafés, galleries & boutiques
Rooms: 7

Baths: private & shared
Meals: full brkfst
Kids: 14 yrs & up welcome
Smoking: no
Rates: $99-169

The Mark Spencer Hotel   Portland

409 SW Eleventh Ave
Portland, OR 97205
503/ 224-3293 800/ 548-3934
www.markspencer.com

Clientele: gay-friendly
Type: hotel; fully equipped kitchens in all rms & 1-bdrm suites; "we offer the best downtown value"
Owned/ Run By: straights
Rooms: 102
Baths: private

Meals: cont'l brkfst
Kids: welcome
Pets: welcome; $200 pet deposit (refundable)
Rates: $89-169 (+ tax)
AC: 10%

Sullivan's Gulch B&B   Portland

1744 NE Clackamas St
Portland, OR 97232
503/ 331-1104
www.sullivansgulch.com

Clientele: mixed gay/ straight
Type: b&b; city-themed rms & suites in a relaxed, easy-going, spa atmosphere; near light rail & restaurants
Owned/ Run By: bisexuals
Rooms: 4
Baths: private & shared
Meals: full brkfst

Amenities: free parking, laundry, hot tub, massage
Kids: over 6 yrs old w/ innkeepers approval
Pets: welcome w/ prior approval
Smoking: no
Rates: $95-135
AC: 10%

DiamondStone Guest Lodge & Gallery   Sunriver

PO Box 4584
Sunriver, OR 97701
541/ 536-6263 866/ 626-9887
www.diamondstone.com

Clientele: gay-friendly
Type: b&b; hotel-style; in a peaceful, rural setting; featured in Northwest Best Places
Owned/ Run By: bisexuals
Rooms: 4
Baths: private & shared
Meals: full brkfst

Amenities: free parking, outdoor hot tub, DVDs/ videos
Kids: welcome
Pets: by arrangement; $20/ night
Smoking: no
Rates: $90-180
AC: 10%

Ocean Odyssey   Yachats

PO Box 491
Yachats, OR 97498
541/ 547-3637 800/ 800-1915
www.ocean-odyssey.com

Clientele: gay-friendly
Type: vacation rental homes; on central Oregon coast from Cape Perpetua to Seal Rock, including Yachats; some homes w/ hot tubs; many pet-friendly
Owned/ Run By: lesbian & straight

Amenities: laundry, outdoor hot tub, DVDs/ videos
Kids: welcome
Pets: please inquire
Smoking: no
Rates: $75-495
AC: 10%

The Oregon House   Yachats

94288 Hwy 101
Yachats, OR 97498
541/ 547-3329
www.oregonhouse.com

Type: peaceful Oregon coast inn, retreat & conference center; unique, private location on a cliff overlooking the Pacific Ocean
Rooms: 11
Baths: private

Wheelchair Access: yes, 1 rm
Amenities: free parking, hot tub, massage
Kids: welcome in certain rms
Pets: no
Smoking: no
Rates: $65-175

See Vue Motel   Yachats

95590 Hwy 101
Yachats, OR 97498
541/ 547-3227 866/ 547-3237
www.seevue.com

Clientele: mixed gay/ straight
Type: motel; on bluff above Pacific Ocean; all w/ ocean views
Owned/ Run By: lesbians
Rooms: 11
Baths: private

Wheelchair Access: yes, 1 rm
Kids: please inquire
Pets: welcome (limit: 2); $10/night
Smoking: no
Rates: $70-170

Shamrock Lodgettes   Yachats

105 Hwy 101 S
Yachats, OR 97498
541/ 547-3312 800/ 845-5028
www.shamrocklodgettes.com

Clientele: gay-friendly
Type: 5-acre resort located in the village of Yachats; overlooking Yachats River & Pacific Ocean; great beach access
Owned/ Run By: gay men
Rooms: 19 (cabins & guest rms)
Baths: private

Meals: coffee/tea only
Amenities: free parking, sauna, indoor hot tub, massage, DVDs/ videos, gym
Kids: welcome
Pets: welcome in certain units
Rates: $59-200
AC: 10%

The Barnyard Inn & Carriage House   Adamstown

2145 Old Lancaster Pike
Reinholds, PA 17569
717/ 484-1111 888/ 738-6624
www.barnyardinn.com

Clientele: mixed gay/ straight
Type: b&b; 150-yr-old German schoolhouse; petting zoo on premises; owner is retired chef
Owned/ Run By: straights
Rooms: 5
Baths: private
Meals: full brkfst

Amenities: free parking, massage, WiFi
Kids: welcome at Carriage House; 12 yrs & up welcome at Inn
Pets: welcome in Carriage House only
Smoking: no
Rates: $85-185
AC: 10%

Battlefield B&B   Gettysburg

2264 Emmitsburg Rd
Gettysburg, PA 17325
717/ 334-8804 888/ 766-3897
www.gettysburgbattlefield.com

Clientele: gay-friendly
Type: b&b; 1809 Civil War home on 30 acres of the Gettysburg Battlefield; daily history demonstrations & Friday night ghost stories
Owned/ Run By: lesbian
Rooms: 8
Baths: private

Meals: full brkfst
Amenities: free parking, DVDs/ videos
Kids: welcome
Pets: no
Rates: $125-250
AC: 10%

Sheppard Mansion B&B
Gettysburg

117 Frederick St
Hanover, PA 17331
717/ 633-8075 877/ 762-6746
www.sheppardmansion.com

Clientele: mixed gay/ straight
Type: b&b-inn; in elegant 1913 neo-classical residence; fully restored w/ modern amenities; minutes from historic Gettysburg & York
Rooms: 7

Baths: private
Meals: full brkfst
Kids: over 12 yrs welcome
Pets: no
Smoking: no
Rates: $140-250

Sweetwater Farm B&B
Glen Mills

50 Sweetwater Rd
Glen Mills, PA 19342
610/ 459-4711 800/ 793-3892
www.sweetwaterfarmbb.com

Clientele: gay-friendly
Type: b&b; on 50 acres in Brandywine Valley; Manor House (circa 1734) has 7 guest rms; 7 private pet-/ child-friendly cottages surround home
Owned/ Run By: straights
Rooms: 14 (7 rms & 7 private cottages)
Baths: private
Wheelchair Access: yes, 2 cottages rms

Meals: full brkfst
Amenities: free parking, pool, outdoor hot tub, massage, DVDs/ videos, gym, WiFi
Kids: in outdoor cottages; $35 per child
Pets: in outdoor cottages; $35 per pet
Smoking: no
Rates: $125-275
AC: 10%

Mountain View Inn
Greensburg

1001 Village Dr
Greensburg, PA 15601
724/ 834-5300 800/ 537-8709
www.mountainviewinn.com

Clientele: gay-friendly
Type: hotel; in Laurel Highlands of W Pennsylvania; 15 miles from antique shopping in Ligonier
Owned/ Run By: straights
Rooms: 90
Baths: private

Wheelchair Access: yes, 10 rms
Meals: full brkfst
Amenities: free parking, pool
Kids: welcome
Pets: no
Smoking: ok
Rates: $69-265

Grim's Manor B&B
Kutztown

10 Kern Rd
Kutztown, PA 19530
610/ 683-7089

Clientele: mixed gay/ lesbian
Type: b&b; 200-yr-old, historical stone farmhouse; on 5 acres; offering wknd accommodations
Owned/ Run By: gay men
Rooms: 4
Baths: private

Meals: full brkfst
Amenities: free parking, indoor hot tub
Kids: no
Pets: no
Smoking: no
Rates: $85-90

Cameron Estate Inn
Lancaster

1855 Mansion Ln
Mount Joy, PA 17552
717/ 492-0111 888/ 422-6376
www.cameronestateinn.com

Clientele: mixed gay/ straight
Type: b&b-inn; elegant, secluded mansion (circa 1805) on 15 acres of lawn & woods
Owned/ Run By: gay men
Rooms: 18
Baths: private
Wheelchair Access: yes, 3 rms

Meals: full brkfst
Amenities: free parking, hot tub, DVDs/ videos
Kids: well-behaved teens welcome
Pets: no
Smoking: no
Rates: $129-299

Candlelight Inn B&B
Lancaster

2574 Lincoln Hwy E
Ronks, PA 17572
717/ 299-6005 800/ 772-2635
www.candleinn.com

Clientele: gay-friendly
Type: b&b; elegantly appointed inn in the heart of PA's Dutch/ Amish countryside
Owned/ Run By: straights
Rooms: 7
Baths: private

Meals: full brkfst
Amenities: free parking, hot tub, massage
Kids: well-behaved & over 8 yrs
Pets: no
Rates: $89-179
AC: 10%

The Noble House B&B   Lancaster

113 W Market St
Marietta, PA 17547
717/ 426-4389 888/ 271-6426
www.thenoblehouse.com

Clientele: mixed gay/ straight
Type: b&b-private home; 1810 Federal-style brick town house
Owned/ Run By: straights
Rooms: 4 (4th rm actually bungalow)
Baths: private
Meals: full brkfst

Amenities: free parking, hot tub
Kids: 1 kid welcome in bungalow
Pets: welcome in bungalow
Smoking: no
Rates: $1115-225
AC: please inquire

The Railroad House B&B, Restaurant & Tavern   Lancaster

280 W Front St
Marietta, PA 17547
717/ 426-4141
www.therailroadhouse.com

Clientele: mixed gay/ straight
Type: b&b-inn; romantic Victorian-style getaway; 1820s Nat'l Historic Register site; patio dining, formal gardens; located on the Susquehana River
Owned/ Run By: gay men
Rooms: 8

Baths: private
Meals: full brkfst
Amenities: laundry, massage, WiFi
Kids: welcome if supervised at all times
Pets: well-behaved pets in cottage only
Smoking: no
Rates: $109-179

Babbling Brook Cottages   Milford

570/ 828-9175
www.babblingbrookcottages.net

Clientele: mixed gay/ straight
Type: cottage; charming, pristine cottages bordering nat'l park; 5 waterfalls/ hiking trails; 2.5 miles to Delaware River w/ canoeing, fishing; near Pocono attractions
Owned/ Run By: women

Rooms: 5
Baths: private
Kids: welcome
Pets: welcome
Smoking: ok
Rates: $99-285

Mt Haven Country Resort   Milford

RD 1 Log Tavern Rd
Milford, PA 18337
570/ 296-7262 800/ 553-1530
www.mthavenresort.com

Clientele: gay-friendly
Type: family run resort in Poconos; beautiful views; jacuzzi tubs; Italian restaurant
Owned/ Run By: straights
Rooms: 35
Baths: private
Wheelchair Access: yes, 15 rms

Meals: full brkfst
Amenities: free parking, pool, massage DVDs/ videos, WiFi
Kids: welcome
Pets: welcome
Smoking: ok
Rates: $130-250

Cordials B&B of New Hope   New Hope

143 Old York Rd
New Hope, PA 18938
215/ 862-3919 877/ 219-1009
www.cordialsbb.com

Clientele: mixed gay/ lesbian
Type: b&b-inn; "it's not only our name, but our way of life"
Owned/ Run By: gay men
Rooms: 6
Baths: private
Wheelchair Access: yes, 2 rms

Meals: expanded cont'l brkfst
Amenities: free parking, outdoor hot tub DVDs/ videos
Smoking: no
Rates: $85-155

Fox & Hound B&B   New Hope

246 West Bridge St
New Hope, PA 18938
215/ 862-5082 800/ 862-5082
www.foxhoundinn.com

Clientele: gay-friendly
Type: b&b; elegant 1840 stone farmhouse on 2 acres; 1/2 mile to center of historic New Hope
Owned/ Run By: straights
Rooms: 8
Baths: private

Meals: full brkfst
Amenities: free parking, hot tub, WiFi
Kids: 17 yrs & up welcome
Pets: no
Smoking: no
Rates: $90-200
AC: 10% (on availability)

The Lexington House

New Hope

6171 Upper York Rd
New Hope, PA 18938
215/ 794-0811
www.lexingtonhouse.com

Clientele: mixed gay/ straight
Type: b&b; circa 1749 home; charming old-world setting, 2 pools, waterfall, fireplaces
Owned/ Run By: gay men
Rooms: 6
Baths: private

Meals: expanded cont'l brkfst
Kids: no
Pets: no
Smoking: no
Rates: $130-200

The Mansion Inn

New Hope

9 S Main
New Hope, PA 18938
215/ 862-1231
www.themansioninn.com

Clientele: mixed gay/ lesbian
Type: b&b-inn; in heart of New Hope's historic district; AAA 4 Diamond Award
Owned/ Run By: gay men
Rooms: 12
Baths: private
Meals: full brkfst

Amenities: pool, hot tub, massage
Kids: no
Pets: no
Smoking: no
Rates: $155-295
AC: 10%

Silver Maple Organic Farm & B&B

New Hope

483 Sergeantsville Rd (Rte 523)
Sergeantsville, NJ 08557
908/ 237-2192
www.silvermaplefarm.net

Clientele: mixed gay/ straight
Type: b&b; charming 200-yr-old farmhouse on 20-acre working farm
Owned/ Run By: gay men
Rooms: 5
Baths: private
Wheelchair Access: yes, 1 rm

Meals: full brkfst
Amenities: pool, outdoor hot tub
Kids: welcome
Pets: welcome
Smoking: no
Rates: $99-159
AC: 10%

The Victorian Peacock B&B

New Hope

309 E Dark Hollow Rd
Pipersville, PA 18947
215/ 766-1356
www.victorianpeacock.com

Clientele: mixed gay/ straight
Type: b&b-inn; romantic Victorian set on 5 acres
Owned/ Run By: lesbians
Rooms: 4
Baths: private
Meals: expanded cont'l brkfst

Amenities: pool, hot tub, DVDs/ videos
Kids: 16 yrs & up, in private rm only
Pets: no
Smoking: no
Rates: $100-190
AC: 10%

The Wishing Well Guesthouse

New Hope

144 Old York Rd
New Hope, PA 18938
215/ 862-8819
www.wishingwellguesthouse.com

Clientele: mixed gay/ straight
Type: b&b; 1840s farmhouse on wooded acre; stream, gazebo, gym & pool passes; walk to town, shops & gay nightlife
Owned/ Run By: gay men
Rooms: 6
Baths: private

Meals: expansive brkfst buffet wknds, cont'l weekdays
Kids: welcome in suite
Pets: no
Smoking: no
Rates: $99-150

Oneida Camp & Lodge

New Milford

PO Box 537
New Milford, PA 18834
570/ 465-7011
www.oneidalodge.com

Clientele: mostly men
Type: campground; several campsites, 12 RV hookups, guest rms & private cabins; also nightclub & lodge; all-male 95% of the time
Owned/ Run By: gay men
Rooms: 24
Baths: private & shared

Meals: coffee/tea only
Amenities: free parking, laundry, pool, sauna, massage, DVDs/ videos, WiFi
Pets: must be leashed; call ahead
Smoking: ok
Rates: $send for brochure
AC: 10%

Alexander Inn 🏳️‍🌈
Philadelphia

Spruce (at 12th St)
Philadelphia, PA
215/ 923-3535 877/ 253-9466
www.alexanderinn.com

Clientele: mixed gay/ straight
Type: hotel; beautifully restored historic bldg; w/ nearby parking; complimentary fitness center, brkfst, guest emails, 8 movie channels
Owned/ Run By: gay men
Rooms: 48

Baths: private
Meals: expanded cont'l brkfst
Amenities: WiFi
Kids: not recommended
Pets: no
Rates: $109-159
AC: 10%

Antique Row B&B
Philadelphia

341 S 12th St
Philadelphia, PA 19107
215/ 592-7802
antiquerowbnb.com

Clientele: gay-friendly
Type: rm & apt; comfortable & attractive; around the corner from Antique Row; convenient Center City location
Baths: private & shared
Meals: full brkfst
Kids: well-behaved welcome on 1st flr

Pets: no
Smoking: ok
Rates: $65-110
AC: 6%

Hampton Inn Center City Philadelphia 🏳️‍🌈
Philadelphia

1301 Race St
Philadelphia, PA 19107
267/ 765-1110 800/ 426-7866
www.hershahotels.com

Clientele: gay-friendly
Type: hotel; 24hr fitness center; function rms & 3,753 square ft of meeting space; internet access
Owned/ Run By: straights
Rooms: 250
Baths: private
Wheelchair Access: yes, 11 rms

Meals: expanded cont'l brkfst
Amenities: laundry, pool, hot tub
Kids: welcome
Pets: under 10 lbs welcome; $25 fee
Smoking: smoking rooms available
Rates: $79+
AC: 10%

Holiday Inn Historic District
Philadelphia

400 Arch St
Philadelphia, PA 19106
215/ 923-8660 800/ 843-2355
www.holiday-inn.com/phlhistoric

Clientele: gay-friendly
Type: hotel; upscale; located in historic district; walk to restaurants, art galleries, cafes, bars, shopping, historic attractions
Owned/ Run By: gay & straight
Rooms: 364
Baths: private

Wheelchair Access: yes, 14 rms
Amenities: laundry, pool, gym, WiFi
Kids: welcome
Pets: welcome; deposit
Smoking: ok
Rates: $99-239
AC: 10%

Shippen Way Inn
Philadelphia

416-18 Bainbridge St
Philadelphia, PA 19147
215/ 627-7266 800/ 245-4873
shippenway.com

Clientele: gay-friendly
Type: b&b-inn; restored 18th-c inn; afternoon wine/tea; close to shops, restaurants & historic district
Owned/ Run By: gay & straight
Rooms: 9

Baths: private
Meals: expanded cont'l brkfst
Kids: 7 yrs & up welcome
Pets: no
Rates: $105-150

Uncles Upstairs Inn
Philadelphia

1220 Locust St
Philadelphia, PA 19107
215/ 546-6660
www.unclesphilly.com

Clientele: mostly men
Type: b&b-inn; in renovated town house in the heart of downtown
Owned/ Run By: gay man
Rooms: 6

Baths: private
Meals: cont'l brkfst
Pets: welcome
Rates: $115
AC: 10%

The Inn at Chester Springs

Philadelphia

315 N Pottstown Pike
Exton, PA 19341

610/ 363-1100
888/ 253-6119

hotel_info@innatchestersprings.com
www.innatchestersprings.com

Clientele: gay-friendly
Type: hotel; full-service hotel & conference center in the heart of the Brandywine Valley; 25 minutes from Philadelphia
Owned/ Run By: gay & straight
Nearby Attractions: Longwood Gardens, QVC Studio Tour, Valley Forge Nat'l Historic Park, The Plaza & The Court at King of Prussia (East Coast's largest mall)
Transit: 25 miles to Philadelphia Int'l Airport
Rooms: 215 total, suites, A/C, color TV, cable, phone (2 per rm w/ 2 data ports, voicemail), rm service, maid service, iron & ironing board
Baths: private, showers, robes, hairdryers
Wheelchair Access: yes, 2 rms
Meals: vegetarian meals available
Amenities: free parking, laundry, WiFi, indoor & outdoor pool, exercise facility, Arthur's full-service restaurant & lounge
Kids: welcome
Pets: must stay w/ owner at all times; $25 per pet

Smoking: ok
Reservations: *Cancellation:* cancel by 1 day prior *Check in/ out:* 3pm/ 11am
Payment: cash, travelers checks, Visa, Amex, MC, Discover

Season: open yr-round
Rates: $89-149
AC: 10%

Arbors B&B

Pittsburgh

745 Maginn St
Pittsburgh, PA 15214-3007

412/ 231-4643

www.arborsbnb.com

Clientele: men
Type: b&b-inn; on historic North Side; near city center, cultural district, stadiums, bike trails, bars
Owned/ Run By: gay men
Rooms: 3 (including 1 suite)
Baths: private

Meals: expanded cont'l brkfst
Amenities: free parking, indoor hot tub, DVDs/ videos
Kids: no
Pets: no
Smoking: no
Rates: $75-95

Camp Davis

Pittsburgh

311 Red Brush Rd
Boyers, PA 16020

724/ 637-2402

campdaviscampground.com

Clientele: mixed gay/ lesbian
Type: cabins & trailer/ tent sites; some electric sites; hot showers & flush toilets (wheelchair accessible); volleyball, hiking trails, 20x40 swimming pool; Sat night dances; $10 membership fee; May thru 2nd wknd in Oct

Rooms: 4 (cabins)
Rates: $17 (tent sites); $25 (cabins); $30 (trailer)

The Inn on the Mexican War Streets

Pittsburgh

604 W North Ave
Pittsburgh, PA 15212

412/ 231-6544

hometown.aol.com/innwarst/collect/index.htm

Clientele: mixed gay/ lesbian
Type: b&b-inn; located in the historic Boggs Mansion & gay-friendly North Side; "Pittsburgh's premier gay b&b"
Owned/ Run By: gay men
Rooms: 8 (6 suites & 2 apts)
Baths: private

Meals: expanded cont'l brkfst
Pets: under 25 lbs welcome; in 1st flr suites only
Smoking: no
Rates: $99-169

The Inns on Negley
Pittsburgh

703 S Negley Ave
Pittsburgh, PA 15232
412/ 661-0631
www.theinnsonnegley.com

Clientele: gay-friendly
Type: b&b-inn; elegant, upscale, suite-style rms; convenient to museums, universities, hospitals, upscale shopping & culture
Owned/ Run By: women
Rooms: 16
Baths: private
Wheelchair Access: yes, 2 rms

Meals: full brkfst
Amenities: free parking, massage, DVDs, videos, WiFi
Kids: no
Pets: no
Smoking: no
Rates: $150-280

The Priory
Pittsburgh

614 Pressley St
Pittsburgh, PA 15212
412/ 231-3338
www.thepriory.com

Clientele: gay-friendly
Type: hotel; restored & renovated European-style hotel; located in historic East Allegheny area; fitness center
Rooms: 24
Baths: private

Meals: cont'l brkfst
Kids: welcome; kids under 13 yrs free
Pets: no
Smoking: ok
Rates: $134-195
AC: 10%

On the Rocks B&B & Lakefront Retreat
Pocono Lake

570/ 643-5377
www.visitontherocks.com

Clientele: mixed gay/ straight
Type: b&b; boats, private black-sand beach, steam rm
Rooms: 3
Baths: private
Wheelchair Access: yes, 3 rms
Meals: full brkfst

Amenities: free parking, laundry, sauna, outdoor hot tub, DVDs/ videos, gym, WiFi
Kids: cribbed infants ok
Pets: no
Smoking: no
Rates: $150-225
AC: 10%

The Arrowheart Inn
Poconos

3021 Valley View Dr
Bangor, PA 18013
610/ 588-0241
www.arrowheartinn.com

Clientele: mixed gay/ straight
Type: b&b; beautiful & secluded mtn setting; convenient to many Pocono attractions
Owned/ Run By: gay men
Rooms: 4
Baths: private & shared

Meals: full brkfst
Amenities: free parking, outdoor hot tub, massage
Kids: must stay in rm w/ private entrance
Smoking: no
Rates: $85-125

Blueberry Ridge
Poconos

RR1 Box 67
Scotrun, PA 18355
570/ 629-5036
ridges@ptd.net

Clientele: women
Type: b&b; romantic accommodations w/ great view of Delaware Water Gap
Owned/ Run By: lesbians
Rooms: 4
Baths: private & shared
Meals: full brkfst

Amenities: free parking, outdoor hot tub, DVDs/ videos
Smoking: no
Rates: $65-100

Frog Hollow
Poconos

570/ 595-2814

Clientele: mixed gay/ lesbian
Type: cottage; secluded 1920s cottage nestled deep in a Pocono Mtn hollow; w/ huge fireplace, screened-in porch, deck & full kitchen; accommodates 4

Owned/ Run By: lesbians
Rooms: 2
Kids: welcome
Pets: dogs & cats only
Rates: $100-150

Rainbow Mountain Resort
Poconos

210 Mt Nebo Rd
East Stroudsburg, PA 18301
570/ 223-8484
www.rainbowmountain.com

Clientele: mixed gay/ lesbian
Type: resort; nestled high atop a Pocono mtn on 26 private wooded acres; w/ spectacular views; also nightclub; special theme wknds
Owned/ Run By: gay men
Rooms: 45
Baths: private & shared

Meals: full brkfst (& gourmet dinner)
Amenities: free parking, pool, sauna, hot tub, massage, DVDs/ videos, gym
Kids: welcome on family wknds only
Pets: welcome in summer
Smoking: ok
Rates: $46-248
AC: 10%

Stoney Ridge
Poconos

RR 1, Box 67
Scotrun, PA 18355
570/ 629-5036
ridges@ptd.net

Clientele: mixed gay/ lesbian
Type: cabin; beautiful new cedar log home; quietly secluded in the woods; sleeps 2-4 people
Owned/ Run By: lesbians
Rooms: 2

Baths: private & shared
Kids: welcome
Pets: welcome
Rates: $250 (for 2) – 350 (for 4) / wknds; $550 (2) – 750 (4)/ week

The Woods Campground
Poconos

345 Vaughn Acres Ln
Lehighton, PA 18235
610/ 377-9577
www.thewoodscampground.com

Clientele: mixed gay/ lesbian
Type: private, clothing-optional campground; disco, bonfires, theme wknds
Owned/ Run By: gay men
Rooms: 5 (cabins)
Baths: shared

Amenities: free parking, laundry, pool, hot tub, massage
Kids: welcome on family-themed wknds only
Pets: welcome
Rates: $15-95

Hillside Campgrounds
Scranton

Creek Rd
Gibson, NY 13902
570/ 756-2007
www.hillsidecampgrounds.com

Clientele: men
Type: campground, RV park; 212 campsites; on 176 acres w/ 45-acre play area; clothing-optional; reservations required; open May 1-Oct 1; "largest men-only one in the world"

Owned/ Run By: gay men
Kids: no
Pets: welcome
Smoking: ok
Rates: $45 (campsite) - 285 (cabin)

Mountain Top Resort
Scranton

570/ 798-0342 877/ 429-3868
www.mountaintopresort.org

Type: lodge; overlooking breathtaking views; lots of space for camping, roaming
Rooms: 7
Baths: private & shared
Amenities: free parking, laundry, DVDs/ videos, gym, WiFi

Kids: no
Pets: welcome outside only
Smoking: no
Rates: $19-160

Blueberry Cove Inn
Narragansett

75 Kingstown Rd
Narragansett, RI 02882
401/ 792-9865 800/ 478-1426
www.blueberrycoveinn.com

Clientele: gay-friendly
Type: b&b-inn; 3 blks from beach & Narragansett Towers; close to Newport & Block Island; whirlpools, fireplaces, A/C; open yr-round
Owned/ Run By: straights
Rooms: 9

Baths: private
Amenities: hot tub
Kids: no
Pets: dogs welcome
Smoking: no
Rates: $110-250

Brinley Victorian Inn
Newport

23 Brinley St
Newport, RI 02840
401/ 849-7645 800/ 999-8523
www.brinleyvictorian.com

Clientele: mixed gay/ straight
Type: b&b-inn; consisting of 2 adjoining Victorian houses (1850 & 1870)
Owned/ Run By: straights
Rooms: 17
Baths: private
Meals: cont'l brkfst

Amenities: free parking, hot tub
Kids: 8 yrs & up welcome; under 12 yrs sta free
Pets: no
Smoking: no
Rates: $119-229
AC: 10%

Francis Malbone House Inn
Newport

392 Thames St
Newport, RI 02840
401/ 846-0392 800/ 846-0392
www.malbone.com

Clientele: gay-friendly
Type: b&b-inn; Colonial mansion circa 1760; beautiful rms, gracious sitting rms, manicured gardens & award-winning hospitality; listed in Nat'l Regiter of Historical Places
Owned/ Run By: gay & straight
Rooms: 20

Baths: private
Wheelchair Access: yes, 1 rm
Meals: full brkfst
Kids: over 12 yrs welcome
Smoking: no
Rates: $165-495
AC: 10%

Hydrangea House Inn
Newport

16 Bellevue Ave
Newport, RI 02840
401/ 846-4435 800/ 945-4667
www.hydrangeahouse.com

Clientele: mixed gay/ straight
Type: b&b-inn
Owned/ Run By: gay men
Rooms: 9
Baths: private
Meals: full brkfst buffet
Amenities: hot tub, DVDs/ videos

Kids: no
Pets: no
Smoking: no
Rates: $250-475
AC: 10%

Inn Bliss B&B
Newport

10 Bliss Rd
Newport, RI 02840
401/ 845-2547
www.innbliss.com

Clientele: mixed gay/ straight
Type: b&b; 1888 Victorian b&b; close walk to beaches & downtown area
Owned/ Run By: gay men
Rooms: 2
Baths: private & shared

Meals: full brkfst
Kids: over age of 14
Pets: no
Rates: $47-175
AC: 15%

The Spring Seasons Inn
Newport

86 Spring St
Newport, RI 02840
401/ 849-0004 877/ 294-0004
www.springseasonsinn.com

Clientele: gay-friendly
Type: b&b; classic 1870s Victorian located in the heart of Newport nightlife; all rms have jacuzzi baths & king- or queen-size beds; short walk to sailing, dining, shopping & attractions
Owned/ Run By: gay & straight

Rooms: 3
Baths: private
Meals: full brkfst
Amenities: hot tub
Kids: ages 1-12 welcome
Pets: no
Rates: $125-275

The Villa
Westerly

190 Shore Rd
Westerly, RI 02891
401/ 596-1054 800/ 722-9240
www.thevillaatwesterly.com

Clientele: gay-friendly
Type: b&b; many amenities & a great location
Owned/ Run By: straights
Rooms: 6
Baths: private
Meals: cont'l brkfst

Amenities: free parking, pool, outdoor ho tub, DVDs/ videos
Kids: no
Pets: no
Smoking: no
Rates: $115-305
AC: 10%

A B&B @ 4 Unity Alley
Charleston

4 Unity Alley
Charleston, SC 29401
843/ 577-6660
www.unitybb.com

Clientele: mixed gay/ straight
Type: b&b; 18th-c warehouse converted to a private home
Rooms: 3
Baths: private
Meals: full brkfst

Kids: welcome sometimes
Pets: dogs under 12 lbs welcome; must be attended at all times
Smoking: no
Rates: $125-245
AC: 10%

Alice's Carriage House B&B
Charleston

22 New St
Charleston, SC 29401
843/ 973-3458
acwhitt@bellsouth.net

Clientele: gay-friendly
Type: b&b; in historical district, near unique architecture, museums & restaurants; private carriage house w/ elegant courtyard; Old World charm & history all around
Owned/ Run By: straights
Rooms: 1
Baths: private

Meals: cont'l brkfst
Amenities: free parking, laundry, pool, outdoor hot tub, WiFi
Kids: no
Pets: no
Smoking: no
Rates: $165-195
AC: 15%

Height of Folly
Charleston

PO Box 716
Folly Beach, SC 29439
843/ 588-6200
BillyMyron@bellsouth.net

Clientele: men
Type: apt; beachfront; w/ hot tub on deck; nude areas; 20 minutes to gay bars; very private
Owned/ Run By: gay men
Rooms: 1 (apt) + 1 (efficiency)
Baths: private

Amenities: free parking, laundry, outdoor hot tub, DVDs/ videos
Kids: no
Pets: welcome
Smoking: ok
Rates: $70-85

Phoebe Pember House
Charleston

26 Society St
Charleston, SC 29401
843/ 722-4186
www.phoebepemberhouse.com

Clientele: gay-friendly
Type: b&b; an oasis in the heart of historic Charleston; yoga studio on property offers classes
Owned/ Run By: straights
Rooms: 6

Baths: private
Meals: expanded cont'l brkfst
Kids: 10 yrs & up
Pets: no
Rates: $185-250
AC: no

Wentworth Mansion
Charleston

149 Wentworth St
Charleston, SC 29401
843/ 853-1886 888/ 466-1886
www.wentworthmansion.com

Clientele: gay-friendly
Type: hotel; built during the Gilded Age, hand-carved marble fireplaces, intricate woodwork, Tiffany stained-glass windows, in historic downtown Charleston; also restaurant

Meals: expanded cont'l brkfst
Amenities: massage, WiFi
Kids: welcome
Smoking: no
Rates: $275-705

Walnut Lane Inn
Greenville

110 Ridge Rd
Lyman, SC 29365
864/ 949-7230 800/ 949-4686
www.walnutlaneinn.com

Clientele: gay-friendly
Type: b&b-inn; reminiscent of the grand plantations of yesterday, this gracious b&b inn is located in a great tourist area
Owned/ Run By: gay men
Rooms: 6

Baths: private
Meals: full brkfst
Kids: welcome
Smoking: no (porch only)
Rates: $125
AC: 10%

The Myrtle Beach Resort   *Myrtle Beach*

518/ 330-1163

Clientele: mixed gay/ straight
Type: oceanview condo at 33-acre, family-friendly resort; 6 pools, lazy river, beach bar, kids' playground
Owned/ Run By: lesbians
Rooms: 2 (bdrms)
Baths: private

Amenities: laundry, pool, sauna, indoor hot tub
Kids: welcome
Pets: no
Smoking: no
Rates: $500-1,200
AC: 6%

Wakpamni B&B   *Batesland*

HC64 Box 43
Batesland, SD 57716
605/ 288-1800
www.wakpamni.com

Clientele: gay-friendly
Type: b&b; unique rms & tipis on Indian reservation; dinner available; gift shop
Rooms: 6
Baths: shared
Meals: full brkfst
Amenities: free parking, hot tub, DVDs/

videos, gym, WiFi
Kids: 12 yrs & up welcome
Pets: no
Smoking: no
Rates: $70-125
AC: 10%

Camp Michael B&B   *Rapid City*

13051 Bogus Jim Rd
Rapid City, SD 57702
605/ 342-5590
www.campmike.com

Clientele: mixed gay/ lesbian
Type: b&b; an amazingly peaceful & serene getaway; nestled in the woods of the Black Hills
Owned/ Run By: gay men
Rooms: 4
Baths: shared

Meals: full brkfst
Amenities: laundry, outdoor hot tub
Kids: welcome
Pets: welcome
Smoking: no
Rates: $60-75
AC: $5 per booking

Camp America   *Salem*

25495 US 81
Salem, SD 57058-1925
605/ 425-9085
www.campsalemsd.com

Clientele: gay-friendly
Type: campground; 1 1/2 miles N of I-90 on US 81; tenting to 50 amp pull-thru sites in a restful rural setting; 52 level, shaded tent sites or RV hookups; meditation labyrinth
Owned/ Run By: lesbians

Kids: welcome
Pets: welcome
Smoking: no
Rates: $14-24

An Appalachian Mountain Vacation   *Bristol*

PO Box 30
Butler, TN 37640
423/ 768-2446 888/ 781-2399
www.ironmountaininn.com

Clientele: gay-friendly
Type: mtn-top b&b or private chalet next to creek; also luxury lakeside cottage (3-bdrm & wheelchair access)
Owned/ Run By: straight woman
Rooms: 4 + 1 cabin + 1 cottage
Baths: private & shared
Wheelchair Access: yes, 2 rms

Meals: full brkfst
Amenities: free parking, laundry, outdoor hot tub, massage, WiFi
Kids: welcome in chalet & cottage
Pets: welcome in chalet & cottage
Smoking: no
Rates: $160-400
AC: 10%

Big Creek Stables & Big Creek Outpost   *Gatlinburg*

5019 Rag Mtn Rd
Hartford, TN 37753
423/ 487-5742 423/ 487-3490
www.bigcreekoutdoors.com

Clientele: mixed gay/ straight
Type: cabin; 10 campsites & 2 RV hookups
Owned/ Run By: straights
Rooms: 4
Baths: private & shared
Wheelchair Access: yes, 1 rm

Meals: coffee/tea only
Kids: welcome
Pets: no
Smoking: ok
Rates: $75-150

Christopher Place, An Intimate Resort
Gatlinburg

1500 Pinnacles Wy
Newport, TN 37821
423/ 623–6555 800/ 595–9441
www.christopherplace.com

Clientele: mixed gay/ straight
Type: b&b-inn; secluded mtn estate w/ panoramic views & Southern hospitality; 30 miles from Gatlinburg
Owned/ Run By: other
Rooms: 9
Baths: private

Wheelchair Access: yes, 1 rm
Meals: full brkfst
Kids: 12 yrs & up welcome
Smoking: no
Rates: $165-330
AC: 10%

Mountain Vista Cabins
Gatlinburg

865/ 712–9897
www.mountainvistacabins.com

Clientele: mixed gay/ lesbian
Type: cabin; near Great Smoky Mtns Nat'l Park, Dollywood, hiking, riding, fishing; w/ grill, fireplace, satellite TV & more
Owned/ Run By: women
Amenities: free parking, laundry, outdoor hot tub, DVDs/ videos

Kids: well-behaved welcome
Pets: well-behaved welcome
Smoking: no
Rates: $120-175

Timberfell Lodge
Greeneville

2240 Van Hill Rd
Greeneville, TN 37745
800/ 437–0118
www.timberfell.com

Clientele: men
Type: resort; 250 acres of mtn trails & streams; clothing-optional; also 40 tent/ campsites & 15 RV hookups
Owned/ Run By: gay men
Rooms: 16
Baths: private & shared
Meals: full brkfst & dinner

Amenities: free parking, pool, sauna, hot tub, massage, DVDs/ videos
Kids: no
Pets: welcome
Smoking: no
Rates: $79-134 (rms); $15 (camping per person)
AC: 3%

Cabin on Twin Pine Lane
Johnson City

423/ 542–8962
www.vrbo.com/62291

Clientele: gay-friendly
Type: cabin; forest setting w/ privacy; great views of mtns & waterfall beside porch; sleeps 5; 4 miles from town
Owned/ Run By: straights
Meals: coffee/ tea only

Amenities: free parking, massage
Kids: welcome
Pets: no
Smoking: no
Rates: $75

Safehaven Farm
Johnson City

436 Stanley Hollow Rd
Roan Mountain, TN 37687
423/ 725–4262
www.safehavenfarm.com

Clientele: gay-friendly
Type: cabin; creekside privacy; w/ fireplace & wraparound porch; stocked pond (fishing poles provided); can perform commitment ceremonies; extremely private
Owned/ Run By: straights

Rooms: 4
Baths: private
Kids: welcome
Pets: by arrangement
Smoking: no
Rates: $90/ night; $450/ week

Madison Hotel
Memphis

79 Madison Ave
Memphis, TN 38103
901/ 333–1200
www.madisonhotelmemphis.com

Clientele: gay-friendly
Type: hotel; combines the intimate service of a b&b w/ all you expect from a first-class boutique hotel
Owned/ Run By: straights
Rooms: 110
Baths: private

Wheelchair Access: yes, 8 rms
Meals: expanded cont'l brkfst
Kids: welcome
Pets: no
Rates: $220+
AC: 10%

Shellcrest Guesthouse

Memphis

671 Jefferson Ave
Memphis, TN 38105
901/ 277-0223
www.shellcrest.com

Clientele: mixed gay/ straight
Type: apt; 2 1,200-sq-ft suites; in downtown Victorian town house circa 1868; w/ garden & skyline views
Owned/ Run By: gay men
Rooms: 2 (suites)
Baths: private

Meals: expanded cont'l brkfst
Amenities: laundry, pool, hot tub, DVDs, videos, WiFi
Kids: no
Pets: no
Smoking: no
Rates: $170-250

Talbot Heirs Guesthouse

Memphis

99 S 2nd St
Memphis, TN 38103
901/ 527-9772 800/ 955-3956
www.talbotheirs.com

Type: inn; located in the heart of downtown; all rms have queen bed & full kitchen
Rooms: 9
Baths: private
Meals: cont'l brkfst

Amenities: laundry, massage, DVDs, videos, WiFi
Kids: welcome
Smoking: no
Rates: $150+
AC: 10%

Lake Fork Resort

Alba

5004 N FM 17
Alba, TX 75410
903/ 765-2987 800/ 230-4367
www.lakeforkresort.com

Clientele: gay-friendly
Type: campground, motel, RV park
Owned/ Run By: straights
Wheelchair Access: yes
Amenities: pool, WiFi

1888 Miller Crockett House

Austin

112 Academy Dr
Austin, TX 78704
512/ 441-1600 888/ 441-1641
www.millercrockett.com

Clientele: gay-friendly
Type: b&b; elegant New Orleans-style; spectacular view; grand rms in main house & 2 private cottages
Owned/ Run By: woman
Rooms: 6
Baths: private
Wheelchair Access: yes, 2 rms

Meals: full brkfst
Kids: welcome
Pets: welcome; in cottages only
Smoking: no
Rates: $139-169
AC: 10%

Austin Folk House

Austin

506 W 22nd St
Austin, TX 78705
512/ 472-6700 866/ 472-6700
www.austinfolkhouse.com

Clientele: mixed gay/ straight
Type: b&b-inn; in newly restored 1880s house; full of antiques & folk art; centrally located
Rooms: 9
Baths: private
Wheelchair Access: yes, 1 rm

Meals: full brkfst
Kids: welcome
Pets: welcome; must be flea-free
Smoking: no
Rates: $95-145

Hotel San Jose

Austin

1316 S Congress Ave
Austin, TX 78704
512/ 444-7322 800/ 574-8897
www.sanjosehotel.com

Clientele: mixed gay/ straight
Type: small boutique hotel; featured in *Flaunt, Texas Monthly* & *Met Home*
Owned/ Run By: gay/ lesbian & straight
Rooms: 40
Baths: private & shared
Wheelchair Access: yes, 2 rms

Meals: expanded cont'l brkfst
Kids: welcome
Pets: welcome
Smoking: no
Rates: $90-315
AC: 10%

Park Lane Guest House
Austin

221 Park Ln
Austin, TX 78704
512/ 447-7460 800/ 492-8827
parklaneguesthouse.com

Clientele: mixed gay/ straight
Type: b&b-private home; Florentine rm in main house w/ private bath; garden cottage w/ kitchen; also carriage house w/ kitchen
Owned/ Run By: lesbians
Rooms: 3

Baths: private
Wheelchair Access: yes, 1 rm
Meals: full brkfst
Kids: under 1 yr or over 12 yrs welcome
Pets: please call first; $25 deposit
Rates: $109-169
AC: 10%

Star of Texas Inn
Austin

611 W 22nd St
Austin, TX 78705
512/ 472-6700 866/ 472-6700
www.staroftexasinn.com

Clientele: gay-friendly
Type: b&b-inn; in neo-classical Victorian; voted best B&B in Austin 1997-2002
Owned/ Run By: gay/ lesbian & straight
Rooms: 10
Baths: private

Meals: full brkfst
Kids: welcome
Pets: welcome; must be flea-free
Smoking: no
Rates: $85-225

Anthony's By The Sea
Corpus Christi

732 S Pearl St
Rockport, TX 78382
361/ 729-6100 800/ 460-2557
anthonys@pyramid3.net

Clientele: mixed gay/ straight
Type: b&b; quiet retreat hidden by live oaks; 4 blks from the water
Owned/ Run By: lesbians
Rooms: 6
Baths: private & shared
Wheelchair Access: yes, 2 rms

Meals: full brkfst
Kids: by arrangement
Pets: by arrangement
Smoking: ok (in 2 rms only)
Rates: $95-115
AC: 10%

Christy Estates Suites
Corpus Christi

3942 Holly Rd
Corpus Christi, TX 78415
361/ 854-1091 800/ 678-4836
www.christyestatessuites.com

Clientele: gay-friendly
Type: hotel; full-size apt suites; furnished w/ full kitchens
Rooms: 261
Baths: private
Wheelchair Access: yes, 1% of rms
Amenities: laundry, pool, hot tub

Kids: welcome; $100 deposit if 21 yrs of age or younger
Pets: some pets welcome; $300 deposit
Smoking: ok (some smokefree rms)
Rates: $89-159
AC: 10% on full rate

Warfield House B&B
Crockett

712 Houston Ave
Crockett, TX 75835
936/ 544-4037
www.warfieldhouse.net

Clientele: mixed gay/ straight
Type: b&b; "turn-of-the-century charm & elegance"; close to Big Piney Woods & antique shopping; 2 hrs from Houston or Dallas
Owned/ Run By: gay men
Rooms: 5

Baths: private
Meals: expanded cont'l brkfst
Amenities: free parking, pool, indoor hot tub, DVDs/ videos
Kids: 5 yrs up & welcome
Pets: no
Rates: $89-99

Amelia's Place
Dallas

1108 S Akard St #13
Dallas, TX 75215-1062
214/ 421-7427
www.ameliasplace.com

Clientele: gay-friendly
Type: apt; "your own completely furnished apt in downtown"; near bus & light rail; quiet, clean; generous Happy Hour & genuine Southern hospitality
Owned/ Run By: straight women
Rooms: 2
Baths: private

Meals: full brkfst
Amenities: free parking, laundry, DVDs/ videos, WiFi
Kids: no
Pets: no
Smoking: ok
Rates: $125
AC: 5%

Holiday Inn Select Dallas Central

Dallas

10650 N Central Expwy
Dallas, TX 75231
214/ 373-6000 888/ 477-STAY
www.sixcontinentshotels.com

Clientele: mixed gay/ straight
Type: hotel; 10-story luxury high-rise; all first-class amenities; centrally located
Owned/ Run By: gay & straight
Rooms: 284
Baths: private
Meals: full brkfst

Kids: welcome
Smoking: ok
Rates: $79+
AC: 10%

Melrose Hotel

Dallas

3015 Oak Lawn Ave
Dallas, TX 75219
214/ 521-5151 800/ 635-7673
www.melrosehoteldallas.com

Clientele: gay-friendly
Type: historic boutique hotel; 3 miles N of downtown in Arts & Central Business District; 4 1/2-star restaurant & popular piano bar
Owned/ Run By: straights
Rooms: 184

Baths: private
Wheelchair Access: yes, 10 rms
Pets: service dogs only
Smoking: ok (some smokefree rms)
Rates: $209-335
AC: 10%

Robinson Rainbow Resort

Dallas

2248 FM55
Waxahachie, TX 75165
972/ 937-5088
www.robinsonrainbowresort.com

Clientele: women
Type: campground; quiet country retreat near Dallas; 30 campsites & 8 RV hookups
Owned/ Run By: lesbians
Rooms: 2
Baths: shared

Meals: full brkfst
Amenities: free parking, DVDs/ videos
Kids: welcome
Pets: welcome in campsites on leash
Smoking: no

The Stoneleigh Hotel

Dallas

2927 Maple Ave
Dallas, TX 75201
214/ 871-7111
www.stoneleighhotel.com

Clientele: gay-friendly
Type: hotel; Dallas landmark since 1923
Rooms: 153
Baths: private
Wheelchair Access: yes, all rms
Amenities: laundry, gym, WiFi

Kids: welcome
Pets: welcome
Smoking: ok
Rates: $109-299
AC: 10%

Best Western InnSuites Hotel

Fort Worth

2000 Beach St
Fort Worth, TX 76103
817/ 534-4801 800/ 989-3556
www.bwsuite.com

Clientele: gay-friendly
Type: 168 suites & 16,000-sq-ft meeting rm space; located minutes from downtown Fort Worth; 1 mile from Best Friends Club gay bar
Rooms: 168
Baths: private

Wheelchair Access: yes, 5 rms
Meals: full brkfst
Amenities: outdoor hot tub
Kids: welcome
Pets: welcome
Smoking: no
Rates: $69-149

Town Creek B&B

Fredericksburg

304 N Edison
Fredericksburg, TX 78624
830/ 997-6848
www.fredericksburg-fun.com

Clientele: mixed gay/ straight
Type: b&b-inn; in historic German home, built in 1898
Owned/ Run By: straights
Baths: private

Meals: full brkfst
Pets: small pets welcome; in cottage only
Rates: $125-190

Cottage by the Gulf

Galveston

810 Ave L
Galveston, TX 77550
409/ 770-9332
cottagebythegulf.com

Clientele: gay-friendly
Type: cottage; w/ kitchen, patio; near shopping & attractions; across from Stewart Beach; pet-friendly
Owned/ Run By: gay men
Rooms: 6 (homes)
Baths: private

Wheelchair Access: yes, 1 rm
Kids: welcome
Pets: welcome; please call first
Smoking: ok
Rates: $90-170+
AC: 15%

Island Jewel B&B

Galveston

1725 Ave M
Galveston, TX 77550
409/ 763-5395 866/ 428-5395
www.islandjewelbnb.com

Clientele: mostly men
Type: b&b; beautifully restored Greek revival home; in historic area; 3 blks from Gulf of Mexico
Owned/ Run By: gay men
Rooms: 3
Baths: private & shared
Meals: expanded cont'l brkfst

Amenities: free parking, laundry, pool, poolside mist, outdoor hot tub, DVDs/ videos, WiFi
Kids: no
Pets: call for arrangement
Smoking: no
Rates: $110-150
AC: 10%

Lost Bayou Guesthouse B&B

Galveston

1607 Ave L
Galveston, TX 77550
409/ 770-0688
www.lostbayou.com

Clientele: mixed gay/ straight
Type: b&b; 1890 Victorian home that survived hurricane of 1900
Owned/ Run By: gay men
Rooms: 5
Baths: private & shared
Meals: expanded cont'l brkfst

Amenities: free parking, laundry, sauna, massage, DVDs/ videos, WiFi
Kids: 12 yrs & up welcome
Pets: no
Smoking: no
Rates: $115-145

Oasis Beach Cottage

Galveston

713/ 256-3000

Clientele: gay-friendly
Type: cottage; gulf breezes & great views from deck off the open kitchen/ dining & living areas
Owned/ Run By: gay men
Rooms: 2

Baths: private & shared
Meals: coffee/tea only
Kids: welcome
Pets: welcome
Smoking: no
Rates: $125-175 & $750-950/ week

Rainbow Ranch Campground

Groesbeck

1662 LCR 800
Groesbeck, TX 76642
254/ 729-8484 888/ 875-7596
www.rainbowranch.net

Clientele: mixed gay/ lesbian
Type: cabin, campground, RV park; fishing, billiards, darts, hiking, horse shoes & more; 74 campsites & 51 RV hookups
Owned/ Run By: gay
Wheelchair Access: yes

Kids: welcome
Pets: must be leashed
Smoking: ok in designated areas
Rates: $10-75

Circle J Ranch & Cattle Co.

Gun Barrel City

903/ 479-4189
www.circlejranchandcattlecompany.com

Clientele: mostly men
Type: gay campground on 100-acre working Texas Longhorn Cattle ranch; swimming lake on-site

Owned/ Run By: gay men
Pets: welcome
Rates: $15

The Lovett Inn
Houston

501 Lovett Blvd
Houston, TX 77006
713/ 522–5224 800/ 779–5224
www.lovettinn.com

Clientele: mixed gay/ straight
Type: b&b-inn; distinctive lodging in historic home of former Houston mayor & Federal Judge
Owned/ Run By: gay men
Rooms: 12
Baths: private
Meals: cont'l brkfst

Amenities: free parking, laundry, pool, outdoor hot tub, DVDs/ videos
Kids: by arrangement
Pets: by arrangement
Smoking: no
Rates: $90-195
AC: 10% (when made by travel agent)

Montrose Guesthouse
Houston

408 Avondale
Houston, TX 77006
713/ 520–0206 800/ 357–1228
www.montroseguesthouse.net

Clientele: mostly men
Type: b&b-inn; our slogan: "Basic & Butch"
Owned/ Run By: gay men
Rooms: 7
Baths: private & shared

Meals: full brkfst
Pets: welcome if well-behaved
Smoking: ok
Rates: $59-89
AC: 10%

Patrician B&B Inn
Houston

1200 Southmore Blvd
Houston, TX 77004-5826
713/ 523–1114 800/ 553–5797
www.texasbnb.com

Clientele: gay-friendly
Type: b&b-inn; 1919 three-story mansion; centrally located between downtown Houston & Texas Medical Center
Owned/ Run By: women
Rooms: 4

Meals: full brkfst
Kids: 11 yrs & up welcome
Rates: $95-150
AC: 10%

Seldom Rest Ranch
Mission

3900 Bentsen Palm Dr
Mission, TX 75874
956/ 585–1215
bobbrixey@aol.com

Clientele: gay-friendly
Type: RV park; 33 hookups; located 10 miles outside of Mexico & 1 hr from the beach; secluded area
Owned/ Run By: gay men
Rooms: 3
Wheelchair Access: yes, 3 rms

Amenities: free parking, laundry, outdoor hot tub, DVDs/ videos
Kids: welcome
Pets: welcome
Smoking: ok
Rates: $10-30/ night; $165-500/ month
AC: 10%

The Veranda
Mt Vernon

3264 County Rd SE 4115
Mt Vernon, TX 75457
903/ 588–2402
www.ourveranda.com

Clientele: mixed gay/ straight
Type: b&b; in spacious luxury accommodations w/ gourmet dining (Fri-Sat); on 68 acres of East Texas scenery w/ 4.5 acres of pond for fishing & boating
Rooms: 3
Baths: private

Meals: full brkfst
Amenities: free parking, pool, hot tub, DVDs/ videos, gym, WiFi
Kids: welcome
Smoking: no
Rates: $150

The Belles by the Sea
Port Aransas

1501 S 11th St
Port Aransas, TX 78373
361/ 749–6138
www.bellespa.com

Clientele: mixed gay/ straight
Type: Euro-style inn w/ a New Orleans flair & a touch of Old Mexico; on dunes of Mustang Island & Port Aransas
Owned/ Run By: women
Rooms: 15
Baths: private

Amenities: pool, hot tub
Kids: welcome; please call first
Pets: welcome
Smoking: no
Rates: $89-145

Adams House B&B
San Antonio

231 Adams St
San Antonio, TX 78210
210/ 224-4791 800/ 666-4810
www.adams-house.com

Clientele: mixed gay/ straight
Type: b&b-private home; 3-story 1902 Italianate-style; in King William Historic District; walk to Alamo, Riverwalk, shopping & nightlife
Owned/ Run By: straights
Rooms: 6
Baths: private

Meals: full brkfst
Amenities: free parking, hot tub, massage, WiFi
Kids: 12 yrs & up welcome
Pets: no
Smoking: no
Rates: $99-169
AC: 8%

Alamo Lodge
San Antonio

1126 E Elmira
San Antonio, TX 78212
210/ 222-9463
www.alamolodge.com

Clientele: gay-friendly
Type: motel; clean & quiet; very close to downtown
Rooms: 70
Baths: private
Meals: coffee/tea only

Amenities: indoor hot tub
Kids: welcome
Pets: welcome
Smoking: ok
Rates: $34-69
AC: 10%

Arbor House Suites B&B
San Antonio

109 Arciniega
San Antonio, TX 78205
210/ 472-2005 888/ 272-6700
www.arborhouse.com

Clientele: mixed gay/ straight
Type: b&b-inn; divided among 4 century-old houses; all share rear courtyard w/ large grape arbor
Owned/ Run By: gay men
Rooms: 8 (suites)
Baths: private

Meals: expanded cont'l brkfst
Amenities: free parking, laundry, hot tub
Kids: welcome
Pets: welcome; $50 deposit
Smoking: no
Rates: $125-150

Fiesta B&B
San Antonio

1823 Saunders Ave
San Antonio, TX 78207
210/ 226-5548 210/ 887-0074
fiestabandb@sbcglobal.net

Clientele: mostly men
Type: b&b-private home
Owned/ Run By: gay men
Rooms: 3
Baths: private & shared
Meals: full brkfst

Amenities: free parking, laundry, WiFi
Kids: welcome
Pets: no
Smoking: no
Rates: $95-125

The Painted Lady Inn on Broadway
San Antonio

620 Broadway
San Antonio, TX 78215
210/ 220-1092
www.thepaintedladyinn.com

Clientele: mixed gay/ lesbian
Type: luxurious downtown inn; in historic 1920s neo-classical apt bldg; 6 blks from the River Walk
Owned/ Run By: lesbians/ gay men
Rooms: 8
Baths: private

Meals: full brkfst
Amenities: free parking, laundry, outdoor hot tub, massage, DVDs/ videos
Kids: welcome
Pets: welcome; $15/ day
Rates: $109-229
AC: 10%

English Bay Marina
Shelbyville

186 D English Ln
Shelbyville, TX 75973
936/ 368-2554
www.toledo-bend.net/englishbay

Clientele: mixed gay/ straight
Type: motel; w/ cabins & 20 RV hookups; marina w/ store, boat ramp & fishing pier
Owned/ Run By: lesbians
Rooms: 7

Baths: private
Kids: welcome
Pets: welcome
Smoking: ok
Rates: $35-50

New Upper Deck Hotel & Bar

South Padre Island

PO Box 2309
South Padre Island, TX 78597

956/ 761-5953

www.upperdeckhotel.com

Clientele: mostly men
Type: resort; on South Padre Island on the Gulf of Mexico; gay beach 1/2 blk away w/ clothing-optional areas
Owned/ Run By: gay men
Nearby Attractions: 30 minutes to nude beach, Mexico, Gladys Porter Zoo; 15 minutes to golf course & wildlife reserve
Transit: 35 minutes to Brownsville, TX; 60 minutes to Harlingen, TX
Rooms: 21 total, 9 kings, 13 queens, A/C, color TV (17), cable TV (17), ceiling fan (20), deck (17), safer sex supplies, rm service, maid service
Baths: private & shared, bathtubs, showers
Wheelchair Access: yes, 3 rms
Meals: expanded cont'l brkfst
Amenities: office hrs: 9am-6pm; free parking, laundry, pool, outdoor hot tub, DVDs/ videos, cocktails, coffee/ tea, restaurant & rm service, community kitchen; hot tub is always clothing-optional
Recreation: steps to gay beach, sailing, parasailing, horseback riding, fishing, dolphin-watching

Pets: welcome
Smoking: ok
Reservations: recommended *Deposit:* required, 1 night, due at booking *Cancellation:* cancel by 1 week prior or forfeit deposit *Minimum Stay:* 3 nights (holidays) *Check in/ out:* 3pm/ 11am

Payment: cash, travelers checks, Visa, Amex, MC, Discover
Season: open yr-round *High season:* June-Aug
Rates: $50-250

Bella Vista

Wimberley

2121 Hilltop
Wimberley, TX 78676
512/ 847-6425
www.texhillcntry.com/bellavista

Clientele: mixed gay/ straight
Type: b&b; beautiful home on hilltop; w/ gorgeous view of the Wimberley Valley & Texas Hill Country
Owned/ Run By: gay men
Rooms: 2

Baths: private
Meals: expanded cont'l brkfst
Kids: special circumstances only
Pets: special circumstances only
Smoking: no
Rates: $95-125

The Red Brick Inn of Panguitch B&B

Bryce Canyon

161 N 100 West
Panguitch, UT 84759
435/ 676-2141 866/ 733-2745
www.redbrickinnutah.com/

Clientele: gay-friendly
Type: b&b-private home; circa 1930s Dutch Colonial brick home was the area's first hospital; very casual atmosphere; close to Bryce Canyon, Zion & lots of hiking
Owned/ Run By: straights
Rooms: 6

Baths: private & shared
Meals: full brkfst
Kids: welcome
Pets: no
Rates: $89-199

Rainbow Country B&B

Escalante

585 E 300 S
Escalante, UT 84726
435/ 826-4567 800/ 252-8824
www.color-country.net/~rainbow/

Clientele: gay-friendly
Type: b&b-private home; scenic, quiet, relaxing & friendly; great location
Owned/ Run By: straights
Rooms: 4
Baths: private
Meals: full brkfst

Amenities: free parking, outdoor hot tub, DVDs/ videos
Kids: welcome
Pets: welcome
Smoking: no
Rates: $60-80
AC: 10%

Los Vados Canyon House
Moab

801/ 971-5304
www.losvados.com

Clientele: mixed gay/ straight
Type: rental home; 15 miles from Moab; in red rock canyon beside yr-round creek; accommodates 1-4 people; tent cabin $25/ night when you rent main cabin
Owned/ Run By: gay men
Rooms: 2

Baths: private
Meals: coffee/tea only
Kids: 11 yrs & up welcome
Smoking: no
Rates: $250
AC: 10%

Mayor's House B&B
Moab

505 Rose Tree Ln
Moab, UT 84532
435/ 259-6015 888/ 791-2345
www.mayorshouse.com

Clientele: gay-friendly
Type: b&b-private home; in heart of canyonlands; near downtown Moab, restaurants & shopping
Owned/ Run By: gay men
Rooms: 6
Baths: private
Meals: full brkfst

Amenities: free parking, pool, outdoor hot tub, DVDs/ videos
Kids: welcome
Pets: no
Smoking: no
Rates: $90-200
AC: 10%

Mt Peale Resort Inn/ Spa/ Cabins
Moab

1415 E Hwy 46 (at mile marker 14.1)
Old La Sal, UT 84530
435/ 686-2284 888/ 687-3253
www.mtpeale.com

Clientele: mixed gay/ straight
Type: b&b-inn; cabins; near Moab/ Arches Nat'l Park & Canyonlands; 93 miles to Telluride
Owned/ Run By: lesbians
Rooms: 6 rms & 6 cabins
Baths: private
Wheelchair Access: yes, 1 rm

Meals: full brkfst
Amenities: free parking, laundry, outdoor hot tub, massage
Kids: welcome in cabins only
Pets: 1 dog-friendly cabin
Smoking: no
Rates: $79-199
AC: 10%

Red Cliffs Lodge
Moab

Hwy 128
Moab, UT 84532
435/ 259-2002 866/ 812-2002
www.redcliffslodge.com

Clientele: gay-friendly
Type: resort; on banks of Colorado River; full-service restaurant, winery
Owned/ Run By: straights
Rooms: 70 (w/ private river patios)
Baths: private
Wheelchair Access: yes, 1 rm

Amenities: free parking, laundry, pool, outdoor hot tub, massage
Kids: welcome
Pets: no
Smoking: no
Rates: $99-269
AC: 10%

North Fork B&B
Ogden

PO Box 809
Eden, UT 84310
801/ 540-5490
www.northforkguesthouse.ourfamily.com

Clientele: mostly men
Type: guesthouse; 4,000-sq-ft mtn home; views of Wasatch Nat'l Forest
Owned/ Run By: gay men
Rooms: 3
Baths: private & shared
Meals: cont'l brkfst

Amenities: free parking, laundry, enclosed outdoor hot tub
Kids: welcome
Pets: please inquire
Smoking: no
Rates: $75-150
AC: 10%

Anton Boxrud B&B
Salt Lake City

57 S 600 E
Salt Lake City, UT 84102
801/ 363-8035 800/ 524-5511
www.antonboxrud.com

Clientele: gay-friendly
Type: b&b-inn; traditional 3-story Victorian: beveled & leaded glass windows, oak fireplaces & lace
Owned/ Run By: women
Rooms: 7

Baths: private & shared
Meals: full brkfst
Amenities: free parking, outdoor hot tub
Kids: 10 yrs & up; must be prearranged
Rates: $72-150
AC: 10%

Hotel Monaco Salt Lake City

Salt Lake City

15 W 200 S
Salt Lake City, UT 84101
801/ 595-0000 877/ 294-9710
www.monaco-saltlakecity.com

Type: hotel; beautifully restored historic landmark; stylish & sophisticated; gracious & upbeat service; welcoming all travelers
Rooms: 225
Baths: private
Wheelchair Access: yes, 9 rms
Meals: coffee/tea only
Kids: welcome
Pets: welcome

Smoking: ok (in designated rms only)
Rates: $109-239
AC: 10%

Parrish Place

Salt Lake City

720 E Ashton Ave
Salt Lake City, UT 84106
801/ 832-0970 888/ 832-0869
www.parrishpl.com

Clientele: mixed gay/ straight
Type: b&b; 1890 historic Victorian mansion; w/ sundeck & conservatory
Owned/ Run By: gay men
Rooms: 5
Baths: private
Meals: expanded cont'l brkfst
Amenities: free parking, outdoor hot tub, DVDs/ videos

Kids: no
Pets: no
Smoking: no
Rates: $99-119
AC: 10%

Peery Hotel

Salt Lake City

110 W 300 S
Salt Lake City, UT 84101
801/ 521-4300 800/ 331-0073
www.peeryhotel.com

Clientele: gay-friendly
Type: hotel; also 2 bars & full bar
Owned/ Run By: straights
Rooms: 77
Baths: private
Meals: cont'l brkfst
Amenities: free parking, laundry, hot tub
Kids: welcome

Pets: $20/ day
Rates: $90-190
AC: 10%

Under the Lindens

Salt Lake City

128 S 1000 E
Salt Lake City, UT 84102
801/ 355-9808
www.underthelindens.com

Clientele: mostly men
Type: studio; all units have private kitchen; some w/ jacuzzi tubs & heated flooring on lower flrs; backyard for commitment ceremonies; DSL hookups
Owned/ Run By: gay men
Rooms: 4 (studios)
Baths: private
Meals: cont'l brkfst

Amenities: free parking, laundry, outdoor hot tub, DVDs/ videos
Kids: no
Pets: no
Smoking: no
Rates: $125-150
AC: 10%

SkyRidge Inn B&B

Torrey

950 E Hwy 24
Torrey, UT 84775
435/ 425-3222 800/ 448-6990
www.skyridgeinn.com

Clientele: gay-friendly
Type: b&b-inn; on 75 acres w/ unparalleled views; 2 rms w/ private hot tubs; rated AAA 4 Diamonds
Owned/ Run By: straights
Rooms: 6
Baths: private
Meals: full brkfst

Amenities: outdoor hot tub, DVDs/ videos
Kids: over 10 yrs welcome in main house; families w/ younger kids in Tumbleweed Suite
Smoking: no
Rates: $95-155

Torrey Inn Econo Lodge

Torrey

600 E Hwy 24
Torrey, UT 84775
435/ 425-3688
www.torreylodging.com

Clientele: gay-friendly
Type: economy lodging
Rooms: 35
Baths: private
Wheelchair Access: yes, 2 rms
Meals: expanded cont'l brkfst
Amenities: free parking, laundry, pool, hot
tub, WiFi

Kids: welcome
Pets: welcome in some rms
Smoking: no
Rates: $39-82

Red Rock Inn

Zion Nat'l Park

998 Zion Park Blvd
Springdale, UT 84767
435/ 772-3139
www.redrockinn.com

Clientele: mixed gay/ straight
Type: b&b, cottage; newly constructed; all
w/ canyon views & spas; brkfst basket
delivered to your door
Owned/ Run By: lesbians
Rooms: 5
Baths: private
Wheelchair Access: yes, 1 rm

Meals: full brkfst
Kids: welcome w/ prior approval
Pets: no
Smoking: no
Rates: $85-225

Canyon Vista B&B

Zion National Park

2175 Zion Park Blvd
Springdale, UT 84767
435/ 772-3801
www.canyonvistabandb.com

Clientele: gay-friendly
Type: b&b; 1.2 acre property on Virgin River
Owned/ Run By: straights
Rooms: 4
Baths: private
Meals: full brkfst
Amenities: free parking, outdoor hot tub,
DVDs/ videos

Kids: no
Pets: no
Smoking: no
Rates: $85-120

Arlington Inn

Arlington

Historic Rte 7-A
Arlington, VT
802/ 375-6532 800/ 443-9442
www.arlingtoninn.com

Clientele: gay-friendly
Type: elegant country inn; fireplaces, jacuzzi
tubs; full-service restaurant & tavern;
country gardens; civil unions & special
events
Rooms: 18
Baths: private
Wheelchair Access: yes, 1 rm
Meals: full brkfst

Amenities: free parking, WiFi
Kids: welcome
Pets: no
Smoking: no
Rates: $125-315
AC: 10%

Hummingbird Haven

Berkshire

956 Richford Rd
Richford, VT 05476
802/ 848-7037
www.hummingbirdhavenvt.com

Clientele: gay-friendly
Type: b&b-inn; elegant 735-square-ft guest
rm w/ views; in beautiful 1843 Greek
Revival nestled at base of Green Mtns
Owned/ Run By: lesbians
Rooms: 1
Baths: private
Meals: full brkfst
Kids: no

Pets: dogs, only in patio rm; $30 charge
Smoking: no
Rates: $90

The Black Bear Inn

Burlington

4010 Bolton Access Rd
Bolton Valley, VT 05477

802/ 434-2126
800/ 395-6335

www.blkbearinn.com

Clientele: mixed gay/ straight
Type: b&b-inn; 28-rm mtn-top country inn; at 2,000 ft above the valley flr; 6,000 private acres to explore; private hot tubs & fireplaces; civil unions performed
Owned/ Run By: straights
Nearby Attractions: 45 minutes to Canada; Ben & Jerry's, historical sites, nightclubs, cider mills, maple sugar houses
Pickup Service: airport pickup; $10-15
Transit: 18 minutes to Burlington Int'l
Rooms: 28 total, 4 suites, 2 kings, 20 queens, A/C (12), color TV, DVD/ VCR, cable, ceiling fan, fireplace, deck, phone, refrigerator, maid service, country decor, homemade quilts, flowering balconies
Baths: private, bathtubs, showers, whirlpools, robes, hairdryers
Meals: full brkfst, also dinner menu
Amenities: pool, indoor & outdoor hot tub, DVDs/ videos, gym, WiFi, snacks, coffee/ tea, private hot tubs, skiing out of slopeside inn, bar & restaurant, kennel
Kids: welcome

Pets: welcome
Smoking: no
Reservations: required *Deposit:* required, 1-3 nights, due at booking *Cancellation:* cancel by 21 days prior or forfeit 1 night + $25 *Check in/ out:* 3:30pm/ 11am

Payment: cash, travelers checks, Visa, MC
Season: open yr-round *High season:* Sept 15-Oct 15
Rates: $104-325
AC: 10%

The Inn at Essex

Burlington

70 Essex Way
Essex, VT 05452
802/ 878-1100 800/ 727-4295
www.VTCulinaryResort.com

Clientele: gay-friendly
Type: hotel; Vermont's culinary resort, featuring acclaimed New England Culinary Institute; on-site golf, tennis
Owned/ Run By: straights
Rooms: 120
Baths: private
Wheelchair Access: yes, 12 rms

Meals: full brkfst
Amenities: pool, massage, gym, WiFi
Kids: welcome
Pets: welcome; $25 refundable deposit
Smoking: ok
Rates: $159-499
AC: 10%

One of a Kind B&B

Burlington

53 Lakeview Terrace
Burlington, VT 05401
802/ 862-5576 877/ 479-2736
www.oneofakindbnb.com

Clientele: mixed gay/ straight
Type: b&b; 2-rm suite w/ view of lake & sunsets; tree swing in back; friendly cat on premises
Owned/ Run By: woman
Rooms: 2
Baths: private & shared

Meals: expanded cont'l brkfst
Amenities: free parking, massage, WiFi
Kids: must be watched
Pets: must be watched
Smoking: no
Rates: $90-120

Wyndham Burlington

Burlington

60 Battery St
Burlington, VT 05401
802/ 658-6500
www.wyndhamburlington.com

Clientele: gay-friendly
Type: full-service hotel; in downtown; lake & mtn views; walk to Church St marketplace & lakeside activities
Owned/ Run By: gay & straight
Rooms: 256
Baths: private
Wheelchair Access: yes, 6 rms

Meals: coffee/tea only
Amenities: laundry, pool, hot tub
Kids: welcome
Pets: no
Smoking: no
Rates: $159-289
AC: 10%

Chester House Inn
Chester

266 Main St
Chester, VT 05143
802/ 875-2205　888/ 875-2205
www.chesterhouseinn.com

Clientele: mixed gay/ straight
Type: b&b-inn; circa 1780; located on village green; close to skiing & other recreation
Owned/ Run By: gay men
Rooms: 7
Baths: private
Wheelchair Access: yes, 1 rm

Meals: full brkfst
Amenities: free parking, WiFi
Kids: welcome
Pets: no
Smoking: no
Rates: $99-195
AC: 10%

Greenhope Farm
Craftsbury Common

2478 Wylie Hill Rd
Craftsbury Common, VT 05827
802/ 586-7577
www.greenhopefarm.com

Clientele: mostly women
Type: lesbian b&b in VT since 1982; horseback riding, kayaking, near lakes & skiing
Owned/ Run By: lesbian
Rooms: 4
Baths: private & shared

Wheelchair Access: yes, 1 rm
Meals: full brkfst
Kids: welcome
Pets: please inquire
Smoking: no
Rates: $75-135

Highland Lodge
Greensboro

1608 Craftsbury Rd
Greensboro, VT 05841
802/ 533-2647
www.highlandlodge.com

Clientele: gay-friendly
Type: resort; open 5/28-10/25 & 12/21-3/15; 50km groomed x-country skiing; private beach & boats
Owned/ Run By: straights
Rooms: 11 rooms & 11 cottages
Baths: private

Wheelchair Access: yes, 2 rms
Meals: full brkfst (also dinner)
Kids: welcome
Pets: no
Smoking: no
Rates: $125-550
AC: 10%

Four Seasons Apartments
Jay Peak

10 Elm St
North Troy, VT 05859
802/ 578-7103
www.jaypeakskiing.com/elm2.htm

Clientele: mixed gay/ straight
Type: apt; affordable, spacious vacation rental; in quaint N Vermont town; just minutes from ski slopes of Jay Peak resort
Owned/ Run By: straights
Rooms: 2-bdrm apt (sleeps up to 6)

Baths: shared
Kids: welcome
Pets: no
Smoking: no
Rates: $100-250
AC: 10%

Grey Gables Mansion
Jay Peak

122 River St
Richford, VT 05476
802/ 848-3625　800/ 299-2117
www.greygablesmansion.com

Clientele: gay-friendly
Type: b&b; 1888 Queen Anne Victorian; on Canadian border; 1 hr from Montréal & Burlington, civil union packages available
Owned/ Run By: straights
Rooms: 5
Baths: private

Meals: full brkfst
Amenities: free parking, DVDs/ videos, WiFi
Kids: welcome
Pets: no
Rates: $79-139
AC: 10%

Donomar Inn
Jeffersonville

916 Rte 108 S
Jeffersonville, VT 05464
802/ 644-2937
www.donomarinn.com

Clientele: gay-friendly
Type: 1865 inn; views of Mt Mansfield; homemade afternoon treats; near theater, galleries, skiing, canoeing
Owned/ Run By: lesbians
Rooms: 6
Baths: private & shared
Meals: full brkfst

Amenities: free parking, laundry, outdoor hot tub, massage, DVDs/ videos, WiFi
Kids: over 13 yrs & w/ adult
Pets: no
Smoking: no
Rates: $80-210
AC: 10%

Cortina Inn & Resort

Killington

Rte 4
Killington, VT 05751
802/ 773-3333 800/ 451-6108
www.cortinainn.com

Clientele: gay-friendly
Type: resort; Vermont's scenic beauty draws visitors from all over New England & beyond
Owned/ Run By: straights
Rooms: 96
Baths: private
Wheelchair Access: yes, 5 rms

Meals: full brkfst
Amenities: free parking, laundry, pool, sauna, indoor hot tub, massage, gym, WiFi
Kids: welcome; $8 for brkfst (14 yrs & under)
Pets: small pets welcome; $10 per pet
Rates: $99-239 double
AC: 10%

Salt Ash Inn

Killington

4758 Rte 100A
Plymouth, VT 05056
802/ 672-3748 800/ 725-8274
www.saltashinn.com

Clientele: mixed gay/ straight
Type: b&b-inn; historic rural inn w/ citified service: DSL & WiFi, CTV, phones in all rms; monthly all-male wknds; full bar
Owned/ Run By: straights
Rooms: 17
Baths: private

Meals: full brkfst
Amenities: outdoor hot tub, DVDs/ videos
Kids: 5 yrs & up welcome
Pets: welcome; 5 rms available
Rates: $109-289
AC: 15%

Cavendish Inn

Ludlow

1589 Main St
Cavendish, VT 05142
802/ 226-7080 877/ 282-7460
www.cavendishinnvt.com

Clientele: gay-friendly
Type: inn; at the historic Glimmerstone Mansion; "refined country atmosphere"; fine dining
Owned/ Run By: gay & straight

Rooms: 9
Baths: private
Wheelchair Access: yes
Rates: $50-260

Happy Trails Motel

Ludlow

321 Rte 103 S
Ludlow, VT 05149
802/ 228-8888 800/ 228-9984
www.happytrailsmotel.com

Clientele: gay-friendly
Type: motel; four seasons; 1 1/2 miles from Okemo Mtn; ski packages; groups welcome
Owned/ Run By: straights
Rooms: 27 (also 2-bdrm cottage)
Baths: private

Meals: coffee/tea only
Amenities: free parking, indoor hot tub
Kids: welcome
Smoking: ok
Rates: $65-425
AC: 10%

Hill Farm Inn

Manchester

458 Hill Farm Rd
Arlington, VT 05250
802/ 375-2269 800/ 882-2545
www.hillfarminn.com

Clientele: gay-friendly
Type: b&b; spectacular views from 50 acres on Battenhill River; romantic country rms, suites & cabins; walking trails, fly-fishing, farm animals
Owned/ Run By: straights

Rooms: 15
Baths: private
Meals: full brkfst
Kids: welcome
Rates: $100-220
AC: 10%

Colonel Williams Inn

Marlboro

Rte 9
Marlboro, VT 05344
802/ 257-1093
www.colonelwilliamsinn.com

Clientele: mixed gay/ straight
Type: b&b-inn; circa 1769 Colonial farmhouse; on 9 acres w/ pond; fine dining; chef-owned & operated
Owned/ Run By: straights
Rooms: 13
Baths: private
Wheelchair Access: yes, 1 rm

Meals: full brkfst
Amenities: outdoor hot tub, DVDs/ videos
Kids: welcome
Pets: welcome in Carriage House rms only
Smoking: no
Rates: $100-250
AC: 10%

Marshfield Inn & Motel
Marshfield

5630 US Rte 2
Marshfield, VT 05658
802/ 426-3383
www.marshfieldinn.com

Clientele: gay-friendly
Type: motel; country lodging in a serene mtn setting; great views of the Green Mtns & Winooski River
Owned/ Run By: lesbians
Rooms: 10
Baths: private

Amenities: free parking, WiFi
Kids: welcome
Pets: welcome in 2 rms; $10 fee
Smoking: no
Rates: $60-95

Phineas Swann B&B
Montgomery Center

195 Main St
Montgomery Center, VT 05471
802/ 326-4306
www.phineasswann.com

Clientele: mixed gay/ straight
Type: b&b-inn; "a light-hearted country b&b offering jacuzzi suites & a gourmet brkfst to die for!"; free telephone & cable TV
Owned/ Run By: gay men
Rooms: 9
Baths: private

Meals: full brkfst
Amenities: hot tub, DVDs/ videos, WiFi
Kids: 6 yrs & up welcome
Pets: welcome w/ prior approval
Smoking: no
Rates: $99-295
AC: 10%

The Inn of the Six Mountains
Rutland

2617 Killington Rd
Killington, VT 05751
802/ 422-4302 800/ 228-4676
www.sixmountains.com

Clientele: gay-friendly
Type: hotel; nestled amid peaks of world-famous Killington; charm of country inn w/ amenities of full-service resort
Owned/ Run By: straights
Rooms: 103
Baths: private
Wheelchair Access: yes, 18 rms

Meals: full brkfst
Amenities: pool, sauna, hot tub, massage
Kids: welcome
Pets: no
Smoking: ok
Rates: $99-249
AC: 10%

Lilac Inn
Rutland

53 Park St
Brandon, VT 05733
802/ 247-5463 800/ 221-0720
www.lilacinn.com

Type: b&b-inn; a leading romantic destination for weddings & civil unions, Middlebury College events, Killington winter & summer recreation & corporate retreats
Rooms: 9

Baths: private
Wheelchair Access: yes, all rms
Meals: full brkfst
Kids: 12 yrs & up welcome
Rates: $145-295
AC: 10%

Maplewood Inn
Rutland

Rte 22A South
Fair Haven, VT 05743
802/ 265-8039 800/ 253-7729
www.maplewoodinn.net

Clientele: mixed gay/ straight
Type: b&b-inn; beautiful 1843 Greek Revival; at base of Green Mtns; "close to all Vermont's treasures & pleasures"
Owned/ Run By: straights
Rooms: 5
Baths: private

Meals: full brkfst
Kids: welcome
Pets: welcome only in patio rm; $30 charge
Smoking: no
Rates: $110-250
AC: 10%

The Inn at Saxtons River
Saxtons River

27 Main St
Saxtons River, VT 05154
802/ 869-2110
www.innsaxtonsriver.com

Clientele: gay-friendly
Type: b&b-inn; historic Victorian inn w/ charming pub & restaurant; located in quaint New England village
Owned/ Run By: gay men
Rooms: 16
Baths: private

Meals: expanded cont'l brkfst
Kids: welcome
Pets: no
Rates: $110-150

The Green Mountain Inn — *Stowe*

18 Main St
Stowe, VT 05672
802/ 253-7301 800/ 253-7302
www.greenmountaininn.com

Clientele: gay-friendly
Type: hotel; restored 1833 private residence in the heart of Stowe Village; some rms w/ canopy beds; fireside jacuzzis; health club; 2 restaurants
Rooms: 105

Wheelchair Access: yes
Amenities: free parking, pool, sauna, hot tub, massage, DVDs/ videos, gym, WiFi
Kids: welcome
Rates: $119-729
AC: 10%

Honeywood Inn — *Stowe*

4527 Mountain Rd
Stowe, VT 05672
802/ 253-4846 800/ 821-7891
www.honeywoodinn.com

Type: b&b-inn; cozy inn w/ antiques, large individually decorated rms; on 9 peaceful acres
Rooms: 10 (includes 2 suites w/ jacuzzi tub)
Baths: private
Meals: full brkfst
Amenities: free parking, pool, outdoor hot

tub, massage, DVDs/ videos
Kids: 11 yrs & up welcome
Pets: no
Smoking: no
Rates: $109-249
AC: 10%

Northern Lights Lodge — *Stowe*

4441 Mountain Rd
Stowe, VT 05672
802/ 253-8541 800/ 448-4554
www.stowelodge.com

Clientele: gay-friendly
Type: b&b-inn; great amenities & location; full-service wedding planners for your civil union commitment
Owned/ Run By: gay men
Rooms: 50
Baths: private

Meals: full brkfst
Amenities: free parking, laundry, pool, sauna, indoor hot tub, DVDs/ videos
Kids: welcome
Pets: welcome
Rates: $58-198
AC: 10%

Timberholm Inn — *Stowe*

452 Cottage Club Rd
Stowe, VT 05672
802/ 253-7603 800/ 753-7603
www.timberholm.com

Clientele: mixed gay/ straight
Type: b&b-inn; nestled on 4 acres of woods overlooking mtns; large common area w/ fireplace; 1 mile from Stowe Village & ski resorts
Owned/ Run By: gay men
Rooms: 10
Baths: private

Meals: full brkfst
Amenities: free parking, outdoor hot tub, DVDs/ videos
Kids: welcome
Pets: no
Smoking: no
Rates: $89-179

Winding Brook, A Classic Mountain Lodge — *Stowe*

199 Edson Hill Rd
Stowe, VT 05672
802/ 253-7354 800/ 426-6697
www.windingbrooklodge.com

Clientele: mixed gay/ straight
Type: rustic mtn retreat, massive fieldstone fireplace, wood flrs, antiques
Owned/ Run By: gay men
Rooms: 15
Baths: private
Wheelchair Access: yes, 1 rm

Meals: full brkfst
Amenities: pool, outdoor hot tub
Kids: welcome
Pets: no
Smoking: no
Rates: $85-195 + 12% service charge
AC: 10%

Grünberg Haus B&B & Cabins — *Waterbury*

94 Pine St, Rte 100 S
Waterbury, VT 05676
802/ 244-7726 800/ 800-7760
www.grunberghaus.com

Clientele: mixed gay/ lesbian
Type: b&b; Austrian chalet on secluded hillside in Vermont's Green Mtns; plus secluded cabins
Rooms: 14
Baths: private & shared

Meals: full brkfst
Kids: 5 yrs & up welcome
Pets: welcome in cabins only
Smoking: no
Rates: $70-185
AC: 10%

Moose Meadow Lodge

Waterbury

507 Crossett Hill
Waterbury, VT 05676
802/ 244-5378
www.moosemeadowlodge.com

Clientele: mixed gay/ straight
Type: b&b; 4,000-sq-ft, Adirondack-style log home; on private 86-acre wooded estate; spectacular mtn views
Owned/ Run By: gay men
Rooms: 4
Baths: private

Meals: full brkfst
Amenities: free parking, indoor hot tub, massage, DVDs/ videos, WiFi
Rates: $129-169

The Gargoyle House

Wells River

3351 Wallace Hill Rd
Wells River, VT 05081
802/ 429-2341
www.gargoylehouse.com

Clientele: men
Type: clothing-optional retreat on a 16-acre forest
Owned/ Run By: gay men
Rooms: 4
Baths: private & shared
Amenities: free parking, laundry, sauna,

DVDs/ videos, gym, WiFi
Pets: in private rooms only
Rates: $40-100

Deerhill Inn

West Dover

PO Box 136
West Dover, VT 05356
802/ 464-3100   800/ 993-3379
www.deerhill.com

Clientele: mixed gay/ straight
Type: inn; restaurant on-site
Rooms: 14
Baths: private
Meals: full brkfst
Kids: 13 yrs & up welcome

Pets: no
Smoking: no
Rates: $130-345

Red Oak Inn

West Dover

45 Rte 100
West Dover, VT 05356
802/ 464-8817
www.redoakinn.com

Clientele: gay-friendly
Type: b&b; country inn on 3 beautifully landscaped acres; also tavern & gamerm w/ billiards; AAA approved
Owned/ Run By: gay men
Rooms: 24
Baths: private

Meals: full brkfst
Kids: welcome
Pets: welcome w/ prior approval; $30 fee (per stay)
Rates: $85-269
AC: 10%

A Stone Wall Inn

Windham

RFD 133
Windham, VT 05359
802/ 875-4238
www.astonewallinn.com

Clientele: mixed gay/ straight
Type: b&b-inn; extensive gardens & ponds; located in the heart of the southern Green Mtns 4-season resort area
Owned/ Run By: gay men
Rooms: 10
Baths: private & shared

Meals: expanded cont'l brkfst
Amenities: free parking, sauna, indoor hot tub
Smoking: no
Rates: $125-175

The Ardmore Inn

Woodstock

23 Pleasant St
Woodstock, VT 05091-0466
802/ 457-3887   800/ 497-9652
www.ArdmoreInn.com

Clientele: gay-friendly
Type: b&b; elegant Greek Revival house; in historic district near covered bridge, shops, attractions
Rooms: 5
Baths: private
Meals: full brkfst

Amenities: free parking, hot tub, WiFi
Kids: no
Pets: no
Smoking: no
Rates: $135-195
AC: 10% (except Sept-Oct)

Cabin in the Woods   *Woodstock*

PO Box 368
Bridgewater Corners, VT 05035
802/ 672–5141 (no calls after 9pm EST)

Clientele: gay-friendly
Type: cabin; luxurious, secluded, fully furnished; for 2 people only; w/ swimming hole & 86' waterfall/ gorge; no neighbors; seasonal May-Oct; phone for color brochure
Owned/ Run By: transgender
Rooms: 1 (5-rm cabin)
Baths: private

Meals: coffee/tea only
Amenities: free parking, indoor hot tub
Kids: no
Pets: welcome w/ prior approval
Smoking: no (except outdoors)
Rates: $225
AC: 10-15%

Deer Brook Inn   *Woodstock*

535 Woodstock Rd
Woodstock, VT 05091
802/ 672–3713
www.deerbrookinn.com

Clientele: gay-friendly
Type: b&b; circa 1820 colonial farmhouse on 5 acres along Ottauquechee River; near skiing, Dartmouth, lakes & antiquing
Owned/ Run By: gay men
Rooms: 5
Baths: private
Meals: full brkfst
Kids: welcome

Pets: no
Smoking: no
Rates: $105-165
AC: 10%

Village Inn of Woodstock   *Woodstock*

41 Pleasant St
Woodstock, VT 05091
802/ 457–1255 800/ 722–4571
www.villageinnofwoodstock.com

Clientele: gay-friendly
Type: restored Victorian inn; romantic rms w/ period antiques
Owned/ Run By: straights
Rooms: 7
Baths: private
Meals: full brkfst
Kids: over 14 yrs of age welcome
Pets: no

Smoking: no
Rates: $120-300

Column Wood B&B   *Bowling Green*

233 N Main St
Bowling Green, VA 22427
804/ 633–5606 866/ 633–9314
www.columnwood.com

Clientele: gay-friendly
Type: b&b; warm, elegant, historic home; spacious rms; modern amenities; queen- or king-size beds; fireplaces; btwn Richmond & Frendricksburg
Owned/ Run By: gay men
Rooms: 4
Baths: private
Meals: full brkfst

Amenities: free parking, DVDs/ videos, WiFi
Kids: no
Pets: please inquire
Smoking: no
Rates: $80-110

Cape Charles House B&B   *Cape Charles*

645 Tazewell Ave
Cape Charles, VA 23310
757/ 331–4920
www.capecharleshouse.com

Clientele: gay-friendly
Type: b&b; elegant 1912 Colonial Revival home filled w/ antiques; featured on Home & Garden TV
Owned/ Run By: straights
Rooms: 5
Baths: private
Meals: full brkfst
Amenities: free parking, hot tub, DVDs/

videos
Smoking: no
Rates: $100-160
AC: 10%

Sea Gate B&B   Cape Charles

9 Tazewell Ave
Cape Charles, VA 23310
757/ 331-2206
www.bbhost.com/seagate

Clientele: gay-friendly
Type: b&b-private home; restored 1912 Colonial Revival house; steps from the beach; afternoon tea served; cable TV; "a perfect place to rest, relax & recharge"
Rooms: 4
Baths: private & shared
Meals: full brkfst
Kids: 7 yrs & up welcome

Pets: no
Smoking: no
Rates: $95-110
AC: 10%

Sterling House B&B   Cape Charles

9 Randolph Ave
Cape Charles, VA 23310
757/ 331-2483
www.sterling-inn.com

Clientele: mixed gay/ straight
Type: b&b; 1913 Craftsman-style beach bungalow just off Chesapeake Bay; "come see our beaches & sunsets!"
Owned/ Run By: gay men
Rooms: 5
Baths: private
Meals: full brkfst
Amenities: outdoor hot tub, DVDs/ videos

Kids: 12 yrs & up welcome
Rates: $110-135

CampOut   Charlottesville

9105 Minna Dr
Richmond, VA 23229
804/ 301-3553
www.campoutva.com

Clientele: women
Type: campground; rustic w/ hot showers in-season; 50 campsites on 100 acres w/ 7-acre stocked lake; hiking, boating, festivals; between Charlottesville & Richmond
Owned/ Run By: women
Wheelchair Access: yes, 1 cabin rms
Kids: girls welcome; males 5 yrs & under

only
Pets: welcome; must be leashed
Smoking: no
Rates: $20 (membership fee)

The Inn at Court Square   Charlottesville

410 E Jefferson St
Charlottesville, VA 22902
434/ 295-2800 866/ 466-2877
innatcourtsquare.com

Clientele: mixed gay/ straight
Type: b&b-inn; oldest house in downtown Charlottesville; antiques throughout; fine dining 11am-2pm Mon-Fri
Owned/ Run By: women
Rooms: 5
Baths: private
Meals: expanded cont'l brkfst
Amenities: free parking, hot tub

Kids: well-behaved welcome
Pets: no
Smoking: no
Rates: $99-299
AC: 10%

The Summer Kitchen B&B   Charlottesville

6482 Dick Woods Rd
Charlottesville, VA 22903
540/ 456-7009
www.summerkitchencottage.com

Clientele: mixed gay/ straight
Type: cottage; beautifully renovated 1820 country cottage; features breathtaking views
Owned/ Run By: lesbians
Rooms: 1 (cottage)
Baths: private
Meals: full brkfst
Amenities: sauna, outdoor hot tub,

massage
Pets: no
Smoking: no
Rates: $125-135
AC: 5%

1848 Island Manor House

Chincoteague Island

4160 Main St
Chincoteague Island, VA 23336-2410
757/ 336-5436 800/ 852-1505
hosts@islandmanor.com
www.islandmanor.com

Clientele: mixed gay/ straight
Type: b&b; historic home; near downtown; minutes from Assateague Island & Nat'l Wildlife Refuge
Owned/ Run By: gay men
Nearby Attractions: artist galleries, shopping, Assateague Nat'l Seashore & Lighthouse, Chincoteague Nat'l Wildlife Refuge, Atlantic Ocean, wineries
Transit: 2 hrs to Norfolk airport; 45 minutes to Salisbury Regional
Rooms: 8 total, 2 kings, 4 queens, 2 fulls, A/C, color TV (1), DVD/ VCR (1), cable TV (1), ceiling fan (2), fireplace (1), maid service, all rms recently redecorated w/ tasteful reminders of coastal life & new beds
Baths: private & shared, bathtubs, showers, robes, hairdryers
Meals: full brkfst
Amenities: office hrs: 9am-9pm; free parking, DVDs/ videos, WiFi, snacks, coffee/ tea, afternoon refreshments, also beach towels, umbrellas & chairs
Recreation: kayaking, biking, boating, fishing, bird-watching, beach, surfing
Kids: 10 yrs & up welcome
Pets: no
Smoking: no
Reservations: *Deposit:* required, 50% or 1 night, due at booking, personal check ok *Cancellation:* cancel by 2 weeks prior or forfeit 50% or 1 night (whichever is greater) *Minimum Stay:* 2 nights (wknds)/ 3 (holidays) *Check in/ out:* 3pm/ 11am
Payment: cash, travelers checks, personal checks, Visa, Amex, MC, Discover
Season: open yr-round *High season:* June-Sept
Rates: $95-250 *Discounts:* 5% Damron Guide users

Chincoteague's most historic and romantic bed-and-breakfast is now gay-owned! This beautiful manor is located on Main Street within easy walking distance of restaurants and shops. We provide off-street parking for all our guests. You are just minutes from the Wildlife Refuge, a bird-watchers' paradise, and the Assateague National Seashore, the beach with the wild ponies.

You can select from eight guest rooms, most with private baths. Wake to the smell of fresh-baked breads, all part of the full Southern breakfast served each morning. Plenty of common space for your enjoyment and pleasure, including a parlor with period antiques, a relaxing living room with modern conveniences, a garden room with a fireplace, and a brick courtyard with a fountain to trickle your worries away.

Let the sea breeze calm your spirit. Enjoy a romantic sunset. Here is the place to celebrate your special occasion!

1848 Island Manor House...Island beauty, coastal charm, Southern hospitality.

Tazewell Hotel & Suites
Norfolk

245 Granby St
Norfolk, VA 23510
757/ 623-6200
www.thetazewell.com

Clientele: gay-friendly
Type: hotel; in heart of downtown; newly renovated w/ a perfect blend of class, style & convenience
Owned/ Run By: gay & straight
Rooms: 72
Baths: private

Wheelchair Access: yes, 5 rms
Meals: full brkfst
Kids: welcome
Smoking: ok
Rates: $120-200
AC: 10%

Neptune Vacation Suites
Onley

21033 Front St
Onley, VA 23418
757/ 630-5193
www.neptuneva.com

Clientele: gay-friendly
Type: apt; suites have retro TV theme, outdoor grill, fireplaces
Owned/ Run By: gay man

Amenities: hot tub, DVDs/ videos, gym
Rates: $95

Walker House B&B
Petersburg

3280 S Crater Rd
Petersburg, VA 23805
804/ 861-5822
www.walker-house.com

Clientele: gay-friendly
Type: b&b-private home; large antebellum farmhouse; exceptional amenities & landscaped gardens; 1 mile off I-95
Owned/ Run By: gay men
Rooms: 4
Baths: private

Meals: full brkfst
Kids: welcome
Pets: no
Smoking: no
Rates: $98-120
AC: 10%

Frog Hollow B&B
Shenandoah Valley

492 Greenhouse Rd
Lexington, VA 24450
540/ 463-5444
froghollowbnb.com

Clientele: mixed gay/ straight
Type: b&b; completely restored 1800s farmhouse; large guest rms; rocking-chair porches, gift shop & patio; also a cottage
Owned/ Run By: gay men
Rooms: 3
Baths: private

Meals: full brkfst
Amenities: free parking, laundry, outdoor hot tub, massage
Kids: no
Pets: no
Rates: $115-155
AC: 10%

Mayneview B&B
Shenandoah Valley

439 Mechanic St
Shenandoah Valley, VA 22835
540/ 743-7921
www.mayneview.com

Clientele: gay-friendly
Type: b&b; Victorian w/ mtn views; near Luray Caverns, wineries & hiking
Owned/ Run By: straights
Baths: private
Meals: full brkfst
Amenities: free parking, outdoor hot tub,

DVDs/ videos
Kids: welcome
Pets: welcome
Smoking: no
Rates: $110-150
AC: 10%

The Olde Staunton Inn
Shenandoah Valley

260 N Lewis St
Staunton, VA 24401
540/ 886-0193 866/ 653-3786
www.oldestauntoninn.com

Clientele: mixed gay/ straight
Type: b&b; restored historic home convenient to downtown restaurants & area attractions
Rooms: 5
Baths: private & shared
Meals: expanded cont'l brkfst

Amenities: free parking, laundry, outdoor hot tub
Kids: welcome
Pets: no
Smoking: no
Rates: $49-120
AC: 10%

Piney Hill B&B
Shenandoah Valley

1048 Piney Hill Rd
Luray, VA 22835
540/ 778-5261 800/ 644-5261
www.pineyhillbandb.com

Clientele: mixed gay/ straight
Type: b&b-inn; 1700s farmhouse in beautiful Shenandoah Valley; also cottage; spectacular mtn views
Owned/ Run By: gay men
Rooms: 5
Baths: private & shared

Meals: full brkfst
Amenities: free parking, outdoor hot tub, massage, DVDs/ videos
Kids: no
Pets: no
Smoking: no
Rates: $109-189

Twelfth Night Inn
Shenandoah Valley

402 E Beverley St
Staunton, VA 24401
540/ 885-1733
www.12th-night-inn.com

Clientele: gay-friendly
Type: b&b; gracious 1904 mansion; 2 blks from downtown & Blackfriars Playhouse on quiet street
Owned/ Run By: straights
Rooms: 3
Baths: private

Meals: full brkfst
Kids: welcome
Pets: welcome; $10 fee
Rates: $89-145
AC: 10%

White Fence B&B
Shenandoah Valley

275 Chapel Rd
Stanley, VA 22851
540/ 778-4680 800/ 211-9885
www.whitefencebb.com

Clientele: gay-friendly
Type: b&b; 1890 Victorian w/ cottages; close to Shenandoah Nat'l Park & Luray Caverns
Owned/ Run By: straights
Rooms: 3
Baths: private
Meals: full brkfst

Amenities: free parking, hot tub, DVDs, videos
Kids: by arrangement
Pets: no
Smoking: no
Rates: $129-195
AC: 10%

Inn at Urbanna Creek
Urbanna

804/ 758-4661
www.innvirginia.com

Clientele: gay-friendly
Type: b&b; 1870s home; walk to unique shops, antique stores, restaurants, marinas, & historic sites; 2 hrs from Washington, DC
Owned/ Run By: straights
Rooms: 4

Baths: private
Meals: full brkfst
Amenities: free parking, hot tub, massage
Smoking: no
Rates: $95-150

Capes Ocean Resort Hotel
Virginia Beach

2001 Atlantic Ave
Virginia Beach, VA 23451
757/ 428-5421 800/ 456-5421
www.capeshotel.com

Clientele: gay-friendly
Type: hotel; all rms oceanfront w/ private balconies
Owned/ Run By: straights
Rooms: 59
Baths: private
Wheelchair Access: yes, 3 rms

Meals: coffee/ tea only
Amenities: free parking, laundry, pool
Kids: welcome
Pets: no
Smoking: no
AC: 10%

Gay Street Inn
Washington

160 Gay St
Washington, VA 22747
540/ 675-3288
www.gaystreetinn.com

Clientele: gay-friendly
Type: b&b
Owned/ Run By: gay men
Rooms: 4
Baths: private
Meals: full brkfst
Amenities: free parking, WiFi

Kids: under 12 yrs only if whole inn reserved
Pets: Shenandoah Suite only
Smoking: no
Rates: $145-215

Lavender Sea B&B
Williamsburg

107 Capitol Landing Rd
Williamsburg, VA 23185-4318
757/ 345-0198
www.lavenderseabandb.com

Clientele: mixed gay/ lesbian
Type: b&b; 1938 home; haven for arts; w/ antiques & inviting gardens; paces from Colonial Williamsburg
Owned/ Run By: lesbians
Rooms: 1
Baths: private

Meals: expanded cont'l brkfst
Kids: welcome; 3 persons max in rm
Pets: no
Smoking: no
Rates: $75-95
AC: 10%

Blackwater Campground
Windsor

651 Whispering Pines Trail
Windsor, VA 23487
757/ 357-7211
www.pagan.com/Blackwater

Clientele: gay-friendly
Type: family-oriented campground that welcomes LGBT family; 300 campsites & 150 RV hookups; pagan, medieval & gay events often occur on wknds
Owned/ Run By: gay & straight
Kids: welcome; must be accompanied by

adult
Pets: welcome; must be attended at all times
Smoking: ok
Rates: $25 (full hookup); $22 (water & electric); $5 per night (primitive camping)

Mary Kay's Romantic Whaley Mansion
Chelan

415 S 3rd St
Chelan, WA 98816
509/ 682-5735 800/ 729-2408
www.whaleymansionbandb.com

Clientele: gay-friendly
Type: b&b-inn; in elegant Victorian; "take someone you love to Mary Kay's Whaley Mansion"
Owned/ Run By: women
Rooms: 6

Baths: private
Meals: full brkfst
Smoking: no
Rates: $95-145

Morris Farmhouse B&B
Coupeville

105 W Morris Rd
Coupeville, WA 98239
360/ 678-0939 866/ 440-1555
www.morrisfarmhouse.com

Clientele: gay-friendly
Type: b&b; restored 1908 farmhouse on 10 acres
Owned/ Run By: lesbians
Rooms: 6

Rates: $75-185

Mt Baker B&B
Glacier

9447 Mt Baker Hwy
Glacier, WA 98244
360/ 599-2299
www.mtbakerbedandbreakfast.com

Clientele: mixed gay/ straight
Type: b&b-private home; chalet-style home on 4 acres in pristine mtn valley; closest to Mt Baker ski area
Owned/ Run By: straights
Rooms: 3
Baths: private & shared

Meals: full brkfst
Amenities: free parking, hot tub, DVDs/ videos
Kids: welcome
Pets: by arrangement
Smoking: no
Rates: $80-100

Mt Baker Cabins
Glacier

9447 Mt Baker Hwy
Glacier, WA 98244
360/ 599-2299
www.mtbakercabins.com

Clientele: mixed gay/ straight
Type: cabin
Owned/ Run By: straights
Rooms: 3
Baths: private & shared
Meals: full brkfst

Amenities: free parking, outdoor hot tub, DVDs/ videos
Kids: welcome
Pets: by arrangement
Smoking: ok
Rates: $80-100

The White Swan Guesthouse

La Conner

15872 Moore Rd
Mt Vernon, WA 98273
360/ 445–6805
www.thewhiteswan.com

Clientele: mixed gay/ straight
Type: cottage; Victorian farmhouse w/ English gardens & private cottage; 6 miles to historic LaConner
Owned/ Run By: other
Rooms: 1
Baths: private

Meals: expanded cont'l brkfst
Kids: welcome in cottage only
Pets: no
Smoking: no
Rates: $160-175
AC: 10%

The Wild Iris

La Conner

PO Box 696
La Conner, WA 98257
360/ 466–1400 800/ 477–1400
www.wildiris.com

Type: inn
Rooms: 19
Baths: private
Wheelchair Access: yes, 1 rm
Meals: expanded cont'l brkfst

Kids: 13 yrs & up welcome
Pets: no
Smoking: no
Rates: $109-199
AC: 10%

Ashingdon Manor Inn & Cottages

Langley

PO Box 869
Langley, WA 98260
360/ 221–2334 800/ 442–4942
www.ashingdonmanor.com

Clientele: gay-friendly
Type: English country inn in idyllic valley setting; reservations required for dining Fri-Sat; jacuzzi in cottage
Owned/ Run By: straights
Rooms: 8
Baths: private

Wheelchair Access: yes, 4 rms
Meals: full brkfst
Kids: 16 yrs & welcome
Pets: no
Smoking: no
Rates: $109-179

Anthony's Home Court

Long Beach Peninsula

1310 Pacific Hwy N
Long Beach, WA 98631
360/ 642–2802 888/ 787–2754
www.anthonyshomecourt.com

Clientele: mixed gay/ straight
Type: cottage; w/ 27 hookups & housekeeping cabins; on beautiful peninsula at mouth of Columbia River
Owned/ Run By: gay men
Rooms: 8
Baths: private

Amenities: free parking, laundry, WiFi
Kids: welcome
Pets: welcome; fee
Smoking: no
Rates: $100-150

The Historic Sou'wester Lodge, Cabins & RV Park

Long Beach Peninsula

Beach Access Rd
Seaview, WA 98644
360/ 642–2542
www.souwesterlodge.com

Clientele: gay-friendly
Type: retreat; historic oceanside Victorian, beach cottages & classic trailers; w/ 8 campsites & 50 RV hookups; on 3 tranquil acres
Owned/ Run By: straights

Rooms: 24
Baths: private
Kids: 5 yrs & up, small kids welcome w/ restrictions
Pets: in cabins & trailers
Smoking: no

Senator TC Bloomer's Mansion

Long Beach Peninsula

1004 41st Pl
Seaview, WA 98644
360/ 642–3471
www.enchantedbluewave.com

Clientele: gay-friendly
Type: rental home; on 5 oceanfront acres
Owned/ Run By: lesbians/ gay men
Rooms: 5
Baths: private & shared

Amenities: free parking, outdoor hot tub, massage, DVDs/ videos
Kids: please call ahead to arrange
Rates: $425+

Shakti Cove Cottages
Long Beach Peninsula

PO Box 385
Ocean Park, WA 98640
360/ 665-4000
www.shakticove.com

Clientele: mixed gay/ straight
Type: cabin; w/ kitchens; nestled in a grove of trees on 3 secluded acres; beach access
Owned/ Run By: lesbians
Rooms: 10 (cabins)
Baths: private

Kids: welcome w/ adult supervision
Pets: welcome; dogs on leash
Smoking: no
Rates: $73-88

Aunt Jenny's Guest House
Port Townsend

504 Root St
Port Townsend, WA 98368
360/ 385-2899
www.auntjennysguesthouse.com

Clientele: mixed gay/ straight
Type: cheerful, small retro cottage in ideal location; walk to town & parks; cozy stove, sweet patio, full kitchen
Owned/ Run By: straight woman
Rooms: 1
Baths: private

Wheelchair Access: yes, all rms
Meals: expanded cont'l brkfst
Kids: welcome
Pets: please call first
Smoking: no
Rates: $65-125/ night & $300-600/ week
AC: 10%

The James House
Port Townsend

1238 Washington St
Port Townsend, WA 98368
800/ 385-1238 360/ 385-1238
www.jameshouse.com

Clientele: gay-friendly
Type: b&b-inn; award-winning grand Victorian mansion on a bluff w/ sweeping views of bay & mtn ranges
Rooms: 12
Baths: private
Meals: full brkfst

Amenities: free parking, massage, DVDs/ videos, WiFi
Kids: 13 yrs & up welcome
Pets: no
Smoking: no
Rates: $120-250
AC: 10%

Ravenscroft Inn
Port Townsend

533 Quincy St
Port Townsend, WA 98368
360/ 385-2784 800/ 782-2691
www.ravenscroftinn.com

Clientele: gay-friendly
Type: b&b-private home; sits high on a bluff overlooking bay & mtns
Owned/ Run By: straights
Rooms: 8
Baths: private

Meals: full brkfst
Amenities: free parking, indoor hot tub, DVDs/ videos
Kids: 14 yrs & up welcome
Smoking: no
Rates: $94-210

Beaverton Valley Farm B&B
San Juan Islands

4144 Beaverton Valley Rd
Friday Harbor, WA 98250
360/ 378-3276 877/ 378-3276
www.beavertonvalley.com

Clientele: gay-friendly
Type: b&b-private home; classic island farmhouse w/ romantic stone fireplace; quiet, country setting
Owned/ Run By: straights
Rooms: 5
Baths: private

Meals: full brkfst
Amenities: free parking, outdoor hot tub
Kids: welcome
Pets: welcome in cabin only
Smoking: no
Rates: $90-170
AC: 10%

Inn on Orcas Island
San Juan Islands

PO Box 309
Deer Harbor, WA 98243
360/ 376-5227 888/ 886-1661
www.theinnonorcasisland.com

Clientele: gay-friendly
Type: b&b-inn; named one of the best seaside getaways by *Sunset* magazine
Owned/ Run By: gay men
Rooms: 8
Baths: private
Wheelchair Access: yes, 1 rm

Meals: full brkfst
Amenities: free parking, hot tub, DVDs/ videos
Kids: no
Pets: no
Smoking: no
Rates: $145-285

Lopez Farm Cottages & Tent Camping

San Juan Islands

555 Fisherman Bay Rd
Lopez Island, WA 98261
360/ 468-3555 800/ 440-3556
www.lopezfarmcottages.com

Clientele: mixed gay/ straight
Type: cottage; new NW Scandinavian cottages in cedar grove; brkfst delivered; also camping; adults only
Owned/ Run By: straights
Rooms: 5 (cottages)
Baths: private

Meals: expanded cont'l brkfst
Amenities: free parking, outdoor hot tub
Kids: no
Pets: no
Smoking: no
Rates: $33 (camping) – 180 (cottages)
AC: 10%

Spring Bay Inn on Orcas Island

San Juan Islands

PO Box 97
Olga, WA 98279
360/ 376-5531
www.springbayinn.com

Clientele: mixed gay/ straight
Type: b&b-inn; secluded retreat on spectacular water frontage; kayak tour included in price
Owned/ Run By: gay & straight
Rooms: 5
Baths: private
Meals: full brkfst

Amenities: free parking, laundry, outdoor hot tub, WiFi
Kids: 2 people max per rm
Pets: no
Smoking: no
Rates: $220-260
AC: $25 per booking

The Ace Hotel

Seattle

2423 1st Ave
Seattle, WA 98121
206/ 448-4721
www.acehotel.com

Clientele: mixed gay/ straight
Type: hotel; sleek, futuristic yet classic accommodations in heart of Seattle; restaurant, bar, barbershop & tailor
Owned/ Run By: gay & straight
Rooms: 28
Baths: private & shared

Amenities: WiFi
Kids: welcome
Pets: welcome
Smoking: ok
Rates: $75-195
AC: 10%

Alexis Hotel

Seattle

1007 1st Ave
Seattle, WA 98104
206/ 624-4844 800/ 426-7033
www.alexishotel.com

Type: hotel; "Seattle's premier luxury hotel"
Rooms: 109
Baths: private
Wheelchair Access: yes, 6 rms
Amenities: free parking, laundry, massage, WiFi

Kids: welcome; under 18 yrs free w/ parent & existing bedding
Pets: owner must sign pet waiver
Smoking: ok
Rates: $299-595
AC: 10%

Bed & Breakfast on Broadway

Seattle

722 Broadway Ave E
Seattle, WA 98102
206/ 329-8933
www.bbonbroadway.com

Clientele: mixed gay/ straight
Type: b&b-private home; elegant accommodations on a tree-lined street near trendy shops & restaurants; near downtown
Owned/ Run By: gay/ lesbian & straight
Rooms: 4

Baths: private
Meals: cont'l brkfst
Kids: no
Pets: no
Smoking: no
Rates: $125-175

Grand Hyatt Seattle

Seattle

721 Pine St
Seattle, WA 98101
206/ 774-1234
grandseattle.hyatt.com

Clientele: gay-friendly
Type: views of Puget Sound, Lake Union & the Olympic & Cascade Mtns
Rooms: 425 total
Baths: private
Wheelchair Access: yes, 10 rms

Amenities: sauna, gym, WiFi
Kids: welcome

Bacon Mansion

959 Broadway E
Seattle, WA 98102

206/ 329-1864
800/ 240-1864

Seattle

info@baconmansion.com
baconmansion.com

Clientele: mixed gay/ straight
Type: b&b-inn; classical Edwardian-style Tudor; w/ original woods, 3,000-crystal chandelier, stained glass & more; located on Capitol Hill in a historic neighborhood
Owned/ Run By: gay/ lesbian & straight
Nearby Attractions: Volunteer Park, downtown, University of Washington, arboretum, Japanese Gardens
Transit: 20 miles to Sea-Tac airport; 2 miles to train; 1 blk to #49 bus
Rooms: 11 total, 3 suites, 11 queens, 2 twins, color TV, wetbar (3), ceiling fan (3), fireplace (2), phone, refrigerator (6), maid service, voicemail & data ports, WiFi
Baths: private & shared, bathtubs, showers, hairdryers
Wheelchair Access: yes, 1 rm
Meals: expanded cont'l brkfst
Amenities: WiFi, coffee/ tea, concierge, piano, patio
Recreation: tennis, sunbathing in park, kayaking, canoeing
Kids: limited to certain rms; charged as extra person

Smoking: no
Reservations: recommended *Deposit:* required, credit card guarantee, personal check ok *Cancellation:* cancel by 1 week prior or forfeit full amount *Minimum Stay:* wknds, holidays & June-Sept

Payment: cash, travelers checks, Visa, Amex, MC, Discover
Season: open yr-round *High season:* May-Oct & holidays
Rates: $94-209 *Discounts:* single, 7+ nights (off-season)

Gaslight Inn

1727 15th Ave
Seattle, WA 98122

206/ 325-3654

Seattle

innkeepr@gaslight-inn.com
www.gaslight-inn.com

Clientele: mixed gay/ straight
Type: b&b-inn; in beautiful Arts & Crafts home
Owned/ Run By: gay men
Nearby Attractions: 4 blks to exciting Broadway; close to Volunteer Park; walking distance to downtown shopping & Pike Place Market
Transit: near public transit; 1 blk to Metro busline
Rooms: 8 total, 6 queens, 2 fulls, A/C (3), color TV, cable, ceiling fan (4), fireplace (1), deck (1), phone, refrigerator (5), maid service
Baths: private & shared, bathtubs, showers, robes, hairdryers
Meals: cont'l brkfst
Amenities: coffee/ tea, seasonal pool
Kids: no
Pets: no
Pets On Premises: 1 dog, 1 cat
Smoking: no
Reservations: required *Deposit:* credit card info requested, due at booking

Cancellation: cancel by 1 week prior or forfeit 1 night *Minimum Stay:* 2 nights (wknds) *Check in/ out:* 3-6pm/ 11am
Payment: cash, travelers checks, personal checks, Visa, Amex, MC

Season: open yr-round *High season:* Memorial Day-Labor Day
Rates: $88-158 *Discounts:* off-season; weekly

Gypsy Arms B&B   *Seattle*

3628 Palatine Ave N
Seattle, WA 98103
206/ 547-8194
www.gypsyarms.com

Clientele: mixed gay/ lesbian/ bisexual/ transgender
Type: b&b; luxury & a dungeon
Owned/ Run By: men
Rooms: 2
Baths: shared
Meals: full brkfst
Amenities: laundry, outdoor hot tub,

DVDs/ videos
Kids: no
Pets: no
Smoking: no
Rates: $100-150

Hotel Vintage Park   *Seattle*

1100 5th Ave
Seattle, WA 98101
206/ 624-8000 800/ 853-3914
www.hotelvintagepark.com

Clientele: mixed gay/ straight
Type: hotel; ultra luxe; in the heart of the city; evening wine-tasting
Rooms: 126
Baths: private
Wheelchair Access: yes, 6 rms
Meals: coffee/tea only
Amenities: WiFi

Kids: welcome
Pets: well-behaved & quiet welcome
Smoking: ok (in designated rms)
Rates: $139-319
AC: 10%

Pioneer Square Hotel   *Seattle*

77 Yesler Wy
Seattle, WA 98104
206/ 340-1234 800/ 800-5514
www.pioneersquare.com

Clientele: gay-friendly
Type: hotel; lovely historic boutique b&b-style hotel in historical downtown
Rooms: 75
Baths: private
Wheelchair Access: yes, 3 rms
Meals: cont'l brkfst
Kids: welcome; under 12 yrs free

Pets: no
Smoking: ok
Rates: $119-239
AC: 10%

Salisbury House B&B   *Seattle*

750 16th Ave E
Seattle, WA 98112
206/ 328-8682
www.salisburyhouse.com

Clientele: gay-friendly
Type: b&b-inn; urban inn on quiet, tree-lined street; phones w/ data port, fireplaces
Owned/ Run By: women
Rooms: 5
Baths: private
Meals: full brkfst
Amenities: free parking, hot tub, WiFi

Kids: 12 yrs & up welcome
Smoking: no
Rates: $89-165

Seattle Suites   *Seattle*

1400 Hubbell Pl
Seattle, WA 98101
206/ 232-2799
www.seattlesuite.com

Clientele: mixed gay/ straight
Type: condo; studio, 1- & 2-bdrms; complete w/ top of the line furnishings & all the amenities; near major downtown attractions
Owned/ Run By: woman
Rooms: 12 (condos)
Baths: private
Wheelchair Access: yes

Meals: coffee/tea only
Amenities: laundry, DVDs/ videos, WiFi
Kids: welcome
Pets: no
Smoking: no
Rates: $128-195

nn at Queen Anne

Seattle

05 1st Ave N
eattle, WA 98109

206/ 282-7357
800/ 952-5043

info@innatqueenanne.com
www.innatqueenanne.com

lientele: mixed gay/ straight
ype: hotel; quaint inn located across from Seattle Center; accessible to the Capitol Hill gay district via hotel courtesy van or bus
wned/ Run By: gay/ lesbian & straight
earby Attractions: Space Needle, Pike Pl Market, Pioneer Square, Boeing Museum of Flight
ransit: near public transit; 15 miles to SeaTac; 2 miles to Union Station; 1 mile to Greyhound
ooms: 68 total, 3 suites, 33 queens, 32 twins, A/C (34), color TV, DVD/ VCR (3), cable, ceiling fan, phone, refrigerator, maid service, walk-in closets, voicemail, kitchenettes w/ cooking supplies, European decor
aths: private, bathtubs, showers
Meals: expanded cont'l brkfst
Amenities: office hrs: 7am-11pm; coffee/ tea, guest laundry, courtesy shuttle service, complimentary wine receptions on selected days
ids: welcome

Pets: no
Reservations: *Cancellation:* cancel by 1 day prior or forfeit 1 night + tax *Check in/ out:* 3pm/ noon
Payment: cash, travelers checks, Visa, Amex, MC, Discover, JCB, Diners Club, Carte

Blanche
Season: open yr-round *High season:* May-Sept
Rates: $99-159 *Discounts:* AAA, AARP, AMEX
AC: 10%

MarQueen Hotel

Seattle

00 Queen Anne Ave N
eattle, WA 98109

206/ 282-7407
888/ 445-3076

info@marqueen.com
www.marqueen.com

lientele: mixed gay/ straight
ype: hotel; features numerous complimentary services & premium amenities; experience upscale service & appointments; conveniently located in Seattle's Theater District
wned/ Run By: gay/ lesbian & straight
earby Attractions: Capitol Hill, Space Needle, Pike Pl Market, Pioneer Square
ransit: 15 miles to airport; 2 miles to bus station; 1 mile to Greyhound
ooms: 56 total, 8 suites, 30 kings, 18 queens, A/C, color TV, DVD/ VCR (4), cable, wetbar, ceiling fan, phone, kitchenette, refrigerator, rm service, maid service
aths: private, bathtubs, showers, whirlpools, robes, hairdryers
Wheelchair Access: yes, 3 rms
Meals: coffee/tea only
Amenities: office hrs: 24hrs; laundry, massage, DVDs/ videos, coffee/ tea, aesthetics & hair salon, espresso bar, conference rm, Ten Mercer restaurant, courtesy shuttle service, complimentary wine reception on selected days

Kids: welcome
Reservations: *Cancellation:* cancel by 1 day prior or forfeit 1 night + tax
Payment: cash, travelers checks, Visa, Amex, MC, Discover, Diners Club, Carte Blanche, JCB

Season: open yr-round *High season:* May-Sept
Rates: $125-325 *Discounts:* AAA, AARP, AMEX
AC: 10%

Wild Lily Ranch B&B

Seattle

PO Box 306
Index, WA 98256
360/ 793-2103
www.wildlilyranch.com

Clientele: mostly men
Type: b&b; on Skykomish River in the Cascades; 1 hr from Seattle; cedar sauna; campsites & authentic Sioux tipis (w/ electricity) also available
Owned/ Run By: gay men
Rooms: 3 (log cabins)

Baths: shared
Meals: cont'l brkfst
Kids: 16 yrs & up welcome
Pets: welcome; $10 per day for dogs
Smoking: no
Rates: $105

Sunset Marine Resort

Sequim

40 Buzzard Ridge Rd
Sequim, WA 98382
360/ 681-4166
www.sunsetmarineresort.com

Clientele: gay-friendly
Type: resort; 6 private waterfront cottages on Sequim Bay (on the Olympic Peninsula)
Owned/ Run By: lesbians
Rooms: 6 (cabins)
Baths: private
Wheelchair Access: yes, 1 rm

Meals: coffee/tea only
Kids: welcome
Pets: up to 2 dogs welcome w/ fee
Smoking: no
Rates: $95-195
AC: 10%

Montvale Hotel

Spokane

1005 W First Ave
Spokane, WA 99201
509/ 747-1919 866/ 668-8253
www.montvalehotel.com

Clientele: gay-friendly
Type: hotel; luxury boutique hotel in downtown Spokane; also restaurant
Owned/ Run By: gay man
Rooms: 36
Baths: private
Wheelchair Access: yes, 4 rms

Meals: cont'l brkfst
Amenities: WiFi
Kids: welcome
Pets: no
Smoking: no
Rates: $145-4,400

Chinaberry Hill

Tacoma

302 Tacoma Ave N
Tacoma, WA 98403
253/ 272-1282
www.chinaberryhill.com

Clientele: gay-friendly
Type: b&b-inn; spacious suites, private jacuzzis, bay views, fireplaces, guest cottage; featured in *Sunset* magazine
Owned/ Run By: straights
Rooms: 5
Baths: private

Meals: full brkfst
Amenities: free parking, hot tub, DVDs/ videos
Kids: welcome in guesthouse only
Smoking: no
Rates: $145-250
AC: 10%

Whidwood Inn

Whidbey Island

360/ 679-7472
www.whidwood.com

Clientele: mixed gay/ straight
Type: b&b; log guesthouse near historic Coupeville; hot tub, library, sunroom & brkfst
Owned/ Run By: gay men
Rooms: 2
Baths: private

Meals: cont'l brkfst
Amenities: free parking, hot tub
Kids: no
Pets: no
Smoking: no
Rates: $76-96
AC: 5%

Chewuch Inn

Winthrop

223 White Ave
Winthrop, WA 98862
509/ 996-3107 800/ 747-3107
www.chewuchinn.com

Clientele: gay-friendly
Type: b&b-inn; country inn w/ 8 rms; also 6 private cabins located in a pine grove w/ seasonal creek
Owned/ Run By: straights
Rooms: 14
Baths: private

Meals: expanded cont'l brkfst
Amenities: free parking, outdoor hot tub, DVDs/ videos
Kids: welcome
Smoking: no
Rates: $70-140
AC: 10%

Lee Street Inn B&B
Lewisburg

200 N Lee St
Lewisburg, WV 24901
304/ 647-5599 888/ 228-7000
www.leestreetinn.com

Clientele: gay-friendly
Type: b&b; built in 1876 & located in the heart of Lewisburg's Historical District
Owned/ Run By: gay men
Rooms: 5
Baths: private & shared

Meals: cont'l brkfst
Amenities: hot tub, DVDs/ videos, WiFi
Kids: 13 yrs & up welcome
Pets: please call first
Rates: $75-125

Guest House at Lost River
Lost River

288 Settlers Valley Wy
Lost River, WV 26810
304/ 897-5707
www.guesthouseatlostriver.com

Clientele: mixed gay/ lesbian
Type: guesthouse
Owned/ Run By: gay men
Rooms: 16
Baths: private
Meals: full brkfst

Amenities: free parking, pool, sauna, hot tub, massage, gym, WiFi
Kids: no
Pets: no
Smoking: no
Rates: $125-150

Roseland Guest House & Campground
Proctor

RD 1, Box 185B
Proctor, WV 26055-9703
304/ 455-3838
www.RoselandWV.com

Clientele: men
Type: resort; clothing-optional gay men's resort w/ guest rms, cabins & camping; 120 campsites & 17 RV hookups
Owned/ Run By: gay men
Rooms: 10
Baths: private & shared
Meals: full brkfst

Amenities: free parking, laundry, pool, hot tub, massage
Kids: no
Pets: welcome if good around people
Smoking: no
Rates: $74-149
AC: 10%

Thomas Shepherd Inn
Shepherdstown

300 W German St
Shepherdstown, WV 25443
304/ 876-3715 888/ 889-8952
www.thomasshepherdinn.com

Clientele: gay-friendly
Type: b&b; comfortably furnished Federal-style b&b in historic town; large common areas
Owned/ Run By: straights
Rooms: 6
Baths: private

Meals: full brkfst
Amenities: free parking, DVDs/ videos, WiFi
Kids: 12 yrs & up welcome
Pets: no
Smoking: no
Rates: $95-155

Wildernest Inn
Upper Tract

HC 32 Box 63V
Upper Tract, WV 26866
304/ 257-9076 888/ 621-2948
www.wildernestinn.com

Clientele: gay-friendly
Type: b&b-inn; lake & mtn views; magnificent sunsets & starry night skies; delicious dining
Owned/ Run By: straights
Rooms: 6
Baths: private

Meals: full brkfst
Amenities: outdoor hot tub, massage
Kids: no
Pets: housebroken only
Smoking: no
Rates: $85-125
AC: 10%

Long Fork Campgrounds
Walton

114 Long Fork Camp Rd
Walton, WV 25286
304/ 577-9347 888/ 598-2267
www.longfork.com

Clientele: mixed gay/ lesbian
Type: campground, resort; 46 tent/campsites & 10 RV hookups; camping along w/ cabin rentals & rms in main lodge
Owned/ Run By: gay men
Rooms: 3
Baths: private
Wheelchair Access: yes, 1 rm

Meals: cont'l brkfst
Amenities: free parking, pool, outdoor hot tub, massage, DVDs/ videos, WiFi
Kids: accompanied by adult; not on some weekends
Pets: welcome
Rates: $12-150

Blacksmith Inn on the Shore

8152 Hwy 57
Baileys Harbor, WI 54202
920/ 839–9222 800/ 769–8619
www.theblacksmithinn.com

Clientele: gay-friendly
Type: b&b; nestled on the shore; charming & private; extraordinary views of the harbor
Owned/ Run By: straights
Rooms: 15
Baths: private

Wheelchair Access: yes, 1 rm
Meals: cont'l brkfst
Amenities: free parking, hot tub, DVDs, videos, WiFi
Smoking: no
Rates: $125-245

Wild Iris Shores

2741 11th St
Cumberland, WI 54829
715/ 822–8594
wildiris@chibardun.net

Type: cabin; new, yr-round log cabins w/ private lake; wheelchair accessible w/ roll-in showers
Owned/ Run By: woman
Rooms: 2 (cabins)
Wheelchair Access: yes, all rms

Meals: coffee/ tea only
Kids: welcome
Pets: welcome
Smoking: no
Rates: $95-120

The Edgewater Inn & Cottages

5054 St Hwy 70 W
Eagle River, WI 54521
715/ 479–4011 888/ 334–3987
www.edgewater-inn-cottages.com

Clientele: mixed gay/ straight
Type: resort; beautiful riverfront accommodations; open yr-round; all are welcome
Owned/ Run By: straights
Rooms: 22
Baths: private
Amenities: free parking, WiFi

Kids: welcome
Pets: welcome if leashed & supervised
Smoking: ok in designated rms
Rates: $65-175
AC: 10%

The Lake House

5793 Division
Stone Lake, WI 54876
715/ 865–6803
www.lakehouse-bb.com

Clientele: mixed gay/ lesbian
Type: b&b-private home; country-style; located on a clear, sand-bottom lake; use of paddleboat or canoe;
Owned/ Run By: lesbians
Rooms: 4
Baths: private

Wheelchair Access: yes, 1 rm
Meals: full gourmet brkfst
Amenities: free parking, hot tub, gym, WiFi
Kids: by arrangement
Pets: no
Smoking: no
Rates: $90-160

Anton-Walsh House

202 Copper St
Hurley, WI 54534–1339
715/ 561–2065
www.Anton-Walsh.com

Clientele: gay-friendly
Type: b&b; 107-yr-old home w/ warm, home-town ambience; in-rm high-speed cable internet connections
Owned/ Run By: gay/ lesbian & straight
Rooms: 3
Baths: private

Meals: full brkfst
Kids: 5 yrs & up welcome
Pets: no
Smoking: limited (not in guest rms)
Rates: $75-115

Whitecap Mountains Ski Resort & Skye Golf

PO Box D
Montreal, WI 54550
715/ 561–2227 800/ 933–7669
www.skiwhitecap.com

Clientele: gay-friendly
Type: resort; hotel-style suites w/ kitchenettes to fully furnished multi-bdrm chalets
Owned/ Run By: gay & straight
Rooms: 75
Baths: private
Wheelchair Access: yes, 53 rms

Meals: full brkfst
Amenities: free parking, laundry, pool, sauna, indoor hot tub
Kids: welcome
Pets: welcome
Rates: $45-475

Rainbow Ridge Farms B&B
La Crosse

N 5732 Hauser Rd
Onalaska, WI 54650
608/ 783-8181
www.rainbowridgefarms.com

Clientele: gay-friendly
Type: b&b; restored farmhouse on 35 scenic acres; working farm; full brkfst wknds
Rooms: 4
Baths: private
Meals: expanded cont'l brkfst

Kids: well-supervised welcome
Pets: no
Smoking: no
Rates: $70-125
AC: 10%

Trillium B&B
La Crosse

608/ 625-4492
www.trilliumcottage.com

Clientele: gay-friendly
Type: cottage; cozy & private; on family farm; near large Amish community & 35 miles from LaCrosse
Rooms: 2 (cottages)
Baths: private

Meals: full brkfst
Kids: welcome
Pets: no
Smoking: no
Rates: $65-105

Allyn Mansion Inn
Lake Geneva

511 E Walworth Ave
Delavan, WI 53115
262/ 728-9090
www.allynmansion.com

Clientele: mixed gay/ straight
Type: b&b-private home; 23 rms of Victorian splendor; fireplaces, great food & great hosts; on Nat'l Register
Owned/ Run By: gay men
Rooms: 8
Baths: private & shared

Meals: full brkfst
Kids: 12 yrs & up welcome
Pets: no
Smoking: no
Rates: $100-150
AC: 10% (Sun-Th)

Eleven Gables Inn on the Lake
Lake Geneva

493 Wrigley Dr
Lake Geneva, WI 53147
262/ 248-8393
www.lkgeneva.com

Clientele: gay-friendly
Type: b&b-inn; lakefront 1847 Gothic residence; antiques, balconies & private entrances; also cottage
Owned/ Run By: straights
Rooms: 12 (includes bridal chamber, 2- & 3-bdrm quaint country cottages)
Baths: private

Wheelchair Access: yes, 1 rm
Meals: expanded cont'l brkfst
Amenities: free parking, DVDs/ videos, WiFi
Kids: by arrangement
Pets: welcome w/ prior approval
Smoking: no
Rates: $109-330
AC: 10%

Hawks Nest Log Home Rentals
Madison

2455 Fairview Rd
Stoughton, WI 53589
608/ 445-7468
hawksnestresort.com

Clientele: mixed gay/ lesbian
Type: rental home; one 3-bdrm & one 2-bdrm; also rustic cottage; fully furnished; by Lake Kegonsa; 20 minutes to Madison
Owned/ Run By: lesbians/ gay men
Rooms: 3 (homes)
Baths: private

Amenities: laundry, DVDs/ videos
Kids: welcome; under 8 yrs free
Pets: small pets welcome; please inquire about fee
Smoking: no
Rates: $150-190 (for 2)
AC: 10%

Prairie Garden B&B
Madison

W 13172 Hwy 188
Lodi, WI 53555
608/ 592-5187 800/ 380-8427
www.prairiegarden.com

Clientele: mixed gay/ lesbian
Type: b&b-inn; near Lake Wisconsin & the nude beach; 30 minutes N of Madison; spectacular views
Owned/ Run By: gay men
Rooms: 5
Baths: private
Wheelchair Access: yes, 1 rm

Meals: full brkfst
Amenities: free parking, outdoor hot tub, massage, DVDs/ videos
Kids: please inquire
Pets: welcome
Smoking: no
Rates: $90-220
AC: 10%

Comfort Inn Suite
Milwaukee

916 E State St
Milwaukee, WI 53202
414/ 276-8800 800/ 328-7275
www.parkeasthotel.com

Type: hotel; theme suites & business flrs; free downtown shuttle service; "Milwaukee's downtown hotel of distinction overlooking Lake Michigan"
Rooms: 159
Baths: private

Wheelchair Access: yes, 6 rms
Meals: cont'l brkfst
Kids: welcome
Smoking: no
Rates: $90-200
AC: 10%

Kilbourn Guesthouse
Milwaukee

2825 W Kilbourn Ave
Milwaukee, WI 53280
414/ 344-3167
www.kilbournguesthouse.com

Clientele: mixed gay/ straight
Type: b&tb; "offers a great environment for both business & leisure travelers visiting Milwaukee"
Owned/ Run By: gay men
Rooms: 5
Baths: private & shared

Meals: cont'l brkfst
Amenities: free parking, WiFi
Kids: no
Pets: no
Smoking: no
Rates: $79-159
AC: 10%

Daughters of the Earth
Norwalk

18134 Index Ave
Norwalk, WI 54648
608/ 269-5301
doejo777@yahoo.com

Clientele: women
Type: campground; private & rustic camping area for women only; 12 campsites; clothing-optional; near state parks, bike trails; groups welcome
Owned/ Run By: lesbians

Wheelchair Access: yes
Kids: girls of any age welcome; boys under 5 yrs only
Pets: welcome w/ responsible owners
Rates: $9-15

Lochnaiar Inn
Racine

1121 Lake Ave
Racine, WI 53403-1924
262/ 633-3300
www.lochnaiarin.com

Clientele: gay-friendly
Type: b&tb; English Tudor in the historic district & overlooking Lake Michigan
Rooms: 8
Baths: private
Wheelchair Access: yes, 2 rms
Meals: full brkfst

Amenities: free parking, hot tub, DVDs, videos
Kids: 12 yrs & up welcome
Pets: no
Smoking: ok (in library only)
Rates: $90-250
AC: 10% at full rack rates

Musky Bay Resort
Rhinelander

3724 N Limberlost Rd
Rhinelander, WI 54501
715/ 365-7004 866/ 855-9971
www.muskybay.com

Clientele: gay-friendly
Type: resort; comfortable cabins on Moen Chain of Lakes; 5 1/2 acres w/ 800 ft of lake frontage, swimming beach & boats for fishing
Owned/ Run By: lesbians
Rooms: 6 (3 cabins)

Baths: private
Kids: welcome
Pets: no
Smoking: no
Rates: $125-140/ night; $575-675/ week

Woodwind Health Spa & Resort
Rhinelander

3033 Woodwind Wy
Rhinelander, WI 54501
715/ 362-8902
www.woodwindspa.com

Clientele: mixed gay/ straight
Type: retreat & spa; gourmet meals; "only destination spa in Midwest"
Owned/ Run By: lesbians
Rooms: 6 (plus dorm for 8)
Baths: private & shared
Wheelchair Access: yes, 4 rms
Meals: full brkfst

Amenities: free parking, pool, sauna, hot tub, massage, DVDs/ videos
Kids: 14 yrs & up welcome w/ adult supervision
Pets: welcome in duplex only
Smoking: no
Rates: $85-110

The Chadwick Inn
Sturgeon Bay

25 N 8th Ave
Sturgeon Bay, WI 54235
920/ 743-2771
www.thechadwickinn.com

Clientele: gay-friendly
Type: b&b-private home; 1890 Queen Anne w/ private suites; 2-person whirlpool bath & fireplace in each suite
Owned/ Run By: lesbians
Rooms: 3
Baths: private

Meals: cont'l brkfst
Kids: no
Pets: no
Smoking: no
Rates: $100-135

The Chanticleer Guest House
Sturgeon Bay

4072 Cherry Rd
Sturgeon Bay, WI 54235

920/ 746-0334
866/ 682-0384

information@chanticleerguesthouse.com
www.chanticleerguesthouse.com

Clientele: mixed gay/ straight
Type: b&b-inn; on 70 private acres of rolling pastures, hiking trails & flower gardens; new in-ground heated pool, sauna & gazebo on property
Owned/ Run By: gay men
Nearby Attractions: 5 minutes to beaches, maritime museums, antique shops, fine dining, winery, brewery, lighthouses
Transit: near public transit; 15 minutes to Cherryland airport
Rooms: 12 total, suites, 9 kings, 5 queens, A/C, color TV, DVD/ VCR, wetbar (4), ceiling fan (10), fireplace, deck, phone (4), kitchenette (4), refrigerator, rm service, maid service, antique-filled suites have double whirpools w/ view of fireplace, balconies, entertainment center
Baths: private, bathtubs, showers, whirlpools, hairdryers
Wheelchair Access: yes, 1 rm
Meals: expanded cont'l brkfst, delivered to your rm
Amenities: office hrs: 8am-10pm; free parking, laundry, sauna, hot tub, DVDs/ videos, snacks, coffee/ tea, heated in-ground pool, hiking trails, firepit, flower gardens & gazebo, hammock
Recreation: 10-25 minutes to 5 state parks w/ x-country & downhill skiing, hiking, biking, gay-owned horse stables, golf,

swimming, horse-drawn carriage rides
Kids: no
Pets: no
Pets On Premises: 20 sheep, all outdoors & 2 horses
Smoking: no
Reservations: required; will take walk-ins if rms available *Deposit:* required, 1 night, due at booking, personal check ok *Cancellation:* cancel by 3 weeks prior or forfeit deposit *Check in/ out:* 2pm-8pm/ 11am

Payment: cash, travelers checks, personal checks, Visa, Amex, MC, Discover
Season: open yr-round *High season:* June-Oct
Rates: $120-320 *Discounts:* midweek discounts, 10-20% off for extended stays

Wilderness Way
Wascott

PO Box 176
Wascott, WI 54890
715/ 466-2635
www.wildernesswaywomen.com

Clientele: women
Type: resort; 5 cabins, 2 camping cabins & 18 campsites (9 w/ electricity); canoes & rowboats w/ each cabin & campsite; lake
Owned/ Run By: lesbians
Rooms: 5 (cabins)
Baths: private
Wheelchair Access: yes, 1 rm

Kids: welcome
Pets: dogs welcome (4 cabins); 2 max
Smoking: ok (in 3 cabins)
Rates: $16 (camping); $65-98 (cabins)

Rainbow Valley Resort
Wisconsin Dells

4125 River Rd
Wisconsin Dells, WI 53965
608/ 253–1818 866/ 553–1818
www.captaindixresort.com

Type: cottage; Midwest's largest gay resort; on 24 private acres; near water & amusement parks
Rooms: 14 + 6 cabins
Baths: private
Wheelchair Access: yes, 1 rm
Meals: full brkfst
Amenities: free parking, pool, massage, DVDs/ videos, WiFi

Kids: call for details
Pets: welcome
Smoking: ok
Rates: $99-239

Bar H Ranch
Jackson

PO Box 297
Driggs, ID 83422
208/ 354–2906 888/ 216–6025
www.tetontrailrides.com

Clientele: mostly women
Type: private ranch; w/ deluxe loft accommodations; fully equipped kitchen, decks w/ sweeping views; also women-only horseback riding trips in Grand Tetons
Owned/ Run By: women
Rooms: 600-sq-ft loft w/ separate sleeping & dressing areas
Baths: private

Pets: welcome w/ prior approval
Rates: $125/ night; $750/ week; 3-night minimum
AC: 10%

Spring Creek Ranch
Jackson

1800 Spirit Dance Rd
Jackson, WY 83001
307/ 733–8833 800/ 443–6139
www.springcreekranch.com

Clientele: gay-friendly
Type: resort; 1,000 feet above Jackson Hole; w/ health club, wilderness adventure spa, Granary restaurant on-site
Rooms: 36 rms (also 1 to 3-bdrm condos & homes)
Baths: private
Amenities: laundry, pool, indoor hot tub
Kids: welcome

Pets: no
Smoking: ok (some smokefree rms)
Rates: $150-310
AC: 10%

Cowgirl Horse Hotel
Laramie

32 Black Elk Trail
Laramie, WY 82070
307/ 745-8794
www.cowgirlshorsehotel.com

Clientele: gay-friendly
Type: b&b-private home; specializing in women travelers & their horses (men welcome)
Owned/ Run By: woman
Rooms: 1
Baths: private
Meals: cont'l brkfst
Kids: welcome

Pets: welcome
Rates: $79

11th Street Lodging
Calgary

403/ 209-1800
www.11street.com

Clientele: mixed gay/ straight
Type: b&b; downtown Calgary's most affordable; w/in walking distance to many attractions
Owned/ Run By: gay men
Rooms: 10

Baths: private & shared
Meals: expanded cont'l brkfst
Kids: 10 yrs & up welcome
Pets: no
Smoking: no
Rates: C$63-170

Calgary Westways Guest House
Calgary

216 25th Ave SW
Calgary, AB T2S 0L1
403/ 229-1758 866/ 846-7038
www.gaywestways.com

Clientele: mixed gay/ straight
Type: b&b-inn; 1912 Arts & Craft heritage home w/ English ambience; walk to downtown & bars; AAA 3 Diamonds
Owned/ Run By: gay men
Rooms: 5
Baths: private
Meals: full brkfst

Amenities: free parking, laundry, outdoor hot tub, DVDs/ videos, WiFi
Kids: by arrangement
Pets: by arrangement
Smoking: no
Rates: C$65-150
AC: 10%

The Foxwood B&B
Calgary

1725 12th St SW
Calgary, AB T2T 3N1
403/ 244-6693
www.thefoxwood.com

Clientele: mixed gay/ lesbian
Type: b&b-private home; 19th-c Edwardian home; great location, great hosts, great value; "Calgary's favorite gay b&b"
Owned/ Run By: gay men
Rooms: 4
Baths: private & shared
Meals: expanded cont'l brkfst

Amenities: free parking, indoor hot tub, DVDs/ videos
Kids: no
Pets: no
Smoking: no
Rates: C$75-175
AC: 10%

Home Plate Comforts B&B
Calgary

917 Drury Ave NE
Calgary, AB T2E 0M3
403/ 263-2442
www.homeplatecomforts.ca

Clientele: women
Type: b&b-private home; "our casual, welcoming & women-centered b&b features private bath, living rm & kitchenette for your exclusive use w/ lovely gardens in quaint inner-city neighborhood"
Owned/ Run By: lesbians
Rooms: 1

Baths: private
Meals: full brkfst
Amenities: free parking, 2-person jacuzzi in bdrm, DVDs/ videos, WiFi
Kids: no
Pets: no (fragrance-free preference)
Smoking: no
Rates: C$85-95

Westpoint Executive B&B
Calgary

101 Westpoint Gardens SW
Calgary, AB T3H 4M4
403/ 248-5668
www.bbcanada.com/westpoint

Clientele: mixed gay/ straight
Type: b&b-private home; beautiful modern home situated in quiet community; close to city center
Owned/ Run By: gay man
Rooms: 3

Baths: private & shared
Meals: expanded cont'l brkfst
Kids: 16 yrs & up welcome
Smoking: no
Rates: C$75-105
AC: 10%

Labyrinth Lake Lodge
Edmonton

Site 2, Box 3, RR 1
Millet, AB T0C 1Z0
780/ 878-3301
www.lablake.ca

Clientele: mixed gay/ straight
Type: two 1,200-sq-ft lodges on 160 acres by a private lake; canoes, badminton, volleyball & horseshoe pits all provided
Rooms: 4

Wheelchair Access: yes, 1 rm
Amenities: outdoor hot tub
Kids: welcome
Pets: welcome
Rates: C$200-250

Northern Lights B&B   *Edmonton*

Main PO Box 515
Edmonton, AB T5J 2K1
780/ 483-1572
www.nlightsbnb.com

Clientele: mixed gay/ lesbian
Type: b&b-private home
Owned/ Run By: gay men
Rooms: 3

Baths: private & shared
Meals: full brkfst
Rates: C$60-70

Birkenhead Resort   *Birken*

Box 369
Pemberton, BC V0N 2L0
604/ 452-3255
www.birkenheadresorts.bizland.com

Clientele: gay-friendly
Type: cabin; rustic resort on a small lake;
also 10 campsites
Owned/ Run By: woman
Rooms: 6 (cabins)

Baths: shared
Amenities: outdoor hot tub
Pets: welcome
Rates: C$80-212

Sky Ranch   *Burns Lake*

C4 Site 20 RR 2
Burns Lake, BC V0J 1E0
250/ 694-3738
www.ngis.ca/~skyranch

Clientele: mixed gay/ straight
Type: cabin; wilderness log-cabin; wood-
stove; outhouse; camping available
Owned/ Run By: lesbians
Rooms: 1
Baths: shared
Wheelchair Access: yes

Meals: coffee/tea only
Kids: welcome
Pets: in cabin only
Smoking: no
Rates: C$150-200/ week
AC: 10%

Copes' Islander Oceanfront B&B   *Comox*

1484 Wilkinson Rd
Comox, BC V9M 4B3
250/ 339-1038 888/ 339-1038
www.bbvancouverisland-bc.com

Clientele: gay-friendly
Type: b&b-private home; beachfront b&b &
vacation rental on Vancouver Island;
spectacular views, tranquil settings &
unforgettable brkfsts
Owned/ Run By: straights
Rooms: 3

Baths: private & shared
Meals: full brkfst
Amenities: free parking, WiFi
Kids: welcome
Pets: welcome w/ prior approval
Smoking: no
Rates: C$75-115

Canoe Pass Seaside Cottage   *Gibsons*

604/ 687-7798 866/ 587-7798
www.bccabin.com

Clientele: mixed gay/ straight
Type: cottage; 2 self-contained waterfront
suites in Pender Harbour; private dock &
beach; panoramic ocean view; secluded
Owned/ Run By: gay men
Rooms: 2 (self-contained suites; whole
cottage can also be rented)
Baths: private

Meals: coffee/tea only
Amenities: free parking, laundry, indoor
hot tub, DVDs/ videos
Kids: please inquire
Pets: no
Smoking: no
Rates: C$100-350
AC: 5%

Anne's Oceanfront Hideaway B&B   *Gulf Islands*

168 Simson Rd
Salt Spring Island, BC V8K 1E2
250/ 537-0851 888/ 474-2663
www.annesoceanfront.com

Clientele: gay-friendly
Type: b&b; ocean views; Canada Select 4 1/2
Stars; evening turndown
Owned/ Run By: straights
Rooms: 4
Baths: private
Wheelchair Access: yes, 1 rm

Meals: full 4-course brkfst, afternoon
snacks
Kids: no
Pets: no
Smoking: no
Rates: C$195-275
AC: 10%

Bellhouse Inn
Gulf Islands

29 Farmhouse Rd
Galiano Island, BC V0N 1P0
250/ 539-5667 800/ 970-7464
www.bellhouseinn.com

Clientele: mixed gay/ straight
Type: b&b; historic waterfront inn on 6 acres; watch eagles & killer whales from the sheltered sandy beach or relax on the lawns in a hammock
Owned/ Run By: straights
Rooms: 3

Baths: private
Meals: full brkfst
Amenities: free parking, hot tub
Smoking: no
Rates: C$85-195
AC: 10%

The Blue Ewe Cabin in the Woods
Gulf Islands

1207 Beddis Rd
Salt Spring Island, BC V8K 2C8
250/ 537-9344
www.saltspring.com/blueewe

Clientele: mixed gay/ lesbian
Type: cabin; 5+ acres of privacy; views; "luxurious for 2, comfortable for 4"
Owned/ Run By: gay men
Rooms: 2
Baths: private
Meals: cont'l brkfst
Amenities: free parking, sauna, outdoor

hot tub, massage, DVDs/ videos
Kids: over 5 & under 16 yrs welcome w/ prior approval
Pets: welcome
Smoking: no
Rates: C$150-175
AC: 10%

Fulford Dunderry Guest House
Gulf Islands

2900 Fulford-Ganges Rd
Salt Spring Island, BC V8K-1X6
250/ 653-4860
fulford-dunderry.ca

Clientele: gay-friendly
Type: b&b; oceanfront guesthouse close to pub, bakery, stores & kayak rental shop
Owned/ Run By: gay men
Rooms: 3
Baths: private

Wheelchair Access: yes, 1 rm
Meals: cont'l brkfst
Amenities: outdoor hot tub
Kids: no
Pets: welcome; in suites

Hawthorne House
Gulf Islands

6436 Porlier Pass Rd
Galiano Island, BC V0N 1P0
250/ 539-5815
www3.telus.net/Hawthorne/

Clientele: mixed gay/ straight
Type: guesthouse; character home on 10 parklike acres; sleeps 10 comfortably; close to beaches, parks & shops; short ferry trip to Vancouver or Victoria
Owned/ Run By: lesbians
Rooms: 3 (+ 2 lofts)

Baths: shared
Wheelchair Access: yes, 3 rms
Kids: welcome
Pets: welcome
Smoking: no
Rates: C$195+

Hummingbird Lodge B&B
Gulf Islands

1597 Starbuck Ln
Gabriola, V0R1X5
250/ 247-9300 877/ 551-9383
www.hummingbirdlodgebb.com

Clientele: gay-friendly
Type: b&b; private, luxurious atmosphere; close to beaches & kayaking; private decks
Owned/ Run By: straights
Rooms: 3
Baths: private
Meals: full brkfst

Amenities: free parking, outdoor hot tub, massage
Kids: welcome
Pets: welcome w/ prior approval
Rates: C$89-139
AC: 10%

Moonshadows Guest House
Gulf Islands

771 Georgeson Bay Rd
Galiano Island, BC V0N 1P0
250/ 539-5544 888/ 666-6742
www.moonshadowsbb.com

Clientele: gay-friendly
Type: b&b-private home; nestled in a quiet, 2-acre pastoral setting; w/ views of meadows, trees, hills & nearby farmlands
Owned/ Run By: straights
Rooms: 3
Meals: full brkfst

Amenities: free parking, outdoor hot tub, massage, DVDs/ videos
Kids: please inquire
Smoking: no
Rates: C$110-145
AC: 10%

Sun Raven Lodge
Gulf Islands

1356 MacKinnon Rd
North Pender Island, BC V0N 2M1
250/ 629-6216
www.sunraven.com

Clientele: mostly women
Type: retreat; outdoor meditation areas; panoramic ocean views; "a special place to reconnect w/ Mother Earth"
Owned/ Run By: lesbians

Rooms: 3
Baths: shared
Meals: full brkfst
Smoking: no
Rates: C$95-125

Tutu's B&B
Gulf Islands

3198 Jemima Rd
Denman Island, BC V0R 1T0
250/ 335-0546 877/ 560-8888
mars.ark.com/~gero/bb4/tutus.html

Clientele: gay-friendly
Type: b&b; peaceful lakefront property; w/ private dock, swimming, canoeing; separate accommodation w/ private patio, cooking facilities
Owned/ Run By: woman

Rooms: 1
Baths: private
Meals: full brkfst
Kids: limited space
Rates: C$50-90

Eagles Nest B&B
Okanagan Lake

15620 Commonage Rd
Kelowna, BC V4V 1A8
250/ 766-9350 866/ 766-9350
www.theeaglesnestbandb.com

Type: luxurious 7,000 sq ft B&B; quiet & clean; nestled between the forest & cherry orchards of BC; unparalleled view of Lake Okanagan
Rooms: 5
Baths: private & shared

Meals: full brkfst
Amenities: free parking, laundry, outdoor hot tub, DVDs/ videos
Smoking: no
Rates: US$80-150
AC: 10%

The Flags B&B
Okanagan Lake

2295 McKinley Rd
Kelowna, BC V1V 2B6
250/ 762-8184 866/ 762-8184
www.the-flags.org

Clientele: men
Type: b&b-private home; mini-resort for gay men in a country setting w/ fireplaces, bbq, recreation rm, gardens; clothing-optional patio
Owned/ Run By: gay men
Rooms: 6
Baths: private & shared

Meals: full brkfst
Amenities: free parking, laundry, pool, sauna, indoor hot tub, DVDs/ videos
Kids: no
Pets: welcome; please call first
Smoking: ok
Rates: C$60-135

Hostelling International—Penticton
Okanagan Lake

464 Ellis St
Penticton, BC V2A 4M2
250/ 492-3992 866/ 782-9736
www.hihostels.ca

Clientele: gay-friendly
Type: hostel; private rms & 4-bed dorms; common areas w/ kitchen; located in Okanagan Valley & close to city center, shops & beaches; "Penticton is famous for its hot sunny weather"
Rooms: 47 (beds)

Wheelchair Access: yes, all rms
Kids: welcome
Rates: C$21-24 (dorms)

Morningside B&B
Okanagan Lake

1645 Carmi Ave
Penticton, BC V2A 7G3
250/ 492-5874
www.bbcanada.com/1712.html

Clientele: mixed gay/ straight
Type: b&b-private home; a comfortable, air-conditioned home; "come try the Life of Ryley"
Owned/ Run By: straights
Rooms: 2
Baths: private & shared

Meals: full brkfst
Kids: no
Pets: no
Smoking: no
Rates: C$65-75

Rainbow's End
Okanagan Lake

8282 Jackpine Rd
Vernon, BC V1B 3M7
250/ 542-4842
rainbowsend@telus.net

Clientele: mixed gay/ lesbian
Type: b&b-private home; also RV parking available (1 hookup); 10 minutes to Silver Star Provincial Park
Owned/ Run By: gay men
Rooms: 2
Baths: private & shared

Wheelchair Access: yes, 1 rm
Meals: full brkfst
Amenities: free parking, laundry, outdoor hot tub
Pets: welcome
Rates: C$45/double ($35 2nd night)

Beacon B&B & Spa
Powell River

3750 Marine Ave
Powell River, BC V8A 2H8
604/ 485-5563 877/ 485-5563
www.beaconbb.com

Clientele: gay-friendly
Type: b&b-private home; relaxing waterfront atmosphere; lots of outdoor recreation & wilderness hiking; "Powell River welcomes you"
Owned/ Run By: straights
Rooms: 3
Baths: private

Wheelchair Access: yes, 1 rm
Meals: full brkfst
Amenities: free parking, laundry, indoor hot tub, massage
Kids: 12 yrs & up welcome
Pets: please inquire
Smoking: no
Rates: C$85-155 (7% tax to be added)

Wilde Road Farm & Guesthouse
Powell River

7420 Wilde Rd
Powell River, BC V8A 4Z3
604/ 483-4923

Clientele: mixed gay/ straight
Type: farm b&b; sunny country retreat w/ timberframe farmhouse & cabin; near town, hikes & ocean
Owned/ Run By: gay/ lesbian & straight
Rooms: 2

Baths: private & shared
Meals: full brkfst
Kids: welcome
Pets: welcome
Rates: C$40-90

Bahari Oceanside Inn
Qualicum Beach

5101 Island Hwy W
Qualicum Beach, BC V9K 1Z1
877/ 752-9278
www.baharibandb.com

Clientele: gay-friendly
Type: b&b-private home; tranquil, elegant home on cliffside overlooking Georgia Strait; also 2-bdrm self-catering apt
Owned/ Run By: straights
Rooms: 5
Baths: private

Meals: full brkfst
Amenities: free parking, laundry, outdoor hot tub
Kids: welcome; pay adult rates
Smoking: no
Rates: C$145-290
AC: 10%

BriMar B&B
Tofino

1375 Thornberg Crescent
Tofino, BC V0B 2Z0
250/ 725-3410 800/ 714-9373
www.brimarbb.com

Clientele: mixed gay/ straight
Type: b&b; in elegant home on spectacular Chesterman Beach; all rms overlook rugged Pacific Ocean; full 3-course gourmet brkfst
Rooms: 3

Baths: private
Meals: full brkfst
Kids: 12 yrs & up welcome
Rates: C$110-200
AC: 10%

West Wind
Tofino

1321 Pacific Rim
Tofino, BC V0R 2Z0
250/ 725-2777
www.tofinoaccommodation.com

Clientele: mostly men
Type: cottage; luxurious private cottage or suite; forested boardwalks, sundecks, garden acreage; clothing-optional; w/in 5-minute walk of ocean; "truly an 'Oasis on the Pacific'"
Owned/ Run By: lesbians/ gay men
Rooms: 2 (1 cottage, 1 suite)

Baths: private
Meals: coffee/ tea only
Amenities: free parking, laundry, outdoor hot tub, DVDs/ videos
Smoking: no
Rates: C$125-245
AC: 10% (except July-Aug)

A Place at Penny's   *Vancouver*

810 Commercial Dr
Vancouver, BC V5L 3Y5
604/ 254–2229
www.pennysplacevancouver.com

Clientele: gay-friendly
Type: b&b-inn; w/ antique-decorated suites
   w/ full kitchens
Owned/ Run By: straights
Rooms: 10
Baths: private

Wheelchair Access: yes, 2 rms
Meals: cont'l brkfst
Kids: welcome
Pets: please inquire first
Smoking: no
Rates: US$45-100

Absolutely Fabulous B&B at Johnson Heritage House   *Vancouver*

2278 W 34th Ave
Vancouver, BC V6M 1G6
604/ 266–4175
www.johnsons-inn-vancouver.com

Clientele: gay-friendly
Type: vacation suite; 1100 sq ft, self-catered,
   fully furnished garden suite in classic 1920
   Craftsman home; full kitchen, living rm w/
   river-rock fireplace; on quiet tree-lined
   avenue
Owned/ Run By: straights
Rooms: 2
Baths: private

Meals: full brkfst
Amenities: free parking, laundry, jacuzzi en
   suite, DVDs/ videos, WiFi
Kids: welcome
Pets: no
Smoking: no
Rates: C$100-155
AC: 10%

Barclay House B&B   *Vancouver*

1351 Barclay St
Vancouver, BC V6E 1H6
604/ 605-1351 800/ 971–1351
www.barclayhouse.com

Clientele: mixed gay/ straight
Type: b&b-inn; classic, late Victorian home
   in the heart of Vancouver's West End;
   steps to the Davie Village & Vancouver gay
   nightlife
Owned/ Run By: gay men
Rooms: 5

Baths: private
Meals: full brkfst
Kids: 12 yrs & up welcome
Pets: no
Smoking: no
Rates: C$175-245
AC: 10%

Columbia Cottage B&B   *Vancouver*

205 W 14th Ave
Vancouver, BC V5Y 1X2
604/ 874–7787
www.columbiacottage.com

Clientele: gay-friendly
Type: b&b-private home; 1920s Tudor
   centrally located in heritage neighborhood; close to city center; 20-minutes to
   airport; great brkfsts!
Owned/ Run By: straights
Rooms: 5

Baths: private
Meals: full brkfst
Kids: welcome
Pets: no
Smoking: no
Rates: C$95-135

Comfort Inn Downtown   *Vancouver*

654 Nelson St
Vancouver, BC V6B 6K4
604/ 605-4333 888/ 605-5333
www.comfortinndowntown.com

Clientele: mixed gay/ straight
Type: hotel; "this is not your typical Comfort
   Inn–you'll be surprised by our great
   service & beautiful rms, which rival many
   of Vancouver's four-star hotels"
Owned/ Run By: gay & straight
Rooms: 82
Baths: private

Meals: cont'l brkfst
Amenities: laundry, hot tub
Kids: welcome
Pets: welcome; C$25 pet charge
Smoking: ok (in smoking rms only)
Rates: C$89-229
AC: 10%

Dufferin Hotel   *Vancouver*

900 Seymour St
Vancouver, BC V6B 3L9
604/ 683-4251 877/ 683-5522
www.dufferinhotel.com

Clientele: mixed gay/ straight
Type: hotel; 3 bars (tavern, pub & lounge)
   on-site
Owned/ Run By: gay & straight
Rooms: 70
Baths: private

Kids: welcome
Pets: no
Smoking: ok
Rates: C$65-105
AC: 10%

English Bay Inn
Vancouver

1968 Comox St
Vancouver, BC V6G 1R4
604/ 683-8002 866/ 683-8002
www.englishbayinn.com

Clientele: gay-friendly
Type: b&b; unexpected hideaway in heart of city; all bdrms furnished w/ antiques, luxurious queen-size beds, bathrobes & duvets dressed w/ crisp Ralph Lauren linens
Owned/ Run By: gay & straight
Rooms: 6

Baths: private
Meals: full brkfst
Amenities: hot tub, DVDs/ videos, WiFi
Kids: no
Pets: no
Smoking: no
Rates: C$130-295
AC: 10%

The Fahrenheit Hotel 🏷
Vancouver

1212 Granville St
Vancouver, BC V6Z 1M4

604/ 685-2615
888/ 685-2615

info@thefahrenheithotel.com
www.thefahrenheithotel.com

Clientele: men
Type: hotel; guests receive free access to M2M Playspace, a steam bath directly below the hotel
Owned/ Run By: gay men
Nearby Attractions: Cruisey T Gay Cruises; Davie & Robson Sts: shopping; Granville Island; Vancouver Aquarium Marine Science Center; VanDusen Botanical Garden; Vancouver Art Gallery
Transit: 14 kilometers to airport; 3 kms to train station
Rooms: 42 total, 4 queens, 20 fulls, 18 twins, color TV, cable, refrigerator, safer sex supplies, maid service, also cotton duvet covers; as w/ other European boutique hotels, our bathrms are private upon entering & located at the ends of the hall
Baths: shared
Meals: cont'l brkfst
Amenities: laundry, sauna, DVDs/ videos, gym, WiFi, large flat-screen TV lounge, cook-it-yourself kitchen
Kids: no
Pets: no
Smoking: no

Reservations: valid credit card necessary to guarantee reservation *Deposit:* required, $50 key deposit always & 1 night for confirmed holidays *Cancellation:* cancel by 7 days prior except 30 days (holidays) & 2 weeks (high season) or forfeit 1 night *Minimum Stay:* on holidays & special events *Check in/ out:* 3pm/ 11am

Payment: cash, travelers checks, Visa, Amex, MC
Season: open yr-round *High season:* May-Oct
Rates: C$69-99
AC: 10%

Inn Penzance
Vancouver

1388 Terrace Ave
North Vancouver, BC V7R 1B4
604/ 681-2889 888/ 546-3327
www.innpenzance.com

Clientele: gay-friendly
Type: b&b
Owned/ Run By: gay men
Rooms: 3
Baths: private
Meals: full brkfst

Amenities: free parking, WiFi
Kids: welcome
Pets: in cottage or suite
Smoking: no
Rates: C$125-250
AC: 10%

The Langtry
Vancouver

968 Nicola St
Vancouver, BC V6G 2C8
604/ 687-7892 800/ 699-7892
www.thelangtry.com

Clientele: mixed gay/ straight
Type: apt; short- & long-term apt rentals in a 1930s building furnished w/ period pieces in Vancouver's vibrant West End
Owned/ Run By: gay man
Rooms: 6
Baths: private

Meals: coffee/ tea only
Kids: welcome
Pets: w/ prior approval; extra charge
Smoking: no
Rates: C$85-300
AC: 10%

The Listel Hotel 📷   *Vancouver*

1300 Robson St
Vancouver, BC V6E 1C6

604/ 684-8461
800/ 663-5491

moreinfo@thelistelhotel.com
www.thelistelhotel.com

Clientele: gay-friendly
Type: hotel; Vancouver's most "art-ful" hotel, featuring original art from the Buschlen Mowatt Gallery; located in the heart of the West End, on Vancouver's most popular shopping & dining street
Owned/ Run By: gay & straight
Nearby Attractions: Stanley Park, English Bay, art gallery, library, aquarium, Gastown, Chinatown, GM Place, Granville Island
Transit: near public transit; 30 minutes to Vancouver Int'l; 5 minutes to Pacific Central Station (train/ bus)
Rooms: 130 total, 10 suites, 60 kings, 60 queens, A/C, color TV, cable, wetbar, deck (3), phone, rm service, maid service
Baths: private, bathtubs, showers, hairdryers
Wheelchair Access: yes, 2 rms
Meals: coffee/tea only, special meals available on request

Amenities: office hrs: 24hrs; indoor hot tub, coffee/ tea
Recreation: tennis, golf, indoor & outdoor swimming, bike rentals, windsurfing, sailing, kayaking, skiing, inline skating
Kids: welcome
Pets: no
Smoking: no
Reservations: recommended *Deposit:* required, credit card guarantee, due at booking *Cancellation:* cancel by 3 days prior or forfeit 1 night + tax *Check in/ out:* 3pm/ noon
Payment: cash, travelers checks, Visa, Amex, MC, Discover, JCB, Diners Club, personal checks w/ Amex
Season: open yr-round *High season:* May-Oct
Rates: C$150-300
AC: 10%

The Manor Guest House 📷   *Vancouver*

345 W 13th Ave
Vancouver, BC V5Y 1W2
604/ 876-8494
www.manorguesthouse.com

Clientele: gay-friendly
Type: b&b-inn; in fully restored Edwardian heritage mansion; in the heart of Vancouver; also apt
Owned/ Run By: women
Rooms: 10
Baths: private & shared

Meals: full brkfst
Amenities: free parking, WiFi
Kids: welcome in garden level rms only
Pets: no
Smoking: no
Rates: C$57-111
AC: 10%

Nelson House B&B   *Vancouver*

977 Broughton St
Vancouver, BC V6G 2A4
604/ 684-9793 866/ 684-9793
www.downtownbandb.com

Clientele: mixed gay/ lesbian
Type: b&b-inn; in handsome 1907 heritage home; in easy-walking location
Owned/ Run By: lesbians/ gay men
Rooms: 6
Baths: private & shared
Meals: full brkfst

Amenities: free parking, indoor hot tub, massage, DVDs/ videos, WiFi
Kids: by arrangement
Rates: C$68-198
AC: 10% (IGLTA)

"O Canada" House B&B   *Vancouver*

1114 Barclay St
Vancouver, BC V6E 1H1
604/ 688-0555 877/ 688-1114
www.ocanadahouse.com

Clientele: mixed gay/ straight
Type: b&b-inn; award-winning heritage home in excellent downtown location; a few minutes walk to shopping, attractions, beaches, restaurants, Robson & Davie Streets
Owned/ Run By: gay & straight

Rooms: 7
Baths: private
Amenities: free parking, DVDs/ videos, WiFi
Kids: 12 yrs & up welcome
Rates: C$135-265
AC: 10%

Opus Hotel ⊤Ⓖ

322 Davie St
Vancouver, BC V6B 5Z6
604/ 642-6787 866/ 642-6787
www.opushotel.com

Clientele: gay-friendly
Type: hotel; "Opus Hotel provides the service & amenities of a luxury hotel w/in a highly personalized & stylish environment"
Rooms: 96
Baths: private
Wheelchair Access: yes, 3 rms

Kids: welcome
Pets: welcome
Smoking: ok
Rates: C$299-1,500
AC: 10%

Vancouver

Pacific Palisades Hotel ⊤Ⓖ

1277 Robson St
Vancouver, BC V6E 1C4
604/ 688-0461 800/ 663-1815
www.pacificpalisadeshotel.com

Clientele: mixed gay/ straight
Type: hotel; sleek, sexy & very "in the now"; interior design inspired by hip South Beach, FL; spacious suites w/ vistas of water, mtns & city lights
Owned/ Run By: straights
Rooms: 233

Baths: private
Amenities: free parking, laundry, pool, sauna, indoor hot tub, massage
Kids: welcome
Pets: welcome
Rates: C$200-350
AC: 10%

Vancouver

Plaza 500 Hotel

500 W 12th Ave
Vancouver, BC V5Z 1M2
604/ 873-1811 800/ 473-1811
www.plaza500.com

Clientele: gay-friendly
Type: minutes from downtown; surrounded by breathtaking views; near shopping, theater & attractions; gym on-site
Owned/ Run By: straights
Rooms: 153
Baths: private

Wheelchair Access: yes
Meals: full brkfst
Kids: welcome
Pets: no
Smoking: ok
Rates: C$109-189
AC: 10%

Vancouver

Quality Hotel (Inn at False Creek) ⊤Ⓖ

1335 Howe St
Vancouver, BC V6Z 1R7
604/ 682-0229 800/ 663-8474
www.qualityhotel.ca

Clientele: gay-friendly
Type: hotel; full-service boutique hotel; in the heart of Vancouver's gay scene, "Davie Village"
Owned/ Run By: gay & straight
Rooms: 157
Baths: private

Wheelchair Access: yes, 2 rms
Amenities: pool, WiFi
Kids: welcome
Pets: welcome
Smoking: ok
Rates: C$89-209
AC: 10%

Vancouver

Sandman Suites on Davie

1160 Davie St
Vancouver, BC
604/ 681-7263 800/ 726-3626
sandmansuites.com

Clientele: mixed gay/ straight
Type: hotel; located in the heart of the West End; many suites w/ spectacular city views
Owned/ Run By: gay & straight
Rooms: 198 (includes 190 1-bdrm suites & 8 deluxe or penthouse suites)
Baths: private

Wheelchair Access: yes, 2 rms
Kids: welcome; under 17 yrs must be accompanied by parent or legal guardian
Pets: welcome; 2 per suite
Smoking: no
Rates: C$119+
AC: 13%

Vancouver

The West End Guest House

1362 Haro St
Vancouver, BC V6E 1G2
604/ 681-2889 888/ 546-3327
www.westendguesthouse.com

Clientele: mixed gay/ straight
Type: guesthouse; 1906 Victorian inn filled w/ antiques & modern conveniences; central downtown location
Owned/ Run By: gay man
Rooms: 8
Baths: private

Meals: full brkfst
Kids: 12 yrs & up welcome
Smoking: no
Rates: C$95-255
AC: 10%

Vancouver

Ambrosia Historic B&B
Victoria

522 Quadra
Victoria, BC V8V 3S3
250/ 380-7705 877/ 262-7672
www.ambrosiavictoria.com

Clientele: gay-friendly
Type: b&b; romantic 5-star b&b 3 blks from Victoria's inner harbor; gas fireplaces; Aveda salon amenities; gourmet 4-course brkfst
Owned/ Run By: straights
Rooms: 4

Baths: private
Meals: full brkfst
Amenities: free parking, hot tub, massage
Smoking: no
Rates: C$110-255
AC: 5-10%

The Consulate, A Historic B&B
Victoria

528 Goldstream
Victoria, BC V9B 2W7
250/ 818-0208
www.theconsulateongoldstream.com

Clientele: gay-friendly
Type: b&b-private home; pagoda-shaped home reputed to have been built as the home & office of the Japanese Consul; tasteful decor, relaxing atmosphere, gracious hosts

Meals: full brkfst
Kids: welcome; please inquire
Pets: welcome: please inquire
Rates: C$80

The Fairmont Empress
Victoria

721 Government St
Victoria, BC V8W 1W5
250/ 384-8111 800/ 257-7544
www.fairmont.com/empress

Clientele: gay-friendly
Type: hotel; Victoria landmark famous for its afternoon tea; award-winning cuisine & signature cocktail lounge; fitness center & full-service Willow Stream Spa
Rooms: 477
Baths: private
Wheelchair Access: yes, 8 rms

Amenities: pool, sauna, indoor hot tub, massage
Kids: welcome
Pets: small pets welcome
Smoking: no
Rates: C$159-479
AC: 10%

Ifanwen B&B
Victoria

44 Simcoe St
Victoria, BC V8V 1K2
250/ 384-3717
www.ifanwen.com

Clientele: mixed gay/ lesbian
Type: b&b-private home; friendly; located in a quiet, safe neighborhood just a short walk to downtown
Owned/ Run By: gay man
Rooms: 2

Baths: private & shared
Meals: full brkfst
Kids: 16 yrs & up welcome
Pets: small & well-behaved welcome
Rates: C$60-99

Oak Bay Guest House
Victoria

1052 Newport Ave
Victoria, BC V8S 5E3
250/ 598-3812 800/ 575-3812
www.oakbayguesthouse.com

Clientele: gay-friendly
Type: b&b-inn; 1912 Tudor-style house; w/ quiet garden setting; located in genteel suburb
Owned/ Run By: straights
Rooms: 11
Baths: private

Meals: full brkfst
Kids: 10 yrs & up welcome
Smoking: no
Rates: C$80-205
AC: 10%

Prior House
Victoria

620 St Charles
Victoria, BC V8S 3N7
877/ 924-3300
www.priorhouse.com

Clientele: gay-friendly
Type: b&b-inn; 5-star inn in historic 1912 manor home; ocean & mtn views; afternoon tea
Rooms: 6
Baths: private
Meals: full brkfst

Kids: 10 yrs old & up welcome
Pets: welcome in 1 rm only
Smoking: no
Rates: C$185-310
AC: 5%

Ryan's B&B
Victoria

224 Superior St
Victoria, BC V8V 1T3
250/ 389-0012 877/ 389-0012
www.ryansbb.com

Clientele: mixed gay/ straight
Type: b&b; in the heart of Victoria; "this romantic heritage home is ideal for a retreat, wedding, anniverary, or simple coronations"
Owned/ Run By: gay men
Rooms: 8
Baths: private

Meals: full brkfst
Amenities: free parking, hot tub, DVDs/ videos
Kids: over 12 yrs welcome
Pets: welcome in cottage only
Smoking: no
Rates: C$109-239

Adara Hotel 🏳️‍🌈
Whistler

4122 Village Green
Whistler, BC V0N 1B4
604/ 905-4009 866/ 502-3272
www.adarahotel.com

Clientele: gay-friendly
Type: "Whistler's first designer boutique hotel"
Rooms: 41
Baths: private
Amenities: pool, hot tub w/ mtn view

Kids: welcome
Pets: welcome
Smoking: no

Coast Whistler Hotel
Whistler

4005 Whistler Wy
Whistler, BC V0N 1B4
604/ 932-2522 800/ 663-5644
www.coastwhistlerhotel.com

Clientele: gay-friendly
Type: full-service resort hotel; mtg rms for catered functions & events; located in the heart of Whistler Village
Rooms: 192
Baths: private
Wheelchair Access: yes, 5 rms

Meals: coffee/ tea only
Amenities: pool, sauna, outdoor hot tub
Kids: welcome; under 16 yrs free
Pets: welcome; $25 charge
Smoking: no
Rates: C$99-359
AC: 10%

Hostelling International—Whistler
Whistler

5678 Alta Lake Rd
Whistler, BC V0N 1B5
604/ 932-5492
www.hihostels.ca/whistler

Clientele: gay-friendly
Type: hostel; shared dorms; common areas w/ kitchen; sauna, fire pit, dock, pool table, huge deck & lounge; "rustic lodge on picturesque Alta Lake, short drive from Whistler & Blackcomb Mtns"
Owned/ Run By: other

Rooms: 32 (beds)
Baths: shared
Kids: welcome
Pets: no
Smoking: no
Rates: C$20-28 (dorms)

Listel Whistler Hotel
Whistler

4121 Village Green
Whistler, BC V0N 1B4
604/ 932-1133 800/ 663-5472
www.listelhotel.com

Clientele: gay-friendly
Type: hotel; "in the heart of Whistler Village"
Owned/ Run By: gay & straight
Rooms: 98
Baths: private
Wheelchair Access: yes, 2 rms
Amenities: laundry, pool, sauna, indoor

hot tub, WiFi
Kids: 18 & under
Pets: 1st flr rms only; $25 per night
Smoking: no
Rates: C$99-449
AC: 10%

A Beach House B&B
White Rock

15241 Marine Dr
White Rock, BC V4B 1C7
604/ 536-5200
www.WhiteRockBedBreakfast.com

Clientele: gay-friendly
Type: b&b; refurbished waterfront beachhouse w/ spectacular views & numerous decks; 5 minutes to USA-Canada border
Owned/ Run By: straights
Rooms: 4
Baths: private & shared

Meals: cont'l brkfst
Kids: no
Pets: no
Smoking: no
Rates: C$75-190
AC: 15%

A Swan in the Town
Winnipeg

170 Kane Ave
Winnipeg, MB R3J 2P2
204/ 832-9773
www.aswaninthetown.ca

Clientele: gay-friendly
Type: b&b-private home; quiet, peaceful, affordable home; close to airport; 15 minutes from downtown
Owned/ Run By: gay men
Rooms: 3
Baths: private & shared

Meals: full brkfst
Amenities: outdoor hot tub, WiFi
Kids: 13 yrs & up welcome
Pets: no
Smoking: no
Rates: C$50-65

Winged Ox Guest House
Winnipeg

82 Spence St
Winnipeg, MB R3C 1Y3
204/ 783-7408
www.gaycanada.com/winged-ox/

Clientele: mixed gay/ lesbian
Type: b&b-private home; hospitable accommodations in a turn-of-the-century brick home
Owned/ Run By: gay men
Rooms: 3

Baths: shared
Meals: full brkfst
Kids: by arrangement
Pets: by arrangement
Smoking: no
Rates: C$40-55

River's Edge Campground
Fredericton

19 Cottage Ln
Durham Bridge, NB E6C 1R9
506/ 459-8675 800/ 370-1644
www.riversedgecamp.ca

Clientele: mixed gay/ lesbian
Type: campground, RV park; LGBT family campground on the Nashwaak River; plenty of outdoor activities
Owned/ Run By: gay men

Kids: welcome
Rates: C$23-32

Kingsbrae Arms Relais & Chateaux
St Andrews

219 King St
St Andrews, NB E3B 1Y1
506/ 529-1897
www.kingsbrae.com

Clientele: mixed gay/ straight
Type: inn; award-winning seaside country inn hotel; brkfst & gourmet dinners
Owned/ Run By: gay & straight
Rooms: 10
Baths: private
Meals: full brkfst
Amenities: free parking, laundry, pool,

sauna, hot tub, massage, DVDs/ videos
Kids: welcome
Pets: welcome in Carriage House w/ prior approval
Smoking: no
Rates: US$600-1,750 (all meals + wine & bar included)
AC: up to 10%

Windsor House of St Andrews
St Andrews

132 Water St
St Andrews, NB E5B 1A8
506/ 529-3330 888/ 890-9463
www.windsorhouseinn.com

Clientele: mixed gay/ straight
Type: b&b-inn; "the most comfortable inn w/ friendly service & great food"
Owned/ Run By: gay men
Rooms: 6
Baths: private
Meals: full brkfst

Kids: please inquire
Pets: welcome
Smoking: no
Rates: C$125-300
AC: 10%

Mahogany Manor
St John

220 Germain St
St John, NB E2L 2G4
506/ 636-8000 800/ 796-7755
www.sjnow.com/mm

Clientele: mixed gay/ straight
Type: b&b; in turn-of-the-century home restored to its classic elegance; located in the heart of uptown Saint John
Owned/ Run By: gay men
Rooms: 5
Baths: private

Wheelchair Access: yes, 1 rm
Meals: full brkfst
Kids: welcome; under 12 yrs free
Pets: please inquire
Smoking: no
Rates: C$95-105

Inn by the Bay
Dildo

78-80 Front St
Dildo, NF A0B 1P0
709/ 582-3170 888/ 339-7829
www.innbythebaydildo.com

Clientele: gay-friendly
Type: b&b-inn; historic circa 1880s oceanside mansions; evening dinner w/ ocean views; service to remember; 4.5 stars
Rooms: 10
Baths: private

Meals: full brkfst
Kids: 7 yrs & up welcome
Pets: no
Smoking: no
Rates: C$99-199
AC: 10%

Abba Inn B&B
St John's

36 Queen's Rd
St John's, NF A1C 2A5
709/ 754-0058 800/ 563-3959
www.abbainn.com

Clientele: mixed gay/ straight
Type: b&b-inn; 4-star luxurious Victorian heritage home; located in the center of downtown; incredible views; large rms
Rooms: 4
Baths: private
Meals: full brkfst

Pets: welcome
Smoking: no
Rates: C$75-185
AC: 5%

Banberry House
St John's

116 Military Rd
St John's, NF A1C 2C9
709/ 579-8006 877/ 579-8226
www.banberryhouse.com

Clientele: mixed gay/ straight
Type: b&b-inn; spacious rms w/ en suite baths, fireplaces, ornate stained glass, hardwood flrs, antiques; downtown location
Rooms: 4

Baths: private
Meals: full brkfst
Kids: welcome
Pets: small pets only
Smoking: no
Rates: C$99-169

Bluestone Inn
St John's

34 Queen's Rd
St John's, NF A1C 2A5
709/ 754-7544 877/ 754-9876
www.thebluestoneinn.com

Clientele: gay-friendly
Type: b&b-inn; near convention center, shopping, boat tours, gay bars; pub located in cellar; also studio apts
Owned/ Run By: gay men
Rooms: 7
Baths: private

Meals: full brkfst
Amenities: free parking, laundry, hot tub
Kids: 2 people max per rm
Pets: welcome; please inquire
Smoking: no
Rates: C$79-149
AC: 15%

Gower House B&B
St John's

180 Gower St
St John's, NF A1C 2A5
709/ 754-0058 800/ 563-3959
www.bbonline.com/can/nf/gower

Clientele: mixed gay/ straight
Type: b&b; in Victorian home in the center of downtown; close to gay bars, restaurants, theater, stadium & ocean
Rooms: 4
Baths: private & shared

Meals: full brkfst
Kids: please inquire
Pets: please inquire
Smoking: no
Rates: C$75-225
AC: 5%

NaGeira House
St John's

7 Musgrave St
Carbonear, NF A1Y 1B4
709/ 596-1888 800/ 600-7757
www.nageirahouse.com

Clientele: gay-friendly
Type: b&b; gracious home nestled in the historic, romantic & adventurous community of Carbonear; quiet elegance, fireplaces, lovely gardens; "whales & icebergs at our doorstep"

Rooms: 4
Baths: private
Meals: full brkfst
Kids: welcome; please call ahead
Smoking: no
Rates: C$99-149

Bailey House B&B
Annapolis Royal

150 St George St
Annapolis Royal, NS B0S 1A0
902/ 532-1285 877/ 532-1285
www.baileyhouse.ca

Clientele: mixed gay/ straight
Type: b&b; circa 1770 historic waterfront home; large water-view rms; tiled en-suite baths; high quality linens; antiques; afternoon refreshments; great in-town location
Owned/ Run By: gay men

Rooms: 3
Baths: private & shared
Meals: full brkfst
Amenities: free parking, DVDs/ videos, WiFi
Kids: please inquire
Smoking: no
Rates: C$80-130

King George Inn
Annapolis Royal

548 Upper St George St
Annapolis Royal, NS B0S 1A0
902/ 532-5286 888/ 799-5464
www.kinggeorgeinn.20m.com

Clientele: mixed gay/ straight
Type: b&b-inn; in grand Victorian sea captain's mansion, circa 1868; honeymoon & family suites; private decks
Owned/ Run By: lesbian & straight
Rooms: 8
Baths: private

Meals: full brkfst
Amenities: laundry, hot tub
Kids: well-behaved welcome
Pets: small pets welcome
Smoking: no
Rates: C$89-299
AC: 10%

The Dunlop Inn
Baddeck

902/ 295-1100 888/ 263-9840
www.dunlopinn.com

Clientele: gay-friendly
Type: b&b-inn; exclusive waterfront accommodations; private sandy beach; waterside deck; w/in walking distance of shops, Alexander Graham Bell museum, sailing, swimming, kayaking, golfing
Owned/ Run By: gay & straight

Rooms: 5
Baths: private
Meals: cont'l brkfst
Kids: welcome
Pets: no
Rates: C$99-160

Harbourview Inn
Digby

25 Harbourview Rd
Smith's Cove, NS B0S 1S0
902/ 245-5686 877/ 449-0705
www.theharbourviewinn.com

Clientele: gay-friendly
Type: b&b-inn; beautiful century-old country inn; in tranquil setting overlooking water
Owned/ Run By: gay men
Rooms: 12
Baths: private

Wheelchair Access: yes, 1 rm
Meals: full brkfst
Kids: welcome
Pets: welcome w/ prior notice
Smoking: no
Rates: US$89-149
AC: 10%

Thistle Down Country Inn
Digby

98 Montague Row
Digby, NS B0V1A0
902/ 245-4490 800/ 565-8081
www.thistledown.ns.ca

Clientele: gay-friendly
Type: b&b-inn; 1904 Edwardian inn on Higby Harbour w/ views of the Annapolis Basin
Owned/ Run By: gay men
Rooms: 12
Baths: private

Meals: full brkfst
Kids: welcome
Pets: welcome
Smoking: no
Rates: C$55-125
AC: 15%

Barrens at Bay Coastal Cottages
Guysborough

6870 RR #2
Guysborough, NS B0H 1N0
902/ 358-2157
www.barrensatbay.com

Clientele: mixed gay/ straight
Type: cottage; custom-built oceanfront cottages in private, rural setting; ideal for quiet getaways
Owned/ Run By: gay men
Rooms: 3
Baths: private

Wheelchair Access: yes, 1 rm
Amenities: free parking, laundry, hot tub, DVDs/ videos
Kids: welcome
Pets: welcome; must be under control
Smoking: no
Rates: C$150-260

DesBarres Manor Inn — Guysborough

90 Church St
Guysborough, NS B0H 1N0
902/ 533-2099
www.desbarresmanor.com

Clientele: gay-friendly
Type: excellent accommodations & dining
Owned/ Run By: straights
Rooms: 10
Baths: private
Meals: full brkfst
Amenities: free parking, WiFi
Kids: welcome
Smoking: no
Rates: C$149-239
AC: yes

Forevergreen House B&B — Halifax

5560 Hwy 1
St Croix, NS B0N 2E0
902/ 792-1692
forevergreen_house@yahoo.ca

Clientele: gay-friendly
Type: b&b; Victorian farmhouse; orchard, gardens
Owned/ Run By: women
Rooms: 3
Baths: private
Meals: full brkfst
Kids: must not disturb others
Pets: welcome; not allowed on furniture
Smoking: no
Rates: C$65-85
AC: 10%

Fresh Start B&B — Halifax

2720 Gottingen St
Halifax, NS B3K 3C7
902/ 453-6616 888/ 453-6616
bbcanada.com/2262.html

Clientele: gay-friendly
Type: b&b-private home; in modest Victorian mansion in the heart of a small, friendly city; informal atmosphere; flexible check-in/out
Owned/ Run By: women
Rooms: 8
Baths: private & shared
Meals: full brkfst
Kids: welcome
Pets: welcome
Rates: C$70-120
AC: 10%

Roosters Glen B&B — Halifax

12 Glen Manor Dr
Dartmouth, NS B3A 3S5
902/ 462-1300 877/ 774-4999
www.roostersglen.com

Clientele: mixed gay/ straight
Type: b&b-private home; quiet & comfortable b&b 8 minutes from downtown Halifax
Owned/ Run By: gay men
Rooms: 3
Baths: private & shared
Meals: full brkfst
Amenities: free parking, laundry, DVDs/ videos, WiFi
Kids: welcome
Pets: no
Smoking: no
Rates: C$99-125
AC: 10%

1860 Kaulbach House Historic Inn — Lunenburg

75 Pelham St
Lunenburg, NS B0J 2C0
902/ 634-8818 800/ 568-8818
www.kaulbachhouse.com

Clientele: gay-friendly
Type: b&b-inn; situated in the center of the historic district; award-winning Victorian mansion w/ a view; gourmet brkfst
Owned/ Run By: gay men
Rooms: 7
Baths: private
Meals: full brkfst
Smoking: no
Rates: C$109-169
AC: 10%

Lighthouse Cottage — New Glasgow

PO Box 904
New Glasgow, NS B2H 5K7
902/ 928-0627
lighthousecottage@logic.bm

Clientele: gay-friendly
Type: rental home; oceanfront cottage; completely private; 1 hr from Halifax airport; "One of the nicest cottage rentals available in Nova Scotia"
Owned/ Run By: gay & straight
Rooms: 2-bdrm
Amenities: free parking, laundry
Kids: welcome
Pets: no
Smoking: no
Rates: C$750-1,900/ week
AC: 10%

The Mermaid and the Cow
West Branch

902/ 351-2714
www.themermaidandthecow.ca

Clientele: mixed gay/ lesbian
Type: cabin & campsites on 57-acre organic farm overlooking Berichon Hills
Owned/ Run By: lesbian
Rooms: 1
Baths: private

Pets: dogs ok on leash
Rates: US$20/ camping, $75/ cabin

Charles C Richards House Historic B&B
Yarmouth

17 Collins St
Yarmouth, NS B5A 3C7
902/ 742-0042
www.charlesrichardshouse.ns.ca

Clientele: mixed gay/ straight
Type: b&b; in Queen Anne Revival (circa 1893) brick mansion; offers elegance & style; situated in the historic district, just minutes from all attractions
Owned/ Run By: gay men
Rooms: 4

Baths: private
Meals: full brkfst
Rates: C$125-150
AC: 10%

Murray Manor B&B
Yarmouth

225 Main St
Yarmouth, NS B5A 1C6
902/ 742-9625 877/ 742-9629
www.murraymanor.com

Clientele: gay-friendly
Type: b&b-private home; beautiful 1820s heritage home; w/ lovely gardens; downtown near shopping, restaurants, ferry, airport & info center
Owned/ Run By: straights
Rooms: 3

Baths: shared
Meals: full brkfst
Kids: welcome
Pets: please inquire
Rates: C$80-95

Ptartan Ptarmigan
Yellowknife

5120 51st St
Yellowknife, NWT X1A 1S7
867/ 669-7222
www.yellowknife.com/Ptartan

Clientele: mixed gay/ straight
Type: b&b; comfortable home downtown; satellite TV; 20-minute walk (5-minute taxi) to floatbases & historic Old Town
Owned/ Run By: gay man
Rooms: 3
Baths: shared

Meals: full brkfst
Pets: no
Smoking: no
Rates: C$65-75

Apple Manor
Brighton

96 Main St, Box 11
Brighton, ON K0K 1H0
613/ 475-0351
www.bbcanada.com/1249.html

Clientele: gay-friendly
Type: b&b-private home; 150-yr-old, Loyalist-styled house; furnished w/ antiques
Owned/ Run By: straights
Rooms: 4
Baths: shared

Meals: full brkfst
Kids: no
Pets: no
Smoking: no
Rates: US$60-80

Butler Creek Country Inn
Brighton

202 County Rd #30
Brighton, ON K0K 1H0
613/ 475-1248 877/ 477-5827
www.butlercreekcountryinn.com

Clientele: gay-friendly
Type: b&b-inn; relax in Victorian home, circa 1905; tastefully decorated rms; on 10 acres w/ stream
Owned/ Run By: gay men
Rooms: 6
Baths: private & shared

Meals: full brkfst
Kids: welcome
Pets: no
Smoking: no
Rates: C$85-115
AC: 10%

The Calico Cat B&B   *Brockville*

93 Brockmere Cliff
Brockville, ON K6V 5T3
613/ 342-0363
www.bbcanada.com/350.html

Clientele: gay-friendly
Type: b&b; waterfront b&b located in the beautiful 1000 Islands
Owned/ Run By: straights
Rooms: 2
Baths: shared

Meals: expanded cont'l brkfst
Kids: welcome w/ prior approval
Pets: no
Smoking: no
Rates: C$80-110

Victoria View B&B Retreat   *Cobourg*

98 Bagot St
Cobourg, ON K9A 3G4
905/ 377-0620
www.victoriaview.ca

Clientele: mixed gay/ straight
Type: b&b; 1874 heritage home; "an elegant & peaceful retreat destination"
Owned/ Run By: gay men
Rooms: 3
Baths: private

Meals: full brkfst
Kids: please inquire
Pets: no
Rates: C$115-145

Log Cabin Heaven   *Elora*

384 Middlebrook Rd
Elora, ON N0B 1S0
519/ 846-9439
www.logcabinheaven.com

Clientele: mixed gay/ straight
Type: gated, secluded, 5-acre hilltop country spa retreat; spa amenities, indoor heated pool, waterfall, gourmet dining by blue ribbon California chef
Owned/ Run By: women
Rooms: 1

Baths: private
Meals: full brkfst
Amenities: free parking, laundry, pool, sauna, hot tub, massage, DVDs/ videos
Smoking: no
Rates: C$195

Boathouse Country Inn & Heritage Boat Tours   *Gananoque*

17-19 Front St, 1000 Islands
Rockport, ON K0E 1V0
613/ 659-2348 877/ 434-1212
www.boathouse-heritage.on.ca

Clientele: mixed gay/ straight
Type: b&b-inn; on St Lawrence River; quiet, rural setting; near Kingston, Ottawa, Montréal & Toronto
Owned/ Run By: gay/ lesbian & straight
Rooms: 10
Baths: private

Wheelchair Access: yes, 1 rm
Meals: full brkfst
Kids: welcome
Pets: no
Smoking: no
Rates: C$75-200
AC: 10%

Rockport Village Cottage   *Gananoque*

1 Front St, 1000 Islands
Rockport, ON K0E 1R0
613/ 659-3845
www.1000islandscottage.com

Clientele: gay-friendly
Type: rental home; riverside English cottage; in the heart of 1000 Islands; private garden; all amenities; quaint & pretty; in a tiny yet busy village; great for kayaking
Owned/ Run By: woman
Rooms: 2

Baths: shared
Kids: welcome
Pets: welcome
Smoking: no
Rates: C$900/ week

Trinity House Inn   *Gananoque*

90 Stone St South, 1000 Islands
Gananoque, ON K7G 1Z8
613/ 382-8383 800/ 265-4871
www.trinityinn.com

Clientele: gay-friendly
Type: b&b-inn; built in 1859; voted "Best Canadian Inn" in *North America Country Inns* magazine's Readers' Choice Survey 2000 & 2001; fireside fine dining
Owned/ Run By: gay man
Rooms: 8 (6 rms & 2 suites)

Baths: private
Meals: expanded cont'l brkfst
Kids: 10 yrs & up welcome in suites only
Pets: call ahead for info
Smoking: no
Rates: C$90-243

Rainbow Ridge Resort · *Grand Valley*

Country Rd 109
Grand Valley, ON
519/ 928-3262
www.geocities.com/rainbowridgeresort/

Clientele: mixed gay/ lesbian
Type: campground & trailer park; summers; located on 72 acres along Grand River; w/ hiking trails, fishing, restaurant, dance hall; day visitors welcome; 1 hr from Toronto

Owned/ Run By: gay men
Pets: welcome
Rates: C$15/ person

Dr WF Savage House B&B · *Guelph*

45 Colborne St
Elora, ON N0B 1S0
519/ 846-5325
www.bbcanada.com/savagehouse

Clientele: mixed gay/ lesbian
Type: b&b; home away from home in scenic village of Elora; w/ private garden, Victorian charm; steps from Elora Gorge; dinners available on request
Owned/ Run By: gay men
Rooms: 3

Baths: private & shared
Wheelchair Access: yes, 1 rm
Meals: full brkfst
Kids: welcome
Smoking: no
Rates: C$75-100

Cedars Campground · *Hamilton*

1039 5th Concession W Rd
Millgrove, ON L0R 1V0
905/ 659-3655 905/ 659-7342
www.cedarscampground.com

Clientele: mixed gay/ lesbian
Type: friendly LGBT campground on 130 unspoiled acres in southern Ontario; w/ dance club, full-service restaurant
Rooms: 10 (cabins, also tent/ trailer camping)
Baths: private & shared

Kids: welcome
Pets: welcome; must be leashed & controlled
Rates: C$65-95 (cabins); C$15 (camping)

Moonlight Point B&B · *Hillier*

613/ 399-5178
www.bbcanada.com/moonlightpoint

Clientele: mixed gay/ lesbian
Type: b&b-private home; modern rancher on 2.5 acres; near Lake Ontario beaches & wineries
Owned/ Run By: lesbians
Rooms: 2
Baths: private

Meals: expanded cont'l brkfst
Amenities: free parking, pool, outdoor ho tub, DVDs/ videos
Kids: no
Pets: please inquire
Smoking: no
Rates: C$90

Wildewood Guesthouse · *Maynooth*

970 Madawaska Rd, Box 121
Maynooth, ON K0L 2S0
613/ 338-3134
www.wildewood.net

Clientele: mixed gay/ lesbian
Type: guesthouse; located on 10 private acres on a hill overlooking pond; dinner also included
Owned/ Run By: gay men
Rooms: 2
Baths: shared

Wheelchair Access: yes, 2 rms
Meals: full brkfst
Amenities: indoor hot tub, DVDs/ videos
Kids: by arrangement
Pets: no
Smoking: no
Rates: C$175

Sunny Rock B&B · *Minden*

1144 Scotts Dam Rd
Minden, ON K0M 2K0
705/ 286-4922 888/ 786-6976
www.sunnyrock.on.ca

Clientele: gay-friendly
Type: b&b; offering upscale accommodations on historic log estate; 2.5 hrs N of Toronto; Haliburton Highlands lake country; sights & sounds of moving water
Owned/ Run By: straights
Rooms: 7

Baths: private & shared
Meals: full brkfst
Amenities: free parking, hot tub, massage DVDs/ videos
Smoking: no
Rates: C$130-250

The Village Antiques & Tea Room B&B
Morrisburg

4326 County Rd 31
Williamsburg, ON K0C 2H0
613/ 535–2463 877/ 264–3281
www.bbtearoom.com

Clientele: gay-friendly
Type: b&b-inn; combination antique shop/ tea rm/ inn; dining rm w/ excellent wine list; packages available
Owned/ Run By: gay men
Rooms: 4

Baths: private & shared
Meals: full brkfst
Kids: no
Pets: no
Smoking: no
Rates: C$65-110

Absolute Elegance B&B
Niagara Falls

5023 Culp St
Niagara Falls, ON L2G 2B6
905/ 353–8522 877/ 353–8522
nebedandbreakfast.com

Clientele: mixed gay/ straight
Type: b&b; beatiful Victorian circa 1855; all rms feature king-size bed, jacuzzi, fireplace, TV/ VCR; 10-minute walk to falls
Owned/ Run By: gay men
Rooms: 3

Baths: private
Meals: full brkfst
Kids: welcome if behaved & quiet
Smoking: no
Rates: US$100-170
AC: 10%

Amelia's
Niagara Falls

15526 Niagara River Pkwy
Niagara-on-the-Lake, ON L0S 1J0
905/ 468–5550
www.canvisit.com/Notlbba.218/

Clientele: mixed gay/ straight
Type: b&b-private home; Colonial-style home facing Niagara River & recreation trails; backs onto vineyards; walk to wineries
Owned/ Run By: gay men

Rooms: 3
Baths: private
Meals: full brkfst
Pets: under 25 lbs & crate-trained welcome
Rates: C$125-145

Bampfield Hall B&B
Niagara Falls

4761 Zimmerman Ave
Niagara Falls, ON L2E 3M8
905/ 353–8522 877/ 353–8522
www.niagaraniagara.com

Clientele: mixed gay/ straight
Type: b&b; in historic Gothic beauty circa 1872; w/ antiques & welcoming wrap-around veranda
Owned/ Run By: gay men
Rooms: 3
Baths: private

Meals: full brkfst
Amenities: free parking, hot tub, DVDs/ videos
Kids: welcome
Smoking: no
Rates: US$65-170
AC: 10%

Britaly B&B
Niagara Falls

7 The Promenade
Niagara-on-the-Lake, ON L0S 1J0
905/ 468-8778
www.britaly.com

Clientele: gay-friendly
Type: b&b; furnished w/ antiques; located in old town close to theater & shops
Owned/ Run By: gay men
Rooms: 3
Baths: private
Meals: full brkfst

Kids: no
Pets: no
Rates: C$95-120

Fairbanks House/ Ellis House
Niagara Falls

965 River Rd
Niagara Falls, ON L2E 3G6
905/ 371–3716 866/ 246–6616
www.mergetel.com/~fbhouse

Clientele: mixed gay/ lesbian
Type: b&b; in restored Victorian overlooking Niagara River, walk to falls; silver service in dining rm; A/C; fireplaces en suite, jacuzzi; also host to same-sex weddings
Owned/ Run By: lesbians/ gay men
Rooms: 8
Baths: private

Meals: full brkfst
Amenities: free parking, hot tub, DVDs/ videos
Kids: welcome
Pets: no
Smoking: no
Rates: C$75-160
AC: 10%

Oasis Niagara B&B
Niagara Falls

4266 Elgin St
Niagara Falls, ON L2E 2X6
905/ 353-0223
www.oasisniagara.com

Clientele: mostly men
Type: b&b; clean, comfortable, affordable rms; clothing-optional areas; near Niagara Falls; "only b&b in Niagara Falls catering exclusively to gay clientele"
Owned/ Run By: gay men
Rooms: 4

Baths: shared
Meals: cont'l brkfst
Kids: no
Pets: no
Smoking: no
Rates: US$55-80 (or C$75-110)
AC: 15%

Sheraton Fallsview Hotel & Conference Centre
Niagara Falls

6755 Fallsview Blvd
Niagara Falls , ON L2G 3W7

905/ 374-1077
800/ 747-9045

sheraton@fallsview.com
www.fallsview.com

Clientele: gay-friendly
Type: hotel; 300 yards from the mystical & enchanting Niagara Falls; "Niagara's most prestigious & award-winning hotel"
Owned/ Run By: straights
Nearby Attractions: casinos, IMAX Theatre, aviary, Maid of the Mist Boat Ride, Clifton Hill, golf, wineries, Shaw Theatre, Niagara on the Lake
Pickup Service: airport pickup; varies w/ airport
Transit: 1 1/2 hour to Toronto, 45 minutes to Hamilton, 45 minutes to Buffalo, NY
Rooms: 402 total, 35 suites, 110 kings, 292 queens, A/C, color TV, cable, deck (18), phone, refrigerator (106), rm service, maid service, enjoy oversized rms w/ warm, contemporary decor & the fabulous Sweet Sleeper Bed
Baths: private, bathtubs, showers, whirlpools, robes, hairdryers

Wheelchair Access: yes, 3 rms
Meals: coffee/tea only, vegetarian, allergy specific
Amenities: pool, sauna, hot tub, gym, coffee/ tea, parking & valet, 3 restaurants, concierge desk, fitness centre, banquet & ballrooms for weddings
Recreation: Niagara Parks
Kids: welcome
Pets: some restrictions apply
Smoking: ok (specified rms & area)
Reservations: required; walk-ins welcome (no guarantee) *Cancellation:* cancel by 2 days prior or forfeit 1 night + tax
Payment: cash, travelers checks, Visa, Amex, MC, Discover
Season: open yr-round
Rates: C$79-599
AC: 10%

Ambiance B&B
Ottawa

330 Nepean St
Ottawa, ON K1R 5G6
613/ 563-0421 888/ 366-8772
www.ambiancebandb.com

Clientele: mixed gay/ straight
Type: b&b; Parliament Hill, Rideau Canal, Byward Market, major attractions, all w/ walking distance
Owned/ Run By: gay
Rooms: 4
Baths: private & shared

Meals: full brkfst
Amenities: free parking, laundry, DVDs, videos, WiFi
Kids: please call
Pets: no
Smoking: no
Rates: C$85-110

Home Sweetland Home B&B
Ottawa

62 Sweetland Ave
Ottawa, ON K1N 7T6
613/ 234-1871
www.homesweetlandhome.ca

Clientele: mixed gay/ straight
Type: b&b; in historic downtown Ottawa home; walking distance of Byward Market, Parliament Hill, museums
Owned/ Run By: gay men
Rooms: 4

Baths: private & shared
Meals: full brkfst
Kids: welcome
Pets: no
Smoking: no
Rates: C$72-120

Inn on Somerset
Ottawa

282 Somerset St W
Ottawa, ON K2P 0J6
613/ 236-9309 800/ 658-3564
www.innonsomerset.com

Clientele: mixed gay/ straight
Type: b&b; Victorian elegance in the heart of Ottawa; close to bars, shopping & Parliament Hill
Owned/ Run By: gay/ lesbian & straight
Rooms: 11
Baths: private & shared

Meals: full brkfst
Kids: welcome
Pets: no
Smoking: no
Rates: C$75-140
AC: 10%

Rideau Inn
Ottawa

177 Frank St
Ottawa, ON K2P 0X4
613/ 688-2753 877/ 580-5015
www.rideauinn.ca

Clientele: mixed gay/ straight
Type: b&b; in elegantly restored Edwardian town house; w/ guests' own living rm, dining rm & kitchen; located in the center of Ottawa
Owned/ Run By: gay men
Rooms: 7

Baths: private & shared
Meals: expanded cont'l brkfst
Kids: 14 yrs & up welcome
Pets: no
Smoking: no
Rates: C$70-110
AC: 10%

Perth Manor
Perth

23 Drummond St W
Perth, ON K7H 2J6
613/ 264-0050
www.perthmanor.com

Clientele: mixed gay/ straight
Type: boutique hotel & reception facility; built in 1878; "Perth Manor is your chance to step back in time, yet still enjoy all of today's luxuries"
Owned/ Run By: gay men
Rooms: 6

Baths: private
Meals: full brkfst
Kids: welcome
Pets: welcome
Smoking: no
Rates: C$135-145
AC: 10%

Henderson House B&B
Picton

116 Main St
Consecon, ON K0K 1T0
613/ 394-5093
www.bbcanada.com/4952.html

Clientele: mixed gay/ straight
Type: b&b; lovely century home in park-like setting on Consecon River in Prince Edward County, Ontario
Owned/ Run By: lesbians
Rooms: 2

Baths: private
Meals: full brkfst
Kids: no
Pets: no
Smoking: no
Rates: C$85-100

Plantation House B&B
Picton

613/ 471-1116
www.plantationhouse.ca

Clientele: mixed gay/ straight
Type: b&b-private home; in Prince Edward County near Toronto; gracious hospitality, beautiful guestrooms; decadent, healthy brkfst
Owned/ Run By: gay men
Rooms: 4

Baths: private & shared
Meals: full brkfst
Amenities: free parking, WiFi
Kids: no
Pets: no
Smoking: no
Rates: C$80-125

Cedarbrook Farm B&B
Puslinch

312 8th Conc Rd W, RR 3
Puslinch, ON N0B 2J0
905/ 659-1566
www.cedarbrookfarm.on.ca

Clientele: mixed gay/ straight
Type: retreat; yr-round; available for overnight accommodations, getaway wknds & special events; 50 minutes W of Toronto; midway between Hamilton & Guelph
Owned/ Run By: lesbians

Rooms: 4 (bldgs)
Baths: private & shared
Meals: full brkfst
Kids: welcome w/ prior approval
Smoking: no
Rates: US$85-150

A Hundred Church Street

Stratford

100 Church St
Stratford, ON N5A 2R2
519/ 272-8845
www.ahundredchurchst.ca

Clientele: mixed gay/ straight
Type: b&b; in newly renovated 1902 home; downtown location
Owned/ Run By: gay men
Rooms: 4
Baths: private & shared
Meals: full brkfst

Amenities: free parking, outdoor hot tub, WiFi
Kids: 10 yrs & up welcome
Pets: no
Smoking: no
Rates: C$85-120

The Maples of Stratford

Stratford

220 Church St
Stratford, ON N5A 2R6
519/ 273-0810
www.bbcanada.com/maplesbb

Clientele: gay-friendly
Type: b&b-private home; in large Victorian, built in 1905; restored to reflect the early century grace & charm w/ a modern touch for your comfort
Rooms: 5

Baths: private & shared
Meals: expanded cont'l brkfst
Kids: please inquire
Pets: no
Smoking: no
Rates: C$65-115

Rainbow Guest House

Sudbury

43 Lorne St
Sudbury, ON P3C 4P1
705/ 688-0561

Clientele: men
Type: guesthouse; clean & quiet; 5 minutes from downtown Sudbury, Science North & Big Nickel Mine
Owned/ Run By: gay men
Rooms: 5

Baths: shared
Meals: coffee/tea only
Kids: welcome
Smoking: ok
Rates: C$30-40

213 Carlton Street—Toronto Townhouse

Toronto

213 Carlton St
Toronto, ON M5A 2K9
416/ 323-8898 877/ 500-0466
www.toronto-townhouse.com

Clientele: mixed gay/ straight
Type: b&b-private home; 130-year-old heritage home; 1999 & 2000 Tourism Toronto Award winner for Best Accommodation sponsored by Diners Club Int'l; "Best of Toronto.com" finalist; steps to the Gay Village; great brkfsts
Owned/ Run By: gay men

Rooms: 8
Baths: private & shared
Meals: full brkfst
Amenities: hot tub, WiFi
Kids: 12 yrs & up welcome
Smoking: no
Rates: C$69-169

A Seaton Dream

Toronto

243 Seaton St
Toronto, ON M5A 2T5
416/ 929-3363 866/ 878-8898
www.aseatondream.ca

Clientele: mixed gay/ straight
Type: b&b-inn; downtown Toronto accommodations; experience casual luxury in the center of the city; enjoy the garden patio, sauna & beautiful rms
Owned/ Run By: gay men
Rooms: 3

Baths: private & shared
Meals: full brkfst
Kids: please inquire
Pets: no
Smoking: no
Rates: C$85-130

B "R" Guest

Toronto

367 Ontario St
Toronto, ON M5A 2V8
416/ 928-0187 866/ 928-0187
www.brguesttoronto.com

Clientele: mixed gay/ straight
Type: 2-bdrm apt
Owned/ Run By: gay men
Kids: welcome
Pets: no

Rates: C$250
AC: 20%

Banting House Inn   *Toronto*

73 Homewood Ave
Toronto, ON M4Y 2K1
416/ 924-1458 800/ 823-8856
www.bantinghouse.com

Clientele: mixed gay/ straight
Type: guesthouse; beautifully restored Edwardian home in heart of lesbian/ gay community; private entrances off secluded garden
Owned/ Run By: gay men
Rooms: 7

Baths: private & shared
Meals: expanded cont'l brkfst
Kids: please inquire
Pets: please inquire
Smoking: no
Rates: C$85-150
AC: 10%

The Bear Foot Inn   *Toronto*

80-A Dundonald St
Toronto, ON M4Y 1K2
416/ 922-1658 888/ 871-2327
www.bearfootinn.com

Clientele: men
Type: b&b; bear-friendly inn in the gay village
Owned/ Run By: gay men
Rooms: 4
Baths: private

Meals: cont'l brkfst
Amenities: sauna, DVDs/ videos, WiFi
Pets: small dogs up to 25 lbs welcome
Smoking: no
Rates: C$115-175

Bent Inn   *Toronto*

107 Gloucester St
Toronto, ON M4Y 1M2
416/ 925-4499
www.bentinn.com

Clientele: men
Type: b&b-inn; masculine, spacious Victorian house; ideal for relaxing or being as wild as you can fantasize in our huge dungeon
Owned/ Run By: gay men
Rooms: 3
Baths: private & shared

Meals: coffee/tea only
Amenities: WiFi
Kids: no
Pets: well-behaved welcome
Smoking: ok
Rates: C$100-175
AC: 3%

Cawthra Square Bed & Breakfast Inns   *Toronto*

416/ 966-3074 800/ 259-5474
www.sleepwithfriends.com

Clientele: mixed gay/ lesbian
Type: b&b-inn; multiple historic homes to choose from; "delight in refined Edwardian charm & Victorian elegance"
Owned/ Run By: gay men
Rooms: 18+
Baths: private & shared

Meals: expanded cont'l brkfst
Amenities: laundry, hot tub, DVDs/ videos
Kids: welcome in some rms
Pets: please inquire
Smoking: no
Rates: C$99+
AC: varies

Dundonald House   *Toronto*

35 Dundonald St
Toronto, ON M4Y 1K3
416/ 961-9888 800/ 260-7227
www.dundonaldhouse.com

Clientele: mostly men
Type: b&b; voted "Best B&B"; 3-5 minute walk to every bar, restaurant, or club in the Village; complimentary touring bikes; work-out rm
Owned/ Run By: gay men
Rooms: 7
Baths: shared

Meals: full brkfst
Amenities: sauna, hot tub, massage,
Kids: no
Pets: no
Smoking: no
Rates: C$85-195
AC: 8% to qualifying agents

House on McGill   *Toronto*

110 McGill St
Toronto, ON M5B 1H6
416/ 351-1503 877/ 580-5015
www.mcgillbb.ca

Clientele: mixed gay/ straight
Type: b&b; elegant, cozy, restored Victorian town house; in the heart of Toronto's vibrant Gay Village; near theatres, restaurants, nightlife
Owned/ Run By: gay men

Rooms: 6
Baths: private & shared
Meals: expanded cont'l brkfst
Kids: 15 yrs & up welcome
Smoking: no
Rates: C$50-110

Pimblett's Rest B&B

Toronto

242 Gerrard St E
Toronto, ON
416/ 929-9525   416/ 921-6896
pimblett.ca

Clientele: mixed gay/ straight
Type: b&b-private home; located downtown in Cabbagetown; "eclectic & not quite normal: the owner is like John Cleese & the house is a veritable Fawlty Towers"
Rooms: 8

Baths: private & shared
Meals: full brkfst
Kids: 12 yrs & up welcome
Smoking: no
Rates: C$85-105
AC: 10%

Toronto Downtown Bed & Breakfast®

Toronto

57 Chicora Ave
Toronto, ON M5R 1T7
416/ 921-3533   877/ 950-6200
www.tdbab.com

Clientele: mixed gay/ straight
Type: b&b-private home; "Toronto's premier luxury boutique accommodation—you deserve nothing less"
Owned/ Run By: gay men
Rooms: 2 (queen rm & family suite)
Baths: private

Meals: full brkfst
Kids: 13 yrs & up welcome
Pets: no
Smoking: no
Rates: C$240-329
AC: 10%

The Point Tent & Trailer Resort

Turkey Point

918 Charlotteville Rd #2, RR 1
Vittoria, ON N0E 1W0
519/ 426-7275
www.get-tothepoint.com

Clientele: mostly men
Type: campground; 75 campsites & 24 RV hookups on 50 acres surrounded by forest & trails; clothing-optional area including pool; open 3rd wknd in April till 3rd wknd in Oct

Owned/ Run By: gay men
Pets: welcome; no aggressive breeds
Rates: C$16-65

Devil Lake B&B

Westport

8991 Perth Rd
Westport, ON K0H 2L0
613/ 273-4001
www.bbcanada.com/9132.html

Clientele: mostly women
Type: romantic lakeside getaway w/ fireplace & claw-foot tub; enjoy kayaking, canoeing, fishing & swimming; use of canoe included
Owned/ Run By: lesbian

Inn on the River

Windsor

3857 Riverside Dr E
Windsor, ON
519/ 945-2110   866/ 635-0055
www.windsorinnontheriver.com

Clientele: gay-friendly
Type: b&b-inn; charming old home built in 1890s; much of original interior intact; fireplace in great rm, dining rm & library; same-gender marriage packages
Owned/ Run By: gay & straight
Rooms: 5
Baths: private & shared

Meals: full brkfst
Amenities: free parking, hot tub
Kids: welcome
Pets: ok (kennel on-site)
Smoking: no
Rates: C$79-179
AC: please inquire

Nunn's Hollow Guest Suites

Woodstock

21 Delatre St
Woodstock, ON N4S 6B6
519/ 539-9780
www.nunnshollow.on.ca

Clientele: mostly men
Type: b&b-inn; in orange double-brick, workingman's Edwardian built in 1905; w/ beautiful, shady gardens; close to Stratford; new self-catering apt
Owned/ Run By: gay men

Rooms: 4
Baths: private
Meals: full brkfst
Amenities: hot tub
Rates: C$80-120

Blooming Breezes Executive Cottage
Charlottetown

108 Lowe Ln
Blooming Point, PE C0A 1T0
902/ 626-4475
www.bloomingbreezes.com

Clientele: mixed gay/ straight
Type: cottage; gorgeous private chalet w/in minutes of white-sand beach w/ great dunes; fully equipped; a great place to relax & get away from it all
Owned/ Run By: gay men
Rooms: 3

Baths: shared
Kids: welcome
Pets: no
Rates: C$140-250/ night; C$1,100-1,600/ week

Rainbow Lodge
Charlottetown

7521 TCH
Vernon Bridge, PE C0A 2E0
902/ 651-2202 800/ 268-7005
www.gaypei.com

Clientele: mixed gay/ lesbian
Type: b&b; in old converted general store that has been in the community for 100 yrs; many artifacts inside & cozy, well-appointed rms
Owned/ Run By: gay men
Rooms: 2

Baths: private
Meals: full brkfst
Kids: welcome
Pets: no
Smoking: no
Rates: C$80

Johnson Shore Inn
Souris

RR #3 Rte16
Souris, PE C0A 2B0
902/ 687-1340 877/ 510-9669
www.johnsonshoreinn.com

Clientele: mixed gay/ straight
Type: b&b-inn; built on 50 acres, this charming country inn offers spectacular ocean views, fireside meals, beautiful sunsets & miles of walking trails along the rugged shore
Owned/ Run By: lesbians

Rooms: 12
Baths: private
Wheelchair Access: yes, 4 rms
Meals: full brkfst
Kids: 10 yrs & up welcome
Rates: C$125-289
AC: 10%

Gîte aux Trois Pains
Baie-des-Sables

3 rue des Pins CP 127
Baie-des-Sables, QC G0J 1C0
418/ 772-6047 877/ 210-2910
www.bbcanada.com/giteauxtroispains

Clientele: mixed gay/ straight
Type: b&b; in nice, old house at the beginning of Gaspesie; near St Lawrence River & Jardins de Métis
Owned/ Run By: gay man
Rooms: 4
Baths: shared

Meals: full brkfst
Kids: welcome
Pets: welcome
Smoking: no
Rates: C$50-100
AC: 5%

Motel Alouette
Drummondville

1975 boul Mercure
Drummondville, QC J2B 3P3
819/ 478-4166 866/ 478-4166
www.motel-alouette.com

Clientele: mixed gay/ straight
Type: motel; 3 stars; 2 terraces & spa & sauna; halfway between Montréal & Québec; "pleasant environment for a moment of relaxation"
Owned/ Run By: gay men
Rooms: 25
Baths: private

Meals: cont'l brkfst
Amenities: free parking, laundry, sauna, outdoor hot tub, DVDs/ videos
Kids: no
Pets: welcome
Smoking: ok
Rates: US$80-140

Le Campagnard B&B
Granby

146 Denison Ouest
Granby, QC J2G 4C8
450/ 770-1424 450/ 777-0245
campagnard.ca

Clientele: gay-friendly
Type: b&b; beautiful location in nature
Rooms: 5
Baths: shared

Meals: cont'l brkfst
Kids: welcome
Smoking: no
Rates: C$100

Auberge de la Gare

1694 chemin Pierre-Peladeau
Ste-Adèle, QC J8B 1Z5
450/ 228-3140
888/ 825-4273 (in Québec only)
www.aubergedelagare.com

Clientele: mixed gay/ lesbian
Type: b&b; in Victorian inn, circa 1880
Owned/ Run By: gay/ lesbian & straight
Rooms: 5
Baths: private & shared
Meals: expanded cont'l brkfst

Pets: no
Smoking: ok (in pool rm)
Rates: C$60-80
AC: 10%

Havre du Parc Auberge

2788 Rte 125 N
St-Donat, QC J0T 2C0
819/ 424-7686
www.havreduparc.qc.ca

Clientele: mixed gay/ straight
Type: inn; in the heart of marvelous Laurentian Mtns; 30-minutes from downhill skiing; "a small & discreet corner of paradise on beautiful Lake Provost"
Owned/ Run By: gay men
Rooms: 9

Baths: private
Meals: full brkfst
Pets: small pet welcome in 1 rm only
Smoking: ok (in 40% of rms)
Rates: C$130-150 + tax
AC: 10%

Le Septentrion B&B

901 chemin St-Adolphe
Morin-Heights/ St-Sauveur, QC J0R 1H0
450/ 226-2665
www.leseptentrion.qc.ca

Clientele: mixed gay/ lesbian
Type: b&b-private home; 6,000-sq-ft Victorian on 3 secluded mtn acres; Canadian gov't rated 5 stars; very luxurious decor
Owned/ Run By: gay men
Rooms: 5 (includes 2 large suites)
Baths: private

Meals: full brkfst
Amenities: free parking, laundry, pool outdoor hot tub, DVDs/ videos
Kids: no
Pets: no
Smoking: no
Rates: C$120-250
AC: 10%

Les Réfugiés

418/ 986-4192
www.bblesrefugies.com

Clientele: gay-friendly
Type: b&b-private home; 2 out of 4 rms have TV; veggie food on demand
Owned/ Run By: gay men
Rooms: 4

Baths: shared
Meals: full brkfst
Smoking: no
Rates: C$60-80
AC: 8%

Au Gîte du Cerf Argenté

2984 chemin Georgeville Rd
Magog, QC J1X 3W4
819/ 847-4264
www.cerfargente.com

Clientele: mixed gay/ straight
Type: b&b; idyllic natural setting in a mid-19th-c farmhouse; wildlife; view of Mt Orford & Lake Memphrémagog; also camping
Owned/ Run By: gay men
Rooms: 5

Baths: private
Meals: expanded cont'l brkfst
Kids: welcome
Pets: please inquire
Smoking: ok
Rates: C$78-115
AC: 10%

The Mascul'inn/ Auberge au Masculin

202 Bolton Pass
Bolton Ouest, QC J0E 1V0
450/ 243-5904
www.aumasculin17.com

Clientele: men
Type: b&b-inn; a relaxing, luxurious French inn w/ English surroundings; 1 hr to Montréal; near fine restaurants & Brome Lake
Owned/ Run By: gay men
Rooms: 4

Baths: private & shared
Meals: full brkfst
Kids: no
Pets: no
Rates: C$90-140
AC: 10%

Abri du Voyageur Hotel   *Montréal*

9 rue Ste-Catherine West
Montréal, QC
514/ 849-2922
www.abri-voyageur.ca

Clientele: gay-friendly
Type: hotel; charming, good-value; in downtown Montréal; 15-minute walk to the Village
Rates: C$42+

Absolument Montréal B&B   *Montréal*

1790 Amherst
Montréal, QC H2L 3L6
514/ 223-0017 866/ 360-1351
www.absolumentmontreal.com

Clientele: mixed gay/ straight
Type: b&b; "enjoy luxury amenities in our cinema-themed rms & a fabulous gourmet brkfst in Montréal's Gay Village!"
Owned/ Run By: gay men
Rooms: 5
Baths: private
Meals: full brkfst

Amenities: outdoor hot tub, massage, DVDs/ videos, WiFi
Kids: 16+ welcome
Pets: no
Smoking: no
Rates: C$89-209
AC: please inquire

Accommodations International B&B   *Montréal*

2002 Champlain #1
Montréal, QC H2L 2T3
514/ 596-2317 888/ 334-0348
perso.b2b2c.ca/bnb

Clientele: men
Type: b&b; "quiet, clean, inexpensive"; walking distance to Gay Village; terrace
Owned/ Run By: gay men
Rooms: 3

Rates: C$49-95

Alcazar B&B   *Montréal*

514/ 223-2622 866/ 589-8964
www.alcazarmontreal.com

Clientele: mostly men
Type: beautiful cozy b&b located in the heart of Montreal's Gay Village
Owned/ Run By: gay men
Rooms: 3
Baths: private & shared

Meals: expanded cont'l brkfst
Smoking: no
Rates: C$75-95

Alexandrie-Montréal   *Montréal*

750 Amherst
Montréal, QC H2L 3L6
514/ 525-9420
www.alexandrie-montreal.com

Clientele: gay-friendly
Type: b&b-inn; rms & apts in the Village; specials for groups or extended stays
Owned/ Run By: gay men
Rooms: 9
Baths: private & shared

Meals: cont'l brkfst
Kids: welcome
Pets: welcome
Rates: C$50-200

Auberge Cosy   *Montréal*

274 Ste-Catherine Est
Montréal, QC H2L 2H2
514/ 525-2151
www.aubergecosy.com

Clientele: men
Type: b&b; sunny terrace; "the best location in the heart of the Gay Village"
Owned/ Run By: gay men
Rooms: 14
Baths: shared
Meals: expanded cont'l brkfst

Amenities: laundry, indoor hot tub
Rates: C$80-140

Auberge de la Fontaine
Montréal

1301 Rachel St est
Montréal, QC H2J 2K1
514/ 597-0166 800/ 597-0597
www.aubergedelafontaine.com

Clientele: mixed gay/ straight
Type: b&b-inn; in magnificent turn-of-the-century stone house overlooking Lafontaine Park; peaceful oasis ideally located; free access to kitchen for snacks
Owned/ Run By: straights
Rooms: 21

Baths: private
Wheelchair Access: yes, 2 rms
Meals: expanded cont'l brkfst
Kids: welcome; under 12 yrs free
Smoking: ok
Rates: C$119-360
AC: 10%

Auberge La Raveaudiere B&B
Montréal

11 Hatley Center
North Hatley, QC J0B 2C0
819/ 842-2554
www.laraveaudiere.com

Clientele: mixed gay/ straight
Type: b&b-inn; in elegant 19th-c country inn; an exquisite vacation destination; guests are amazed by its size, warm ambience & sophisticated decor; 1.5 hrs from Montréal

Owned/ Run By: gay men
Rooms: 7
Baths: private
Meals: full brkfst
Rates: C$105-165

Aux Studios Montcalm—Guesthouse
Montréal

902 Rene-Levesque E #201
Montréal, QC H2L 2L5
514/ 815-6195
www.auxstudiosmontcalm.com

Clientele: mostly men
Type: guesthouse; "your home away from home!"; w/in walking distance from all of Montréal's hottest tourist attractions
Owned/ Run By: gay men
Rooms: 3

Baths: private
Kids: welcome
Pets: welcome
Smoking: ok
Rates: C$75+

B&B L'escogriffe
Montréal

1264 rue Wolfe
Montréal, QC H2L 3J3
514/ 523-4800 877/ 523-6105
www.lescogriffe.com

Clientele: men only
Type: b&b; 6 well-appointed rms located in an elegant guesthouse; in heart of Gay Village; A/C, Cable TV
Owned/ Run By: gay men
Rooms: 6
Baths: shared

Meals: full brkfst
Amenities: DVDs/ videos, WiFi
Kids: no
Pets: no
Smoking: ok
Rates: C$60-150

B&B Le Terra Nostra
Montréal

277 Beatty
Montréal, QC
514/ 762-1223 866/ 550-5235
www.leterranostra.com

Clientele: gay-friendly
Type: b&b; affordable luxury; on St-Lawrence River; near city life; stylish rms w/ spacious bathrms, heated floor, award-winning garden
Owned/ Run By: straights
Rooms: 3

Baths: private
Meals: full brkfst
Amenities: free parking, DVDs/ videos
Kids: welcome
Pets: please inquire
Smoking: no
Rates: C$85-135

B&B Le Cartier
Montréal

1219 rue Cartier
Montréal, QC H2K 4C4
514/ 917-1829 877/ 524-0495
www.bblecartier.com

Clientele: mixed gay/ straight
Type: b&b; 100-yr-old stone house in Gay Village; stylish rms w/ back terrace; fun host!; close to all tourist attractions
Owned/ Run By: gay men
Rooms: 5
Baths: private & shared
Meals: expanded cont'l brkfst

Amenities: free parking, WiFi
Kids: welcome; please inquire about kids under 15 yrs of age
Pets: no
Smoking: no
Rates: C$60-125
AC: negotiable

Big Boys Guesthouse

Montréal

1478 de Maisonneuve Est
Montréal, QC H2L 2A9
514/ 525-4222 866/ 889-2697
www.bigboysguesthouse.com

Clientele: men
Type: b&b-private home; Chinese, Arabic, Victorian & Roman-themed rms; in the heart of the Gay Village
Owned/ Run By: gay men
Rooms: 5
Baths: shared
Meals: expanded cont'l brkfst
Amenities: laundry, outdoor hot tub,

massage, WiFi
Kids: welcome
Pets: welcome
Smoking: no
Rates: C$90-170

Le Bliss

Montréal

282 rue Panet
Montréal, QC H2L 2Y8
514/ 277-0170
www.lebliss.com

Clientele: mixed gay/ straight
Type: apt; elegant & comfortable boutique-apt in the heart of the Village; close to downtown & historic district; short- or long-term stays
Owned/ Run By: gay man
Rooms: 3

Baths: private
Kids: no
Pets: no
Smoking: no

Cachet Accommodations Network (CAN)

Montréal

514/ 355-4636 (9am-noon EST)
www.can-reservations.htmlplanet.com

Clientele: mixed gay/ lesbian
Type: reservation service; "Montréal's only gay & lesbian service for rm bookings & short-term lodging reservations; since 1984; mention Damron when calling for details
Owned/ Run By: gay man
Wheelchair Access: yes
Meals: cont'l brkfst
Amenities: free parking, WiFi

Kids: no
Pets: welcome
Smoking: no
Rates: please inquire

Le Chasseur B&B

Montréal

567 rue St-André
Montréal, QC H2L 3T5
514/ 521-2238 800/ 451-2238
www.lechasseur.com

Clientele: mixed gay/ straight
Type: b&b; charming Victorian row house; large rm, quiet & clean; near everything; "best prices in the Village"
Owned/ Run By: gay men
Rooms: 8
Baths: private & shared
Meals: cont'l brkfst

Kids: welcome
Pets: welcome
Smoking: ok (in smoking lounge)
Rates: C$34-209
AC: 10%

Chez Philippe

Montréal

457 rue Ste-Catherine Est
Montreal, QC H2K 2J9
514/ 890-1666 877/ 890-1666
www.chezphilippe.info

Clientele: mixed gay/ straight
Type: b&b; w/in walking distance to Gay Village; vegan brkfst; large terrace
Owned/ Run By: gay men
Rooms: 3
Baths: shared
Meals: full vegetarian brkfst
Kids: no

Pets: no
Rates: C$55-135

La Conciergerie Guest House

Montréal

1019 rue St-Hubert
Montréal, QC H2L 3Y3
514/ 289-9297
www.laconciergerie.ca

Clientele: mostly men
Type: b&b; beautiful Victorian built in 1885; in the summer, tan on the rooftop sundeck; enjoy the indoor jacuzzi yr-round; gym on-site
Owned/ Run By: gay men
Nearby Attractions: Old Montréal, casino, amusement park, museums, galleries, antiquaries, botanical gardens, Olympic Village
Transit: near public transit; 15 minutes to airport (cab); 5-minute cab ride to train station; 3 blks bus station; 2 blks to métro (subway)
Rooms: 17 total, 1 suite, 21 queens, A/C, color TV (1), cable TV (1), ceiling fan (1), refrigerator (1), safer sex supplies, maid service, uncluttered & well-appointed
Baths: private & shared, bathtubs, showers
Meals: expanded cont'l brkfst
Amenities: office hrs: 8am-11pm EST; laundry, indoor hot tub, gym, on-street parking, massage by appointment, free wireless connections & PC to check email, sundeck; nudity ok at sundeck, hot tub
Recreation: biking & inline skating trails, ice-skating, nature walks in Mont Royal Park
Kids: 16 yrs & up welcome
Pets: by arrangement
Pets   On Premises: 1 dog
Smoking: no
Reservations: required *Deposit:* required, 1 night (nonrefundable), due w/in 1 week of booking *Cancellation:* cancel by 3 days prior or forfeit deposit *Minimum Stay:* 3-5 nights (holiday wknds & special events) *Check in/ out:* flexible/ noon
Payment: cash, travelers checks, Visa, MC
Season: open yr-round *High season:* April-Dec
Rates: C$99-200 *Discounts:* 10% (off-season)
AC: 10%

La Conciergerie is Montréal's premier guesthouse. Since our opening in 1985, we have gained an ever-growing popularity around the world.

This beautiful Victorian home built in 1885 offers a total of 17 rooms, with shared bath, and 9 with private bath. All of our rooms are furnished with comfortable queen-size beds and duvet comforters. The rooms are air conditioned for your comfort.

The house is centrally located, within walking distance of most major points of interest.

In summer months, you can take advantage of our private rooftop sun deck to work on your tan. All year round there is a warm Jacuzzi to relax in and we have a gym on-site for your workouts.

We offer free wireless connections and a PC to check up on your email. Our European-style breakfast is served from 8am to noon.

Le Cottage B&B
Montréal

1415 de la Visitation
Montréal, QC H2L 3B7
514/ 678-9638
www.lecottage.ca

Clientele: mixed gay/ straight
Type: b&b; inspired by boutique hotels
Owned/ Run By: gay men
Rooms: 3
Baths: shared
Meals: full brkfst

Amenities: WiFi
Kids: no
Pets: no
Smoking: no
Rates: C$87-99
AC: 10%

Delta Montréal
Montréal

475 Ave President Kennedy
Montréal, QC H3A 1J7
514/ 286-1986 877/ 286-1986
www.deltahotels.com

Clientele: gay-friendly
Type: hotel; 4-star hotel in great downtown location; close to gay area, underground shopping, restaurants, bars & museums
Owned/ Run By: straights
Rooms: 456
Baths: private
Wheelchair Access: yes, 6 rms

Amenities: free parking, laundry, pool, sauna, indoor hot tub, massage
Kids: welcome
Pets: welcome if supervised
Smoking: ok
Rates: C$129-259
AC: 10%

Gay Bed
Montréal

1002 Champlain #1
Montréal, QC H2L 2T3
514/ 596-2317 888/ 334-0348
www.gaybed.ca

Clientele: mostly men
Type: b&b; in Gay Village; amenities include TV, VCR, cable, "gay XXX," A/C
Owned/ Run By: gay men
Rooms: 4
Baths: shared
Meals: expanded cont'l brkfst

Amenities: free parking, laundry, DVDs/ videos, WiFi
Kids: no
Pets: no
Smoking: no
Rates: C$$49-69+

Hotel du Fort
Montréal

1390 rue du Fort
Montréal, QC H3H 2R7
514/ 938-8333 800/ 565-6333
www.hoteldufort.com

Clientele: mixed gay/ straight
Type: 4-star European boutique hotel built in 1992; high-speed internet access in all rms
Owned/ Run By: gay & straight
Rooms: 127

Baths: private
Wheelchair Access: yes, all rms
Meals: expanded cont'l brkfst
Kids: welcome
Rates: C$135-275
AC: 10%

Hotel Dynastie
Montréal

1723 St-Hubert
Montréal, QC H2L 3Z1
514/ 529-5210 877/ 529-5210
www.hoteldynastie.com

Clientele: mixed gay/ straight
Owned/ Run By: gay men
Rooms: 6
Baths: private

Rates: C$58-88

Hotel le St-André
Montréal

1285 rue St-André
Montréal, QC H2L 3T1
514/ 849-7070 800/ 265-7071
www.hotelsaintandre.ca

Clientele: mixed gay/ straight
Type: hotel; clean, quiet & comfortable; very reasonable rates; located in downtown Montréal on the edge of Gay Village; w/in walking distance of many attractions, including Old Montréal
Owned/ Run By: gay & straight
Rooms: 62

Baths: private
Meals: cont'l brkfst
Kids: welcome
Pets: no
Smoking: ok
Rates: C$68-148
AC: 10%

Hotel Lord Berri

Montréal

1199 rue Berri
Montréal, QC H2L 4C6
514/845-9236 888/363-0363
www.lordberri.com

Clientele: gay-friendly
Type: hotel; located in the heart of a charming, cosmopolitan city; w/ European character that brings out all of its charming beauty
Owned/ Run By: straights
Rooms: 154

Baths: private
Wheelchair Access: yes, most rms
Kids: welcome
Pets: no
Smoking: ok
Rates: C$99-159
AC: 10%

Hotel Manoir des Alpes

Montréal

1245 rue St-André
Montréal, QC H2L 3T1
514/ 845-9803 800/ 465-2929
www.hotelmanoirdesalpes.qc.ca

Clientele: gay-friendly
Type: hotel; a comfortable 3-star hotel reminiscent of a French Alpine inn; located in downtown Montréal
Rooms: 29
Baths: private
Meals: cont'l brkfst

Amenities: free parking, jacuzzi (in some rms)
Kids: welcome
Pets: no
Smoking: ok
Rates: C$60-90+

The House of Angels B&B

Montréal

1640 rue Alexandre de Sève
Montréal, QC H2L 2V7
514/ 527-9890
pages.videotron.com/anges

Clientele: mostly men
Type: b&b-private home; comfortable rms in cosy & quiet apt; access to terrace; brkfst buffet; great location: 1 blk from all the action
Owned/ Run By: gay men

Rooms: 2
Baths: shared
Meals: expanded cont'l brkfst
Rates: C$50-90
AC: 10%

Le Houseboy B&B

Montréal

1281 rue Beaudry
Montréal, QC H2L 3E3
514/ 525-1459 866/ 525-1459
www.lehouseboy.com

Clientele: men
Type: b&b; nice cozy rms; outdoor jacuzzi; garden & patio; right in the Gay Village; 1 minute walking distance from Sainte-Catherine St & subway
Owned/ Run By: gay men
Rooms: 7
Baths: shared

Meals: full brkfst
Amenities: outdoor hot tub, DVDs/ video, WiFi
Kids: no
Pets: no
Smoking: no
Rates: C$70-120

Immeuble Avenue Lacombe

Montréal

3536 av Lacombe
Montréal, QC H3T 1M1
514/ 738-5787 (fax only)
www.aptmontreal.com

Clientele: gay-friendly
Type: beautiful, fully furnished apts (bachelor, 1- & 2-bdrm); 4km from downtown, subway station next door; restaurants, gourmet grocery close by
Rooms: 3 apts

Baths: private
Kids: welcome
Pets: no
Smoking: no
Rates: C$100-150+ (also monthly & weekly rates)

Jade Blue B&B

Montréal

1225 de Bullion
Montréal, QC H2X 2Z3
514/ 878-9843 800/ 878-5048
www.jadeblue.net

Clientele: mixed gay/ straight
Type: b&b-inn; 3-story 1890 Victorian; between the Gay Village, the Old City & downtown; given 4-star rating from Quebec Tourism
Rooms: 5
Baths: private

Meals: full brkfst
Amenities: free parking, laundry, DVD videos, WiFi
Kids: welcome
Pets: no
Smoking: no
Rates: C$75-155
AC: 10%

Lindsey's B&B for Women
Montréal

974 Laval Ave
Montréal, QC H2W 2J2
14/ 843-4869 888/ 655-8655
lindseys.ca

Clientele: women
Type: b&b-private home; restored Victorian greystone in the heart of the "cool" plateau Mont-Royal; walk to everything
Owned/ Run By: lesbians
Rooms: 3
Baths: private & shared

Meals: full brkfst
Amenities: free parking, massage, WiFi
Kids: by arrangement
Pets: no
Smoking: no
Rates: C$75-145
AC: 5%

Loews Hotel Vogue
Montréal

425 rue de la Montagne
Montréal, QC H3G 1Z3
14/ 285-5555 800/ 465-6654
www.loewshotels.com

Type: hotel; Montréal's most fashionable address; upscale service, boutique style; all rms w/ comfy duvets, oversize spa baths w/ jacuzzi tubs & separate showers
Rooms: 126
Baths: private
Wheelchair Access: yes, 2 rms

Amenities: jacuzzi (in rm)
Kids: welcome
Pets: welcome
Smoking: ok
Rates: C$169+
AC: 10%

Les Lofts de L'Apothicaire
Montréal

623 rue Amherst
Montréal, QC H2L 3L4
14/ 998-2056
www.lesloftsdelapothicaire.com

Clientele: mostly men
Type: apt; luxurious loft in heart of the Gay Village; private entrance
Owned/ Run By: gay men
Rooms: 2
Baths: private

Amenities: laundry, WiFi
Kids: no
Pets: no
Smoking: no
Rates: C$299/ night, C$1,900/ week

Montréal Boutique Suite Guesthouse
Montréal

269 rue de Champlain
Montréal, QC H2L 2R9
14/ 521-9436 514/ 521-3523
www.montrealboutiquesuite.com

Clientele: mixed gay/ lesbian
Type: guesthouse; stylish village guesthouse suite; alternative to shared b&b facilities or a commercial hotel
Owned/ Run By: gay men
Rooms: 1
Baths: private

Meals: expanded cont'l brkfst
Amenities: laundry, hot tub, massage
Kids: no
Pets: no
Smoking: no
Rates: C$118-160

Petite Auberge Les Bons Matins
Montréal

401 Argyle Ave
Montréal, QC H3G 1V5
14/ 931-9167 800/ 588-5280
www.bonsmatins.com

Clientele: gay-friendly
Type: b&b-inn; award-winning establishment; in the heart of downtown; antique-furnished rms; some rms w/ fireplaces or jacuzzis
Owned/ Run By: gay men
Rooms: 23
Baths: private

Meals: full brkfst
Amenities: jacuzzi, WiFi
Kids: welcome; under 12 yrs free
Pets: no
Smoking: no
Rates: C$119-229
AC: 10%

Le Roy d'Carreau Guest House
Montréal

537 rue Amherst
Montréal, QC H2L 3L4
14/ 524-2493 877/ 527-7975
www.leroydcarreau.com

Clientele: mixed gay/ lesbian
Type: guesthouse; 1870 restored townhouse, centrally located in the Village; stunning courtyard terrace; 4 sun rated
Owned/ Run By: gay men
Rooms: 5
Baths: private & shared

Meals: cont'l brkfst
Amenities: laundry, indoor hot tub, WiFi
Kids: welcome; must be quiet after 11pm
Pets: with restrictions; call ahead
Smoking: no
Rates: C$95-300
AC: 10%

Le St-Christophe

Montréal

1597 rue St-Christophe
Montréal, QC H2L 3W7
514/ 527-7836 888/ 521-7836
www.stchristophe.com

Clientele: men
Type: guesthouse; an attractive escape from the bustle of the outside world
Owned/ Run By: gay men
Rooms: 5
Baths: private & shared

Meals: full brkfst
Amenities: indoor hot tub, massage, DVDs, videos
Smoking: no
Rates: C$79-160

St-Lawrence Apartments

Montréal

65 René-Lévèsque Est
Montréal, QC H2X-1N2
514/ 998-0047
www.apartments-montreal.com

Clientele: mixed gay/ straight
Type: 3 luxurious fully equipped apts; in heart of Montréal; queen-size bed; walking distance to Gay Village & entertainment
Owned/ Run By: straights
Rooms: 2 (apts)

Baths: private
Amenities: laundry, DVDs/ videos, WiFi
Kids: welcome
Pets: no
Smoking: ok
Rates: US$695-895/ week
AC: 10%

W Montréal T&G⊕

Montréal

901 Square Victoria
Montréal, QC H2Z 1R1
514/ 395-3100
877/ WHOTELS (reservations only)
www.whotels.com/montreal

Clientele: gay-friendly
Type: hotel; "tucked away in the heart of the unique, up-&-coming Quartier International District, close to downtown & Old Montréal"
Rooms: 152
Baths: private
Wheelchair Access: yes, 7 rms

Amenities: laundry, massage, DVDs, videos, WiFi
Kids: welcome
Pets: welcome
Smoking: ok (1 smoking flr)
Rates: C$249-5,000
AC: 10%

Le Zebre B&B

Montréal

514/ 528-6801
www.bblezebre.com

Clientele: mixed gay/ straight
Type: b&b; elegant Victorian house in front of Park Lafontaine, near Village
Owned/ Run By: gay men
Rooms: 4
Baths: private & shared

Meals: full brkfst
Amenities: indoor hot tub
Kids: welcome w/ restrictions
Pets: no
Rates: C$87-175
AC: no

Auberge le Flamant et la Tortue

Morin Heights

796 Ch St-Adolphe
Morin Heights, QC J0R 1H0
450/ 226-2009 877/ 616-2009
www.aubergeleflamantetlatortue.ca

Clientele: mixed gay/ straight
Type: on river near Montréal; fireplaces
Owned/ Run By: lesbians
Rooms: 12
Baths: private

Meals: full brkfst
Kids: welcome
Pets: no
Smoking: no
Rates: C$90

Le Coureur des Bois Guest House

Québec City

15 rue Ste-Ursule
Québec City, QC G1R 4C7
418/ 692-1117 800/ 269-6414
gayquebec.net/hebergement.html

Clientele: mixed gay/ lesbian
Type: guesthouse; located in historic stone house
Owned/ Run By: gay men
Rooms: 6
Baths: shared

Meals: expanded cont'l brkfst
Kids: no
Pets: no
Smoking: no
Rates: C$65-135
AC: 10%

Dans les Bras de Morphée
Québec City

225 chemin Royal,
St-Jean-De-L'Ile d'Orléans
Québec City, QC G0A 3W0
418/ 829-3792
www.danslesbrasdemorphee.ca

Clientele: gay-friendly
Type: b&b; in Normandy-style hilltop estate overlooking St Lawrence River; 15 minutes from old Québec; sublime landscapes; outdoor trails; separate guesthouse available
Owned/ Run By: straights

Rooms: 4
Baths: private
Meals: full brkfst
Kids: welcome
Pets: no
Smoking: ok
Rates: C$115-140

Domaine Vagabond
Québec City

878 rang 5 Ouest
oly, QC G0S 1M0
18/ 728-5522
f.geocities.com/domainevagabond/
ndex.html

Clientele: men
Type: campground; w/ 100 campsites; 3 trailers & a chalet; also full bar & restaurant
Meals: full brkfst

Rates: US$22-32 (camping); $40-95 (trailers & chalet)

Hôtel Dominion 1912
Québec City

26 rue St-Pierre
uébec City, QC G1K 4A8
18/ 692-2224 888/ 833-5253
www.hoteldominion.com

Type: hotel
Rooms: 60
Baths: private
Wheelchair Access: yes, 2 rms

Meals: expanded cont'l brkfst
Smoking: ok
Rates: C$169-265
AC: 10%

Hôtel Germain Des Prés
Québec City

200 av Germain des Prés
ainte-Foy, QC G1V 3M7
18/ 658-1224 800/ 463-5253
www.germaindespres.com

Clientele: gay-friendly
Type: hotel; "unequalled comfort, exquisite decor"; read under the quilt or spend your day online w/ no concern for tomorrow
Owned/ Run By: women
Rooms: 126
Baths: private

Wheelchair Access: yes, 1 rm
Meals: expanded cont'l brkfst
Kids: welcome
Smoking: ok
Rates: C$129-250
AC: 10%

Hotel Le Clos Saint-Louis
Québec City

9 Saint-Louis
uébec City, QC G1R 3Z2
18/ 694-1311 800/ 461-1311
www.clossaintlouis.com

Clientele: mixed gay/ straight
Type: hotel; small Victorian-style boutique hotel; located in historic district near shops & restaurants; "the most romantic small hotel in Québec City"
Owned/ Run By: women
Rooms: 18
Baths: private

Meals: cont'l brkfst
Amenities: free parking, laundry, massage, WiFi
Kids: no
Pets: no
Rates: C$165-255
AC: 10%

Hôtel-Motel Le Voyageur
Québec City

250 boul Sainte-Anne
uébec City, QC G1J 1Y2
18/ 661-7701 800/ 463-5568
www.motel-voyageur.com

Clientele: mixed gay/ straight
Type: hotel; suburban atmosphere 5 minutes from activities; restaurant & 2 bars
Owned/ Run By: gay & straight
Rooms: 64
Baths: private

Meals: cont'l brkfst
Kids: welcome
Pets: no
Smoking: ok
Rates: C$70-120
AC: 10%

Le Moulin de St-Laurent Chalets

Québec City

754 chemin Royal
St Laurent, Ile d' Orleans, QC G0A 3Z0

418/ 829-3888
888/ 629-3888

info@moulinstlaurent.qc.ca
www.moulinstlaurent.qc.ca

Clientele: mixed gay/ straight
Type: cottage; fully equipped luxury riverfront chalets along the St Lawrence on beautiful Ile d'Orleans; 20 minutes from Old Québec City; also fine-dining restaurant
Owned/ Run By: straights
Nearby Attractions: 15 miles to Old Québec City & Ste-Anne deBeaupré; 8 miles to Montmorency Falls; located on beautiful Island of Orleans
Transit: near public transit; 25 miles to airport; 15 miles to bus/ train station
Rooms: 8 (chalets) total, 1 suite, 1 king, A/C (2), color TV (4), DVD/ VCR (4), cable TV (4), ceiling fan (4), fireplace (4), deck, maid service, full kitchens, private entrances, 3 chalets w/ washer/ dryer; all chalets have queen beds & some also have doubles & singles
Baths: private, bathtubs, showers, whirlpools, hairdryers
Wheelchair Access: yes, 1 rm
Meals: expanded cont'l brkfst, restaurant offers fine regional cuisine (sweetbreads, wild game, fish)
Amenities: office hrs: 9am-5pm; free parking, laundry, pool, coffee/ tea, waterfront sites, stereo

Recreation: tennis courts, x-country & alpine skiing, snowmobiling, golf, cycling paths (rollerblading)
Kids: welcome
Pets: welcome in some chalets
Smoking: ok
Reservations: required *Deposit:* credit card guarantee *Cancellation:* cancel by 15 days prior or forfeit 15% (full amount if w/in 24hrs) *Check in/ out:* 3pm/ noon

Payment: cash, travelers checks, Visa, Amex, MC
Season: open yr-round *High season:* July Aug
Rates: C$50-100/ person
AC: 8%

Bain de Nature

St-Alphonse-de-Granby

127 rue Lussier
St-Alphonse-de-Granby, QC J0E 2A0
450/ 375-4765
www.baindenature.qc.ca

Clientele: men
Type: guesthouse; private home & 20 campsites; near a beautiful small lake (great for swimming) surrounded by rocks, flowers & forest
Owned/ Run By: gay men
Rooms: 3

Baths: shared
Meals: full brkfst
Amenities: free parking, sauna, indoor h tub, DVDs/ videos
Rates: C$90

Domaine Gay Luron

St-François-du-Lac

263 Rte Grande Terre
St-François-du-Lac, QC J0G 1M0
450/ 568-3634
www.gayluron.com

Clientele: men
Type: full-service campground w/ restaurant & bar, chalet, cabins, apts & RV hookups
Owned/ Run By: gay men
Wheelchair Access: yes, some rms
Meals: full brkfst

Pets: please inquire
Rates: US$19+

Auberge à l'Arrêt du Temps

Ste-Anne-de-la-Pérade

965 boul de Lanaudière
Ste-Anne-de-la-Pérade, QC G0X 2J0
418/ 325-3590 877/ 325-3590
www.laperade.qc.ca/arretdutemps

Clientele: mixed gay/ straight
Type: b&b-inn; 18th-c mansion; French garden, 2 gazebos, spa & solarium
Owned/ Run By: gay men
Rooms: 4
Baths: private & shared
Meals: full brkfst

Kids: welcome
Smoking: no
Rates: US$55-146

L' Auberge Ste-Catherine-de-Hatley

Ste-Catherine-de-Hatley

2 rue Grand
Ste-Catherine-de-Hatley, QC J0B 1W0
819/ 868-1212
www.interlinx.qc.ca/~gagnony

Clientele: gay-friendly
Type: b&b-inn; w/ terrace-bar w/ breath-taking views
Owned/ Run By: lesbian & straight
Rooms: 6
Baths: shared

Meals: coffee/ tea only
Kids: welcome
Rates: C$72/ couple
AC: 10%

Camping Plein Bois

Ste-Marthe

650 chemin St-Henri
Ste-Marthe, QC J0P 1W0
450/ 459-4646 888/ 459-4646
www.campingpleinbois.com

Clientele: men
Type: campground; 350 campsites (30 clothing-optional) & 200 trailer sites; also nightclub, bar & restaurant w/ terrace; open May-Sept
Owned/ Run By: gay men
Baths: shared

Meals: full brkfst
Pets: welcome
Smoking: ok

Spring Valley Guest Ranch

Ravenscrag

Box 10
Ravenscrag, SK S0N 0T0
306/ 295-4124
www.springvalleyguestranch.com

Clientele: mixed gay/ straight
Type: b&b; 1913 character home & log cabin; in pleasant wooded valley w/ 1,100 acres of hills & prairie to explore
Owned/ Run By: gay man
Rooms: 8
Baths: shared
Meals: full brkfst

Kids: welcome; under 6 yrs free; 6-10 yrs half price
Pets: welcome
Smoking: no
Rates: C$50-70

Inn on the Lake

Whitehorse

PO Box 10420
Whitehorse, YT Y1A 7A1
867/ 660-5253
www.exceptionalplaces.com

Clientele: gay-friendly
Type: b&b-inn; in luxury lakefront log inn; private setting; Canada Select 4 1/2 stars; featured on *Martha Stewart Living*
Owned/ Run By: straights
Rooms: 12
Baths: private
Meals: expanded cont'l brkfst
Amenities: free parking, laundry, sauna, outdoor hot tub, gym, WiFi

Kids: no
Pets: welcome
Smoking: no
Rates: C$135-290
AC: 10%

Fort Recovery Villa Beach Resort

Tortola, British Virgin Islands

Road Town, Tortola, British Virgin Islands
284/ 495-4467
800/ 367-8455 (wait for ring)
www.fortrecovery.com

Clientele: gay-friendly
Type: resort; luxury Caribbean seaside villas on private beach; intimate & romantic
Owned/ Run By: women
Rooms: 30
Baths: private
Wheelchair Access: yes, 15 rms
Meals: expanded cont'l brkfst

Amenities: free parking, laundry, pool, massage, DVDs/ videos, gym
Kids: welcome
Pets: no
Smoking: ok
Rates: US$165-879
AC: 10%

Alberto House

Habana, Cuba

53-7/ 863-4834
www.w-i-t.com

Type: guesthouse; "comfortable rms in a bourgeois apt"
Rooms: 3
Meals: coffee/ tea only
Amenities: laundry

Kids: welcome
Pets: welcome
Smoking: ok
Rates: US$25-30

Hotel Arcos

Puerto Plata, Dominican Republic

Jardin Deportivo
Cabarete, Dominican Republic
809/ 571-0586
www.fonthot.com/arcos

Clientele: men
Type: resort
Owned/ Run By: gay men
Rooms: 20
Baths: private
Wheelchair Access: yes, 2 rms
Meals: full brkfst

Amenities: pool
Kids: no
Pets: no
Smoking: ok
Rates: US$120-225
AC: 20%

Isla Verde

Puerto Plata, Dominican Republic

Jardin Deportivo
Cabarete, Dominican Republic
809/ 571-0586
www.fonthot.com/isla

Clientele: mixed gay/ straight
Type: hotel; surrounding a beautiful garden w/ 2 swimming pools
Owned/ Run By: straights
Rooms: 62
Baths: private
Wheelchair Access: yes, 17 rms

Meals: full brkfst
Amenities: laundry, pool, massage
Kids: welcome
Pets: no
Smoking: ok
Rates: US$20-72

La Plantacion

Puerto Plata, Dominican Republic

Jardin Deportivo
Cabarete, Dominican Republic
809/ 571-0586
www.fonthot.com/plantacion

Clientele: men
Type: new hotel exclusively for gay men at the heart of Cabarete's gay village
Owned/ Run By: gay men
Rooms: 20
Baths: private
Wheelchair Access: yes, 8 rms
Meals: full brkfst

Amenities: pool
Kids: no
Pets: no
Smoking: ok
Rates: US$50-59
AC: 20%

Tropix Hotel

Puerto Plata, Dominican Republic

809/ 571-2291
www.tropixhotel.com

Clientele: mixed gay/ straight
Type: hotel; friendly, relaxed ambience; garden setting close to center of town, beach & all activities
Owned/ Run By: gay & straight
Rooms: 13
Baths: private

Meals: full brkfst
Amenities: laundry, pool, massage
Kids: welcome
Pets: welcome
Smoking: ok
Rates: US$55-70
AC: 10%

Casa New Yorker

Santo Domingo, Dominican Republic

102 Calle Canela esq. Estrelleta
Santo Domingo, Dominican Republic
809/ 689-3017
www.casanewyorker.com

Clientele: mixed gay/ lesbian
Type: b&b-inn; art deco b&b located in Zona Colonial: hub of nightlife & history
Owned/ Run By: gay men
Rooms: 10
Baths: private
Wheelchair Access: yes
Meals: expanded cont'l brkfst
Amenities: outdoor hot tub

Kids: no
Pets: welcome
Smoking: no
Rates: US$50-60
AC: 10%

Enchanting Encounters B&B

Santo Domingo, Dominican Republic

Av Isabel de Torres #17
Santo Domingo, Dominican Republic
809/ 472-4488
www.enchantingencounters.net/ gay_hotels.html

Clientele: mostly men
Type: b&b; tropical garden; home theater; gym; 24hr security
Owned/ Run By: gay men
Rooms: 10
Baths: private
Meals: full brkfst

Amenities: free parking, laundry, pool, hot tub, DVDs/ videos, gym
Smoking: ok
Rates: US$40-50 + tax
AC: 10%

Residencial El Candil

Santo Domingo, Dominican Republic

Calle el Candil #2
Boca Chica,
809/ 523-4252 809/ 523-4253
www.comdata.nl/hotel-boca-chica-candil

Clientele: mixed gay/ straight
Type: hotel; beautiful apt-hotel in Boca Chica; 30 minutes to Santo Domingo; 5 minutes to beach
Owned/ Run By: gay men
Rooms: 24 (apts)
Baths: private
Meals: full brkfst

Amenities: pool
Kids: welcome
Pets: welcome
Smoking: ok
Rates: US$28-84
AC: 10%

Little David B&B

Aruba, Dutch & French West Indies

Seroe Blanco 56L
Oranjestad, Dutch & French West Indies
297/ 58-38-288
www.littledavidaruba.com

Clientele: men
Type: b&b; private guesthouse w/ tropical garden; clothing-optional by the pool
Owned/ Run By: gay men
Rooms: 5
Meals: full brkfst
Amenities: free parking, laundry, pool,

massage, DVDs/ videos
Kids: no
Pets: no
Smoking: no
Rates: US$65

Coco Palm Garden/ Casa Oleander

Bonaire, Dutch & French West Indies

Kaya Statius van Eps 9
Bonaire, Dutch & French West Indies
599/ 717-2108
www.cocopalmgarden.com

Clientele: gay-friendly
Type: cottage; Bonaire vacation homes w/ private tropical gardens; studios, apts & houses
Owned/ Run By: straights
Wheelchair Access: yes, 3 rms
Amenities: free parking, pool
Kids: welcome

Pets: welcome
Smoking: ok
Rates: US$66-86
AC: 10%

Ocean View Villas

Kaya Statius van Eps 6
Bonaire, Dutch & French West Indies

599/ 717-6105

www.oceanviewvillas.com

Clientele: mixed gay/ straight
Type: apt; tastefully furnished in pickled oak w/ pastel accents, our luxury accommodations have secluded, intimate patios & outdoor showers
Owned/ Run By: gay man
Pickup Service: airport pickup; free
Transit: near public transit; 3 minutes to airport
Rooms: 3 total, queens, A/C, color TV, DVD/ VCR, cable, ceiling fan, phone, kitchenette, refrigerator, DVD player
Baths: private, showers, hairdryers
Amenities: office hrs: 8am-10pm; free parking, massage, WiFi, snacks, coffee/ tea
Recreation: scuba diving, snorkeling, swimming, kayaking
Pets On Premises: 1 dog, 1 cat
Smoking: ok
Reservations: required

Payment: cash, travelers checks, Visa, MC
Season: open yr-round *High season:* Dec-April
Rates: US$80-140 *Discounts:* groups & extended stays
AC: 10%

Juliana's Hotel

Windwardside, Dutch & French West Indies
599/ 416-2269 888/ 289-5708
www.julianas-hotel.com

Clientele: mixed gay/ straight
Type: ocean & garden views; also apt suite & Saban-style cottages
Owned/ Run By: gay & straight
Rooms: 12
Baths: private
Meals: full brkfst
Amenities: free parking, laundry, pool, outdoor hot tub, WiFi

Kids: welcome
Pets: no
Smoking: ok
Rates: US$85-255
AC: 15%

Hotel le Village St-Jean

PO Box 623
St Barthélemy, 97098 CEDEX
590-590/ 27-61-39 800/ 651-8366
www.villagestjeanhotel.com

Clientele: gay-friendly
Type: hotel & cottages; Caribbean hideaway of cottages amid lush foliage; privacy & views of sparkling bay below
Owned/ Run By: straight family
Rooms: 6 (plus 20 cottages)
Baths: private
Meals: full brkfst
Amenities: free parking, laundry, pool, hot tub, massage
Kids: welcome

Pets: welcome
Smoking: ok
Rates: € 110-850

Delfina Hotel

PO Box 5305
St Maarten, Netherlands Antilles 00000

599/ 545-3300

St Maarten, Dutch & French West Indies

www.delfinahotel.com

Clientele: mostly men
Type: resort; built in original Caribbean gingerbread style; large tropical garden w/ clothing-optional pool & jacuzzi
Owned/ Run By: gay men
Nearby Attractions: 37 beaches, 370 restaurants of all kinds of cuisine, tax-free shopping
Transit: 3 miles to airport
Rooms: 12 total, 8 kings, 4 fulls, A/C, cable, ceiling fan, phone, refrigerator, maid service, coffeemaker
Baths: private, showers, hairdryers
Meals: expanded cont'l brkfst
Amenities: free parking, laundry, pool, hot tub, massage, gym, spa w/ massages, facials, yoga, water aerobics
Recreation: Cupecoy Beach, clothing-optional gay beach w/ cruising area
Kids: no
Pets: no
Smoking: ok

Reservations: required *Deposit:* required, 1 night, due at booking *Cancellation:* cancel by 2 weeks prior or forfeit full amount *Minimum Stay:* 3 nights *Check in/ out:* noon

Payment: cash, travelers checks, Visa, Amex, MC
Season: open yr-round
Rates: US$79-149
AC: 10%

Orient Bay Hotel & Jardins de Chevrise

Mont Vernon 1
St Martin, Dutch & French West Indies
9-0590/ 87-31-10
www.orientbayhotel.com

St Martin, Dutch & French West Indies

Clientele: gay-friendly
Type: studios & villas (up to 5 people); "exceptional setting offering all the calm & privacy you may wish & easy access to all island's activities"
Rooms: 60
Baths: private
Wheelchair Access: yes, 1 rm
Amenities: free parking, laundry, pool

Kids: welcome
Pets: welcome
Smoking: ok
Rates: US$115-395
AC: 10%

Seagrape Villas

The Cliffs, West End Rd
Negril, Jamaica
31/ 625-1255 (US#)
www.seagrapevillas.com

Negril, Jamaica

Clientele: mixed gay/ straight
Type: rental home; 3 seafront villas (each sleep up to 6); features privacy, cable; walk to many restaurants; chef on premises; massage available
Owned/ Run By: straights
Rooms: 3 (villas)
Baths: private
Meals: cont'l brkfst
Amenities: free parking, laundry

Kids: kids 13 & up welcome
Pets: no
Smoking: ok
Rates: US$120-275
AC: 10%

Golden Clouds Villa

Ocho Rios, Jamaica

941/ 922-9191 888/ 625-6007
www.sunvillas.com/golden.htm

Clientele: gay-friendly
Type: rental home; fully staffed waterfront estate in picturesque banana port village; sleeps up to 18
Owned/ Run By: gay men
Rooms: 9
Baths: private

Wheelchair Access: yes, 4 rms
Meals: full brkfst
Amenities: laundry, pool, hot tub
Kids: welcome
Smoking: ok
Rates: US$960-49,500/ week
AC: 10%

Hotel Mocking Bird Hill

Port Antonio, Jamaica

PO Box 254
Port Antonio, Jamaica
876/ 993-7267 876/ 993-7134
www.hotelmockingbirdhill.com

Clientele: gay-friendly
Type: hotel; romantic, comfortable, environmentally friendly hideaway close to the beach
Owned/ Run By: lesbians
Rooms: 10
Baths: private

Wheelchair Access: yes, 2 rms
Amenities: laundry, pool, massage
Kids: welcome
Pets: no
Smoking: ok
Rates: US$135-260
AC: 10-12%

Moun Tambrin Retreat

Westmoreland, Jamaica

876/ 437-4353 876/ 357-6363
www.mountambrin.com

Clientele: mixed gay/ straight
Type: retreat; art deco estate furnished & built from tropical woods; formerly owned by Alex Haley
Rooms: 5 (includes 3 suites each w/ private solarium)

Baths: private & shared
Kids: no
Pets: no
Smoking: no (outdoors only)
Rates: US$100-150 per person
AC: 10%

Le Carbet B&B

Les Trois Ilets, Martinique

18 rue des Alamandas
Les Trois Ilets, Martinique
596/ 660-331
www.lecarbet-gaybandb.com

Clientele: mixed gay/ lesbian
Type: b&b-private home; quiet & private location; rooftop jacuzzi & nude sunbathing; near beach, restauraunts & watersports
Owned/ Run By: gay men
Rooms: 3
Baths: shared

Meals: full brkfst
Amenities: outdoor hot tub, DVDs/ video
Kids: no
Pets: no
Smoking: ok
Rates: €42-53
AC: 15%

A Boqueron Bay Guest House

Boqueron, Puerto Rico

10 Quintas del Mar
Boqueron, Puerto Rico 00622-9702
787/ 847-4325
www.boqueronbay.com

Clientele: mixed gay/ lesbian
Type: guesthouse; views bay, beach, sea & mtns in SW Puerto Rico
Owned/ Run By: gay men
Rooms: 3
Baths: private & shared
Meals: coffee/ tea only

Amenities: free parking, laundry, pool, ho tub, DVDs/ videos
Pets: dogs, cats, birds & fish welcome onl
Smoking: ok
Rates: US$100
AC: 10%

Coqui Villa

Luquillo, Puerto Rico

PMB 343, PO Box 7005
Fajardo, Puerto Rico 00738-7005
787/ 889-2098
www.coquivilla.com

Clientele: mixed gay/ straight
Type: rental home; tropical paradise on 3 gorgeous acres in the rain forest foothills; no neighbors
Owned/ Run By: bisexuals
Rooms: 2
Baths: private

Amenities: pool, outdoor hot tu massage, DVDs/ videos
Kids: welcome
Pets: no
Smoking: no
Rates: US$750-1,000/ week
AC: 10%

Caribe Playa Beach Resort

Patillas, Puerto Rico

Road #3, Km 112.1 Guardarraya
Patillas, Puerto Rico 00723
787/ 839-6339
www.caribeplaya.com

Clientele: gay-friendly
Type: inn; small & secluded beachfront property w/ all the amenities for a truly relaxing & romantic getaway
Owned/ Run By: straights
Rooms: 32
Baths: private

Amenities: free parking, laundry, pool, outdoor hot tub, massage
Kids: welcome
Pets: small pets; please inquire
Smoking: ok
Rates: US$79-104
AC: 10%

Club Bon-Accord

Rincon, Puerto Rico

Barrio Buntas Carr 413, km 3.3 Int
Sector Sandy Beach
Rincon, Puerto Rico 00677
787/ 823-2525 866/ 461-8936
www.bonaccordinn.com

Clientele: mixed gay/ straight
Type: hotel; jacuzzi, also restaurant, near beach
Rooms: 10
Baths: private

Wheelchair Access: yes, 1 rm
Meals: full brkfst
Amenities: pool, hot tub
Kids: 12 yrs & up up welcome
Rates: US$110-200

Lemontree Oceanfront Cottages

Rincon, Puerto Rico

PO Box 200
Rincon, Puerto Rico 00677
787/ 823-6452 888/ 418-8733
www.lemontreepr.com

Clientele: mixed gay/ straight
Type: cottage; fully equipped beach home; private oceanfront deck; "relax-renew-reawaken your senses & deepen your relationships"
Owned/ Run By: straights
Rooms: 6
Baths: private

Wheelchair Access: yes, 1 rm
Meals: coffee/ tea only
Amenities: massage, WiFi
Kids: welcome
Pets: no
Smoking: no
Rates: US$140-310
AC: 5%

Villa Orleans Beachfront Vacation Home

Rincon, Puerto Rico

787/ 433-6013
www.villaorleanspr.com

Clientele: gay-friendly
Type: rental home; on one of the most secluded beaches in the area
Owned/ Run By: bisexuals
Rooms: 3
Baths: private

Amenities: free parking, laundry, WiFi
Kids: welcome
Pets: no
Smoking: no
Rates: US$250-350

Andalucia Guesthouse & Vacation Rentals

San Juan, Puerto Rico

2011 McLeary St
San Juan, Puerto Rico 00911
787/ 309-3373
www.andalucia-puertorico.com

Clientele: mostly men
Type: guesthouse; comfortable rms near beach; quiet, gay-friendly neighborhood
Owned/ Run By: gay men
Rooms: 2
Baths: private
Meals: coffee/ tea only

Amenities: free parking, laundry
Kids: welcome w/ prior approval
Pets: welcome w/ prior approval
Rates: US$50-65

Caribe Mountain Villas

San Juan, Puerto Rico

Carr 857, km 6.0
Carolina, Puerto Rico 00985
787/ 769-0860
www.caribevillas.com

Clientele: gay-friendly
Type: resort; in outer foothills of rain forest (25 minutes from Old San Juan); spacious, clean; beaches, nightlife & shopping nearby
Owned/ Run By: gay men
Rooms: 7 (villas)
Baths: private

Wheelchair Access: yes, 1 rm
Amenities: free parking, laundry, pool, massage, DVDs/ videos
Kids: welcome
Pets: welcome
Smoking: ok
Rates: US$100-225

Casa del Caribe Guest House
San Juan, Puerto Rico

Calle Caribe 57, Condado
San Juan, Puerto Rico 00907
787/ 722-7139 877/ 722-7139
www.casadelcaribe.net

Clientele: gay-friendly
Type: guesthouse; a Caribbean b&b in the heart of Condado; wraparound veranda; tropical garden & patio
Owned/ Run By: straights
Rooms: 13
Baths: private

Wheelchair Access: yes, 1 rm
Meals: cont'l brkfst
Kids: welcome
Pets: by arrangement
Smoking: no
Rates: US$50-125
AC: 10%

Condado Inn
San Juan, Puerto Rico

Av Condado 6
San Juan, Puerto Rico 00907
787/ 724-7145
canadianpet@yahoo.com

Clientele: mostly men
Type: guesthouse; gay bar on premises
Owned/ Run By: gay men
Rooms: 8
Baths: private
Amenities: DVDs/ videos

Kids: no
Pets: only small dogs welcome
Smoking: ok
Rates: US$59-79

L' Habitation Beach Guesthouse
San Juan, Puerto Rico

Calle Italia 1957, Ocean Park
San Juan, Puerto Rico 00911
787/ 727-2499
www.habitationbeach.com

Clientele: mixed gay/ lesbian
Type: guesthouse; warm, serene, yet lively atmosphere to suit your style; directly on the beach
Owned/ Run By: gay men
Rooms: 10
Baths: private

Meals: expanded cont'l brkfst
Amenities: free parking, laundry, massage
Pets: welcome
Smoking: ok
Rates: US$70-111
AC: 10%

The San Juan Water & Beach Club Hotel
San Juan, Puerto Rico

2 Tartak St
Carolina, Puerto Rico 00979
787/ 728-3666 888/ 265-6699
www.waterbeachclubhotel.com

Clientele: gay-friendly
Type: "San Juan's only boutique hotel on the beach"; luxury environment
Owned/ Run By: gay & straight
Rooms: 84
Baths: private
Wheelchair Access: yes, 2 rms

Amenities: laundry, pool, massage, gym, WiFi
Kids: welcome
Pets: welcome
Smoking: no
Rates: US$229-695
AC: 10%

Bravo!
Vieques Island, Puerto Rico

North Shore Rd
Vieques Island, Puerto Rico 00765
787/ 741-1128
www.bravobeachhotel.com

Clientele: mixed gay/ straight
Type: hotel; Vieques' "first true beachside designer hotel" w/ beautiful ocean views
Owned/ Run By: gay men
Rooms: 11
Baths: private & shared
Meals: expanded cont'l brkfst

Amenities: pool, DVDs/ videos
Kids: no
Pets: small dogs welcome w/ prior approval
Rates: US$175-475
AC: 10%

Casa de Amistad
Vieques Island, Puerto Rico

27 Benitez Castano
Vieques Island, Puerto Rico 00765
787/ 741-3758
www.casadeamistad.com

Clientele: mixed gay/ straight
Type: guesthouse; in heart of Isabel Segunda, close to everything in town; garden courtyard
Owned/ Run By: gay men
Rooms: 7

Baths: private
Amenities: free parking, pool, WiFi
Kids: welcome
Pets: no
Smoking: no
Rates: US$65-90

Crow's Nest Inn

Vieques Island, Puerto Rico

PO Box 1521
Vieques Island, Puerto Rico 00765
787/ 741-0033 877/ 276-9763
www.crowsnestvieques.com

Clientele: gay-friendly
Type: inn
Owned/ Run By: gay & straight
Rooms: 17
Baths: private
Meals: cont'l brkfst

Amenities: free parking, laundry, pool, massage
Kids: 12 yrs & up
Pets: welcome (no large dogs please)
Smoking: no
Rates: US$114-225

Hix Island House

Vieques Island, Puerto Rico

HC-02 Box 14902
Vieques Island, Puerto Rico 00765
787/ 741-2302
www.hixislandhouse.com

Clientele: mixed gay/ straight
Type: guesthouse; quiet retreat in the Caribbean; wonderful views; yoga available
Owned/ Run By: gay & straight
Rooms: 12
Baths: private
Wheelchair Access: yes, 1 rm

Meals: expanded cont'l brkfst
Amenities: free parking, laundry, pool, massage
Kids: 13 yrs & up welcome
Pets: small pets welcome
Smoking: ok
Rates: US$185-295
AC: 10% w/ approval

Inn on the Blue Horizon

Vieques Island, Puerto Rico

PO Box 1556
Vieques Island, Puerto Rico 00765
787/ 741-3318
www.innonthebluehorizon.com

Clientele: gay-friendly
Type: tropical country inn & cottages; w/ beach access, gym; also bar & restaurant
Rooms: 10
Baths: private
Meals: cont'l brkfst

Amenities: free parking, pool
Pets: welcome (May through mid-Dec)
Smoking: in designated areas only
Rates: US$125-375

La Posada Vista Mar

Vieques Island, Puerto Rico

300-A Calle Almendro
Esperanza, Puerto Rico 00765
787/ 741-8716
PosadaVistaMar@aol.com

Clientele: mixed gay/ straight
Type: hotel; charming small guest hotel; on Carribean side of island; 2 blks to beach
Owned/ Run By: gay & straight
Rooms: 5
Baths: private
Meals: coffee/ tea only

Amenities: free parking
Kids: welcome
Pets: welcome
Smoking: no
Rates: US$60-70

Grafton Beach Resort

Tobago, Trinidad & Tobago

PO Box 25
Scarborough, Trinidad & Tobago
868/ 639-0191 888/ 790-5264
www.grafton-resort.com

Clientele: gay-friendly
Type: resort; surrounded by 5 acres of lush, tropical hills & fronted by the sparkling Caribbean Sea; includes 2 restaurants & bar; 2 blks to beach
Rooms: 78
Baths: private

Meals: full brkfst
Amenities: pool
Kids: welcome
Rates: US$200-344
AC: 10%

Kariwak Village Hotel & Holistic Haven

Tobago, Trinidad & Tobago

Store Bay Local Rd, Crown Point
Tobago, Trinidad & Tobago
868/ 639-8442 868/ 639-8545
www.kariwak.co.tt

Clientele: mixed gay/ straight
Type: independently owned holistic hotel; w/ fully fitted rms, open-air restaurant & bar; beach shuttle
Owned/ Run By: straights
Rooms: 24
Baths: private
Wheelchair Access: yes, 4 rms

Amenities: free parking, laundry, pool, hot ozone bath, massage, WiFi
Kids: welcome
Pets: no
Smoking: ok
Rates: US$108-150
AC: yes

Sand Castle on the Beach

127 Smithfield	340/ 772-1205
Frederiksted, Virgin Islands 00840	800/ 524-2018

St Croix, Virgin Islands
info@sandcastleonthebeach.com
www.sandcastleonthebeach.com

The original Caribbean gay resort for over 30 years on St. Croix, US Virgin Islands. All of the hotel's 22 accommodations are newly refurbished. The hotel grounds are lush and common areas inviting! The award-winning Beach Side Cafe, the hotel's on-site restaurant/bar, is open 5 days a week and features an eclectic menu to satisfy all palates. The hotel property has expanded on the southern edge and now includes a Fitness Center for the "muscularly-inclined," a spa with massage services to erase your aches and pains and offer you the opportunity to pamper yourself, and a retreat center overlooking the Caribbean Sea!

Visit this tropical, gay- and straight-friendly, Caribbean paradise any time of the year for incredible sunshine, magnificent beach, water sports–sail, scuba dive, snorkel, swim, float right outside the hotel's beachfront door! Experience for yourself the freedom and celebrate completely on your vacation! Build friendships and community amongst the visiting guests and locals as you get acquainted with Frederiksted, the west end of the island where the sun sets, the stars beam, and the moon shines over the sea.

Explore the Cruzan shores and get acquainted with our attentive staff who will guide you along your way. Plan to celebrate your next special occasion at the Sand Castle on the Beach, St. Croix, United States Virgin Islands! We will assist you in every way we can to make this vacation your most outstanding to date!

Clientele: gay, lesbian & straight-friendly

Type: resort; on a magnificent beach; 2 pools (1 clothing-optional)

Owned/ Run By: lesbians/ gay men

Rooms: 22 total, 10 suites, 12 kings, 11 queens, 3 twins, A/C, color TV, DVD/ VCR, cable, ceiling fan, deck (17), kitchenette, refrigerator, maid service, "all sizes to fit all budgets"

Baths: private, showers, hairdryers

Meals: cont'l brkfst, complimentary welcome drink/ cocktail on arrival

Amenities: laundry, pool, massage, DVDs/ videos, gym, WiFi, cooler, iron & ironing board

Kids: welcome off season

Pets: $250 refundable deposit

Smoking: ok

Reservations: required *Deposit:* required, 3 days or 50%, due at booking, personal check ok *Cancellation:* cancel by 60 days prior or forfeit 15%

Payment: cash, travelers checks, Visa, Amex, MC, personal checks for deposit only

Season: open yr-round *High season:* Dec-March

Rates: US$89-399 + 10% VI hotel tax *Discounts:* travel agents, airline & cruiseline employees

AC: 10%

The Palms at Pelican Cove

St Croix, Virgin Islands

4126 La Grande Princesse
St Croix, Virgin Islands 00820
340/ 778-8920 800/ 548-4460
www.palmspelicancove.com

Clientele: mixed gay/ lesbian
Type: resort; "the best small hotel in the American Virgin Islands" is now gay-owned & operated; full-size gym
Owned/ Run By: gay men
Rooms: 40
Baths: private
Meals: full brkfst

Amenities: free parking, pool, massage, DVDs/ videos
Kids: welcome; please call first
Pets: small pets welcome
Smoking: ok
Rates: US$110-265
AC: 10%

Pink Fancy Hotel

St Croix, Virgin Islands

27 Prince St
Christiansted, Virgin Islands 00820
340/ 773-8460 800/ 524-2045
www.pinkfancy.com

Clientele: gay-friendly
Type: hotel; 4-bldg complex including 1780s Danish town house; became hotel in 1950s, owned by Ziegfeld Follies star & frequented by artists & writers like Noel Coward; totally restored
Baths: private

Meals: cont'l brkfst
Amenities: pool
Kids: welcome
Rates: US$85-175

Island's End

St John, Virgin Islands

Hanson Bay
St John, Virgin Islands
800/ 341-2532 340/ 693-8692
www.islandsendstjohn.com

Clientele: mixed gay/ straight
Type: rental home; in octagonal vacation villa w/ panoramic views; snorkeling; near beautiful beaches
Owned/ Run By: lesbian
Rooms: 5
Baths: private

Amenities: free parking, laundry, pool, DVDs/ videos
Kids: 5 yrs & up welcome
Pets: please call
Smoking: no
Rates: US$2,240-7,800/ week
AC: 10%

Maho Bay Camps & Harmony Studios

St John, Virgin Islands

PO Box 310
St John, VI 00830
340/ 715-0501 800/ 392-9004
www.mahobay.com

Clientele: gay-friendly
Type: campground; tent-cottages, studios & condos combining comfort w/ environmental sensitivity; 7-night minimum stay during some holidays
Owned/ Run By: straights
Rooms: 114 (tent-cottages plus 12 studios & 18 eco-tents)

Baths: private & shared
Amenities: free parking, laundry, massage
Kids: welcome
Pets: no
Smoking: not in public areas
Rates: US$75-230
AC: 10%

St John Inn

St John, Virgin Islands

PO Box 37
St John, Virgin Islands 00831
800/ 666-7688 340/ 693-8688
www.stjohninn.com

Clientele: gay-friendly
Type: inn; completely refurbished units; all have A/C, cable TV; some rms w/ kitchenettes; courtyard; bar w/ 61" TV; 5 minutes to town & main port of entry
Owned/ Run By: straights
Rooms: 13

Baths: private & shared
Amenities: pool, DVDs/ videos
Kids: welcome
Smoking: no
Rates: US$75-295
AC: 10%

Danish Chalet Guest House

St Thomas, Virgin Islands

PO Box 4319
9E Gamble Nordsidevej
St Thomas, VI 00803
340/ 774-5292 877/ 407-2567
www.danishchaletinn.com

Clientele: mixed gay/ straight
Type: b&b-inn; tucked away on the hill above Charlotte Amalie, St Thomas, the Danish Chalet Inn is one of the island's best-kept secrets
Owned/ Run By: straights
Rooms: 15

Baths: private & shared
Meals: cont'l brkfst
Amenities: hot tub
Rates: US$98-160
AC: 10%

Pavilions & Pools Hotel

St Thomas, Virgin Islands

6400 Estate Smith Bay
St Thomas, Virgin Islands 00802
340/ 775-6110 800/ 524-2001
www.pavilionsandpools.com

Clientele: gay-friendly
Type: resort; 1-bdrm villas each w/ its own private swimming pool
Owned/ Run By: straights
Rooms: 25 (villas)
Baths: private
Meals: cont'l brkfst
Amenities: free parking, pool, massage
Kids: 6 yrs & up; $25 per night

Pets: welcome; $25 per night
Smoking: ok
Rates: US$190-350
AC: 10%

Bequia Beachfront Villas

Bequia, St Vincent & the Grenadines

La Pompe, Friendship Bay Beach,
Bequia, St Vincent & the Grenadines

284/ 495-4467
800/ 367-8455 (wait for ring)

bequia@fortrecovery.com
www.bequiabeachfrontvillas.com

Clientele: gay-friendly
Type: resort; 1-4-bdrm villas located on Friendship Bay Beach on Bequia, St Vincents & the Grenadines; "the only AAA-approved villa/ hotel on Bequia"
Owned/ Run By: straight women
Nearby Attractions: botanical gardens, La Soufriere (volcanic phenomenon), site where *Pirates of the Caribbean* was filmed, shopping, ferries to nearby islands
Pickup Service: airport pickup
Transit: near public transit; 10 minutes to airport
Rooms: 7 villas (1-, 2-, 3/4-bdrm) total, 6 kings, 1 queen, A/C, color TV, DVD/ VCR, cable, ceiling fan, deck, phone, kitchenette, refrigerator, maid service, all w/ sleek, modern design, high ceilings, oversized rms, large decks
Baths: private, showers
Wheelchair Access: yes, 5 rms
Meals: cont'l brkfst, special meals available on request
Amenities: office hrs: 8am-7pm; free parking, laundry, massage, on the beach, lounge chairs, beach towels

Recreation: fishing, snorkeling, boating
Kids: welcome
Pets: no
Smoking: ok
Reservations: required *Deposit:* required, 20%, due at booking *Cancellation:* cancel by 90 days prior (except Dec 18-April 14; nonrefundable) *Check in/ out:* 3pm/ 11am

Payment: cash, travelers checks, Visa, Amex, MC
Season: open yr-round *High season:* Dec 18-April 14
Rates: US$207-879
AC: 10%

Acapulco Las Palmas Resort Hotel

Acapulco, Mexico

Av Las Conchas 155, Fracto Farralón
Acapulco, Mexico 39690
52-744/ 487-0843
www.acapulco-laspalmas.com

Clientele: men
Type: resort; upscale, luxury Colonial-style gay resort; clothing-optional; located in the "Gay Golden Zone"
Owned/ Run By: gay men
Rooms: 16
Baths: private
Meals: cont'l brkfst

Amenities: free parking, laundry, pool, poolside mist, hot tub, massage, DVDs/ videos
Pets: welcome
Smoking: ok
Rates: US$85-300
AC: 10%

Acapulco–Villa Roqueta

305/ 677-3525 (US#)
52-744/ 483-8503

Clientele: men
Type: resort; luxury gay guesthouse in former estate of disco queen Gloria Gaynor on the cliffs of Acapulco; beautiful views
Owned/ Run By: gay men
Nearby Attractions: Acapulco cliff divers, walk to beach & restaurants
Pickup Service: airport pickup
Transit: near public transit; 10 miles to Acapulco Int'l; 25-minute ride to airport
Rooms: 7 total, 1 suite, 6 kings, 1 queen, 1 full, A/C, color TV, DVD/ VCR, cable, ceiling fan, rm service, maid service, white slip-covered furniture, down comforters, stereos, safes
Baths: private, showers, hairdryers
Meals: brkfst, lunch & dinner

Amenities: office hrs: 8am-midnight; free parking, laundry, pool, sauna, hot tub, massage, gym, cellular phones & private chauffeur available
Pets: by arrangement
Smoking: ok (in some rms)
Reservations: required *Deposit:* required, 1 night, due at booking *Cancellation:* cancel by 1 week prior or forfeit deposit *Minimum Stay:* 3 nights *Check in/ out:* 2pm/ noon
Payment: cash, travelers checks, Visa, Amex, MC, Discover
Season: open yr-round *High season:* Nov-April
Rates: US$125-375
AC: 15%

Alberto's of Acapulco

Calle Juan Sebastián Elcano 355
Acapulco, Mexico 39850
52-744/ 481-2027
aca@aca.cableonline.com.mx

Clientele: men
Type: b&b; close to restaurants, shopping, beaches & bars; "splash" pool under construction
Owned/ Run By: gay men
Rooms: 7
Baths: private

Meals: cont'l brkfst
Kids: 18 yrs & up only
Pets: no
Smoking: no
Rates: please inquire
AC: 10%

Casa Condesa

Bella Vista 125
Acapulco, Mexico 39361
52-744/ 484-1616
800/ 816-4817 (US & Canada)
www.casacondesa.com

Clientele: mostly men
Type: b&b; your private Shangri-la in a lush, tropical setting; 2 blks to Condesa (gay) Beach
Rooms: 8 (includes suite & studio apt)
Baths: private & shared
Meals: full brkfst

Amenities: pool
Kids: no
Pets: no
Smoking: ok
Rates: US$75-150

Las Brisas

52-744/ 469-6900
888/ 559-4329 (US#)
www.brisas.com.mx

Type: resort; individual bungalow-style casitas & suites; each w/ private or semi-private pool
Rooms: 263 (casitas)
Baths: private
Wheelchair Access: yes, 1 rm
Meals: cont'l brkfst

Amenities: free parking, laundry, pool, sauna, massage
Kids: welcome; 2 kids under 12 yrs free w/ parents
Smoking: ok
Rates: US$330-1,520

Quinta Encanto
Acapulco, Mexico

Privada Roca Sola 108, Col. Club Deportivo
Acapulco, Mexico 39690
310/ 276–0752 310/ 659–5384 (night)
rentalo.com/2711/quintaencanto.html

Clientele: gay-friendly
Type: rental home; secluded villa; sleeps up to 6; full staff w/ gourmet cook; 1 1/2 blks to Condessa (gay) Beach & bars; palapa w/ bar & balcony
Owned/ Run By: gay man
Rooms: 3

Baths: private
Amenities: pool
Kids: 13 yrs & up welcome
Pets: no
Smoking: ok
Rates: US$200-325

Villa Estrella
Acapulco, Mexico

169 Anahuac
Acapulco, Mexico 39850
52–744/ 460–1112
www.acavio.com/villaestrella.html

Clientele: gay-friendly
Type: rental home; hilltop villa w/ 180° views of Acapulco Bay; rent 4 rms or whole villa; pool & jacuzzi w/ views; fully staffed
Rooms: 6
Baths: private

Amenities: pool, outdoor hot tub
Kids: welcome
Pets: no
Smoking: ok (some nonsmoking rms)
Rates: US$400-1,000

Cabo Villas Resort
Cabo San Lucas, Mexico

Callejon del Pescador s/n
Cabo San Lucas, Mexico 23400
52–624/ 143–9199
877/ 382–2932 (reservations US only)
www.cabovillasresort.com

Clientele: gay-friendly
Type: resort w/ condo suites on Medano Beach; w/ 2 restaurants
Baths: private
Amenities: pool, outdoor hot tub

Kids: welcome
Rates: US$140-450

Solmar Suites
Cabo San Lucas, Mexico

Av Solmar 1
Cabo San Lucas, Mexico 23410
800/ 344–3349 310/ 459–9861 (US#)
www.solmar.com

Clientele: gay-friendly
Type: resort; secluded oceanfront suites at southernmost tip; tennis court, horseback riding on beach, 2 swimming pools w/ swim-up bar
Rooms: 120

Baths: private
Amenities: pool, outdoor hot tub
Kids: welcome
Rates: US$145-330

The Todos Santos Inn
Cabo San Lucas, Mexico

Calle Legaspi #33
Todos Santos, Mexico 23305
52–612/ 145–0040
www.todossantosinn.com

Clientele: mixed gay/ straight
Type: colonial inn; a grand old hacienda in heart of Todos Santos' historic district; also bar
Owned/ Run By: gay men
Rooms: 8
Baths: private
Meals: cont'l brkfst

Amenities: free parking, laundry, pool, massage
Kids: no
Pets: small pets welcome
Smoking: no
Rates: US$125-225
AC: 12%

Akul Hotel
Cancún, Mexico

Blvd Kukulcán 5
Cancún, Mexico 77500
52–998/ 838–330 or 619/297–0897
800/ 765–4370
mexhotels.8m.net/photo5.html

Clientele: mixed gay/ straight
Type: hotel
Rooms: 70
Baths: private
Amenities: pool
Kids: no

Pets: no
Smoking: ok (some nonsmoking rms)
Rates: US$99-119

Cancún Beach House
Cancún, Mexico

212/ 598-0469 (US#)
members.aol.com/corredorpr

Clientele: mixed gay/ straight
Type: rental home; spacious 2-story Mayan beach house; bohemian community; in tranquil fishing village 15 minutes S of Cancún
Owned/ Run By: women
Rooms: 6

Baths: private & shared
Wheelchair Access: yes, 1 rm
Amenities: free parking
Kids: 10 yrs & up welcome
Pets: welcome w/ prior approval
Smoking: no (ok on outdoor decks)
Rates: US$120-140

Cancún Luxury Villas
Cancún, Mexico

Palenque #17 #1-B, SM 29
Cancún, Mexico
877/ 482-3758 x122 (reservations, TX #)
52-998/ 892-4102
www.cancunluxuryvillas.com

Clientele: gay-friendly
Type: rental home; group of individually owned, beautiful, private, beachfront villas that allow you the freedom to pursue your pleasures
Owned/ Run By: straights
Amenities: pool

Kids: welcome
Pets: each villa's owner has different policy

Casa de los Amigos
Cancún, Mexico

Isla Mujeres, Mexico
52-998/ 44-01-877-1169
islamujeresescape.com

Clientele: mixed gay/ straight
Type: cottage; quiet; on Mexican Caribbean; great view of ocean; short bus or taxi ride to center of town & best beach on the island
Owned/ Run By: gay men
Rooms: 1 (cottage)

Baths: private
Amenities: WiFi
Kids: no
Pets: no
Smoking: ok
Rates: US$55-60 (4-day minimum)

Rancho Sak Ol
Cancún, Mexico

52-998/ 871-0181
www.ranchosakol.com

Clientele: gay-friendly
Type: b&b; beachfront palapa-style accommodations w/ hammock beds; low-key pace & ambience; 30 minutes S of Cancún
Owned/ Run By: straights
Rooms: 13
Baths: private

Meals: cont'l brkfst
Amenities: massage
Kids: please inquire
Pets: welcome
Smoking: ok
Rates: US$45-95

El Cid La Ceiba Beach Hotel
Cozumel, Mexico

Carretera a Chankanaab km 4.5
Cozumel, Mexico 77600
52-987/ 872-0844 800/ 435-3240
www.elcid.com

Clientele: gay-friendly
Type: resort; 5-star w/ oceanview rms; beach area, dive shop, sauna, tennis courts, 2 swimming pools, bar & restaurants
Owned/ Run By: straights
Rooms: 98
Baths: private

Wheelchair Access: yes, 2 rms
Amenities: free parking, laundry, pool, sauna, outdoor hot tub, massage
Kids: welcome
Pets: no
Smoking: ok
Rates: US$93-200+

Sol Cabañas del Caribe
Cozumel, Mexico

52-987/ 872-9871
888/ 956-3542 (US#)
www.solcabanasdelcaribe.solmelia.com

Clientele: gay-friendly
Type: small resort; white sandy beach; "beach bum's paradise"; restaurant & bar
Rooms: 48 (including 9 private beach cabins)
Baths: private

Amenities: pool
Rates: US$86-195

Villa Las Anclas

Cozumel, Mexico

S 5th Ave #325
Cozumel, Mexico
52-987/ 872-5476   52-987/ 872-6103
www.lasanclas.com

Clientele: gay-friendly
Type: suites-hotel; 2-story villas surrounding serene garden; gated & secure; owners live on-site; excellent personal service; 1 blk to main plaza
Owned/ Run By: straights
Rooms: 7 (suites)
Baths: private

Meals: expanded cont'l brkfst
Amenities: free parking, laundry, massage, DVDs/ videos, WiFi
Kids: 12yrs & up welcome
Pets: no
Smoking: ok
Rates: US$80-120
AC: 10-15%

Casa del Angel

Cuernavaca, Mexico

Calle de Helechos #206
Cuernavaca, Mexico 62160
52-777/ 364-6319
www.hotelangelmexico.com

Clientele: gay-friendly
Type: guesthouse w/ cooking school & spa; can rent whole house (sleeps 6) & comes w/ housekeeper/ cook & gardener/ pool boy; tours available
Owned/ Run By: gay men

Rooms: 3
Baths: shared
Amenities: pool
Rates: US$60-125 & $1,000 (whole house)

Hostería Las Quintas Resort Spa

Cuernavaca, Mexico

9 Diaz Ordaz Blvd
Cuernavaca, Mexico 62240
52-777/ 362-3949   800/ 990-1888
www.hlasquintas.com

Clientele: gay-friendly
Type: resort; includes spa & eco-spa (day hikes to Mayan ruins); bar & restaurant; 3 pools & outdoor jacuzzi
Rooms: 86

Baths: private
Amenities: pool, outdoor hot tub
Rates: US$200-360

La Nuestra

Cuernavaca, Mexico

Calle Mesalina 18
Cuernavaca, Mexico 62330
52-777/ 315-2272   404/ 806-9694
www.lanuestra.com

Clientele: mixed gay/ straight
Type: b&b-private home; 1 1/2 hrs from Mexico City; ideal for studying Spanish, sight-seeing or just relaxing
Owned/ Run By: lesbians
Rooms: 4
Baths: private
Wheelchair Access: yes, all rms

Meals: full brkfst
Amenities: laundry, pool, WiFi
Kids: welcome; must be quiet after 10pm
Pets: no
Rates: 60-75 pesos

Quinta Las Flores

Cuernavaca, Mexico

Tlaquepaque 1
Cuernavaca, Mexico 62050
52-777/ 314-1244   52-777/ 312-5769
www.quintalasflores.com

Clientele: gay-friendly
Type: small hotel set among sprawling lawns & gardens; also restaurant & bar
Baths: private
Amenities: pool

Kids: welcome
Smoking: ok
Rates: US$100-165

La Villa Hidalgo

Cuernavaca, Mexico

52-777/ 317-3777
www.lavillahidalgo.com

Clientele: mixed gay/ lesbian
Type: boutique hotel & social club w/ array of pampering amenities for the discriminating traveler
Owned/ Run By: gay men
Rooms: 4
Baths: private & shared
Wheelchair Access: yes, all rms

Meals: full brkfst
Amenities: laundry, pool, massage
Kids: no
Pets: no
Smoking: ok
Rates: US$100-200
AC: 10-12%

Best Western El Cid

Ensenada, Mexico

Av Lopez Mateos 993
Ensenada, Mexico
52-646/ 178-2401
www.hotelelcid.com.mx

Clientele: gay-friendly
Type: hotel; overlooking Ensenada Bay; free high-speed internet; secured parking; centrally located
Rooms: suites
Baths: private
Meals: cont'l brkfst
Amenities: free parking, laundry, pool,

DVDs/ videos, WiFi
Kids: welcome
Pets: no
Smoking: ok (15 nonsmoking rms available)
Rates: US$52-150
AC: 15% (no commission on certain dates)

Casita GDL

Guadalajara, Mexico

Calle 68 A #312 SL
Guadalajara, Mexico 44730
310/ 890-8377 (US #)
www.CasitaGDL.com

Type: b&b-private home
Rooms: 3
Baths: private
Meals: full brkfst
Amenities: laundry, sauna, hot tub, DVDs/ videos

Kids: welcome
Pets: welcome
Smoking: no
Rates: US$50-70

Hotel Casa Campos B&B

Guadalajara, Mexico

Francisco de Miranda 30-A
Colonia Centro
Tlaquepaque, Mexico 45500
52-33/ 3838-5296 52-33/ 3838-5297
www.hotelcasacampos.com

Clientele: gay-friendly
Type: hotel; 15 minutes SE of Guadalajara; also lounge/ restaurant & bar
Rooms: 12
Baths: private
Meals: cont'l brkfst

Amenities: free parking, laundry, WiFi
Kids: welcome
Pets: welcome
Rates: 850-1,250 pesos

Hotel Puerta del Sol

Guadalajara, Mexico

Av López Mateos Sur 4205
Col. Loma Bonita
Zapopan, Mexico 45087
52-33/ 3133-0808,
52-33/ 3133-0852 & 0862
www.hotelpuertadelsol.com.mx

Clientele: gay-friendly
Type: hotel; "truly gay-friendly hotel where everything is different"
Rooms: 54
Baths: private
Amenities: pool, outdoor hot tub
Pets: no

Smoking: ok
Rates: 450-790 pesos

Hotel San Francisco

Guadalajara, Mexico

Degollado 267
Guadalajara, Mexico
52-33/ 3613-8954
52-33/ 3613-8971

Clientele: gay-friendly
Type: hotel; Colonial-style hotel w/ Old World charm, balconies & courtyards; close to many gay bars; also restaurant
Rooms: 76
Baths: private & shared

Amenities: free parking
Rates: US$55+

Old Guadalajara B&B

Guadalajara, Mexico

Belén 236
Guadalajara, Mexico 44100
52-33/ 3613-9958
www.oldguadalajara.com

Clientele: mixed gay/ straight
Type: b&b- elegant private 16th-c home in downtown historic district; safe; gay owners always available
Owned/ Run By: gay men
Rooms: 4
Baths: private

Meals: full brkfst
Kids: no
Pets: no
Smoking: no
Rates: US$100

La Perla B&B
Guadalajara, Mexico

Prado 128, Col. Americana
Guadalajara, Mexico
52-33/ 3826-6961
www.prado128.com

Clientele: mixed gay/ straight
Type: b&b-inn; lavishly furnished mansion in the heart of Guadalajara
Owned/ Run By: gay men
Rooms: 6
Baths: private
Meals: full brkfst

Amenities: free parking, laundry, massage, DVDs/ videos, WiFi
Kids: no
Pets: no
Smoking: no (ok on rooftop terrace & balconies)
Rates: US$100-200

La Casa Mexicana Inn
La Paz, Mexico

Calle Nicolas Bravo 106
La Paz, Mexico 2000
52-612/ 125-2748
www.casamex.com

Clientele: mixed gay/ straight
Type: b&b-inn; secure & intimate Spanish-Moorish-Deco retreat; bay views, center of town
Owned/ Run By: woman
Rooms: 5
Baths: private
Wheelchair Access: yes, 1 rm

Meals: expanded cont'l brkfst
Amenities: massage, WiFi
Kids: 10 yrs & up welcome
Pets: no
Smoking: no
Rates: US$65-95
AC: 5%

Hotel Mediterrane
La Paz, Mexico

Allende 36
La Paz, Mexico 23000
52-612/ 125-1195
www.hotelmed.com

Clientele: mixed gay/ straight
Type: hotel; privacy & tranquility in the heart of La Paz; Mykonos & Mexican ambience; also bar & restaurant
Owned/ Run By: gay men
Rooms: 9
Baths: private

Wheelchair Access: yes, 3 rms
Meals: full brkfst
Amenities: laundry, WiFi
Pets: welcome
Smoking: no
Rates: US$60-83
AC: 10%

Casa Mora B&B Malinalco
Malinalco, Mexico

Calle de la Cruz 18
Malinalco, Mexico 52440
52-714/ 147-0572
www.casamora.net

Clientele: gay-friendly
Type: hacienda-style b&b in charming, historic town; decorated w/ authentic Mexican & European antiques; extraordinary views
Owned/ Run By: straight
Rooms: 5 (4 jr & 1 master suite)
Baths: private

Meals: full brkfst
Amenities: pool, massage
Kids: no
Pets: no
Smoking: ok
Rates: US$125-260
AC: 10%

Mexico's Villa Montaña Adventure Outpost
Manzanillo, Mexico

PO Box 16343
Seattle, WA 98116
206/ 937-3882
www.choice1.com/villamontana.htm

Clientele: gay-friendly
Type: b&b-private home; 2-bdrm hilltop villa in sleepy fishing village of La Manzanilla; 1/2 hr N of Manzanillo; bay & ocean views
Owned/ Run By: straights
Rooms: 5

Baths: private
Wheelchair Access: yes, all rms
Kids: welcome
Pets: welcome
Smoking: no
Rates: US$65-139
AC: 5%

Red Tree Melaque Inn
Manzanillo, Mexico

Primaveras
Melaque-Villa Obregon, Mexico
52-315/ 355-8917
www.redtreemelaque.com

Clientele: gay-friendly
Type: cottage; small, intimate bungalows a few blks from the ocean
Owned/ Run By: gay men
Rooms: 3
Baths: private
Meals: coffee/ tea only

Amenities: free parking, laundry, pool, DVDs/ videos, WiFi
Kids: welcome
Pets: welcome
Smoking: no
Rates: US$35-50
AC: 10%

Los Sueños del Mar

Manzanillo, Mexico

Calle Almendros 98
Manzanillo, Mexico
52-314/ 335-0482
800/ 316-9032 (reservations only)
www.lossuenosdelmar.com

Clientele: mixed gay/ straight
Type: b&b; perched on a cliff above Pacific Ocean; incredible view
Owned/ Run By: gay men
Rooms: 2 private guesthouses & 2 bdrms in main villa
Baths: private

Meals: full brkfst
Amenities: free parking, laundry, pool, massage, DVDs/ videos, WiFi
Kids: no
Pets: no
Smoking: no (ok on outdoor terraces)
Rates: US$150-220

Los Arcos B&B

Mérida, Mexico

Calle 66
Mérida, Mexico
52-999/ 928-0214
www.losarcosmerida.com

Clientele: gay-friendly
Type: b&b; Colonial home from 1800s; in heart of Mérida's Centro
Owned/ Run By: gay men
Rooms: 3
Baths: private
Wheelchair Access: yes, all rms

Meals: cont'l brkfst
Amenities: laundry, pool, massage
Kids: no
Pets: no
Smoking: ok (nonsmoking rms available)
Rates: US$75-95

Angeles de Mérida

Mérida, Mexico

Calle 74-A, #495-A x 57 y 59-A
Mérida, Mexico 97000

52-999/ 923-8163
713/ 208-2482 (US#)

angelesdemerida@sbcglobal.net
www.angelesdemerida.com

Clientele: mixed gay/ straight
Type: b&b-private home; 18th-c home restored & renovated in 2004; on the quietest streets in Merida
Owned/ Run By: gay men
Pickup Service: airport pickup; $15
Transit: 15 minutes to airport; 7 blks to bus station; 2 blks to taxi stand
Rooms: 5 total, 1 king, 4 fulls, A/C, ceiling fan, maid service, all custom-decorated guest rms w/ own bath; 4 rms overlook pool & garden
Baths: private, showers, hairdryers
Meals: full brkfst, free beer/ wine & snacks; lunch is available for $10-15
Amenities: laundry, pool, massage, cocktails, coffee/ tea, 2 houseboys, 1 chef, 1 masseur, 1 driver; by winter 2006 ADM will have rooftop terrace for nude sunbathing, hot tub & steam rm; also have beach house, "Casa de Angeles de Chicxulub," located 45 minutes from Mérida
Kids: no
Pets: no

Pets On Premises: 1 cat
Smoking: no
Reservations: required *Deposit:* required, 100%, due at booking *Cancellation:* cancel by 2 weeks prior or forfeit 50% cancellation fee *Minimum Stay:* 2 nights
Payment: cash, Visa, Amex, MC, PayPal

Season: open yr-round *High season:* Oct 1-April 30
Rates: US$85-130 *Discounts:* stay 3 nights & 4th is free (May-Sept)
AC: 20%

Casa Ana B&B

Mérida, Mexico

Calle 52 #469
Mérida, Mexico
52-999/ 924-0005
www.casaana.com

Clientele: mixed gay/ straight
Type: b&b; in Colonial home; tropical garden; natural rock pool; palapa; homemade muffins & marmalades; homecooked dinners available
Owned/ Run By: women
Rooms: 4

Baths: private
Meals: cont'l brkfst
Amenities: laundry, pool, massage
Kids: please call first
Pets: please call first
Smoking: no (outside only)
Rates: US$30-45

Casa San Juan B&B

Mérida, Mexico

545-A Calle 62
Mérida, Mexico 97000
52-999/ 986-2937 305/ 394-9551 (US #)
www.casasanjuan.com

Clientele: mixed gay/ straight
Type: b&b-private home; a true b&b located in historical center of Mérida; large rms, A/C
Owned/ Run By: gay man
Rooms: 8
Baths: private
Wheelchair Access: yes, 5 rms

Meals: cont'l brkfst
Amenities: free parking, laundry
Kids: welcome
Pets: welcome w/ prior approval
Smoking: no
Rates: US$35-55
AC: 20%

Best Western Majestic Hotel

Mexico City, Mexico

Madero 73, Col. Centro
Mexico City, Mexico 06000
52-55/ 5521-8600 800/ 528-1234
www.majestic.com.mx

Clientele: gay-friendly
Type: 4-star hotel on the Zócalo Plaza; rooftop restaurant; bar
Rooms: 85
Baths: private
Wheelchair Access: yes
Amenities: laundry

Kids: welcome
Smoking: ok (some nonsmoking rms)
Rates: US$115+

Hostal San Sebastian

Mexico City, Mexico

Havre 41
Mexico City, Mexico
52-55/ 5208-6528

Clientele: gay-friendly
Type: hostel
Owned/ Run By: gay man
Meals: cont'l brkfst

Rates: US$23-34

Hotel Gillow

Mexico City, Mexico

Isabel la Católica 17
Mexico City, Mexico
52-55/ 5518-1440 52-55/ 5510-2636
www.hotelgillow.com

Clientele: gay-friendly
Type: hotel; close to Zócalo & museum; also restaurant, bar & travel agency; internet access
Rooms: 103
Baths: private

Amenities: laundry
Rates: US$42-90

Hotel Polanco

Mexico City, Mexico

Edgar Allan Poe 8
Mexico City, Mexico
52-55/ 5280-8082 800/ 221-9044
www.hotelpolanco.com

Clientele: gay-friendly
Type: hotel; posh location steps from Paseo de la Reforma; high-speed internet in all rms; gym; business center; restaurant
Rooms: 71

Baths: private
Rates: 1,150-1,606 pesos

NH Mexico City

Mexico City, Mexico

Liverpool 155
Mexico City, Mexico
52-55/ 5228-9928
www.nh-hotels.com

Clientele: gay-friendly
Type: hotel; upscale; 2 restaurants
Rooms: 302
Baths: private

Amenities: pool
Rates: US$85-210

W Mexico City

Mexico City, Mexico

Campos Eliseos 252
Mexico City, Mexico
52-55/ 9138-1800
www.whotels.com/mexicocity

Clientele: gay-friendly
Type: hotel; Mexico City's most ultracool hotel in trendy Polanco neighborhood; 2 restaurants & bar
Rooms: 237

Baths: private
Amenities: WiFi
Kids: welcome
Rates: US$199+

Casa Montana

Mineral de Pozos, Mexico

Plaza Principal, Jardin Juarez #4A
Mineral de Pozos, Mexico 37910
52-442/ 293-0032 & 0033
www.casamontanahotel.com

Clientele: gay-friendly
Type: b&b-inn; boutique hotel in stone villa; w/ high-beamed ceilings, fireplaces, cozy sitting area, hand-carved & antique furniture; patio & inside dining; town a Colonial gem w/ growing artists colony
Owned/ Run By: straights
Rooms: 5

Baths: private
Meals: full brkfst
Kids: welcome
Pets: welcome
Smoking: ok
Rates: US$78-105 + tax
AC: 10%

Casa Camelinas B&B

Morelia, Mexico

Jacarandas 172
Morelia, Mexico
52-443/ 324-5194 707/ 942-4822 (US#)
www.cimarron.net/mexico/camelinas.html

Clientele: gay-friendly
Type: b&b-inn; mostly women; 3 1/2 hrs from Mexico City; also Spanish classes
Owned/ Run By: women
Rooms: 4
Baths: private

Meals: cont'l brkfst
Kids: 12 yrs & up welcome
Pets: no
Smoking: no
Rates: US$75

Casa Adobe B&B

Oaxaca, Mexico

Independencia 11
Tlalixtac de Cabrera, Mexico
52-951/ 517-7268
www.casaadobe-bandb.com

Clientele: mixed gay/ straight
Type: b&b; 15 minutes from center of Oaxaca; "experience Old Mexico"
Owned/ Run By: gay men
Rooms: 4
Baths: private & shared
Meals: full brkfst

Amenities: free parking, laundry, DVDs/ videos, WiFi
Kids: please inquire
Pets: no
Rates: US$37-65

La Casa de Mis Recuerdos

Oaxaca, Mexico

Pino Suárez 508
Oaxaca, Mexico
52-951/ 515-5645
www.misrecuerdos.net

Clientele: gay-friendly
Type: charming b&b that is "classic Oaxaca"; decorated w/ handmade art & owner's paintings
Rooms: 10
Baths: private & shared

Meals: full brkfst
Kids: 16 yrs & up welcome
Pets: no
Smoking: no
Rates: US$57-96 (3-night minimum)

Casa Machaya B&B

Oaxaca, Mexico

Sierra Nevada 164, Col. Loma Linda
Oaxaca, Oaxaca, Mexico 68024
52/ 951-1328203
www.oaxacadream.com

Clientele: gay-friendly
Type: b&b-private home; private level w/ patio & valley views
Owned/ Run By: straights
Rooms: 1
Baths: private
Meals: full brkfst

Amenities: free parking, laundry
Kids: welcome
Pets: no
Smoking: no
Rates: US$50-75

Aventura Mexicana Resort

Playa del Carmen, Mexico

Avenida 10 y Calle 22
Playa del Carmen, Mexico 77710
52-984/ 873-1876
www.AventuraMexicana.com

Clientele: gay-friendly
Type: resort; 2 blks from beach, 1 blk from 5th Ave; gay bar & restaurant at hotel
Owned/ Run By: gay man
Rooms: 25
Baths: private
Meals: cont'l brkfst

Amenities: free parking, laundry, pool, 2 hot tubs, massage
Kids: no
Pets: no
Smoking: ok
Rates: US$50-225
AC: 10%

Casa Cúpula

Puerto Vallarta, Mexico

Callejon de la Igualdad 129, Col. Amapas
Puerto Vallarta, Mexico 48300
52-322/ 223-2484 866/ 261-3516
www.casacupula.com

Clientele: men
Type: luxury gay guesthouse; walk to gay beach, bars & restaurants; concierge service
Owned/ Run By: gay men
Rooms: 12
Baths: private
Meals: expanded cont'l brkfst

Amenities: free parking, laundry, pool, massage, DVDs/ videos, WiFi
Kids: no
Pets: welcome
Smoking: no
Rates: US$145-355
AC: 10%

Casa de los Arcos

Puerto Vallarta, Mexico

Calle las Hortencias 168
Puerto Vallarta, Mexico 48300
52-322/ 222-5990 212/ 561-5795 (US#)
www.casadelosarcos.com

Clientele: mixed gay/ straight
Type: rental home; 3 suites in private villa; stunning views; private sun terraces; in-house water purification system
Rooms: 4
Baths: private

Amenities: free parking, laundry, pool
Kids: please inquire
Pets: please inquire
Smoking: ok
Rates: US$100-600

Abbey Hotel

Puerto Vallarta, Mexico

Pulpito 138
Puerto Vallarta, Mexico 48380

52-322/ 222-4488

abbeyhotelvallarta@yahoo.com
www.abbeyhotelvallarta.com

Clientele: men
Type: hotel; newly established cozy hotel w/ comfortable rms & intimate areas; near beach; in center of romantic gay quarter; also restaurant & lounge
Owned/ Run By: gay & straight
Nearby Attractions: Rio Cuale, Gallery District & famous church built in the 1900s
Pickup Service: airport pickup; yes
Rooms: 55 total, 12 suites, 42 kings, A/C, color TV, deck, phone, maid service, cozy, clean, intimate rms; suites include kitchenette & dining area
Baths: private, showers, hairdryers
Meals: full brkfst, complimentary cocktail upon arrival
Amenities: laundry, pool, outdoor hot tub, massage, reserved beach area w/ restaurant & bar service
Recreation: fishing, golf, scuba diving, tennis, horseback riding, mtn tours, Abbey Sailboat Tour
Kids: no
Pets: no
Smoking: ok

Reservations: *Deposit:* required, 50%, due at booking *Cancellation:* cancel by 2 weeks prior Dec-May & 1 week (June-Nov) (30 days special events & holidays) or forfeit $25 service fee (whole deposit if under 14 days) *Minimum Stay:* 3- to 4-night minimum (Dec 23 - April 15); longer holidays & special events

Payment: Visa, MC, personal checks must clear before arrival
Season: open yr-round
Rates: US$117-222 + 17% tax
AC: 18%

Blue Chairs Beach Resort

Puerto Vallarta, Mexico

229/ 336-9979 (US#)
866/ 514-7969 (US & Canada)
bluechairsresort@aol.com
www.bluechairs.com

Clientele: mixed gay/ lesbian
Type: resort; only gay beachfront resort in Mexico; rooftop pool
Pickup Service: airport pickup; US$18
Transit: near public transit
Rooms: 40 total, A/C, color TV, cable, ceiling fan, deck, phone, kitchenette, refrigerator, rm service, maid service, many rms & suites w/ ocean views, memory-foam mattresses
Baths: private, showers
Wheelchair Access: yes, 10 rms
Amenities: free parking, laundry, massage, rooftop pool, restaurant & bar
Recreation: on Los Muertos Beach, the gay beach; also gay cruise every Th, gay horseback riding tours
Kids: no
Pets: no
Smoking: ok
Reservations: *Check in/ out:* 3pm/ noon
Payment: travelers checks, Visa, Amex, MC
Season: open yr-round
Rates: US$59-229
AC: please inquire

On behalf of the staff and senior management at Blue Chairs Beach Resort we welcome you to our little piece of paradise and we are ready to host you in gay-friendly Vallarta.

We run a clean, professional operation that welcomes gay, lesbian, and transgender travelers, and we're even "straight-friendly" for those with good attitudes. Our hotel has been inspected by the Mexican Tourism Authority and has been awarded a 4-star rating. Our property is well maintained, clean, and offers all the services and amenities you would expect of 4-star accommodations–best of all, we're in the heart of the daytime gay and lesbian scene in Vallarta.

The men and women guests at the hotel mix very well since the ones in the gay community who are "allergic" to their gay brothers or sisters tend not to book with us. Our entire operation is designed to give all guests a great experience and value, and isn't that what you're looking for in a vacation? Come and let your hair down, let your guard down, relax and just be yourself–we will take care of the rest.

Casa Las Brisas

Puerto Vallarta, Mexico

Playa Careyeros, Punta de Mita
Nayarit, Mexico
52-329/ 298-4114
www.casalasbrisas.com

Clientele: mixed gay/ straight
Type: hotel; all-inclusive oceanfront villa-style resort w/ 6 guest suites; secluded & romantic
Owned/ Run By: gay men
Rooms: 6
Baths: private
Meals: full brkfst

Amenities: free parking, pool, massage, DVDs/ videos
Kids: welcome only if entire villa rented by same group
Pets: please inquire
Smoking: no
Rates: US$355-595
AC: please inquire

Casa Mariposa

Puerto Vallarta, Mexico

270 Belleveu #181
Newport, RI 02840
401/ 849-8597 866/ 849-8597
visitnewport@aol.com

Clientele: mostly men
Type: colorful condo w/ balcony 1 blk from Los Muertos Beach; 10-minute walk to restaurants
Owned/ Run By: lesbians/ gay men
Amenities: pool
Kids: welcome

Pets: no
Rates: US$65-100
AC: 20%

Los Cuatro Vientos

Puerto Vallarta, Mexico

Matamoros 520
Puerto Vallarta, Mexico
52-322/ 222-0161
www.cuatrovientos.com

Clientele: gay-friendly
Type: hotel that's home to popular El Nido rooftop bar & Chez Elena restaurant; sponsors annual weeklong Women's Getaway; also commitment ceremonies
Rooms: 14

Baths: private
Meals: cont'l brkfst
Amenities: pool

Hotelito Desconocido

Puerto Vallarta, Mexico

Playon de Mismaloya
La Cruz de Loreto, Tomatlán, Mexico
52-322/ 281-4010 800/ 851-1143
www.hotelito.com

Clientele: mixed gay/ straight
Type: hotel; luxurious eco-resort w/ 40 miles of pristine beach; 1 1/2 hrs S of Puerto Vallarta
Owned/ Run By: gay/ lesbian & straight
Rooms: 24
Baths: private
Meals: full brkfst
Amenities: free parking, laundry, pool,

poolside mist, sauna, hot tub, massage
Kids: 12 yrs & up welcome in summer
Pets: please inquire
Smoking: ok
Rates: US$302-697
AC: 10%

Paco's Hidden Paradise

Puerto Vallarta, Mexico

Pino Suarez 583
Puerto Vallarta, Mexico 48380
52-322/ 227-2189
www.pacopaco.com

Clientele: mixed gay/ lesbian
Type: condo; secluded gay-run beach resort; w/ restaurant & bar; swimming, snorkeling, kayaking & nature trails; accessible only by boat
Owned/ Run By: gay man
Rooms: 4 (condos)
Baths: private

Kids: no
Pets: welcome
Smoking: ok
Rates: US$40-80
AC: 15%

Hotel Mercurio

Puerto Vallarta, Mexico

52-322/ 222-4793
202/ 292-4250

reservations@hotel-mercurio.com
www.hotel-mercurio.com

Clientele: mixed gay/ lesbian
Type: gay/ lesbian hotel in Vallarta's Gayborhood; outstanding service; clean, quiet, well-appointed rms; English-speaking staff; overnight guests welcome w/ valid ID
Owned/ Run By: gay man/ gay staff
Nearby Attractions: walking distance to gay nightlife; restaurants, shopping, galleries steps from hotel; ATV tours, gay nude beach (private)
Pickup Service: airport pickup; $30 for up to 3 passengers
Transit: near public transit; 20 minutes to airport; 25 minutes to bus station
Rooms: 28 total, 9 kings, 5 queens, 6 fulls, A/C, color TV, cable, ceiling fan, kitchenette (9), refrigerator, safer sex supplies, maid service, luxury-quality bedding & linens; also 8 double rms for up to 4 people
Baths: private, showers
Meals: brkfst buffet
Amenities: laundry, massage, WiFi, coffee/ tea, heated pool
Kids: no

Pets: small pets welcome w/ prior approval
Pets On Premises: small dog (daytime only)
Smoking: ok
Reservations: required *Deposit:* required, 1 night, due at booking *Cancellation:*

cancel by 1 week prior or forfeit deposit
Payment: cash, travelers checks, Visa, Amex, MC, Discover, US$ & pesos ok
Season: open yr-round *High season:* Dec-April
Rates: US$60-110

Villa Safari Condo

Puerto Vallarta, Mexico

Francisca Rodriguez 203
Puerto Vallarta, Mexico 48351

269/ 469-0468 (US #)

info@bluefishvacations.com
www.villasafari.com

Clientele: mixed gay/ straight
Type: condo; new 2-bdrm condo; on hillside just 2 short blks from Los Muertos Beach, PV's most sought-after area; close to beaches, shopping & best restaurants
Owned/ Run By: gay men
Nearby Attractions: in the heart of Old Town or the Zona Romantica
Transit: near public transit; 15 minutes to airport
Rooms: 1 (condo) total, 1 queen, 2 twins, A/C, color TV, DVD/ VCR, cable, ceiling fan, deck, phone, kitchenette, refrigerator, maid service, plus sleeper sofa
Baths: private, bathtubs, showers, hairdryers
Amenities: free parking, laundry, gym, largest infinity (swimming) pool in the area, sundeck, snack bar
Recreation: surfing, sailing, beaches, golfing, scuba, snorkeling, jet-skiing, fishing
Kids: welcome
Pets: welcome w/ prior approval

Smoking: no
Reservations: required *Deposit:* required, 50%, due at booking *Cancellation:* cancel by 30 days prior or forfeit $50 + condo needs to be rebooked *Minimum Stay:* 5

nights–1 week *Check in/ out:* 3pm/ 11am
Payment: Visa, Amex, MC
Season: open yr-round *High season:* Jan-May
Rates: US$125-200

Villa del Cielo
Puerto Vallarta, Mexico

Paseo de los Delfines 121
Puerto Vallarta, Mexico
206/ 285-3503 (US#)
www.villadelcielo.com

Clientele: mixed gay/ straight
Type: rental home; private villa (sleeps 10-12) on Conchas Chinas hillside; walk to gay beaches & downtown; maid & houseman
Owned/ Run By: gay men
Rooms: 5
Baths: private & shared

Wheelchair Access: yes
Amenities: free parking, laundry, pool, DVDs/ videos
Kids: welcome
Pets: welcome
Smoking: ok
Rates: US$395-750
AC: 15%

Villas David B&B
Puerto Vallarta, Mexico

Calle Galeana 348
Puerto Vallarta, Mexico
877/ 832-3315 (US#)
52-322/ 223-0315
www.villadavidpv.com

Clientele: gay men only
Type: b&b; located in the heart of beautiful Old Puerto Vallarta; rooftop jacuzzi & pool w/ nude sunbathing; balconies
Owned/ Run By: gay men
Rooms: 10
Baths: private

Meals: full brkfst
Amenities: pool, hot tub, massage, DVDs/ videos, WiFi
Smoking: no
Rates: US$59-159
AC: 10%

Rosarito Beach Hotel
Rosarito Beach, Mexico

Blvd Benito Juárez 31
Rosarito Beach, Mexico
52-661/ 612-0144 or 1111
800/ 343-8582 (reservations)
www.rosaritobeachhotel.com

Clientele: gay-friendly
Type: historic hotel that's hosted stars & royalty; ocean views; also restaurant & full-service spa
Rooms: 280
Baths: private

Amenities: pool
Kids: welcome
Pets: no
Rates: US$70-350

RosaritoRental.com
Rosarito Beach, Mexico

La Paloma Beach & Tennis Club
Rosarito Beach, Mexico
760/ 318-9652 (US#)
www.rosaritorental.com

Clientele: gay-friendly
Type: condo; 1- & 2-bdrm rentals at oceanside La Paloma Beach & Tennis Club; 24hr gated community; private beach
Amenities: free parking, pool, outdoor

hot tub
Kids: welcome
Rates: US$79-229

Casa Gayceta
San Miguel de Allende, Mexico

Quebrada 24
San Miguel de Allende, Mexico
52-415/ 152-0710
www.casagayceta.com

Clientele: mixed gay/ lesbian
Type: charming b&b; in historic house in downtown San Miguel de Allende
Rooms: 4
Baths: private

Rates: US$60-150

Casa Schuck Boutique B&B
San Miguel de Allende, Mexico

Garita #3, Apdo 180
San Miguel De Allende, Mexico 37700
52-415/ 152-0657 937/ 684-4092 (US#)
www.casaschuck.com

Clientele: gay-friendly
Type: boutique hotel; w/ private gardens & rooftop deck; intimate colonial charm & friendly atmosphere
Rooms: 6 (suites)
Baths: private
Meals: full American or Mexican brkfst

Amenities: free parking, laundry, pool, massage, DVDs/ videos
Kids: no
Pets: no
Smoking: no
Rates: US$140-199

Dos Casas
San Miguel de Allende, Mexico

Calle Quebrada 101
San Miguel de Allende, Mexico
52-415/ 154-4073
www.livingdoscasas.com

Clientele: gay-friendly
Type: luxury b&b 3 blks from main square; rent one of the deluxe rms (including rm w/ jacuzzi, sauna & private terrace) or the whole house
Rooms: 5

Baths: private
Meals: full brkfst
Amenities: sauna, hot tub
Rates: US$195-315

Las Terrazas San Miguel
San Miguel de Allende, Mexico

Santo Domingo 3
San Miguel de Allende, Mexico 37700
52-415/ 152-5028 707/ 534-1833 (US#)
www.terrazassanmiguel.com

Clientele: mixed gay/ straight
Type: rental home; walled compound of 4 unique casas (houses) on a terraced hillside in Centro San Miguel de Allende, Mexico; health club w/ pool, sauna, gym next door
Owned/ Run By: gay men
Rooms: 4 (houses: studio to 2-bdrm)

Baths: private
Meals: pastries, juice, milk & coffee
Amenities: laundry, WiFi
Kids: please inquire
Pets: no
Smoking: no
Rates: US$770-1,225/ week

Casa de la Luz
Veracruz, Mexico

Bernardino Aguirre 15
Tlacotalpan, Veracruz, Mexico
52-288/ 884-2331
www.geocities.com/casadelaluz_mexico/index.htm

Clientele: gay-friendly
Type: charming studio apt; also rms in guesthouse; 4 blks from town center
Rooms: 3 (2 guest rms & 1 apt)
Baths: private & shared
Amenities: free parking, laundry

Kids: welcome
Pets: welcome
Rates: US$35 (guesthouse) & $65 (apt)

Hotel Las Palmas
Zihuatanejo, Mexico

335 W Virginia Ave
Phoenix, AZ 85003
52-755/ 557-0634 (cell)
www.hotellaspalmas.net

Clientele: gay-friendly
Type: b&b-inn; small specialty boutique hotel w/ quiet, remote setting right on beach; beautiful natural surroundings; for mature adults
Owned/ Run By: straights
Rooms: 6
Baths: private

Meals: full brkfst
Amenities: laundry, pool, massage
Kids: no
Pets: welcome w/ prior notice
Smoking: ok
Rates: US$225
AC: 10%

Parrot Cove Resort
Hopkins Village, Belize

501/ 523-7225 877/ 207-7139 (US #)
www.parrotcoveresort.com

Clientele: gay-friendly
Type: resort; on miles of sandy beach surrounded by rain forest, rivers, lagoons, waterfalls & mtns
Owned/ Run By: straights
Rooms: 5
Baths: private
Meals: full brkfst

Amenities: free parking, laundry, pool, massage, DVDs/ videos
Kids: no
Pets: no
Smoking: ok
Rates: US$120-250
AC: 15%

Rum Point Inn
Placencia, Belize

501/ 523-3239 888/ 235-4031
www.rumpoint.com

Clientele: gay-friendly
Type: resort on Placencia Peninsula, also tours & scuba diving
Owned/ Run By: straights
Rooms: 22
Baths: private

Amenities: laundry, pool, massage
Kids: welcome
Smoking: ok (some rms)
Rates: US$139-209
AC: 10% (agent) & 20% (wholesalers)

Casa Ramon

Dominical, Costa Rica

100 meters from Cuna de Angel
Portocita, Dominical, Costa Rica
www.casaramoncr.com

506/ 882-7687
506/ 787-8378 (ask for Fateh)

Casa Ramon–Ultimate in Tropical Coastal Living
Gazing toward an immense expanse of azure South Pacific...Caño Island on the horizon...and the alluring palm-lined tropical beaches nearby...you watch the dolphins and the whales on their way north...all from Casa Ramon.

Designed to accommodate groups of like-minded people in harmony, Casa Ramon contains three luxury apartments. Each apartment is a completely sufficient private abode with its own trendy balance of indoor and outdoor living spaces. Casa Ramon is the ultimate statement in tropical style, contemporary flair, and comfort.

To ensure your total enjoyment, Casa Ramon's concierge service offers you a hassle-free itinerary. The service includes tours, therapeutic massage, private yoga class, and an in-home chef.

Located 9 kilometers south of Dominical in southern Costa Rica, Casa Ramon features several packages and weekly seasonal rates.

Please see our website for contact information and for reservations at: www.casa-ramoncr.com.

Clientele: gay-friendly
Type: apt; 3 luxury apts that can be rented individually or as a whole building
Owned/ Run By: gay & straight
Pickup Service: airport pickup; $150-200 (depends on # of people)
Transit: 100 miles to San Jose Int'l airport; 25 miles from Palmar Sur Airstrip
Rooms: 3 (apts) total, suites, includes following properties: Casita Ramon: 2 flrs, king, full kitchen, 2 baths; Deluxe Suite: 2 beds (1 king, 1 guest), 3 baths, kitchen; Grand View Apt: 2 bedrooms (1 king, 1 guest)

Baths: private
Meals: each apt w/ full kitchen & a chef can be appointed to suit any such diet (see Epicurian Package)
Amenities: hot tub, coffee/ tea, jacuzzi, pool, spa, lookout point w/ 200° ocean view, 3 luxe outdoor baths & showers, semi-private beach, jungle walks
Kids: over 16 yrs welcome
Pets: no
Smoking: no

Reservations: required; *Deposit:* required, $1,000, due 15 days after booking, personal check ok *Cancellation:* cancel by 15 days prior or forfeit 50% *Minimum Stay:* 1 week
Payment: cash, travelers checks, personal checks, Visa, Amex, MC, Discover
Season: open yr-round *High season:* Nov 15–April 15
Rates: US$4,200-6,800/ weekly *Discounts:* packages, low season, whole house

Cabinas Alma
Dominical, Costa Rica

Costarena Hwy, Hatillo de Aguirre
Puntarenas, Costa Rica
506/ 850–9034
www.cabinasalma.com

Clientele: gay-friendly
Type: b&b-inn; yoga/ meditation rm in rain forest; exercise rm; ocean view from pool & jacuzzi
Owned/ Run By: women
Rooms: 8
Baths: private
Wheelchair Access: yes, 1 rm

Meals: full brkfst
Amenities: laundry, pool, outdoor hot tub, massage, DVDs/ videos
Kids: welcome
Pets: welcome
Rates: US$45-60
AC: 10%

Key Lime Cottage
Guanacaste, Costa Rica

612/ 362–0763

Clientele: mixed gay/ lesbian
Type: rental home; beautiful, new Spanish-style home nestled amongst tropical gardens; walk to award-winning beach, Playa Hermosa
Owned/ Run By: lesbians
Rooms: 2

Baths: private
Meals: coffee/ tea only
Amenities: laundry, DVDs/ videos
Smoking: no
Rates: US$1,400-2,500/ week

Sela's Condo & B&B
Guanacaste, Costa Rica

Valle Escondido 8
Guanacaste, Costa Rica
506/ 293–6430
sixta@ice.co.cr

Clientele: mixed gay/ lesbian
Type: modern, 10-condo complex; 1 blk from the beach; near restaurants, bars, shopping
Owned/ Run By: lesbians
Rooms: 2
Baths: shared

Wheelchair Access: yes, 1 rm
Amenities: free parking, pool
Kids: welcome
Pets: no
Smoking: no
Rates: US$$25 (condo); $20 (B&B)
AC: 10%

Casa Dome
Jaco, Costa Rica

Los Sueños Resorts
Jaco, Costa Rica
804/ 726–6500
www.lossuenosrentals.com

Type: luxury rental home in resort setting
Rooms: 6
Baths: private & shared
Wheelchair Access: yes, 4 rms
Amenities: laundry, pool, poolside mist, hot tub, massage

Kids: welcome
Pets: not recommended
Smoking: no
Rates: US$1,295-1,400
AC: 20%

Big Ruby's La Plantacion
Manuel Antonio, Quepos, Costa Rica

Pacific Coast
Manuel Antonio, Quepos, Costa Rica
506/ 777-1332 or 506/ 777-1115
800/ 477-7829 (US#)
www.bigrubys.com

Clientele: mixed gay/ lesbian
Type: guesthouse; tropical paradise over-looking the Pacific; minutes from gay beach; full bar in high season
Owned/ Run By: gay men
Rooms: 25
Baths: private
Wheelchair Access: yes, 1 rm

Meals: full brkfst
Amenities: laundry, pool, hot tub, massage, DVDs/ videos
Kids: no
Pets: no
Smoking: ok
Rates: US$149-1,050
AC: 10%

Casa Romano
Manuel Antonio, Quepos, Costa Rica

4586 Paper Mill Road
Marietta, GA 30067
770/ 226-0054
www.casaromano.net

Clientele: mixed gay/ straight
Type: vacation rental home in preserved rain forest; gay beach is less than a mile away
Owned/ Run By: gay men
Rooms: 8
Baths: private & shared

Wheelchair Access: yes, 2 rms
Amenities: laundry, pool, massage
Kids: kids over 8 yrs welcome
Rates: US$150+ (also weekly rates)
AC: 10%

Gaia Hotel & Reserve
Manuel Antonio, Quepos, Costa Rica

km 2.7
Carretera Quepos a Manuel Antonio
Manuel Antonio, Quepos, Costa Rica
506/ 777-9797 800/ 226-2515
www.gaiahr.com

Clientele: gay-friendly
Type: luxury boutique hotel; all-jacuzzi tubs; member of Small Luxury Hotels of the World; 5-star restaurant
Owned/ Run By: gay men
Rooms: 16
Baths: private

Wheelchair Access: yes, 8 rms
Amenities: free parking, laundry, pool, massage, DVDs/ videos, WiFi
Kids: no
Pets: under 25 lbs welcome
Smoking: ok
AC: 20%

Hammocks & Eggs B&B
Manuel Antonio, Quepos, Costa Rica

150 meters E of Amigos del Rio
Manuel Antonio, Quepos, Costa Rica
506/ 777-4909
www.hammocksandeggs.com

Clientele: mostly men
Type: b&b; 2 private homes overlooking the jungle of Manuel Antonio; 5 minutes from gay beach; 2 campsites & tent rental
Owned/ Run By: gay men
Rooms: 4
Baths: shared

Meals: full brkfst
Amenities: free parking, massage
Kids: welcome
Pets: welcome
Smoking: yes
Rates: US$75

Hotel Casa Blanca
Manuel Antonio, Quepos, Costa Rica

apdo 194 Entrada La Mariposas
Manuel Antonio, Quepos, Costa Rica 6350
506/ 777-0253 506/ 777-1790
www.hotelcasablanca.com

Clientele: mixed gay/ lesbian
Type: hotel; gay & lesbian hotel overlooking the nat'l park & Pacific Ocean; walk to nude/ gay beach
Owned/ Run By: lesbians/ gay men
Rooms: 11
Baths: private

Wheelchair Access: yes, 4 rms
Meals: expanded cont'l brkfst
Amenities: free parking, laundry, pool
Kids: welcome
Smoking: ok
Rates: US$50-180
AC: 10%

Hotel Del Mar
Manuel Antonio, Quepos, Costa Rica

apdo 6350-31
Manuel Antonio, Quepos, Costa Rica
506/ 777-0543
www.gohoteldelmar.com

Clientele: mixed gay/ straight
Type: hotel; clean, comfortable & affordable rms nestled in the jungle; walk to beach
Owned/ Run By: gay men
Rooms: 12
Baths: private
Wheelchair Access: yes, 1 rm

Meals: cont'l brkfst
Amenities: free parking, laundry, massage
Kids: 12 yrs & up welcome
Pets: welcome; please call first
Smoking: ok
Rates: US$50-110
AC: 10%

Kekoldi Beach Hotel (El Dorado Mojado)
Manuel Antonio, Quepos, Costa Rica

main rd to Manuel Antonio Nat'l Park
Manuel Antonio, Quepos, Costa Rica
506/ 248-0804 786/ 221-9011 (from US)
www.kekoldi.com

Clientele: mixed gay/ straight
Type: hotel; rms & villas w/ full kitchens; resemble modernized banana plantation houses
Owned/ Run By: gay man
Rooms: 8 (includes 4 villas)
Baths: private

Amenities: free parking, laundry, pool
Kids: please inquire
Pets: welcome
Smoking: no
Rates: US$40-105
AC: 10%

Las Aguas Resort
Manuel Antonio, Quepos, Costa Rica

813/ 784-7930 (US#)
www.lasaguas.com

Clientele: mostly men
Type: new resort in the jungle in the mtns of Costa Rica
Owned/ Run By: gay man
Rooms: 12 (cottages/ rms)
Baths: private
Meals: full brkfst

Amenities: free parking, pool, outdoor hot tub, DVDs/ videos, gym, WiFi
Kids: no
Pets: no
Smoking: ok
Rates: US$79-129
AC: 10%

La Mansion Inn

506/ 777-3489
www.lamansioninn.com

Manuel Antonio, Quepos, Costa Rica

Type: 5-star elegance in heart of coastal rain forest; friendly, polite staff; short walk to gay beach & other gay-friendly establishments
Owned/ Run By: gay & straight
Rooms: 15
Baths: private
Meals: full brkfst
Amenities: free parking, pool, outdoor hot tub, massage
Kids: over 12 yrs welcome
Pets: welcome
Smoking: yes
Rates: US$125-1,600
AC: 25%

Banana Azul

506/ 750-0212
www.BananaAzul.com

Puerto Viejo de Limon, Costa Rica

Clientele: mostly men
Type: guesthouse; "beaches, nature, culture & so much more await you on the Carribean side of Costa Rica"
Owned/ Run By: gay men
Meals: full brkfst
Amenities: free parking, laundry
Kids: no
Pets: please inquire
Smoking: no
Rates: US$35-50

Bohemian Paradise Hotel

Calle 3
San José, Costa Rica
506/ 258-9683
www.seecentralamerica.com

San José, Costa Rica

Clientele: mostly men
Type: small, friendly hotel in the heart of San José; centered among gay clubs & restaurants
Owned/ Run By: gay men
Rooms: 8
Baths: private
Meals: coffee/ tea only
Amenities: laundry, hot tub, DVDs/ videos
Kids: welcome
Pets: please inquire
Rates: US$25-200
AC: 10%

Canyon House

Brasil de Santa Ana
San José, Costa Rica
506/ 249-3722
www.thecanyonhouse.com

San José, Costa Rica

Clientele: men
Type: b&b; luxury clothing-optional b&b for gay men only; airport transportation, gourmet brkfst, fine amenities, heated pool
Owned/ Run By: gay men
Rooms: 5
Baths: private
Meals: full brkfst
Amenities: laundry, pool, jacuzzi, massage, DVDs/ videos, WiFi
Kids: no
Pets: no
Smoking: no
Rates: US$105-149
AC: 10%

Hotel Kekoldi

Av 9
San José, Costa Rica
506/ 248-0804
786/ 221-9011 (from US)
www.kekoldi.com

San José, Costa Rica

Clientele: mixed gay/ straight
Type: the only hotel in downtown San José w/ a secluded garden; in beautiful art deco bldg
Owned/ Run By: gay man
Rooms: 10
Baths: private
Meals: expanded cont'l brkfst
Amenities: laundry
Smoking: ok
Rates: US$60-105
AC: 10%

Colours Oasis Resort

San José, Costa Rica

506/ 232-3504 & 506/296-1880
877/ 932-6652 or 954/ 241-7472

newcolours@colours.net
www.colours.net

Clientele: mostly men
Type: resort; newly expanded w/ complete travel- & tour-planning; bar, lounge, orchid garden, attentive service; great location in the center of gay life in exciting capital city
Owned/ Run By: gay men
Pickup Service: airport pickup; $30 (round trip)
Transit: near public transit; 20 minutes to airport, 2 blks to local bus
Rooms: 14 total, 3 suites, 5 kings, 4 queens, 6 fulls, DVD/ VCR, cable, ceiling fan, phone, kitchenette (2), refrigerator (2), maid service, updated & improved rm layouts
Baths: private, showers, robes
Meals: full brkfst, full-service bar & limited food service on premises
Amenities: laundry, pool, hot tub, massage, DVDs/ videos, sundeck, mini-gym, massage rm, bar & dining rm, concierge
Recreation: rafting, hiking, volcano tours
Kids: no
Pets: no

Smoking: ok
Reservations: required *Deposit:* required, 50%, due at booking *Cancellation:* cancel by 30 days prior or forfeit $25
Payment: cash, travelers checks, Visa, Amex, MC, Discover

Season: open yr-round *High season:* Dec-April
Rates: US$59-189 *Discounts:* weekly repeat guest, prepay
AC: 10-15+%

Hotel Santo Tomas

San José, Costa Rica

Av 7, btwn Calles 3 & 5
San José, Costa Rica

506/ 255-0448

info@hotelsantotomas.com
www.hotelsantotomas.com

Clientele: gay-friendly
Type: hotel; in beautiful 1908 home; awarded Frommers Best Value Star & Lonely Planet's Excellence Recommendation
Owned/ Run By: straights
Pickup Service: airport pickup; $20 in & $15 out (per person)
Transit: 20 minutes to airport
Rooms: 19 total, 8 suites, 13 queens, 6 fulls, color TV, cable, ceiling fan, phone, rm service, maid service, Louis XV furniture, high ceilings, safety box, Persian rugs, alarm clock/ radio, high-speed internet, free in-country calls
Baths: private, bathtubs, showers, hairdryers
Meals: expanded cont'l brkfst w/ fresh fruit, chefs can prepare whatever guests wish w/ advance notice at poolside restaurant (El Oasis)
Amenities: laundry, pool, outdoor hot tub, coffee/ tea, gift shop, free travel- & tour-planning, 4 computers in lobby, waterfall, on-site poolside restaurant (El Oasis)

Kids: welcome
Smoking: no (ok outside)
Reservations: required *Deposit:* required, due at booking *Cancellation:* cancel by 2 days prior or forfeit 1 night
Payment: cash, travelers checks, Visa, MC

Season: open yr-round *High season:* Dec-April
Rates: US$60-105 *Discounts:* please call
AC: 20%

Joluva Guesthouse
San José, Costa Rica

Calle 3-Bis, Aves 9 y 11
Barrio Amón
San José, Costa Rica
506/ 223-7961
www.joluva.com

Clientele: mixed gay/ lesbian
Type: guesthouse; in central location; proudly gay; catering to the gay & lesbian traveler since 1993
Owned/ Run By: gay men
Rooms: 7
Baths: private & shared

Meals: cont'l brkfst
Amenities: laundry, DVDs/ videos
Kids: no
Pets: no
Smoking: ok
Rates: US$30-50
AC: 10%

Angel Valley Farm B&B
San Ramon, Costa Rica

506/ 456-4084 506/ 308-7357
angelvalleyfarmbandb.com

Clientele: mixed gay/ straight
Type: b&b; on a farm in Costa Rica's central valley; "relax & re-energize your body & soul!"
Owned/ Run By: gay & straight
Rooms: 6
Baths: private & shared

Wheelchair Access: yes, 6 rms
Amenities: free parking, massage, DVDs/ videos
Smoking: no
Rates: US$35-65
AC: 10%

Inn at Coyote Mountain
San Ramon, Costa Rica

329 W Buffalo St
Ithaca, NY 14850
506/ 383-0544 902/ 482-8360
www.cerrocoyote.com

Clientele: mixed gay/ straight
Type: retreat; neo-colonial-style; overlooking 50 miles of ocean & coast; gourmet food & impeccable service; near beaches, Monteverde & San Jose
Owned/ Run By: gay men
Baths: private

Wheelchair Access: yes, 1 rm
Meals: full brkfst
Amenities: laundry, pool, sauna, massage
Kids: no
Pets: no
Rates: US$110-450

Cala Luna Hotel & Villas
Tamarindo, Costa Rica

Apdo 85-1000
San José, Costa Rica
506/ 653-0214
www.calaluna.com

Clientele: gay-friendly
Type: hotel; some rms w/ private terraces; also 2- & 3-bdrm villas
Owned/ Run By: gay & straight
Rooms: 41
Baths: private
Meals: cont'l brkfst

Amenities: free parking, laundry, pool, massage
Kids: welcome
Pets: welcome w/ prior approval
Smoking: ok
Rates: US$155-440
AC: 20%

Hotel Sueño del Mar
Tamarindo, Costa Rica

Playa Langosta, Tamarindo
Guanacaste, Costa Rica
506/ 653-0284
www.sueno-del-mar.com

Clientele: gay-friendly
Type: b&b-inn; private hacienda on the beach; w/ exquisite ocean views
Owned/ Run By: straights
Rooms: 5
Baths: private
Meals: full brkfst

Amenities: free parking, laundry, pool, hot tub, massage, WiFi
Kids: 12 yrs & up welcome
Pets: no
Smoking: no
Rates: US$145-295
AC: 15%

Tucan Hotel
Uvita, Costa Rica

506/ 743-8140
www.tucanhotel.com

Clientele: gay-friendly
Type: hotel; w/ covered rancho w/ hammocks; 1 rm w/ full kitchen; close to natural waterfalls
Owned/ Run By: bisexuals
Rooms: 5
Baths: private & shared

Meals: coffee/ tea only
Amenities: laundry
Kids: welcome
Pets: welcome
Rates: US$8-10 (dorm-style)-$15-35 (rms)
AC: 10%

Posada Del Angel
La Antigua, Guatemala

A-006 PO Box 669004
Miami Springs, FL 33266
502/ 7832-5303 305/ 677-2382 (US #)
www.posadadelangel.com

Clientele: gay-friendly
Type: 5-star colonial inn; each suite w/ fireplace, remote-control cable TV, fresh flowers, views of 3 volcanoes; hosted President Clinton in 1999
Owned/ Run By: straights
Rooms: 5 (suites)

Baths: private
Meals: cont'l brkfst
Amenities: laundry
Kids: no
Pets: no
Rates: US$190-240

The Lily Pond Guest House
Roatan, Bay Islands, Honduras

Half Moon Bay
Roatan, Bay Islands, Honduras
504/ 403-8204
www.lilypondguesthouse.com

Clientele: mixed gay/ straight
Type: guesthouse; yoga sessions on roof garden, sea views, near beach
Owned/ Run By: gay men
Rooms: 4
Baths: private
Wheelchair Access: yes, 1 rm

Meals: full brkfst
Amenities: free parking, laundry, WiFi
Kids: over age 15
Pets: no
Smoking: no
Rates: US$95-120
AC: yes

Joluva Granada
Granada, Nicaragua

Calle Cuiscoma
Granada, Nicaragua
505/ 844-2317
www.joluvanicaragua.com

Clientele: mostly men
Type: b&b; king- & queen-sized beds
Owned/ Run By: gay men
Rooms: 5
Baths: private
Meals: cont'l brkfst

Amenities: laundry, massage, WiFi
Kids: welcome
Pets: welcome
Smoking: ok
Rates: US$20
AC: 10%

Nicaragua Guesthouse
Managua, Nicaragua

Bello Horizonte VI, Etapa 217
PO Box 3701
Managua, Nicaragua 0000
505/ 249-8963
www.3dp.ch/nicaragua

Clientele: gay-friendly
Type: guesthouse; TV, cable, internet; "stay at our family-owned & run guesthouse in an elegant suburb of Managua"
Owned/ Run By: straights
Rooms: 6
Baths: private & shared
Wheelchair Access: yes, 2 rms

Meals: full brkfst
Amenities: free parking, laundry
Kids: welcome
Pets: no
Smoking: ok
Rates: US$15-35
AC: 15%

Cabañas B&B Momentum
Boquete, Panama

Apdo 4-092
Boquete, Panama 00413-00092
507/ 720-4385
www.momentum-panama.com

Clientele: gay-friendly
Type: mtn-top resort; nestled in greenery on secluded plateau at 1,000 meters; heated pool, gym; spectacular views
Owned/ Run By: gay & straight
Rooms: 10
Baths: private
Wheelchair Access: yes, all rms

Meals: coffee/ tea only
Amenities: laundry, pool, gym, WiFi
Kids: welcome under supervision of responsible parents
Pets: welcome on leash or in cabin
Smoking: no
Rates: US$55 (b&b); $70 (cabins)
AC: 15%

The Purple House Int'l Backpacker's Hostel
David, Panama

Calle C Sur & Avenida Sexta Oeste
David, Chiriqui, Panama 00000
507/ 774-4059
www.purplehousehostel.com

Clientele: gay-friendly
Type: small & homey hostel for backpackers, travelers, surfers; free internet access
Owned/ Run By: straights
Rooms: 5

Baths: private & shared
Meals: coffee/ tea only
Amenities: free parking, DVDs/ videos
Rates: US$7-30

Solarte del Caribe Inn
Isla Solarte, Panama

507/ 6488-4775 507/ 6593-2245
www.solarteinn.com

Clientele: gay-friendly
Type: b&b-inn; "tropical island paradise"; meals available; hotel bar; minutes from Bocas del Toro
Owned/ Run By: gay men
Rooms: 7
Baths: private

Meals: full brkfst
Amenities: laundry
Pets: no
Rates: US$80-210
AC: 10%

Casa Blanca
Puerto Lindo, Panama

507/ 508-5541

Clientele: mixed gay/ straight
Type: guesthouse; view of the Caribbean & rain forest; great courtyard w/ bar & restaurant
Owned/ Run By: gay men
Rooms: 4
Baths: private & shared

Meals: full brkfst
Amenities: free parking, laundry, massage
Kids: welcome
Pets: welcome
Smoking: ok
Rates: US$40-50

1555 Malabia House
Buenos Aires, Argentina

Malabia 1555, Palermo Viejo
Buenos Aires, Argentina C1414DME
54-11/ 4832-3345
www.malabiahouse.com.ar

Clientele: gay-friendly
Type: b&b; in old "San Vincente Ferrer Home for Ladies"; located in Palermo Viejo, the Soho of Buenos Aires
Owned/ Run By: straights
Rooms: 15
Baths: private

Meals: expanded cont'l brkfst
Amenities: laundry, DVDs/ videos, WiFi
Pets: welcome
Smoking: ok
Rates: US$100-170
AC: 10%

Bayres B&B
Buenos Aires, Argentina

Av Córdoba 5842
Buenos Aires, Argentina
54-11/ 4772-3877
www.bayresbnb.com

Clientele: mostly men
Type: b&b; art deco house; modern decor; friendly atmosphere
Owned/ Run By: gay men
Rooms: 5
Baths: private & shared
Meals: cont'l brkfst

Amenities: DVDs/ videos
Pets: quiet pets welcome
Smoking: ok
Rates: US$30-50

The Cocker
Buenos Aires, Argentina

Av Juan de Garay 458
Buenos Aires, Argentina 1153
54-1/ 1436-28451
www.thecocker.com

Clientele: mixed gay/ straight
Type: hotel; 5 suites surrounded by roof gardens in newly restored art nouveau townhouse
Owned/ Run By: gay men
Rooms: 5
Baths: private

Meals: full brkfst
Amenities: laundry, DVDs/ videos, WiFi
Kids: no
Pets: welcome
Smoking: ok
Rates: US$60-70

Como en Casa B&B
Buenos Aires, Argentina

Gurruchaga 2155
Buenos Aires, Argentina 1425
54-11/ 4831-0517
www.bandb.com.ar

Clientele: gay-friendly
Type: b&b; located in a bohemian area w/ period architecture, bistros, designer stores & art galleries
Owned/ Run By: straights
Rooms: 11
Baths: private & shared

Meals: cont'l brkfst
Amenities: laundry
Kids: welcome
Pets: please inquire
Smoking: no
Rates: US$30-80
AC: 10%

Don Sancho Youth Hostel

Buenos Aires, Argentina

Constitucion 4062
Buenos Aires, Argentina 1254
54-11/ 4923-1422
www.hostaldonsancho.com.ar

Clientele: mixed gay/ straight
Type: hostel; cozy & friendly; in traditional area of the city, surrounded by tango everywhere; new & spacious; full kitchen; solarium
Owned/ Run By: gay & straight
Rooms: 8
Baths: shared

Meals: full brkfst
Amenities: laundry, hot tub, DVDs/ videos, WiFi
Kids: welcome
Pets: no
Smoking: ok (restricted areas)
Rates: US$7-15
AC: 10%

Lugar Gay B&B

Buenos Aires, Argentina

54-11/ 4300-4747
www.lugargay.org

Clientele: men
Type: b&b; located downtown in historical quarter of city (San Telmo, bohemian & chic)
Owned/ Run By: gay men
Rooms: 8
Baths: private & shared

Meals: cont'l brkfst
Amenities: laundry, sauna, hot tub, massage, DVDs/ videos
Kids: no
Pets: no
Rates: US$35-65
AC: 10%

Palermo Viejo B&B

Buenos Aires, Argentina

Niceto Vega 4629
Buenos Aires, Argentina 1414
54-11/ 4773-6092
www.palermoviejobb.com

Clientele: mostly men
Type: b&b; in typical home in traditional & well-located neighborhood; close to shopping & gay nightlife
Owned/ Run By: gay men
Rooms: 7
Baths: private & shared

Meals: expanded cont'l brkfst
Amenities: DVDs/ videos, WiFi
Kids: no
Pets: no
Smoking: no
Rates: US$45-65
AC: 10%

Solar Soler B&B

Buenos Aires, Argentina

Soler 5676
Buenos Aires, Argentina
54-11/ 4776-3065
www.solarsoler.com.ar

Clientele: gay-friendly
Type: b&b; located on a quiet street in Palermo Hollywood area; "ideal place to rest after a whole day visiting our beautiful city"
Owned/ Run By: straight
Rooms: 7
Baths: private

Meals: cont'l brkfst
Amenities: laundry, indoor hot tub
Kids: welcome
Pets: please inquire
Smoking: no
Rates: US$45-75

Casas Brancas

Búzios, Brazil

Alto do Humaitá 10
Búzios, Brazil
55-22/ 2623-1458
www.casasbrancas.com.br

Clientele: gay-friendly
Type: hotel; terrace, ocean views, spa, also restaurant
Owned/ Run By: straights
Rooms: 32

Baths: private
Meals: full brkfst
Amenities: pool

Glenzhaus Lodge

Búzios, Brazil

Rua 1, Quadra F, Lote 27/28
Búzios, Brazil
55-21/ 2239-9933 55-22/ 2623-2823
www.glenzhaus.com.br

Clientele: gay-friendly
Type: hotel; near beaches
Owned/ Run By: straights
Meals: full brkfst

Amenities: laundry, pool, massage, DVDs/ videos

Our House

Búzios, Brazil

Ferradura area
55-22/ 2623-1913
55-22/ 9222-5672 (cell)
www.ourhousebrazil.com

Clientele: mixed gay/ lesbian
Type: verandas, ocean views, guided hiking
& biking, near beach
Owned/ Run By: lesbians
Meals: full brkfst

Amenities: pool
Rates: US$95-125

Majestic Palace

Florianópolis, Brazil

Avenida Beira-Mar Norte 2786
Florianópolis, Brazil 88015-010
55-48/ 3231-8000
www.majesticpalace.com.br

Clientele: gay-friendly
Type: hotel; near beaches
Owned/ Run By: straights
Meals: full brkfst

Amenities: laundry, pool, massage, gym

Ponta Dos Ganchos

Florianópolis, Brazil

Gov Celso Ramos
Santa Catarina, Brazil 88190-000

55-48/ 3262-5000
800/ 643-3346

reservas@pontadosganchos.com.br
www.pontadosganchos.com.br

Clientele: gay-friendly
Type: resort; bungalows on private beach;
access to canoes, tennis, gym & diving
Owned/ Run By: straights
Nearby Attractions: city tours,
shopping
Pickup Service: airport pickup; US$65
Transit: near public transit; 50 minutes to
aiport; we provide private transfer
Rooms: 20 total, suites, kings, A/C, color TV,
DVD/ VCR, cable, ceiling fan, fireplace, deck
(15), phone, refrigerator, rm service, maid
service, 4 types of bungalows available
Baths: private, bathtubs, showers, robes,
hairdryers
Meals: full brkfst, special meals available;
must be requested 24hrs in advance
Amenities: office hrs: 9am-4pm; free
parking, laundry, pool, indoor hot tub,
massage, DVDs/ videos, gym, WiFi, snacks,
coffee/ tea, cinema, games rm
Recreation: golf, diving
Kids: no
Pets: no
Smoking: ok

Reservations: required; email at
reservas@www.pontasdosganchos.com.br
Deposit: required, 50%, due 2 days after
booking *Cancellation:* cancel by 30 days
prior *Minimum Stay:* 2 nights (4 Jan-Feb)
Check in/ out: 2pm/ noon

Payment: cash, Visa, Amex, MC
Season: open yr-round *High season:* Dec-
April
Rates: US$490-1,075
AC: 10%

Copacabana Panorama

Rio de Janeiro, Brazil

3806 Av Atlantica
Rio de Janeiro, Brazil
617/ 803-9164
martyinrio@yahoo.com

Clientele: mostly men
Type: condo; oceanfront w/ gorgeous view
of Copacabana Beach; short walk to gay
nightlife
Owned/ Run By: gay men
Rooms: 1
Baths: private

Wheelchair Access: yes, 1 rm
Amenities: DVDs/ videos
Kids: welcome
Pets: no
Smoking: ok
Rates: US$70-125
AC: 15%

MyRioCondo.com

Rio de Janeiro, Brazil

PO Box 223
Hauula, HI 96717

808/ 536–4263 (HI #)
888/ 236–0799

www.myriocondo.com

Clientele: mixed gay/ straight
Type: condo; views of Copacabana Beach; near Le Boy & gay nightlife of Rio
Owned/ Run By: gay men
Nearby Attractions: steps away from cafes, art galleries & more; Le Boy, Le Girl, bath houses & more just a few blocks away; 1 blk to Help Disco
Pickup Service: airport pickup; $40
Transit: near public transit; 45 minutes to GIG airport; 20 minutes to Santos-Dumont airport
Rooms: 3 total
Amenities: office hrs: 8am-8pm & 10am-6pm wknds Hawaiian Standard Time; laundry, WiFi, complimentary washer & dryer, VOIP phone w/ free int'l calls, digital TV w/ English-speaking channels, 24hr doorman
Kids: welcome
Pets: no
Smoking: no

Reservations: required; book online at www.myriocondo.com *Deposit:* required, 30%, due at booking, personal check ok *Cancellation:* cancel before final payment or fee varies, see policies *Minimum Stay:* 3 nights *Check in/ out:* 3pm/ 11am

Payment: cash, travelers checks, personal checks, Visa, MC, Discover
Season: open yr-round *High season:* Dec-March
Rates: US$180-375
AC: 5-10%

Nice Condos in Rio

Rio de Janeiro, Brazil

rua Barata Ribeiro 669/ 604
Rio de Janeiro, Brazil 22051-000
55-21/ 2227-5658 55-21/ 9416-2665
www.globecondos.com

Clientele: mostly men
Type: newly renovated condos; close to famous Copacabana & Ipanema beaches
Owned/ Run By: gay men
Rooms: 1-3
Wheelchair Access: yes, 1 rm

Amenities: free parking, laundry, pool, sauna
Kids: welcome
Pets: welcome
Smoking: ok
Rates: US$20-100
AC: 10%

O Veleiro B&B

Rio de Janeiro, Brazil

CP 62601 Praia de Botafogo
Rio de Janeiro, Brazil 22251-020
55-21/ 2554-8980
www.oveleiro.com

Clientele: mixed gay/ straight
Type: b&b-private home; rustic home in forested urban setting; minutes from Copacabana, Ipanema beaches, clubs & bars
Owned/ Run By: gay men
Rooms: 7

Baths: private & shared
Meals: full brkfst
Amenities: laundry, pool, sauna, DVDs/ videos
Kids: welcome
Pets: no
AC: 10%

Itacaré Eco Resort

Salvador, Brazil

BA 001 Km 64
Itacaré, Brazil
55-73/ 3251-3133
www.ier.com.br

Clientele: mixed gay/ straight
Type: resort; surrounded by mangrove trees, tropical forest & the beach; 25 campsites
Owned/ Run By: bisexuals
Rooms: 25
Baths: private
Meals: full brkfst

Amenities: laundry, pool, sauna, hot tub, massage
Kids: welcome
Pets: welcome
Rates: US$120-263
AC: 10%

Hotel Castillo

Santiago, Chile

Pio Nono 420
Santiago, Chile
56-2/ 735-0243
www.moteles.cl/stgo1/scl1.htm

Clientele: mixed gay/ lesbian
Type: hotel; 1920s building w/ ornate interior decor
Baths: private
Meals: full brkfst
Rates: US$25-47

Hosteria Papagayo

Machachi, Ecuador

Panamericana Sur, Km 43
Pichincha, Ecuador
593-2/ 231-0002 593-9/ 946-2268
www.hosteria-papagayo.com

Clientele: mixed gay/ straight
Type: hotel; restored 200-yr-old hacienda manor near impressive volcanoes; organized tours
Owned/ Run By: gay & straight
Rooms: 10
Baths: private & shared

Meals: full brkfst
Amenities: free parking, indoor hot tub, WiFi
Kids: welcome
Pets: welcome
Smoking: ok

Hostal El Cipres

Quito, Ecuador

Lerida 381
Quito, Ecuador
593-2/ 549-561
el_cipres_hostel.tripod.com/Quito

Clientele: mixed gay/ straight
Type: b&b; located in nice residential area of Quito
Owned/ Run By: gay men
Rooms: 9
Baths: private & shared
Meals: cont'l brkfst

Amenities: free parking, laundry
Kids: welcome
Pets: no
Smoking: no
AC: 10%

Hotel Cafe Cultura

Quito, Ecuador

Robles 513 y Reina Victoria
Quito, Ecuador
593-2/ 222-4271 593-2/ 256-4956
www.cafecultura.com

Clientele: gay-friendly
Type: hotel; 2-story post-colonial home w/ whitewashed walls & terracotta-tiled roof
Rooms: 26
Baths: private
Meals: cont'l brkfst

Amenities: free parking, laundry, hot tub, massage
Kids: welcome
Pets: welcome
Smoking: no
Rates: US$69-99
AC: 10%

Ariosto Hotel

Lima, Peru

Avenida La Paz 769
Miraflores
Lima, Peru
511/ 444-1414
www.hotelariosto.com.pe

Clientele: gay-friendly
Type: hotel; in shopping district of Lima; short walk to folk markets, 3 Lima gay bars, 1 gay sauna & Gold's Gym; "only hotel in Lima w/ free airport shuttle"
Owned/ Run By: gay man
Rooms: 125
Baths: private

Meals: full brkfst
Amenities: free parking, laundry
Kids: welcome but 95% mature clientele
Pets: welcome; small pets only
Smoking: ok
Rates: US$55-140
AC: 20%; rates negotiable

Ayllu B&B

Lima, Peru

José Gavez 711
Lima, Peru
51-1/ 243-0276 310/ 341-3933 (US #)
www.ayllu-peru.com

Clientele: mixed gay/ straight
Type: b&b-inn; stylish & modern decor; in Miraflores near thriving commercial area
Owned/ Run By: gay men
Rooms: 5
Baths: private & shared
Meals: expanded cont'l brkfst

Amenities: free parking, laundry, massage
Kids: welcome
Pets: no
Smoking: ok
Rates: US$15-50

Arcotel Wimberger
Vienna, Austria

Neubaugürtel 34–36
Vienna, Austria A-1070
43-1/ 521–650
www.arcotel.at

Clientele: gay-friendly
Type: hotel; 4-stars; centrally located; restaurant & bar on premises; fitness club & Turkish bath

Rooms: 225
Rates: €59+

Pension Wild
Vienna, Austria

Lange Gasse 10
Vienna, Austria A-1080
43-1/ 406-5174
www.pension-wild.at

Clientele: mixed gay/ straight
Type: hotel; small, friendly pension; close to "gay area" at Wienzeile; nice, clean, newly restored rms
Owned/ Run By: gay men
Rooms: 22 (includes 3 apts, 3 singles, 16 doubles)

Baths: private & shared
Meals: expanded cont'l brkfst
Amenities: sauna
Kids: welcome
Pets: welcome
Smoking: ok
Rates: €37-102

Résidence les Ecrins
Brussels, Belgium

rue du Rouleau 15
Brussels, Belgium 1000
32-2/ 219-3657
www.lesecrins.com

Clientele: mixed gay/ lesbian
Type: hotel; comfortable & hospitable; in large century-old building in heart of Brussels; near monuments & best-known restaurants

Baths: private & shared
Rates: €50-95

Cuberdon B&B
Ghent, Belgium

Wolterslaan 76
Flanders, Belgium 9000
32-4/ 7668-3109
www.cuberdon.be

Clientele: gay-friendly
Type: b&b; "have sweet dreams at our b&b in the historical city of Ghent"
Owned/ Run By: gay men
Rooms: 3
Baths: private & shared
Meals: expanded cont'l brkfst

Amenities: free parking
Kids: welcome
Pets: no
Smoking: no
Rates: €38-59

Best Western New Hôtel de Lives
Namur, Belgium

Chaussée de Liège 1178
Namur, Belgium B-5101
32-81/ 580-513
www.newhoteldelives.com

Clientele: mixed gay/ straight
Type: hotel; renovated 19th-c hotel w/ modern conveniences
Owned/ Run By: bisexuals
Rooms: 20
Baths: private & shared
Wheelchair Access: yes, 5 rms

Meals: full brkfst
Amenities: free parking, laundry, WiFi
Kids: welcome
Pets: welcome
Smoking: ok
Rates: €61-150
AC: 8-21%

Scottys Hotel
Sofia, Bulgaria

Ekzarh Iosif St
Sofia, Bulgaria 1000
36-309/ 32-33-34
www.gaystay.net/Scottys

Clientele: mixed gay/ straight
Type: Sofia's first gay hotel
Owned/ Run By: gay men

Amenities: WiFi
Rates: €45-85

Robinsone home Blue Dreams

Zadar, Croatia

Tkon 18
Zadar, Croatia 23262
385/ 9891-79591
www.islandpasman.com

Clientele: mostly men
Type: rental home
Owned/ Run By: gay & straight
Rooms: 2
Baths: shared
Amenities: free parking

Kids: welcome
Pets: welcome
Smoking: ok
Rates: €70-90
AC: 10%

Arco Guest House

Prague (Praha), Czech Republic

Voronézská 24
Prague (Praha), Czech Republic 100 00
36-309/ 323-334 (English & German)
www.gaystay.net/Arco/

Clientele: mostly men
Type: rms & apts in Prague Vinohrady, popular neighborhood for gay Czechs & immigrants; also Arco cafe
Owned/ Run By: gay men
Rooms: 8
Baths: private

Meals: cont'l brkfst
Amenities: free parking
Kids: welcome
Pets: dogs & cats welcome
Smoking: ok
Rates: €39-69
AC: on request

Hotel Villa Mansland Prague

Prague (Praha), Czech Republic

Stepnicná 9, Liben
Prague (Praha), Czech Republic 182 00
420/ 286-884-405
www.villa-mansland.com

Clientele: mostly men
Type: hotel; "the leading gay hotel in Prague"
Owned/ Run By: gay men
Rooms: 11
Baths: private & shared
Meals: full brkfst

Amenities: free parking, laundry, pool, sauna, massage, DVDs/ videos
Kids: no
Pets: welcome
Smoking: ok
Rates: €55-110
AC: 10%

Italska Apartment

Prague (Praha), Czech Republic

44-7802/ 225-917 (UK#)
www.GayPrague.biz

Clientele: mostly men
Type: apt; centrally located; near tourist sights & gay scene; also offers general travel advice & gay guide; sleeps 1-8
Owned/ Run By: gay men
Rooms: 2

Baths: shared
Wheelchair Access: yes, some rms
Amenities: laundry
Kids: welcome; no toddlers or young kids
Rates: US$50-179

Old Town Apartments

Prague (Praha), Czech Republic

36/ 309-323-334
www.gaystay.net/OldTown

Clientele: mostly men
Type: apt
Owned/ Run By: gay men

Prague Accommodations

Prague (Praha), Czech Republic

Vlasska 8
Prague, Czech Republic 110 00
420/ 251-512-502
www.pragueaccommodations.com

Clientele: gay-friendly
Type: reservation service; "offering beautiful apts in historic buildings in center of Prague"
Rooms: 12 (apts)
Baths: private
Wheelchair Access: yes, 2 (apts) rms

Amenities: WiFi
Kids: welcome
Pets: welcome
Smoking: ok
Rates: €65-160
AC: 10%

Prague Center Guest Residence

Prague (Praha), Czech Republic

Stepanska Street
Prague (Praha), Czech Republic 110 00
36–309/ 323–334
gaystay.net/PragueCenter

Clientele: mixed gay/ lesbian
Type: apt; 4 apts located in central Prague near famous Wenceslas Square & at river; American owner extremely helpful
Owned/ Run By: gay men
Rooms: 4 (apts)
Baths: private
Meals: coffee/ tea only

Kids: please inquire
Pets: please inquire
Smoking: ok
Rates: €44-99
AC: on request

Ron's Rainbow Guest House

Prague (Praha), Czech Republic

Bulharska 4
Prague (Praha), Czech Republic 101 00
420/ 271–725–664
www.gay-prague.com

Clientele: mixed gay/ straight
Type: b&b; quiet & friendly; next to city center; native English-speaking manager offers tourist info to guests
Owned/ Run By: gay man
Rooms: 4
Baths: private
Meals: cont'l brkfst

Amenities: laundry, hot tub, DVDs/ videos
Smoking: ok
Rates: US$50-75

Studio Henri

Prague (Praha), Czech Republic

Jeseniova 52
Prague (Praha), Czech Republic 130 00
420/ 271–773–837
www.studiohenri.cz

Clientele: mostly men
Type: new apt; quiet, spacious, sunny & private; top floor w/ great view of Old Town Prague
Owned/ Run By: gay men
Rooms: 2
Amenities: free parking, hot tub

Kids: welcome
Pets: welcome

Vodickova Apartments

Prague (Praha), Czech Republic

Vodickova 38
Prague (Praha), Czech Republic 110 00
420/ 222–242–431
www.pragueapartment.cz

Clientele: gay-friendly
Type: apt; fully equipped flats w/ kitchen; central location
Owned/ Run By: gay & straight
Rooms: 20
Baths: private
Wheelchair Access: yes, 10 rms
Meals: cont'l brkfst
Amenities: laundry, DVDs/ videos, WiFi

Kids: welcome
Pets: welcome
Smoking: ok
Rates: €50-150
AC: 15%

Carstens Guesthouse

Copenhagen, Denmark

Christians Brygge 28, 5th flr
Copenhagen, Denmark 1559
45/ 3314–9107 45/ 4050–9107 (cell)
www.carstensguesthouse.dk

Clientele: mixed gay/ lesbian
Type: b&b-private home; youth hostel & holiday apts; 5-minute walk to gay area; guest kitchen; roofdeck
Owned/ Run By: gay men
Rooms: 14
Baths: private & shared
Amenities: laundry, sauna, DVDs/ videos,

WiFi
Kids: welcome w/ prior approval
Pets: welcome w/ prior approval
Smoking: ok
Rates: DKK165-1,250

Copenhagen Rainbow Guest House B&B
Copenhagen, Denmark

"Stroeget" Frederiksberggade 25 C
Copenhagen, Denmark 1459 K
45/ 3314-1020
www.copenhagen-rainbow.dk

Clientele: men
Type: guesthouse; very centrally located penthouse (w/ lift); on the main shopping/ pedestrian street ("stroeget"); near City Hall, Tivoli Gardens, gay bars & clubs
Owned/ Run By: gay men
Rooms: 5
Baths: private & shared

Wheelchair Access: yes, all rms
Meals: full brkfst
Amenities: laundry, WiFi
Kids: no
Pets: no
Smoking: ok (partly)
Rates: DKK750-940

First Hotel Skt. Petri
Copenhagen, Denmark

Krystalgade 22
Copenhagen, Denmark 1172
45/ 3345-9100
www.firsthotels.com/sktpetri

Clientele: gay-friendly
Type: hotel; w/ private & dorm-style rms; located downtown
Owned/ Run By: gay & straight
Rooms: 21

Baths: shared
Meals: expanded cont'l brkfst
Amenities: massage, gym
Kids: welcome
Smoking: ok

Hotel Fox
Copenhagen, Denmark

Jarmers Plads 3
Copenhagen, Denmark 1551
45/ 3395-7755 45/ 3313-3000
www.hotelfox.dk

Clientele: mixed gay/ straight
Type: hotel
Rooms: 61
Baths: private
Meals: expanded cont'l brkfst

Smoking: no
Rates: DKK945-1,620

Hotel Jørgensen
Copenhagen, Denmark

Rømersgade 11
Copenhagen, Denmark 1362
45/ 3313-8186
www.hoteljoergensen.dk

Clientele: gay-friendly
Type: hotel; w/ private & dorm-style rms; located downtown
Owned/ Run By: gay & straight
Rooms: 21
Baths: private & shared

Meals: expanded cont'l brkfst
Kids: welcome
Smoking: ok
Rates: DKK140-700

Hotel Windsor
Copenhagen, Denmark

Frederiksborggade 30
Copenhagen, Denmark 1360
45/ 3311-0830
www.hotelwindsor.dk/

Clientele: mostly men
Type: hotel; in the center of Copenhagen; walking distance to gay scene; "Copenhagen's only gay-owned & operated hotel"
Owned/ Run By: gay men

Baths: shared
Meals: cont'l brkfst
Smoking: ok
Rates: €59-86

Women's Summercamp on Femø
Femø, Denmark

Gothersgade 37
Copenhagen, Denmark 1123
45/ 3391-1557 45/ 2191-0461
www.kvindelejren.dk

Clientele: women
Type: campground; women's camp since 1971; 1-2 weeks July-Aug only; must enroll; near seaside; communal cooking; hot showers; no electricity
Owned/ Run By: women

Kids: girls welcome; boys up to 11 yrs only
Pets: no
Rates: DKK700-1,600/ week

Hos Ole og Per
Skagen, Denmark

Fyrbrovej 9
Skagen, Denmark 9990
45/ 9844–6017
www.sitecenter.dk/per

Clientele: mixed gay/ straight
Type: b&b-private home; great new rms; private balcony, garden, ocean view; perfect location close to Grenen & beach; cash only
Owned/ Run By: gay men
Rooms: 3
Baths: shared
Meals: cont'l brkfst

Amenities: free parking
Kids: 12 yrs & up welcome
Pets: no
Smoking: no
Rates: DKK250-400

The Amsterdam
Brighton, England

11-12 Marine Parade
Brighton, England BN2 1TL
44–01273/ 688–825
www.amsterdam.uk.com

Clientele: mostly men
Type: hotel; spacious & minimalist rms; seaview terrace; also sauna & popular gay bar on-site
Owned/ Run By: gay men
Rooms: 24
Baths: private & shared
Meals: cont'l brkfst

Amenities: sauna
Smoking: ok
Rates: £50-160

Hudsons Guest House
Brighton, England

22 Devonshire Pl
Brighton, England BN2 1QA
44–01273/ 683–642
www.hudsonshotel.com

Clientele: mixed gay/ lesbian
Type: guesthouse; converted from 19th-c town house; some non-smoking rms; exclusively gay & lesbian
Rooms: 7
Baths: private & shared
Meals: cont'l brkfst

Smoking: ok
Rates: £50-85

The Old Bridge House Hotel
Cornwall, England

The Quay, West Looe
Looe, England PL13 2BU
44–(0)1503/ 263–159
www.theoldbridgehouse.com

Clientele: mixed gay/ straight
Type: b&b; centrally located; river views; also bar & seasonal cafe
Owned/ Run By: gay men
Rooms: 9
Baths: private
Meals: full brkfst
Amenities: WiFi
Kids: welcome

Pets: no
Smoking: no
Rates: £30-45

Central London Guestrooms & Apts
London, England

44–(0)20/ 7497–7000
www.apartment-centre.co.uk

Clientele: mixed gay/ lesbian
Type: self-catering apts & rms in the heart of London & Soho's gay village; near shopping, theater, dining, nightlife & tourist attractions
Owned/ Run By: gay & straight
Rooms: 10
Baths: private & shared
Amenities: laundry

Kids: welcome
Pets: no
Smoking: no
Rates: £75-185
AC: 10-15%

Checkin Accommodation London

London, England

Charing Cross Rd
London, England WC2
44-(0)78/ 0874-4847
www.checkin.se/london

Clientele: mixed gay/ straight
Type: apt; "most centrally located luxury apt & rms w/ great views over Covent Garden/ Soho"; in the middle of all the action; rent a rm or the whole apt
Owned/ Run By: gay men
Rooms: 3

Baths: private & shared
Amenities: WiFi
Kids: welcome
Smoking: no
Rates: £60-185
AC: 10%

Clone Zone Luxury Apts

London, England

64 Old Compton St
London, England W1
44-(0)20/ 7287-3530
www.clonezone.co.uk

Clientele: mixed gay/ lesbian
Type: apts; located in London's West End; studio apt has kitchenette
Rooms: 3 (apts)
Baths: private

Smoking: ok
Rates: £85-130

Comfort Inn Kensington

London, England

22-32 West Cromwell Rd
London, England SW5 9QJ
44-(0)20/ 7373-3300
www.hotels-kensington.com

Type: ideally located for business & leisure traveler; 5-minute walk to Earl's Court tube station
Rooms: 125
Baths: private
Meals: cont'l brkfst

Amenities: laundry
Kids: welcome
Pets: companion animals only
Smoking: ok (certain areas only)
Rates: £65-160

Garth Hotel

London, England

69 Gower St
London, England WC1E 6HJ
44-(0)20/ 7636-5761 866/ 548-8653
www.garthhotel-london.com

Clientele: gay-friendly
Type: hotel; elegant Georgian town house; peaceful, clean & friendly; in center of London's West End
Owned/ Run By: gay & straight
Rooms: 17
Baths: private & shared

Meals: full brkfst
Kids: welcome
Pets: welcome
Rates: £45-120
AC: 10%

George Hotel

London, England

58-60 Cartwright Gardens
London, England WC1H 9EL
44-(0)20/ 7387-8777
www.georgehotel.com

Type: w/in easy walking distance of Soho & the West End; internet access
Rooms: 40
Baths: private & shared
Meals: full brkfst

Kids: welcome
Pets: no
Smoking: ok (some restrictions)
Rates: £38-99
AC: 10%

Lincoln House Hotel

London, England

33 Gloucester Pl, Marble Arch
London, England W1U 8HY
44-20/ 7486-7630
www.lincoln-house-hotel.co.uk

Clientele: mixed gay/ straight
Type: b&b; Georgian town house b&b hotel in London's West End; 3-minute walk to Oxford St & Marble Arch tube
Owned/ Run By: gay/ lesbian & straight
Rooms: 23
Baths: private

Meals: full brkfst
Amenities: free parking, WiFi
Kids: welcome
Pets: guide dogs only
Smoking: ok
Rates: £58-135
AC: 15%

London Gay Accommodation
London, England

near Bond St, Mayfair
London, England W1
44-(0)20/ 7486-0855
www.londongay.co.uk

Clientele: mixed gay/ lesbian
Type: b&b-private home; rm in private apt; quality gay holiday accommodations in London's West End; close to Baker St
Baths: shared

Amenities: laundry, hot tub
Pets: welcome

London Holiday Accommodation Bureau
London, England

44-(0)20/ 8800-5908
44-(0)79/ 1405-5999
www.londonholiday.co.uk

Type: apt; self-catering apts in London's West End; also shared & hosted apts in gay homes; "incredible value"
Owned/ Run By: lesbian
Baths: private & shared
Amenities: free parking, laundry
Kids: welcome

Pets: welcome in some flats
Smoking: ok
Rates: £35-50 (shared) & £35-200 (self-contained)
AC: 10%

Manors & Co
London, England

1 Baker St
London, England W1M 1AA
44-(0)20/ 7486-5982 800/ 454-4385
www.londonapartment.co.uk

Clientele: gay-friendly
Type: luxury fully furnished apts in the heart of London; "the perfect hotel alternative"
Owned/ Run By: straights
Rooms: 85
Baths: private

Wheelchair Access: yes
Amenities: laundry, DVDs/ videos
Kids: welcome
Pets: no
Smoking: ok
Rates: please call or email
AC: 10%

The Philbeach Hotel
London, England

30-31 Philbeach Gardens
London, England SW5 9EB
44-20/ 7373-1244 44-20/ 7244-6884
www.philbeachhotel.co.uk

Clientele: mostly men
Type: gay hotel complex; located in London's vibrant gay scene: clubs, bars, discos
Rooms: 35
Baths: private & shared
Meals: expanded cont'l brkfst

Kids: no
Pets: no
Smoking: ok
Rates: £35-95
AC: 10%

The Town House
London, England

44-(0)20/ 7609-9082
www.sbr22.dircon.co.uk

Clientele: mostly men
Type: b&b-private home; ideally situated in central London, offering accommodations on b&b basis
Owned/ Run By: gay men

Rooms: 4
Baths: private
Wheelchair Access: yes, 3 rms
Meals: cont'l brkfst
Rates: £55-60

Merchants Hotel
Manchester, England

33 Back Piccadilly
Manchester, England OL158LX
44-(0)161/ 236-2939
www.smoothhound.co.uk/hotels/
merchantshotel.html

Clientele: mixed gay/ straight
Type: hotel; modern & comfortable; centrally located only 5 minutes from Gay Village & its host of clubs, bars, restaurants
Owned/ Run By: bisexuals
Rooms: 35
Baths: private & shared

Meals: cont'l brkfst
Kids: welcome
Pets: welcome (no lions)
Smoking: ok
Rates: £30-60
AC: 10%

The New Union Hotel

Manchester, England

111 Princess St
Manchester, England M1 6JB
44–(0)161/ 228–1492

Clientele: mixed gay/ straight
Type: hotel; in heart of Gay Village; above very popular gay bar
Baths: private & shared

Meals: expanded cont'l brkfst

The Rembrandt Hotel

Manchester, England

33 Sackville St
Manchester, England M1 3LZ
44–(0)161/ 236–1311
www.rembrandtmanchester.com

Clientele: mostly men
Type: hotel; in heart of Gay Village; 2 bars & bistro on-site; "Manchester's oldest gay pub & hotel"
Rooms: 20

Baths: private & shared
Smoking: ok
Rates: £35-60

Frognel Hall Hotel

Torquay, England

Higher Woodfield Rd
Torquay, England TQ1 2LD
44–(0)18/ 0329–8339
www.frognel.co.uk

Clientele: gay-friendly
Type: hotel; Victorian villa close to harbor & beach; specializes in Murder Mystery wknds; also restaurant & bar
Owned/ Run By: straights
Rooms: 27
Baths: private
Wheelchair Access: yes, 4 rms
Meals: full brkfst

Amenities: laundry
Kids: welcome
Pets: small, well-behaved dogs welcome
Smoking: no
Rates: £32-45
AC: 5%

Bloomsbury Hotel

York, England

127 Clifton
York, England YO30 6BL
44–(0)1904/ 634–031
www.bloomsburyhotel.co.uk

Clientele: gay-friendly
Type: guesthouse; in Victorian town house; 12-minute walk to the medieval city center of historic York
Owned/ Run By: gay men
Rooms: 9
Baths: private
Meals: full brkfst
Amenities: free parking

Kids: welcome
Pets: welcome
Rates: £40-120

Padaste Manor

Muhu Island, Estonia

Muhu Island
Saare Maakond, Estonia
372–(0)/ 454–8800
www.padaste.ee

Clientele: gay-friendly
Type: resort; small luxury resort on island of Muhu, 2 hrs from Tallinn; suites w/ balconies overlooking Baltic Sea
Owned/ Run By: gay & straight
Rooms: 13
Baths: private
Wheelchair Access: yes, all rms
Meals: full brkfst
Amenities: free parking, laundry, sauna, hot tub, massage, DVDs/ videos

Kids: welcome
Pets: very small pets only
Smoking: ok (in lobby only)
Rates: €104-850
AC: 10%

Big Ruby's La Villa Mazarin Aigues-Mortes

Aigues-Mortes, France

35 Blvd Gambetta
Aigues-Mortes, France 30220

33-4/ 6673-9048
0800/ 666-919

france@bigrubys.com
www.bigrubys.com

Clientele: gay-friendly
Type: guesthouse; in the S of France on the Mediterranean coast; renovated & restored
Owned/ Run By: gay men
Nearby Attractions: 15-45 minutes to Arles, Avignon, Orange, Nimes, Aix-en-Provence; located in the city of Aigues-Mortes
Transit: near public transit; 20km to Montpellier-Méditerranée airport (€40 taxi ride)
Rooms: 20 total, 12 kings, 4 queens, 2 twins, A/C, color TV, DVD/ VCR, phone, refrigerator, safer sex supplies, all furnished in 17th-c style & Provençal colors
Baths: private, bathtubs, showers, robes
Wheelchair Access: yes, 1 rm
Meals: cont'l brkfst (€12.5)
Amenities: office hrs: 8am-1pm; laundry, pool, poolside mist, hot tub, massage, DVDs/ videos, gym, sunset drinks, pool rm w/ steam rm, sauna; also large ground-flr salon opening onto conservatory courtyard & terrace
Recreation: 10-15 minutes to Espiguette, one of largest natural beaches
Kids: no

Pets: small pets under 4 kg w/ approval; must be clean & on leash
Pets On Premises: 2 cats
Smoking: ok
Reservations: required *Deposit:* required, due 35% at booking, remainder on arrival *Cancellation:* cancel by 30 days prior (less $25 cancellation fee) or forfeit deposit *Check in/ out:* 2pm/ 11am

Payment: cash, Visa, Amex, MC
Season: *High season:* June-Sept *Closed:* mid-Oct to end of March
Rates: €89-234 *Discounts:* please inquire
AC: 10%

Historic Rentals

Annecy, France

813/ 765-4701 (US#)
800/ 537-5408 (US#)
www.annecy.historicrentals.com

Clientele: mixed gay/ straight
Type: condo; 1-bdrm apt; view overlooking Annecy's Old Town, lake & Alps; easy access to Paris & Geneva
Owned/ Run By: gay & straight
Rooms: 1
Baths: private
Meals: coffee/ tea only

Amenities: laundry
Kids: welcome
Pets: no
Rates: US$700-1,100/ week
AC: 5%

Mas du Petit Grava

Arles, France

Hameau de Moules
Arles, France 13200
33-(0)4/ 9098-3566
www.masdupetitgrava.net

Clientele: mixed gay/ straight
Type: b&b; 300-yr-old country home; also cottage; surrounded by orchards; near Arles; traditional Provençal hospitality
Owned/ Run By: gay couple
Rooms: 4 (plus 2-bdrm cottage)
Baths: private
Wheelchair Access: yes, 1 rm
Meals: full brkfst
Amenities: free parking, pool, gym

Kids: welcome
Pets: welcome; in the cottage
Smoking: no
Rates: €100-120
AC: 10%

Sans Souci
Beziers, France

Impasse de la Placette
Cebazan, France 34360
718/ 633–0367
www.le-guide.com/sanssouci

Clientele: mixed gay/ lesbian
Type: rental home; full modernized century-old village house; full kitchen; located in wine region
Owned/ Run By: lesbians
Rooms: 2

Baths: private
Amenities: free parking, laundry
Kids: welcome
Rates: €285-400/ week

Domaine Grand Guilhem
Cascastel, France

Chemin du Col de la Serre
Cascastel, France 11360
33–4/ 6845–8667
www.grandguilhem.com

Clientele: gay-friendly
Type: guesthouse; 19th-c mansion; also rental home
Owned/ Run By: straights
Rooms: 8 (includes 6 b&b rms & 2 bdrms in rental house)
Baths: private
Meals: full brkfst

Amenities: free parking, laundry, pool, hot tub, DVDs/ videos
Kids: welcome
Smoking: ok
Rates: €72+/ night (b&b); €490-1,940/ week (private houses)
AC: 8%

Les Ruisseaux
Cauterets, France

Route de Pierrefitte
Cauterets, France 65110
33/ 562–92–2802
www.lesruisseaux.com

Clientele: mixed gay/ straight
Type: b&b-private home; tranquil location in High Pyrenees near skiing, hiking & rafting
Owned/ Run By: gay men
Rooms: 4
Baths: private

Meals: cont'l brkfst
Amenities: free parking
Kids: welcome
Pets: no
Smoking: no
Rates: €49

L'Hutentyque
Crissay sur Manse, France

1 rue de Chinon
Crissay sur Manse, France
33–02/ 4758–5811
www.hotentyque.com

Clientele: mostly men
Type: inn; located in beautiful, rural village; 15 minutes from Chinon & Azay; 30 minutes from Villandry
Owned/ Run By: gay man

Rooms: 4
Baths: private
Rates: €90-160

Le Rocher
Gacé, France

rue de Rouen
Gacé, France 61230
33–(0)2/ 3312–5184
www.lerocher.biz

Type: b&b-private home; newly restored 15th-c château; ideal location to explore southern Normandy
Rooms: 4
Baths: private
Meals: expanded cont'l brkfst

Amenities: free parking
Kids: no
Pets: welcome
Smoking: no
Rates: €65
AC: 10%

Itsara Suites & Spa
Le Touquet, France

21 rue de Moscou
Le Touquet, France 62520
33–3/ 2105–4922
www.itsara-touquet.com

Clientele: gay-friendly
Type: b&b-private home; charming place for trendy guests; Asian- & Moroccan-themed suites; also spa
Owned/ Run By: bisexuals
Rooms: 4
Baths: private

Meals: full brkfst
Amenities: sauna, indoor hot tub, massage
Pets: no
Smoking: no
Rates: €96-160

Hotel Le Cassini
Les 2 Alpes, France

Le Freney d'Oisans, France 38142
33–(0)476/ 800–410
www.gayski.fr

Clientele: mixed gay/ straight
Type: hotel; charming gay-owned hotel in the French Alps for your winter & summer holidays; also restaurant & bar
Owned/ Run By: gay men
Rooms: 10
Baths: private

Meals: expanded cont'l brkfst
Amenities: free parking, laundry
Kids: welcome
Pets: no
Smoking: ok
Rates: €51-73

La Grande Maison d'Arthenay
Les Verchers Sur Layon, Maine et Loire, France

rue de la Cerisaie
Les Verchers Sur Layon, Maine et Loire, France 49700
33/ 241–403–506
www.lagrandemaison.net

Clientele: gay-friendly
Type: b&b; walled farmhouse surrounded by vineyards in the Loire Valley
Owned/ Run By: lesbian
Rooms: 4
Baths: private

Meals: cont'l brkfst
Amenities: free parking, DVDs/ videos
Kids: no
Pets: welcome
Rates: €80-100

Le Roc
Limoges, France

33–5/ 5597–1986
www.cottages4two.com

Clientele: gay-friendly
Type: 2 cottages in converted barn, woodburning stoves, private gardens, kitchens
Owned/ Run By: straights
Rooms: 2 cottages
Baths: private

Meals: cont'l brkfst
Amenities: free parking, laundry, outdoor hot tub
Kids: no
Pets: no
Smoking: no
Rates: €60-150

Moulin Bregeon
Linieres Bouton, France

Le Moulin Bregeon
Linieres Bouton, France 49490
33–241/ 823–054
www.moulinbregeon.com

Clientele: mixed gay/ straight
Type: resort; a beautifully renovated water mill in Loire Valley
Owned/ Run By: gay men
Rooms: 5
Baths: private
Wheelchair Access: yes, 1 rm

Meals: expanded cont'l brkfst
Amenities: free parking, massage
Kids: welcome
Pets: welcome w/ prior approval
Smoking: ok
Rates: €140-180
AC: 15%

Bay Ouest Guesthouse
Mont St-Michel, France

St-Seliac
Quebriac, France 35190
33–299/ 230–723
www.bayouest.com

Clientele: gay men only
Type: guesthouse; 100% gay; 40 minutes from Mont St-Michel; garden; sundeck; clothing-optional; cash or check only
Owned/ Run By: gay men
Rooms: 4
Baths: private & shared

Meals: expanded cont'l brkfst
Amenities: free parking, laundry, pool, DVDs/ videos, WiFi
Kids: no
Pets: welcome w/ prior approval
Smoking: no
Rates: €69

Guesthouse Sandeh
Montpellier, France

12 ave de Fontes
Neffies, France 34320
33–4/ 6724–0981 33–6/ 8046–1479
www.guesthouse-sandeh.com

Clientele: mixed gay/ straight
Type: guesthouse; fully equipped apts & rms in village home; private courtyard; terrace overlooking vineyard
Owned/ Run By: gay men
Rooms: 6
Baths: private & shared

Meals: expanded cont'l brkfst
Amenities: laundry, WiFi
Kids: welcome
Pets: welcome; extra fee
Smoking: ok
Rates: €38-48 (b&b); €280-402 (apt) week

Hôtel Canal
Montpellier, France

33-(0)466/ 805-004
www.hotelcanal.fr

Clientele: gay-friendly
Type: newly restored 1950s "design" hotel; 5 miles from largest gay beach in France
Owned/ Run By: gay men
Rooms: 25
Baths: private

Wheelchair Access: yes, 2 rms
Meals: full brkfst
Pets: under 10 kg (22 lbs) welcome
Smoking: ok
Rates: €60-125

Les Salamandres
Montreuil-Bonnin, France

Le Melier
Montreuil-Bonnin, France 86470
33-5/ 4918-2462
www.les-salamandres.com

Clientele: mixed gay/ lesbian
Type: b&b; "whether you're visiting Poitou-Charentes or you wish to make a stop during your vacations, we'll be happy to accommodate you all year round in calm & restful surroundings"
Owned/ Run By: lesbians
Rooms: 5 total

Baths: private
Meals: cont'l brkfst
Amenities: free parking, DVDs/ videos, gym
Kids: no
Pets: no
Smoking: no
Rates: €40-45

Hi Hôtel
Nice, France

3 ave des Fleurs
Nice, France 06000
33-497/ 072-626
www.hi-hotel.net

Clientele: mixed gay/ straight
Type: hotel; 200 meters from sea; designed by Matali Crasset; organic meals
Owned/ Run By: gay & straight
Rooms: 38
Baths: private
Wheelchair Access: yes, 3 rms
Meals: full brkfst

Amenities: laundry, pool, hammam/ steam rm & outdoor jacuzzi in 2 rms, massage
Kids: welcome
Pets: welcome; no cats
Smoking: ok
Rates: €190-680
AC: 10%

Hôtel des Deux Amis
Nice, France

Chemin des Philippons
Les Adrets de l'Esterel, Var, France 83600
33-494/ 441-342
www.hotel2amis.com

Clientele: gay-friendly
Type: hotel; spacious rms w/ balconies/ terraces; sea view; friendly atmosphere; bbq evenings
Owned/ Run By: gay men
Rooms: 8
Baths: private

Meals: full brkfst
Amenities: free parking, pool, massage
Kids: no
Pets: welcome
Smoking: no
Rates: €75-115

Hôtel Du Centre
Nice, France

2 rue De Suisse
Nice, France 06000
33-493/ 888-385
www.nice-hotel-centre.com

Clientele: gay-friendly
Type: hotel; open yr-round; located in city center near shopping, beach & train station
Owned/ Run By: straights
Rooms: 28
Meals: cont'l brkfst

Amenities: outdoor hot tub
Kids: welcome
Pets: welcome
Smoking: ok
Rates: €55-100
AC: 10%

Hôtel Splendid
Nice, France

50 bd Victor Hugo
Nice, France 06048
33-493/ 164-100
www.splendid-nice.com

Clientele: mixed gay/ straight
Type: hotel; exclusive 4-star boutique hotel; located in the city center; only 400 meters from the beach
Owned/ Run By: straights
Rooms: 128
Baths: private

Meals: full brkfst
Amenities: laundry, pool, sauna, hot tub, DVDs/ videos
Kids: welcome
Pets: welcome
Rates: €175-350
AC: 10%

Mas des Oliviers

Nice, France

350 Chemin de Crémat
Nice, France 06200
33-(0)493/ 522-260
www.masdesoliviers-nice.com

Clientele: gay-friendly
Type: b&b-private home; 4 large &
comfortable rms; on the hills overlooking
Nice; 10-minute drive to airport; terraces;
tennis club nearby
Owned/ Run By: gay men
Rooms: 4

Baths: private
Meals: expanded cont'l brkfst
Amenities: free parking, pool, gym, WiFi
Kids: welcome
Pets: no
Smoking: no
Rates: €115-205

Un ange passe...

Nice, France

419 Chemin de Montgros
La Colle sur Loup, France 06480
33-493/ 326-039
www.unangepasse.fr

Clientele: mixed gay/ straight
Type: b&b-private home; in 18th-c former
sheep farm surrounded by parkland
Owned/ Run By: gay men
Rooms: 6
Baths: private
Wheelchair Access: yes, 1 rm
Meals: cont'l brkfst

Amenities: free parking, pool, DVDs/
videos
Kids: 12 yrs & up welcome
Pets: welcome; please inquire
Smoking: ok
Rates: €85-185
AC: 5-10%

A B&B Gay Paris Center

Paris, France

place de la République
Paris, France 75003
33-6/ 6453-6450
bnbparis.free.fr

Clientele: mostly men
Type: b&b; in a historical area on the edge
of Le Marais, the gay center
Owned/ Run By: gay men
Rooms: 2
Baths: private & shared
Meals: cont'l brkfst

Amenities: laundry, DVDs/ videos
Kids: no
Pets: no
Smoking: ok
Rates: €55-65

Absolu Living

Paris, France

236 rue St Martin
Paris, France 75003

33-1/ 4454-9700

info@absoluliving.com
www.absoluliving.com

Clientele: mixed gay/ lesbian
Type: apt; superior, contemporary furnished
apts; from small studios to designer lofts;
w/ TV, internet, stereo; warm & lovely atmosphere in the most popular gay district
of Paris; short or long-term rentals
Owned/ Run By: gay men
Nearby Attractions: located near all
major gay venues & in the heart of Paris
Pickup Service: airport pickup
Transit: near public transit; we provide our
own shuttle from the airport
Rooms: 100 (apts) total, color TV, DVD/ VCR,
cable, deck, safer sex supplies, all our apts
feature contemporary interiors, equipped
kitchen & all modern conveniences
Baths: private, bathtubs, showers,
hairdryers
Amenities: office hrs: 9am-7pm; high-
speed internet connection
Kids: welcome

Reservations: required *Deposit:* required,
30% of total rental, due at booking
Cancellation: cancel by 40 days prior
Minimum Stay: 4 days *Check in/ out:* 2pm/
noon

Payment: cash, travelers checks, Visa, MC
Season: open yr-round
Rates: €65-259

A Pink Froggy Gay/ Lesbian B&B Paris
Paris, France

rue du Faubourg du Temple
Paris, France 75010
33-6/ 2561-4944
www.apinkfroggy.org

Clientele: exclusively gay/ lesbian
Type: b&b; cozy & affordable gay/ lesbian b&b located in heart of Paris; useful tips about Parisian gay scene & weekly gay/ lesbian programs
Owned/ Run By: lesbians
Rooms: 1

Baths: shared
Meals: full French brkfst
Kids: no
Pets: no
Smoking: no
Rates: €50

Adorable Apartment in Paris
Paris, France

415/ 397-6454 (US#)
www.adorableapartmentinparis.com

Clientele: gay-friendly
Type: apt; truly charming 2-bdrm flat in heart of the Marais; sleeps 4-6 (no hidden taxes or costs); near the Picasso Museum, Carnavalet & Pompidou Center
Owned/ Run By: lesbians/ gay men
Rooms: 2

Baths: private
Amenities: laundry
Kids: welcome
Pets: no
Smoking: no
Rates: US$1,800/ week

Big Ruby's La Villa Mazarin Paris
Paris, France

6 rue des Archives
Paris, France 75004
33-1/ 5301-9090
www.villamalraux.com

Clientele: mixed gay/ straight
Type: hotel; 4-star; charming, beautiful hotel in the Marais district; like a small residence
Owned/ Run By: straights
Rooms: 30
Baths: private

Meals: expanded cont'l brkfst (€12)
Amenities: WiFi
Kids: welcome but no extra beds or cots
Pets: no
Smoking: no
Rates: €190-350
AC: 8-10%

Historic Rentals
Paris, France

100 W Kennedy Blvd #260
Tampa, FL 33602
800/ 537-5408 (US#)
www.historicrentals.com

Clientele: gay-friendly
Type: apt; fully equipped 1- & 2-bdrm apts in heart of Marais & Latin Quarter
Owned/ Run By: gay & straight
Rooms: 3 (apts)
Baths: private

Amenities: laundry, WiFi
Kids: no
Pets: no
Smoking: no
Rates: US$850-1,100/ week
AC: please inquire

Hôtel Central Marais
Paris, France

2 rue Ste-Croix-de-la-Bretonnerie
Paris, France 75004
33-1/ 4887-5608
www.hotelcentralmarais.com

Clientele: mostly men
Type: hotel; small all-gay hotel in 17th-c building in the center of the Marais Historic Quarter; also gay bar
Owned/ Run By: gay men
Rooms: 7
Baths: private & shared

Amenities: WiFi
Kids: no
Pets: no
Smoking: ok
Rates: €87

Hotel Louvre Richelieu
Paris, France

51 rue de Richelieu
Paris, France 75001
33-1/ 4297-4620
www.louvre-richelieu.com

Clientele: mixed gay/ straight
Type: hotel; ideally located near the Louvre, Opera House & shopping; one of the best value hotels in this prestigious area
Owned/ Run By: gay & straight
Rooms: 14

Baths: private & shared
Kids: no
Pets: no
Smoking: ok
Rates: €65-136

Hotel Louvre Saint-Honoré

Paris, France

141 rue Saint-Honoré
Paris, France 75001
33-1/ 4296-2323
www.regetel.com

Clientele: mixed gay/ straight
Type: hotel; modern 3-star; great central location; short walking distance to Louvre, Notre Dame, Champs Elysées & Le Marais, the large gay district
Owned/ Run By: gay & straight
Rooms: 40
Baths: private

Wheelchair Access: yes, 2 rms
Meals: full buffet brkfst
Amenities: laundry, WiFi
Kids: welcome but no triple rms or extra beds
Pets: small pets welcome
Smoking: ok (in some rms)
Rates: €150-215

Hôtel Mondia

Paris, France

22 rue du Grand-Prieuré
Paris, France 75011
33-1/ 4700-9344
www.hotel-mondia.com

Clientele: gay-friendly
Type: hotel; small & charming; situated on quiet street near Place de la République— a lively area w/ many shops
Owned/ Run By: woman
Rooms: 23
Baths: private

Meals: cont'l brkfst
Kids: welcome
Pets: small pets welcome
Smoking: ok
Rates: €54-80
AC: 10%

Paris Latin Quarters

Paris, France

rue des Ursulines
Paris, France 75005
33-1/ 4325-2903
www.parislatinquarters.com

Clientele: mixed gay/ lesbian
Type: apt; full-service 2- & 3-bdrm apts; antiques & modern appliances; in heart of Latin Quarter; live like a Parisian
Owned/ Run By: gay men
Rooms: 7 (apts)
Baths: private

Meals: coffee/ tea only
Amenities: laundry, massage, DVDs/ videos, WiFi
Kids: please inquire
Pets: please inquire
Smoking: no
Rates: US$100-165

Parisian Dream

Paris, France

6 cour Berard
Paris, France 75004
33-6/ 7117-0169
www.parisiandream.com

Clientele: mixed gay/ straight
Type: apt; 1-bdrm; 400 square ft; w/ fully equipped kitchen, telephone, iron & ironing board, hairdryer; located in Marais district a short walk from gay Paris
Owned/ Run By: gay men
Rooms: 1 (apt)

Baths: private
Meals: coffee/ tea only
Amenities: laundry
Kids: welcome
Pets: no
Rates: €324-400 (for first 4 nights)

Studio in Paris

Paris, France

87 avenue du Lac
Villiers sur Marne, France 94350
33-1/ 4930-0702
www.studioinparis.com

Clientele: mixed gay/ straight
Type: studio; for 2-4 persons; charming; w/ kitchenette; located in the Bastille area, close to the gay section of Paris; cash only
Owned/ Run By: gay men
Rooms: 1 (studio)

Baths: private
Kids: no
Pets: no
Smoking: ok
Rates: €75

Mas d'En Coste

Perpignan, France

66300 Camelas
Perpignan, France
33-4/ 6853-6640
www.masdencoste.com

Clientele: mixed gay/ lesbian
Type: b&b-private home; secluded home near Mediterranean; friendly English owners; informal atmosphere (2-night minimum)
Owned/ Run By: gay men
Rooms: 3

Baths: private
Wheelchair Access: yes, 2 rms
Meals: cont'l brkfst
Amenities: free parking, pool, DVDs/ videos
Smoking: ok
Rates: €44-65

Le Vieux Donjon Gay Resort

Pressigny les Pins, France

6 place du Bourg
Pressigny les Pins, France 45290
33-2/ 3894-9756
www.gayresort.fr

Clientele: men
Type: resort; located 6 miles from Montargis & 1.5 hrs from Paris; splendid park area; nudity ok
Owned/ Run By: gay men
Rooms: 6
Baths: private
Wheelchair Access: yes, 6 rms
Meals: cont'l brkfst

Amenities: laundry, pool, poolside mist, sauna, indoor hot tub, massage,
Kids: no
Pets: welcome
Smoking: no
Rates: €45-85
AC: 10%

Domaine de l'Amerique

Provence, France

13129 Salin de Giraud
Camargue, France
33-4/ 4248-8080
33-6/ 7537-7983 (cell)
www.gitesdecharme.fr

Clientele: gay-friendly
Type: apts, studios, B&B rms & suites in Provence country estate; kitchenettes; 10 minutes from sea by car
Owned/ Run By: gay men
Rooms: 5
Baths: private
Meals: cont'l brkfst

Amenities: laundry, pool, hot tub
Kids: welcome
Pets: €23/ week
Smoking: ok
Rates: €50-220

Les Espagnols

Provence, France

Lagarde d'Apt
Provence, France 84400
33-4/ 9075-0360
www.gay-provence.org

Clientele: women
Type: guesthouse; comfortable "loft" in ancient barn; for animal/ nature-lovers only; hidden in hilltop forest; w/ equipped kitchen; terrace w/ bbq; 1 hr drive from Avignon
Owned/ Run By: lesbians/ gay men
Rooms: 1
Baths: private

Meals: coffee/tea or glass of wine
Amenities: free parking, laundry
Kids: welcome; but rm only for 1
Pets: no
Smoking: no
Rates: €350/ week

Historic Rentals

Provence, France

813/ 765-4701 (US#)
800/ 537-5408 (US#)
www.historicrentals.com

Clientele: mixed gay/ straight
Type: rental home; 2 charming 1-bdrm houses in hilltop village of Menerbes, subject of Peter Mayles' *A Year in Provence*; available individually or together for lovers of Provence; great base to visit southern France
Owned/ Run By: gay & straight
Rooms: 2 (houses)

Baths: private
Meals: coffee/ tea only
Amenities: laundry
Kids: welcome
Pets: no
Rates: US$700-2,000/ week
AC: 5%

The Lotus Tree

Provence, France

La Micocoule
Montclus, France 30630
33-4/ 6682-7609
www.thelotustree.com

Clientele: mostly men
Type: guesthouse; in farmhouse & barn; w/ luxury rms & apts; secluded grounds in stunning valley; clothing-optional pool; English-run
Owned/ Run By: gay men
Rooms: 7
Baths: private & shared
Meals: expanded cont'l brkfst

Amenities: free parking, laundry, pool, DVDs/ videos
Kids: welcome w/ prior approval
Pets: dogs only
Smoking: no
Rates: €50+
AC: 10%

Le Mas de la Treille
Provence, France

33-(0)4/ 6650-6229
www.masdelatreille.com

Clientele: mixed gay/ straight
Type: rental home; renovated farmhouse in the vineyards w/ gardens & shady courtyards
Owned/ Run By: gay men
Rooms: 8
Baths: private

Meals: cont'l brkfst
Amenities: pool, indoor hot tub
Kids: welcome
Pets: welcome
Smoking: ok
Rates: €80-190
AC: 10%

Endless Summer
Soustons, France

36 av d' Azur
Soustons, France 40140
33-5/ 5841-5631
www.endlesssummer.fr

Clientele: mixed gay/ straight
Type: apt; 2 luxury duplex apts; fully equipped; 5 miles from gay beach, great surfing & bike trails
Owned/ Run By: gay men
Rooms: 2
Baths: private

Meals: cont'l brkfst
Amenities: free parking, laundry
Kids: welcome
Pets: no
Smoking: no
Rates: €35-65

Comfort Hotel Strasbourg Montagne Verte
Strasbourg, France

14 rue des Corroyeurs
Strasbourg, France 67200
33-388/ 290-606
www.comfort-strasbourg.com

Clientele: mixed gay/ straight
Type: hotel; 10-minute walk from historic center
Owned/ Run By: gay men
Rooms: 66
Baths: private
Wheelchair Access: yes, 4 rms

Meals: full brkfst
Amenities: free parking, WiFi
Kids: welcome
Pets: welcome
Smoking: ok
Rates: €45-66
AC: 10%

Château de Mauran
Toulouse, France

Mauran, Haute-Garonne, France
33-(0)561/ 986-060
www.chateau-mauran.com

Clientele: mixed gay/ straight
Type: b&b-private home; 45 minutes SW of Toulouse; also gym & gay club on-site
Owned/ Run By: gay men
Rooms: 5
Baths: private
Meals: cont'l brkfst

Amenities: free parking, pool, DVDs/ videos
Kids: welcome
Pets: small dogs welcome
Smoking: ok
Rates: €52-72

La Treille
Vic-Fezensac, France

4 rue de la Treille
Vic-Fezensac, France
33-(0)5/ 6206-3517
www.latreille.fr

Clientele: gay-friendly
Type: friendly, small country hotel w/ shaded terrace; restaurant; in the heart of Gascony
Owned/ Run By: gay men
Rooms: 9
Baths: private & shared

Meals: cont'l brkfst
Amenities: free parking
Kids: welcome
Pets: welcome
Smoking: no
Rates: €30-54

La Vigne du Pont
Vieux Chateau, France

14 rue de Eglise
Vieux Chateau, France
33-380/ 963-223
www.lavignedupont.com

Clientele: gay-friendly
Type: b&b; in a charming village 2 hrs from Paris; near hiking & rock climbing
Owned/ Run By: gay men
Rooms: 2
Baths: private
Meals: cont'l brkfst

Amenities: free parking
Kids: no
Pets: no
Rates: €40-47

Arco Hotel
Berlin, Germany

Geisbergstr 30
Berlin, Germany 10777
49-30/ 235-1480
www.arco-hotel.de

Clientele: mixed gay/ straight
Type: b&b-inn; very central & right in the gay area; quiet, modern rms w/ internet access; idyllic garden
Owned/ Run By: gay men
Rooms: 22

Baths: private
Meals: expanded cont'l brkfst
Kids: welcome
Pets: welcome
Smoking: ok
Rates: €57-102

Art-Hotel Connection
Berlin, Germany

Fuggerstr 33
Berlin, Germany D-10777
49-30/ 2102-18800
www.arthotel-connection.de

Clientele: men
Type: small, strictly gay hotel in the heart of gay Berlin will "refresh your soul"
Owned/ Run By: gay men
Rooms: 17
Baths: private & shared
Wheelchair Access: yes
Meals: expanded cont'l brkfst

Amenities: laundry, hot tub, massage, DVDs/ videos, WiFi
Kids: no
Pets: no
Smoking: ok
Rates: €54-140
AC: please inquire

Artemisia Women's Hotel
Berlin, Germany

Brandenburgischestr 18
Berlin, Germany D-10707
49-30/ 873-8905 49-30/ 869-9320
www.frauenhotel-berlin.de

Clientele: women
Type: hotel; a real bargain; enjoy quiet rms, a drink at the bar & the sundeck w/ an impressive view
Owned/ Run By: lesbians
Rooms: 12 (includes 8 twins & 4 singles)
Baths: private & shared

Meals: cont'l brkfst
Kids: welcome; boys under 14 yrs ok
Pets: no
Smoking: ok (nonsmoking rms available)
Rates: €49-104
AC: 10%

Berlin B&B
Berlin, Germany

49-30/ 2648-4756
www.k37.de

Clientele: mixed gay/ lesbian
Type: b&b-private home; central guestrms w/ gay or lesbian hosts
Owned/ Run By: gay men
Rooms: 4
Baths: private & shared

Meals: full brkfst
Amenities: laundry, WiFi
Kids: no
Pets: welcome
Smoking: ok
Rates: €20-50

Berlin Vacation Rental
Berlin, Germany

49-30/ 2196-9595
www.apartment_berlin.info

Clientele: mixed gay/ straight
Type: reservation service; clean, friendly & inexpensive apt rentals in central & W Berlin
Owned/ Run By: gay men
Rooms: 4

Baths: private
Kids: welcome
Pets: no
Smoking: ok
Rates: €65-100
AC: 10%

Enjoy B&B
Berlin, Germany

Bülowstr 106
Berlin, Germany
49-30/ 2362-3610
www.ebab.com

Clientele: mixed gay/ lesbian
Type: reservation service; for more than 300 b&bs in all districts of Berlin; hosts chosen very carefully; also in 50 other cities Europewide
Rooms: 300

Baths: private
Meals: coffee/ tea only
Kids: please inquire
Pets: please inquire
Smoking: ok
Rates: €18-30+

Hotel Hansablick

Flotowstr 6
Berlin, Germany D-10555
49–30/ 390–4800
www.hotel-hansablick.de

Clientele: gay-friendly
Type: hotel; quiet but centrally located; near the River Spree; tourist sights easy to reach by public transit
Owned/ Run By: gay & straight
Rooms: 29
Baths: private

Meals: full brkfst
Amenities: free parking, laundry
Kids: welcome
Pets: welcome
Smoking: ok
Rates: €82-121
AC: 10%

Hotel Kronprinz Berlin

Kronprinzendamm 1
Berlin, Germany 10711
49–30/ 896–030
www.kronprinz-hotel.de

Clientele: gay-friendly
Type: cozy, boutique hotel; in a restored 1894 Berlin town house; also bar
Rooms: 80
Baths: private
Wheelchair Access: yes, 1 rm
Meals: full brkfst
Amenities: free parking, laundry

Kids: welcome; free in parents' rm up to 12 yrs
Pets: please inquire
Smoking: ok
Rates: €115-250
AC: 10%

Hotel Transit Loft

Greifswalder Str 219
Berlin, Germany 10405
49–30/ 4849-3773
www.hotel-transit.de

Clientele: gay-friendly
Type: hotel; in restored 19th-c yellow-brick factory; loft-style; 24hr reception & bar service; "ideal for families w/ children & groups"
Rooms: 47 (1-5 beds per rm)

Baths: private
Kids: welcome
Smoking: ok
Rates: €19-59

Kunstlerheim Luise

Luisenstr 19
Berlin, Germany
49–30/ 284–480

Clientele: gay-friendly
Type: hotel; former palace w/ rms re-imagined by local artists; near River Spree

Rooms: 46
Rates: US$58+

Pension Niebuhr

Niebuhrstr 74
Berlin, Germany 10629
49–30/ 324-9595 49–30/ 324-9596
www.pension-niebuhr.de

Clientele: mixed gay/ straight
Type: b&b-inn
Owned/ Run By: gay men

Rates: €40-75
AC: 10%

RoB Play 'n Stay Leather Apartments

Fuggerstr 19
Berlin, Germany 10777
49–30/ 2196-7400
www.rob.nl/html/berlin_apartments.html

Clientele: men
Type: self-catering apts in the heart of Berlin's gay scene; playrm suited to the needs of today's leather/ rubber traveler
Owned/ Run By: gay men
Rooms: 2
Baths: private

Meals: coffee/ tea only
Kids: no
Pets: no
Smoking: ok
Rates: €120-140

Schall & Rauch Pension
Berlin, Germany

Gleimstr 23
Berlin, Germany 10437
49-30/ 443-3970 49-30/ 448-0770
www.schall-und-rauch-berlin.de

Clientele: mixed gay/ lesbian
Type: pension; also bar & restaurant (WiFi in restaurant)
Baths: private
Meals: expanded cont'l brkfst

Pets: welcome; €10 fee
Rates: €36-110

Winterfeldt
Berlin, Germany

Pallasstr 10-11
Berlin, Germany 10781
49-30/ 2191-5252
www.winterfeldtberlin.com

Clientele: mixed gay/ straight
Type: b&b-private home; landmark bldg; postmodern furniture; internet access in 1 rm; near gay center
Owned/ Run By: gay men
Rooms: 2 dbl; 1 single room
Baths: shared

Amenities: laundry
Kids: welcome
Pets: welcome
Smoking: ok
Rates: €30-50

Marsil
Cologne, Germany

Marsilstein 27
Cologne, Germany 50676
49-221/ 469-0969
www.marsil.de

Clientele: mixed gay/ straight
Type: guesthouse; located in the gay center of Cologne
Owned/ Run By: gay men
Rooms: 6
Baths: private

Meals: coffee/ tea only
Kids: welcome
Pets: welcome
Smoking: ok
Rates: €50-75

Hotel am Rathaus
Freiburg, Germany

Rathausgasse 4-8
Freiburg, Germany 79098
49-761/ 296-160
www.am-rathaus.de

Clientele: gay-friendly
Type: hotel; modern & friendly; in the center of this lovely town at the border of the Black Forest & the Rhine Valley
Owned/ Run By: gay & straight
Rooms: 39
Baths: private
Meals: full brkfst

Amenities: free parking, DVDs/ videos, WiFi
Kids: welcome
Pets: welcome
Smoking: ok
Rates: €79-89
AC: 10%

Galerie Hotel Sarah Petersen
Hamburg, Germany

Lange Reihe 50
Hamburg, Germany 20099
49-40/ 249-826
www.ghsp.de

Clientele: gay-friendly
Type: hotel; famous little hotel w/ art gallery; located in gay area of Hamburg; transgender-friendly
Owned/ Run By: women
Rooms: 5
Baths: private

Meals: expanded cont'l brkfst
Kids: no
Pets: no
Smoking: ok
Rates: €45-225
AC: 10%

Hotel Konigshof
Hamburg, Germany

18 Pulverteich
Hamburg, Germany 20099
49-40/ 284-0740
www.koenigshof-hamburg.de

Clientele: mostly men
Type: hotel; located in the middle of Hamburg's gay district, St Georg
Owned/ Run By: gay men
Rooms: 22
Baths: private & shared
Meals: cont'l brkfst

Amenities: free parking, massage, DVDs/ videos
Kids: welcome
Pets: small pets only
Smoking: ok
Rates: €45-119
AC: 10%

Gîte Les Deux Marie
Munich, Germany

Schwabenstrasse 49
Ebenhofen, Bavaria, Germany 87640
08342/ 899-266
www.lesdeuxmarie.de

Clientele: women
Type: b&b; studio; fully equipped kitchenette, private entrance, terrace, garden; reflects Bavarian country life
Owned/ Run By: lesbians
Rooms: 1
Baths: private

Meals: full brkfst
Amenities: free parking, massage
Kids: welcome
Pets: welcome
Smoking: no
Rates: €50

Hotel Rio Athens
Athens, Greece

13 Odysseos St, Karaiskaki Square
Athens, Greece 10436
30-210/ 522-7075
www.hotel-rio.gr

Clientele: mixed gay/ straight
Type: hotel; located in center of Athens on quiet pedestrian street; restored neoclassic bldg
Owned/ Run By: bisexuals
Rooms: 41
Baths: private
Wheelchair Access: yes, 3 rms

Meals: cont'l brkfst
Amenities: free parking, laundry, pool, DVDs/ videos
Kids: welcome
Pets: small pets welcome
Smoking: ok
Rates: €70-155
AC: 15%

Ochre & Brown Boutique Hotel
Athens, Greece

7 Leokoriou St
Athens, Greece 10554
30-210/ 331-2940
www.ochreandbrown.com

Clientele: mixed gay/ straight
Type: hotel; across from the Parthenon, at the hub of Athenian nightlife; ultra-comfortable suites, cozy penthouse; lounge bar; stylish, relaxing environment
Owned/ Run By: gay & straight
Rooms: 11
Baths: private

Meals: full brkfst
Amenities: free parking, laundry, massage, DVDs/ videos, indoor hot tub
Kids: no
Pets: no
Smoking: ok
Rates: €178-300
AC: 8%

Papadakis Apartments
Crete, Greece

30-283/ 105-4588
www.beepworld.de/members37/papadakis

Clientele: gay-friendly
Type: apt; nice view of the White Mtns; close to sandy beaches
Owned/ Run By: straights
Rooms: 30
Baths: private

Amenities: free parking
Kids: in some apts
Pets: no
Smoking: ok
Rates: varies

Villa Ralfa
Crete, Greece

30-289/ 702-2827
www.villaralfa.com/ghome.html

Clientele: mixed gay/ straight
Type: b&b-private home; on N coast of Crete; near the airport, main tourist sites, nightlife, beaches & cruising
Owned/ Run By: gay men
Rooms: 3
Baths: private & shared

Meals: expanded cont'l brkfst
Amenities: free parking, laundry, DVDs/ videos, WiFi
Kids: well-behaved kids welcome
Pets: please inquire
Rates: €25
AC: please inquire

Jhoanna Studios
Lesbos, Greece

12 Highfield Rd
Blackpool, England FY4 2JA
44-(0)1253/ 400-033
www.skalaeressos.co.uk

Clientele: gay-friendly
Type: apt; self-catering studios close to the beach
Owned/ Run By: straights
Rooms: 18
Baths: private

Kids: welcome
Smoking: ok
Rates: £130-160
AC: 8%

Krinelos Pension
Lesbos, Greece

12 Highfield Rd
Blackpool, England FY4 2JA
44–(0)1253/ 400–033
www.skalaeressos.co.uk

Clientele: gay-friendly
Type: guesthouse; some rms w/ kitchenette; A/C available for extra fee
Owned/ Run By: straights
Rooms: 20
Kids: welcome

Pets: welcome
Smoking: ok
Rates: £110-160
AC: 8%

Sappho Hotel
Lesbos, Greece

12 Highfield Rd
Blackpool, FY4 2JA
44–(0)1253/ 400–033
www.skalaeressos.co.uk

Clientele: women
Type: guesthouse; situated in the center of Skala Eressos on the beach; 50 meters from main square; offers bar & beachfront restaurant
Owned/ Run By: lesbians
Rooms: 17

Baths: private
Meals: cont'l brkfst
Rates: £140-180
AC: 8%

Geranium Apartments
Mykonos, Greece

Ano Skoli Kalon Technon
Mykonos, Greece 84600
30–22890/ 22867 30–22890/ 24620
www.geraniumhotel.com

Clientele: mostly men
Type: hotel & apt complex 250 meters from center of Mykonos' nightlife; on a hill overlooking Aegean Sea; all w/ balconies, terraces & private entrances; nude sunbathing permitted at pool
Owned/ Run By: gay men

Rooms: 16 (units; includes 6 one- & two-bdrm apts & 2 studio suites)
Baths: private
Amenities: free parking, pool

Hotel Cavo Tagoo
Mykonos, Greece

30–22890/ 23692
www.cavotagoo.gr

Clientele: gay-friendly
Type: superior hotel w/ rms & suites; 10-minute walk to bars; "discover authentic elegance!"
Owned/ Run By: straights
Rooms: 77
Baths: private

Meals: full brkfst
Amenities: laundry, pool, massage
Kids: welcome
Pets: welcome
Smoking: ok
Rates: €135-850
AC: 10%

Villa Konstantin
Mykonos, Greece

Agios Vassilis
Mykonos Town, Greece 84600
30–22890/ 25824
www.villakonstantin-mykonos.gr

Clientele: gay-friendly
Type: guesthouse; apts & studios; in Mykonos Town; 10 minutes from nightlife; panoramic sea views
Owned/ Run By: straights
Rooms: 12
Baths: private

Amenities: free parking
Kids: welcome
Pets: welcome
Smoking: ok
Rates: US$60-160
AC: 10-15%

Kavalari Hotel
Santorini Island, Greece

PO Box 17, Fira
Santorini Island, Greece 84700
30–22860/ 22455 30–22860/ 22347
www.kavalari.com

Clientele: mixed gay/ straight
Type: hotel; the island's traditional architectural style includes exterior stairways that wind down the cliff of the volcano's rim to various flower-decked terraces
Owned/ Run By: gay & straight

Rooms: 20
Baths: private
Meals: cont'l brkfst
Kids: welcome
Rates: €70-240

Zoe-Aegeas Traditional Houses — *Santorini Island, Greece*

30–0286/ 71466
www.zoe-aegeas.gr

Clientele: gay-friendly
Type: seasonal studios & apts overlooking volcano; each w/ kitchen & traditionally furnished & decorated; near beaches
Owned/ Run By: gay men
Rooms: 11 (houses)
Baths: private

Amenities: laundry, massage
Kids: welcome
Pets: welcome
Smoking: ok
Rates: €70-270
AC: 10%

Asteri Villa — *Zakynthos Island, Greece*

149 Maries
Maries, Greece
510/ 409-2294
www.astertivilla.com

Clientele: gay-friendly
Type: 3 private rms w/ kitchenette, bathrms, verandas; 3 bungalow tent cabins
Owned/ Run By: straights
Rooms: 6 (including 3 tent bungalows)
Baths: private & shared
Meals: cont'l brkfst

Amenities: free parking, laundry, pool, outdoor hot tub, massage, WiFi
Kids: welcome
Pets: leashed house pets welcome
Smoking: no
Rates: €35-220

Daphnes Villas & Apartments — *Zakynthos Island, Greece*

Tsilimigras
Vassilikos, Greece 29100
30–26950/ 35319
www.daphnes-zakynthos.com

Type: cottage; country-style summer houses next to the sea for relaxing & peaceful holidays in Greece
Owned/ Run By: straights
Rooms: 22
Baths: private
Wheelchair Access: yes, 6 rms

Amenities: free parking, laundry
Kids: quiet hrs 2pm-6pm & 11pm-9am
Pets: no
Smoking: no
Rates: €450-880/ week
AC: 10%

A1 The Andrassy Apartments — *Budapest, Hungary*

Sziv utca 64
Budapest, Hungary 1063
36–20/ 470-7737
www.a1-apartments.com

Clientele: mostly men
Type: apt; modern rms on the roof of an art deco building
Owned/ Run By: gay men
Rooms: 3
Baths: private & shared
Meals: coffee/ tea only

Amenities: massage, WiFi
Kids: no
Pets: no
Smoking: no
Rates: €25-60
AC: 10%

BudaBaB — *Budapest, Hungary*

Akacfa u. 18 IV/24
Budapest, Hungary 1072
36–1/ 267-5240
www.budabab.com

Clientele: mostly men
Type: b&b-private home; large, newly remodeled apt; shared kitchen & living rm; owners speak English only
Owned/ Run By: gay men
Rooms: 2
Baths: private & shared

Meals: expanded cont'l brkfst
Amenities: laundry, WiFi
Kids: no
Pets: small housebroken animals only
Smoking: ok
Rates: €35-50
AC: 20%

Dembinszky Street Apartment — *Budapest, Hungary*

Dembinszky utca 21
Budapest, Hungary 1071
36–309/ 323-334
gaystay.net/Dembinszky

Clientele: mixed gay/ lesbian
Type: apt; completely renovated; in the center of the Pest side; sleeps up to 3; satellite TV, full kitchen; near gay bars & clubs; cash only
Owned/ Run By: gay men
Rooms: 1

Baths: private
Amenities: free parking, laundry
Kids: welcome
Pets: welcome w/ prior approval
Smoking: ok
Rates: €60-80
AC: 10%

Kapital Inn

30 Aradi utca
Budapest, Hungary 1062

36-30/ 931-1023

Budapest, Hungary
kapitalinn@kapitalinn.com
www.kapitalinn.com

Clientele: mixed gay/ lesbian
Type: on top floor of charming 19th-c bldg w/ large, private terrace
Owned/ Run By: gay men
Nearby Attractions: Heroes Square, Museum of Fine Arts, Andrassy Boulevard, Liszt Ferenc Square, opera house, Museum of Terror, West End shopping mall, Palace of Arts
Transit: 25 minutes to airport; 5-minute walk to tram; 2-minute walk to major subway line; 1-minute walk to trolley
Rooms: 5 total, 4 queens, 1 twin, A/C, DVD/ VCR (2), safer sex supplies, phone, maid service, satellite TV (flat-screen TV w/ DVD in 2 deluxe rms)
Baths: private & shared, showers, robes, hairdryers
Meals: expanded cont'l brkfst, vegetarian options available

Amenities: DVDs/ videos, WiFi, snacks, sunset drinks, coffee/ tea, full concierge service & business services, safe for valuables, evening turndown service, kitchen-ette, laundry (for fee)
Kids: welcome
Pets: welcome
Smoking: no
Reservations: reservation & deposit requested *Cancel-lation:* cancel by 2 weeks prior or forfeit 1 night *Check in/ out:* 2pm/ noon
Payment: cash, Visa, MC, Eurocard for securing reservations
Season: open yr-round *High season:* May-Sept
Rates: €35-80 *Discounts:* for 3-night & 6-night stays

KM Saga Guest Residence

36-309/ 323-334
gaystay.net/Kmsaga

Clientele: mixed gay/ lesbian
Type: guesthouse; 1890s environment w/ up-to-date comfort; near Danube, Szabadság Bridge, Gellert Bath & gay bars; multilingual
Owned/ Run By: gay man
Rooms: 8
Baths: private & shared
Meals: cont'l brkfst

Amenities: free parking, laundry, hot tub
Kids: welcome
Pets: please inquire
Smoking: ok
Rates: €42-165
AC: please inquire

Kristof Square Studios

Kristof Square
Budapest, Hungary 1052
36-309/ 323-334
gaystay.net/KristofSquare

Clientele: mixed gay/ lesbian
Type: apt; studio near the Danube & the famous Vaci Utca; short walk to several gay bars & clubs
Owned/ Run By: gay men
Rooms: 2
Baths: private
Amenities: free parking, laundry

Kids: welcome
Pets: welcome
Smoking: ok
Rates: €60-110
AC: on request

101 Hotel

Reykjavik, Iceland

Hverfisgata 10
Reykjavik, Iceland 101
354/ 580-0101 354/ 861-4710 (cell)
www.101hotel.is

Clientele: mixed gay/ straight
Type: boutique design hotel; also restaurant & bar
Rooms: 38
Baths: private

Amenities: indoor hot tub, gym, WiFi
Rates: 27,900-69,900 Króna

Room with a View

Reykjavik, Iceland

Laugavegur 18
Reykjavik, Iceland 101

354 / 896-2559
354 / 552-7262

www.roomwithaview.is

Clientele: mixed gay/ straight
Type: penthouse apts on main street of charming downtown area; walk to all attractions
Owned/ Run By: gay men
Nearby Attractions: Hallgrimskirkja Church, Iceland Nat'l Museum, Nat'l Gallery, shopping, dining & nightclubs right outside your door
Transit: near public transit; 40 minutes to airport
Rooms: 25 total, suites, color TV, DVD/ VCR, deck (10), kitchenette, refrigerator, maid service, sleek, modern self-catering apts that sleep 2-8
Baths: private, bathtubs, showers, whirlpools, hairdryers
Amenities: office hrs: 9am-5pm; free parking, laundry, indoor & outdoor hot tub, DVDs/ videos, WiFi, coffee/ tea
Recreation: excursions to many natural wonders outside Reykjavik; whale-watching, horseback riding & birding; thermal pools & spas in & around the city
Kids: welcome
Pets: no (cannot bring pets to Iceland)

Smoking: no (ok on balcony)
Reservations: required *Deposit:* credit card guarantee *Cancellation:* see website for policies *Check in/ out:* 2pm/ 10am
Payment: cash, travelers checks, Visa, Amex, MC

Season: open yr-round *High season:* April-Oct
Rates: US$130-345 *Discounts:* 7 nights +
AC: 10%

Arctic Sun

Reykjavik, Iceland

Ingolfsstraeti 12
Reykjavik, Iceland 101
354/ 587-2292
www.arcticsunguesthouse.com

Clientele: mixed gay/ straight
Type: centrally located
Amenities: free parking, WiFi
Rates: 6,500-32,500 Króna

Hotel Fron

Reykjavik, Iceland

Laugavegi 22A
Reykjavik, Iceland 101
354/ 511-4666
www.hotelfron.is

Clientele: mixed gay/ straight
Type: centrally located
Rooms: 71
Baths: private
Rates: €87-240

Tower Guesthouse
Reykjavik, Iceland

Grettisgata 6
Reykjavik, Iceland 101
354/ 896-6694
www.tower.is

Clientele: mixed gay/ straight
Type: view of city & bay
Rooms: 8
Baths: private
Amenities: hot tub

Rates: US$130-470

Emerson House
Cork, Ireland

2 Clarence Terrace
Cork, Ireland
353-21/ 450-3647 353-86/ 834-0891
www.emersonhousecork.com

Clientele: mixed gay/ lesbian
Type: guesthouse; in late 18th-c town house a few minutes walk from city center; large rms, excellent views
Owned/ Run By: gay man
Rooms: 5
Baths: private

Meals: full brkfst
Amenities: free parking
Kids: no
Pets: no
Rates: €35+

Roman House
Cork, Ireland

3 St John's Terr, Upper John St
Cork, Ireland
353-21/ 450-3606
www.interglobal.ie/romanhouse

Clientele: mixed gay/ lesbian
Type: b&b; in period town house, located in historic part of Cork; 4-minute walk from city center; a lively gay scene w/ bars, sauna, bookshop, cafe & club nearby
Owned/ Run By: gay men
Rooms: 4

Baths: private
Meals: cont'l brkfst
Amenities: free parking
Pets: small dogs welcome
Rates: €65+

Templenoe House
Cork, Ireland

353-(0)25/ 82978 (0)86/ 889-5253
www.templenoehouse.com

Clientele: mixed gay/ lesbian
Type: guesthouse; Georgian country house on the Blackwater River; set on 20 acres of private organic gardens, lush pasture & mature woodlands; "an oasis of relaxation & romance"
Owned/ Run By: women
Rooms: 3
Baths: private

Meals: full brkfst
Amenities: free parking, DVDs/ videos
Kids: no
Pets: welcome w/ prior approval
Smoking: ok
Rates: €75-150

Frankie's Guest House
Dublin, Ireland

8 Camden Pl
Dublin, Ireland 2
353-1/ 478-3087 (Reservations #)
353-1/ 475-2182
www.frankiesguesthouse.com

Clientele: mostly men
Type: guesthouse; 150-yr-old Georgian mews-style building; also apt that sleeps 3-4
Owned/ Run By: gay men
Rooms: 12
Baths: private & shared

Wheelchair Access: yes
Meals: full brkfst
Amenities: free parking, WiFi
Kids: no
Pets: no
Smoking: ok
Rates: €40-120

Nua Haven Gay Guesthouse
Dublin, Ireland

353-87/ 686-7062
www.nua.cc

Clientele: mixed gay/ lesbian
Type: b&b; modern, spacious accommodations; 10 minutes from downtown Dublin; on beautiful square
Rooms: 3
Baths: private

Meals: expanded cont'l brkfst
Amenities: free parking, WiFi
Rates: €100

Side By Side B&B
Galway, Ireland

Salthill
Galway, Ireland
353–91/ 592-760
353–087/ 204–6285 (Toll Free)
www.sidebysideb-b.50megs.com

Clientele: women
Type: b&b-private home; in quiet cul de sac; 5 minutes from center of Galway
Owned/ Run By: lesbians
Rooms: 6
Baths: private & shared
Wheelchair Access: yes, 1 rm

Meals: full brkfst
Amenities: laundry, DVDs/ videos
Kids: welcome
Pets: welcome; please inquire about details
Smoking: ok
Rates: €30-60
AC: 5%

Kilgraney House
Kilkenny, Ireland

353/ 503-75283
www.kilgraneyhouse.com

Clientele: gay-friendly
Type: guesthouse; late Georgian house overlooking valley, between Carlow & Kilkenny; wooded & secluded gardens
Owned/ Run By: gay men
Rooms: 6 (plus self-catering apts & cottages)
Baths: private

Meals: full brkfst
Amenities: free parking
Kids: under 6 months & over 12 yrs
Pets: no
Smoking: ok (but not in bdrms or dining rm)
Rates: €65-120
AC: 10%

Dunbrody Country House Hotel & Spa
Wexford, Ireland

Arthurstown, Ireland
353–51/ 389–600 800/ 323–5463
www.dunbrodyhouse.com

Clientele: gay-friendly
Type: privately-owned country house hotel; cookery school & spa; member of Small Luxury Hotels of the World
Owned/ Run By: straights
Rooms: 22
Baths: private
Wheelchair Access: yes, 3 rms

Meals: full brkfst
Amenities: laundry, sauna, massage
Kids: welcome; not allowed in restaurant after 8pm
Pets: no
Smoking: no
Rates: US$250-500
AC: 10%

Agriturismo Savorgnano
Arezzo, Tuscany, Italy

39–057/ 542-2010
www.agriturismosavorgnano.com

Clientele: mostly men
Type: b&b; rms in typical 18th-c stone-walled farmhouse situated in eastern Tuscany countryside
Owned/ Run By: gay men
Rooms: 6
Baths: private

Meals: expanded cont'l brkfst
Amenities: free parking, pool, hot tub
Pets: small & medium dogs welcome
Smoking: no
Rates: €75-120
AC: 10%

Casa Portagioia—Tuscan Breaks
Arezzo, Tuscany, Italy

39/ 0575-650154
www.gaytuscany.com

Clientele: mixed gay/ straight
Type: b&b-inn; also apts
Owned/ Run By: gay men
Rooms: 7
Baths: private
Meals: cont'l brkfst

Amenities: laundry, pool, WiFi
Kids: 12 yrs & up welcome
Pets: no
Smoking: ok (non-smoking rms)
Rates: €140-250
AC: 10%

Priello B&B
Arezzo, Tuscany, Italy

Localita Priello 244, Caprese Michelangelo
Arezzo, Tuscany, Italy 52033
39–0575/ 788–103
www.priello.com

Clientele: mostly men
Type: b&b-inn; luxury accommodations on working Tuscan farm; incredible setting; outstanding views; fun company
Owned/ Run By: gay men
Rooms: 5
Baths: private & shared

Meals: full brkfst
Amenities: free parking, laundry, pool, massage, DVDs/ videos
Kids: welcome
Pets: no
Rates: €60-100

Hotel Suite Duomo
Bologna, Italy

Via Corso Porta Reno 17
Ferrara, Italy 44100
39-0532/ 793-888
www.hirners.com/hotel/suiteduomo

Clientele: mixed gay/ lesbian
Type: romantic hotel located in historic center; jacuzzis in all rms
Owned/ Run By: lesbians/ gay men
Rooms: 16
Baths: private
Wheelchair Access: yes, 1 rm

Meals: cont'l brkfst
Amenities: free parking, laundry, WiFi
Kids: welcome
Pets: welcome
Smoking: ok
Rates: €65-180
AC: 10%

Giardina Cose di Calzata B&B
Campofelice di Roccella, Sicily, Italy

c. da Calzata
Campofelice di Roccella (Pa)
Sicily, Italy 90010
39-320/ 778-2109
www.cosedicalzata.com

Clientele: gay-friendly
Type: b&b; on northern coast, in olive & orange groves between Campofelice di Roccella & Lascari; 48 km from Palermo; near sea; "enjoy a real alternative holiday in a traditional Sicilian environment"
Owned/ Run By: women

Meals: cont'l brkfst
Amenities: free parking
Kids: welcome
Pets: welcome
Smoking: ok
Rates: €40-420

Hotel Capri
Capri, Italy

Via Roma 71
Capri, Italy 80073
39-081/ 837-0003
www.htlcapri.it

Clientele: gay-friendly
Type: hotel; in one of Capri's oldest buildings; most rms w/ sea views & some w/ jacuzzi; restaurant & bar
Rooms: 17 (includes 4 suites)
Baths: private

Meals: cont'l brkfst
Kids: welcome
Pets: no
Rates: €80-500

B&B
Florence, Italy

Borgo Pinti 31
Florence, Italy 50121
39-055/ 248-0056
www.bnb.it/beb

Clientele: women
Type: exclusive b&b for women; located on the top flr of a palazzo in the historic center of Florence; the rms overlook inner gardens
Owned/ Run By: lesbians
Rooms: 4

Baths: shared
Meals: expanded cont'l brkfst
Kids: welcome; boys up to 10 yrs only
Pets: please inquire
Smoking: no
Rates: €47-83
AC: 10%

Casa le Tuje
Florence, Italy

via del Fantone 22
Florence, Italy 50050
39-055/ 872-9113
www.casaletuje.it

Clientele: mixed gay/ lesbian
Type: b&b-private home; 17th-c Tuscan house on a hill surrounded by olive trees & vineyards; 15 minutes from city center
Owned/ Run By: gay men
Rooms: 3
Baths: private & shared

Meals: expanded cont'l brkfst
Amenities: WiFi
Kids: no
Pets: keep off beds
Smoking: ok
Rates: €60/ night (room) & €850/ week (apt)

Il Gallo Rosso (The Red Rooster)
Florence, Italy

Contrada Bagno16
Orvieto, Parrano, Italy 05010
39-076/ 383-8084
www.ilgallorosso.com

Clientele: mixed gay/ straight
Type: guesthouse; stylish, self-contained apts in 18th-c farmhouse in unspoiled rural environment; convenient to sites in central Italy (Tuscany & Umbria)
Owned/ Run By: gay men
Rooms: 3

Baths: private
Amenities: free parking, laundry, pool
Kids: no
Pets: no
Smoking: no
Rates: €110

Hotel Cellai

Florence, Italy

Via 27 Aprile 14
Florence, Italy 50129
39-055/ 489-291
www.hotelcellai.it

Clientele: mixed gay/ lesbian
Type: boutique hotel; w/ cozy atmosphere, antiques, contemporary art, roof garden; English-speaking staff
Rooms: 50
Baths: private

Meals: full brkfst
Amenities: free parking
Kids: welcome
Pets: welcome
Smoking: ok
AC: 10%

Holiday in Naples

Naples, Italy

39-081/ 544-3281
www.holidayinnaples.it

Clientele: gay-friendly
Type: apt; recently renovated, small, 2-level holiday apt in liveliest city on the Mediterranean; full of light; view of citrus groves of Materdei; a few steps from Nat'l Museum & Capodimonte Museum; 2-night minimum; no credit cards

Rooms: 1 (apt)
Baths: private
Meals: cont'l brkfst
Rates: €75-100
AC: 15%

Podere Fontegallo Luxury Farmhouse

Perugia, Italy

La Villa 18A
Castiglione del Lago, Italy 06061
39-340/ 894-3895
www.fontegallo.com

Clientele: gay-friendly
Type: apt; in 17th-c farmhouse perched on a hill in the Umbrian countryside; spectacular panoramic view
Owned/ Run By: straights
Rooms: 4
Baths: private

Amenities: free parking, laundry, pool, DVDs/ videos
Kids: welcome
Pets: no
Smoking: no
Rates: €40-60/ night; €400-1,400/ week

58 Le Real de Luxe

Rome, Italy

Via Cavour 58, 4th flr
Rome, Italy 00184
39-06/ 482-3566
39-399/ 805-2485 (cell)
www.bed-and-breakfast-rome.com

Clientele: mixed gay/ straight
Type: b&b-inn; small exclusive b&b/ hotel in the center of Rome, a few steps from Colosseum
Owned/ Run By: straights
Rooms: 9
Baths: private

Wheelchair Access: yes, 5 rms
Meals: cont'l brkfst
Amenities: hot tub, DVDs/ videos, WiFi
Kids: welcome
Pets: no
Smoking: ok
Rates: €65-150

Accommodation Rome

Rome, Italy

39-06/ 481-8788   39-49/ 565-4606
www.accommodationservice.it

Clientele: mixed gay/ straight
Type: reservation service; accommodations in Rome's historic center; fully furnished/ equipped tourist apts, studios & b&bs
Owned/ Run By: gay men
Meals: cont'l brkfst

Amenities: laundry
Kids: welcome
Pets: welcome
Smoking: ok
Rates: €29-99

Albergo Del Sole al Pantheon

Rome, Italy

Piazza della Rotonda 63
Rome, Italy 00186
39-06/ 678-0441
www.hotelsolealpantheon.com

Type: luxury hotel; since mid-1400s; hosted many famous guests from Ariosto to Jean-Paul Sartre & Simone de Beauvoir
Rooms: 31
Baths: private
Meals: cont'l brkfst

Amenities: laundry, DVDs/ videos
Kids: welcome
Smoking: ok
AC: 8%

Bologna B&B
Rome, Italy

Piazza Bologna, 6
Rome, Italy 00162
39-06/ 4424-0244
39/ 34781-04781 (cell)
www.beb-bologna.it

Clientele: gay-friendly
Type: b&b; "gay-friendly b&b in a central area of the Eternal City"; speak English, French, Spanish, Portuguese & Italian (of course!)
Rooms: 7
Baths: private & shared

Meals: cont'l brkfst
Kids: welcome; under 2 yrs free
Pets: small pets welcome
Smoking: ok (not in common area or 3 nonsmoking rms)
Rates: €45-95
AC: 10%

Daphne Veneto
Rome, Italy

Via di san Basilio 55
Rome, Italy 00187
39-06/ 4782-3529 39-06/ 8745-0086
www.daphne-rome.com

Clientele: gay-friendly
Type: b&b-inn; small family-owned & gay-friendly inn in Rome's historic center; free internet access; hosts Roman & American; also Daphne Trevi across plaza at via Degli Avignonesi 20
Owned/ Run By: straights
Rooms: 15

Baths: private & shared
Meals: expanded cont'l brkfst
Amenities: laundry
Kids: welcome
Pets: no
Smoking: no
Rates: €80-280
AC: 10-12%

Domus International
Rome, Italy

Vicolo delle Palle 25
Rome, Italy 00186
39-06/ 6889-2918
www.domusintl.com

Clientele: mixed gay/ straight
Type: apt; offers a wide range of furnished apts in the historic center of Rome for short-term rental
Rooms: 100
Baths: private

Amenities: laundry, hot tub, DVDs/ videos
Kids: welcome
Pets: welcome
Smoking: ok
Rates: weekly rates
AC: 10-15%

Gayopen B&B
Rome, Italy

Via dello Statuto 44, Apt 18
Rome, Italy 00185
39-06/ 482-0013
www.gayopen.com

Clientele: mixed gay/ straight
Type: b&b; near Colosseum, Roman Forum & the gay street w/ bars, pubs, discotheques & saunas, metro downstairs
Owned/ Run By: lesbians/ gay men
Rooms: 2
Baths: shared

Wheelchair Access: yes, 2 rms
Meals: full brkfst
Kids: welcome
Pets: welcome
Smoking: ok
Rates: €60-90
AC: 12%

Hotel Derby
Rome, Italy

Via Vigna Pozzi 7
Rome, Italy 00145
39-06/ 513-4955 39-06/ 513-6978
www.hotelderby.it

Clientele: gay-friendly
Type: hotel; warm, tidy, small hotel well connected w/ the Colosseum & the heart of Rome
Owned/ Run By: gay & straight
Rooms: 37
Baths: private
Wheelchair Access: yes, 1 rm

Meals: expanded cont'l brkfst
Amenities: laundry
Kids: welcome
Pets: welcome
Smoking: ok
Rates: €91-124
AC: 8%

Hotel Eden
Rome, Italy

Via Ludovisi 49
Rome, Italy 00187
39-06/ 478-121 800/ 543-4300(US#)
www.hotel-eden.it

Type: hotel; 5-star; founded in 1889; one of the oldest & most exclusive hotels in Rome; stylishly furnished w/ marble bathrms; award-winning roof-garden restaurant
Rooms: 121
Baths: private

Wheelchair Access: yes
Amenities: laundry, massage
Kids: welcome
Pets: small pets welcome
Smoking: ok
Rates: €460-3,600 + VAT 10%
AC: 10% on net rm rate

Italy-Accom

Via Dei Greci 26
Rome, Italy 00187
39-06/ 3600-1394
www.italy-accom.com

Clientele: mixed gay/ lesbian
Type: reservation service; serves Venice, Rome, Florence, Positano, Sicily, Calabria & Tuscany; also tours, apt shares, guides gay maps; percentage of booking cost donated to AIDS charity; amenities vary
Owned/ Run By: lesbians/ gay men
Wheelchair Access: yes

Meals: expanded cont'l brkfst
Amenities: free parking, laundry, pool, sauna, massage, DVDs/ videos, gym, WiFi
Kids: welcome
Pets: welcome
Smoking: ok
AC: 4%

Nicolas Inn

Via Cavour 295
Rome, Italy 00184
39-06/ 9761-8483
www.nicolasinn.com

Clientele: gay-friendly
Type: b&b; elegant rms located near the Colosseum & Roman Forum; owned/ operated by native English speaker
Owned/ Run By: straights
Rooms: 4
Baths: private

Meals: cont'l brkfst
Amenities: WiFi
Kids: welcome; ages 5 & up
Pets: no
Smoking: no
Rates: €100-160 (double)

Rainbow B&B

Via Accademia Ambrosiana 41
Rome, Italy 00147
39-34/ 8710-8320
www.aimone1.com

Clientele: gay-friendly
Type: condo; penthouse condo w/ great view; tastefully furnished w/ fully equipped kitchen; private entrance; up to 4 guests
Owned/ Run By: gay men
Rooms: 2

Baths: private
Meals: coffee/ tea only
Amenities: hot tub
Kids: 13 yrs & up welcome
Pets: small pets only welcome
Rates: €410-600/ week

Relais le Clarisse

Via Cardinale Merry del Val 20
Rome, Italy 00153
39-06/ 5833-4437
www.leclarisse.com

Clientele: mixed gay/ straight
Type: hotel; jacuzzis, Mediterranean garden, on historic site in central Rome
Owned/ Run By: lesbian
Rooms: 5
Baths: private
Meals: cont'l brkfst

Amenities: laundry, indoor hot tub, WiFi
Kids: welcome
Pets: well-behaved dogs under 20lbs welcome
Smoking: no
Rates: €130-290
AC: 10%

Roman Reference

Via dei Capocci 94
Rome, Italy 00184
39-06/ 4890-3612
www.romanreference.com

Clientele: gay-friendly
Type: well-furnished vacation apt rentals; from economic studios to luxurious penthouse
Owned/ Run By: straights
Rooms: 110

Baths: private
Amenities: laundry
Kids: welcome
Pets: no
Smoking: ok

Sandy Hostel

Via Cavour 136
Rome, Italy
39-06/ 488-4585
www.sandyhostel.com

Clientele: gay-friendly
Type: hostel; great location near Colosseum, Roman Forum & Spanish Steps
Rooms: 35

Rates: €12-35

Scalinata di Spagna
Rome, Italy

Piazza Trinità dei Monti 17
Rome, Italy 00187
39-06/ 6994-0896
39-06/ 679-3006 (booking #)
www.hotelscalinata.com

Clientele: mixed gay/ straight
Type: hotel; at the top of the Spanish Steps; charming & delightful; cordial & refined atmosphere; wonderful rooftop view of the city
Rooms: 16
Baths: private

Meals: expanded cont'l brkfst
Amenities: laundry, WiFi
Kids: welcome
Pets: welcome
Smoking: no
Rates: €150-420
AC: 8%

Valadier
Rome, Italy

Via della Fontanella 15
Rome, Italy 00187
39-06/ 361-1998 800/ 448-8355
www.hotelvaladier.com

Type: modern art deco hotel; 2 restaurants, piano bar
Rooms: 60
Baths: private
Meals: cont'l brkfst
Amenities: WiFi

Kids: welcome
Pets: no
Smoking: ok
Rates: €110-750
AC: 10%

Tuscan Rental
San Gimignano, Tuscany, Italy

646/ 220-0389
www.Tuscanrental.com

Clientele: gay-friendly
Type: rental homes & apts in Tuscany; majestic backdrop for the Tuscan sunset w/ silhouettes of the towers of San Gimignano & Volterra
Owned/ Run By: straights
Rooms: 2

Baths: shared
Amenities: free parking
Kids: welcome
Pets: small pets welcome
Smoking: ok
Rates: US$600-1,050/ week

Il Chiostro
Siena, Tuscany, Italy

241 W 97th St #13-N
New York, NY 10025
212/ 666-3506 800/ 990-3506
www.ilchiostro.com

Clientele: mixed gay/ straight
Type: guesthouse; unique arts & spiritual workshops in Tuscany & Venice
Owned/ Run By: lesbians/ gay men
Rooms: 6
Baths: shared
Meals: expanded cont'l brkfst

Amenities: free parking, pool
Kids: no
Pets: no
Smoking: no
Rates: US$1,500-2,395
AC: 10%

Il Palazzotto Country Inn
Siena, Tuscany, Italy

Loc La Befa 36
Murlo, Italy 53016
39-0577/ 707-068
800/ 844-6939 (US booking agent)
www.tuscanhouse.com/palazzotto/villa.htm

Clientele: mixed gay/ straight
Type: rental home; villa sleeps 13; located in a small village; surrounded by historical towns, monasteries & castles; 30 minutes S of Siena
Owned/ Run By: gay men

Rooms: 7
Baths: private & shared
Kids: welcome
Pets: small pets only
Rates: €4,400-5,250/ week

Villa Piccola Siena
Siena, Tuscany, Italy

Via Petriccio Belriguardo 7
Siena, Tuscany, Italy 53100
39-0577/ 588-044
www.villapiccolasiena.com

Clientele: mixed gay/ straight
Type: hotel; near art/ historical attractions, public transportation & beautiful Sienese countryside
Owned/ Run By: bisexuals
Rooms: 13
Baths: private

Wheelchair Access: yes, 6 rms
Meals: full brkfst
Amenities: free parking, laundry, massage
Kids: welcome
Pets: welcome
Rates: €90-180
AC: 10%

Mulino Dello Zoppo

Val di Chio, Tuscany, Italy

Santa Cristina Loc 92
Castiglion Fiorentino, Italy 52043
39/ 0575-650324
www.tuscanretreat.com

Clientele: gay-friendly
Type: rental home; secluded mill house surrounded by lovely gardens & vineyard; sleeps 8; rental of house or fully hosted experience available
Owned/ Run By: straights
Rooms: 3
Baths: shared
Meals: full brkfst

Amenities: free parking, laundry, pool, DVDs/ videos
Kids: welcome
Pets: welcome
Smoking: ok
Rates: £700-2,500/ week

Alle Guglie B&B

Venice, Italy

Cannaregio 1308
Venice, Italy
39-320/ 360-7829
www.alleguglie.com

Clientele: gay-friendly
Type: b&b; cozy, elegant b&b in historic center of Venice
Owned/ Run By: gay & straight
Rooms: 1
Baths: shared
Meals: expanded cont'l brkfst

Amenities: laundry
Kids: welcome
Pets: no
Smoking: ok
Rates: €70-95
AC: yes

BBVenezia

Venice, Italy

Calle Bainsizza 3-S Elena
Venice, Italy 30132
39-041/ 520-0529
www.bbvenezia.com

Clientele: gay-friendly
Type: b&b; located a couple of minutes from San Marco town center; free internet access; sundeck
Owned/ Run By: straights
Rooms: 3

Baths: private
Meals: cont'l brkfst
Kids: welcome; 3 yrs & up
Pets: no
Smoking: no
Rates: €55-100

Casa de Uscoli

Venice, Italy

San Marco 2818
Venice, Italy 30124
39-349/ 794-1393 39-041/ 241-0669
www.casadeuscoli.com

Clientele: mixed gay/ straight
Type: b&b; in restored 15th-c palace on grand canal
Rooms: 4

Baths: private
Meals: cont'l brkfst
Kids: welcome

Locanda al Mercante

Venice, Italy

39-041/ 275-0158 39-348/ 339-0843
www.alloggialmercante.com

Clientele: gay-friendly
Type: relax in quiet Venetian atmosphere; near the historic Rialto market; minutes to San Marco Square
Rooms: 6
Baths: private

Meals: coffee/ tea only
Kids: no
Pets: no
Rates: €100-180
AC: please inquire

Aero Hotel

Amsterdam, Netherlands

Kerkstraat 45-49
Amsterdam, Netherlands 1017 GB
31-20/ 662-7728
www.aerohotel.nl

Clientele: mostly men
Type: hotel; situated in heart of Amsterdam; 5 minutes from world-famous gay bars & clubs, the Royal Palace, Jordaan, museum quarter; also Camp Cafe & Aero bar

Baths: private & shared
Amenities: WiFi
Rates: €55-200

AMS Toro Hotel
Amsterdam, Netherlands

Koningslaan 64
Amsterdam, Netherlands 1075 AG
31-20/ 673-7223
www.ams.nl

Clientele: gay-friendly
Type: small chic hotel in refurbished mansion; minibar; fax; parking; next to Vondelpark & walking distance of all well-known museums & fun shopping streets
Rooms: 22
Meals: expanded cont'l brkfst

Kids: welcome
Pets: by arrangement
Smoking: ok (some nonsmoking rms)
Rates: €89-210
AC: 8%

Amsterdam B&B
Amsterdam, Netherlands

Roeterstraat 18
Amsterdam, Netherlands 1018 WD
31-20/ 624-0174
www.amsterdambedandbreakfast.com

Clientele: gay-friendly
Type: b&b; in the historic center, near museums, shops & nightlife; own private floor; WiFi & broadband internet; computer & fax available
Owned/ Run By: gay men
Rooms: 2

Baths: private & shared
Meals: full brkfst
Amenities: WiFi
Kids: welcome
Pets: no
Smoking: no
Rates: €90-200

Amsterdam B&B Barangay
Amsterdam, Netherlands

Droogbak 15
Amsterdam, Netherlands 1013 GG
31-6/ 2504-5432
www.barangay.nl

Clientele: mixed gay/ straight
Type: b&b; your tropical hideaway in the heart of historic Amsterdam center; just 3-minute walk from Centraal Station
Owned/ Run By: gay men
Rooms: 2
Baths: private

Meals: expanded cont'l brkfst
Amenities: WiFi
Kids: 10 yrs & up welcome
Pets: please contact first
Smoking: no
Rates: €69-129
AC: 5%

Amsterdam Canal Apartments
Amsterdam, Netherlands

Kloveniersburgwal 55
Amsterdam, Netherlands 1011 JX
31-20/ 471-0272
www.amsterdamcanalapartments.com

Clientele: mostly men
Type: apt; 3 canal apts in old city center; close to museums, shops & nightlife
Owned/ Run By: gay men
Rooms: 3
Baths: private
Meals: coffee/ tea only

Amenities: DVDs/ videos, WiFi
Kids: no
Pets: no
Smoking: ok
Rates: €139 (3-night minimum) or €875/ week

Amsterdam Central B&B
Amsterdam, Netherlands

Oudebrugsteeg 6-II
Amsterdam, Netherlands 1012 JP
31-62/ 445-7593
www.amsterdamcentralbedandbreakfast.nl

Clientele: mixed gay/ straight
Type: cozy b&b owned by young gay couple; 3-minute walk to Centraal Station; in 16th-c guesthouse in middle of main gay area (Warmoesstraat); also apts
Owned/ Run By: gay men
Rooms: 2

Meals: full brkfst
Kids: welcome
Pets: no
Smoking: ok
Rates: €75-225

Anco Hotel-Bar
Amsterdam, Netherlands

OZ Voorburgwal 55
Amsterdam, Netherlands 1012 EJ
31-20/ 624-1126
www.ancohotel.nl

Clientele: men
Type: guesthouse; 1-star hotel-bar; also studio & hostel; in Red Light District near leather bars; mostly leather men; clothing-optional
Owned/ Run By: gay men
Rooms: 14

Baths: private & shared
Meals: cont'l brkfst
Amenities: DVDs/ videos, WiFi
Kids: no
Pets: no
Smoking: ok
Rates: €43-135

Between Art & Kitsch

Amsterdam, Netherlands

Ruysdaelkade 75-2
Amsterdam, Netherlands 1072 AL
31-20/ 679-0485
www.between-art-and-kitsch.com

Clientele: gay-friendly
Type: b&b; "sleep between art & kitsch near the Amsterdam museums"
Owned/ Run By: straights
Rooms: 2
Baths: private

Smoking: ok
Rates: €80-100

The Black Tulip Hotel

Amsterdam, Netherlands

Geldersekade 16
Amsterdam, Netherlands 1012 BH
31-20/ 427-0933
www.blacktulip.nl

Clientele: men
Type: full leather & S/M hotel, deluxe rms w/ private bathrms combine luxury & lust; extensive play equipment; in a monument on a central Amsterdam canal; near railway station, the leather district, restaurants & shops
Owned/ Run By: gay men

Rooms: 9
Baths: private
Meals: expanded cont'l brkfst
Amenities: hot tub, massage, DVDs, videos, WiFi
Smoking: ok
Rates: €115-190

The Brownstone B&B

Amsterdam, Netherlands

Rozengracht 158
Amsterdam, Netherlands 1016 LN
31-20/ 612-9320
www.brownstone.nl

Clientele: gay-friendly
Type: b&b; charmingly restored turn-of-the-century bldg overlooking Rozengracht Street; quiet hours 9pm-9am; 2-night minimum; also apts
Owned/ Run By: gay men

Baths: private
Meals: cont'l brkfst
Smoking: no
Rates: €89+ & €135+ (apts)

Chico's Guesthouse

Amsterdam, Netherlands

Sint Willibrordusstraat 77
Amsterdam, Netherlands 1073 VA
31-20/ 675-4241
www.chicosguesthouse.tk

Clientele: gay-friendly
Type: guesthouse; in De Pijp; 10-15-minute walk to Rembrandtplein; tramstop Ceintuurbaan on corner; 10 minutes to Centraal Station

Rooms: 4
Kids: welcome when quiet
Pets: welcome when quiet
Smoking: ok
Rates: €50-90

The Collector B&B

Amsterdam, Netherlands

De Lairessestr 46 hs
Amsterdam, Netherlands 1071 PB
31-6/ 1101-0105 (cell) 31-20/ 673-6779
www.the-collector.nl

Clientele: gay-friendly
Type: b&b-private home; art deco; rms decorated w/ different collections; balcony; internet access; near the Concertgebouw, museums, the Vondelpark & nightlife
Owned/ Run By: gay men
Rooms: 2

Baths: private
Meals: full brkfst
Kids: welcome
Pets: no
Smoking: ok (on balcony)
Rates: €80-110

Country & Lake

Amsterdam, Netherlands

IJsselmeerdijk 26
Warder, Netherlands 1473 PP
31-299/ 372-190 31-299/ 372-295
www.countryandlake.nl

Clientele: mixed gay/ straight
Type: apt; 2 beautiful apts in countryside 15 miles outside Amsterdam; one lakeview apt; 3-night minimum
Owned/ Run By: bisexuals & straights
Rooms: 3
Baths: private & shared
Meals: coffee/ tea only

Amenities: free parking, laundry, sauna, outdoor hot tub, DVDs/ videos, gym, WiFi
Kids: welcome
Pets: welcome; dogs cannot be loose outside
Smoking: no
Rates: €100-160

Downtown Guesthouse
Amsterdam, Netherlands

Sint Jorisstraat 12
Amsterdam, Netherlands 1017 BC
31-6/ 5087-2220 (cell)
www.coffeeshopdowntown.nl

Clientele: mostly men
Type: guesthouse; in middle of Amsterdam's gay nightlife; rms have all the comforts: cable TV, DVD, video
Owned/ Run By: gay men

Rooms: 2
Baths: shared
Rates: €70+

Flatmates Amsterdam
Amsterdam, Netherlands

31-20/ 620-1545
www.flatmates.nl

Clientele: mixed gay/ lesbian
Type: apts, studios, house boats & b&bs in the old city center; different locations for different tastes & budgets
Owned/ Run By: gay men
Rooms: 1-3
Baths: private
Wheelchair Access: yes, 2 rms

Meals: cont'l brkfst
Amenities: free parking, laundry
Pets: no
Smoking: no
Rates: €110-275
AC: 10%

Flynt B&B Amsterdam
Amsterdam, Netherlands

Eerste Helmersstraat 34
Amsterdam, Netherlands 1054 DH
31-20/ 618-4614
31-(0)6/ 5260-1160 (cell)
www.flynt.nl

Clientele: mixed gay/ lesbian
Type: b&b; located in cultural center of Amsterdam; 250 meters from Vondelpark near Rijksmuseum & Van Gogh Museum; close to restaurants & nightlife; internet
Owned/ Run By: lesbians/ gay men
Rooms: 2

Baths: private
Meals: expanded cont'l brkfst
Amenities: WiFi
Kids: no
Pets: no
Rates: €70-120

The Grand Sofitel Demeure Amsterdam
Amsterdam, Netherlands

OZ Voorburgwal 197
Amsterdam, Netherlands 1012 EX
31-20/ 555-3111
www.thegrand.nl

Type: 5-star ultraluxe hotel located in the former City Hall; all rms w/ canal or courtyard views
Rooms: 182 (also 16 apts)
Baths: private
Meals: expanded cont'l brkfst

Amenities: free parking, laundry, pool, sauna, hot tub, massage
Kids: welcome
Rates: €440-1,495
AC: 10%

Hotel Aadam Wilhelmina
Amsterdam, Netherlands

Koninginneweg 169
Amsterdam, Netherlands 1075 CN
31-20/ 662-5467
www.hotel-aadam-wilhelmina.nl

Clientele: gay-friendly
Type: hotel; charming; centrally located downtown
Owned/ Run By: straights
Rooms: 24
Baths: private & shared
Meals: full brkfst

Amenities: free parking
Kids: welcome
Pets: no
Smoking: restricted
Rates: €45-215
AC: 8%

Hotel Amistad
Amsterdam, Netherlands

Kerkstraat 42
Amsterdam, Netherlands 1017 GM
31-20/ 624-8074
www.amistad.nl

Clientele: mostly men
Type: hotel; thoroughly renovated; modern art & furniture appeal to the young, hip & sexy patrons
Owned/ Run By: gay men
Rooms: 8
Baths: private & shared
Wheelchair Access: yes, 1 rm

Meals: cont'l brkfst
Amenities: free parking, laundry
Kids: no
Pets: no
Smoking: ok
Rates: €72-180
AC: 5%

Hotel Arena

Amsterdam, Netherlands

Gravesandestraat 51
Amsterdam, Netherlands 1092 AA
31-20/ 850-2400
www.hotelarena.nl

Clientele: gay-friendly
Type: hotel; huge hotel in former orphanage; popular nightclub in former chapel; also restaurant, café/ bar; rms come w/ Playstation 2 & internet

Rooms: 121
Baths: private
Rates: €180-275

Hotel New Amsterdam

Amsterdam, Netherlands

Herengracht 13-19
Amsterdam, Netherlands 1015 BA
31-20/ 522-2345
www.hotelnewamsterdam.nl

Clientele: gay-friendly
Type: b&b; great location at quiet canal; 5-minute walk from Centraal Station; all rms have toilet & either shower or bath
Rooms: 25
Baths: private
Wheelchair Access: yes, 1 rm

Meals: full brkfst
Amenities: laundry, WiFi
Kids: welcome
Pets: no
Smoking: no
Rates: €100-145
AC: 10-14%

Hotel Orlando

Amsterdam, Netherlands

Prinsengracht 1099
Amsterdam, Netherlands 1017 JH
31-20/ 638-6915
www.hotelorlando.nl

Clientele: gay-friendly
Type: guesthouse; design hotel in 17th-c canal house in the heart of Amsterdam; friendly staff & beautifully appointed rms
Owned/ Run By: gay men
Rooms: 5

Baths: private
Wheelchair Access: yes
Meals: cont'l brkfst
Smoking: ok

Hotel Pulitzer

Amsterdam, Netherlands

Prinsengracht 315-331
Amsterdam, Netherlands 1016 GZ
31-20/ 523-5235
www.luxurycollection.com/pulitzer

Clientele: gay-friendly
Type: hotel; luxurious hotel in city center, consisting of 25 17th- & 18th-c canal houses, creating a unique 5-star property
Rooms: 230
Baths: private

Amenities: laundry, massage, DVDs/ videos, gym
Kids: welcome
Pets: welcome; daily fee
Smoking: ok
Rates: €215-1,000
AC: 10%

Hotel The Golden Bear

Amsterdam, Netherlands

Kerkstraat 37
Amsterdam, Netherlands 1017 GB
31-20/ 624-4785
www.goldenbear.nl

Clientele: mostly men
Type: hotel; in center of the city; friendly multilingual staff; "the oldest gay hotel in Amsterdam, since 1948"
Owned/ Run By: gay men
Rooms: 18
Baths: private & shared

Meals: coffee/ tea only
Amenities: DVDs/ videos, WiFi
Kids: no
Pets: no
Smoking: ok
Rates: €62-130
AC: 5%

ITC Hotel

Amsterdam, Netherlands

Prinsengracht 1051
Amsterdam, Netherlands 1017 JE
31-20/ 623-0230
www.itc-hotel.com

Clientele: mixed gay/ lesbian
Type: hotel; w/ "the prettiest location of any of the gay hotels in Amsterdam"; overlooking a quiet stretch of Amsterdam's grandest canal; in gay area
Owned/ Run By: lesbians/ gay men
Rooms: 30

Baths: private & shared
Meals: full brkfst
Kids: no
Pets: no
Smoking: ok
Rates: €55-130
AC: 10%

Johanna's B&B

Van Hogendorpplein 62
Amsterdam, Netherlands 105 1DA
31-(0)62/ 413-3056
home.planet.nl/~johannas

Amsterdam, Netherlands

Clientele: mostly women, but gay men welcome
Type: b&b-private home; small, clean & comfortable; no more than 4 people; w/in walking distance of the Jordaan
Owned/ Run By: woman
Rooms: 2

Baths: shared
Meals: full brkfst
Kids: 13 yrs & up welcome
Pets: no
Smoking: no
Rates: €90

Lloyd Hotel

Oostelijke Handelskade 34
Amsterdam, Netherlands 1019 BN
31-20/ 561-3636
www.lloydhotel.com

Amsterdam, Netherlands

Clientele: gay-friendly
Type: hip hotel for all budgets in cool Eastern Harbor area; each rm is different— from 5 stars to 1; 2 restaurants
Rooms: 116

Baths: private & shared
Rates: €80-300

Maes B&B

Herenstraat 26 hs
Amsterdam, Netherlands 1015 CB
31-20/ 427-5165
www.bedandbreakfastamsterdam.com

Amsterdam, Netherlands

Clientele: mixed gay/ straight
Type: b&b; small, cozy, home-like b&b in city center; near all major attractions
Owned/ Run By: gay men
Rooms: 4 (2 b&b rms, 2 apts)
Baths: private

Meals: expanded cont'l brkfst
Kids: welcome
Pets: no
Smoking: no
Rates: €95-285

NH City Centre Hotel

Spuistraat 288-292
Amsterdam, Netherlands 1012 VX
31-20/ 420-4545
www.nh-hotels.nl

Amsterdam, Netherlands

Clientele: gay-friendly
Type: superior first-class hotel; walk to attractions & gay bars; rms specially adapted for disabled
Owned/ Run By: gay/ lesbian & straight
Rooms: 209
Baths: private
Wheelchair Access: yes, 1 rm

Amenities: laundry
Kids: welcome
Pets: welcome; must be attended at all times
Smoking: ok
Rates: €129-149
AC: 8%

NH Grand Hotel Krasnapolsky

Dam 9
Amsterdam, Netherlands 1012 JS
31-20/ 554-9111
www.nh-hotels.com

Amsterdam, Netherlands

Type: hotel; located in Amsterdam's center, opposite Royal Palace; also apts; business center & 5 restaurants (Winter Garden is historic landmark)
Rooms: 468 (includes 36 apts)
Baths: private
Meals: cont'l brkfst

Amenities: free parking, laundry, massage, DVDs/ videos
Kids: welcome; 0-2 yrs free; 2-12 yrs 50%
Pets: welcome
Smoking: ok (nonsmoking rms available)
Rates: €189-850

The Orfeo Hotel

Leidsekruisstraat 14
Amsterdam, Netherlands 1017 RH
31-20/ 623-1347
www.hotelorfeo.com

Amsterdam, Netherlands

Clientele: mostly men, exclusively gay
Type: hotel; exclusively gay (since 1969!); 2-night minimum wknds (3 high season); also bar & restaurant
Baths: private & shared

Meals: cont'l brkfst
Rates: €47-165

Prinsen Hotel
Amsterdam, Netherlands

Vondelstraat 36-38
Amsterdam, Netherlands 1054 GE
31–20/ 616–2323
www.prinsenhotel.nl

Clientele: gay-friendly
Type: hotel; near the Centre; has a bar, garden & internet access; 2-night minimum wknds
Owned/ Run By: gay & straight
Rooms: 45
Baths: private

Meals: cont'l brkfst
Kids: welcome
Pets: welcome
Smoking: ok
Rates: €110-210

Rembrandt Park Guesthouse
Amsterdam, Netherlands

31–62/ 502–0858
www.rembrandtparkhouse.com

Clientele: mixed gay/ straight
Type: b&b; in quiet residential area overlooking Rembrandt Park; 10 minutes by bike to clubs & gay venues in the heart of Amsterdam
Owned/ Run By: gay men
Rooms: 3
Baths: private & shared

Meals: full brkfst
Amenities: laundry
Kids: welcome
Pets: no
Smoking: no
Rates: €60-80
AC: 20%

Simply Amsterdam Apartments
Amsterdam, Netherlands

31–20/ 620–6608
www.simplyamsterdam-apartments.nl

Clientele: gay-friendly
Type: apt; quality 17th- & 18th-c apts, studios, canal houses, houseboat
Owned/ Run By: gay men
Rooms: 25 (apts)

Baths: private
Amenities: DVDs/ videos
Kids: welcome
Pets: welcome
Rates: €120-280

Sunhead of 1617
Amsterdam, Netherlands

Herengracht 152
Amsterdam, Netherlands 1016 BN
31–20/ 626–1809
www.sunhead.com

Clientele: mixed gay/ straight
Type: b&b; beautiful circa 1617 canal house along Amsterdam's Herengracht; very central yet quiet location
Owned/ Run By: gay men
Rooms: 3 (also 7 canal apts in heart of Amsterdam)

Baths: private
Meals: full brkfst
Amenities: WiFi
Kids: welcome
Pets: small, well-trained pets welcome
Smoking: no
Rates: €99-250

The Townhouse B&B
Amsterdam, Netherlands

Akoleienstraat 2
Amsterdam, Netherlands 1016 LN
31–20/ 612–9320
www.townhouse.nl

Clientele: gay-friendly
Type: b&b; 19th-c town house on quiet residential street in The Jordaan; quiet hrs 9pm-9am; check-in at The Brownstone
Owned/ Run By: gay men
Rooms: 2

Baths: private
Meals: cont'l brkfst
Smoking: no
Rates: €99-125

Triple Five Guesthouse
Amsterdam, Netherlands

Prinsengracht 555
Amsterdam, Netherlands 1016 HS
31–20/ 428–3809
www.triplefive.nl

Type: luxury guesthouse on canal; some rms w/ canal views; also apt (for 4+ people); fully equipped kitchen; close to many gay bars & nightlife; cash only
Owned/ Run By: gay men

Baths: private
Rates: €95-175

Boerderij "La Cagnotte"
Bourtange, Netherlands

1e Pallertweg 5
Bourtange, Netherlands 9545 TV
31-59/ 935-4274
www.lacagnotte.com

Clientele: mixed gay/ lesbian
Type: campground; w/ 25 campsites; also cabins & bungalow-tents; in SE of Groningen Province, along the German border; premises visited by deer, pheasants, hares, etc
Owned/ Run By: lesbians

Meals: cont'l brkfst
Amenities: free parking
Kids: no
Pets: no
Smoking: ok
Rates: €7-50

Bed & Breakfast Bordine
Leeuwarden, Netherlands

Bordineweg 113
Leeuwarden, Friesland, Netherlands 8931AN
31-(0)/ 8719-01877
www.bordine.nl

Clientele: gay-friendly
Type: b&b; 80 miles N of Amsterdam; all studios & rms w/ shower & kitchenette; free internet access; free use of bicycles
Owned/ Run By: gay men
Rooms: 5
Baths: private & shared

Meals: cont'l brkfst
Amenities: free parking, laundry, DVDs/ videos
Kids: welcome; limited; please inquire
Pets: no
Smoking: ok
Rates: €20-30

Sanden Pensjonat
Laerdal, Norway

Oyragata 9
Laerdal, Norway 6887
47-57/ 666-404
www.sandenpensjonat.no/Home.html

Clientele: gay-friendly
Type: b&b-private home; in Laerdal by Sognefjord; newly renovated 1840 bldg; decorated w/ art & period furniture; sunny garden
Owned/ Run By: gay men
Rooms: 4

Baths: shared
Meals: cont'l brkfst
Amenities: free parking, laundry
Kids: welcome
Pets: welcome
Rates: NOK300-500

Friends Guest House
Krakow, Poland

Wrzesinska St
Krakow, Poland
39-309/ 323-334
gaystay.net/Friends/Cracow

Clientele: mixed gay/ lesbian
Type: guesthouse; in center of Krakow; 5-minute walk to Old Town Market & Wawel Castle; all gay clubs w/in 3-10 minutes walk
Owned/ Run By: gay men
Rooms: 3

Baths: private
Amenities: free parking
Kids: welcome
Pets: welcome
Smoking: ok
Rates: €50-60
AC: please inquire

Friends Guest House
Warsaw, Poland

Ulica Sienkiewicza
Warsaw, Poland 00015
36-309/ 323-334
www.gaystay.net/Friends/Warsaw

Clientele: mixed gay/ lesbian
Type: guesthouse; next to Centralni railway station, Centrum metro station & famous Palace of Culture & Science; close to Fantom Club & Sauna; cash only; "Warsaw's first gay-owned & operated guesthouse"
Owned/ Run By: gay men

Rooms: 3
Baths: private
Meals: cont'l brkfst
Amenities: free parking, laundry
Kids: welcome
Smoking: ok
Rates: €44-55
AC: please inquire

Casa da Lenterna
Azores, Portugal

351/ 296-911-128
www.casadalenterna.com

Clientele: mixed gay/ straight
Type: b&b-private home; cozy b&b on the island of Sao Miguel in the Azores; located in a farming/ fishing village close to capital city of Ponta Delgada
Owned/ Run By: gay men
Rooms: 3

Baths: private & shared
Meals: full brkfst
Amenities: free parking
Kids: no
Pets: no
Smoking: no
Rates: €45-55

Anjo Azul/ Hotel Blue Angel
Lisbon, Portugal

Rua Luz Soriano, 75
Lisbon, Portugal 1200-46
351-21/ 347-8069
www.anjoazul.com

Clientele: mostly men
Type: hotel; in renovated 18th-c town house set on narrow street in Barrio Alto; walking distance to popular gay bars & discos as well as city center; "Portugal's first gay hotel"
Rooms: 20

Baths: private & shared
Pets: welcome
Smoking: ok
Rates: €40-75

Belem32
Lisbon, Portugal

351-1/ 962-523-073
www.belem32.com

Clientele: mixed gay/ straight
Type: apt; superb gay-friendly apt in historical district of Belem
Owned/ Run By: gay & straight
Rooms: 1

Baths: private
Kids: no
Pets: welcome
Smoking: no

Ardmor House
Edinburgh, Scotland

74 Pilrig St
Edinburgh, Lothian, Scotland EH6 5AS
44-(0)131/ 554-4944
www.ardmorhouse.com

Clientele: mixed gay/ lesbian
Type: guesthouse; restored city center Victorian; all rms en suite; great Scottish brkfst; near center of gay life; 4-star grading
Owned/ Run By: gay men
Rooms: 5
Baths: private

Wheelchair Access: yes, 1 rm
Meals: full brkfst
Amenities: free parking
Kids: welcome
Pets: by arrangement
Smoking: no
Rates: £50-110
AC: 5%

Ayden Guest House
Edinburgh, Scotland

70 Pilrig St
Edinburgh, Scotland EH6 5AS
44-0131/ 554-2187
www.acorn-edinburgh.com

Clientele: mixed gay/ straight
Type: guesthouse; newly refurbished, comtemporary guesthouse in quiet, central location; in-house chef
Owned/ Run By: lesbians
Rooms: 5
Baths: private

Meals: full brkfst
Amenities: free parking
Kids: welcome
Pets: no
Smoking: no
Rates: £25-45/ person

Garlands
Edinburgh, Scotland

48 Pilrig St
Edinburgh, Scotland
44-(0)131/ 554-4205
www.garlands.demon.co.uk

Clientele: mixed gay/ straight
Type: b&b; 4-story Georgian town house; "we are a no-smoking house about 10-minute walk to the bars, etc."
Rooms: 6
Baths: private
Meals: full Scottish brkfst

Amenities: free parking
Kids: well-behaved kids welcome
Pets: well-behaved welcome
Smoking: no
Rates: £30-53/ person
AC: 10%

The Freedom of the Glen Family of Hotels
Fort William, Scotland

Creag Dhu House
Onich
nr Fort William, Scotland PH33 6RY
44-0871/ 222-3415
www.freedomglen.co.uk

Clientele: gay-friendly
Type: hotel; 3 renowned hotels; offering outstanding service, lochside locations, leisure facilities
Owned/ Run By: straights
Rooms: 140
Baths: private
Wheelchair Access: yes, 8 rms

Meals: full brkfst
Amenities: free parking, laundry, pool, sauna, hot tub, massage
Kids: welcome; except in At the Lodge on the Loch Hotel
Pets: welcome
Smoking: ok

Belhaven Hotel
Glasgow, Scotland

15 Belhaven Terr
Glasgow, Scotland G12 0TG
44-(0)141/ 339-3222
www.belhavenhotel.com

Clientele: mixed gay/ straight
Type: hotel; phone, TV & tea/ coffeemaker; also lounge/ bar serving drinks & light food
Owned/ Run By: straights
Rooms: 16
Baths: private & shared

Meals: full brkfst
Amenities: free parking, indoor hot tub
Kids: welcome
Pets: no
Smoking: ok
Rates: £35-95

Charing Cross Guest House
Glasgow, Scotland

310 Renfrew St
Glasgow, Scotland G3 6UW
44-0141/ 332-2503
www.glasgow-guesthouse.net

Clientele: gay-friendly
Type: guesthouse; affordable b&b in the heart of Glasgow
Owned/ Run By: straights
Rooms: 26
Baths: private & shared

Wheelchair Access: yes, 7 rms
Kids: welcome
Pets: welcome
Smoking: no
Rates: £28-66

Devoncove Hotel
Glasgow, Scotland

931 Sauchiehall St
Glasgow, Scotland G3 7TQ
44-0141/ 334-4000
www.devoncovehotel.com

Clientele: gay-friendly
Type: 3-star boutique hotel
Owned/ Run By: straights
Rooms: 45
Baths: shared
Wheelchair Access: yes, 45 rms
Meals: full brkfst

Amenities: free parking
Kids: no
Pets: welcome
Smoking: ok
Rates: £65-105

Kirkintilloch Apartment
Glasgow, Scotland

41 Kerr St, Kirkintilloch
Glasgow, Scotland G66 1LF
44-0141/ 079909-38815
www.beds2let.com

Clientele: gay-friendly
Type: apt; canal-side; sleeps up to 4
Owned/ Run By: gay & straight
Rooms: 1
Meals: coffee/ tea only

Amenities: DVDs/ videos
Smoking: in kitchen

The Victorian House Hotel
Glasgow, Scotland

212 Renfrew St
Glasgow, Scotland G3 6TX
44-0141/ 332-0129
www.victorianhotel-glasgow.co.uk

Clientele: gay-friendly
Type: b&b; quiet, comfortable, tastefully furnished
Owned/ Run By: straights
Rooms: 60
Baths: private
Meals: full brkfst

Kids: no
Pets: welcome
Smoking: ok
Rates: £32-99

Gay Guesthouse Belgrade
Belgrade, Serbia

Resavska St 8
Belgrade, Serbia 11000
36-30/ 685-2643
www.belgrade-gay.com

Clientele: men
Type: guesthouse
Owned/ Run By: gay men
Rooms: 3
Baths: private
Meals: coffee/ tea only
Amenities: free parking, laundry, indoor

hot tub, WiFi
Smoking: ok
Rates: €40

Barcelona City Centre
Barcelona, Spain

34/ 625–303–005
www.barcelonacitygay.com

Clientele: mostly men
Type: guesthouse; newly built; in the heart of the Eixample district
Owned/ Run By: gay men
Rooms: 10
Baths: private & shared

Amenities: WiFi
Kids: welcome
Pets: welcome
Smoking: ok
Rates: €45-70

BarcelonaMarinaFlat.com
Barcelona, Spain

Carrer Sant Miquel 52
Barcelona, Spain 08003
34/ 677–368–305
www.barcelonamarinaflat.com

Clientele: gay-friendly
Type: apt; beautifully furnished flat near beach for up to 4 people; in center of Barcelona
Owned/ Run By: gay men
Rooms: 3
Baths: shared

Meals: full brkfst
Amenities: laundry
Kids: welcome; quiet building
Pets: welcome
Smoking: ok
Rates: €95+

Beauty & the Beach B&B
Barcelona, Spain

34/ 93–266–0562
www.beautyandthebeach.net

Clientele: exclusively gay (mostly men but women welcome)
Type: b&b-private home; "exclusively gay comfort & service unequaled in Barcelona or Spain"
Owned/ Run By: gay men
Rooms: 4
Baths: shared

Wheelchair Access: yes, 1 rm
Meals: full brkfst
Amenities: laundry, WiFi
Kids: no
Pets: no
Smoking: no
Rates: €80-110
AC: 10%

California Hotel
Barcelona, Spain

Carrer Rauric 14
Barcelona, 08002
34/ 93–317–7766
www.hotelcaliforniabcn.com

Clientele: mixed gay/ straight
Type: hotel; superbly situated in city-center; only 30 meters to The Ramblas; 5 minutes to beaches & 15 minutes to port & more beaches

Rooms: 31
Baths: private
Meals: cont'l brkfst
Amenities: laundry
Rates: €49-115

Catalonia Duques de Bergara
Barcelona, Spain

Bergara 11
Barcelona, Spain 08002
34/ 93–301–5151
www.hoteles-catalonia.es

Type: hotel; 4-star; in the heart of old Barcelona
Rooms: 56
Baths: private
Amenities: free parking, laundry, WiFi

Kids: welcome
Rates: €143-242
AC: 10%

Central Town Rooms & Apartments
Barcelona, Spain

Ronda San Pau 51
Barcelona, Spain 08015
34/ 93–442–7057 24/ 677–802–040
www.centraltown.com

Clientele: mostly men
Type: guesthouse; new & elegant; nice rms w/ balconies & beautiful apts w/ terraces
Owned/ Run By: gay men
Rooms: 8
Baths: private & shared
Wheelchair Access: yes, 4 rms
Meals: cont'l brkfst

Amenities: laundry, indoor hot tub, massage, DVDs/ videos
Kids: welcome in apts only
Pets: no
Smoking: ok
Rates: €30-80
AC: 10%

Éos
Barcelona, Spain

Gran Via de los Corts Catalanes 575
Barcelona, Spain 08011
34/ 93-451-8772 34/ 617-931-439
www.pensioneos.com

Clientele: mostly men
Type: b&b; located in the gay district; close to gay bars, discos, city center
Owned/ Run By: gay men
Rooms: 5
Baths: shared

Meals: cont'l brkfst
Amenities: laundry
Kids: no
Pets: no
Smoking: ok
Rates: €30-60

Gran Hotel Catalonia
Barcelona, Spain

Balmes 142-146
Barcelona, Spain 08008
34/ 93-415-9090
www.hoteles-catalonia.es

Type: hotel; beautiful 4-star; in the heart of Barcelona; close to many gay bars
Rooms: 84
Wheelchair Access: yes, 3 rms
Amenities: laundry

Kids: welcome
Smoking: ok
Rates: €129-242
AC: 10%

Hostal Absolut Centro
Barcelona, Spain

Calle Casanova #72
Barcelona, Spain 08011
34/ 649-550-238
www.absolutcentro.com

Clientele: mostly men
Type: hostel; w/ nice, clean, comfortable rms; friendly atmosphere; right in the heart of the gay district; 5 minutes to Ramblas
Owned/ Run By: gay men
Rooms: 24

Baths: private & shared
Meals: cont'l brkfst
Kids: no
Pets: no
Smoking: ok
Rates: €35-85
AC: 10%

Hostal Que Tal
Barcelona, Spain

Mallorca 290
Barcelona, Spain 08037
34/ 93-459-2366
www.quetalbarcelona.com

Clientele: mostly men
Type: hotel; a 15-minute walk from the gay area & old downtown of city; "a lovely place to stay on your holidays in Barcelona"
Rooms: 14

Baths: private & shared
Meals: coffee/ tea only
Kids: no
Pets: welcome
Smoking: ok
Rates: €39-74

Hotel Axel
Barcelona, Spain

Aribau 33
Barcelona, Spain 08011
34/ 93-323-9393
www.axelhotels.com

Clientele: mixed gay/ lesbian
Type: in the "Gayxample," in Barcelona's gay scene; comfort & design blended w/ cosmopolitan ambience
Owned/ Run By: gay & straight
Rooms: 66
Baths: private
Wheelchair Access: yes, 10 rms

Meals: full brkfst
Amenities: laundry, pool, sauna, hot tub, massage, gym, WiFi
Kids: welcome
Pets: no
Smoking: ok
Rates: €90-300

Hotel Majestic Barcelona
Barcelona, Spain

Paseo de Gracia 68
Barcelona, 08007
34/ 93-487-3939
www.hotelmajestic.es

Clientele: gay-friendly
Type: hotel; 5-star; in heart of Barcelona's shopping district; rooftop pool
Rooms: 303
Baths: private
Wheelchair Access: yes, 4 rms
Amenities: laundry, pool, sauna, massage, gym

Kids: welcome
Pets: no
Smoking: ok (in some rms + bar)
Rates: €189-400
AC: 10%

Suite Gaudi Barcelona B&B
Barcelona, Spain

Rambla de Cataluña, 103, 1°-A
Barcelona, Spain 08008
34/ 93-215-0658
www.suitegaudibarcelona.com

Clientele: gay-friendly
Type: b&b; near Gaudi's famous Casa Mila & Casa Batllo; also near shops, restaurants, & bars
Owned/ Run By: lesbians
Rooms: 7
Baths: private & shared

Meals: cont'l brkfst
Amenities: WiFi
Kids: welcome
Pets: welcome
Smoking: ok
Rates: €50-95

The Third Floor
Barcelona, Spain

430 Avenida Diagonal
Barcelona, Spain 08037
34/ 93-217-3774
www.el-tercero.com

Clientele: mixed gay/ lesbian
Type: b&b-private home; 2 stylish private suites & deluxe double rm in the privacy of W & E wings of luxurious 3,000-sq-ft Bella Epoque apt
Owned/ Run By: gay men
Rooms: 3

Baths: private & shared
Meals: expanded cont'l brkfst
Amenities: massage, DVDs/ videos
Kids: no
Pets: no
Rates: €130-180

Vilanova Property Services
Barcelona, Spain

Carrer Major 1 Bis
Vilanova i la Geltru, Spain 08800
34/ 675-498-229
www.vilanovapropertyservices.com

Clientele: mixed gay/ straight
Type: 1 luxury apt sleeps 2 people, another sleeps up to 5 in 3-bdrm/ 2-bath
Owned/ Run By: lesbians
Rooms: 2
Baths: shared

Kids: no
Pets: no
Smoking: no
Rates: €65-150

Casa Don Juan
Benidorm, Spain

Santa Faz 28
Benidorm, Spain 03501
34/ 96-680-9165
www.gaybenidorm.com/casadonjuan

Clientele: mixed gay/ lesbian
Type: hotel
Owned/ Run By: gay/ lesbian & straight
Rooms: 13 (includes 8 rms, 5 apts)
Baths: private

Kids: welcome in apts only
Pets: small dogs welcome in apts only
Smoking: ok
Rates: €30-48

Villa de los Sueños
Benidorm, Spain

Apartado 2114
Benidorm, Spain 03500
34/ 96-586-8824
www.villadelossuenos.com

Clientele: men
Type: guesthouse; "only exclusive & private gay men's guesthouse on the Costa Blanca"; on mtnside w/ sea views; tropical garden; gym
Owned/ Run By: gay men
Rooms: 10

Baths: private
Meals: full brkfst
Amenities: free parking, laundry, pool, hot tub, massage, DVDs/ videos
Kids: no
Pets: welcome w/ prior approval
Rates: €44-549

Pasion Tropical
Canary Islands, Spain

Calle las Adelfas, 6 San Augustin
Gran Canaria, Playa del Ingles, Spain 35100
34/ 928-770-131
www.pasion-tropical.com

Clientele: mostly men
Type: resort; beachfront bungalows; rooftop terrace w/ ocean views, pool bar, gym; clothing-optional poolside
Owned/ Run By: gay men
Rooms: 15 (studios & apts)
Baths: private
Meals: cont'l brkfst
Amenities: free parking, pool, outdoor

hot tub, massage
Kids: no
Pets: welcome (up to 5 kilos) w/ prior approval
Smoking: ok
Rates: €68-160 (7-night minimum)
AC: 15%

Posada La Fontana
Cantabria, Spain

34/ 94-289-5920

Clientele: mixed gay/ straight
Type: b&b; in stone house in the heart of Cantabria; 2 km from Santillana del Mar & 6 km from beaches; dinner available; bar; also 4-5 campsites
Owned/ Run By: lesbians
Rooms: 5
Baths: private

Wheelchair Access: yes, 1 rm
Meals: cont'l brkfst
Amenities: free parking, laundry, indoor hot tub
Kids: welcome
Pets: welcome
Smoking: ok
Rates: €40-57 + 7% VAT

Cactus Azul
Cuevas del Almanzora, Spain

Paraje de Zutijar 12
Cuevas del Almanzora, Spain 04610
34/ 95-045-6559
www.cave-holidays.com

Clientele: gay-friendly
Type: guesthouse; unique "Hostal Rral" offering caves for rent & normal en-suite hotel rms; bar & restaurant on-site
Owned/ Run By: straights
Rooms: 6
Baths: private

Meals: cont'l brkfst
Amenities: free parking, pool
Kids: no
Pets: no
Smoking: no
Rates: €65-110
AC: 10%

Apartamentos Galeria
Ibiza, Spain

44-(0)870/ 220-1705
www.gayholidayplaces.com

Clientele: mixed gay/ lesbian
Type: self-catering apts (sleep 6-10); special long-stay winter rates; 1 minute to beach & gay nightlife
Owned/ Run By: gay & straight

Kids: no
Pets: no
Smoking: no
Rates: €33-220 per person per week

Casa Alexio
Ibiza, Spain

Barrio Ses Torres 16
Ibiza, Spain 07819
34/ 97-131-4249
www.alexio.com

Clientele: mostly men
Type: guesthouse; located on a small hill overlooking the bay of Talamanca; 5 minutes to beach & center of Ibiza; sunbathing terraces, bar & swimming pool open 24hrs
Rooms: 16
Baths: private

Wheelchair Access: yes, 12 rms
Meals: full brkfst
Amenities: free parking, laundry, pool, hot tub
Smoking: ok
Rates: €35-219
AC: 5%

Chueca Pension
Madrid, Spain

Gravina 4, 2nd flr
Madrid, Spain 28004
34/ 91-523-1473
www.chuecapension.com

Clientele: mostly men
Type: hostel; small, cozy & modern hostel in the heart of Madrid's gay & lesbian district; free internet access
Owned/ Run By: gay & straight
Rooms: 8
Baths: private

Meals: coffee/ tea only
Amenities: laundry
Kids: welcome
Pets: well-trained, quiet dogs welcome
Smoking: ok
Rates: €40-70

Gay Hostal Puerta del Sol
Madrid, Spain

Plaza Puerta del Sol 14, 4°
Madrid, Spain 28013
34/ 91-522-5126
www.hostalpuertadelsol.com

Clientele: mostly men
Type: hostel; located in the center of Madrid & close to the gay nightlife & many tourist sights
Owned/ Run By: gay men
Rooms: 17
Baths: private & shared

Wheelchair Access: yes, all rms
Amenities: laundry
Kids: no
Pets: no
Smoking: ok
Rates: €60-100
AC: 12%

Hostal la Zona
Madrid, Spain

Calle Valverde 7, 1 & 2
Madrid, Spain 28004
34/ 91-521-9904
www.hostallazona.com

Clientele: mostly men
Type: hostel; balconies overlooking street; free internet
Owned/ Run By: gay men
Rooms: 14
Baths: private
Meals: full brkfst

Kids: no
Pets: no
Smoking: ok
Rates: €50-65
AC: 10%

Hostal Odesa
Madrid, Spain

Hortaleza 38, 3rd flr
Madrid, Spain 28004
34/ 91-521-0338
www.hostalsonsodesa.com/odesa.htm

Clientele: mostly men
Type: guesthouse; premier gay guesthouse in Madrid; in heart of vibrant Chueca District, steps from many gay bars & attractions; small & friendly

Rooms: 15
Baths: private & shared
Rates: €25-52

Hotel A Gaudí
Madrid, Spain

Gran Vía 9
Madrid, Spain 28013
34/ 91-531-2222
www.hoteles-catalonia.es

Type: hotel; 4-star; in the heart of the city
Rooms: 185
Baths: private
Wheelchair Access: yes, 3 rms
Amenities: laundry, sauna, hot tub, massage
Kids: welcome

Pets: no
Smoking: ok
Rates: €126-204
AC: 10%

Hotel Villa Real
Madrid, Spain

Plaza de Las Cortes, 10
Madrid, Spain 28014
34/ 91-420-3767
www.derbyhotels.es

Clientele: mixed gay/ straight
Type: hotel; 5-star; in the heart of Madrid; exclusive hotel; member of the Small Luxury Hotels of the World
Rooms: 115
Baths: private
Amenities: free parking, laundry, sauna, massage, WiFi
Kids: welcome
Pets: welcome
Smoking: ok
AC: 10%

The Westin Palace
Madrid, Spain

Plaza de Las Cortes 7
Madrid, Spain 28014
34/ 91-360-8000 800/ 325-3589
www.westinpalacemadrid.com

Type: hotel; built in 1912, the Palace Hotel is located in front of the Prado Museum, between the Thyssen Museum & the Parliament; we've hosted princesses, prime ministers & presidents
Rooms: 440
Baths: private

Meals: cont'l brkfst
Amenities: free parking, laundry, DVDs/ videos
Kids: welcome
Pets: welcome
Rates: please inquire

Hotel Rosamar
Mallorca, Spain

Av Joan Miró 74
Palma de Mallorca
Islas Baleares, Spain 07015
34/ 971-732-723
www.rosamarpalma.com

Clientele: mixed gay/ straight
Type: hotel; small, clean, privately run; cosmopolitan clientele, relaxed atmosphere; rooftop terraces w/ views; near beach & city; in middle of gay scene
Owned/ Run By: gay men
Rooms: 40

Baths: private
Meals: cont'l brkfst
Kids: no
Pets: no
Smoking: ok
Rates: €45-85
AC: 10%

Petit Hotel Cas Comte

Mallorca, Spain

Plaza España, s/n
Lloseta-Mallorca, Baleares, Spain 07360
34/ 97-187-3077
www.cascomte.com

Type: hotel; restored 18th-c nobleman's country-house
Rooms: 8
Baths: private
Meals: full brkfst

Amenities: free parking
Kids: welcome
Smoking: ok
Rates: €100-140
AC: 15%

Scott's

Mallorca, Spain

Plaza de la Iglesia 12
Binissalem, Spain 07350
34/ 97-187-0100
www.scottshotel.com

Clientele: gay-friendly
Type: hotel; luxurious small hotel in restored 18th-c seignorial house; 2 terraces & inner patio & courtyard; in wine country; also bistro
Owned/ Run By: straights
Rooms: 18
Baths: private
Meals: expanded cont'l brkfst

Amenities: free parking, pool, hot tub
Kids: 12 yrs & up welcome
Pets: no
Smoking: no
Rates: €175-330
AC: 10%

Hotel El Molino Santisteban

Marbella, Spain

A366, Km 52-53
Guaro, Malaga, Spain 29108
34/ 95-245-3748
www.hotelmolino.com

Clientele: gay-friendly
Type: hotel; located on the banks of the Rio Grande in Sierra de las Nieves Nat'l Park; central courtyard w/ waterways & fountain
Owned/ Run By: straights
Rooms: 6
Baths: private

Meals: cont'l brkfst
Amenities: free parking, pool, WiFi
Smoking: no
Rates: €75-85 + 7% VAT

Hotel La Buhardilla

Pamplona, Spain

Av Serapio Huici n°15
Villava, Spain 31610
34/ 94-838-2872
www.labuhardilla.com

Clientele: gay-friendly
Type: small hotel w/ a homey atmosphere; 4 rms & 1 suite w/ solarium, jacuzzi & gym
Owned/ Run By: lesbians
Rooms: 5
Baths: private

Amenities: free parking, pool
Smoking: ok
Rates: €70-240
AC: 8%

Catalonia Emperador Trajano

Seville, Spain

José Laguillo, 8
Seville, Spain 41003
34/ 95-441-1111
www.hoteles-catalonia.es

Type: hotel; modern 4-star; in the historic & commercial heart of the city
Rooms: 76
Baths: private

Amenities: free parking, laundry, WiFi
Kids: welcome
Rates: €64-154

Catalonia Giralda

Seville, Spain

Sierra Nevada, 3
Seville, Spain 41003
34/ 95-441-6661
www.hoteles-catalonia.es

Type: hotel; 4-star; in the heart of the city
Rooms: 98
Baths: private
Amenities: laundry
Kids: welcome

Rates: €64-154
AC: 10%

Antonio's Guesthouse
Sitges, Spain

Passeig Vilanova 58
Sitges, Spain 08870
34/ 93-894-9207
www.antoniossitges.com

Clientele: mostly men
Type: guesthouse; sample style & comfort in 6 double rms w/ en suite; enjoy brkfst in the garden
Owned/ Run By: gay man
Rooms: 6
Baths: private
Meals: self-made brkfst in rm

Amenities: free   parking,   laundry, massage, WiFi
Kids: no
Pets: no
Smoking: ok
Rates: €80-110
AC: 10%

Go Gay Sitges
Sitges, Spain

Balmes 28
Barcelona, Spain 08007
34/ 93-301-9341
www.gogay-sitges.com

Clientele: mostly men
Type: apt
Rates: €104-200

Hotel Liberty
Sitges, Spain

Isla de Cuba 45
Sitges, Spain 08870
34/ 93-811-0872
www.hotel-liberty-sitges.com

Clientele: mixed gay/ lesbian
Type: hotel; renovated 3-star; also 2- & 3-bdrm apts (www.staysitges.com); well appointed & luxurious
Owned/ Run By: gay men
Rooms: 14 (plus 10 apts)
Baths: private

Wheelchair Access: yes, 2 rms
Meals: expanded cont'l brkfst
Amenities: WiFi
Pets: please contact first
Smoking: no
Rates: €72-155
AC: 10%

Hotel Romàntic
Sitges, Spain

Carrer de Sant Isidre 33
Sitges, Spain 08070
34/ 93-894-8375
www.hotelromantic.com

Clientele: mixed gay/ straight
Type: historic & artistic hotel in 19th-c villa; also full bar
Owned/ Run By: straights
Baths: private & shared
Meals: full brkfst

Kids: welcome
Pets: welcome
Rates: €49-111
AC: 10%

Masia Casanova
Sitges, Spain

Pasaje Casanova 8
Canyelles, Spain 08811
34/ 93-818-8058
www.masiacasanova.com

Clientele: mostly men
Type: guesthouse; luxurious suites; nude sunbathing ok; terraces w/ beautiful view over mtns; "hetero-friendly" Oct 1–June 1
Owned/ Run By: gay men
Rooms: 5
Baths: private

Meals: full brkfst
Amenities: free parking, laundry, pool, sauna, hot tub, massage, DVDs/ videos, WiFi
Smoking: ok
Rates: €120-140
AC: 10%

El Pintor
Sitges, Spain

34/ 93-814-6541
34/ 68-774-3567 (cell)
www.elpintor.se

Clientele: mostly men
Type: guesthouse
Owned/ Run By: gay men
Rooms: 3
Baths: private
Meals: full brkfst

Smoking: no
Rates: €45-75

Sitges Holiday Apts
Sitges, Spain

Francisco Gum 25
Sitges, Spain 08870
34/ 93-894-1333
www.holasitges.com/apartment

Clientele: gay-friendly
Type: apt; 5 very nice 1-bdrms; centrally located & close to the beach
Owned/ Run By: straights
Rooms: 5 (apts)
Pets: welcome

Smoking: ok
Rates: €266-1,140/ week

Sitges on the Beach
Sitges, Spain

34/ 93-894-1391
www.sitgesonthebeach.com

Clientele: mostly men
Type: 1- or 2-bdrm guesthouse on the beach
Owned/ Run By: gay men
Rooms: 4
Baths: private & shared
Meals: cont'l brkfst

Amenities: laundry, pool, hot tub, DVDs/ videos, WiFi
Smoking: no
Rates: €136-280

El Unicornio
Sitges, Spain

Av Mas den Puig 51
Sitges, Spain
34/ 93-811-3407
www.elunicorn.com

Clientele: mixed gay/ straight
Rooms: 4
Baths: private
Meals: coffee/ tea only

Rates: €80-100

Checkin Apartments
Stockholm, Sweden

Oxenstiernsgatan 33
Stockholm, Sweden 115 27
46-8/ 658-5000
www.checkin.se

Clientele: mixed gay/ straight
Type: apt; outstanding rental accommodations in Stockholm; all centrally located close to gay scene & decorated w/ trendy contemporary Scandinavian design
Owned/ Run By: lesbians/ gay men
Kids: welcome
Pets: no

Smoking: no
Rates: SEK800

Hotel Rival
Stockholm, Sweden

Mariatorget 3
Stockholm, Sweden
46-8/ 5457-8900
www.rival.se

Clientele: gay-friendly
Type: boutique hotel w/ funky, modern interior design; located in the heart of Stockholm's fashion district; also theater, cafe & restaurant
Rooms: 99
Baths: private

Amenities: DVDs/ videos
Rates: SEK1,240-3,090

Pensionat Oden North
Stockholm, Sweden

Odengaten 38
Stockholm, Sweden
46-08/ 796-9600
www.pensionat.nu

Clientele: gay-friendly
Type: guesthouse; charming & cosy yet elegant; rms w/ century-old style & feel; located in heart of Vasastan near Hard Rock Kaffe & many restaurants & shops; near Vanadis Park
Owned/ Run By: gay man

Baths: private & shared
Rates: SEK790-1,295

Pensionat Oden Södermalm
Stockholm, Sweden

Hornsgatan 66B
Stockholm, Sweden 118 49
46-08/ 612-4349
www.pensionat.nu

Clientele: gay-friendly
Type: guesthouse; charming & cosy yet elegant; rms w/ century-old style & feel; near Folkoperan; many restaurants & galleries nearby
Owned/ Run By: gay man
Rooms: 21

Baths: private & shared
Rates: SEK730-1,295

Chalet Alpstein
Grindelwald, Switzerland

Im Kehr
Grindelwald
Berner Oberland, Switzerland 3818
41-33/ 853-0844
www.grindelwaldapartments.com

Clientele: gay-friendly
Type: apt; in cosmopolitan ski village; sports center w/ pool, sauna, gym next door
Owned/ Run By: straights
Rooms: 17
Baths: private & shared
Amenities: free parking, laundry,

massage, WiFi
Kids: welcome
Pets: no
Smoking: no
Rates: 30-65Sfr

Rainbow Inn
Lausanne, Switzerland

41-(0)21/ 311-6969
www.rainbowinn.ch

Clientele: men
Type: guesthouse; near Lake Geneva; free admission to Pink Beach sauna
Owned/ Run By: gay men
Amenities: sauna, DVDs/ videos
Kids: no
Pets: welcome

Smoking: no
Rates: 85-130Sfr

Hotel Goldenes Schwert
Zürich, Switzerland

Marktgasse 14
Zürich, Switzerland 8001
41-44/ 250-7080
www.gayhotel.ch

Clientele: mostly men
Type: hotel; located in the center of Old Town
Owned/ Run By: gay & straight
Rooms: 24
Baths: private
Meals: cont'l brkfst

Amenities: DVDs/ videos
Smoking: ok
Rates: US$109-315
AC: 10%

Eklektik Galata
Istanbul, Turkey

Serdari Ekrem St
Istanbul, Turkey 34420
90-544/ 294-2807 90-212/ 243-7446
www.eklektikgalata.com

Clientele: mostly men
Type: first gay hotel in Istanbul; in city center; near every gay venue
Owned/ Run By: gay men
Rooms: 7
Baths: private & shared
Wheelchair Access: yes, 8 rms

Meals: full brkfst
Amenities: sauna, massage
Kids: no
Pets: no
Smoking: no
Rates: €70
AC: 12%

Sarniç Hotel
Istanbul, Turkey

Kucuk Ayasofya Caddesi 26
Sultanahmet, Istanbul, Turkey 34400
90-212/ 518-2323
www.sarnichotel.com

Clientele: gay-friendly
Type: in the heart of the old city; rooftop bar & terrace w/ fabulous view of the famous Blue Mosque
Owned/ Run By: gay & straight
Rooms: 16
Baths: private

Meals: full brkfst
Amenities: free parking, laundry
Kids: welcome
Pets: welcome: please inquire
Rates: €45-90
AC: 20%

Silverweed B&B
Carmarthen, Wales

Parc-Y-Rhos, Cwmann
Lampeter, Wales SA48 8DZ
44–(0)1570/ 423–254
www.silverweedforwomen.com

Clientele: women
Type: b&b-private home; quiet rural accommodations in 1870s stone cottage; offers jewelry-making courses to women
Owned/ Run By: lesbians
Rooms: 1
Baths: shared
Meals: expanded cont'l brkfst
Amenities: free parking, laundry

Kids: girls only
Smoking: no
Rates: £15–17/ person

Pennant Hall
Conwy, Wales

Beach Rd
Penmaenmawr, Wales LL34 6AY
44–(0)1492/ 622–878
www.gaypennanthall.co.uk

Clientele: mostly men
Type: hotel; in Edwardian villa on secluded grounds on the North Wales coast; non-smoking rms available; bar & restaurant
Owned/ Run By: gay men
Rooms: 11
Baths: private
Meals: full brkfst
Amenities: free parking, sauna, hot tub

Pets: please inquire
Smoking: ok
Rates: £35-60

Diana's Gay B&B
Jerusalem, Israel

10 Hulda Ha-Neviah St
Jerusalem, Israel 95110
972-2/ 628-3131
dr-adiv@zahav.net.il

Clientele: mixed gay/ straight
Type: b&b-private home; lavishly decorated apt; Arab-style stone house in a historic, central & quiet neighborhood; view of Mt of Olives & Old City; "Israel's 1st gay b&b!"
Owned/ Run By: gay men
Rooms: 4 (2 studios)
Baths: private & shared
Wheelchair Access: yes, 2 rms

Meals: cont'l brkfst
Amenities: laundry, hot tub
Kids: welcome
Pets: welcome
Smoking: no
Rates: US$52 (single)-74 (double)

Hopefield Country House & Guest Farm
Addo, South Africa

off R336
Addo, South Africa 6115
27-42/ 234-0333
www.hopefield.co.za

Clientele: mixed gay/ straight
Type: guesthouse; luxury accommodation near big 5 game viewing at Addo Elephant National Park
Owned/ Run By: gay men
Rooms: 5
Baths: private
Meals: full brkfst

Amenities: free parking, pool, DVDs/ videos
Kids: 12 & up welcome
Pets: by arrangement
Smoking: no
Rates: US$40-60
AC: 20%

Tradouw Guesthouse & Restaurant
Barrydale, South Africa

46 Van Riebeek St
Barrydale, South Africa 6750
028/ 572-1434
www.home.intekom.com/
tradouwguesthouse

Clientele: gay-friendly
Type: guesthouse; 100-yr-old Karroo-style house; previously an old trading store; private garden rms
Owned/ Run By: gay men
Rooms: 6
Baths: private
Meals: full brkfst
Amenities: free parking, laundry, DVDs/

videos
Kids: welcome
Pets: no
Rates: ZAR185-220
AC: 5%

4 on Varneys

4 Varneys Rd, Green Point
Cape Town, South Africa 8005

27–(0)21/ 434–7167

Cape Town, South Africa
info@4onvarneys.co.za
www.4onvarneys.co.za

Clientele: mixed gay/ straight
Type: guesthouse; "stylish, top value for quality retreat in the heart of Cape Town's most vibrant quarter"
Owned/ Run By: gay men
Nearby Attractions: 30 minutes to Cape Point; 10 minutes to Table Mtn, V&A Waterfront, city center; 5 minutes to Gay Village
Pickup Service: airport pickup; ZAR160
Transit: near public transit; 20 minutes to Cape Town Int'l
Rooms: 6 total, 3 kings, 3 queens, 3 twins, A/C (2), color TV, cable, ceiling fan, fireplace (2), safer sex supplies, maid service
Baths: private, showers, hairdryers
Meals: full brkfst
Amenities: office hrs: 9am-6pm; free parking, laundry, pool, WiFi, coffee/ tea
Recreation: 10 minutes to beaches of Clifton, Camps Bay; 5 minutes to golf course & gym
Kids: 14 yrs & up welcome
Pets: no

Smoking: ok
Reservations: required *Deposit:* required, 50%, due at booking *Cancellation:* see cancellation policy on website *Check in/ out:* 1pm/ 11am

Payment: cash, Visa, MC
Season: open yr-round *High season:* Oct-March
Rates: ZAR550-850
AC: 15%

30 Fiskaal Rd Guest House

Cape Town, South Africa

30 Fiskaal Rd
Cape Town, South Africa 8005
27–(0)21/ 438–1206
www.30fiskaal.com

Clientele: gay-friendly
Type: guesthouse; 4-star; in Mediterranean-style villa overlooking Camps Bay & Table Mtn; each rm opens onto garden patio
Owned/ Run By: gay men
Rooms: 7
Baths: private

Meals: full brkfst
Amenities: free parking, pool, WiFi
Kids: 13 yrs & up welcome
Pets: no
Smoking: ok
Rates: ZAR550-2,200
AC: 10%

Amsterdam Guest House

Cape Town, South Africa

19 Forest Rd
Cape Town, South Africa 8001
27–(0)21/ 461–8236
www.amsterdam.co.za

Clientele: men
Type: guesthouse; luxury 4-star; centrally located w/ stunning views; winner of *Exit's* "Best Gay Accommodation in South Africa"
Owned/ Run By: gay men

Rooms: 10
Meals: full brkfst
Amenities: free parking, laundry, pool, sauna, outdoor hot tub, DVDs/ videos
Smoking: ok
Rates: ZAR395+

Buçaco Sud & Buçaco Sea Guest Houses

Cape Town, South Africa

2609 Clarence Dr (Main Rd)
Betty's Bay, South Africa 7141
27–(0)28/ 272–9750
www.bucacosud.co.za

Clientele: gay-friendly
Type: guesthouse; set w/in a world biosphere reserve w/ stunning views; comfortable home w/ well-traveled hosts; also restaurant
Owned/ Run By: gay men
Rooms: 6
Baths: private

Wheelchair Access: yes, 2 rms
Meals: full brkfst
Amenities: free parking, pool, massage
Kids: 12 yrs & up welcome
Pets: no
Rates: ZAR215-185
AC: 10%

Camps Bay Beach Village
Cape Town, South Africa

59 Victoria Rd
Cape Town, South Africa
27-(0)21/ 438-4444 27-(0)21/ 438-3972
www.campsbayvillage.com

Clientele: mixed gay/ straight
Type: self-catering cottages & apts; minutes from the beach
Owned/ Run By: gay & straight
Rooms: 40
Baths: private & shared

Amenities: free parking, laundry, pool
Kids: welcome
Smoking: ok
Rates: ZAR280-3,080
AC: 10%

Capsol Property & Tourism Solutions
Cape Town, South Africa

15576 Vlaeberg
Cape Town, 8018
27-(0)21/ 422-3521
www.capsol.co.za

Clientele: mixed gay/ straight
Type: rental home
Owned/ Run By: gay & straight
Rooms: 5
Baths: private
Wheelchair Access: yes, 2 rms

Kids: welcome
Pets: no
Smoking: ok
Rates: ZAR500-6,000+
AC: 5%

Clarence House
Cape Town, South Africa

6 Obelisk Rd
Cape Town, South Africa 7708
27-(0)21/ 683-0307
www.chchouse.co.za

Clientele: gay-friendly
Type: guesthouse; 4-star; in "Beverly Hills" of Cape Town; near Kirstenbosch Gardens & Cavendish Square; views of Table Mtn; bright & luxurious
Rooms: 5
Baths: private
Meals: cont'l & English brkfst

Amenities: free parking, laundry, pool
Kids: 12 yrs & up welcome
Pets: no
Smoking: ok in reception rms but not bdrms
Rates: ZAR390-720
AC: 20% (for overseas agencies)

Drop Anchor
Cape Town, South Africa

7 Flamingo St
Saldanha, South Africa 7395
27-(0)22/ 714-1207
www.dropanchor.co.za

Clientele: gay-friendly
Type: guesthouse; beachfront; upmarket but very different; in town where men outnumber women by 16-1 (Army, Air Force & Navy colleges)
Owned/ Run By: gay men
Rooms: 5

Baths: private & shared
Meals: full brkfst
Amenities: laundry, pool, DVDs/ videos
Kids: ages 12 & up welcome
Smoking: ok
Rates:

The Glen Boutique Hotel
Cape Town, South Africa

3 The Glen
Cape Town, South Africa 8005
27-(0)21/ 439-0086
www.glenhotel.co.za

Clientele: mostly men
Type: hotel; stunning 4-star colonial mansion w/ individually styled suites set in mature tropical garden; close to beaches, shops & clubs
Owned/ Run By: gay men
Rooms: 10
Baths: private

Meals: full brkfst
Amenities: free parking, laundry, pool, sauna, hot tub, massage
Kids: no
Pets: no
Rates: ZAR550-1,840
AC: 10%

Guest House One Belvedere
Cape Town, South Africa

1 Belvedere Ave
Cape Town, South Africa 8001
27-(0)21/ 461-2442
www.onebelvedere.co.za

Clientele: men
Type: beautiful & luxurious circa 1914 Victorian villa; stunning views of city center & Table Mnt; centrally located near beaches & gay hotspots
Owned/ Run By: gay men
Rooms: 6

Baths: shared
Meals: full brkfst
Amenities: free parking, laundry, pool, sauna, hot tub, DVDs/ videos
AC: 10%

Huijs Haerlem
Cape Town, South Africa

25 Main Dr
Cape Town, South Africa 8001
27–(0)21/ 434–6434
www.huijshaerlem.co.za

Clientele: mixed gay/ straight
Type: guesthouse; enjoy breathtaking sunsets in our spacious gardens or on terrace or relax by the heated saltwater pool
Owned/ Run By: gay men
Rooms: 9

Baths: private
Meals: full brkfst
Amenities: free parking, laundry, pool
AC: 20%

Mediterranean Villa
Cape Town, South Africa

21 Brownlow Rd
Cape Town, South Africa 8001
27–(0)21/ 423–2188
www.medvilla.co.za

Clientele: gay-friendly
Type: guesthouse; courtesy bar & internet access available; meditation room; close to major tourist attractions
Owned/ Run By: straights
Rooms: 8
Baths: private
Wheelchair Access: yes, 2 rms
Meals: full brkfst

Amenities: laundry, pool
Kids: 5 yrs & up welcome
Pets: no
Rates: ZAR410-860
AC: 10%

Metropole Luxury Boutique Hotel
Cape Town, South Africa

38 Long St
Cape Town, South Africa 8001
27–(0)21/ 424–7247
www.metropolehotel.co.za

Clientele: gay-friendly
Type: luxury boutique hotel; also M-Bar lounge & Veranda restaurant
Meals: full brkfst
Amenities: hot tub
Rates: ZAR715-2,090

Newlands Guest House
Cape Town, South Africa

4 Alcis Rd
Newlands, South Africa 7700
27–(0)21/ 686–0013
27–(0)83/ 251–7274 (cell)
www.newlandsguest.co.za

Clientele: mixed gay/ straight
Type: guesthouse; beautifully appointed, quiet, accessible old Cape homestead; cats on premises; Classic Cape Tours on-site
Owned/ Run By: gay man
Rooms: 6
Baths: private
Meals: full brkfst
Amenities: free parking, laundry, pool, DVDs/ videos

Kids: 14 yrs & up welcome
Pets: no
Smoking: no
Rates: ZAR300-525
AC: 20%

Oceantide Apartments
Cape Town, South Africa

38 London Rd
Cape Town, South Africa 8005
27–(0)21/ 433–0303
27–(0)82/ 670–4317
www.oceantide.co.za

Clientele: mixed gay/ straight
Type: apt; luxury self-catering units; near beaches, restaurants, shops & V&A Waterfront; gay village nearby; 20 minutes to nudist beach
Owned/ Run By: gay men
Rooms: 6
Baths: private
Wheelchair Access: yes, 4 rms

Amenities: free parking, laundry, pool
Kids: no
Pets: no
Smoking: ok
Rates: ZAR245+
AC: 10%

Parker Cottage
Cape Town, South Africa

3 Carstens St
Cape Town, South Africa 8001
27-(0)21/ 424-6445
27-(0)83/ 702-5743 (cell)
www.parkercottage.co.za

Clientele: gay-friendly
Type: b&b; in stylishly renovated Victorian w/ formal garden; at foot of Table Mtn; centrally located to gay bars, clubs, restaurants
Owned/ Run By: gay men

Rooms: 8
Baths: private
Meals: cont'l brkfst
Kids: 14 yrs & up welcome
Pets: no

Romney Park Luxury Suites & Wellness Centre
Cape Town, South Africa

corner of Hill Rd & Romney Rd
Cape Town, South Africa 8005
27-(0)21/ 439-4555
www.romneypark.co.za

Clientele: gay-friendly
Type: hotel; apts; sea-facing suites w/ private terraces & full kitchens; on-site wellness center
Owned/ Run By: gay & straight
Rooms: 18
Baths: private
Wheelchair Access: yes, 1 rm

Meals: coffee/ tea only
Amenities: free parking, laundry, pool, massage
Kids: welcome; 12 yrs & up
Pets: no
Rates: ZAR850-3,500
AC: 20%

Sunset House Greyton
Cape Town, South Africa

19 Caledon St
Cape Town, South Africa 7233
27-28/ 254-9895
27-82/ 778-0070 (cell)
www.sunsethousegreyton.co.za

Clientele: mixed gay/ straight
Type: guesthouse; self-catering cottage w/ outdoor French kitchen, private courtyard & mtn views
Owned/ Run By: gay men
Rooms: 3
Baths: private

Wheelchair Access: yes, 2 rms
Meals: full brkfst
Amenities: free parking, laundry
Kids: no
Pets: no
Rates: ZAR160-600
AC: 10%

The Twelve Apostles Hotel
Cape Town, South Africa

PO Box 32117
Camps Bay, South Africa 8040
27-(0)21/ 437-9000
www.12apostleshotel.com

Clientele: mixed gay/ straight
Type: hotel; intimate 5-star, stunning hotel; poised on the Atlantic edge & flanked by the majestic Table Mtn & her Twelve Apostles
Owned/ Run By: gay men
Rooms: 70
Baths: private

Wheelchair Access: yes, 1 rm
Meals: full brkfst
Amenities: free parking, laundry, pool, hot tub, massage, DVDs/ videos
Kids: welcome
Pets: welcome
Smoking: ok (in bar-lounge)
Rates: ZAR3,470-13,900

Verona Lodge
Cape Town, South Africa

11 Richmond Rd
Cape Town, South Africa 8005
27-(0)21/ 434-9477
www.veronalodge.co.za

Clientele: gay-friendly
Type: guesthouse; in 1910 Edwardian terrace house at foot of Signal Hill; near bars, clubs, Victoria & Alfred Waterfront & beaches; few minutes to Cape Town by public transit
Rooms: 5

Baths: private
Meals: full brkfst
Amenities: laundry
Kids: no
Pets: no
Rates: ZAR295-400

Petersfield Farm Cottages
Cederberg, South Africa

27-22/ 921-3316
www.petersfieldfarm.co.za

Clientele: mixed gay/ straight
Type: cottage; self-catering storybook cottages on mtn farm; private w/ own plunge pools; Cederberg mtn area 2 hrs drive from Cape Town
Owned/ Run By: gay men
Rooms: 4

Baths: private & shared
Meals: coffee/ tea only
Amenities: free parking, laundry, pool
Kids: welcome
Pets: welcome w/ prior approval
Smoking: ok
Rates: ZAR400-800

La Cabriere Country House

Franschhoek, South Africa

Park Lane
Franschhoek, South Africa
27-(0)21/ 876-4780
www.lacabriere.co.za

Clientele: gay-friendly
Type: guesthouse; luxury accommodations in restored 1870 home; in vineyard area near village center
Rooms: 4
Baths: private

Meals: full brkfst
Amenities: free parking, laundry, pool
Kids: 15 yrs & up welcome
Rates: ZAR750-950+
AC: 15%

Farm 215

Gansbaai, South Africa

27-28/ 388-0920
www.farm215.co.za

Clientele: mixed gay/ straight
Type: secluded retreat on a private nature reserve
Owned/ Run By: gay men
Rooms: 6
Baths: private

Meals: full brkfst
Amenities: pool
Kids: welcome
Pets: no
Rates: ZAR1100-1700
AC: 20%

Die Seemeeue B&B

Hermanus, South Africa

60 Ghwarrieng Crescent, Vermont
Hermanus, South Africa 7201
27-28/ 316-2479 27-83/ 763-6572
www.seemeeue.co.za

Clientele: mixed gay/ straight
Type: b&b; cozy; wide views over ocean & mtns; nature reserves & beaches of unspoilt beauty; sundeck & restaurant
Owned/ Run By: gay men
Rooms: 4
Baths: private

Meals: cont'l brkfst
Amenities: free parking, laundry, pool
Kids: welcome in 1 rm downstairs
Pets: welcome in 1 rm downstairs
Smoking: no
Rates: ZAR170-230
AC: 10-15%

Trogon Guest House B&B

Knysna, South Africa

PO Box 2057
Knysna, South Africa 6570
27-44/ 384-0495
27-83/ 728-8208 (cell)
www.geocities.com/jfmvanwyk/trogon.html

Clientele: mixed gay/ straight
Type: b&b-private home; on the forested mtn slopes of Knysna overlooking lagoon; near Knysna Heads, golf courses & tennis courts
Owned/ Run By: gay men
Rooms: 3 + self-catering apt
Baths: private

Wheelchair Access: yes, 3 rms
Meals: full brkfst
Amenities: free parking
Kids: no
Pets: welcome w/ prior approval; please inquire
Smoking: ok
Rates: ZAR265-460 & ZAR485 (flat)

Annie's Cottage

Springbok, South Africa

4 Kingstreet
Springbok, Northern Cape
South Africa 8240
27-(0)27/ 712-1451
www.springbokinfo.com

Clientele: gay-friendly
Type: b&b-inn; serene ambience in restored colonial home; oasis-like garden; rms w/ private entrances onto veranda or into garden; TV w/ MNET; bar-fridges in all rms
Rooms: 11
Baths: private
Wheelchair Access: yes, 1 rm

Meals: full brkfst
Amenities: free parking, laundry, pool, hot tub
Kids: welcome
Pets: please inquire
Smoking: no
Rates: ZAR500-600
AC: 10%

Fraai Uitzicht 1798

Winelands, South Africa

PO Box 97
Robertson, Western Cape
South Africa 6705
27-(0)23/ 626-6156
www.fraaiuitzicht.com

Clientele: gay-friendly
Type: resort; 4-star superior accommodations overlooking vineyards & mtns; award-winning restaurant
Rooms: 8
Baths: private
Wheelchair Access: yes, 3 rms

Meals: expanded cont'l brkfst
Amenities: free parking, laundry, pool, massage
Kids: no
Pets: no
Rates: ZAR420-1,050
AC: 20%

Elements Hostel
Chennai, India

26-A Wallace Garden, 3rd St
Chennai, India 600034
91-44/ 5214-2552
www.elementshostel.com

Type: hostel; int'l flavor; safe & comfortable; ideal for backpackers; in exciting tourist/ commercial area of the city
Rooms: 1 single or dbl; 3 dorm-style
Baths: private & shared
Meals: full brkfst
Amenities: free parking, laundry

Kids: welcome
Pets: no
Smoking: ok in restricted areas
Rates: 375-1,100 rupees
AC: 10%

Hotel Umaid Bhawan
Jaipur, India

Behari Marg via Bank Rd Bani Park
Jaipur, India 302016
91-141/ 220-6426
www.umaidbhawan.com

Type: heritage, family-run hotel
Rooms: 30
Baths: private
Meals: full brkfst
Amenities: free parking, laundry, pool

Rates: US$40-65
AC: 10%

Umaid Mahal
Jaipur, India

B20B2 Behari Marg Bani Park
Jaipur, India 302016
91-141/ 220-1952 91-141/ 220-4470
www.umaidmahal.com

Clientele: gay-friendly
Type: hotel; classic heritage castle welcomes you to the world of traditional Rajasthani hospitality
Owned/ Run By: other
Rooms: 404
Baths: private & shared
Wheelchair Access: yes, 3 rms

Amenities: free parking, laundry, pool
Kids: welcome
Pets: welcome
Smoking: ok
Rates: US$40-65
AC: 10%

Fifu Guest House
Jaisalmer, India

Opp: Nagarpalika
Jaisalmer, India 345001
91/ 2992-252656 91/ 2992-254317
www.fifutravel.com

Clientele: gay-friendly
Type: hotel; on a quiet street; view of Jaisalmer Fort from the terrace
Owned/ Run By: straights
Rooms: 8
Baths: private
Wheelchair Access: yes, 4 rms

Meals: full brkfst
Amenities: free parking, laundry
Kids: no
Pets: no
Smoking: ok
Rates: 400-1,250 rupees

Hotel Monsoon Palace
Jaisalmer, India

On Fort
Jaisalmer, India 345001
91/ 2992-254317
www.indiamart.com/monsoonpalace

Clientele: gay-friendly
Type: hotel; 600-year-old building in Jaisalmer Fort
Rooms: 4
Baths: private & shared
Meals: full brkfst

Amenities: laundry
Kids: no
Pets: no
Smoking: ok
Rates: 1,200-2,050 rupees
AC: 10%

Naari Women's Guesthouse
New Delhi, India

00 91 11/ 2613-8316 (booking #)

Clientele: women
Type: guesthouse; homey & warm atmosphere; situated in quiet residential area of South Delhi; 25 minutes from city center
Owned/ Run By: lesbian & straight
Rooms: 2
Baths: private & shared

Amenities: free parking, laundry, massage, DVDs/ videos
Kids: welcome; boys under 11 yrs only
Pets: no
Smoking: ok
Rates: 850-950 rupees

Villa Jacaranda   Varkala, India

00 91/ 470–261–0296 (pin: 695 141)
www.villa-jacaranda.biz

Clientele: gay-friendly
Type: guesthouse; verandas, sea views, gardens & terraces; 5 minutes to beach; tranquil setting; friendly owners & staff
Owned/ Run By: gay men
Rooms: 5
Baths: private

Amenities: laundry
Kids: over 6 yrs welcome
Pets: no
Smoking: ok
Rates: 3,300-4,400 rupees
AC: 10%

Kyoto Gion Apartments   Kyoto, Japan

380-1 Yamazaki-cho, Gojo-agaru
Yamato-oji, Higashiyama-ku
Kyoto, Japan 605-0841
415/ 990–6716 (US #)
www.vrbo.com/105639

Clientele: gay-friendly
Type: apt; modern, fully equipped; excellent location in historic Gion geisha district in center of Kyoto; near sights, shopping & transit
Owned/ Run By: gay & straight
Rooms: 5 (apts; can sleep 2-3)

Baths: private
Wheelchair Access: yes
Kids: welcome
Rates: US$90/ night for (7-night minimum); $110/ night for 3

Kyoto Gion House   Kyoto, Japan

563-12 Komatsu-cho, Hanamikoji-sagaru
Gion, Higashiyama-ku
Kyoto, Japan
415/ 990–6716 (US #)
www.vrbo.com/105505

Clientele: gay-friendly
Type: rental home; recently renovated traditional "machiya"-style house; located in Kyoto's historic Gion geisha district; traditional Japanese design details combined w/ luxurious modern amenities
Owned/ Run By: gay & straight

Rooms: 2 (bdrms; can sleep up to 4)
Baths: private
Amenities: WiFi
Rates: US$220/ night for 2 persons (7-night minimum); $20/ night each additional person

Gayana Island EcoResort   Kota Kinabalu, Malaysia

Lot G16, Wisma Sabah
Kota Kinabalu, Malaysia 88000
60-88/ 245–158 60-88/ 245–168
www.gayana-resort.com

Clientele: gay-friendly
Type: resort; a unique water village off the coast of Kota Kinabalu; great for relaxation, hiking, kayaking
Owned/ Run By: straights
Rooms: 44
Baths: private

Meals: expanded cont'l brkfst
Amenities: laundry, pool
Kids: welcome
Smoking: ok
Rates: MYR520-680
AC: 10% to TAs & 20% to wholesalers

238 Guest House   Bangkok, Thailand

238 Pahurat Rd, Wangburapa, Prankorn
Bangkok, Thailand 10200
66-2/ 623–9287
www.east-thai.com/238guesthouse

Clientele: mostly women
Type: guesthouse; in middle of Old Town Bangkok; near major tourist attractions & shopping centers
Owned/ Run By: lesbians
Rooms: 14
Baths: shared

Meals: coffee/ tea only
Amenities: laundry
Kids: welcome
Pets: welcome
Smoking: ok
Rates: 400-600Baht
AC: 10%

Old Bangkok Inn   Bangkok, Thailand

607 Pra Sumen Rd
Bangkok, Thailand 10200
66-2/ 629–1787
www.oldbangkokinn.com

Clientele: gay-friendly
Type: b&b-inn; boutique inn; "set in the heart of Bangkok's yesteryears;" environmentally-friendly "green hotel"
Owned/ Run By: straights
Rooms: 8
Baths: private

Meals: full brkfst
Amenities: laundry
Kids: welcome
Pets: welcome
Smoking: no
Rates: US$79-99

Bangkok Rama Place, City Resort & Hotel

Bangkok, Thailand

1546 Pattanakarn Rd
Bangkok, Thailand 10250

66–2/ 722–6602–10

www.bangkok-hotel.com

Clientele: gay-friendly
Type: hotel; comfortable deluxe bungalows & rms; recommended for enjoyable stay in Bangkok; 24hr hospitality, efficient service, airport pickup
Owned/ Run By: lesbians
Nearby Attractions: ancient city at Bang Phu, Prasart Museum, crocodile farm (Samutphrakarn)
Pickup Service: airport pickup
Transit: near public transit; 20 minutes to airport; 3 km to train; 20 meters to bus
Rooms: 150 (includes 85 hotel rms, 65 resort bungalows) total, 79 kings, A/C, color TV, cable, phone, kitchenette, refrigerator, rm service, maid service, carpeted flrs (hotel) & ceramic tile flrs (bungalow)
Baths: private, bathtubs, showers, hairdryers
Wheelchair Access: yes, all rms
Meals: full brkfst
Amenities: office hrs: 24hr front office; free parking, laundry, pool, hot tub, massage, DVDs/ videos, coffee/ tea, steam rm; also 40, 65, 140 & 200 sq meters of dancing flr for practice & exercise, both standard & Latin American ballroom dancing

Recreation: 7 km to public park; 5 km to golf courses
Kids: welcome
Pets: no
Pets On Premises: cats
Smoking: ok (in smoking rms, bungalows)
Reservations: required *Deposit:* required *Cancellation:* cancel by 1 week prior *Minimum Stay:* 2 nights (for free aiport pickup) *Check in/ out:* noon

Payment: cash, travelers checks, Visa, Amex, MC
Season: open yr-round *High season:* Oct-March
Rates: US$46-106 *Discounts:* ask for promotion package or long-term stay rates
AC: 10%

Omyim Lodge

Bangkok, Thailand

72-74 Naratiwat Rd Silom
Bangkok, Thailand 10500
66–8/ 1300–1778
www.omyimgroup.com

Clientele: mixed gay/ straight
Type: guesthouse; all rms double ensuite w/ safe, fridge, phone, tea & coffee; 24hr security
Owned/ Run By: lesbians/ gay men
Rooms: 12
Baths: private

Meals: full brkfst
Amenities: free parking, laundry, WiFi
Kids: welcome
Pets: no
Smoking: no
Rates: 600-900Baht

Plaza Hotel Bangkok

Bangkok, Thailand

178 Surawong Rd
Bangkok, Thailand 10500
66–2/ 677–6240
www.asiatravel.com/plaza

Clientele: gay-friendly
Type: hotel
Rooms: 175
Baths: private
Amenities: free parking, laundry, pool

Kids: welcome
Rates: 1,299-1,999Baht

Regency Park Hotel

Bangkok, Thailand

66–2/ 259–7420
www.accorhotels-
asia.com/hotel/sof/index.asp?hc=1605

Clientele: gay-friendly
Type: hotel; located in the heart of Bangkok; close to Sky Train, shops & restaurants
Meals: full brkfst

Amenities: free parking, laundry, pool, sauna
Rates: 1,850-4,000Baht

Tarntawan Place Hotel

Bangkok, Thailand

119/5–10 Surawong Rd
Bangkok, Thailand 10500
66–2/ 238-2620
www.tarntawan.com

Clientele: mixed gay/ straight
Type: hotel; new boutique-style; "THE gay-friendly hotel in Bangkok"
Owned/ Run By: gay & straight
Rooms: 75
Baths: private
Wheelchair Access: yes, all rms

Meals: expanded cont'l brkfst
Amenities: laundry, massage
Kids: welcome
Pets: no
Smoking: ok
Rates: 2,500-7,000Baht
AC: 10%

Tower Inn

Bangkok, Thailand

533 Silom Rd
Bangkok, Thailand
66–2/ 237-8300 66–2/ 635-0378
www.towerinnbangkok.com

Clientele: gay-friendly
Type: hotel; also restaurant & bar
Rooms: 175
Baths: private

Amenities: pool, sauna, gym
Rates: 2,200-3,000Baht

Lotus

Chiang Mai, Thailand

2/25 Viangbua Rd, Changphuak
Chiang Mai, Thailand 50300
66–53/ 215-376
www.lotus-hotel.com

Clientele: mostly men
Type: boutique hotel; restaurant, bar & club on-site; "the hub of Chiang Mai's premier gay entertainment center"
Owned/ Run By: gay men
Rooms: 11
Baths: private
Wheelchair Access: yes, 2 rms

Meals: full brkfst
Amenities: free parking, laundry, massage, DVDs/ videos
Kids: no
Pets: no
Smoking: ok
Rates: 800-2,600Baht
AC: 10%

PJ's Place

Chiang Mai, Thailand

19 Soi Plobplueng
Chiang Mai, Thailand 50300
66–53/ 404-894
www.pjs-place.com

Clientele: mostly men
Type: guesthouse; custom-built & set in own private garden; a haven of tranquility only a few moments from Chiang Mai's finest attractions; price includes brkfst & airport transfers
Owned/ Run By: gay men
Rooms: 6

Baths: private
Meals: full brkfst
Amenities: laundry, massage, WiFi
Kids: no
Pets: no
Smoking: no
Rates: 1,500Baht
AC: 10%

CC Blooms's Hotel

Karon, Thailand

84/21 Patak Rd Soi 10
Karon, Phuket, Thailand 83100
66–076/ 333-222
www.ccbloomshotel.com

Clientele: mixed gay/ straight
Type: resort; on a secluded hillside overlooking Kata Beach on Phuket Island; quiet, yet close to all activity
Owned/ Run By: gay men
Rooms: 20
Baths: private
Wheelchair Access: yes, 20 rms

Meals: cont'l brkfst
Amenities: free parking, laundry, pool, massage, DVDs/ videos, WiFi
Kids: welcome
Pets: welcome
Smoking: ok
Rates: US$65-110
AC: 15-20%

Baans Shadis Samui

Koh Samui, Thailand

45/3 Moo 3, Soi 5
Maenam, Thailand 84330
66–77/ 427-793
www.sawadee.com/samui/shadis/details

Clientele: mixed gay/ straight
Type: small, peaceful resort surrounded by coconut palms & jungle; located at the foot of the Samui Hills
Owned/ Run By: gay men
Rooms: 5

Baths: private
Wheelchair Access: yes, 2 rms
Meals: full brkfst
Amenities: free parking, pool, massage
Smoking: ok
Rates: 1,250-2,150Baht

Mana's Home B&B
Koh Samui, Thailand

42/26 Moo 6, Tambon Bophut
Koh Samui, Thailand 84320
66/ 1899-1767
www.premiumwanadoo.com/
atmanasamui

Clientele: mixed gay/ lesbian
Type: b&b-private home; view from the hills of Chaweng; personalized & private atmosphere; 15 minutes to beach; cash only
Owned/ Run By: gay men
Rooms: 2
Baths: shared

Meals: full brkfst
Amenities: free parking, laundry, pool, hot tub, DVDs/ videos
Kids: no
Pets: no
Smoking: ok
Rates: 1,200-2,400Baht

Ao Nang Pearl
Krabi, Thailand

362 Ao Nang Soi 7
Krabi, Thailand
66-72/ 645-014
www.aonangpearl.com

Type: guesthouse; charming, newly renovated rms; private balconies; enjoy your brkfst or evening drinks in the vast lush garden
Rooms: 10
Baths: private
Meals: cont'l brkfst

Amenities: free parking, laundry
Kids: welcome
Pets: no
Smoking: ok
Rates: 400-800Baht
AC: 20%

Le Cafe Royale
Pattaya, Thailand

325/102-109 Pattayaland Soi 3
South Pattaya, Chonburi, Thailand 20260
66-38/ 423-515 66-38/ 428-303
www.caferoyale-pattaya.com

Clientele: mixed gay/ straight
Type: hotel; in the heart of Boyz Town; 24hr restaurant & piano bar on premises (from 7:30pm); plunge pool in gym
Rooms: 33
Baths: private
Amenities: laundry, sauna, massage

Kids: not recommended
Pets: no
Smoking: ok (not in restaurant)
Rates: 1,100-3,000Baht
AC: 10% (except Dec 10-Jan 15)

The Flamingo Hotel
Pattaya, Thailand

20/182 Soi 2, Day-Night Plaza
South Pattaya Rd
Pattaya City, Thailand
66-38/ 427-1613
www.flamingohotelthailand.com

Clientele: gay-friendly
Type: hotel; small, European-managed hotel located in the heart of Pattaya City; conference facilities; travel desk
Rooms: 32
Baths: private
Amenities: free parking, laundry, sauna,

hot tub, massage
Kids: welcome
Pets: small pets welcome
Smoking: ok
Rates: 1,100-2,850Baht
AC: 10%

Siam Thani Resort & Spa
Pattaya, Thailand

391/54 M. 10, Soi 11
Pattaya, Thailand 20160
66-7/ 834-33-10
www.siamthani.com

Clientele: men
Type: resort; authentic Thai pavilions; only 5 minutes to gay beach or Boyz Town; European/ Thai restaurant, cafe & bar
Owned/ Run By: gay men
Rooms: 10
Baths: private

Meals: cont'l brkfst
Amenities: free parking, pool, sauna, hot tub, massage, DVDs/ videos
Pets: welcome
Smoking: ok
Rates: US$80-95
AC: 15%

Aquarius Guesthouse & Sauna
Phuket, Thailand

127/17 Rat-U-Thit Rd, Paradise Complex
Patong Beach, Thailand 83150
66-76/ 346-142
www.aquarius-sauna.com

Clientele: men
Type: guesthouse; upmarket suites & rms located in the middle of the gay area; 5-minute walk to the beach
Owned/ Run By: gay men
Rooms: 9
Baths: private

Meals: full brkfst
Amenities: free parking, laundry, pool, sauna, hot tub, massage, DVDs/ videos, WiFi
Pets: welcome
Smoking: ok
Rates: 600-8,000Baht

Club Bamboo Resort   *Phuket, Thailand*

247/ 1-8 Nanai Rd
Patong Beach, Thailand 83150
66-76/ 345-345
www.clubbamboo.com

Clientele: gay-friendly
Type: resort; on the slopes of old rubber tree & coconut plantations; overlooks Patong Bay
Rooms: 33 (includes rms, suites & bungalows)
Baths: private

Amenities: free parking, laundry, pool, hot tub, massage
Kids: welcome
Smoking: ok
Rates: 1,150-6,075Baht
AC: 10%

Connect Guesthouse   *Phuket, Thailand*

125/ 8-9 Rath-U-Thit Rd
Patong Beach, Thailand 83150
66-76/ 294-195
www.gaypatong.com/connect/guesthouse

Clientele: mixed gay/ lesbian
Type: guesthouse; Swedish-owned gay guesthouse in the middle of the gay area; restaurant, internet access, bar; join our weekly Gay Day Tour to a small island; all guests have access to Aquarius gay sauna/ gym
Owned/ Run By: gay men

Rooms: 25
Baths: private
Meals: cont'l brkfst
Amenities: laundry, WiFi
Kids: no
Rates: 450-2,550Baht
AC: 10-15%

Aloha Mana   *Raratonga, Cook Islands*

808/ 573-5488
www.aloha-mana.com

Clientele: gay-friendly
Type: rental home; renovated/ furnished 125-year-old colonial near beautiful beach, "a true paradise"
Owned/ Run By: woman
Rooms: 2
Baths: shared

Meals: coffee/ tea only
Amenities: laundry, hot tub
Kids: welcome
Pets: no
Rates: NZ$1,500/ week
AC: 15%

Fijian Waters   *Pacific Harbour, Fiji*

PO Box 393
Pacific Harbour, Fiji
679/ 345-0766
www.fijianwaters.com

Type: guesthouse; only gay guesthouse in Fiji; safe & private guesthouse fronts the pool & river
Rooms: 2
Baths: shared
Meals: coffee/ tea only
Amenities: free parking, laundry, pool,

DVDs/ videos
Kids: welcome
Pets: no
Rates: US$100
AC: 5%

Bali Villa Kelapa   *Bali, Indonesia*

Raamgracht 23
Amsterdam, Netherlands 1011 KJ
31-20/ 627-3684 (Netherlands)
www.bali-villa-kelapa.com

Clientele: gay-friendly
Type: rental home; located in the tranquil Balinese village of Seminyak on SW coast; about 1 mile from Legian Beach
Owned/ Run By: straights
Rooms: 3

Baths: private
Meals: expanded cont'l brkfst
Amenities: laundry, pool
Kids: welcome
Rates: €570-670/ week

Gubah Bali Exclusive Villas   *Bali, Indonesia*

62-361/ 948-390
www.gubahbali.com

Clientele: gay-friendly
Type: resort; flowers, fruit plate & a drink upon arrival; free shuttle to Ubud & a tour around Bedulu Village
Owned/ Run By: gay & straight
Rooms: 6
Baths: private
Meals: full brkfst

Amenities: free parking, laundry, pool, hot tub, massage
Kids: welcome
Pets: welcome
Smoking: no
Rates: US$75-190
AC: 10%

Laki Uma Villa

Bali, Indonesia

Umalas-Kerobokan
Kuta, Bali, Indonesia 80361
62-811/ 388-681
lakiuma@hotmail.com

Clientele: men
Type: guesthouse; luxurious traditional Balinese furnishings; "the only gay-only, clothing-optional resort in Bali"
Owned/ Run By: gay men
Rooms: 5
Baths: private & shared
Meals: full brkfst

Amenities: free parking, laundry, pool, sauna, hot tub, massage, DVDs/ videos
Kids: no
Pets: no
Smoking: ok
Rates: US$25-70
AC: upon request

Princess Nusa Dua Resort

Bali, Indonesia

Jl. Pratama 101 Tanjung Benoa
Nusa Dua, Bali, Indonesia 80363
62-361/ 771-604
salan@indo.net.id

Clientele: gay-friendly
Type: hotel; private 3-star hotel in peaceful area of Nusa Dua
Owned/ Run By: straights
Rooms: 50
Baths: private
Meals: expanded cont'l brkfst

Amenities: free parking, laundry, pool, indoor hot tub, massage
Kids: welcome
Smoking: ok
Rates: US$31-296
AC: 10%

Josephine House

Jakarta, Indonesia

J1. Iskandarsyah II/91
South Jakarta, Indonesia
62-21/ 725-0017
www.josephinehouse.com

Clientele: gay-friendly
Type: guesthouse; homey atmosphere; central location
Rates: US$30-52

Dusun Jogja Village Inn

Yogyakarta, Indonesia

Menukan St #5
Yogyakarta, Indonesia 55153
62-274/ 373-031 800/ 537-8483
www.jvidusun.co.id

Clientele: mixed gay/ lesbian
Type: hotel; a tranquil guesthouse in a landscaped environment; private terraces; also restaurant, bar & cafe
Owned/ Run By: straights
Rooms: 24
Baths: private

Meals: full brkfst
Amenities: free parking, laundry, pool, hot tub, massage, DVDs/ videos
Kids: welcome
Smoking: ok
Rates: US$70-160
AC: 10%

Manta Ray Bay Hotel & Yap Divers

Yap, Micronesia

1 Mantaray Ave, Colonia
Yap, Micronesia 96943
691/ 350-2300
www.mantaray.com

Clientele: gay-friendly
Type: one of top 10 dive resorts in the world; on-site bistro & bar; Yap is home to some of the friendliest & most accommodating people in the world
Owned/ Run By: straights
Rooms: 23
Baths: private

Wheelchair Access: yes, 7 rms
Meals: full brkfst
Amenities: laundry, hot tub, massage
Kids: welcome
Pets: welcome
Smoking: ok
Rates: US$150-300
AC: 10%

Rochdale B&B

Adelaide, Australia

349 Glen Osmond Rd
Glen Osmond, Australia 5064
61-8/ 8379-7498
www.go.to/rochdale

Clientele: mixed gay/ lesbian
Type: b&b-private home, art deco influences; enclosed pool; near city, wineries & beaches; friendly & relaxing
Owned/ Run By: gay men
Rooms: 3
Baths: private

Meals: full gourmet brkfst
Amenities: free parking, pool
Kids: welcome w/ prior approval
Pets: welcome w/ prior approval
Smoking: no
Rates: A$90+
AC: 10%

Sportsman Hotel ("Sporties") *Brisbane, Australia*

130 Leichardt St, Spring Hill
Brisbane, Australia 4000
61-7/ 3831-2892
www.sportsmanhotel.com.au

Clientele: men
Type: hotel; "Visiting Brisbane? Don't want to drive home tonight? Embarrassed to take that 'friend' home to Mother? Then 'Stay Gay' at the Sportsman!"
Owned/ Run By: gay men
Rooms: 10
Baths: shared

Rates: A$50-60

Mengyuan B&B *Bundaberg, Australia*

200 Woodswallow Drive
Gin Gin, Australia 4671
61-7/ 4157-3024
www.mengyuan.com.au

Clientele: mixed gay/ lesbian
Type: b&b; in large, modern country home
Owned/ Run By: gay men
Rooms: 4
Baths: shared
Wheelchair Access: yes, all rms
Meals: cont'l brkfst
Amenities: free parking, laundry, pool, hot tub, massage, DVDs/ videos

Kids: welcome
Pets: welcome
Smoking: no
Rates: A$120-140; cash only
AC: 10%

18-24 James *Cairns, Australia*

18-24 James St
Cairns, Australia 4870
61-7/ 4051-4644 800/ 621-824
www.skinnydips.com.au

Clientele: mostly men
Type: hotel; resort-style property; bar & restaurant open onto pool area
Owned/ Run By: gay men
Rooms: 21
Baths: private
Wheelchair Access: yes, 1 rm
Meals: expanded cont'l brkfst

Amenities: free parking, laundry, pool, sauna, outdoor hot tub, massage, DVDs/ videos, gym
Kids: no
Pets: no
Smoking: ok
Rates: A$126-195
AC: 20%

Boyz on the Beach *Cairns, Australia*

1 Coogee Close, Kewarra Beach
Cairns, Australia 4879
61-7/ 4055-6462
www.boyzonthebeach.com.au

Clientele: men
Type: b&b; on Kewarra beach, 15 minutes N of airport; near Cairns best gay beach; many yrs in hospitality industry
Owned/ Run By: gay men
Rooms: 3
Baths: private & shared
Meals: cont'l brkfst
Amenities: free parking, laundry, pool

Kids: no
Pets: no
Smoking: no
Rates: A$86-126
AC: 10%

Mai Tai Resort *Cairns, Australia*

Lot 78 Rex Range Rd
Port Douglas, Australia 4873
61-7/ 4098-4956
www.maitai-resort.com.au

Clientele: mixed gay/ straight
Type: exclusive Balinese-style boutique resort; 10 minutes from Port Douglas & 4 minutes from Mile Beach; easy access to Great Barrier Reef, Daintree Rain Forest
Owned/ Run By: gay men
Rooms: 4
Baths: private
Meals: full tropical brkfst

Amenities: free parking, laundry, pool, massage
Kids: no
Pets: no
Smoking: no
Rates: A$265-795 (3-night minimum)
AC: 15%

Bush House

Gold Coast, Australia

PO Box 282
West Burleigh, Australia 4219
61-7/ 5533-8408
www.bushhouse.net

Clientele: men
Type: b&b-private home; secluded retreat for men inland from central Gold Coast; clothing-optional; transfers from airport included
Owned/ Run By: gay men
Rooms: 2
Baths: private

Wheelchair Access: yes, 1 rm
Meals: full brkfst
Amenities: free parking, laundry, pool, outdoor hot tub, DVDs/ videos
Kids: no
Pets: dogs preferred, but other animals considered
Rates: A$85-125

Columbia Tower Apts

Gold Coast, Australia

19 Fern St
Surfers Paradise, Australia 4217
61-7/ 5570-2088
www.columbiatower.com.au

Clientele: gay-friendly
Type: apt; self-contained; great views; near surfing, 5-star restaurants & shopping; "not a resort—more like a visit w/ old friends"
Owned/ Run By: straights
Rooms: 17
Baths: private

Meals: cont'l brkfst
Amenities: free parking, laundry, pool, sauna
Kids: welcome
Smoking: ok
Rates: A$210+ (2-night minimum)
AC: 10-15%

Paradise Towers

Gold Coast, Australia

3049 Gold Coast Hwy
Surfers Paradise, Australia 4217
61-7/ 5592-3336
www.paradisetowers.com

Clientele: mixed gay/ straight
Type: apt; in the heart of Surfers Paradise; 1 minute to all gay venues
Owned/ Run By: gay man
Rooms: 22
Baths: private

Amenities: free parking, laundry, pool
Kids: welcome
Pets: no
Rates: A$80-250
AC: 10%

Corinda's Cottages

Hobart, Australia

17 Glebe St
Hobart, Australia 7000
61-3/ 6234-1590
www.corindascottages.com.au

Clientele: gay-friendly
Type: cottages created from outbuildings, gardener's residence, servants' quarters & coach house of stately Victorian overlooking Sullivans Cove & Hobart's city center; extensive gardens

Owned/ Run By: gay men
Rooms: 3 (cottages)
Baths: private
Amenities: laundry
Rates: A$195-250

169 Drummond Street

Melbourne, Australia

169 Drummond St, Carlton
Melbourne, Australia 3053
61-3/ 9663-3081
www.169drummond.com.au

Clientele: mixed gay/ lesbian
Type: b&b; beautifully restored terrace house in central Melbourne; exclusively lesbian & gay; gay-friendly folk welcome
Owned/ Run By: gay men
Rooms: 4
Baths: private
Meals: expanded cont'l brkfst

Amenities: free parking, laundry, DVDs/ videos
Kids: welcome
Pets: no
Smoking: no
Rates: A$120-145
AC: please inquire

Cotterville Homestay B&B

Melbourne, Australia

204 Williams Rd
Melbourne, Australia 3142
61-3/ 9826-9105
www.cotterville.com

Clientele: mixed gay/ straight
Type: b&b-private home; gourmet dinners prepared upon request; ask to try on the pair of Liz Taylor's satin pumps on display!
Owned/ Run By: gay men
Rooms: 2
Baths: shared

Meals: full brkfst
Amenities: laundry, DVDs/ videos
Kids: no
Pets: no
Smoking: ok
Rates: A$130-160

The Friendly Backpacker
Melbourne, Australia

197 King St
Melbourne, Australia 3001
61-3/ 9670-1111 800/ 671-115
www.friendlygroup.com.au

Clientele: mixed gay/ straight
Type: hostel; backpacker accommodations: singles, doubles & dorms
Owned/ Run By: straights
Rooms: 50
Baths: shared
Wheelchair Access: yes

Meals: cont'l brkfst
Amenities: laundry, DVDs/ videos
Kids: welcome
Pets: no
Smoking: no
Rates: A$26-70
AC: booking fee

The Gatehouse
Melbourne, Australia

c/o 10 Peel St
Collingwood, Australia 3066
61-3/ 9417-2182
www.club80.net/gateinfo.html

Clientele: men
Type: guesthouse; all rms are equipped for sleep & play; "Melbourne's first designed specifically for the male S/M scene"
Owned/ Run By: gay men

Rooms: 4
Baths: shared
AC: 10%

The Greenhouse Backpacker
Melbourne, Australia

228 Flinders Ln
Melbourne, Australia 3001
61-3/ 9639-6400 800/ 249-207
www.friendlygroup.com.au

Clientele: gay-friendly
Type: hostel; excellent facilities & friendly local staff; kitchen & rooftop garden
Owned/ Run By: straights
Rooms: 50
Baths: shared

Wheelchair Access: yes, all rms
Meals: cont'l brkfst
Amenities: laundry, DVDs/ videos
Kids: welcome
Smoking: no
Rates: A$27-70

Hesket House Retreat
Melbourne, Australia

1201 Romsey Rd
Romsey, Australia 3434
61-03/ 5427-0608
www.heskethouse.com.au

Clientele: mixed gay/ straight
Type: guesthouse; on 150 acres of private forest; luxurious yet rustic; less than 1 hr from Melbourne
Owned/ Run By: gay men
Rooms: 7
Baths: private & shared

Wheelchair Access: yes, 7 rms
Meals: full brkfst
Amenities: free parking, indoor hot tub, massage
Kids: no
Pets: no
AC: 10%

The Laird Hotel & Guest House
Melbourne, Australia

149 Gipps St
Abbotsford, Australia 3067
61-3/ 9417-2832
www.lairdhotel.com

Clientele: men
Type: hotel; above 2 bars & beer garden; also 3 rms in cottage across the street; "home of Melbourne's leather scene & its only male-only venue"
Owned/ Run By: gay men
Rooms: 9
Baths: private & shared

Meals: cont'l brkfst
Amenities: laundry
Kids: no
Pets: no
Smoking: no
Rates: A$90-160
AC: 10%

Horizons at Peregian
Peregian Beach, Australia

45 Lorikeet Dr
Peregian Beach, Noosa Heads
Australia 4573
61-7/ 5448-3444
www.horizons-peregian.com

Clientele: mostly men
Type: exclusive beachfront resort; luxury self-contained apts & penthouses; on Queensland's Sunshine Coast, 60 miles N of Brisbane
Owned/ Run By: gay men
Rooms: 15 (apts)
Baths: private

Wheelchair Access: yes, 5 rms
Amenities: free parking, laundry, pool, hot tub, massage, DVDs/ videos
Kids: welcome
Pets: small dogs only welcome
Smoking: no
Rates: US$170-240
AC: 10%

Abaca Palms
Perth, Australia

34 Whatley Crescent, Mt Lawley
Perth, Australia 6050
61-8/ 9271-2117
www.abacapalms.com

Clientele: men
Type: guesthouse; 1930s art deco character house; 10-man saltwater jacuzzi; "feel pampered at Perth's only exclusively gay premier guesthouse"
Owned/ Run By: gay men

Rooms: 6
Baths: shared
Meals: full brkfst
Amenities: free parking, sauna, hot tub, DVDs/ videos
Rates: A$60-80

Hotel Grand Chancellor Perth
Perth, Australia

707 Wellington St
Perth, Australia 6000
61-8/ 9327-7000
www.ghihotels.com

Type: hotel; near city center & Northbridge, Perth's nightlife area; "Perth's best 4-star hotel located in the West End of the CBD"
Rooms: 275
Baths: private
Wheelchair Access: yes, 1 rm

Amenities: free parking, laundry, pool, sauna, massage, gym
Kids: welcome
Smoking: ok
Rates: A$200-760
AC: 10%

Pension of Perth
Perth, Australia

3 Throssell St, Northbridge
Perth, Australia 6000
61-8/ 9228-9049
www.pensionperth.com.au

Clientele: mostly men
Type: b&b; magnificently renovated 1897 home overlooking Hyde Park; gourmet brkfst; gym; GATLA member & AAA 4 Stars
Rooms: 4
Baths: private
Meals: full brkfst

Amenities: free parking, laundry, pool, massage, WiFi
Kids: no
Pets: no
Smoking: no
Rates: US$115-165

Swanbourne Guest House
Perth, Australia

5 Myera St, Swanbourne
Perth, Australia 6010
61-8/ 9383-1981
www.swanbourneguesthouse.com.au

Clientele: gay-friendly
Type: guesthouse; set in tranquil garden between city & surf; Swanbourne is a beachside suburb; minutes to gay nude beach & best beaches in the world
Owned/ Run By: gay/ lesbian & straight
Rooms: 4

Baths: private & shared
Meals: expanded cont'l brkfst
Amenities: free parking, laundry, massage, DVDs/ videos
Smoking: ok
Rates: A$95
AC: 10%

Great Ocean Road Beachfront Motel
Peterborough, Australia

9 Irvine St
Peterborough, Australia 3270
61-03/ 5598-5251
www.greatoceanroadbeachfrontmotel.com.au

Clientele: mixed gay/ straight
Type: motel; on the Great Ocean Rd across from the southern ocean; minutes from Port Campbell & the 12 Apostles
Owned/ Run By: gay men
Rooms: 12
Baths: private

Meals: full brkfst
Amenities: free parking, laundry, pool, hot tub
Smoking: no
Rates: US$79-154
AC: 10%

Dreamcatcher Apartments
Port Douglas, Australia

26-28 Reef St
Port Douglas, Australia 4877
61-7/ 4099-1800
www.dcapd.com

Clientele: gay-friendly
Type: apt; standard/ luxury studios; "all of the conveniences needed to ensure your holiday is a pleasure"
Owned/ Run By: bisexuals
Rooms: 11
Baths: private
Wheelchair Access: yes, 1 rm

Meals: coffee/ tea only
Amenities: free parking, laundry, pool, hot tub, DVDs/ videos
Kids: no
Pets: no
Rates: A$140-350
AC: 10%

Azura Beach House
Port Macquarie, Australia

109 Pacific Dr
Port Macquarie, Australia 2444
61-2/ 6582-2700
www.azura.com.au

Clientele: mixed gay/ straight
Type: b&b; near unspoilt beaches & spectacular coastal scenery; your private retreat in Port Macquarie
Rooms: 4
Baths: private & shared
Meals: expanded cont'l brkfst

Amenities: free parking, pool, hot tub, DVDs/ videos
Kids: 1 welcome w/ prior arrangement
Pets: no
Smoking: no
Rates: A$100-145
AC: 10%

Rainbow Retreat
St Mary's, Australia

Lot 1 Gillies Rd
St Mary's, Australia 7215
61-3/ 6372-2168
www.rainbowretreat.com.au

Clientele: gay-friendly
Type: eco-lodge & cabins on private nature reserve at St Patrick's Head
Owned/ Run By: gay men
Kids: no

Apartment Hotel East Sydney
Sydney, Australia

61/ 404-793-159
www.apartmenthotel.com.au

Clientele: gay-friendly
Type: apt; spacious 2-bdrm apts w/ outdoor terraces & gourmet kitchens
Owned/ Run By: gay & straight
Rooms: 13
Baths: private
Meals: coffee/ tea only

Amenities: free parking, laundry, DVDs/ videos
Kids: welcome
Smoking: no
Rates: A$254-759
AC: 10%

Bandusia Country Retreat
Sydney, Australia

1056 Upper MacDonald Rd, St Albans
Sydney, Australia 2775
61-2/ 4568-2036
www.bandusia.com.au

Clientele: gay-friendly
Type: guesthouse; luxurious country retreat; in wonderful bush & farm surroundings; AAA-rated 4.5 stars
Owned/ Run By: straights
Rooms: 11
Baths: private & shared
Meals: full brkfst

Amenities: free parking, pool, sauna, outdoor hot tub, massage, DVDs/ videos
Kids: welcome w/ prior arrangement
Pets: dogs only welcome
Smoking: no
Rates: A$165-295
AC: 5%

Brickfield Hill B&B Inn
Sydney, Australia

403 Riley Street
Surry Hills, Australia 2010
61-2/ 9211-4886
www.brickfieldhill.com.au

Clientele: mixed gay/ lesbian
Type: b&b-inn; restored Victorian terrace-house in the Oxford St District; friendly & inviting; near downtown
Owned/ Run By: gay men
Rooms: 5
Baths: private & shared

Amenities: free parking, laundry, WiFi
Kids: welcome by arrangement
Pets: no
Smoking: no
Rates: A$85-125
AC: 10%

Chelsea Guest House
Sydney, Australia

49 Womerah Ave
Darlinghurst, Australia 2010
61-2/ 9380-5994
www.chelsea.citysearch.com.au

Clientele: mixed gay/ straight
Type: guesthouse; recently renovated Victorian situated around a formal Italianate courtyard
Owned/ Run By: gay men
Rooms: 13
Baths: private & shared

Meals: cont'l brkfst
Amenities: laundry
Kids: no
Pets: no
Smoking: no
Rates: A$94-195
AC: 10%

Citigate Sebel Sydney

Sydney, Australia

28 Albion St
Sydney, Australia 2010
61-2/ 9213-3820 800/ 024-231
www.mirvachotels.com.au

Clientele: gay-friendly
Type: hotel; 4.5-star; recently refurbished; excellent facilities; near Oxford St
Owned/ Run By: straights
Rooms: 270
Baths: private
Wheelchair Access: yes, 3 rms

Amenities: laundry, pool, sauna, hot tub, massage, DVDs/ videos
Kids: welcome
Pets: no
Smoking: ok (on certain flrs)
Rates: A$105-249
AC: 10%

Echo Point Holiday Accommodation

Sydney, Australia

36 Echo Point Rd
Katoomba, Australia 2780
61-2/ 4782-3275
www.echopointvillas.com.au

Clientele: gay-friendly
Type: 5 self-contained rental villas & 3 cottages; 2-night minimum stay; near Three Sisters & Jenolan Caves
Owned/ Run By: straights
Rooms: 8
Baths: private

Kids: welcome
Smoking: no
Rates: A$115-165

Footprints Westend

Sydney, Australia

412 Pitt St
Sydney, Australia 2000
61-2/ 9211-4588 1800/ 013-186
www.footprintswestend.com.au

Clientele: gay-friendly
Type: hostel; budget/ backpacker's accommodations; winner of the "Best Backpackers 2003, 2004 & 2005" HMAA
Rooms: 79
Baths: private & shared
Wheelchair Access: yes, 79 rms
Meals: cont'l brkfst

Amenities: laundry
Kids: welcome; under 18 yrs old must be w/ an adult
Pets: no
Smoking: no
Rates: A$30-85
AC: 15%

Governors on Fitzroy B&B

Sydney, Australia

64 Fitzroy St
Surry Hills, Australia 2010
61-2/ 9331-4652
www.governors.com.au

Clientele: mostly men
Type: b&b; in Victorian w/ garden courtyard; 3 blks from Oxford St, the heart of the gay area
Owned/ Run By: gay men
Rooms: 6
Baths: shared

Meals: full brkfst
Amenities: outdoor hot tub
Kids: no
Pets: no
Smoking: no
Rates: A$100-130
AC: 10% (IGLTA agents when pre-paid)

Manor House Boutique Hotel

Sydney, Australia

86 Flinders St
Darlinghurst, Australia 2010
61-2/ 9380-6633
www.manorhouse.com.au

Clientele: mixed gay/ straight
Type: boutique hotel in 1850 Victorian mansion; "offers an oasis of calm elegance & sophistication for discerning travellers"; w/ on-site lounge bar & indoor plunge pool
Rooms: 20

Baths: private
Meals: cont'l brkfst
Amenities: free parking, laundry, DVDs/ videos, WiFi
Smoking: no
Rates: A$140-290
AC: 10%

Medusa

Sydney, Australia

267 Darlinghurst Rd
Darlinghurst, Australia 2010
61-2/ 9331-1000
www.medusa.com.au

Clientele: gay-friendly
Type: "a dramatic blend of the legendary & the cutting edge"
Rooms: 18
Baths: private

Amenities: pool, DVDs/ videos, gym, WiFi
Pets: welcome in certain rms; 2 dogs max per rm
Rates: A$270-385

Oasis on Flinders
Sydney, Australia

106 Flinders St
Darlinghurst, Australia 2010
61-2/ 9331-8791
www.oasisonflinders.com.au

Clientele: men
Type: b&b; offers gay naturist men B&B accommodations in a grand 3-story Victorian; 20 minutes to nude beach; walk to most gay bars, Taylor Square, Oxford Street & restaurants
Owned/ Run By: gay men

Rooms: 6
Baths: private & shared
Meals: cont'l brkfst
Amenities: outdoor hot tub
Kids: 19 yrs & up only
Pets: no
Rates: A$120-210

Park Lodge Hotel
Sydney, Australia

747 S Dowling St
Moore Park, Australia 2016
61-2/ 9318-2393
www.parklodgesydney.com

Clientele: mixed gay/ lesbian
Type: hotel; close to Oxford St & bars; exceptional staff; "Sydney's friendliest gay-owned & operated 3-star boutique hotel"
Owned/ Run By: lesbians/ gay men
Rooms: 20
Baths: private

Wheelchair Access: yes, 1 rm
Meals: cont'l brkfst
Amenities: free parking, laundry, massage, DVDs/ videos
Kids: welcome
Smoking: ok
Rates: US$82-198
AC: 10%

Simpsons of Potts Point
Sydney, Australia

8 Challis Ave
Potts Point, Australia 2011
61-2/ 9356-2199
www.simpsonshotel.com

Clientele: mixed gay/ straight
Type: b&b; boutique hotel in restored circa 1892 mansion; walk to city or to Oxford St
Rooms: 14
Baths: private
Wheelchair Access: yes, 3 rms
Meals: expanded cont'l brkfst

Amenities: free parking
Kids: welcome; on request
Pets: no
Smoking: ok
Rates: A$175-330
AC: 10%

Sydney Star Accommodation
Sydney, Australia

273-275 Darlinghurst Rd
Darlinghurst, Australia 2010
61-2/ 9358-1445
www.sydneystar.com.au

Clientele: mixed gay/ straight
Type: hotel; stylish & private; relaxed personal attention; in heart of colorful Darlinghurst, Sydney's gay/ lesbian capital
Owned/ Run By: gay/ lesbian & straight

Rooms: 18
Baths: private & shared
Amenities: laundry
Rates: A$20-100
AC: 10%

Victoria Court Hotel Sydney
Sydney, Australia

122 Victoria St
Sydney, Australia 2011
61-2/ 9357-3200
1800/ 630-505 (in Australia)
www.victoriacourt.com.au

Clientele: gay-friendly
Type: b&b-inn; in elegant Victorian house; charming; central, quiet location in the heart of Sydney's gastronomic precinct; close to Opera House, Oxford St & beaches
Owned/ Run By: straights
Rooms: 25

Baths: private
Meals: full brkfst
Amenities: free parking, laundry
Rates: US$37-130
AC: 10%

Wattle Hotel
Sydney, Australia

108 Oxford St
Sydney, Australia 2010
61-2/ 9332-4118
www.sydneywattle.com

Clientele: gay-friendly
Type: boutique hotel in heart of Oxford St gay life; 2 rms w/ balconies overlooking Mardi Gras
Owned/ Run By: straights
Rooms: 12

Baths: private
Meals: cont'l brkfst
Amenities: laundry
Rates: A$100-259

881 Homestay
Auckland, New Zealand

881 Tuakau Bridge-Port Waikato Rd,
Franklin
Auckland, New Zealand 2693
64-9/ 232-8581
www.881homestay.co.nz

Clientele: mostly women
Type: b&b-private home; eco-friendly hideaway; generous hospitality; 15 minutes to Port Waikato Beach; 5-minute drive to New Zealand's longest fishing river; short distance from Nikau Caves
Owned/ Run By: lesbians
Rooms: 1

Baths: private
Meals: organic brkfst
Amenities: free parking, laundry, DVDs/ videos
Kids: welcome
Pets: welcome
Rates: NZ$90+

The Brown Kiwi Travellers Hostel
Auckland, New Zealand

7 Prosford St, Ponsonby
Auckland, New Zealand
64-9/ 378-0191
www.brownkiwi.co.nz

Clientele: mixed gay/ straight
Type: hostel; refurbished 1910 Colonial; full kitchen; in Auckland's trendiest inner-city multicultural suburb
Owned/ Run By: gay men
Rooms: 8 (includes 2 double rms, 2 triples, 2 quad-share for up to 4 people & 2 dorm

rms for up to 8 people)
Baths: shared
Amenities: laundry
Kids: welcome
Pets: no
Smoking: no
Rates: NZ$19 (dorm) - 72 (triple)

Great Ponsonby B&B
Auckland, New Zealand

30 Ponsonby Terrace
Ponsonby, New Zealand
64-9/ 376-5989
www.ponsonbybnb.co.nz

Clientele: gay-friendly
Type: b&b-inn; in restored chic 1898 villa; near attractions, bars & cafes; sumptuous brkfst; numerous decks
Rooms: 11
Baths: private
Meals: full brkfst

Amenities: free parking, laundry, DVDs/ videos
Kids: no
Pets: no
Smoking: no
Rates: NZ$180-350
AC: 10%

Dorothy's
Christchurch, New Zealand

2 Latimer Square
Christchurch, New Zealand
64-3/ 365-6034
www.dorothys.co.nz

Clientele: mixed gay/ straight
Type: hotel; boutique hotel in restored Edwardian mansion; award-winning restaurant & bar; "100% pure New Zealand hospitality"
Owned/ Run By: gay men
Rooms: 7
Baths: private

Meals: cont'l brkfst
Amenities: free parking, laundry
Kids: welcome
Pets: no
Smoking: no (except in bar)
Rates: NZ$180-250
AC: 10%

Kew Homestay
Christchurch, New Zealand

4/ 23 Bishop St, St Albans
Christchurch, New Zealand
64-3/ 365-2436
homepages.paradise.net.nz/qhouse

Clientele: mixed gay/ straight
Type: homestay; stylish, modern home in garden setting; on northside of Christchurch; walk to bars, clubs & restaurants
Owned/ Run By: gay men
Rooms: 2

Baths: private & shared
Meals: cont'l brkfst
Amenities: laundry
Kids: no
Pets: no
Smoking: ok
Rates: NZ$45-70

Spa Motel & Homestay
Christchurch, New Zealand

15 Harrogate St
Hanmer Springs, New Zealand
64-3/ 315-7129 0800/ 446-644
www.spalodgehanmer.co.nz

Clientele: gay-friendly
Type: older-style motel of studios, 1- & 2-bdrms; also 2 rms in b&b; 2 friendly dogs in house; close to village thermal pools
Owned/ Run By: gay men
Baths: private & shared
Meals: full brkfst

Amenities: free parking, laundry, pool, outdoor hot tub, massage, DVDs/ videos
Kids: welcome
Pets: no
Smoking: no
Rates: NZ$89-160
AC: please inquire

Sweet & Simply Spectacular

Christchurch, New Zealand

707/ 962-0297 (US #)
www.holidayhouses.co.nz/
properties/6375.asp

Clientele: mixed gay/ straight
Type: rental home; comfortable vacation home overlooking Christchurch; all amenities; spectacular views
Owned/ Run By: women
Rooms: 2

Meals: coffee/ tea only
Amenities: free parking, laundry, WiFi
Kids: no
Pets: no
Smoking: no
Rates: NZ$100

Redwood Lodge

Methven, New Zealand

5 Wayne Pl
Methven, New Zealand 8353
64/ 302-8964
www.snowboardnz.com

Clientele: gay-friendly
Type: hostel; 1 hr from Christchurch int'l airport; community kitchen; discounts on ski & snowboard equipment; internet access
Owned/ Run By: straights
Rooms: 15

Baths: private & shared
Amenities: free parking, laundry, DVDs/ videos
Kids: welcome
Pets: no
Smoking: no
Rates: NZ$23-105

Ngatahi Lodge

Napier, New Zealand

172 St Andrews Rd
Havelock North, New Zealand 4201
64-6/ 877-1525
www.ngatahi.com

Clientele: men
Type: large country garden; near art deco architecture, beaches & wineries; clothing-optional; kayaks & bikes available; 10 campsites
Owned/ Run By: gay men
Rooms: 3
Baths: private & shared

Wheelchair Access: yes, 2 rms
Meals: expanded cont'l brkfst
Amenities: outdoor hot tub
Kids: no
Pets: no
Smoking: no
Rates: NZ$20-25/ tents, NZ$60-120/ beds
AC: please inquire

Floosie Gardens

Nelson, New Zealand

64-3/ 545-9122
www.floosiegardens.co.nz

Clientele: women
Type: guesthouse; peaceful, secluded guestrms & studio; close to galleries, cafes, markets, a river & more
Owned/ Run By: women
Rooms: 3

Baths: private & shared
Meals: coffee/ tea only
Amenities: free parking, laundry
Kids: no
Pets: no
Rates: NZ$60-75

Kamahi Cottage

Otorohanga, New Zealand

229 Barber Rd RD5
Otorohanga, Waikato, New Zealand 3975
64-7/ 873-0849
www.kamahi.co.nz

Clientele: gay-friendly
Type: b&b
Owned/ Run By: straight woman
Rooms: 1
Baths: private
Meals: full brkfst

Amenities: free parking, laundry, WiFi
Kids: welcome
Pets: no
Smoking: no
Rates: NZ$250
AC: 10%

Te Manapouri

Palmerston North, New Zealand

32 Manapouri Crescent
Palmerston North, New Zealand 4410
64-6/ 357-0120
www.gaystay.co.nz/palmerstonN.htm

Clientele: mostly men
Type: b&b; quiet 1930s house on a Heritage Street; bdrms sensuously furnished; close to CBD
Owned/ Run By: gay men
Rooms: 2
Baths: shared
Meals: cont'l brkfst

Amenities: free parking, laundry, hot tub, massage, DVDs/ videos
Kids: no
Pets: no
Smoking: no
Rates: NZ$70-120
AC: 10%

Waihoihoi Lodge
Waipu, New Zealand

239 Massey Rd, Rd 2
Waipu, Northland, New Zealand 0254
64-9/ 432-1234
www.waihoihoi.co.nz

Clientele: women
Type: b&b-inn; less than 2 hrs N of Auckland; fabulous views; organic garden; "affordable luxury for women travellers"
Owned/ Run By: lesbians
Rooms: 4
Baths: private
Wheelchair Access: yes, 1 rm

Meals: expanded cont'l brkfst
Amenities: free parking, laundry, indoor hot tub, DVDs/ videos
Kids: welcome in studio only
Pets: welcome in studio only
Smoking: no
Rates: NZ$50-150

The Gatehouse B&B
Wellington, New Zealand

57 Cheviot Rd
Wellington, New Zealand
64-4/ 568-7600
www.thegatehouse.co.nz

Clientele: gay-friendly
Type: b&b; luxury 1-bdrm villa; near beach, restaurants, cafes & galleries; 15 minutes to Wellington
Owned/ Run By: straights
Rooms: 1
Baths: private

Meals: full brkfst
Amenities: free parking, laundry, pool, hot tub, DVDs/ videos
Kids: welcome
Rates: NZ$425-485 (double)
AC: 20%

Koromiko Homestay
Wellington, New Zealand

64-4/ 938-6539
www.koromikohomestay.co.nz

Clientele: mixed gay/ straight
Type: b&b-private home; on quiet street near city & university; harbor views; 3 decks & lawn for sunning; internet access
Owned/ Run By: gay men
Rooms: 3
Baths: shared

Meals: cont'l brkfst
Kids: no
Pets: no
Smoking: no
Rates: NZ$70 (single) - 110 (double)
AC: 10%

The Mermaid
Wellington, New Zealand

1 Epuni St, Aro Valley
Wellington, New Zealand
64-4/ 384-4511
www.mermaid.co.nz

Clientele: women
Type: guesthouse; full kitchen available; near tourist attractions, cafes, restaurants & universities
Owned/ Run By: lesbian
Rooms: 4

Baths: private & shared
Meals: cont'l brkfst
Kids: welcome
Pets: no
Rates: NZ$80-120
AC: 10%

Qbissima
Wellington, New Zealand

#2S, QBA Apts, 51-75 Webb St
Wellington, New Zealand
64-4/ 384-4511
www.mermaid.co.nz/qbissima

Clientele: mixed gay/ straight
Type: 2nd-flr & sun-filled apt w/ full kitchen & original art deco & '50s furniture; self-catering; in central downtown Wellington on hip Cuba St; walking distance of waterfront & Te Papa Museum
Owned/ Run By: lesbian

Rooms: 1 (apt)
Baths: private
Meals: coffee/ tea only
Amenities: laundry, DVDs/ videos
Kids: welcome w/ prior approval
Rates: NZ$160/ night; NZ$800/ week
AC: 10%

Tinakori Lodge B&B Guest House
Wellington, New Zealand

182 Tinakori Rd, Thorndon
Wellington, New Zealand
64-4/ 939-3478
www.tinakorilodge.co.nz

Clientele: gay-friendly
Type: b&b; 1868 home in historic Thorndon; w/ large conservatory lounge; walking distance to Parliament, Te Papa Nat'l Museum, harbour & gay attractions; NZGLTA member

Rooms: 8
Baths: private & shared
Meals: expanded cont'l brkfst
Kids: 13 yrs & up welcome
Smoking: no
Rates: NZ$99-170

Accommodations for Men

Accommodations for Men

Accommodations for Women

Accommodations That Are LGBT-Owned

Accommodations That Are LGBT-Owned

Accommodations That Are LGBT-Owned

Accommodations That Are LGBT-Owned

Accommodations That Are LGBT-Owned